Harrison E. Salisbury

A Journey for Our Times

A MEMOIR

A Cornelia & Michael Bessie Book

HARPER & ROW, PUBLISHERS, New York

Cambridge, Philadelphia, San Francisco, London

Mexico City, São Paulo, Sydney

Designed by Ruth Bornschlegel

This book is set in 10½ point Divinne. It was composed by ComCom division of Haddon Craftsmen, Inc., and printed and bound by Haddon Craftsmen, Inc.,

Library of Congress Cataloging in Publication Data

Salisbury, Harrison Evans, 1908–
A journey for our times.

   "A Cornelia & Michael Bessie book."
   Includes index.
   1. Salisbury, Harrison Evans, 1908–   . 2. Journalists—United States—Biography. I. Title.
PN4874.S266A34   1983   070'.92'4 [B]   81–47904
ISBN 0–06–039006–9

83 84 85 86 87 10 9 8 7 6 5 4 3 2

For my parents,
Percy Pritchard Salisbury and Georgiana Evans Salisbury,
for my wife, Charlotte,
my sister, Janet,
and my sons, Michael and Stephan

Contents

Illustrations follow page 116.

Acknowledgments

More than to any living person, I am indebted in the writing of these memoirs to my father and mother, Percy and Georgiana Salisbury, and to my aunt Sue M. Salisbury, for creating the family archive and writing the letters that enabled me to reconstruct so much of my early life, and to my sister, Janet, who has preserved that archive and whose trustworthy memory and ingenuity has illuminated many obscure passages.

And my thanks go to my sons, Michael and Stephan, who helped me greatly, and to my wife, Charlotte, for her guidance and forbearance.

I have approached my memoirs like a reporter and have drawn on many sources to refresh, correct and extend my recollections. I discovered through the Freedom of Information Act and the records I retrieved from the FBI, the State Department and the Defense Department many things I did not know and could not have imagined, a side of my life that had been almost totally concealed from me over many years.

For my early years I have been aided by the recollections of my old friends Ruben Reseen, Reuben Berman, Kit Roth, Francis Bosworth, Mrs. Wilson Stone, Judson and Lillian Anderson, Nordau Schoenberg, K. V. Bjornson, Wolf Larson and Hillier Krieghbaum. My cousins Eleanor Clifford and Lucille Khayyam filled in some details.

For the London and pre-London years I was assisted by Joan Dickinson, Harold Hutchinson, Storm Jameson, Robert Musel, Bernard Geis, Claud Cockburn, Eleanor Ungerland and Walter Cronkite.

No one was more helpful on Moscow—and many other matters —than my close friend Tom Whitney. I thank Ludmilla Shapiro and Henry Shapiro for special help, as well as Sir Frank Roberts, Sir John Russell, Paul Winterton and Ann Lauterbach.

I owe a particular debt to Hans Von Herwarth, Yuri Nosenko, Will Lissner, Dr. A. McGee Harvey, Yevgeny Yevtushenko and several Russian friends whose names I will not mention here.

The Minneapolis Public Library, the Minnesota State Historical Society and *The New York Times* archives have provided assistance. For many details about Minnesota in World War I and the Lindbergh episodes I wish to thank Professor Carol L. Jenson of the University of Wisconsin–LaCrosse, Bruce L. Larson of the University of Minnesota–Mankato and Walter Hoffman of the University of Minnesota–Minneapolis.

My special thanks to Simon Michael Bessie, editor, friend and source. And a bouquet to Ruth Strauss, who faithfully typed this manuscript, as she has many others over the years.

Not least I wish to thank Dr. Anna Von Helmholtz Phelan for her efforts to teach me how to write, to Oscar W. Firkins, who tried to teach me how to think, and to Sir Bernard Pares, who convinced me I should put Russia into my life.

A Journey
for Our Times

1 | Child of War

To a workingman, head tucked into collar against the wind, hurrying home in the dark Minnesota November, the figure of a small boy slowly stomping across the snowy lawn beyond the yellow arc of gaslight was almost invisible, a blur against the crepuscular shadows of the gabled house. A flint-edged wind discouraged curiosity, but if, despite wind, and cold, and winter twilight, the man had taken note, he would perhaps have been puzzled at the boy's movements, trudging a dozen paces toward the naked thorn apple hedge, feet squeaking on the dry snow, abruptly reversing and repeating his maneuver again and again, almost as though he was standing guard.

The small boy was myself, and in fact I *was* standing guard. It was late November 1917. The Revolution had triumphed in Petrograd and that evening I was a member of the Children's Regiment. I wore my high-peaked Budenny helmet of gray felt with its red star, and a long-skirted uniform coat over Cossack boots. I thrust my hands deep into black gauntlets and on my shoulder I bore a Berdan rifle. Back and forth I paced before the Winter Palace; back and forth beside the parapet beyond which lay the expanse of Palace Square and the shaft of the monument to Alexander I. Occasionally, I glanced at the glowing windows of the palace and saw my silhouette on the crust of snow: the peak of my helmet, the long point of my bayonet, black against the white. The scene was more real than life. I was a boy soldier on sentry duty.

Then, as I knew it would, came the voice of my mother at the kitchen door. "Bunny! Bunny!" she called. "Time to come in. You'll catch your death of cold."

I hesitated a moment to show that I was not hungry, not cold, not beginning to get a bit frightened by my fantasy, then I turned, left the parapet of snow I had built, and with a last look to the dark curve of Royalston Avenue, where the enemy lay hidden off toward the coalyards, I hurried to the house which my grandfather had built and where I had lived since I was born, on November 14, 1908. Stacking beside the door the rifle I had fashioned from a two-by-four, I brushed the snow from my feet and passed into the radiant sphere of the kitchen, with its coal range and the copper sink so veined with solder it looked like a relief map of Europe. The room was filled with smells: beans and molasses bubbling in an earthen crock, the scent of brown bread, coffee heating in a granite pot and the spice of fresh gingerbread pinching my nostrils.

I hung up my helmet, a white-and-red stocking cap, and my uniform greatcoat, a sheep-lined mackinaw, and put away my gauntlets of rabbit fur with the skin outside. I stood there a nine-year-old fourth grader, wearing itchy wool union suit, flannel shirt, dark brown corduroy britches, long black stockings, heavy wool socks neatly folded over the tops of my soft elkskin boots, suddenly hungry and cold, cheeks chapped, nose running, Petrograd, the Winter Palace, the Children's Regiment vanishing as I sat down at table with my father, my mother and my seven-year-old sister, Janet, to a steaming plate of pork and beans.

"What were you doing out in the yard?" my father asked.

"Just playing," I said, keeping my eyes down and reaching for the ruby red flask of ketchup.

I've looked back a hundred times at that nine-year-old youngster, particularly during my long years in Russia, wondering whether, in fact, I was "just playing."

I think I first heard the names of Lenin and Trotsky a month or two later, in early February 1918, about the time Trotsky submitted to the astonished German plenipotentiaries at Brest Litovsk his proposal of no war, no peace. I could not have guessed that they would run through my life like a red thread.

Afternoons now were growing longer in Minneapolis, and one day when I came home from school I saw a new boy outside a house across the street, a verandaed house of fading red which was being rented to rooms, the original owners, the Dericksons, who like my grandfather had bought a lot in the fashionable Oak Lake Addition in the 1880s, having, as had most of the others, sold their place and moved away.

On this afternoon I was busy behind my snow fort, laying by a supply of icy snowballs with which to repel attack by youngsters passing down Royalston Avenue or issuing from the alley which was my left flank. I glanced occasionally at the boy across the street, a slight youngster, dark, olive-skinned, a bit taller and older than myself, wearing tan muffler, black cap and a torn red sweater over a dark blue woolen work shirt. On his feet were rubber boots, the thin knee-high glossy kind that kids wore when the ice melted in spring. He was fashioning the snow figure of a slender young girl, and even to my rude eye it had a grace that set it apart from the slushy yard, the dingy house, the stains of yellow horse piss and brown droppings from the heavy teams of sledges that passed by.

A sense of envy seized me. I picked up a snowball and threw it across the street. It scudded into the snow and the boy went on working. I threw another. No response. I threw a third. It hit the slender figure, smashing away her shoulder. The boy turned and cried: "Why did you do that?" I saw tears in his brown eyes. Filled with shame, I stood a moment, then crossed the street. "Maybe we can fix it," I said. "No," the boy said. "No. It can't be fixed." He gave a kick and the snow maiden crumpled. "What's your name?" I asked. "Reuben," he said. "What's yours?" "My name is Bunny," I said. I hated that name. I hated it when my mother and sister called me Bunny. I fought any boy who called me Bunny, but now I gave it to the boy as a kind of penance. "Bunny," I said, "that's my name." The glance he gave me burned into my mind, and years later, describing him in a sketch which I called "Christ Was Born in Asia," I wrote that he looked like the figure of Jesus in a Pre-Raphaelite painting.

"Would you like a glass of tea?" he asked. "My father is up-stairs."

I had never heard of drinking tea from a glass. "Yes," I said. "I'd like that a lot."

Reuben's father was Nathan Rosen. He told me about Lenin and Trotsky and Russia and the Revolution and the Czar and the Jews and the pogroms and so many things that my head almost burst. He had fled Russia to escape the pogroms and the Czar's twenty-five-year term of military duty and more importantly because he had become a revolutionary. He had been born in a village in Belorussia between the rivers Dnieper and Sozh, names that meant nothing to me until I went to Russia during World War II. Fierce battles were fought there in 1941 near Gomel, at the hinge of Belorussia, the Ukraine and Russia proper.

Nathan Rosen, slim, dark, lively, had a talent for painting. A local aristocrat offered to send him to St. Petersburg to study, but his family could not spare him. It was the time of the pogroms. Young Nathan looked more Italian than Jewish. He hung about the teahouses where police agents and Black Hundred toughs gathered and he tipped off Jewish self-defense groups about their plans. When he was conscripted for the war against Japan, his regiment mutinied. He made his way to London, where his fiancée joined him. They were married at a registry office on Piccadilly Circus and came to Winnipeg. When war broke out in August 1914, they moved to Minneapolis, Nathan fearful that he might again be conscripted.

Now he was starting to work as a painter—houses, signs, decorations, paperhanging. They lived in three rooms on the second floor, Nathan and his wife, Edith, baby Harold, Reuben and his sister, Bessie, whose sculpture in snow Reuben had been making.

That afternoon we sat in a kitchen crowded with a tall armoire and a magnificent chair that had carved griffins, claw feet and a black leather seat. Reuben loved to run his hands over the silken sheen of the mahogany. I imagined it must have come from Russia. A kettle simmered on the stove, the air was filled with steam and the windows had glazed with frost. A huge brass engine hissed away, a samovar, the first I'd seen. Everything was mysterious and foreign and unknown. I felt very brave to be sitting in so strange a place. Mr. Rosen poured me a glass of black tea and gave me a lump of sugar. "Here," he said, "drink it the Russian way. Put the sugar in your mouth." He took a lump and sucked the tea through it. I had never tasted tea. Children weren't supposed to drink tea. It stunted their growth. So did coffee. Children drank milk and cocoa. Mr. Rosen didn't seem to know this. Nor did he care whether I drank my tea or not; he was too excited, talking about Russia in words and accent that I didn't always understand.

"Enormous things are happening," he said. "The world is changing. The Czar is finished. So is Kerensky. Trotsky and Lenin are changing the world. When the war ends, revolution will sweep Europe—Germany first, then France and England. Even here in America. You'll read about it in the newspapers." I could see that Reuben was a little embarrassed at the torrent of his father's words. "Maybe not here, Papa," he said quietly. "You wait," Mr. Rosen said. "You read the papers. Even here.

The Revolution has started. Nothing will be the same again. Remember what Karl Marx said, and Engels too."

I wanted to tell Mr. Rosen how I had stood guard at the Winter Palace, but he was talking about the *real* Revolution. He came from the *real* Russia. He was a *real* revolutionary. I had just been playing, making up a story from the dispatches of Floyd Gibbons, the *Chicago Tribune* man who wore a black patch over one eye. Gibbons was my hero, along with General Blackjack Pershing, Lord Kitchener (my favorite—I could not believe he had been lost on the *Hampshire*), Edith Cavell, the King of Belgium and Colonel George E. Leach of Minnesota's own 151st Field Artillery, who had gone to Central High with my mother, very handsome but very dumb, she said. At exam time she had had to whisper the answers to him. Later George Leach would become mayor of Minneapolis, campaigning in his uniform, very handsome, but he still didn't know the answers.

World War I was my life. I learned to read sitting in Unk's lap, picking out headlines about the battle on the Marne in the *Minneapolis Journal.* Unk was James Pritchard, my father's uncle, and he had fought at Shiloh and endured the hell of Andersonville prison. It left him a little fuzzy and sometimes he put sugar in his soup, thinking it was oatmeal. He was a gentlehearted man who lived with us and looked after the furnaces—two because the house was so big—until one day when he kept starting fires in the toilets, complaining that somehow they didn't draw very well. After that he went to live in a nursing home.

When I launched my literary career in 1918, my first work was a historical treatise called "The Great War." It filled seven pages (including penciled illustrations and maps) of my old green copybook. I began with these words: "1914—Germany declared war on France August 1, 1914. All France was astire."

I didn't stay long that day at the Rosen flat. I refused the garlic sausage, the spiced cakes, the dill pickles encrusted with salt, the black bread and herring. My mother had laid down a strict rule. I was never, never to visit a boy's house without first getting permission. Quickly I retreated outside, across the street past the lamp, its gas mantle glowing soft and yellow, and into my house. I had had my first experience of Russia. I guess I was a Bolshevik before I was ten, but by the time I was eleven I was wearing a Pershing for President button.

When I finally found myself in Russia in 1944 and began a long career as correspondent, a specialist in Soviet affairs and a historian, I came to realize that nowhere in that gray wasteland would I ever taste the wine of the Revolution as pungent and pure as that of my childhood in the Oak Lake Addition.

I was born a Victorian child. Edward had ascended the throne by the time of my birth, but Victoria still reigned at 107 Royalston Avenue. My grandmother, Mary Pritchard Salisbury, dressed my father in a black velvet suit with gold embroidery like Little Lord Fauntleroy's and had Mr. Schuesler, the photographer on Hudson Street in Mazomanie, Wisconsin, take his picture on a little rattan chair, looking woeful. My father dressed me in the same suit and took my picture. I hated that Fauntleroy outfit, but when the time came, I dressed my son Michael in it, posed him on the curlicued walnut sofa that had stood in the parlor at 107 and took his picture. Continuity.

In his heart, my father never left the house on Royalston Avenue. There are times when I wonder whether I have. Father sold the house just before I went to college and we moved to Kenwood Hill, but when Father walked home from the factory at night, his legs occasionally took him over the Seventh Street bridge, across the railroad tracks, past the coalyards and up to 107 before he realized that he didn't live there anymore. It was home for him and home for me and hardly a day of my life was to pass without my thinking about it. In strange cities I put myself to sleep walking through the rooms at 107, remembering the long yellow Dagestan runner on the hall floor, the red of the Khiva in the parlor, my mother's favorite picture, "The Age of Innocence," over the sofa, the seven-branched candelabra on the mahogany table that had belonged to my great-great-aunt in Cincinnati (or was it Philadelphia?), the gentle head of a deer (how could my father have shot it?) over the fireplace in the dining room; remembering my grandfather's cherrywood library, the folios of Shakespeare lying flat under Milton's *Paradise Lost* with the Doré engravings. Later I was to discover plain-brown-wrapper copies of *What Every Boy Should Know* and *What Every Girl Should Know* hidden back of Milton; the juxtaposition of Doré's naked men and women amid the flames, and the giddy perils of adolescence, convinced me, for a time, that hell was real.

On the library shelves stood volumes of *Scribner's, Harper's* and *Century* magazines, bound in black leather by my grandfather. He was a doctor and he read these volumes, sitting in the carved cherrywood rocking chair where he spent the last year of his life, knowing from his own diagnosis that his heart had worn out, reading and drowsing and waiting for it to stop beating, as soon it did. Here were Gibbon's Rome and Green's history of England, Grant's memoirs, Charles Dickens and William Makepeace Thackeray, John Greenleaf Whittier and Henry Wadsworth Longfellow, Louisa May Alcott and Ralph Waldo Emerson, Henry Thoreau, James Fenimore Cooper and William Cullen Bryant, a nineteenth-century litany. I read them all, serially, in continuous wonder, shelf by shelf, between the ages of nine and thirteen. I grew up knowing what culture was—it was the books on the walls of my grandfather's study.

On New Year's Day in 1966, I found myself in the North Vietnam countryside, eighty-five miles south of Hanoi. It had been a long day, spent driving down narrow bomb-pitted roads, with the threat of more American bombers at any moment. Now I was spending the night on a slat-bottomed bed with a straw mattress in a barracks with open sides and clay floor. I was too tired to sleep. I thought I could hear the rustle of people moving past the compound and wondered what was happening. I was an enemy deep behind the lines. I did not even know the name of the place where I was staying. It was cold under the thin blanket and I lay half awake and a little frightened. Finally, I turned my mind away from Hanoi, away from the war and the bombs, and back to the security of Royalston Avenue. I sat again in our light carriage, the black-painted trap, my father driving Dolly, our old bay, I sitting beside him, my mother and Janet in the rear, clop-clop, neatly around the curve under the elms, Dolly's hooves falling rhythmically on the soft brown earth of the street freshly watered by a yellow sprinkling wagon. My father, dark and handsome, pulled up at 107, the reins taut in his hands, and my mother, broad-brimmed straw hat with mauve veil sheltering her blond hair and pale complexion from the sun, alighted to the granite stepping-stone, Janet and I following her, scrambling up the five wooden steps of the veranda, overhung with grapevines, bursting through the double oak doors with their brass fittings and into the entry, past the half-glass doors, etched with flowers, into the front hall with its elk's head, shot by my uncle Scott

Evans on his way to the Klondike in 1900, grim, menacing and sprinkled so heavily with red pepper against moths that I could not come close without sneezing. A crystal-faceted chandelier sparkled over the oak staircase with its polished newel and banister, whose smooth surface first gave me a warm masturbatory pleasure and made me think of my girl cousin Eleanor Evans, who liked to slide down the rail, thin legs clenching its rotundity, short skirt pulled back and panties riding up narrow thighs.

That night in the Vietnam countryside, I walked through the house on Royalston Avenue as I had so often, and finally I sat on the floor beside the window box in my grandfather's library, pulling out of its depths the architectural journals my father kept there, looking at the plans for the house on the Mississippi riverbank which he dreamed of but never built, taking out the Frederic Remington engravings and the lithographs of the Philadelphia Exposition, and finally a worn purple-and-gold book, *Dick Whittington,* my father's childhood favorite. I listened again to the words: "turn, turn again, Dick Whittington, Lord Mayor of London Town," and at that moment the Bow Bells sounded as they had for Dick Whittington. I awoke. It was not yet dawn, but the iron bells in the shattered tower of the bombed-out Cathedral of St. François Xavier across the rice paddies were calling black-pajamaed peasants to mass before daylight, before the first flight of American bombers appeared in the sky. Pulling aside the mosquito net, shivering in the early coldness, I saw the peasants moving along the willow-lined roadway almost without sound on inner-tube sandals, shuffling past the barracks on their way to pray. In an instant I was transported from my Victorian dream to the reality of grass-cutter bombs, of napalm and Agent Orange, to the deadly imposition by my loved America of pain and horror on an ancient Asian people.

2 | The Making of a Patriot

War was the glory of my childhood. I must confess there was not a hint of moral outrage in my being, nor have I ever been a pacifist. I could say with FDR: "I hate war"; I can say that I have feared war and have opposed war, notably the Vietnam war; but until nuclear war was born, I never believed in a world without war. Now no other kind of world is imaginable.

As a youngster I surrounded myself with lead soldiers, guns, toy cannon, cap pistols. I compelled my complaisant sister, Janet, to play war with me, once keeping her so long in the shallow trenches we had dug in the hot sun that she almost suffered sunstroke.

(I was amused later to learn that Vladimir Lenin and his brothers and sisters played war endlessly in the parlor of their house high on the Volga River bluff at Simbirsk.)

After supper each evening, our family gathered with my uncle Andrew and aunt Mary, who lived on the second floor of our house. We wound up the mahogany Victrola and played "Madelon," "Tipperary," "Over There" and the rest. My father and uncle gravely discussed military strategy.

A Red Cross unit headed by my mother and my aunt met at our house to roll bandages, the ladies in white uniforms and turbans. They rolled hundreds of muslin bandages, knitted 1,194 pairs of socks, 1,003 sweaters and twelve dozen face masks. We children learned to knit too. I shudder to think of the soldiers who had to wear our socks.

I dreamed of Allied victory. My aunt Sue Salisbury was in France with the YMCA. Letter after letter flowed back from Paris, full of the *Boche* and his bestiality. I began to feel ashamed that my father was not Over There; that he was in the Home Guard—in uniform, true, but no tin hat, drilling on Monday evenings and on Wednesdays serving ice cream cones and sodas to Our Boys at the Army and Navy Club. He would come home tired on Wednesday evenings but lugging a gallon of leftover ice cream, a consolation for not being at the Front.

I was totally chauvinistic. When I saw in the atlas the enormous globs of British Empire red spread over the continents, it made me angry that the American green covered only Hawaii, the Canal Zone, Puerto Rico, Alaska and the Philippines. I yearned for an American Empire on which the sun never set. My father was a Teddy Roosevelt Republican, a Bull Mooser, and so was I. In 1916, at the age of seven, I was against "Yellow Dog" Wilson, who was "too proud to fight." I agreed with my father and my uncle Andrew, who said that Wilson was *afraid* to fight.

I could not believe my ears when I heard my uncle John Dort, sitting on the porch of his house in St. Paul (living in St. Paul was bad enough in those days of Twin City rivalry), tell my father that he was voting for Woodrow Wilson. John Dort—a locomotive engineer, a hero—a Wilson Democrat? I was stunned. Only town drunks and Irishmen were Democrats.

When we entered the war, no one was more vigilant than I against the "pros," that is, the pro-Germans, secret enemies of Our Cause. Minnesota had a large population of Scandinavians, many Germans and a small Irish minority. The war was not a "Crusade for Democracy" to them. Many of the Germans and Scandinavians were socialists. They believed the war reflected the rivalry of capitalists eager to grab each other's wealth.

None of this was perceived by me. I listened with rabbit's ears to my elders talking about the "pros"; about old German friends who were suspect, especially a prosperous family that ran a big liquor store. The test was Liberty Bonds. If you didn't buy bonds, you were a "pro." Even if you did buy bonds, you might be trying to mask your secret sympathy for Kaiser Bill. I visioned the Kaiser as a death's head, bony fingers dripping blood, a necklace of skulls, wolf's teeth, spiky helmet, devil's tail. My image may have derived from one of John McCutcheon's cartoons in the *Chicago Tribune*. I believed every atrocity story invented by the British—the nuns used as bell clappers, the little girls with hands chopped off (because they threw stones at German soldiers), the martyrdom of Edith Cavell. God knows what I didn't believe. Every letter of Aunt Sue's from Paris told of horrors—destruction of the Rheims cathedral, desecration of Louvain, *Schreckenskrieg,* poisoned chocolates dropped by zeppelins (I was instructed never to accept chocolate from a stranger on the street), Big Berthas shelling orphanages.

Friday was War Savings Stamp day at Sumner School and I took a quarter to buy a big purple stamp and paste it into my stamp book. When I got one hundred purple stamps, I could turn the book in for a twenty-five-dollar Liberty Bond. Each Friday morning, I glanced around the classroom to see if anyone didn't buy stamps. The children who attended Sumner School were mostly poor. Nickels and dimes were scarce, quarters they never had. But on Friday, each had a coin or two, often pennies carefully tied up by their mother in the corner of a handkerchief. One boy (myself) had a small black leather coin purse with a metal clasp. There was a Swedish girl named Marie in my class who always seemed a bit older than the rest of us (in fifth grade she had real breasts). One Friday she had no money: "My mother said she didn't have any money for savings stamps," and she tossed her blond braids defensively. When I brought this news home, my mother and my aunt Mary exchanged looks. My father started to say something, but was shushed by my mother. I knew this meant a scandal not fit for children's ears and kept mine fine-tuned. Later that evening, I overheard a whispered exchange about Marie's mother. She kept a rooming house on Sixth Avenue around the corner from us. One of the roomers was a black man. "What do you expect from her kind?" my aunt remarked. "Something ought to be done." My mother solemnly agreed: "For the children's sake." The next evening, my father, dressed in his Home Guard uniform, and my uncle Andrew, solemn in a black suit, left the house. They returned a bit later looking pleased and closeted themselves with my mother and aunt. The following Friday, Marie appeared in class with a dollar bill and pushed to the head of the line, saying, "Put four purple stamps in my book. A whole dollar's worth!"

My mother and father and aunt often went to houses door to door, to be sure people were buying Victory Bonds. There were signs in front windows, saying: "We subscribed." And Red Cross stickers too. My father and my uncle Andrew thought well of the board of directors of the Minneapolis Symphony Orchestra when they drove from his position the respected conductor Emil Oberhoffer, who refused to drop German composers from the repertoire.

Of course, I ate spareribs with liberty cabbage instead of sauerkraut, and when I got sick it was with liberty measles. No voice was raised in dissent in our house when the teaching of German was banned by the Minneapolis public schools. My father and my uncle were fluent in German, enjoyed reading German novels and switched to German if they were speaking of "naughty" matters (like the Swedish lady and her black roomer). But they abandoned the language except for an occasional *Donner und Blitzen, Dummkopf* or *Gott im Himmel.*

All this seemed right as rain to the small chauvinistic patriot who was me. I was not a thoughtful child and I enthusiastically joined the chorus of hate. I had never, I am certain, heard of the Bill of Rights or the First Amendment. I loved parades, especially military parades with lots of guns and bands, such as the Stars and Stripes Parade of August 16, 1917, not just an ordinary flag-waving demonstration. The Stars and Stripes Parade touched off—and was designed to touch off—a violent wave of xenophobic, prowar vigilantism in Minneapolis and in the state of Minnesota.

Its leader was a man named Fred B. Snyder. There were bands galore—the Donaldson's department store drum corps, Captain Sinclair and his bagpipe corps, the white-uniformed young women's marching corps of Dayton's department store, led by George D. Dayton himself, the Zurah Temple band, the Maccabees, Modern Woodmen, Shriners, uniformed firemen, the Pillsbury Flour Company band and the band of Glencoe, Minnesota, somewhat crippled because the bass drummer had beat his drum so vigorously both drumheads broke.

The martial music was matched by the martial oratory. On the parade grounds, Snyder whipped up the crowd against the officials of New Ulm, Minnesota, a German community in the southern part of the state, where a temperate attitude toward the war prevailed. "What shall we do with the copperheads?" Snyder demanded. "Shoot 'em! Hang 'em!" the crowd roared. Snyder wound up by pleading that "nothing should be left undone to win this war even though it requires harsh treatment of friends and neighbors."

The hit of the day was William H. Morris, described as "colored" by the *Minneapolis Journal.* He spoke for the "Black Sammies." He declared that the "Black Sammies" already in France and those about to follow would prove that "no braver, better, more patriotic loyal soldiers" had ever lived than the Sammies and that their guns and swords would "always be true to the country that has given them a voice in government for the first time."

Minnesota's governor, a lumbering Republican, J. A. A. Burn-
quist, had set up a Commission of Public Safety, which could
supersede local officials and mayors. It was empowered to do
anything it pleased with persons it accused of disloyalty. The
powers of the commission make those of the late Senator Joseph
McCarthy look like a kindergarten teacher's. Three days after
the Stars and Stripes Parade, the commission ousted the town
officers of New Ulm "so that liberty, equality and humanity
might endure."

There was no pretense of constitutionality about the commission. One of its sponsors privately wrote Minnesota's Senator
Knute Nelson: "The bill has teeth in it eighteen inches long.
There are provisions in it that are unconstitutional and palpably
so."

The commission closed saloons and dance halls in working-class
areas. Soon it had created the Home Guard, in which my father
enlisted, to "protect private property in this period of unrest and
disorder."

My father's finest hour came when the Home Guard was ordered to break a streetcar strike in 1917. Issued a long oak ax
handle and a nickel-plated pistol, he rode with strikebreaking
motormen and, as he swore, cracked the skulls of strikers who
tried to interfere. Put him in uniform, give him a weapon, issue
an order, and even a gentle man like my father obeyed.

The commission published a weekly called *Minnesota in the
War,* which was circulated to the public schools. The issues were
loaded with atrocity stories and incitements against "pros,"
"traitors," "treason." No wonder my mind reverberated with the
sadism of the Huns.

After the war, case after case came to light in which the Home
Guard had led mobs against supposed traitors, particularly A. C.
Townley's Nonpartisan League and the IWW. I grew up believing that the Nonpartisan League was a branch of the Kaiser's
war apparatus and that the initials IWW stood for "I won't
work."

So it was that the liberal state of Minnesota was transformed
into a pre-fascist fief. The powers vested in the Minnesota Public
Safety Commission were totalitarian powers; the commission established a dictatorship in Minnesota; the ideology of hatred,
racism, xenophobia, was as naked as in Nazi Germany.

As a child, I understood nothing of this. Nor, so far as I can see, did my father and mother and their friends. They believed the propaganda. My aunt Sue wrote my father that German agents every night were shooting American soldiers in the training camps, that spies were dug in so deep it would take years to root them out. These good people believed in the threat of "subversion from within." It never entered their minds that a groundwork for authoritarian rule was being laid under the cloak of "protection of democracy and liberty," as Fred B. Snyder so often declaimed.

The lesson of the Minnesota dictatorship is a frightening one, and it was not until I was preparing to write this book that I took a clear look at what was going on behind those red-white-and-blue banners of which I was so proud. It would have served me well if at least I had paid some heed to Fred B. Snyder, for he was to appear dramatically in my life during my years at the University of Minnesota. He was then, had been since 1914, and would until 1950 continue to be chairman of the University Board of Regents.

This lay to the future. With war's end, the hysteria slowly died, leaving me only a faint perception that something had been wrong, but I did not yet understand that it was America's own principles that had been savaged. I was beginning to be influenced by Henry Mencken, George Jean Nathan and *The American Mercury,* and I found in the banning of Heine, Schiller and Goethe, the silencing of Mozart, Beethoven and Bach, a comedy of the absurd which demonstrated the banality of the American booboisie. I never thought to question my own bigotry.

A decade after the war, I had become a cub reporter on the *Minneapolis Journal* and my first out-of-town assignment was to report a convention held at Austin, a small town in southern Minnesota. Not long before this, I had stood one afternoon in May 1927 beside a Morse telegraph operator in the city room of the *Journal* and listened as the sounder clicked away, a Prince Albert tobacco tin wedged against it to enhance the sound, and the operator typed out the news that Minnesota's Slim Lindbergh had made it to Le Bourget field in Paris. It was an extraordinary moment, the biggest moment for me since the armistice of November 7, 1918, the "false" armistice which I and everyone in Minneapolis thought had ended World War I. Now came this remarkable adventure of the skinny young serious-eyed boy from Little Falls, Minnesota, flying alone across the Atlantic, landing precisely where he said he would, thirty-three hours and twenty-nine minutes after takeoff at Roosevelt Field, Long Island, carrying letters of introduction so that people in Paris would know who he was.

Lindbergh was light-years older than myself—that is, he was twenty-seven and I was eighteen—but I experienced a surge of empathy. But for . . . well, let's face it: I could never have flown across Lake Minnetonka, let alone the Atlantic, but my emotion was there, never quite to vanish.

On this hot evening in August 1928, I was sitting in a breeze-less room of the Fox Hotel at Austin with half a dozen men in their upper thirties or forties, elderly in my eyes, members of the American Legion. These were Prohibition days and some had plain pint bottles of Minnesota Thirteen, the best moonshine whiskey in the state, distilled from a corn called Minnesota 13, developed by the State Agricultural Experiment Station. The rest of us were drinking spiked beer, that is, near beer, spiked with grain alcohol—hospital alcohol, we always called it. We poured off an inch of beer, poured in an inch of alcohol, put a thumb to the top, shook the bottle and drank.

The legionnaires were telling stories, mostly stories about the broads they had bedded—the Frenchwomen they claimed to have laid in Paris, whores in Chicago and Minneapolis, gang fucking in the nearby countryside and other brutalities. Lynchings—well, they hadn't actually killed a nigger. There weren't any niggers or hardly any niggers in Minnesota, but once, during the war, they had "run ol' man Lindbergh outa town."

I listened as they talked, tilting back the clean glass pints of Minnesota Thirteen, capping the near beer with a thumb, drain-ing the brown bottles into gullets, sitting on the sagging beds, shirts unbuttoned, shirttails out, belching and farting, sitting and sweating and talking. Yup, old man Lindbergh had come to town, the election was on, shee-it, we wuzzin gonna let him get away with that shee-it, that goddamn commie pro bastud passa-fist. Agin the war. The boys got tugetha, got some tar and feath-ers, good olfashioned taranfeathers, chicken feathers, came up to the hotel, dragged that olbastud down to the street, pulled his pants right off, poured the tar on him, put the feathers on him and run him outa town, right outa town. Took him on a truck down the road bout three miles and dumped him and that was the end of Lindbergh. Yup. That wuz plumb the end. He juskinda wentoff his rocker afta that, never made anutha speech, never heard anutha yip outa that olpassafist bastud.

What about Charley, what about Slim? I heard myself asking. One of the legionnaires took a long swig. Charley was justa kid. Can't blame his olman's craziness on Charley Lindbergh. Charley Lindbergh, he's one of the greatest. The greatest, fact of matter. The greatest. Was he here in town with the old man that night? I asked. Another pause. Damif I know, the legionnaire said. Seems to me he wuz. Course he wuz justa kid then. Yup. I kinda think he wuz here. Seems to me I remember him, cussin', cryin' and throwin' his fists around, and one of the boys had to take him aside an quieten him down. Yup. Kinda think that's what happened that night.

I woke up the next morning early. I had a black taste in my mouth. The sun was shining into my room and it was Sunday morning, the hotel very quiet. I still had the smell in my nostrils of vomit and sweat and alcohol and beer, and the noise of the legionnaires shouting, glasses smashing on the sidewalk outside, women giggling and screaming and the thumping of beds in the rooms next door, hours and hours of it after I left the old veterans with their bragging of great days, the fucking in Paris, the tarring and feathering in Minnesota.

I have searched out the records and they show that mobs trailed Charles Lindbergh, Sr., during his 1918 campaign for the Republican nomination for the Minnesota governorship. He was arrested on charges of conspiracy along with the Nonpartisan Leaguers; a rally at Madison, Minnesota, was broken up with fire hoses; he was hanged in effigy in Red Wing, dragged from the speaking platform, threatened with lynching, and he escaped from one town amid a volley of shots. I could find no record of an incident exactly matching the tale of the legionnaires; probably they exaggerated. What the record does show is the vicious, vituperative, life-threatening mob action against a man who had fought against the war but once we got into it had said: "A few would destroy democracy to win the war and the rest of us would win the war to establish democracy."

The image of the beer-bellied bullies of Austin floods back in my mind each time I hear patriotic flannelmouths ranting against those whose protection is the sacred function of our democracy.

Ten years passed. The kidnapping, the Hauptmann trial, the self-exile to Europe, the trip to Moscow, dinners with Göring, the long days with Alexis Carrel, the Astors, Cliveden, and the speeches against America getting into World War II—people couldn't understand Lindbergh now. He didn't seem like the man who flew to Le Bourget, didn't seem like the kid who grew up in Little Falls, Minnesota, and quit the University of Wisconsin to be an aviator. The Lindbergh who joined General Robert E. Wood of Sears, Roebuck in the America First Committee, who belittled England's chances against Germany, who thought the Luftwaffe would smash Russia in six weeks, who made remarks about Jewish bankers and Jewish influence—this didn't sound like our American hero who rode up Broadway in the greatest ticker tape parade of all and then married Anne Morrow, the ambassador's daughter.

I did not get to know Lindbergh until the last years of his life. Lindbergh hated newspapers and reporters. He never forgave their scrofulous treatment of his family and himself at the time of the kidnapping, the Hauptmann trial and the afteryears, but for a long while he made an exception for *The New York Times.* Adolph Ochs had taken him up; the *Times* had exclusive rights to his articles about the flight and gave him all the profits; Deak Lyman, the *Times*'s aviation writer, became his personal friend and worked with him in the terrible kidnap days; but Lindbergh had not been in the Times Building since Mr. Ochs's death in 1935, until he lunched with me and Alden Whitman there a few times in the late sixties. He came only because he wanted to talk privately about conservation. There had been something mystical, almost pagan, in his relationship to the earth, his feeling for the sea, for continental space, for the crystalline upper air. No one had a more precise, exact, scientific and practical mind. It was this that made him a magnificent flier and gave him his remarkable grasp of aeronautic technology. He was both a theorist and a craftsman. He checked out a Hertz rental car at La Guardia Airport with the meticulous care he gave to the controls of a Boeing 707.

But science and technology were not enough. His mind was forever pushing the unknown regions that lay beyond demonstrable fact. Now, at least partly through the stimulation of his son, Jon, he had come to see the threat man had brought upon his environment and particularly the danger implicit in aeronautics. His sense of concern had been raised to a pitch by the supersonic aircraft, with its potential for irreversible desiccation of the atmosphere.

Lindbergh was never a man to turn from cruel facts. He had made his decision. What was left of his life (very little, as it turned out), and all his determination (enormous) and world prestige (great), would be thrust into a struggle to save the earth he worshiped.

It was, I thought, a heroic decision, consistent with the heroic image he possessed of his role in society. He was prepared, if necessary, to go against the whole of that aviation which had been his life. It was the radical decision of a radical man, a man almost too complex to analyze but one whom I believed I understood. I was nourished in the same soil as he. I had lived close to those giants in the earth of which Rölvaag wrote, the giants that hurled and clawed at the generations which came first to Minnesota and the Dakotas from Sweden, Norway, Denmark and Iceland. I knew now a good deal about Lindbergh's father, about the socialist agrarians of Sweden and Germany, the Nonpartisan League, the Farmer-Labor party, the passions, prejudices and hatreds that swept Minnesota in 1917 and after. I understood, I thought, why Slim Lindbergh, America's fair hero of 1927, had taken the same implacable stand against the majority, against war in 1939, that his father had taken against war in 1917. Others could assess the influences of Carrel, of the Astors, of Munich and Göring, of Truman Smith, of Hoover, Borah and Byrd, of the American politicians who sought to use Lindbergh. To me, he did not seem so different from the teenager who had watched his father, humiliated, defiled, run out of town by bully boys, driven to nervous breakdown because he had dared to stand up for his socialist principles and say what few other men in that day would say: that war was wrong, that America had no business entering Europe's quarrels, that it was, after all, a feud among greedy empires, a contest of lordly jackals over the corpses of ordinary men and women.

3 | 107 Royalston Avenue

To me, 107 Royalston Avenue was more than a house. It was the architecture of the legends that shaped my life.

I took a child's delight in the fact that each principal room of the house was finished in a different wood—oak for front hall and upstairs sitting room, cherry for Dr. Salisbury's library and consulting rooms (which my parents made their bedroom), ash for the dining room, white-painted pine for the parlor. And I took even more delight in the built-in cabinets, bookcases, mantels, cupboards and window seats. The heart of the house was my grandfather's library. At the age of five, I could circle the room without touching the floor, starting with the box couch, covered with a light kilim, hopping to a black wicker chair where my father sat when reading the paper or giving my sister and myself French lessons, then to an easy chair, upholstered in threadbare crimson, always called "the library chair." From its back I clambered to the bookcase where Shakespeare and Milton were kept and worked my way to a built-in writing desk, cluttered with bottles of black, blue and red ink, small pots of glue and paste. I dropped down to a seat below a window looking out on Royalston Avenue, then climbed a pyramid of bookcases, making toeholds by pushing back volumes of the *Encyclopaedia Britannica,* ninth edition, in its handsome dark red binding, not yet beginning to peel. The cases were high and scary. It was like skirting a mountain cliff. Then a second window seat, the one where my father kept his architectural publications, another high case, and across to the fireplace mantel.

The mantel was a realm of magic—carved columns, beveled mirror, nooks and recesses. Above, almost beyond sight, stood a plaster bust of William Shakespeare with a small dent in his nose that always made me feel guilty, but I have no recollection of breaking it. The mantel was narrow and dangerous. The mirror, I believed, was the same as that through which Alice ventured in *Through the Looking Glass.* To me there was no barrier between the world of 107 Royalston Avenue and that of Alice, of *The Land of Oz,* of *Heidi* and *Back of the North Wind,* of *Pi-*

nocchio or Selma Lagerlöf's goose girl. I never gave up hope that if I twisted the right cherry knob, a passage would open to the Emerald City, the land of the little people, the roof of the world, the path to China. Possibly an echo of this fantasy was to spur me to the corners of the world—Siberia, the Gobi, Karakoram, Tibet and the high roads of the Himalayas, the Back of Beyond.

I believed in magic then. I believed in it, I suspect, as firmly as a medieval dweller in London or Bologna or Changan. Nothing suggested to me that magic was not logical. All I needed were the passwords, the keys, the ciphers, the incantations, the powders. Magic powders! The house at 107 Royalston had almost as many mansards as Hawthorne's house had gables. The vanes, the crenellated chimneys, the millwork turned 107 into poetry. Who could doubt secret passages, hidden doors, veiled mysteries?

Sometimes I explored the house, room by room, floor by floor (adults never realize what raccoons children are), but I never found the magic powders. The attic was a grotesque of cobwebs, cubbyholes, iron-bound chests, leather valises. There was a cabinet of curios, collected by my father—Indian peace pipe, feather headdress, tomahawk, opium pipe, bits of amethyst and a pair of buffalo horns. The buffalo horns, mounted on a walnut plaque, were the only remnant of the herds my father had seen stretching across the high-grass prairies as far as eye could see when he accompanied his father on a trip to the badlands of Dakota. He saw buffalo hides stacked like cordwood at the raw new stations of the Jim Hill railroads. By my birth, they had vanished almost as totally as the passenger pigeon, whose passing in 1914 saddened my youth. For years I kept hoping I might discover a survivor.

I loved the attic. On the Fourth of July, waking very early, sunlight embroidering the wall of my bedroom, I would go with my father to the attic, fit the American flag onto its wooden pole and, carefully edging it out the window, I paying out the Stars and Stripes into the cool air, Dad setting the pole into the iron flanges on the floor, we would dress the house for the great holiday, the Glorious Fourth. This was *the* holiday, the only holiday, really, and years later when I came to read the journal kept by my great-great-uncle Hiram in the first years of the nineteenth century, I was delighted to discover that the Fourth was the only day that he regularly celebrated—the New Year, sometimes; Christmas, never.

Once I discovered in the attic a box of bones and a human skull. My mother was not amused. The bones had belonged to Dr. Salisbury. They were not, she said, the bones of anyone; they were the bones of an Indian. That put them in a different category, not really human. In the afterglow of frontier days, I grew up in Minnesota accepting the doctrine that the only good Indian was a dead Indian. What a little atavistic pig I was!

The basement of 107 was a kingdom of darkness. When my mother sent me to fetch potatoes, onions or rutabagas kept in sand bins in the coldroom, I would steel my nerves, scurry down, swiftly enter the dark vegetable chamber, root out the potatoes and scramble back as fast as I could.

All through childhood I had violent dreams, dreams of falling from the tops of buildings (I suffered from acrophobia) and other terrors; often I fell from bed in my struggles to escape the terrors. One night I dreamed that I had been sent on an errand to the cellar. It was an hour before supper, the cellar was dark. I forced myself down the steps. As I reached the bottom, I saw stalking from behind the ash mountain that built up winter-long beside the furnaces a demonic figure—white beard, the hair of a prophet, a figure that, as I realized in later years, resembled John Brown in the John Steuart Curry painting. My feet were rooted to the spot. I was rigid with terror, vocal cords paralyzed. Closer and closer the demon approached. His bony hands reached for my throat.

I awoke, screaming, bathed in perspiration, falling to the floor in a clot of blankets, the icy air piercing my addled brain and bringing it back to reality. I pulled myself into bed, but I kept awake all night lest the dream return.

It did return, again and again and again, for more nights and more years than I care to remember. Finally came a time when I was able to recognize within the dream that it *was* a dream and struggle to free myself, sometimes succeeding. When I went to London in World War II, the old man in the cellar did not cross the Atlantic. Instead I began to dream of being trapped in an open park (as I had been one London midnight), unable to run, to move, to take cover, as the planes came over and the bombs began to fall. It was, I thought, a case of psychological adaptation to geographic and technological change. But the terror was the same.

Christmas was the joy at 107. It began with subtle changes in noises, movements, moods. Mother and Father became more busy. There were comings and goings, openings and closings of doors and closets, whisperings, heads close together, frequent glances at my sister and myself, unexpected hugs and kisses, giggles and mumblings. Christmas was coming and that meant Holtzermann's. Holtzermann's was what generations of children may have imagined Santa's North Pole workshop to have been. It *was* Christmas. I was six years old when I was taken there for the first time, early in World War I, before feelings about the Germans had become strong. We drove in our Studebaker Super-Six, with its jump seats, isinglass side curtains and running boards. Two steamer robes. No heater. The temperature was fifteen degrees above zero and the streets had a footing of packed snow. (Minneapolis did not begin to clear snow from the streets until the mid-1930s because of the heavy horse-drawn sledges.)

Holtzermann's was located in a region beyond Seven Corners, a German and Scandinavian working-class section. I thought it the end of the world.

We walked down a scuffed linoleum staircase into fairyland, miniature Christmas trees made of green fabric, greener than real trees and glittering like stars, mounds of ornaments, red, silver, green and blue, pendants of silver and insets of rose, spun glass suns and moons, forests of red and green and silver birds with real tails (they weren't real at all—they were spun glass, too, but I didn't know the difference). This dazzled my eyes so that I ran a mittened hand across them.

Slowly we made our way past counters filled with lead soldiers; a bin of grenadiers, a bin of cavalrymen, artillerymen with mounted guns, French regiments on parade, the Kaiser's own uhlans, Austrian soldiers in red waistcoats, red-jacketed English guards with high shakos, Russian generals in gold braid and ermine—every soldier in the world except, I think, American. I grasped my father's hand so tightly he smiled at me. On the shelves were sailing ships and dreadnaughts, even tin submarines. Arms for Christmas, guns for the Christ child's birthday.

Years later, I would come upon a statement the Kaiser made to William Bryan Hale of *The New York Times* in the year of my birth, 1908, but not published for two generations. He spoke of the early Christians who propagated the faith by the sword among Teutonic tribes. "The greatest soldiers," said Wilhelm II, "have been Christians." Holtzermann's, I now understood, had constituted a temple to the military-Christian ideology. I loved it. How easy it is to turn children into eager cannon fodder.

We walked and walked and finally arrived in the land of cuckoo clocks, the walls dripping with clocks, long iron chains, pine cone weights, carved Black Forest huts, cuckoos crying the hours in hoarse voices. There, too, were weather vanes with Bavarian men and women who came in and out with the rise and fall of the barometer; bundles of heavy skis (no fancy equipment in those days) and piles of snowshoes; toy trains running through snow passes and halting at Swiss stations, electric headlights gleaming, engine bells ringing, signal towers with red and green lights; turreted castles of Anchor blocks and skyscrapers of Erector steel. My head spun. My mind could not consume it— the piles of *Lebkuchen,* the dark brown, almost black, sugar-shellacked bells with German saints pictured in blues and browns, the pastry wreaths, the barrels of *Pfeffernuesse.*

Finally we came to a simple vault—no decorations, no glitter, no festoons, just bins of wooden shoes: big wooden shoes for men, smaller for women, still smaller for children, pale, unadorned, naked as bones, wooden shoes, the kind Hans Brinker wore when he was not on his silver skates. There was nothing in the world I wanted more than a pair of these shoes. I never got them.

How, in 1914 and 1915, the war going on, Holtzermann's had stocks of German toys I can't imagine. How did they get through the British blockade? For a while I clung to the romantic idea that the toys had been brought in by Captain Boy-Ed, the German blockade runner who slipped into New York harbor with a cargo of analine dyes and German drugs, which in those simplistic days American manufacturers didn't make—things like aspirin for headaches and Salvarsan for syphilis.

It never occurred to me that we should boycott Holtzermann's. Nor did it, I think, occur to my father. We went every year, war or no war. I've no idea what Mr. Holtzermann's sentiments were in World War I, but I do know that his nephew who was running the store at the time of World War II was a strong supporter of America First and Charles Lindbergh.

Our Christmas tree was placed in the bay window of the parlor, which was my observation post from the time I was able to pull myself to the sill and look out the corner where a big air bubble embedded in the glass stared back at me. Here I watched in joy and terror as three bay horses pulled the lurching, smoke-belching fire engine, the steamer, around the curve of Royalston Avenue from the firehouse built by my Grandfather Evans, Evan D. J. Evans, Evan Evans Straightback as he was called to distinguish him from a dozen other Evan Evanses in Jackson County, Ohio, where he grew up, my mother's father, a patriarch and tyrant, believer in hellfire and damnation, dead long before I was born, dead of pneumonia in the epidemic of 1890, his spirit broken by the loss of his favorite son, Miller, and his beloved daughter, Emma, victims with several neighbors of typhoid contracted from the "sweet water" of the well he dug for the red-brick castle he built for his family at 524 Russell Avenue North.

In the bay window where the Christmas tree stood, stiff lace curtains hung. Father had had candles on his tree since childhood in Mazomanie, and he had them as long as we celebrated Christmas at 107 Royalston, small candles of red, white, blue, green and yellow affixed to the branches with snap holders.

The tree was lighted at evening. Mother presided over a pail of water. Dad, matches in hand, climbed a stepladder and lighted the candles, one by one, until the tree sparkled with captured stars. Almost immediately the aroma of pine filled the room as the candles warmed the needles. Janet and I sat beside the tree in delight edged by fear communicated by Mother. Dad seemed oblivious of the moment, his gray-blue eyes distant, a smile on his face such as I never saw at other times. Mother hovered beside the water pail, nervously calculating the distance between herself and the tree, an exercise in emotional geometry. Hardly were the candles lighted than she said: "Perce—that's enough, don't you think?" Dad would stare at the tree. He was years away from the present. God knows what thoughts were passing through his mind. He would not answer. Possibly he did not hear. He sat and watched the play of lights, the reflected image on the plate-glass window. Three or four minutes passed. Mother spoke again: "Really, Percy, I think we'd better put them out. They're beginning to burn down." Soon, very quickly, she would stride to the tree and begin to snuff out the candles, and Dad, with reluctance that slowed every muscle in his body, rose and helped at the task. Christmas was over.

Christmas was Dad's ritual, more his than ours. I was in love with toy trains and so was he. One Christmas he gave me an electric train (in those days they were rare and expensive). He had spent weeks laying out, on a green-baize-covered board which fitted over the dining room table, a whole track system.

Another Christmas, a very cold one (all Christmases were cold), he gave me a miniature steam engine, a genuine engine that made its own steam with a little boiler and an alcohol flame. I had never been so delighted. Nor, perhaps, had he. After breakfast we sat on the dining room floor in front of a hot coal fire, trying out the engine. It worked like a charm. The house was smoky that morning, as it often was, the furnaces balking, and Dad went to attend them. When he got back, the engine had stopped. "Something happened," I told him. It had. The boiler had burned out and it never ran again. I saw that look in Dad's eyes, the look of despair. I had, I knew, failed him and there was nothing I could say. Nothing he could say. My eyes turned away, welling up in tears. Within the hour I was in bed with a high fever. An attack of flu, the doctor said.

What Christmas meant to my father, so I finally understood, was an occasion to play good fairy; on this day he could make dreams come true. For the rest of the year the iron of economics held him prisoner. On Christmas he broke the bonds. As money grew tighter and tighter, Christmas meant more and more to him. Beyond the things he gave Mother, Janet and myself, there must be one surprise—the "big present," the present no one expected or could imagine. Perhaps his big presents sound mundane today—a Stromberg-Carlson table radio, an ice cream freezer, bicycles for Janet and myself, a player attachment for the old piano. These presents were expensive. They cost fifty or a hundred dollars, sometimes more. He smuggled them home at the last moment and put them in a corner by the tree, wrapped not in tissue and ribbons but in brown kraft paper direct from the wholesale house.

On Dad's Christmas, everything had to fall into place, mistletoe in the doorway, the tree touching the ceiling. There must be a bottle of good bourbon whiskey for the Tom and Jerrys, three-star brandy burning on the plum pudding. The pudding must be made by Grandmother Salisbury's recipe, which her mother had brought from St. Ives—suet and brown sugar, real plums, raisins, citron, a little flour, very little, blanched almonds, candied fruit peel. It must be steamed for hours in a wash boiler, as it always had been. We put the puddings up in November, just before Thanksgiving, the whole family taking part, Dad chopping the fruit and suet, setting up the boiler with a wooden platform inside so the water would not splash into the pudding tins, we children decorating the puddings with a star of white almonds and jewels of candied fruit. This was ceremony, custom to be preserved, tradition which bound the present with the past. Continuity.

By the late 1920s, my father was hopelessly hard-pressed for money, much more hopelessly than I or even Mother had an idea. But Christmas was as usual. Dad struggled home with the "big present," a new Crosley cabinet radio to replace the tabletop model. As always, we were surprised, delighted, impressed. I, a little knowledgeable now about our finances (I had dropped out of school and was working on the *Minneapolis Journal* to earn money to continue at the University of Minnesota), wondered a bit. I knew Dad had been borrowing on his life insurance; that his pay at the factory had been cut and cut again; that he was barely hanging on to his job.

A few days later, I was rummaging for a collar button in the leather box he kept on top of his chiffonier, and found the forty-five-dollar pawn ticket. It was for Grandfather Salisbury's gold watch, the watch Dad carried for years, the one with the case engraved with birds, the open face and delicate hands, the heavy gold chain which he had worn across his vest. About the time I got out of high school, my sister, my mother and I had given Dad a slim, stylish, modern (and much less beautiful) watch, which he obligingly began to wear in his watch pocket. The fine old Elgin (I think it was an Elgin) went into the leather box along with his gold stick pins, his gold cuff links, his gold studs, his gold watch fobs, his father's gold-and-enamel Masonic emblems. Now the old gold fobs were gone. So were two heavy rings and all but one set of cuff links. So I knew. Christmas must be Christmas. I felt like crying. I thought of the five dollars I had spent for a bottle of Minnesota Thirteen; of the ten dollars for tickets to a university dance; of all the trivia I had wasted money on. What could I do? Never could I mention the pawn ticket. I waited until the day I was going back to school. Then I took fifty dollars of my savings and told my father I wanted to start reimbursing him for what he had paid for my first two years in college; that I would be earning money regularly now and this was the first installment on my debt. I had two new twenty-dollar bills and a new ten-dollar bill. He looked at the bills in surprise. "Do you really want to do this?" he asked. I said I did. He gave me a sharp glance, but apparently I passed muster. Thanks, he said, and put the money in his pocket. A couple of weeks later, I looked in the leather box. Grandfather's watch was back.

4 | The Ghetto

If anyone had told me that I was growing up in a ghetto, I would not have known what they meant. When I came home from my first day at Sumner School, my mother asked me about the children in my class. I said there were "five Sullivans." She was skeptical. So was my father. There were, in fact, five Solomons in my class. I knew no more of Jews than did my aunt Mary, growing up thirty years before in the Welsh community of the Western Avenue M.E. Church. She had a handsome young suitor, of whom she was very fond. One day a friend asked her, a bit hesitantly, if she knew that the young man was Jewish. "What do you mean?" my aunt asked. "Is that some kind of disease?"

In Miss MacPherson's first-grade classroom there were probably twenty-four children, of whom I suppose twenty were Jewish, one was black—a handsome boy named Booker T. Washington, who later became a professional singer—two were blond Scandinavian girls and one was myself. I do not believe any of us felt differences of creed, color or national origin. We wouldn't have understood that. Sumner School was about 95 percent Jewish, but years later, former classmates told me that neither they nor their parents had thought of it as a "Jewish" school. Nor did I. No one noticed that there were no Jewish teachers until, in 1918, Miss Levy appeared and took over grade three.

We all enjoyed the usual holidays—Christmas vacation, Lincoln's and Washington's birthdays, Easter vacation and, later on, Armistice Day, November 11. But the Jewish children got extra holidays—Rosh Hashanah, Yom Kippur and Passover. On those days, our little band of four or five goyim huddled in the deserted classroom while our teacher tried to find a way to occupy us. Outside on Sixth Avenue, my friends walked with their parents in their best clothes, or played shinny and marbles. It wasn't fair. When I grew a bit older, three of us would be selected as "writers" and go to the big Keneseth Israel Temple, very Orthodox, escorted by serious men in black suits. There we would record the financial pledges, the names, addresses and amounts. Writing was forbidden on the high holy days. For this we got a dollar. Almost every holiday, a worried old grandmother —a babushka, as I would come to say in Russia—would encounter me as I was walking home from school, grasp my wrist and ask me to light the stove in her kitchen. It was forbidden to light a fire until sundown, but if the little goy would do it she could get supper going. For this I got a nickel.

The nickels and dollars did not wash away the discrimination. I was a member of a small minority amid a large and powerful majority. We were friends, but there were lines I could not cross. School ended at three o'clock. I came home, had a glass of milk and a butter-and-sugar sandwich, and was ready to play. But my friends who went to *keder,* the Hebrew school, weren't free until five. I could see no reason, nor did they, why I shouldn't go to *keder* too. Finally, my mother went to the school and asked if I could be admitted. The rabbi was outraged. Positively not. This was not a school for the goyim.

In time I came to know a great deal about discrimination, about anti-Semitism in American country clubs and in the higher ranks of the Soviet government, about *numerus clausus* at Harvard and in the Academy of Science in Moscow. One of my childhood friends adopted a new, "non-Jewish" name and several of my Russian friends conveniently "lost" their internal passports and got new ones which specified their nationality as Russian, not Jewish. I had walked across the neatly kept ghetto in Warsaw, its carefully piled bricks and fresh-swept rubble marking where the streets and houses had been. I had met survivors of Auschwitz. I knew the results of the dirty little game that starts with "some of my best friends are Jews" and ends with extermination ovens. I went south in 1960 for the opening of the great struggle to bring America to live under the reality of our Constitution. I knew Malcolm X before he was murdered. I learned a good bit about the rawest edges of racism.

I hesitate to mention trivial childhood experiences in the context of the atrocities of our pseudo-civilized twentieth century, the rape and ravage of humanity which we have inflicted. Even so, let me say that it did me no harm and possibly a little good to suffer a teaspoon of discrimination. It was only a whiff, but it stuck in my nostrils and I grew up perhaps a fraction less racist than I would have been. I do not think it hurts to stand in the other fellow's shoes for a time. One of the glories of America is that we do mix; we can't help it. We are a restless, transient people. We arrive as aliens, each with his own tongue, religion, color. There is no American accent. A Frenchman who goes to Germany is French to the end of his life. If he comes here, he is American from the moment he asks a New York cop the way to the subway. It is fashionable now to denigrate the melting pot; now we are all ethnics and we fight to preserve our ethnicity. Good. I am proud of the mixture and oddity of my ethnic background, the English, the Welsh, the Scots, the Dutch and heaven knows what else, but I bless fate for letting me grow up in the most alien corner of that most Middle Western city of Minneapolis.

That corner was bisected by Sixth Avenue North, the Broadway of our Russian-Jewish quarter. It began with Rappaport's grocery at Sixth Avenue and Royalston, the store where my mother sent me for a loaf of bread (five cents), a quart of milk (five cents), a dozen eggs (twenty cents). The bread came unwrapped, the milk in a bottle and the eggs in a brown bag. In winter, Rappaport's windows were plated with frost. Beside the nickeled cash register stood a jar as big as Sinbad's, filled with dill pickles swimming in brine like small carp. There were barrels of flour and barrels of crackers, bushels of potatoes, onions and turnips, which began to sprout toward the end of winter. I didn't like Rappaport's, possibly because my playmates said the Rappaports yelled at children about their parents' bills. Next door was a tailor. When my uncle Scott Evans made trips to Minneapolis, stopping at our house, I took his suits to be pressed— twenty-five cents for pants, fifty cents for a suit. I didn't like this shop either, its air one-half naphtha, one-half steam. Nor did I like my uncle when he threw me a bright half dollar as tip. I didn't like being treated as a bellboy and I liked myself even less for keeping the money.

The center of our neighborhood was the "Yiddish store," Brochin's, at the corner of Sixth Avenue and Lyndale, across from the synagogue. Mr. Brochin was Orthodox, a strong Zionist with gray beard and black skullcap. His store breathed garlic—I could smell it when I passed by—and was renowned for its peppered corned beef sandwiches an inch thick, its garlicky Bobruisk sausage, its white-and-green dill pickles and sharply spiced green tomatoes. There were wooden bins of fresh-baked matzohs at Passover time; dried herring and sausage hung always from the ceiling. To the rear of the store were shelves of religious books, prayer shawls, mezuzahs and phylacteries. At Rosh Hashanah, Jewish New Year cards festooned the window. In this store I felt an alien. Here everyone spoke Yiddish and I was a goy. Here, I thought, were real Jews, Jews in black yarmulkes, with sidelocks and gray beards, women in gray shawls and black dresses who might have walked in from any village in the Pale. I could stand at the counter for ten minutes and no one would notice my blond presence. I didn't go into Brochin's often. Beyond it was Belzer's. A couple of years earlier Mr. Belzer had peddled fruit and vegetables door to door. Now he had his own store. In a room above was the Yiddish school. Then there was Hecker's, the kosher butcher. I watched Nathan Rosen letter the signs in Hecker's windows, carefully outlining and filling in with gold paint the Hebrew letters for "kosher," and later I watched the ritual slaughter of chickens. Farther up Sixth was Garfinkel's, where women brought in fresh horseradish roots and had them ground for Passover. That cost a nickel.

Down the street from Sumner School was Volkert's candy store. Volkert wore a beard and spoke fiercely, but no one was afraid of him. He lived off our pennies—penny candy, penny sticks of licorice, a penny handful of jelly beans, a penny's worth of horehound, penny grab bags. He sold "Brazil drink," a bit like cola, which I was forbidden to drink because my mother said it contained something very bad, by which she meant cocaine. Brazil drink cost two cents. You could buy valentines for a penny and miniature ice cream cones for three cents. Small bags of nibs or clay marbles cost two cents, aggies a nickel.

Beyond Sumner School was the Liberty Theater, where I saw the Pearl White serial, *The Perils of Pauline,* the whole sequence, almost peeing in my seat when Pearl was left until next week bound and gagged in the path of the onrushing express; or Pearl bound and gagged and about to be hurled from the railroad trestle; or Pearl with a revolver to her head and the police pounding at the door; or Pearl about to be thrown into the harbor, a weight tied to her feet. Poor Pearl! Lucky children! The Liberty Theater, ten cents admission, five cents for children plus one cent war tax. Charlie Chaplin in *Shoulder Arms,* Mary Pickford and Douglas Fairbanks and Bill Hart. All the greats. And more for my classmates—Molly Picon and stars of the Yiddish theater,

Jewish recitals and concerts. Out farther on Sixth Avenue was the Labor Lyceum, the socialist center, where debates took place about Russia, about the Bolsheviks, the Mensheviks and the Socialist Revolutionaries, about Samuel Gompers and the U.S. labor movement, about the political role of the immigrants. Of this I knew nothing, but later I was told by my old schoolmates that their families were divided into Reds and Whites, the Reds supporting the Revolution, the Whites against it. But their memories were muted. They could not recall being interested in these disputes; nor could they remember the arguments which embroiled their parents.

What they did remember and what I remembered was the life of the street: hitching my sled to the back of the horse-drawn sledges, running after the ice wagon in summer to pick up slivers, trailing the sprinkler wagons and letting the cold water spray over bare feet, picking soft tar from the pavement in the hot sun and chewing it (in place of Spearmint), my friends filling gunny sacks in winter with bits of coal dropped from the sledges.

In summer, the popcorn wagon came slowly around the curve, the steam whistle sounding, the popcorn man up to his waist in popcorn, endlessly shaking his wire basket over the gas flame, the horse halting as the kids gathered, a nickel a big white paper bag. And the waffle man. *The waffle man!* This was the event of my summer. He came seldom. Perhaps he was the only waffle man in town. I knew he was coming when I heard the sound of his bugle, silver and clear, beyond the corner; then the wagon came slowly into view, bigger than the popcorn wagon, nickel plate around the glass windows and a coal fire to heat the griddles. He made the waffles as we waited, dredging them in powdered sugar, we clutching our fifteen cents, clinging to the open window, observing his white surgeon's apron, his tall chef's cap, taller than the cap of the man who made pancakes in the window of Child's restaurant on Nicollet Avenue.

The street was alive even at night, when the bushwhackers came, the men crying: Extra! The first I remember was the *Titanic,* in the middle of the night, the terrible cry of the newsmen, the six-inch headlines, fat and black, the excitement of my father and mother, awakened after they had gone to bed. My God! Colonel Astor! Not his wife too! Not Mr. Guggenheim! Oh, Lord! The Strausses! Lord! I think I remember all that. I know I remember the *Lusitania.* A terrible sound. Extra! Extra! Ah, cover, cover the eyes of the newspaper, as Mayakovsky said. The bushwhackers were the Cassandras of my childhood, the criers of terrible tidings.

With hardly an exception, my friends and playmates in grammar school were boys and girls of Russian-Jewish origin—the Rosens, the Ravitskys, the Besners, children of the tidal wave that after 1905 poured out of the Pale of Settlement, the area of forced Jewish residence in Belorussia, the western Ukraine, eastern Poland. The families were poor. They ate potatoes and cabbage. Not much meat. In winter, mothers "sewed in" their children, in long underwear. They wore little cotton bags of foul-smelling asafetida around their necks to ward off colds. Once a week we were taken to the basement of Sumner School and inspected for nits—that is, lice. The school nurse ran a steel-tooth comb through our hair. If nits were discovered, the hair was doused in kerosene and inspected daily for a week.

Poor the youngsters were, but the Czar's Russia could have given America no greater gift. The more I came to know Russia in my long years in that country, the more profligate I realized she was. Ivan the Terrible expelled from Russia his favorite, the Danish ambassador, for daring to ask permission to marry a Russian woman. No foreign infidel could take from the homeland Russia's pride, her Russian souls. The same was true under Stalin and even under Brezhnev. Yet no land had on a scale so colossal driven people out—native Slavs, Catholics, Jews. Millions of Jews had fled: physicists, composers, writers, philosophers—an asset without price. No people has contributed more to the progress, enlightenment and evolution of America than these outcasts. What Russia might have been had she not savaged her best children, driven them out, committed genocide against herself, generation after generation, regime after regime, time without end! Russia's tragedy, America's fortune.

The brightest boy in my class was a wizened child named Solomon Wasserman. Every day Mrs. MacPherson allowed us to choose one song to sing. Solomon would always propose "The Worst Is Yet to Come." His father was a junkman, who came down the alley with a small cart and a bony horse, a brass bell jangling, crying: "Rags! Old rags! Iron! Old iron!" Before World War I was over, he had his own business. His son became a brilliant attorney, first in his class at the University of Minnesota. Most parents of my friends were tailors or handymen, or ran small stores. First they worked for someone and then they struck out on their own.

My mother thought our neighborhood was becoming a slum, but I don't believe she ever convinced my father of this. He saw Oak Lake as he had seen it with his father, planting the arborvitae tree and the red cedars on the lawn, putting in the thorn apple hedge, playing in amateur theatricals, the girls in Oriental costume and slant eyes, the boys in blackface, strumming their mandolins. To my playmates and their families, Oak Lake was a land beyond dreams. They had seen nothing like the Victorian houses, the lawns, the curving streets, the sidewalks and the elms in Bialystok or Pinsk. In the villages, they had lived in *izbas* of mud and reeds, with thatched roofs and clay floors. Now they occupied three thousand square feet in a mansion, bigger than the landlord's house. If your house backed up on the railroad yards, was anything more exciting?

They were right and Mother was wrong. Oak Lake was not a slum. True, the houses began to run down. They needed paint and the front steps sagged. The "best" families no longer lived here. The houses were divided into duplexes and then divided again. Ragged children played in the street and their parents spoke broken English. But what is a slum? A place of degradation, decay and despair? A den of crime? A breeder of disease of body and soul? Oak Lake was none of these. It acquired a character of its own. Certainly it was no longer the lace-curtain neighborhood it had been when my grandfather built his house, although at dusk it might look much the same. Gloom veiled the scars as I watched out the bay window and saw the lamplighter swing down Highland Avenue, pause at the lamp beside our lawn, snake his long pole under the glass and flip on the gas. Now the lamplighting of Oak Lake was let by contract to the Besikof family, poor, very recent immigrants who ran a tiny store on Lyndale Avenue. The lamplighting contract gave them status and they began their upward move. Soon there were two Jewish policemen on the force, named Cohen and Ginsberg, assigned to our neighborhood. But there was little crime. Oh, yes, occasionally a kid would swipe an apple or a banana at Belzer's or a handful of candy at Volkert's. There were family quarrels and Saturday night drunks.

Sumner was one of fifteen or twenty Minneapolis schools built in the 1880s of cream brick. We pupils considered it a very good school and I think it was, tough but not bad. The "bad" schools were Blaine and Grant, just adjacent. Probably the kids at these schools thought Sumner "very bad." I was small and wiry and tried to steer clear of bigger, tougher boys. There was a pecking order, based on size and strength. Big boys picked on me; I picked on kids my size or smaller and on a boy named Sam, who was bigger but slightly feeble of mind. We threw small stones or cinder at each other—the bigger boys at me; I at Sam and smaller kids, and so on. One afternoon, the worm turned. As I was dodging the pebbles of the older boys, Sam threw one and hit me on the forehead. This was lèse majesté. I threw a stone at Sam and hit a big boy. The big boys joyfully chased me from the schoolyard, over a fence and down a long alley. None of their stones caused any damage; Sam's had given me a good whack. It was O.K. for the older boys to go after me; but Sam had violated the rules. Unless I put him down, I would drop below him in the pecking order. I insisted that Reuben join me in ambushing Sam. Sam had to be given a lesson. Reuben couldn't understand, but came along because I was so excited. Soon Sam appeared, on his way home. We showered him with stones and he ran off crying. That settled the matter—so I thought. But the bruise on my face brought questions at home and I had to confess I had been fighting with Sam, deleting the rest of the story. My mother was outraged. She was not going to have her angel child assaulted by a ruffian. Father donned his Home Guard uniform. Uncle Andrew put on his black suit (by this time I knew it was his bill-collecting suit—he worked for a collection agency). Off they went "to have a little talk"—that is, to intimidate the parents of the addle-witted Sam. The mission was successful; Sam and I never fought again; but to this day I have a guilty conscience.

By now I was beginning to make discoveries. I got very good grades in school. I was held in high regard by my family. But on the street, it was wit and fists that counted. In the Jewish community of my friends I was a minority of one, but actually a cherished minority. Despite my separateness, I was protected. Over and above this was another level of protection, that of my family, and this stemmed from intangibles which I could only faintly perceive— something to do with our prestige. It was not wealth, although in the neighborhood of the poor we were rich. It had to do with being a symbol of the greater community. In the city of Minneapolis our family was not distinguished. But in Oak Lake we were first.

By the time I was in third grade, I usually walked to school through the alley that bisected our block. Ice-clogged in winter and muddy in summer, it was my favorite route. Some families kept horses in their barns and many had chickens or pigeons. A rooster woke me every morning. There were several cows and two or three goats. And Smellakahorse. Smellakahorse was a stableman, but I don't think he worked for anyone. He lived in the alley and I never heard him called anything but Smellakahorse. He was a shifty, red-eyed man dressed in a ragged half-coat, horseman's breeches and patched boots. He slept with the horses in a stable and came down the alley with a bowlegged gait, and I suppose he was usually drunk. He was the only unclassified unemployed person I encountered regularly in my childhood. That does not count tramps. Tramps were normal. They came to the back door and offered to do chores for a handout. Sometimes, if Mother was in the mood, she would let them chop some wood, fix a storm door or rake the lawn, then let them sit in the kitchen and eat a plate of bacon and eggs or a sandwich. Sometimes she would give them a half loaf of bread and send them on their way. Sometimes she just slammed the door. Tramps were not men to be frightened of. They came and went and sometimes you were sorry for them, sometimes not. Gypsies were different. Gypsies were dangerous. They kidnapped children. They stole. They had camps, traveled in canvas-covered wagons and spoke a language of their own. When Gypsies appeared in the neighborhood, we ran home and told Mother and she locked the door.

I loved the alley. I liked backyards better than front yards; they gave me a feel of things. One afternoon in 1920, I saw the initials BYOL lettered in chalk on a back fence. I was disappointed to learn that they only meant Bring Your Own Liquor (Prohibition had set in). I had hoped they were a secret code. About the same time, I saw the initials KKK. I knew what they meant. The Klan was on the move in the Midwest. I had not been permitted to see *The Birth of a Nation*. Probably my mother thought it cheap and sensational. My mother's movie censorship was puzzling. She refused to let me see any Charlie Chaplin pictures. He was "vulgar." I was permitted to see Buster Keaton and Harold Lloyd. Fatty Arbuckle was "cheap." Pola Negri was "too exciting for children." So was Erich von Stroheim. That meant too sexy. *Orphans of the Storm* was O.K.

When I saw the initials KKK on the fence, I began to look for Klan activity: robed men, burning crosses, night riders. I was disappointed. None appeared in our neighborhood. This did not mean I was anti-black, anti-Jewish or anti-Catholic; it reflected my passion for secret societies. I yearned to belong, as my grandfather Salisbury had, to the Masonic order and used to dress up in the attic in his Knights Templar embroidered hat, wear his ceremonial sash and silver-plated sword. I started a secret society and called it Kappa Kappa Kappa. I was the only non-Jewish member. We had a codebook, passwords and secret meetings. It was a bust. There wasn't any "secret," my friend Reuben couldn't remember the password and we had nothing to do at our meetings.

One winter day after I had started at North High, I was kicking through the slush in the alley and found a photograph on cardboard lying under an abandoned wagon frame. I picked it up and almost burned my fingers. It was a picture of a dark-haired young woman, bare to the waist. I had never seen a photograph of a naked woman and was so excited I almost jumped up and down. I hadn't imagined that such photos existed. I studied the full bare breasts, the nipples, the navel, in painful ecstasy. I didn't dare take it home. Nor did I want to lose it. I hid it carefully under the wagon box. The next day it was gone.

Sex had become an obsession to me and to my classmates. At Boy Scout camp that summer, one boy in my tent lay in bed all day and all night, playing with his penis. He didn't get up for reveille. He didn't go swimming. He didn't go to meals. He wore an embarrassed grin and told us he couldn't stop himself. It went on and on. We marveled at him. Boys from neighboring tents came to see. Finally, he was taken to the hospital. We shook our heads. It was an extreme case, but there was some of him in all of us.

In the study hall at North High, the pages of the big Webster's dictionary where the "dirty words" were located were grimy with our finger marks. I was an ardent Boy Scout and attended meetings of Troop 2 every Friday at the Church of the Redeemer, the Universalist church. Now the meetings acquired a new attraction. They were usually finished by a quarter to nine.

We—that is, four or five of the older boys—would run top speed a half mile across town to the Gayety burlesque theater on Washington Avenue. The oldest-looking boy bought second-balcony tickets and we raced up to "nigger heaven," looking straight down on the stage, and waited for Carrie Finnell, our idol. Carrie Finnell was a robust woman, the epitome of the beef trust. She came on stage, a shimmering sequin cape covering her extensive anatomy. To the traditional beat she began the classic divestiture, first the cape, revealing an equally sequined gown, slit to her hips, which were richly proportioned. Then off came elbow-length gloves and all the rest, until she stood center stage, as we Scouts, saliva dripping from our mouths, preposterously excited, held our breaths. She stood, the music silent, in a dazzling sequined cache-sexe, with glittering red-tasseled cones glued to the nipples of her great bosoms. She stood, an utterly magnificent woman, all haunch and paunch, belly and breast, shoulder and buttocks, thighs and pelvis and mane of peroxide hair. This was what we came for. The band struck up and Carrie Finnell did her bumps and grinds. Then, slowly at first, but with mounting speed, she began to gyrate her breasts, the glittering tassels whirling like spinning tops. Around and around the circumferential bosoms spun—clockwise. Then came a sharp break in the music. Another moment of silence. Around and around the breasts spun—counterclockwise. It was unreal, unbelievable, a miracle. We gasped for breath. A quick flash and she was gone. We Boy Scouts scampered down the stairs, with flushed faces, tumescent bodies, glazed eyes, numbed brains, to run full tilt to our comfortable, quiet, middle-class homes and apologize to our mothers for being a bit late because we had had to stay for some extra practice at making fire by friction.

The world I've written about is gone—gone with Oak Lake. The Liberty Theater is gone. Not a brick remains of Sumner School. There is no evidence that Brochin's store existed. The house where my friend Reuben lived disappeared long ago. So did the fire station Grandfather Evans built, the belching steamer and the troika of gray horses. All of it gone. And 107 Royalston lives only in my imagination. Not a stick, stone, tree, shrub. Not a gingerbread cornice or a granite block from the foundation. Even the alley is gone. Royalston Avenue survives in one signpost which leads nowhere. There is no street. The Rus-

sian-Jewish neighborhood today could be the landscape of Anywhere, U.S.A.—flat-top manufacturing plants, a warehouse or
two, acres of blacktop, and vacant land grown up to weeds. The
bulldozers came one day and left nothing. Well, that is not quite
true. I did find a few feet of the old brick paving where Royalston Avenue began, warm red brick, the kind they don't use anymore.

One building survives. It is a vaguely Gothic structure set
back from Floyd B. Olson Boulevard, the artery whose construction destroyed Sixth Avenue. It stands four blocks west of where
Sumner School used to be. It is a building I know well and have
known since a year or two after it was built, in 1915, and I began
to visit it on Saturday mornings. This is the Sumner Branch
Library.

In 1965, I went back to the library and spoke at its fiftieth
anniversary. Mae Wessberg, long since Mrs. W. H. Hamilton of
Dayton, Ohio, was there. She was the first librarian. Mayor
Naftalin was there. So were many survivors of the old days. "It
was our university," one man said. It was, too. Here they
learned English in special classes and read the papers, both English and Yiddish. Here they learned to be Americans. A small
building. It cost the Carnegie people $25,000.

I talked a bit that night about how the other kids and I used to
struggle home with armloads of books. There was nothing like a
library to us. A friend of mine in high school named Alice Gates
wouldn't say yes when her husband-to-be proposed until he had
answered positively her question: "Do you have your library
card?" I talked to my old friends, so many of whom had roots in
Russia, of my years in the Soviet Union and what a remarkable
institution was our public library with its open shelves, no locks,
no bars. I explained that in Moscow the libraries were closed institutions. The Lenin Library, the equivalent of the Library of
Congress, was a citadel of security. Libraries there were like the
three circles of hell. No ordinary person could use them, but a
student or scholar with a certificate had access to ordinary
books. That was the outer ring. Then there was a category of
books for which you had to get special permission. That was the
second ring. Then there were the books only those with security
clearance could use, the third ring, books about Russia's own
past, the political disputes and controversies of the Soviet years,
books of the disgraced, the nonpersons—Khrushchev after his

fall, Stalin after his fall, anything about Trotsky or Bukharin or Radek or Zinoviev or Kamenev, the great figures of the Revolution. And to anything sensitive about Lenin or great areas of prerevolutionary history, there was no access. It was, I said, as though they had cut the great oak of Russian history at the base and then sawed off the limbs, one by one.

Here in the United States, you could walk into the Sumner Branch Library and read what you wanted. No questions asked. If they didn't have the book you wanted, they would get it. That, I said, was one of the elements of American strength and the genius of the American idea.

I surprised my old friends whose fathers and mothers had come from Russia. They knew the Sumner Library was an institution of marvels. But they had not realized how savagely Russia had crippled itself. I could not help thinking of the library's origin, the grant from the funds of the immigrant millionaire Andrew Carnegie. No matter what evils he committed in amassing his fortune, he had planted the best of acorns in the American soil. The Sumner Library had not cost enough to buy the wheels of a super-superbomber today or a thimbleful of nuclear explosive. But to me the contribution of the library to America's security outweighed all the MX's we might build. It had staying power. So did the people who learned to be Americans within its modest walls.

5 | Dr. Salisbury's Son

It was a crisp February Saturday, sun shining on a white world of snow new fallen, sky blue, no wind—the best of Minnesota days. I watched at the bay window for my father. Saturday was a half day at the factory, the Northern Bag Company, where he would work his whole life, starting out dark, thin, aristocratic, looking very young, working until, gray, worn, thin, tired, sad, bent, he died June 6, 1944, D-Day in Normandy, lingering only a few days after the stroke felled him as he walked out of the factory. I was at an American shuttle bombing base at Poltava, deep in the Ukraine, the cherry trees in blossom, hopelessly distant, when I got the news that he was ill; a few days later I was in Moscow, trying to figure out how to get back to Minneapolis. It was midafternoon and I was whiling away the time playing poker in the Metropol Hotel with my friends Bill Lawrence of *The New York Times,* Ed Angly of the *Chicago Sun,* Dave Nichol of the *Chicago Daily News* and Dick Lauterbach of *Life* magazine. Mike Handler, my UP colleague, walked into the room, motioned me over and said: "Your father is dead. The cable just came." "Thanks," I said, turned, picked up my hand and threw a chip into the pot.

Back on that diamond of a February day I saw my father coming around the curve of Royalston Avenue, walking fast, a steady countryman's gait, his head high, wearing a dark winter fedora and a velvet-collared black overcoat. All his life he wore fedoras, a woolly fedora in winter, a sleek gray fedora in spring and autumn; in June he donned a panama with black band and wore it until Labor Day. He was a Victorian in dress, and wore striped cambric shirts with detachable collars and starched cuffs, brass collar buttons, plain gold cuff links, and a small gold lion's head stickpin with a tiny ruby eye in dark blue, dark purple or dark, dark carmine figured silk ties. He preferred pin-stripe suits, and I never saw him with his coat and vest off in the office, even in steamy August. In summer he changed to tan linen suits, never baggy, never wrinkled. I thought he was very handsome with his Indian high cheekbones, aquiline nose, black hair,

41

blue eyes, set chin. When he grew older he looked like Lincoln, not so tall, but with Lincoln's deep-set eyes and melancholy, the melancholy of a man who believed he had failed—failed his wife, his family, his heritage. He could not have been more wrong.

On this particular bright Saturday as he rounded the curve, his step was that of a comfortable paterfamilias who soon would experience his greatest pleasure, reunion with his wife and children in his own home. I saw that he was carrying a small packet and I knew what it contained. I jumped from the window, away from the bubble that stared back at me, and I ran to my mother: "Daddy's coming!"

Then he was at the front door being kissed by his wife, herself happy and gay, her waist-long hair a golden mass, blue eyes sparkling behind golden pince-nez attached to gold button on frothy white shirtwaist. He put the packet in Mother's hands, reached into an inner pocket, extracted a small manila envelope sealed with waxed red string, handed this to her, then looked at Janet and myself in mock surprise as we jumped up and down, shouting: "What's for us?"

This was the Saturday ceremonial. It occurred every two weeks. We went into the dining room, the sun sweeping through the stiff Brussels curtains and pocking highlights on the black carved furniture. Mother's quick fingers untwisted the red twine and out sparkled a handful of golden coins, six of them, six twenty-dollar gold pieces, heavy, almost greasy to the touch, rolling out on the sunlit table, my father's salary at the factory. No one was paid by check, it was always by cash—factory people once a week in big green bills and silver coins, office heads twice a month in gold. Class-conscious money. Mother turned to the packet. "And what is this?" she asked as she always asked. "Open it! Open it!" Janet and I demanded. Slowly she pulled away the white paper, exposing a box covered in crinkly gold imprinted with the name "Ivy." It was, as we all knew it would be, the pound of chocolate which Dad brought home from Ivy's shop on Nicollet Avenue every two weeks. We were permitted one chocolate each, one for Janet, one for me. This was grownups' candy. When we were put down for naps, Dad came into the room. We appealed for candy. He had none. Then, mysteriously, he pulled back the pillow and a gumdrop was discovered; doodle candy I called it, God knows why. How did he do it? I never figured it out.

The plant closed at 1 P.M. on Saturday. Every day the factory shift went to work at seven. You could hear the seven o'clock factory whistles all over town. The office started at seven-thirty. Dad's day ended at five. He spent his life on that schedule. I do not believe there was a single day in fifty years of work that gave him pleasure.

The Northern Bag Company was an extension of the flour-milling industry. Minneapolis was two things: lumber and flour. It was the biggest milling center in the world. I grew up to the smell of sawdust burning, mountains of sawdust endlessly burning at the Camden Place mills above St. Anthony's Falls, the pungent pitch itching my nostrils. One cold spring day in 1919, I watched the last log drive down the Mississippi, the logs filling the river bank to bank, great booms to corset them, the jacks leaping log to log, timber to timber, jam to jam, spikes on heels, peaveys and cant hooks in hand. The air was thick in spring with the smoke of sawdust fires and thicker in autumn with the smoke of forest fires, the Hinckley fire (which my mother narrowly escaped—it killed more than four hundred people—riding out on the Northern Pacific train; the train carried three hundred fifty people, and engineer Jack Root's hands were burned to the throttle when they got to Duluth), the Moose Lake–Cloquet fire, which darkened Minneapolis and drove deer, bear and birds a hundred miles south, a horned owl sitting one morning in the oak tree, staring in my window. My father's Home Guard regiment went north and he helped stack burned bodies on the railroad platform. The smell of the charred corpses haunted him for years.

Before I was born, northern Minnesota had been cut over, burned over, ravaged by the timber barons. Minnesota was the happy land of barons: timber barons, Shevlin, Heffelfinger, Walker, Weyerhaeuser; milling barons, Washburn, Crosby, Bell, Pillsbury; railroad barons, Jim Hill, who fought Jay Gould and E. H. Harriman to a standstill; iron barons, Gary, Frick, Carnegie. The timber barons beat all. They slashed away the lordly Norway pine which mantled northern Minnesota, Wisconsin and Michigan, slamming the logs down rivers to the mills, leaving behind the raddled earth, a ruin that had no equal until our petrochemicals turned the forests of Vietnam into hell. So technology advances. Forty years after the devastation, I began to canoe in the North Woods along the Canadian border. My friends and I had to pick our trails with care to bypass tamarack swamps, log-choked streams, square miles of stumps that looked like Belleau Wood, a monument to the Almighty Dollar.

The milling business was different. No one thought badly of milling wheat. No one thought badly of turning the prairie, of bringing the plow to the soil. This was man's duty. Man lived by the sweat of his brow and bread was the stuff of life. No one regretted the high grass that extended like a sea from the Mississippi to the Missouri and beyond, the grass that nourished the buffalo, the Sioux, the Chippewa, in a symbiotic life. No one thought of that. To bring plow to prairie, to break the sod (and break the men)—this, as I grew up to understand, was civilization, progress, turning land to use; *use* was the word. I could not have imagined dust bowls, erosion, red gullies that bloodied the hills, irrevocable annihilation of earth and plant and animal. To be American, I understood, was to be hell-bent for change. Away with the prairie that stretched to the horizon and on to the next horizon. Bring in the plow. Rip the earth. Endure in a sod hut with your bone-skinny wife and the bone-skinny children. Build a log cabin. Bury your wife and get another, a strong young one. Work. Work. Work.

This was the philosophy on which I was raised, the pioneer spirit, boosterism, as Sinclair Lewis called it, the American way, as Henry Luce would say. Not until I read the novels of Willa Cather, O. E. Rölvaag and Frank Norris did I begin to see what was wrong. The grain poured into the mills at St. Anthony's Falls. I remember my pride, my wonder and my fear when my father showed me the falls, turbulent brown water, and the gray mills that lined the river like battlements. (St. Anthony's Falls does not turn a wheel today; not a flour mill, not one, remains; water power is out; Washburn Crosby is General Mills, big on fast foods, toys, electronics and frosted cornflakes.) St. Anthony's Falls ground the wheat of Minnesota, the Dakotas, Montana, all bound together by Jim Hill's iron rails, the Northern Pacific, the Great Northern, the Burlington. Into Minneapolis poured the wheat and from the mills flour flowed to the world.

The North Dakota farmers took a different view of all this. They saw the millers as part of a crooked combine with the railroads, the elevator men, the bankers, the speculators of the Chicago wheat pit, an unholy alliance that rigged prices and drove the farmers to the wall. The monopoly was the blight of humanity, capitalists ruled the world by money, by money-love. The oratory of the Populists, the Nonpartisan League, was florid but it made the point.

Untimely thoughts. So these would have seemed in the living

room at 107 Royalston, where my father and my uncle smoked their cigars and pondered the state of the world. Untimely? Revolutionary! But the blood sagas of the barons were ready meat for my greedy ears. These were told and relished: the seven Merritt brothers, who discovered the Mesabi iron range, and the steel barons who stole it and sent them to ruin; Jim Hill, sitting in his St. Paul castle and hurling back the challenge of Jay Gould, devils condemning each to perdition and Archbishop Ireland saving Jim Hill's soul on his deathbed, a pretty penny for the Church; the bold young logger who married the old timber baron's daughter and then tossed the old man into the river with a twist of his peavey, deaf to his cries, and inheriting the fortune. What was truth? Did it matter? These were tales of giants that illuminated the lust, the greed, the plunder.

I do not suppose a man less apt at business existed than my father, an artist; not a great artist, but a wonderfully satisfying one, with a sure hand, an eye for likeness. He enjoyed sketching still lifes, dogs, cats, horses and children, and made a hobby of rather elaborate wood carving, for he loved the textures of woods. He enjoyed the work of William Morris and the handicrafts of the Oneida community. He liked color and succumbed to the 1880s rage for Rosa Bonheur, Edwin Landseer, Delacroix, Henri Rousseau; he collected exotica: Persian rugs, Armenian brasses, Turkish water pipes. He pored over architectural journals and books and planned every detail of the house he hoped to build on the Mississippi riverbank. His bent was well developed before he entered the University of Minnesota in 1889, son of a moderately well-to-do and popular doctor, an attractive young man with attractive friends, men and women. He was a sensitive amateur photographer, and left a collection of plates that exquisitely illuminate the life of Oak Lake Addition and the early years of his marriage, not unlike Leonard Dakin's record of Cherry Valley, New York. He developed and printed his own work. His pictures were tart, simple, evocative, often humorous. He had a good voice, loved to sing, strummed a good banjo and a sentimental mandolin. Later he taught himself to play a squeaky violin to accompany my mother's rather boisterous piano. She played the "Warsaw" Concerto with such gusto that I grew up thinking it portrayed the Battle of Warsaw. Dad took romantic leads in amateur theatricals. He was very fond of pretty girls. He was a fine hunter, spending afternoons in the nearby countryside shooting partridge and ducks. He owned a beautiful English shotgun, which he sold when he was desperate for money. He taught me to shoot and shoot well. He believed in guns and would stand for no nonsense where they were concerned, a lesson I learned from him. He never raised his voice.

He told me once that he had expected to study medicine and go into partnership with his father, but when Dr. Salisbury fell ill he told Percy that the life of the doctor was too hard. You could not do your duty to your patients without neglecting your family. He forbade his son to take up medicine. So Percy Pritchard Salisbury, a little solemn, shy, reticent, twenty-one years old, standing in the red cherry library where Dr. Salisbury spent his last year of life, swore to his father that he would not become a doctor. I think he would have been a grand doctor. His gray-blue eyes could see into your soul. But I think his father was right. A family doctor ninety years ago needed an iron constitution and an iron will. My father was not made of steel. The profession would have killed him as it did his father.

Now my father was free to follow his bent, to become an architect. But Grandfather Salisbury's death coincided with the panic of '93. His money was tied up in two Minneapolis banks which failed. The money his patients owed him was in the same closed banks. My father took up the unpleasant task of bill collecting. He did not do well. Mary Pritchard Salisbury was a demanding woman in the Victorian tradition. With the death of her husband, she took to her bed and never emerged, placing her son Percy in thrall for seven years until she died, in 1900. He turned away from the mandolin, blackface theatricals, sketching still lifes, picnics in the country with saucy Maude Derickson or pretty Josie Mann. He spent a year or two trying to collect bills and then found a job with a firm run by an upstate New Yorker and a handful of men from Dundee. They had set up a bag business in Minneapolis. Dundee was the milling center of Scotland; Minneapolis, of the U.S.A. There was bound to be a profit, and indeed, there was a smart ha'penny and a deal more for the Christians, the Falconers and the Skinners. They knew their business to the last strand of jute, the toughest hemp and the stoutest cotton. Into the ranks of this cold-eyed company Percy Salisbury entered and there he was to remain for the rest of his life. There could not have been a greater misfit.

I didn't know that. I was fascinated by my father; by the six doubloons twice a month; by the miniature flour samples he gave us, doll sacks bearing the Gold Medal label just like the big sacks; by the curious stamps ripped off letters from Scotland and India. Mother loved the lengths of Osnaburg Dad brought home, seconds, and the misprints, the flour sacks with wrong labels or bled colors. Bleach them and they made dish towels or even curtains. I loved the mill: the pounding of the presses, the huge stamping machines, the automatic sewing machines, the looms, the smell of jute and Osnaburg and ink.

Very early I knew that my father was different from other men. My uncle Andrew, handsome, brown-haired, pipe-smoking, loved to talk about his receiverships; sometimes he brought home a suitcase of dress materials, thread, ribbon, buttons, buckles, linings, from a bankrupt shop for my aunt Mary, who was a dressmaker. He talked of crooks and crookedness, of sly tricks and coups. John Dort would talk all afternoon about the Milwaukee railroad, and Charley Gaskill, who sold coats and jackets on the road, couldn't wait, relaxing in the front porch swing, lighting up his seegar, to begin talking of "conditions." "Conditions" were never, never good, but they were always expected to get better. Dad loved a good Havana cigar. He smoked with the rest. But I never heard him say one word about "conditions" or the bag business. He listened. More likely he didn't listen, his mind far away in that secret place I never penetrated.

I think the men from New York State and Scotland with whom he worked liked my father in their dry, dusty way. Of course, they would have been the last to say it. I think they liked him because he was totally loyal, totally conscientious. He did everything he was asked and did it promptly and accurately. I don't think he ever initiated anything.

I believe the men from Dundee knew that Dad didn't belong with them, that he marched to another tune, but they respected him because he never complained, and could be depended upon. I don't know how many times he told me: "If a thing is worth doing, it is worth doing well." Usually he said this after I had made a mess of something—splitting the wood I was driving a nail into or failing to shake out the clinkers before putting coal on the fire. He was not given to aphorisms and this is the only one I remember his repeating. I think he lived by it and the Scots respected him for it.

To this day I do not know what Dad did at the factory. Oh, I know one thing: He locked up the safe at night. The safe was

Dad's responsibility. He closed it in the evening and opened it in the morning, last man out, first man in. A responsible job—well, a servitor's job, as became clear after they put him out on the factory floor, on his feet all day at nearly seventy and made to understand it was just a matter of charity, keeping him on. I never knew what he did in the factory. I didn't want to ask, because I knew he didn't want me to know. But he continued to lock the safe at night and open it in the morning. At 2 A.M. he would awaken, possessed with certainty that he had not locked the safe. He could see it standing open. He would slip from bed, quickly dress and walk to the plant, a three-mile walk in the dead of night, often in the dead of winter, temperature twenty below zero. He would walk to the plant, let himself in with his passkey, check with the night watchman and visit the big safe. It was always locked. So he would sit in the office from 3 A.M. or 4 A.M., shivering in his overcoat until the first shift began arriving and he could get a cup of coffee. Dear, dear man.

The gold pieces. The war years were golden for the millers. For the farmers, as well. Wheat two dollars a bushel. Before the war it had been fifty cents, and there were times when you couldn't give wheat away. Two-dollar wheat! Minneapolis couldn't ship enough flour to match the U-boat sinkings. Grain poured like a golden river into the elevators, siphoned from the boxcars, the chaff filling the air. Wheat, wheat, wheat, the combines working through the night, migrant labor in Gateway Square, shipping by the thousands to North Dakota and the Red River of the North, every empty freight car filled with the 'boes, going north to work the harvest, to Fargo, to Bismarck, to Great Falls, golden grain pouring into Pillsbury A, pouring into Washburn Crosby Main, twenty-four hours a day, bags, bags, bags, never enough, bags for flour, bags for grain, bags for the army, three shifts a day, the money rolled in. Yes. By now there must have been another gold piece or two in the manila envelope.

One day I heard my father telling my mother the news. Old George H. Christian had died, the founder of the mill. He had left the business to the "boys," all the stock, and Dad along with the others. "We will never have to worry again." I can hear the sound of his voice. Bubbling. Happy. "How much? How much?" Mother asked. Dad's reply meant nothing. It was—what?—fifteen thousand, twenty thousand, a little more, a little less. It was just grand. I don't know what Mother and Dad did that night.

Probably they went to Rogers' Café, *the* night spot in Minneapolis, the only one, the one with the artificial waterfall and the mirror as you went downstairs from the street, and they drank champagne.

That night Dad laughed. Well, you know, he said, George H. was a skinflint to the last. He didn't *give* us the stock, as he could have just as well. What he did was to let us *buy* the stock. Not that it makes any difference. It pays for itself from the dividends. Isn't that like him? Mother couldn't understand. I couldn't. But it didn't make any difference. Don't bother. It's just a technicality. The dividend is so high it will buy the stock in three years. It's just one last Scots touch—from beyond the grave. Dad laughed. He loved the Scots that night.

Dad was easy, relieved. We'll pay off the mortgage on 107, the one Dr. Salisbury took out, he said, and he began looking over the plans for the Mississippi River house. The house would be a clean white colonial. I was disappointed. I had fallen in love with England and I longed for a house of exposed beams, plaster and fake thatch, Anne Hathaway's cottage.

Happy days. There must have been more gold pieces in the envelope. I heard all the talk and then it stopped. Just like that. The grain boom burst. In Minnesota, 1929 happened in 1920. The mills ground to a halt. You couldn't give bags away. Government contracts were canceled. Business—there was no business. But what difference did it make? The stock put Dad on easy street and it paid for itself, didn't it? Just an old man's whim against giving something away, wasn't it?

Like hell it was. There were no dividends. Not in 1920. Not in '21. Not in '22. If you wanted your stock, you put up your money. If you didn't have the money—too bad. You couldn't expect the company to go broke paying for stock that was supposed to be bought, could you? That busted it. No more dream. Oh, it was 1929, all right, but nobody yet knew there would be a 1929. For Minnesota it would be 1929 until 1929, and then 1929 would go on forever.

What was a man to do? The look that came to my father's face would stay there for the rest of his life. It just settled down. Not a mask, just a tiredness, a terrible tiredness.

6 | My Son the Writer

There were two strands in my early life. Dad's philosophy was hard work and plain talk. He permitted himself few illusions and no complaints. He was descended from a line of diligent countrymen, farmers one generation after another since the Salisburys made their way to Rhode Island around 1640, marrying wives of the same English yeoman stock. True, there had been two great-great-uncles who went into the book-and-newspaper business in upstate New York, and my favorite ancestor, my great-great-uncle Hiram, a peddler, carpenter, farmer, man of all trades and diarist, a true Yankee—but these were exceptions. My grandfather Augustus Harrison Salisbury, for whom I was, alas, named (his birth having occurred in the year of William Henry Harrison's election to the presidency, 1840), was the first to break the pattern of yeomanry.

My father discovered that the Salisbury family motto was *Fractes non flectes,* which he translated to mean "We break before we bend." He liked that. He was not a bender. He stood by his principles, mistaken as they sometimes might be. It didn't matter to him that the motto had belonged to some other Salisbury family. He made it his own and painted a fine coat of arms, a lion on a red background, enamel paint on black walnut cut from an old table leaf. Very handsome. And he painted one for his mother's family, the Pritchards, as well, though he disliked the Pritchards; they were Welsh and he believed in the nursery rhyme "Paddy was a Welshman, Paddy was a thief." Nonetheless, he painted a handsome Pritchard coat of arms, a glorious green dragon with red blood on its claws. No one I knew had coats of arms. I delighted in showing them off. So did Dad.

With his plainspoken, rather puritanical background (the Salisburys probably were Puritans when they left England), my father had never expected a ship to come in for him. Anything he got he would have to work hard for. When old George Christian willed him the stock, it threw him off balance. For a while he tried to believe that fortune had blessed him, but the 1920 panic brought him back to reality, to that despond which would govern the rest of his life.

I do not want to suggest that my father was a latter-day Puritan. Indeed, he had no religious beliefs. I discovered by accident one day that he was an atheist, a devotee of Tom Paine, whose *Age of Reason* he thrust into my hands when I raised some question about God. He did not believe in God or the hereafter, he said, although to that moment he had never mentioned this and, as a matter of form, at my mother's urgent bidding, he had permitted himself to join the Universalist Church at the same Easter service during which Janet and I did. Once when he was convalescing in the hospital after a prostate operation, a minister wandered in to "give him comfort." "Get out of my room this minute," Dad responded, "or I'll throw this at you." He delighted in telling the story. "This" was a urine jar connected to him by a long rubber tube.

I was quick to share my father's skepticism. I attended Sunday school and baited our patient teacher about the biblical fables. Later, in Moscow, I fell in love with the Russian Orthodox service, the magnificent ceremonials at Easter midnight, the chanting, the incense, the censers, the icons, the banners, the robes of golden thread, the beauty and piety of the peasant believers. I thought it a faith totally suitable to Russia, even to Bolshevik Russia. When I finally came to St. Peter's in Rome, very late in life, I knew with no doubt that this was the seat of the earth's power. I could feel the waves of magnetism radiating from the great dome, the pillars that reach to heaven, the very walls. But belief was another thing. I was glad there were people who believed; I thought belief had, despite many evils, been a positive force in the world. But I have always felt more comfortable standing outside looking in.

My father's acceptance of the unpromising hand that life was bound to deal him was not the style of my mother. She, too, was half Welsh and she shared Dad's distaste for the race. She hated her Welsh father, the Welshiness of him, his hymn-singing, his Sabbath-keeping, prayer meetings, hellfire and damnation. Only one thing she conceded to the Welsh—the singing. She and her family loved to sing and spent hours around the piano in the red-brick castle on Russell Avenue and, after her father's death, in a modest house not far from the Western Avenue M.E. Church.

For all her hatred of the Welsh, particularly of her father and his friends who used to sit around the table talking Welsh, roaring in laughter at Welsh jokes, making snide remarks about the non-Welsh, she and her brothers and sisters had absorbed much of the Welsh poetry, the music, the belief in magic, the Celtic wonders which were preserved in that impossible land under the lock of its impossible tongue—a belief in treasure, lost and found, in pots of gold at the end of the rainbow (how often I ran and ran across fields and through the woods as a youngster to see if I could find where the rainbow ended), in titles and prince-doms, in kingdoms seized by rude and savage Angles, Saxons, Normans, in hidden wills, missing ships' captains and their cargoes, mysterious prophecies.

And of the Courts of Chancery—above all, of the Courts of Chancery. I did not have to read Dickens to learn about Chancery. Of the Courts I heard at my mother's knee. She firmly believed lost fortunes lay hidden there, bound in the red cord of the solicitors' files in the Inner Temple, sleeping through decades and centuries, waiting for a bold, brave discoverer (myself) to appear and make good the claim.

It was not clear to me then nor is it today exactly whose fortune had been hidden in the dusty documents, but I never doubted it was there. When in 1942 I was assigned to London for United Press, a light came into Mother's eyes. Of course I would be too busy at first, and of course the documents might not have survived the blitz—but at least I would be on the scene, a stone's throw from the Courts (she had looked at the map and knew that Bouverie Street where the UP offices were located was just a step from the Law Courts). When the moment came, she would send me the evidence and I could have a look.

I do not think she hoped to find any fortune in Chancery from her Evans ancestors. I think that even she believed the Evanses were plain, hard-working people, miners in Wales as they were miners in America when they first came over. She was, after all, an Evans, born in Moriah Township, Jackson County, Ohio, in the old log cabin her grandfather built. But she had hopes of the Pritchards, for had not Grandmother Salisbury's mother come with her children from England, from St. Ives, had not her fa-ther been a wealthy ship's captain, a knight, no less, Sir James Davies, who had sailed away and vanished, but who no doubt had left a magnificent pile which to this day lay unclaimed, awaiting the proper heirs in Chancery?

The Courts of Chancery. What dreams they brought, what remarkable stories! I loved them. I was fascinated by the "Agony" column of the London *Times.* I read its complicated messages with wide eyes and open mouth. Maybe *there* the clue was to be found. It fed my child's love of secrets, codes, cryptograms.

There was, too, the fortune of Barent Johnson. Barent Johnson was one of mother's Dutch ancestors, an early settler who was possessed, so family tradition had it, of vast estates in what is now Brooklyn and perhaps Staten Island as well. (The estates seemed to move about a bit geographically, but that may be only a small boy's lack of attention to detail.) Johnson was a loyalist during the Revolutionary War and went to Montreal, or was it the West Indies?

To Brooklyn and Montreal, Mother felt sure, the family held a claim—if only it could be proved. But Aunt Charlotte "burned the papers." Aunt Charlotte was a formidable lady married to a gentleman called "Doctor" Lovejoy. Once, as a little girl, my mother was stricken with a nosebleed, the blood gushing in torrents as she walked across the lonely prairie, south of Minneapolis, picking pasqueflowers in early spring with Aunt Charlotte and Doctor Lovejoy. The doctor found an old puffball, blew the dust into her nose and the bleeding halted. Her life was saved, a miracle she never forgot.

Aunt Charlotte's action was the family tragedy. When Grandfather Evans died, Maria, my grandmother, collapsed. The strong-willed Charlotte took over, getting the family out of the red-brick castle, settling its affairs, packing up for the move to a modest house on Western Avenue. It was then that she "burned the papers," dumping the old trunk with the precious claims into a bonfire.

To the end of her life, Mother engaged in a fitful search for evidence. When I went to London during World War II, I resumed my habit of scanning the Agony column. I would pick up *The Times* each morning like an addict and quickly look for the magic words "Seeking heirs of Pritchard," "Seeking heirs of Salisbury." I never saw them.

My mother's brother Scott Ford Evans embodied the Welsh romantic fallacy. He lived the romances my mother dreamed. He was her hero. That of my aunt Mary too. And of my father. I hated my uncle, but I couldn't have told you why.

He it was who had gone to the Klondike in 1900, not to hunt gold but to install coaling stations on the White Pass & Yukon

Railroad, a difficult task and one that brought him a good deal more than panning for yellow dust would have. At twenty-three, he had made a name as a swashbuckling construction engineer, builder of the world's largest grain elevator, the Calumet K in Chicago, amid a swinging fight with the labor unions, an epic recorded in a novel called *Calumet K,* by Henry Kitchell Webster. He was bright, arrogant, sarcastic, and determined to become a millionaire before he was thirty. He was sure he would make it, nimble as quicksilver, a devil for the main chance, cutting every corner, a gambler. He had no common sense and was possessed by all the perversities of the Welsh. He and my father bought their first automobile together, a secondhand 1908 Packard, and spent every Sunday taking it apart, putting it together, gathering their harassed wives and children and going for "joyrides" and picnics in the country, always, always coming back after two, three, four or five blowouts, one or more wheels "riding on the rim."

Scott had married a conventional, rather stupid young woman from Council Bluffs, Iowa, where he happened to be building a grain elevator. He thought she would inherit a million dollars. Or at least half a million. She did neither. It was one of the many gambles he lost. He put up with the "Madam," as he called her, because she produced a daughter with whom he was totally, fatally in love.

About the time of World War I, Scott got the break he thought would bring his million. An old Baltimore company picked him to run its affairs. He left Minneapolis in grand style, bought a marble-stoop house at 1217 Cathedral Street, joined the Episcopal Church, drank whiskey with the worldly bishop, put his wife into society, put his daughter into a good school, joined the clubs, ran the company, became a dollar-a-year man in Herbert Hoover's Food Administration in Washington, driving back and forth daily in a new Packard Twin-Six, once in his predawn enthusiasm driving right up the steps of the U.S. Capitol.

I don't know what happened. I heard much talk, all painting him a hero, painting the others as villains. What I think happened—and I know something very much like this would have had to happen—was that some stockholders discovered he was putting his hand into the till in a complicated and clever way. Before they could act he acted and, perhaps for fear of scandal, perhaps because of his cleverness, no one laid a glove on him. He skimmed out of Baltimore with—how much?—possibly $100,000 in gold and gold certificates, as he proudly boasted, safe in a money belt which he wore next to his skin, a Colt .32 automatic in his alligator gladstone along with a pint of bonded whiskey (he would carry the bag, the Colt and the whiskey to the end of his days), made a hasty and costly settlement with his wife, began to live with his attractive and intelligent secretary, lavished money and affection on his daughter (she married at seventeen and not many experiences that can befall a woman failed to come her way), and chased his million for the remaining years of his life, of which there were to be five.

In his restless journeys across the United States, he more and more often came back to his sisters in Minneapolis (even then I understood that this was touching base, a brief King's X from the devils that haunted him). He lived on a diet of whiskey, peanuts and cottage cheese, nothing else. He insisted it was the perfect diet. He suffered from boils on the back of his neck.

He would sit at the dining room table telling story after story of how he would get his million. Once a man had come to him with a tale of shipwreck on the coast of Chile. He washed ashore, half drowned. The ship sank and all the others were lost. When he came to his senses, he saw that the beach was glistening. The glisten was gold dust, fabulous deposits. The man walked to the nearest village, got help from the Indians and made his way back to the United States. Now, if Scott could finance him, he would reveal the location. They would go partners. "There are millions there," Scott said, his blue, blue eyes shining with excitement and greed, his face flushed by the bonded whiskey. He was a big, full-bodied man with a handsome head, silvered now, and a petulant, stubborn mouth. These were Prohibition days; he always bought whiskey-in-bond on medical prescriptions; got it in such quantities that it went to my father's head; he dozed through most of Scott's fantasies. Why didn't Scott finance the expedition to Chile? I don't know. Perhaps without the whiskey he knew it was fool's gold. But his sisters believed every word he spoke. At the age of fifteen, I turned Scott's tale into my first long piece of fiction. I called it "Jack Hopewood's Story." It ran thirty-eight penciled pages.

Then there was the diamond field. This, too, in South America. A prospector had gone up the Amazon and spotted a gravelly stream flowing into the great river. It was not just gravel; it was diamonds. Probably the richest field any man had ever seen. This required not only capital but stealth. If the diamond cartel discovered that Scott was exploiting the field . . . They would buy it. Or eliminate Scott. These men played for keeps.

Millions in it, Scott said, but how to get the diamonds out was a puzzle he could not solve.

He believed in the claims to Brooklyn and to Montreal. He believed in Chancery and often called on old cousins in Philadelphia and Cincinnati to see if by any chance they had family papers that might be used to support the case.

In the last two years of his life, he found the bonanza he had been seeking, the discovery that was going to bring him a million dollars—or so he said, there always being the possibility, I am afraid, that he was laying the groundwork for a bunco game. Somehow in his rambles he had heard of Dahlonega, a small town in the hills of Georgia, once the site of gold mines, where until the Civil War the U.S. government had maintained a mint. Long since, the mines had been abandoned. But Scott had a hunch. He believed they had not been worked out; that there was a shaft where rich gold deposits lay untouched. With conspiratorial cunning, he took options on the old mining properties. He went into the hills near Dahlonega and built a cabin. With his secretary-mistress, he began to explore the diggings. He bought two Mannlicher heavy-caliber rifles, equipped with telescopic sights, two Colt six-shooters and two sawed-off shotguns. He trained his secretary to use the weapons. He set up trip wires and electrified gates to warn of the approach of strangers. It was, as he told it, as dangerous and dramatic a venture as he had ever embarked upon. He was taking no chances. He warned his sisters to investigate instantly if they did not hear from him or if anything seemed wrong.

Then, at noon one February day, a telegram came from New York, from the secretary. Scott had suffered a heart attack and died instantly in the lobby of the Imperial Hotel as he was talking with some businessmen.

Dad took the first train. The secretary didn't know what had happened. Everything had been going as usual. They were living quietly at the Dahlonega cabin. No threats. No alarms. She could not have been more loyal, more in love with this frustrated, romantic man, but she had not thought the situation so dangerous, so desperate, as had Scott. Perhaps, too, she had not really believed in the big casino. Suddenly Scott announced they must leave. Immediately. Back to New York. No explanation. She did not know whether they had come back so that he could arrange financing or because he finally knew that Dahlonega was a dry hole. He never said.

Dad brought Scott's body back to Minneapolis in the baggage coach. There were headlines in the *Minneapolis Journal* and a big funeral at the Scottish Rite Temple. The Madam and Scott's daughter, Eleanor, attended the funeral. So did I. It was the first funeral I ever went to. When Unk died and when my grandmother Maria Evans died, I had not been permitted to attend. Too young. I didn't mind. The idea of a funeral frightened me, as Unk and Maria Evans had in life. She used to sit in the parlor in a rocking chair and shout when I went to the toilet: "Leave that door open, boy." She always called me "boy." Everyone else told me to close the door. I couldn't understand. I didn't know until I was grown up and Dad once said to Mother: "Well, your mother was nutty as a fruitcake." And she agreed. It had never occurred to me. I thought all old people were like that.

Scott's body rested in an open coffin on an apricot satin cushion, the face lightly powdered, a wisp of an arrogant grin still on his lips. I couldn't hate my uncle that afternoon. I only felt sorry for him. I knew that one way or another, the Welsh dream he lived by had turned to dust.

It took a long time to understand why I hated my uncle. In part, I realized it was because he treated me like a bellhop, confident that for his half dollars and crisp dollar bills I would run any errand he sent me on, and he was right. That was big money, even though I had to crawl for it. Later I understood something else. He was a man of physical self-confidence, a man of the world, sophisticated (so I believed), courageous and cocksure. He had come through the dangers of the Klondike, the labor battles of Chicago and the perils of Baltimore's blue-blooded society. He was an adventurer, a man of the world, just what I wanted to be. He came right out of the novels of Frank Norris and he made me feel like a gawky kid. Of course I hated him.

I suppose there was a will. I suppose that Scott's daughter got whatever he didn't leave to his secretary. Dad felt sorriest for her. She couldn't come to the funeral. It wouldn't have been right, she felt, and he had to agree. He liked her very much and they corresponded for several years. He did bring back Scott's alligator bag, the .32 Colt and a pint of bonded whiskey. I don't know what became of the Mannlicher guns and the telescopic sights. I ultimately inherited the alligator bag and the .32. I guess Dad drank the bonded pint.

My mother dreamed of being a writer. Perhaps it was the Welsh in her. She grew up a dreamer. Youngest in the family, she was both babied and bossed. Her brothers, Scott and Wesley, just older than she, took turns commanding her. At table they would say: "Bread." She would pick up a slice. "Butter." She would butter it. "Eat." She would pop it in her mouth. There it would rest between locked jaws until the command: "Chew." I don't know if they continued this rigmarole to "Swallow." They probably did. Her brothers were a year apart, look-alikes, sarcastic, saucy, each out for his million. Scott came closest, but died without it at fifty-two. Wesley didn't even come close. He lost his way while still in his twenties, deserted his wife and two girls, took to drink, went down the Mississippi and, alone, alcoholic, a flophouse bum, shot himself one New Year's Eve in New Orleans.

The brothers loved their little sister, loved to tease her until she fled in tears, climbing a narrow ladder to the tower room of the castle. She pulled the ladder up through the trapdoor and was safe despite every call and appeal, reading the hours away, oblivious of anything but the perils of Clarissa or the struggles of Vanessa. She read until her eyes gave out and she had to have glasses: romance, poetry, most of all English novels—the Brontës, Jane Austen—and later W. D. Howells and still later Booth Tarkington (Julia, not Penrod). All her life she read novels and dreamed of writing them. She was a writer manquè with a certain gift for light verse. To her a writer was a special person, and her son must be a writer—not a novelist, not a poet, but the editor of *The Times,* by which she meant *The Times* of London. She had been introduced to the London *Times* by her brother-in-law Andrew, a prodigious reader, a man steeped in England, English politics, English criticism, whose favorite author was Anthony Trollope. He read before breakfast. He read in the long hours he spent in the bathroom. He read before lunch, after lunch, before dinner and all evening. No wonder he barely managed to earn a living. He was the source of mother's fantasy about *The Times* of London. It was *the* paper, so far as Andy was concerned. *The New York Times,* he felt, was a little parvenu.

There was no love between my mother and Sue, my father's sister. She regarded Mother as a woman of dubious origin who had stolen her beloved brother's affections. Perhaps had Sue married, she would not have been so acerbic.

Sue had her own small literary pretensions, very small. She worked as an editor of an obscure children's magazine called *Everyland,* and for years wrote and edited a column of letters, signed "Aunt Helen." She was an indefatigable letter writer and insisted on receiving frequent letters from her nephew. I spent my childhood being hounded to "answer Aunt Sue's letter." Sue was proud of Janet and me, but she was convinced she must direct and guide our development because of our mother's ineptitude.

To this end she invoked precept and model. Her favorite model was Sally Fisher, daughter of her friend the novelist Dorothy Canfield Fisher.

When Sue joined Dorothy in Paris during World War I, she began to include in her letters remarks about Sally. At the age of nine, Sally was already following in her mother's footsteps, a precocity that was phenomenal. A pity that neither Janet nor Harrison had such talent!

These comments nettled me and I decided to try my hand at writing, not understanding, of course, that I was the shuttlecock of two frustrated lady writers. My history of "The Great War" was my first venture. Years later I discovered that my father had written about it to my aunt, citing it as evidence of industry if not creative skill. "I don't think he has any literary ability," my father wrote, "but the 'history' is at least original. He has got it pretty straight considering it is all out of his head."

I don't think this argument convinced my aunt. She wrote that a submission I sent to the St. Nicholas League, the writing club of *St. Nicholas* magazine, displayed a "style not so developed as that of most children his age." It was called "A Message to the Front" and told of a captain who sent a message by a soldier and, fearing he would not make it, duplicated it by courier pigeon. The soldier was killed, the pigeon got through. *St. Nicholas* enrolled me in the League and said the story "deserved high praise."

Next came a contest sponsored by the DAR, an essay on Alexander Hamilton. Mother did a lot of research and my manuscript was heavily "edited" by my uncle Andrew. It ran a staggering three thousand words and won the prize, even though I had to cut it back to the specified limit of three hundred words. A big score for me.

I glowed in the praise of my mother and aunt. Each felt she had put me on the track. Their cozening was enjoyable and I got into the habit of writing. I knew how to do it. I liked it. When I went to high school I wrote, a bit languidly, always getting high marks in English composition, joining *The Polaris,* the North High weekly, sometimes writing satiric verse (very poor), more often editorials and essays (not too bad). In my senior year in high school, I made a fateful decision. Despite the embarrassment of sitting, the only male, in a room with sixty prospective young female secretaries, I took a course in typewriting and learned the touch system. This was probably my only achievement of those years. It would stand me in good stead all my life. When I went to Washington for United Press in the early New Deal days, I could write copy at sixty to seventy words a minute, fast enough to keep up with the teleprinter machines. No one in the bureau could do that. Don't ask me what I wrote at sixty words a minute. I wrote anything.

North Side High was not a ghetto school like Sumner School. Sumner had been a segregated school, segregated by religion, in a sense, but really by income. Everyone in the Sumner neighborhood was low income or poverty line. North High was not poor. It was a working-class school, a blue-collar school with a tincture of white collar. Here Scandinavian children predominated, Swedish, Norwegian, Danish, Icelandic, a few Finnish and a good many Germans. Jewish pupils formed an enclave, possibly of twenty-five percent; "old Americans" maybe ten percent. There were two blacks in my 1925 class. Two. Perhaps fifteen in a student body of eighteen hundred. "Integration" had not yet been thought of, and the tiny band of blacks in Minneapolis was, let us say, smothered by white students and white schools.

At North High as at Sumner, I was in a minority, having automatically joined the Jewish bloc. I didn't know any non-Jewish kids. In my senior year, through working on *The Polaris,* I met some Scandinavians who were to become lifelong friends. The most important member of my class and surely the most interesting I did not get to know for fifty years. To be certain, neither he nor I in 1925 had any notion that I would, as he wrote in my high school yearbook, actually become "a journalist and editor," and that he would become a revolutionary and a three-time candidate for the U.S. presidency. This classmate was Farrell Dobbs, who grew up near Keegans Lake, to the west of the Oak Lake Addition, his father a driver for the Pittsburgh Coal Company, whose yards lapped at the edge of Royalston Avenue. When we signed each other's yearbooks, I was a pimply kid just out of knee pants; he was a lanky young man who could hardly wait to get his graduation certificate and be on his own, earning money, marrying his high school sweetheart, Marvel Scholl, starting a family and beginning to climb the American ladder of success.

By a quirk of fate (of course, no good Marxist would put it that way), the Great Depression and a chance meeting with one of the Dunne brothers, the Trotskyite Teamsters Union leaders, Farrell, who didn't know what a trade union was, was swept up in the Minneapolis teamsters strike of 1934 and plunged into the wilder edges of revolutionary struggle. Farrell was the first presidential candidate I was to meet, but it was not until his career was over, the FBI at long last exposed in its undercover harassment of the Socialist Workers party (it beat anything I ever read about the Okhrana, the Czar's police, which used similar tactics against the Social Revolutionary party in Russia), and Trotsky long since murdered by Stalin's assassin—possibly because Trotsky resolutely ignored Farrell's sensible warnings about security—that I finally sat down with him and Marvel in their quiet home in Berkeley, California, and began to untangle the fifty years that had sent us along such differing paths.

There was something elusive here, some Minnesota connection that I still haven't quite figured out. Farrell Dobbs entered revolution on an absolutely flat trajectory. He came from a working-class family. He married young and he was out of a job. A strike started and before he knew it, he and Grant Dunne were leading one of the most revolutionary strikes ever conducted in the United States, all the other leaders having been arrested. On the spot they invented tactics never used before or since—flying squadrons, field headquarters that moved hour by hour, and even oftener, from one suddenly commandeered filling station to another. It was the high spot of Trotskyite action in the United

States—and Farrell had not even heard Trotsky's name a few weeks before. It was a passionate experience, and fifty years after the event, Marvel was still capable of flying into a rage against Eric Sevareid, or Arne, as he was still known in Minneapolis, because he and some other reporters didn't take her seriously. And she and Farrell never lost their anger at what they regarded as the equivocal ("traitorous") attitude of Minnesota's radical governor Floyd B. Olson toward the strike. I was a great supporter of Olson, which may be why when the strike was settled, in August 1934, I wrote from Washington a "plague on both your houses" letter to my parents in Minneapolis, commenting on the six deaths, the millions of dollars of business lost and the beating up of one of my friends, a reporter named Wiley Maloney, adding: "I trust that both employees and employers figure they won the honors and that all will be peaceful ever after." Or perhaps I was being tactful because I knew my father thought civil war was breaking out. He came close to being right.

I wish that more of my letters of this period had survived. I am not entirely satisfied that I stood so aloof from the social and political confrontations of Depression and early New Deal. In a letter written to an old UP friend, Wolf Larson, six days after Roosevelt's inauguration on March 4, 1933, I spoke of the violence, the Dearborn riots and many others, that had swept the country, and added that "even the arch-capitalists (with the exception of the *Chicago Tribune*) are tinged with at least the first faint blush of socialism and many of them openly admit it."

I expressed hope that "the suffering and starvation" of the people had not been in vain and that "a definite change in the system" would emerge. But I added that the UP was "a grand seat for viewing things over the world from the grandstand" and that "I think that after all the grandstand is the place I would rather view them from."

"I have been in the arena and close enough to smell the hot blood and it is not a pleasant thing," I added. This sounds as though, regardless of my feelings—my sympathies for the radicalism of Floyd B. Olson, for the underdogs of depression, for the demonstrators whom I had seen beaten and clubbed down by the Chicago police—I had taken my place on the sidelines. I was to be a reporter of events, not a participator in them. It was a role I would adhere to throughout my long journalistic career.

But it was not thoughts of revolution, not social or political issues, that filled my mind as I came to the end of my high school days. I was looking forward to the University of Minnesota, but had no clear idea of what I wanted to do. My father was not impressed with my writing. He was very hard up. He had sold 107 Royalston and it had been a disaster. He had had to take Saskatchewan farmlands in exchange; the land, in turn, had been traded for two run-down Minneapolis houses; he had mortgage payments on our Kenwood house and he didn't know where to turn. Tuition at the university was not high, fifteen dollars a quarter plus another three dollars in fees. But there were textbooks, streetcar fare, lunches, incidentals. It mounted up. Since I didn't know what I wanted to do and he didn't know what talent I had, he suggested that I go to work for a while or possibly enter the Dunwoody Institute where I could learn metalworking, carpentry or automobile maintenance. Not a bad idea. But Mother would have none of it. Her boy must go to the university. She threw a tantrum. Her tantrums were no small affairs. They were hurricanes, dangerous, deadly, chilling outbursts which scarred her life and that of my father. The hysterics went on for hours: frantic weeping, pounding against the bed, turning her back to her husband or anyone who tried to comfort her, a paroxysm totally without control. The attacks came like clockwork. One happened every Sunday, just about the time we were ready to sit down to dinner. There was one every holiday. There was one whenever a decision (such as my going to the university) was to be made. Or they could come out of a clear sky. She would just drop a dishrag while washing dishes and slam into her bedroom. She would get up from the dinner table and slam into her bedroom. She would be reading in the living room, get up and slam into the bedroom. It could be a word from me, a word from Janet, a word from her sister Mary, a word from Uncle Andy. But usually it was a word from my father. My sister and I often talked in secret about our mother. We decided Dad was too nice, too polite, too long-suffering. He should stamp his foot, slam the door himself, slap her in the face, walk out of the house. But these were useless prescriptions. His mother and father had hammered it into him (as he was once to tell me) that women suffered as men did not (I suppose he meant in childbearing and child rearing), and that men must be sympathetic, kind and gentle because they did not understand women's pain. Neither Janet nor I thought Mother had anything to suffer about. I didn't know then that the "saying" written under my father's name in the Central High yearbook for 1889 quoted Chaucer's "And of his porte as meke as is a mayde."

One night I awoke to the sound of sobbing. I was so deeply asleep I did not at first understand. Then I realized it was my mother, that she had flung herself on my bed, crying hysterically. I did not move a muscle, but I was instantly wide awake. I heard my father's voice, deep and quiet. He was kneeling beside the bed, one arm around her, stroking her gently. "Listen," he said in the saddest voice I ever heard, "listen to me, Georgie. Just listen for once. Stop this. You know why I bought my pistol and you know what I will do with it unless you stop this." My mother's sobs quickly faded away. She slipped from the bed and they were gone. I knew that she knew (as I knew) that my father meant what he said. If she did not stop he would kill himself. That must have happened during my first year in high school. A little later I went to my father's chiffonier one afternoon when there was no one in the house. I took the cartridge holder out of his gun and hid it. Not long after this my mother was in the hospital for a mysterious operation. She had a private nurse, an enchanting girl with whom Dad fell in love and she with him. Janet and I adored her. She felt about Dad as we did. How could Janet and I persuade our father to divorce our mother and marry this lovely woman with the sparkling eyes, the warm smile, the ready adoration? There was no way, not the faintest chance. All we could do was to bless her for giving him a few weeks of happiness.

There had to be a deep psychological explanation for all this. In the early twenties, Mother began to read Freud and Jung. I was sure she was trying to understand something about herself, but it never came clear. The older my father grew, the more depressed, the more vulnerable he became, and the worse my mother's attacks. Finally and thankfully, Dad began to grow deaf. It was his only protection.

Mother's hysteria poisoned our family life. So long as my father lived, my sister later told me, she lived in dread that he would take his life to escape the cruel harangues and weeping that went on night after night. Janet and I became fiercely protective of our father. I turned antagonistic, contemptuous, sarcastic toward my mother and sometimes deliberately provoked her hysteria, telling myself that I was turning her against me and not Dad. Today I don't believe that. I think it was a kind of sadism which I justified as "punishment" of my mother. I even launched a study of her symptoms for a course I took at the university in abnormal psychology—not a very scientific exercise, I must say. All of this strengthened within me a resolve that when I married, it must be to the most "normal" girl I could possibly find.

If there had been any question whether I would go to the university, Mother's hysterics resolved it. In September 1925, I took the streetcar to the campus and one hot autumn day registered as a freshman. I didn't know where I was headed, but inspired by childhood dreams of alchemy, I enrolled as a prechemistry student. In five years off and on at Minnesota, I would never take a course in chemistry. Before my first month was over, I had been hooked as a cub reporter on the campus newspaper, the *Minnesota Daily*.

7 | Growing Up

I was sixteen years old when I entered the university, five feet ten inches tall, weight 138 pounds; I had blue eyes and blond hair, with a cowlick I had been trying for three years to suppress with the aid of brilliantine and a nightcap made of one of my mother's old black stockings. (Fifty years later, I still had the cowlick.) I was skinny—bony knees, bony elbows, bony chest, bony face. I could run a mile without catching my breath and was the best freshman breast stroke on the swimming team. I had been out of the state of Minnesota twice, once at the age of six on an automobile odyssey to my cousins near Madison, Wisconsin, and in 1922 with my mother and sister on a journey east "to see the sights": the Washington monument, Times Square, Montauk Point, Beacon Street, Niagara Falls. The trip east was my only claim to sophistication. No one else in my class had walked the length of Broadway from the Battery to the Bronx. Just before we boarded the *Pioneer Limited* at the Milwaukee station to take our berths in the sleeping car, my father had handed me a big white envelope marked "Sealed Orders." It contained his deputation. For the duration of the trip, I was in charge of the well-being of my mother and my sister. He put them in my responsibility. I had taken my "orders" with utter seriousness.

Now, as I stripped down for the physical examination that was compulsory before enrolling at the "U," I was in tiptop physical condition, mentally O.K., shy almost to the blush point. I had worn knee britches in high school and had never gone out with a girl. I have lived through many hells in my life, but never, I swear, one like my last two high school years. It was a matter of age. I had been late going to primary school, entering the September before my seventh birthday in November. But I was early leaving Sumner School because the teachers had the custom of skipping bright children through grades. It was a pernicious practice. All my life, my handwriting has been abominable. I have never spelled or punctuated properly. I don't know the rules of grammar. I skipped the grades where these subjects were practiced. I was skipped two full grades. It made no sense.

I entered high school in 1921, two years younger than my classmates. Nothing could have been worse. I was a schoolboy among
adolescents. There are no longer years in life for a boy surrounded by older youngsters than the two years between twelve
and fourteen. There was no escape from the tyranny of age. I did
not dance. The rest did. I did not date. The rest did. I did not
drink. Many others did. I never kissed a girl in all my high
school years. Nor would any girl I would have liked to kiss
thought of kissing a juvenile like me.

I turned my back on high school and threw myself into the
companionship of my friends outside school, my chums of summer camps and scouting, giving myself up to the outdoors, hik-
ing and swimming summer-long, exploring the Minnesota wilderness, beginning to know it and love it—the pure lakes, the
streams, the deep, deep silence of the woods, the white snow of
winter, the fierce cold of harvesting ice, the bite of the zero wind,
the swiftness of skis, all cross-country in those days, the smell of
fresh perch frying on a wood fire, the iron taste of water in the
northern lakes, waking up in a blanket roll buried in snow, fresh
snow blinding my eyes, snow filling my ears, the plunge into deep
water, the ecstasy of a dive from the high board, lungs pounding
in a long underwater swim. A substitute, but not a bad substitute. It bonded me to the wilderness with a passion that would
never leave, a passion I felt at sixty below zero on the Mongolian
steppe, in the winter wastes of Siberia, Lake Baikal boiling with
frost in December before sinking into frozen solitude, in the perfumed deserts of northwest China or southeast Persia, in the
blue, blue heavens of Tibet. It is not geography; it is the wilderness implanted in me by Minnesota: Minnetonka, still wild at the
north end when I was young; Mille Lacs, that saucer in the sand;
the St. Croix as it meanders north of Taylors Falls; the Gunflint
Trail, Grand Marais and the Arrowhead country.

I came to feel totally at home in the wilderness. I used a compass, but I did not need one to tell my way by stars and moss. I
carried matches, but I could light my fire with flint and steel or
by twirling a stick in dry moss. Nothing delighted me like a
canoe and the boundary waters of Canada. To this day I am jealous of Eric Sevareid for his canoe trip from Rainy Lake to Hudson's Bay, the adventure of my adolescent dream.

I could fish and shoot and trap, and I had begun to think of
the big woods as sanctuary, as refuge from the world, a place to

escape—God knows from what. A superstition was implanted in my mind. I never wanted to live too far from the big woods, too far from the network of trails and streams that led north through the glaciated country of Minnesota or the other lands of the Laurentian belt to the real forests. I still have it. I sometimes wonder if it comes down from the old generations that lived at the edge of the frontier, never farther than a day's march from the unknown.

At the end of August, after the temporary summer jobs of college years, my friends and I loaded up the old model A and headed north. It would be fall now, cold, often the snow coming in, deerflies gone, summer campers gone. We would take off from the forest trails and canoe to Canada; no one in the whole woods but ourselves, waking beside bronze lakes to the cry of a loon, watching a moose drinking at misty dawn, looking up at the bluest sky in the world, hot at midday, freezing at sundown. Happiness. Then we would bundle up our gear, venture into Canada, hole up in a cheap room in Port Arthur, buy a few quarts of whiskey (it was still Prohibition), get ragingly drunk, too drunk to carry out the adventure we had plotted of finding lonely beautiful Canadian girls. Instead we would awake in our own vomit with gruesome hangovers, stagger back to the model A and start the long, long drive homeward, sometimes halted by the customs men, who removed surplus quarts of whiskey we had carefully hidden in the car or hospital-taped to our flat-muscled bellies. Not even the nausea of Port Arthur could erase the smell of pines from our nostrils, the gold of sunrise over blue-gray waters, the flash of a canvasback rising from the pickerel grass one hundred yards distant.

Years later, I went back to the north country with my two boys, Michael and Stephan. There are ten thousand lakes in Minnesota, hundreds of them named Long Lake or Mud Lake. Governor Orville Freeman decided to rename them for Minnesotans who had won some fame. One of the lakes had been christened Lake Salisbury. I decided to take my youngsters to see it and to let them savor a tang of my youth. We rented a car and spent several days in northern Minnesota. We went to Grand Marais and the Gunflint Trail: cabins, boat rentals, commercialization, but not too bad. The boys seemed to enjoy it. We never found Lake Salisbury, though. Nobody in the vicinity had heard of it.

There was a Long Lake and a Mud Lake. Someday, I told the boys, I'll come back and find our lake. I wonder.

Perhaps, after all, being twelve years old in high school had its compensations. Perhaps I would not have fallen in love with the wilderness if I had been old enough to credibly fall in love with a high school beauty. At the university, the age margin narrowed, and I said, Thank God, I'm through with puberty. I'm growing fast and I'm big enough to take girls out. I did too, although I wasn't very good at it. Besides, I knew what I wanted to do and I was doing it every day. I was a cub reporter for a newspaper and I knew that I would be reporting for the rest of my life.

I cannot remember the first story I wrote for the *Minnesota Daily,* and it's just as well. It could not have been of any consequence. It was not the subject, it was the milieu that captured me. The *Daily* world was self-consciously irreverent, nonconformist, hell-raising. We took our cue from *The Front Page.* We played Hildy Johnson and Walter Burns. The *Daily* was printed at the plant of the *Minneapolis Tidende,* a Swedish-language daily. Two or three of us went to the plant each night and made up the pages with the printers. They drank alcohol. Grain alcohol, 144 proof. You had a choice. You could have it with hot water. Or cold. Only by downing a glass in which two ounces of alcohol was combined with an equal quantity of water, downing it with half a dozen tough Swedish typographers looking on, did you pass your maturity rites.

Our bible was the *New York World* (the *World,* we would say, a bit testily, not the *Evening World*). Our gods were Donald Mellett, editor of the *Canton* (Ohio) *Repository,* who was gunned down in the midst of an investigation of corruption; Lincoln Steffens, Ida Tarbell, Upton Sinclair and Frank Norris, the muckrakers; Paul Y. Anderson of the *St. Louis Post-Dispatch,* for his Teapot Dome exposé. We read *The Brass Check, The Shame of the Cities, The Jungle,* and when it came out, Vincent Sheean's *Personal History.* We read *Time* magazine ("backward run the sentences in *Time* until reels the mind," we liked to repeat), *The New Yorker,* Frank Crowninshield's *Vanity Fair* and Mencken's *The American Mercury.* We had contempt for the local papers.

Politics? We were "aginners," against whatever was the prevailing opinion, iconoclasts in the traditional pattern of youth. Not principled critics. I turned with glee against my Republican heroes, Hughes, Harding, Coolidge, Hoover. But not against TR. I delighted in outrageous declarations, but not to my father. I held my tongue with him and he with me, although he knew what kind of nonsense I was spouting.

I wish I could claim that when the American dream was roaring happily toward 1929 I stood on the ramparts crying disaster. I did not. Social criticism bored me. I knew nothing of economics, nothing of life. I worshiped at the shrine of Thomas Beer, a slightly older iconoclast, who wrote a fleeting work about the 1890s called *The Mauve Decade*.

My new passions, just replacing John Galsworthy, whose *The Forsyte Saga* I had followed breathlessly in *Scribner's* magazine, were F. Scott Fitzgerald and Ernest Hemingway. Toward Fitzgerald I had a touch of condescension. He did, after all, come from St. Paul. I had friends whose older brothers remembered him at St. Paul Central, and of course, he had written his famous story about the Ice Palace. He was a holy wonder, I thought, but I did not understand how much he differed from the other *Saturday Evening Post* writers.

Of Hemingway there was no question. From the moment I read "The Killers" I had to *be* Hemingway. I had to *write* Hemingway. I had to *live* Hemingway. I don't think anyone in Anna Von Helmholtz Phelan's writing seminar felt differently, except for one girl who was locked in imitational embrace with Edna St. Vincent Millay. I and my friends became Hemingway—monosyllabic, repetitive, cynical, the Lost Generation. I could not believe anything had ever been so true, so passionate, so tragic as *A Farewell to Arms*. I ached for Catherine. Poor Dr. Anna. We were all third-rate Hemingways.

A dozen years later, I met Hemingway in London during World War II, no longer lean, handsome, dark, young, romantic; not the tragic hero of *For Whom the Bell Tolls* but blowsy, drink-ridden, grizzled, a character from the poorest of his novels, warming over his youth, a man who should never have grown old, a man who should have died in Italy. Or in Spain. Oh, I know that makes no sense. He could not have written *Farewell* if he had died on the Arno, nor *Bell* had he died in Spain. But there is a time for life and a time for death, and I felt Hemingway must understand this. He would struggle another fifteen years before he took matters into his hands on the ranch in Idaho. When you have an image in your heart, as I did, when you have been totally possessed by the exactness, the absolute pitch, of his ear and his emotion—well, to meet him in a London pub, to see him in his paunch, his jowls, putting his life through summer reruns . . . I wished he could be killed in a jeep accident, a parachute jump or in some other ridiculous manner. But quickly.

Perhaps I have that all wrong. But I do not have anything wrong about the Hemingway of the late 1920s and his effect on me and my generation. He wiped us out. I think, perhaps, he wiped out Dr. Anna as well, although I never did know what she felt deep within her great generous heart. She was a phenomenon, immensely tall, tall as a Grenadier Guard, six feet four, a Brunhild come to earth, in pince-nez, dark blue professional-cut serge suit and white shirtwaist, only letting her small girl's wonderment run riot in hats of magnificent diameter and plumage. She took each of us with total seriousness, total assumption that we were *writers* and that writing was the only thing in existence, and by that assumption confirmed us in the profession. She inspired us to perform miracles. Most of all, each week, she encouraged us, sitting around the oblong table, to devour each other, to read and criticize each other's work with a ferocity that sent young women to tears and young men to the verge of blows. It was jungle war. We learned how to survive. We had to if we were to remain in the seminar. I spent two years in that golden circle and anything I ever acquired of style or taste was born there. Imitation was always present, but toward the end some of us began to work our way through Hemingway, through Fitzgerald, through Dreiser, Lardner, Van Vechten, O'Neill, Dorothy Parker and that miraculous, long-faded Algonquin crowd, into something closer to the reality of our lives.

I began to write of Oak Lake. I wrote about the Sixth Avenue rooming house and its black boarder. I was very proud of this absurdity and included it in a collection that five of us published privately, called *Broken Mirrors;* there were eighty-two copies, some in purple velour, some in gold-and-black wrapping paper, set and printed at the Fairbault School for the Deaf, where the parents of one of us, Gordon Roth, taught. *Broken Mirrors* reeked of Dostoyevsky, incest, murder, lust, insanity, delirium tremens, miscegenation, suicide, hangings. It would be many, many years before I turned back seriously to creative writing.

Anna Von Helmholtz Phelan. In appearance, accent, bearing, breeding, education, she was a caricature of the "Good German," the German who could be depended upon not to make a revolution because the sign said: "Don't Walk on the Grass." You could see her silver helmet and her breastplate and almost hear the doom tones of Wagner. One young man took the girl he hoped to marry to meet Dr. Anna. Years later, the girl remembered the cats—a row of them, each named for a medieval poet, crouched on a railing above eye level, looking down at her with cruel green eyes. Another young man asked Dr. Anna after his first daughter was born: "How long will it be before I feel any love for her?" How could this woman inspire a room of anarchistic young men and women, leavened by a few perfumed, eye-shadowed Sapphos and Beardsleys who drank wine and formed a society which met by cloistered candlelight? I do not know now nor did I then. We Hemingways used to debate the question over our mugs of home brew. I expect the wine drinkers did the same. I do not think Anna Phelan ever had a student who did not leave her seminar with a deep debt of gratitude. The University of Minnesota rewarded this remarkable woman in exemplary academic style. When she retired in 1949 at the age of sixty-nine, after forty years of teaching, she still held the lowly title of assistant professor.

The University of Minnesota in the 1920s was a meat and potatoes institution; it gave you the facts and figures. If you wanted to become a dentist, a doctor, a pharmacist, a chemist, an engineer or a farmer, this was the place. Athens it was not and the regents and the state legislature had no intention of its being Athens. But the football teams were pretty good. These were the days of Alexander Meiklejohn at the University of Wisconsin. At the University of Chicago, Robert Hutchins was stirring up a tempest. A revolution was sweeping the academic world, but not in Minnesota under the stewardship of the improbably named Lotus Delta Coffman, as the *Minnesota Daily* was fond of pointing out. Not that this should be blamed entirely on President Coffman. Excellence, brilliance, initiative were not the Minnesota style. I came to know Coffman quite well (for a student) because he was on my beat as a reporter for the *Daily*. I saw him once a week to jot down his pedantic pronouncements. He was a cautious, conservative, don't-rock-the-boat man. If he hadn't been, Fred B. Snyder, chairman of the Board of Regents, would never have permitted him to take the job.

If one thing could be said for Minnesota, at least it provided a seat for Oscar W. Firkins. (He was never called Oscar Wilde Firkins, even in his obituary.) The presence of Firkins, I thought, justified the existence of the university. He was sui generis. He lived in an 1860s clapboard house, built by an early St. Anthony farmer, a few blocks from the university. He was, in the opinion of many playwrights, actors and directors, the best serious critic of the American theater in his day. He did not possess the savagery of Nathan nor the joie de vivre of Woollcott nor the authority of Percy Hammond. What he had was taste, knowledge, love, style, humor, analysis and devotion to the theater—the whole theater from the Greeks to Broadway. He was a bachelor and lived with his three sisters, Ina, Orra and Frances, all unmarried. Ina was librarian of the university. Frances helped her brother in research and reading. Orra kept house. Oscar Firkins's vision was so poor he could not see beyond the first row of his classes. How he managed to see performances in the theater I do not know. He went to New York twice a year, at Christmas and in the spring. He saw all the plays. Then he returned and delivered his lecture on the current theater. There were sixty students in each of his classes (he offered two), the capacity of the classroom. For the twice-yearly theater talks there might be twice that number, including faculty and people from outside. I do not know whether, with his poor vision, he realized the tremendous crowds he attracted.

A visit to his house, a rare privilege for a student, was like stepping into a New England play by O'Neill (whom Firkins regarded as the playwright of our day). Firkins in black worsted wool suit with starched wing collar, his three sisters equally prim and severe, the housekeeping Orra a little less so, a neat coal fire in the grate, tea, quite a high English tea, the tea poured from a fine silver pot into very thin cups, very tasty scones—all this in a small parlor of black walnut and mahogany, very mannered, I sitting on the edge of my chair, hoping that I would not make a gaffe, certain that I would, dependent on Firkins's charity not to mention it.

Conversation was no problem. Oscar Firkins liked to talk and uttered, in a rather nasal Yankee tone, periodic sentences as though he had memorized his lines. Perhaps he had. His memory was phenomenal and he could quote whole plays by Shakespeare or Sophocles. He spoke in epigrams about events in the morning paper, prefacing his lectures each day with a few minutes of commentary, invariably sardonic, about a political event that had caught his eye or a campus oddity. He was in many respects a radical, with a sharp nose for the underdog and no tolerance for the frailties of his fellow academics, which was why the university had created a department for him of which he was the sole member, not even a clerk or secretary. Would that he had been alive during the Vietnam war; I do not believe Lyndon Johnson could have survived his merciless tongue.

Firkins knew all the gossip of the New York theater and actresses like Florence Reed, Blanche Yurka, Ina Claire were dedicated to him. He watched over them carefully, even tenderly, giving advice on roles, on the plays they should choose, the playwrights whose work best suited them, the most interesting directors. He was for many, many years the inside critic of the American theater, known within the theater but unknown to the public, a secret man, almost a mysterious man, offering his advice cryptically as Pasternak offered his to Stalin.

Oscar Firkins had no use for most of the formalities of academia. Once, it was said, he gave every one of his students an A without reading their papers because his colleagues had criticized his grading methods. He dictated to his students an outline of his lectures because, as he said, he could give them better notes than they would take. Then they could sit back and enjoy the lecture. He didn't care a whit if students brought their books and notes to class for use in examinations, but one hot day when many students removed their jackets and loosened their ties, he announced: "I am not accustomed to giving lectures to stableboys." It was his view that students came to the university to obtain an education. They were adults. If they were too stupid to make use of their opportunity, if they did not study or attend classes, that was their loss. He was not a policeman or a guardian of morals. Students rushed to sign up for his classes. Being in Firkins's classes was like being admitted to a secret society.

What did I learn from Oscar Firkins? The virtue of independence: the virtue of using my mind, of not taking anyone's word, of going back to the source, of trying to work out a philosophy of existence; he taught me the wonders of the classics, the eternal and absolute wonder of the Greeks. No one taught me more. And to rebel. Never to accept banality. That was the main thing.

For whatever reason, possibly because, being a rebel, Oscar Firkins sensed a fellow spirit, I was privileged to share his friendship, talking with him in his office, visiting at his house and on two occasions being invited for very formal Sunday dinners.

There were occasions when efforts were made to persuade Oscar Firkins to move to New York and become a resident critic. Twice he took leaves of absence to serve as critic for New York literary reviews and he contributed over the years to *The Nation,* the *Atlantic Monthly,* the *Yale Review* and the *Saturday Review of Literature* (then a literary journal of some merit), criticism, essays, reviews written in that finest of tongues, the English language. Firkins was flattered by and enjoyed the attention that was paid to him in New York, but he always returned to Minnesota. I think he was right. He carried a furled umbrella every day of his life and he never entered an automobile. He rode streetcars. I do not believe he could have existed outside the circle of his three sisters and their New England house in southeast Minneapolis. He died in 1932, and soon the three sisters died too, one after the other.

My father got me my first job. It was in the pancake mill of the Pillsbury Flour Company across St. Anthony's Falls from the old bag company plant. I had to earn money if I was to stay in school, so one morning in June 1926, I showed up at the mill at seven o'clock, hung my clothes in a locker, put on khaki coveralls and went to work as a sweeper at $21.50 a week. By the time I had swept the three floors, the flour had coated them again. No one wore face masks, not even the girls. They wore dustcaps to keep the flour out of their hair, but by quitting time they looked like Martha Washington.

This was my introduction to the proletariat, as Lenin would have called it. I had grown up in the poorest of neighborhoods, but the parents of the children at Sumner School were not proletarians. They were artisans, craftsmen, small traders, petty bourgeoisie. They wore blue collars and many held blue-collar jobs, but they did not intend to go on working with their hands. They were not, by and large, factory workers. The pancake mill was a blue-collar society, of Swedes, Finns and many Poles, particularly among the women. This was their life and they did not, by and large, expect to move out of it. It was days before any of them even said hello. I was not part of their world. No one in the mill spoke very much. Too much noise from the machinery. I got to know the men when I began to work night shifts and Saturdays. The pace was slower and we sat outside the mill in the cool evening, eating our box lunches. The only subject discussed was women—women and the clap, the two were indivisible. The clap stories were monotonous. All but one of the men had had it. "No worse than a bad cold," was the classic phrase, but they didn't believe that. Neither did I. One dour Norwegian told over and over of a whore he had had in France during the war, a remarkable creature, never heard of anyone like her. She had special muscles so that she actually milked him when he bedded her. "Just like you milk a cow's tits," he said. "So help me God. She milked me. I don't know how she did it."

I sat with prurient ears, chewing an American-cheese sandwich, drinking a pint of milk, eating my banana, all brought from home. The story brought a hush of wonderment over the little group, half a dozen of us. Then one of the men would take a tin of Copenhagen snoose from his pocket, put a dab under his lip and say, "Huh. Women. God knows what women can do. Beats me." Another would add wistfully, "Yeh, you can't live with 'em and you can't live without 'em." There would be a fainthearted, unconfident chuckle. Then someone would rise. The others would get up, loose a genial fart or two, pat their thighs, rub their crotches, pick up their lunch pails, stow them in the lockers and go to work.

There were no women on the night shift. Daytimes there were half a dozen, four "older women"—that is, over thirty—and two young women, one extremely thin, blond, tubercular. The prime mover was a woman named Angela, Polish, a certain accent, full of boister and rough jokes, robust, strong, large-breasted. The butt of her jokes was Tony, a loader with whom I worked, dark, rather handsome and pimply. The jokes were variations on a single concept: what Angela would do with Tony in bed; how he had better not muck around with any other woman. She would turn to her crew and say: "We know how to fix this young bastard, don't we? We'll screw that prick of his right off, we'll wear it down until he hasn't got any left for the rest of his life."

This drew gales of laughter. I could see that Tony didn't think it was entirely funny. "Wait till Saturday night," Angela would say. "How about it, girls? Shall we give it to him? How about tying him down, locking him in a room and going to work? You watch out, Tony. We'll show you what a real woman is."

This talk frightened me. I had never imagined women could talk like this, was surprised to see that even the tubercular girl's eyes sparkled when Angela described what they would do with Tony. I was even more surprised that women of an advanced age were still interested in "it." When, occasionally, Angela's eyes turned speculatively on me, I would hurriedly begin to stack boxes farther down the line. I didn't want to be a prisoner of love in a pancake mill. On Monday morning, when Tony showed up, pale, hung over, hangdog, facing a barrage of jokes about the weekend, I wondered whether he had really been captured by these ferocious females.

The talk was not just banter. A year earlier on a Saturday night (and this, perhaps, was why no women now worked on the night shift), a jug of moonshine had been smuggled in. Tony's predecessor as loader had got tight. So had the women. At quitting time they began a rambunctious game. The women pinned the young man down and pulled off his trousers. The man cursed and fought. Someone, no one would say who, ran for the air hose. "We'll show the son of a bitch," she shouted. They stuck the hose in the man's anus and blew him up like the Michelin tire man. He died in the hospital. No wonder Tony paled.

There was a casualty while I worked at the pancake mill—another loader fell from a window to the railroad track and broke his back. Officially it was an accident. Not in Angela's version. Ole, she said, had been putting his prick into the hole of Oscar's woman. Oscar was Ole's partner on the shift. "You know," she said, "a few drinks and Ole falls or is pushed. Who'll say? Nobody seen it. At least, nobody admits it." She turned to Tony. "You better watch that prick of yours, Tony."

I worked ten weeks that summer and had two hundred dollars to start the school year with. I was rich.

8 | Coming of Age

Rich—but not rich enough. Before the end of the 1926–27 term, I knew that I would have to drop out of school and put by more money, not just for college but to help my father. I went to Leslie M. Harkness, city editor of the *Minneapolis Journal,* and talked him into giving me a job. It didn't take much talk. He said through thin lips: "You know, you ought to be paying us. You'll get a better education on the *Journal* than at the university." In a way, he was right. So at eighteen I became a full-time newspaperman at fifteen dollars a week and took up the trade at which I would work the rest of my life.

The reason I had no difficulty in talking Leslie Harkness into hiring me was that I had already had a front-page banner headline in the *Journal,* an exclusive report that the St. Paul airport was flooded and out of service, which fact St. Paul had managed to conceal. My friend Jim Brown, as hard up as myself, had been trying to get a job with a brickyard located on the Mississippi flats next to the airport. We couldn't get to the brickyard; the whole area was flooded. I raced to the *Journal* and told Harkness. It was a scoop at a time when rivalry between the two cities was intense.

Harkness was a small, dyspeptic man. I think he hated all reporters, hated the *Journal,* hated newspapers, hated himself. I never saw him smile. The managing editor was Neil H. Swanson, a flashy young man who delighted in coming to the office in riding boots and breeches. We young reporters were sure he slept with one of the stenographers, a gorgeous platinum blonde, and were very jealous.

The best thing about the *Journal* for a cub reporter was the low pay—so low that only a few older men stayed very long. Cubs advanced rapidly. After a week or two of writing obituaries and traffic accidents, I began to cover big stories—tornadoes, bank robberies (very, very frequent in small Minnesota and Dakota towns) and three-legged races at the annual Grocers Picnic at Minnehaha Falls. I interviewed the Irish poet AE (George William Russell), and was surprised to find he was an agriculturist, more interested in cows than in culture. When Calvin Coolidge came to Minnesota, I got to ride on his special train from Cannon Falls to St. Paul; I met the governor; I covered the mayor; I covered the U.S. federal attorney's office and the U.S. courts and I covered the American Legion convention at Austin, my first out-of-town assignment. By autumn I was number two rewrite man. I wore a felt hat, a cigarette (a Camel) dangled from the left corner of my mouth, and I shot craps on Friday nights in newspaper alley between the *Journal* and the *Tribune,* side by side on Fourth Street, old white-faced buildings, miniatures of the *Tribune* and the *Herald* buildings on Park Row in New York. I got a raise to eighteen dollars and then to twenty-one. I was on my way. But though I remember the events, I don't remember a word of any story I wrote. Just as well.

Money was very tight in 1928 in Minnesota. I ran into Nordau Schoenberg, my best friend on the *Daily,* outside the First National Bank building as he was making the rounds. He would do anything. Look, I said, this is campaign year, they have to need publicity men. Go and brace the Republicans—they have more money. He got a job and later he got another good friend on the payroll. So it was that Nordau Schoenberg and Gordon Roth, two men from the *Daily,* two men who shared wildly non-Republican ideas, went to work for the Republican State Committee and in 1932 invented a "Black Hand" slogan for use against Floyd B. Olson, Minnesota's Farmer-Labor, self-described radical governor, whom both secretly favored. They stole the "Black Hand" from a *Vanity Fair* cover. *Vanity Fair* was running a "Red Hand" campaign against Prohibition. "They imported the Black Hand of the Mafia in an attempt to destroy me," Olson said. He was of Swedish, Norwegian and Danish ancestry, spoke Yiddish like a Jew, and won in a walk. The "Black Hand" kept my friends alive. And it didn't hurt Olson.

I loved the *Journal.* I despised its stuffy politics, but I couldn't wait to get to work each morning, to see what story I would cover. Leslie Harkness kept telling us that there were more good stories in a city block than a newspaper could print in a year; he meant human comedies and tragedies à la Balzac. It was a good philosophy, but the *Journal* would not have printed those stories if it had had them. It was the kind of paper that forbade the use of the word "blizzard" because it might give people the idea that it got cold in Minnesota. The same psychology caused St. Paul for many years to give up its magnificent Winter Carnival. In the *Journal,* blizzards were always "million-dollar snowfalls," a big boost for the crops.

Harkness was not exactly an inspired editor, and soon enough a Hearst city editor named Bill Mason showed up. Mason was about as unsuited to run the *Journal* as a racehorse to pull a brewery truck. But it was fun while he lasted. He brought *The Front Page* into the placid *Journal* city room. He tilted his hat back on his head, tilted his chair back on its rear legs and put his feet on his desk, a real Chicago newspaperman.

Then a twelve-year-old girl named Dorothy Aune was murdered in south Minneapolis, her body tossed in a gutter, tied up in a gunnysack. Mason pulled in all the reporters, everyone except old Charley Cheney, who had been covering state politics since the McKinley era, every last man and woman (the *Journal* had only one woman reporter, a sob sister named Florence Lehmann), and put them on the Aune case. The *Journal* was going to break it, Mason said, come hell or high water. Screw the police! We would do it, if we had to take the town apart. God! What excitement! We had our orders. Go to every house. Talk to everyone. Ring every doorbell. Look into every alley. Check the garbage cans. The first day, I found a bloody rag in a gutter, picked it up by the edge, dropped it in a paper bag and rushed back to the city room. Mason looked at my find a moment, then tossed it into the wastebasket. "Wrong kind of rag, kid," he said, turning away. I was mortified. I didn't know much about menstruation.

Before I could leave the office, Bill had another assignment for me. "Get out to this place as fast as you can," he said, giving me the name and address of a man who lived near the Aune home. "He's got a record," Bill said. "A known child molester. Find out everything you can. Talk to the neighbors. See what they know. Talk to him. See if he has an alibi. *Make him talk.*"

I caught the streetcar and, filled with apprehension, hurried to south Minneapolis. I didn't know how to talk to a murderer. I tried the neighbors. No luck; they either weren't home, didn't know anything or didn't want to get involved. I squared my shoulders and rang the man's doorbell. A gaunt woman in her fifties appeared. I introduced myself and asked if I could come in. With reluctance, she admitted me. I hadn't any notion whether you could ask a woman if her husband was a child molester. I said we were investigating the Aune case and perhaps she could help, perhaps she knew of something that might bear on the murder. She fixed me with a cold eye and said she didn't. I said I was calling on all the homes in the vicinity to see if anyone had seen anything suspicious. No response. I asked if I could talk to her husband. He wasn't home. When might he be coming? She didn't know. I was at the end of my short tether when in walked the husband, a middle-aged man with fear-filled eyes, gray face and baggy trousers. The wife gave him a stony stare, said I was a reporter and left the room.

I wondered what a reporter did next. Should I ask the man if he had committed murder? The man sat down. I looked at him. He looked at me. He looked exactly as I expected a murderer to look. A chill went down my back. I started through my short routine of questions. He replied nervously, but not that nervously. He had confronted these questions before. Suddenly I was convinced that he had already talked to the police, perhaps had just come back from being questioned and they had let him go. That's why Bill knew about him. Have you talked to the police? I asked. Yes, he said, and they know I had nothing to do with it. Well, I said, I suppose you can tell me what you were doing on the night of August 6. He flushed and had begun to reply when his wife reappeared.

"Now, young man, you just get out of here," she said. "We've had enough trouble and we are not going to have any more."

I got up, two pair of eyes following me to the door. Jesus Christ, I thought, what is it like for a woman to live with a man who molests children and what is it like to live with a woman who knows you molest children? I went back and told Bill Mason it was a washout. He nodded sourly. "Yeh, we got that from the cops. Now, tomorrow I want you to take another area." This went on for a week. We found no clue to the Aune killing.

By the time I returned to the university the next year, I considered myself a real-time reporter. I had learned the mechanics of the trade. I knew my way around. I had another summer stint on the *Journal* and then in the autumn of 1929 I began to run the *Minnesota Daily*—"the world's largest college daily," as we called ourselves, circulation eight thousand, six times a week—for a salary of seventy-five dollars a month. I had been more or less self-supporting for two years and was finally helping my father a bit.

The American dream blew up that autumn. Black Friday tore our world apart and even a smart-ass youngster like myself had to realize something had changed. I had grown up believing the stock market was the devil's kitchen. My father never owned a share of stock except in the bag company. The only member of the family who had any stock was my New York aunt, Sue. She thought she was a sophisticated investor. She bought French and Italian bonds and saw them fall to cut-rate levels. Then she bought Kreuger and Toll, blue chip. She gave me ten shares of Kreuger and Toll for a graduation present. A bit later, Ivar Kreuger put a bullet in his head and that was the end of my poor aunt's nest egg. When Black Friday hit, I had no idea what it meant, but I was pleased to have a front-row seat. I was editor of the *Daily,* a senior at the university, and I had fallen in love. I was supporting myself, doing exactly what I wanted. Depression? The word hadn't been coined.

The *Daily*'s editorial line—caustic, adolescent, antagonistic to the university administration, to the Board of Regents, still headed by the durable Fred Snyder, and to the state legislature, controlled, as always, by bumpkin Republicans and lobbyists for big interests—had been set by Gordon Roth, who preceded me as editor. Roth was my hero. He was tough, cynical, courageous. He had worked the lumber mills in Snowqualmie Falls, Washington, and the copper smelters in Alaska. The day he graduated, he secretly eloped, leaving his bride to finish school, set off for China, riding the rods to Seattle, working his way across the Pacific, writing for the China coast papers, and then, at Christmas, returning, Kit meeting his train in St. Cloud. He regarded the whole lot—President Coffman, the regents, the legislature—as Yahoos. So did I. I thought the *Daily*'s position was very strong. I did not understand that power will use any weapon to preserve itself. This lesson would have to be dinned into my head again and again.

The *Daily* was the creature of a student Board of Publications, which possessed unlimited authority. It was not subordinate to the university. So I thought. The board was controlled by my friends, a quasi-secret political society of which I was a leading member. To my mind, my position as editor was beyond challenge. What the *Daily* said was true and I believed truth was a terrible swift sword.

Our Grey Friars society held a commanding position in student affairs, largely due to the political sense of the man who had built up the coalition, Harold Stassen. Harold was the second future presidential aspirant whom I came to know. Unlike Farrell Dobbs's, his rise was no surprise. The surprise was his fall.

I still regard Stassen as the outstanding young political figure of his day. Extraordinary for his hard work (he put himself through law school as a night Pullman conductor on the St. Paul–Chicago run), a first-class student and debater, the winner of speech medals, strong and rugged (though he came down with TB the summer after leaving Minnesota), articulate, personable, shrewd, he built a political system which monopolized the Minnesota campus. For him, the university was a dry run for adult politics. In his day the Friars never lost an election. We picked attractive candidates, carefully welded interest groups together, did our spadework at the grass roots. Plus dirty tricks. The dirty tricks were just like Richard Nixon's, schoolboy skulduggery and just as needless. We not only got out the vote, we counted it and if necessary, as in the case of an unfortunate business school election, flushed the ballots down the toilet so that they would not reveal our candidate had lost. We planted spies in the enemy camp, stole the opposition secrets.

This makes Stassen sound like Nixon. He wasn't. For all the hijinks, he was a serious politician. He had a set of values in the liberal mode of Minnesota Republican politics which developed in the wake of World War I chauvinism.

Stassen represented something new, able, vigorous. He had set his sights high. In his later years he seemed an oddball (which he was), a nut who campaigned into his seventies for the presidency, wearing an unlovely wig to cover the baldness he had had before he left the university.

But that looks at his life wrong end to. I was present at the beginning and I watched Stassen get off to the fastest kind of start. In no time, he had skyrocketed into the governor's mansion and was headed for national leadership. After serving in the Pacific with Admiral Halsey, he came back to pick up his career. One morning in 1946, I bumped into him in the coffee shop of the Mayflower Hotel in Washington. He told me his plans, full of confidence, good sense and intelligence about the postwar world. He had been a member of the U.S. delegation to the United Nations founding conference in San Francisco and was ready to remake the world and the country. Four Roosevelt terms had left the Republican party a shambles, and Stassen hoped to take it over. I believed he had more than a chance of pulling it off, until one evening in the spring of 1948 when he engaged in a radio debate in Portland, Oregon, against Thomas Dewey, his rival for the Republican presidential nomination. Stassen's career ended that night although he spent another life-time trying to pull it back together. I still cannot understand why Stassen, the champion debater, the silver-tongued boy ora-tor, floundered in the presence of Tom Dewey, who sounded like old blotting paper. But it happened. Harold did yeoman service for President Eisenhower. He was the first national politician to understand, take seriously and accomplish something in the field of disarmament. With a dime's worth of luck and one clear pat from Eisenhower, he could have had a second shot at the presi-dency and elbowed Richard Nixon aside. Had he done so, I think he would have beaten John Kennedy in 1960. He could have made the Republican party the vehicle for progress and intelli-gent change instead of a swamp of opportunism and recurrent know-nothingism under Goldwater, Nixon and Reagan. Stassen would have made it the party of Willkie, Vandenberg, Warren, Aiken, Hatfield and Mathias—my kind of Republicanism.

This did not happen. Twenty years of eccentricity drove out of people's minds the quality of the early Stassen, the Stassen I knew and admired, youngest governor ever elected, farsighted in his views of the world and of his country. We will never reckon the national loss suffered through Stassen's political degrada-tion. He once stood head and shoulders above every man who had a run for the presidency after Eisenhower, with the possible ex-ception of the two Kennedys. He was the first of a succession of Minnesota disappointments, men who came out of the old North-west and fell short on the national scene—McCarthy, Humphrey, possibly Mondale.

I embarked upon editing the *Minnesota Daily* with no deep po-litical convictions. That was true of all of us on the *Daily*. We grew up as naïfs. There may have been a socialist among us, but

I don't remember one. And I never heard of a Communist on the campus. Communists were in Russia or possibly China, not in Minnesota. We on the *Daily* thought of ourselves as muckrakers. I was beginning to read Thorstein Veblen and was captivated by his theory of the leisure class, but when I was twenty-one I registered as a Republican. I have never changed.

I guess you could call us the last generation of the Ski-U-Mahs, crazy about football, Red Grange, the Four Horsemen, Bronko Nagurski, the Little Brown Jug, Stutz Bearcats (there wasn't one on the campus), John Held, Jr., girls, "Soft Shoulders," "Dangerous Curves," pom-poms, rumble seats, homecoming bonfires and booze—the last of the 1920s. Europe was still Paris via cattle boat. We hadn't heard of Hitler. Mussolini was a comic tin soldier, we didn't know about Matteotti. We worked part time (some of us full time) for Captain Billy Fawcett, who had conceived his famous *Whiz-Bang* while in the trenches of France, a doughboy's jokebook of outhouse and farmyard humor. It had roared up to circulate a million or two copies in the early twenties. Now Captain Billy had a string of Hollywood, confession and Western magazines and a north woods resort at Breezy Point, Gull Lake, complete with slot machines, roulette tables, illegal liquor and fly-in Hollywood starlets. I went there once on an assignment for the *Journal* and it blew my mind.

My attention, I'm afraid, was more drawn to froth than the Sacco-Vanzetti case and Stalin's drive against the kulaks.

I thought the university administration was dumpy, maybe even rotten. I knew the Board of Regents was violently reactionary, dictatorial and geriatric (I knew nothing of Fred Snyder's World War I behavior). I regarded the legislature as the creature of the big lobbies—public utilities, railroads, shipping interests, milling—and I think I was right.

Armed with Bill Mason's expertise, I set out in the *Daily* to show them up. We were hard diggers. If you had asked me our objective, I would have said that we wanted a better university, we wanted to expose the shoddy system and lay the foundation for a university dedicated to good teaching, good research, high standards. Yes, that was so. But there was also the chase, the scoop, the fast action, the headlines. I was going to make the *Daily* the talk of the town. Well, I succeeded.

Hardly a day passed without a *Daily* exposé landing on page one of the Twin City newspapers. Soon I was invited to talk with Lotus Delta Coffman, who spoke of his hope for a more healthy attitude by the *Daily*. The dean of students, Edward E. Nicholson (whose long, sad face later would be recalled to me by John Foster Dulles), expressed his concern to the Board of Publications. Warning signals flew. I paid no heed. I knew it was legislative year, the year when the university budget must be approved. I knew the university trembled at each new story splashed onto the front pages. I delighted in it. We would show them! Warnings? Threats? Dangers? We were armored with the Truth, and besides, we controlled the Board of Publications. Before Christmas vacation in December, someone close to the administration passed on word that unless the *Daily* quieted down, there would be trouble. Fred Snyder was on the warpath. I shrugged. No one could intimidate me.

The state legislature convened in January. I opened the month with another *Daily* crusade, directed against a new rule posted by the administration which forbade smoking in the vestibule of the library on penalty of a year's suspension. A student who wanted a quick fag would have to brave twenty-below-zero cold on the outer steps. A trivial issue, a silly issue, but the banality of it—a year's suspension for one cigarette. Ridiculous! So thundered the *Daily*. I sent reporters to violate the new rule and write sarcastic stories. One cold morning, my friend John Moorhead, business manager of the university yearbook, said: "What will you do if the dean throws one of your reporters out of school?" This had not occurred to me. I donned my camel's hair coat, which reached to my ankles. For the first time in my life I was sporting a current fad; the coat was my pride and joy. I had bought it wholesale for forty dollars from Charley Gaskill. John and I went to the library vestibule, smoked our cigarettes, exchanged a casual word with a janitor named George Sundy and hiked back to the *Daily*, where I wrote an account of the episode which ended with the words: "Thus far all attempts to secure an arrest and a test of the legality of an arrest have failed due to the backwardness of the prohibition officer (Sundy) to exercise his legal rights." I felt a lot better. Now if the university wanted a culprit it would be me, the editor of the *Daily*, not some fresh·man cub. Four days later, Dean Nicholson suspended me from the university. My camel's hair coat had been a giveaway to my identity. I could not have better served the interests of Lotus Delta Coffman and Fred Snyder.

There was a tremendous stink. We published an extra called the *Vigilante,* with headlines six inches high. I made the front page of *The New York Times,* a three-paragraph box at the top of column two. The only result was to get poor John Moorhead suspended, as well.

To my father, my expulsion was more trouble in a life of trouble. For him, no trumpets of the free press, no political cadenzas; just his son being unfairly treated. I had offered the dean a public apology. That, said Dad, would have been an appropriate punishment for what he regarded as an inexcusable violation of university regulations. But the university, to his mind, was even more in the wrong. As he wrote Coffman: "The severe punishment inflicted takes on the color of persecution rather than prosecution."

There was something else the university had done. In defense of his action, the dean said that John and I had blown smoke into the face of Janitor Sundy, had used foul language and thrown our cigarette butts at him. This was a lie. It took my breath away. That the dean could be sore—that I could understand; that he and the others would lie was beyond imagination. I was desperate lest Oscar Firkins believe these calumnies. He suffered from such an allergy to tobacco that he could not enter a room in which a cigarette had been smoked. I thought I had lost him. Two days after my suspension, he wrote:

"My Dear Mr. Salisbury: I wish to say that in the recent difficulty, penalty seems to me to be altogether disproportionate to offense, that my sympathies are with you and that my regard for you is unchanged."

He invited me to Sunday lunch and arranged for me to attend his winter lecture on the New York theater. That was better than a diploma.

I had a telephone call from Hillier Krieghbaum, manager of the United Press office in St. Paul. He had an opening in his bureau and it had occurred to him that I might be at liberty. I was. Within the week I went to work for UP.

I was suspended on January 13, 1930. On January 19, 1955, twenty-five years later, I stood on the platform of Northrop Auditorium and received the University of Minnesota's Outstanding Achievement Award for my career in journalism. As I told the audience, I long since had given up smoking and the library long since had abolished restrictions on smoking. I should have added that Fred Snyder, Lotus Delta Coffman and Dean Nicholson had done me the favor of my life. The cigarette I smoked in the library vestibule plunged me into fifty years of turbulent world history. I owed them more than I could ever repay.

But it didn't seem so at the time. I had been tossed out of school for a foolish stunt, I had disappointed my father and I had just lost the girl with whom I had fallen in love, my first, wild romantic love. Jean was an intellectual, all A's, *Lebkuchen* hair, green eyes, snub nose, serious face, slim figure, light foot, a high-tension girl, a nervous girl, not much humor. She was a sophomore, I a senior, and she thought of me as an "older man." She was the daughter of a newspaperman, an erratic genius, long separated from Jean's mother, a Hearst man who, assigned to a story about Aimee Semple McPherson, had become her acolyte. Perhaps that was why Jean sometimes turned her clear eyes on me with skepticism. I could not bear to be separated from her. I sat around the parlor, talking to her mother, while Jean studied. Once she burst out: "You've been talking so much I've done three extra pages of Latin!" We went to the prom and stayed up for breakfast. I thought she was the most beautiful girl in the world. There was nothing I would not do to be in her company. I even persuaded her to go to work for the *Daily* as a reporter. One soft summer evening, we paddled down to the Minnesota River, past the sandy bars and cottonwoods. At dusk we made a landing, built a driftwood fire, lay on a blanket and talked about poetry—and biology—as we watched the stars come out. Poetry was not Jean's thing. She was a budding scientist, filled with excitement over experiments with fruit flies. I put my arm around her and we kissed. It was the first time I had kissed a real girl, not a cousin or a sister. I was careful to kiss her with coolness. Passion, I thought, would offend her. Her lips had a clean, fresh, salty taste that surprised me. I mustered more courage and gently, ever so gently, put my hand around her breast. I had never done anything so daring. It felt so round, so firm, so soft, so warm, so globular, I almost went out of my mind. I could feel her heart beat and mine began to race like an engine. I held myself apart so that she would not know how excited I was. I thought that would shock her. I was sure no good girl wanted to feel *that*. We lay on the sandbar until it began to grow chilly, then we got into the canoe, she resting against the thwart, looking at me, I thought, quizzically. I paddled silently, slipping the paddle into the water without a sound, and swiftly brought us to the landing. A little shakily, I helped Jean out of the canoe and we got into the old Packard and drove back to St. Paul, sitting very close, her head on my shoulder, her hair flowing in my face. I had never had such an evening. I never imagined what it might be to love a girl. I took Jean out as often as she would go. Occasionally we parked by Lake Como and held hands, kissing gently. I never whispered to Jean that I loved her. Why? I think I sensed that she did not love me and I could not bear the shock of hearing her say it. I wanted to go on drifting. Sometimes it was dawn when I took her home. Then I would get into the Packard, roar west on Lake Street and watch the speedometer climb to sixty miles an hour, twin-six engines throbbing, the air fresh in my face, the sun coming up, the clouds all golden, the fading night air fragrant with roses and bridal wreath. I could hardly contain myself. Once toward dawn I lost self-restraint. I kissed Jean passionately, drew her to me, crushed her thin body to mine and we kissed wildly. Then suddenly I pulled away, saying, "That's enough! I must be a man!" Jean looked at me, her face a puzzle. "Why did you say that?" And she slipped out of the car. To this day I don't know what I meant.

She had made up her mind to leave Minnesota and transfer to the University of Texas. She had a chance to work with Dr. Hermann Muller, the great geneticist, who would win the Nobel Prize in 1946. Nothing I could say turned her intention. She was strong-willed and I was not part of her plan of life.

I told Jean I would follow her to Texas, to the ends of the earth. She thought I was joking. "You're crazy," she said. I said I could not live without her. She laughed. "That's silly." When she saw that I was serious, she shook her head in wonderment. "I never thought you felt like that. Why didn't you say something?" It was, she made plain, too late. Off she did go, three young men escorting her to the St. Paul Union Station. We saw her aboard the train, watched it pull out and separated abruptly. For weeks I dreamed of getting into the Packard and heading south at sixty miles an hour, driving day and night until I reached Austin, bursting in on her, showing the depths of my love. I got the road maps, traced out the route, but never went. I wrote every day, she much less often.

It was years before we met again. Muller was a Soviet sympathizer, probably for a time a Communist party member (on the tenth anniversary of Lenin's death, he delivered in Moscow an address entitled "Lenin's Teachings in His Attitude Toward Genetics"). He was a close friend and colleague of Vavilov, the great Russian geneticist, who worked with him in Austin. In 1933, Muller went to Moscow, where he collaborated with Vavilov until 1937; then he went to Spain to aid the Spanish Loyalists. He left Moscow just in time. Two Soviet biologists who had worked in Austin vanished into Stalin's purges that year. The next year, Vavilov was arrested. He starved to death in a Soviet prison in 1943. The whole Soviet genetics world was wiped out. Jean came within a hair's breadth of being caught up in the maelstrom. Muller asked her to accompany him to Moscow. Fortunately, she fell in love with a young American scientist and decided instead to marry and stay in Austin.

9 | Newspaperman

Gradually the pain began to ease, helped by my new love, the UP. The UP hired very young men, paying them a bare minimum, tossed story after story at them, and advanced them with startling rapidity. Within a year or so we became "young veterans," that is, we were doing jobs normally handled by men ten or twenty years older and doing them with flair, dash and energy, although occasionally not with total accuracy or mature judgment. Our watchword was "Beat Rox." "Rox" was patois for the AP, our rival. International News Service, the Hearst agency, was called "Jits." No one knew the origin of these nicknames. I came to UP in the last years of the Morse telegraph operators. The system was rapidly switching to teleprinters, but in 1930 there were still parallel Morse lines along the trunks. The St. Paul office had one Morse operator, named Markham, and one teleprinter operator, a woman named Erickson. Markham got more money than the bureau chief and three times as much as I did. He was the one who lent me five dollars when I needed it to see me through the week. The Morse wire provided constant communication around the continent, the operators chattering among themselves or relaying messages bureau to bureau.

Though short on pay, the UP was long on praise. We dealt in competitive breaks measured in minutes or even in seconds, and a stream of congratulations and complaints emanated from New York (NX) to spur us on. This traffic was handled in now-forgotten Phillips telegraphic code, in which Supreme Court became "Scotus," White House "WHU," the State Department "DOS." Messages were signed off "73's," which meant "Regards." Every person in the system was addressed by initials. I acquired a new nickname, "HES."

Our coverage out of St. Paul was catch-as-catch-can. The office had only seventy-five dollars a month for string correspondents, and often "downholds" would cut this to sixty dollars or even to zero. We were responsible for everything that happened in Minnesota, North and South Dakota, eastern Montana, western Wisconsin and western Canada (through an under-the-counter arrangement with the Winnipeg Free Press).

I don't remember where the idea came from. Possibly from Earl J. Johnson, the UP's news director, possibly from my chief, Hillier Krieghbaum. It grew out of the lengthening shadow of Depression. Already UP was carrying a daily column of "Good News," items of business upturns, sales increases, new plants, rehirings, and the like. Sometimes we could collect only four or five paragraphs from the whole country. The Depression was clamping down on a nation that didn't know what was happening to it. UP was beginning to run stories exploring the situation, and I was assigned to do one about Minneapolis. We didn't then know that the story was the same everywhere, only the details were different. I found that the city was dead; nothing was moving; each day more haunted men lost their jobs. My father was lucky. His pay had been cut to a pittance, but he had a place to go to work.

Minneapolis, having felt only the faintest blush of the boom, was sliding into the pit. The mills were grinding to a halt. The great distributive businesses were drying up. Utilities, especially 1920s stock promotions like that of W. B. Foshay, who had built the tallest and newest and almost the only skyscraper in town, were tottering.

I was delighted with the assignment. I went down to the Gateway, to skid row, the traditional migrant-labor market. Here were the hiring halls for the north woods, the grain fields, the railroads, the mines. I went to the labor exchanges. There wasn't a job posted in the windows. The men sat on the curbs, row on row, silent, desperate, not a drink to pass around, no grain alcohol, no filtered wood alcohol, no ginger jake, not even Copenhagen snuff. They sat and stared blankly into space, each man in his denim work clothes an island to himself, beyond communication, beyond hope, sitting on the curb and sometimes shifting a bit, when his legs or his ass got stiff. The Salvation Army was feeding those who got fed. Many didn't have twenty-five cents for a flophouse. They slept on the sidewalk or in the parks. They were seedy and thin and hungry. Nothing to pawn. I went to the IWW hall on Western Avenue, up a worn staircase to the second floor. It smelled of thirty years of Edgeworth and Prince Albert, generations of cut plug and snoose. A dozen men sat at tables, playing pinochle. There were no young men, no one my age. They looked at me with suspicion. What did a reporter want, talking to them? They had been through it before, the provocations, the beatings, the police harassment, the jails. They were gun-shy. I had sense enough not to ask questions, just listened. They had, they said, hopes. The IWW would make a comeback. This was their hour. The IWW was putting itself at the head of the jobless. They were not going to ask for jobs. They would take them. I didn't believe a word of it. I felt sorry for these broken men. If these were dangerous revolutionaries, there would be no revolution. They were leftovers, bitter, crushed, castrated.

I talked to the chamber of commerce people. They had no answers. They were frightened. I talked to businessmen. They were no more eager to see me than the IWW was. Their eyes were angry and puzzled. Why was this happening? Hadn't they done all the right things—worked hard, invested their money, tried to make a decent profit? Everything had been so good, and now out of a clear sky—this.

There were, of course, no welfare agencies. No relief. No social security. No unemployment insurance. No federal work programs. I put it together and the story went on the wire. Almost instantly I got congratulations. "Fine yarn" was the message from HX, the Chicago bureau. I felt very proud.

But within an hour, Hillier Krieghbaum had a telephone call from New York. New York—my God! It was the first time since I had gone to work for UP that we had had a call from New York. It was not a pleasant call. The *Minneapolis Journal* had telephoned. Either the UP would kill that story and fire its author or the *Journal* would cancel the service. Who was this Salisbury, New York asked, what did he mean, putting a defamatory story on the wire? Kill that story; kill it fast; call the *Journal* and go to see them. Hold their hand. Fire Salisbury if he's to blame.

I was appalled. So was Krieghbaum. So was Chicago, which had already congratulated me on the story. Somehow Krieghbaum smoothed it all down. He mollified the *Journal.* They didn't quit, but they muttered a lot about the UP hiring "that goddamn radical kid from the university." I dug out a letter of recommendation I had got when I left the *Journal,* which said I was "careful, accurate and efficient" and "one of the best men that came to the *Journal."* Krieghbaum sent that on to Earl J. Johnson, who said, Well, O.K., but keep his name off the wire until the

Journal calms down, and for chrisake put the fear of God into him.

It put the fear of God into me, all right. Twice in six months I had been given a demonstration of the power of the press. I had brought the university down on me and now I had aroused the *Journal* and the power structure of Minneapolis. It caused me to think a bit. I had written nothing more than the truth. There wasn't a word in my vignette of Minneapolis that wasn't true. It was a "careful, accurate" story. Even the *Journal* didn't challenge that. But the truth was not what the *Journal* wanted. The truth might hurt business more than the Depression already had. The *Journal* feared that other cities would say, look, Minneapolis is where the Depression is—not Milwaukee, not St. Louis, not Kansas City. Depression is in Minneapolis. Didn't you see that story by UP?

Not, of course, that things were O.K. in Milwaukee. The whole country was in the same boat, but each businessman, each city, was fighting for that little edge over the other fellow. Fear was at the root of the *Journal*'s outrage, just as fear had been what moved Dean Nicholson, Lotus Delta Coffman and Fred Snyder. It wasn't that the *Daily* was printing lies. It was that the *Daily* was printing truth. So sit on the truth. Put down the editor. Plaster it over. The *Journal* gave me the same lesson. Don't think that truth is a defense. The hell with the truth. Give us varnish. No blizzards ever hit Minneapolis in the *Journal,* and no Depression is going to hit it either. If UP doesn't agree, rip the wires out.

Did I get the message? Not really. A hundred lessons lay ahead of me—in Moscow; in Birmingham, Alabama; in Hanoi. The geography changed. The country changed. The society and the politics changed. Sometimes it was the administration of a Midwestern university, sometimes the city fathers of my own city; President Lyndon Johnson or the rulers of the Kremlin; World War II generals or Bull Connor in Birmingham; but the message was always the same: Shut up! Don't rock the boat. Keep those unpleasant truths to yourself. The truth, I was ultimately to learn, is the most dangerous thing. There are no ends to which men of power will not go to put out its eyes.

On my way to Chicago! Goodbye, Minneapolis! On the way to the big city, the city of brawny shoulders, tough Chicago. I sat up a little straighter in the night coach, fare $8.20, the midweek excursion, paid by myself, the condition of my transfer by UP from WS (St. Paul) to HX (Chicago). The date was January 13, 1931, one year to the day from my expulsion from Minnesota. I sat drowsing against the worn red plush of the heated coach, my uncle Scott's alligator gladstone by my side, on my way to Chicago. I was scared, but more excited than scared. Dreams wandered through my head. I had never lived away from home. I kept thinking in capital letters. The Big Test. Sandburg's Chicago, Frank Norris's Chicago, Colonel McCormick's Chicago, Al Capone's Chicago. The Big Time. I dozed at the window, got up, went to the toilet, came back, smoked a cigarette. Everyone was asleep, even the sickly baby who had cried in his mother's arms for the first two hours. The train rattled through the little towns, just a blur of a station, a blur of a lighted window. It had been snowing, perhaps still was, and the train moved in a whirl of powdery snow. I heard the clack-ity-clack as we went over the grade crossings, on and on, the windows thick with frost, the red and green lights of the signals aureoled on the panes as we roared through the night. The Chicago train. Chicago. Chicago. *Chicago.* The wheels beat the rhythm into my dull brain. The umbilical cord was cut. I was on my own now; never again Minneapolis.

Oh, I would go back, but the house on Kenwood Hill wasn't home and home was gone. Home was 107 Royalston Avenue. But I knew on that night train to Chicago that I would carry 107 within me like a cave to crawl in when lonely or distant or fearful.

The sky had hardly grayed when we pulled into Chicago at 7 A.M., the long nights of winter still holding us in their grasp. I put on my camel's hair coat, my throat sore from the hot air, the feverish naps, the cigarettes. I picked up my bags and walked through the great waiting room and out over the bridge, dirty ice floating on the green puke of the Chicago River, men and women, mostly men, hurrying head down against the wind, I hurrying too, under the "L" and up Monroe Street to the Great Northern Hotel. I got a room, paid in advance, three dollars. I gave the bellhop a dime tip, my first tip. I remember coming down to the street and out into the cold, the wind blowing off Lake Michigan. Not eight o'clock yet and on my way to the office, my throat ached, my eyes ached, my head ached. I breathed in the cold air, big breaths, threw back my shoulders, put my head up, held it high and walked east toward the lake. I leaned into the wind and walked through the crowds pouring down from the "L," starting their day's work. They did not know me. They did not know who I was. They did not know what I was going to do. I stepped forward with sharp, hard steps, my heels slamming on the icy pavement, across State Street, the wind stronger, red streetcars rattling by, past the Palmer House, on to Wabash, under the "L" and on to Michigan Avenue, and the plain of snow where lay Lake Michigan, frozen, the wind gathering strength from miles and miles and smiting the great barrier buildings, the monuments to Jenney, to Louis Sullivan, to Frank Lloyd Wright, the Tribune Tower, the Wrigley Building, the Union Carbide Building, black and shiny, the bulky stones of the public library, the Museum of Art, the Auditorium, the Congress Hotel, the Blackstone, the Stevens. Nothing could hurl them down, nothing could move them. Chicago was built for eternity.

I walked down the avenue, tall and skinny, six feet tall, 142 pounds, a long cantering gait, my ankle-length coat swirling around me, a comic figure, likely to be splintered by the wind, but not splintering, not aware of the comedy, deathly serious, stalking Chicago like a camel-coated panther. I was going to *take* this city. I was going to take Chicago. Words out of some book I had read. Well, that was my fantasy. I was wearing Unk's old brown sealskin cap, very soft, very worn, very seedy, the earflaps not down—hell, I didn't feel the cold, the blood raced too strongly in my veins. So I had said as I left the Great Northern. But now I was slapping at my ears. They had lost sensation. My cheeks were numb, and so were my thighs above my knees. Enough. I had laid my challenge. I turned off the avenue, scuttled once more under the "L" and over to State Street. There, kitty-cornered across from Carson Pirie Scott, was the Consumers Building, creamy white tile, at 220 South State Street, home of the Chicago bureau of United Press. I crossed the street, swung through the brass-bound revolving doors, and took an open-cage elevator to the eighth floor.

Chicago. The near North Side. East Ohio Street. The Berkshire Hotel, twin to the Devonshire Hotel, standing side by side. They still stood fifty years later, now the East Ohio and the New Tokyo. I had a broom-closet room in the Berkshire, $7.57 a week, with a Murphy bed. When it was down, the room was full. There was a window on an air shaft, and across the air shaft, two windows. At night sometimes I turned out the light and watched an old actress (I *knew* she was an old actress) with dangling tits tumble a young actress (I *knew* she was a young actress), skinny, almost titless. I was revolted. I could not pull my eyes away.

The first friend I made was Tom Sweeney—it was a year before he told me his real name was Tony Segala—who would wear a jaunty gray felt hat, a camel's hair coat as bulky as mine, his with reinforced inner pockets. He could carry eight quarts. Gin was three dollars a quart and he would put on any label you fancied. If you saved the bottle, he'd knock off fifty cents, two quarts for five dollars, day or night, delivery in five minutes. Weekends were pretty busy. A young man named Emil helped Tom on weekends. Then Emil went into business for himself. Tom didn't mind. "There's plenty of business," he said. One Sunday, Tom and Emil had lunch in the greasy spoon at Ohio and State. They finished about 2 P.M. and Emil said, "Well, I guess I'll go and mix a bit." He was getting ready for the late Sunday afternoon rush. He went back to his room on the third floor of a red-brick flat at 644 North State. An hour later, something happened. "Probably it was a cigarette," Tom said. "I always told him, Never smoke when you're mixing." The alcohol went up in a flash. Emil was trapped, the flame between him and the door. He jumped from the window, not noticing the iron pickets along the sidewalk, which impaled his skull. "It's a pity," Tom said. "Emil was a nice young man. He had a good future."

Tom was very philosophical.

He worried a lot about Ray Black, who came to UP a year after I went to Chicago. He was a veteran newspaperman who had worked on Bonfils's *Denver Post*. Once, after an argument at the Denver Athletic Club, Ray had stepped out a window. A glass portiere broke his fall. He fractured his ankles and quite a few bones.

One night, Ray Black stomped into the UP office leaving a red trail behind him. "What happened?" I asked. "My shoe is full of blood," Ray said. "The goddamn night watchman didn't come, so I kicked in the plate-glass door."

Ray had a friend named Miss Featherstonehaugh. He ordered three bottles of gin at a crack from Tom Sweeney. "I brought him two," Sweeney said. "But he got mad. He said I was trying to get him to go on the wagon. I wish he would."

Just up State Street from the Berkshire was Holy Name, the diocesan cathedral. On summer evenings I liked to stroll by the little flowershop across the street, the one that did a big business in funeral wreaths, the flowershop where Dion O'Banion was shot to death in 1927. I was fascinated by O'Banion and liked to think there was a touch of Dublin, Easter Sunday, 1916, about his murder. But it was all fake. O'Banion carried three guns, and traded in women, booze and "protection." My head swam with gang lore and my ears reverberated to the gang bombings. The gang was "organizing" cleaning shops on the near North Side, the protection racket. Almost every evening at the Berkshire, I would hear the rumble of a bomb or two. I felt cheated at having missed the 1929 St. Valentine's Day massacre at a garage a few blocks away, and the shoot-up that turned Cicero, on Chicago's outskirts, into a war zone.

I walked to work each night just before eleven o'clock, down State Street, very dark, and over the drawbridge. Waiting most nights just at the draw were two black whores, big, brawny women. They stood close together, and as I got to the bridge, half averting my head, half transfixed, they would throw up their broad skirts, revealing black thighs, all hairy and crawling with crabs and oozing with clap, so I was sure. They gave off great guffaws that sent me scurrying over the bridge. "Only a dollah, boy," they would shout, "only a dollah for you. Come and get it."

I got to the Consumers Building at eleven, checked the file, hurried out for lunch, past the Rialto burlesque house, where I sometimes paid fifty cents for a balcony seat on Saturday night, under the "L" and up Jackson Street to the B/G sandwich shop, just as the Rainbow Dance Palace was closing, the girls, tired, starved, feverish, faces streaked with rouge and smudged powder, skinny legs and shoulders, jostled down from the second-floor hall, into the street with their ponces. My mind rang with sentimentality: Ten Cents a Dance, Ten Cents a Dance. I suppose the girl kept a nickel. I slouched into the B/G, clean, lighted, wholesome, ordered my BLT (seventeen cents), my coffee (five cents), my cherry pie (eleven cents); a nickel tip for the all-American waitress in her crisp green uniform. I ate quickly, my mind imagining the little Polack girls, the little Hunky girls, the fat stomachs and fat pricks of middle-aged men pressing their flat thighs, fat hands rubbing their flat breasts, meeting at quitting time for a quick one in the alley, the girls hurrying home with a couple of dollars in a little beaded snap purse—well, my scenario was maudlin, and it was true. Sometimes I walked on the dance hall side of the street, brushing through the cluster of chattering girls smelling of sweetish cheap powder and sweat, all of them so small I wondered whether the dance hall insisted on that, small girls, small faces, fifteen years old, sixteen, maybe seventeen. This was deep Depression time. No kidding about it. Not now, the girls supporting their families, hurrying to catch the "L" and turn the money over to a hard-faced mother eager to get her girl back into the house and the money out of the beaded bag before the old man found out that she had turned her daughter into a whore.

10 | Depression

Back to 220 South State, back to my night's work, the 1 A.M. editions of the *Trib* and the *Examiner,* a bulletin or two, hot news, Chicago news!—the UP lived on angles, banner headlines, black and bold, about Gang Wars and Capone. Capone was the best headline.

I was in seventh heaven. I wrote notes to my friends in Minneapolis in Ben Hechtese. I dreamed of Charles MacArthur and *The Front Page.* I reread Carl Sandburg and Dreiser, *Sister Carrie* and Stephen Crane's *Maggie: A Girl of the Streets.* One Sunday I walked down South Michigan to Twenty-third Street, hoping to see Al Capone come out of his bulletproof headquarters in the Metropole Hotel, where he received supplicants like a pope, extending his diamond-studded pinkie to courtiers. But he didn't emerge and I didn't have the courage to go into the hotel. I walked back to the Berkshire ashamed of my cowardice, but soon I forgot all that in the excitement of my new assignment—an assignment to cover the Big Guy, Mr. Brown, Al Capone himself.

Capone turned out to be a small, soft man with layers of fat over his shoulders and neck, his arms rounded like a woman's, his face steel blue—I think he shaved three times a day—smelling of barbershop cologne, with pudgy hands, manicured nails, radishy fingers. He had his $135 suits tailored by the best Italian tailors in Chicago—dark, striped, thin stripes, very close-fitting, shoulders padded, jacket constructed so that his breast gun did not bulge, the waist slightly broadened so there was no bulge from his hip gun, the trousers pockets reinforced so there was no sag from the gun weight. He wore a heavy gold wristwatch, a heavenly blue silk shirt ($25), a dark polka-dot necktie, a purple-edged silk handkerchief, dabbed at his forehead again and again. He sweated easily, as I was to learn, for I sat two feet from him for twelve days while he was tried on income tax charges before Judge Wilkerson at the old Federal Building. Capone, a beady-eyed man, a rather dignified man, agile on the balls of his feet, had no small talk, spoke not a word except to his lawyer, Michael

Ahearn. Ahearn was Irish handsome, a high flush in his cheeks, haunted, eloquent, reciting the litany of Marcus Cato to the Roman Senate: *Delenda est Carthago.* Carthage must be destroyed. So, said Ahearn, the government thundered: Capone must be destroyed. It was eloquent in Ahearn's rich baritone. It moved me. I thought the government's case was repugnant. Admittedly they could not put together the evidence to convict Capone on charges of violating the Volstead Act, although he and his men broke the law a thousand times a day. So they brought suit for not paying income taxes on his illegal gains—sleazy politics, I thought. I had no sympathy for Capone. He was a killer and a pig, but by this time I understood that Prohibition was a cozy conspiracy, everyone in it for the bucks, everyone in on the payoff—the gangs, the government, the police, the businessmen, the banks, the quiet and respectable interests that owned those fine old breweries where the beer was brewed. And what about the thousands of speakeasies, open and operating everywhere? To whom did they pay the protection—and the rent? What about the world's largest building, the new Chicago Merchandise Mart, echoingly vacant except for a block-long speakeasy and restaurant; who was this New York operator Joseph Kennedy, who owned it all? One night, very drunk, some friends and I visited the Working Man's Exchange, that unique juxtaposition of one hundred feet of bar and one hundred parallel feet of pissoir. A man could open his fly, take two steps and relieve his bladder while the bartender was drawing the next stein. This functional miracle was the genial creation of those quintessential Chicagoans Michael ("Hinky Dink") Kenna and John ("The Bathhouse") Coughlin, now and forever aldermen of the First Ward. The First Ward was where it all came together—the Four Deuces, the Metropole and the famous house of the Everleigh sisters. After drinking at the Working Man's Exchange I insisted on visiting the Everleigh establishment, but when we arrived I refused to go in. The next morning my patient friend Bill Deighton said: "What the hell was that about last night? First you insist on going to the Everleigh house and then you refuse to go in." I couldn't answer Bill. The fact was I didn't even remember going to the Working Man's Exchange.

What I did know by this time was that everything in the First Ward and everything in the Capone racket was connected with Big Business, Big Banks and Big Politics, a partnership in greed. Even Big Press had a stake in it. Colonel McCormick and William Randolph Hearst and their bloody circulation wars used the same plug-uglies who provided manpower for the gangs—in fact, some said the Chicago gangs had their birth in the circulation wars, the whole raucous schmeer in which the Annenberg brothers played so prominent a role.

There had to be something wrong with our system if it produced such outrages. All this came together for me as I sat in the courthouse during the Capone trial. Who would profit by Capone's conviction? I thought Capone had the same question in his mind. I knew what Dwight Green, the federal D.A., hoped to get —a run for the governorship on the Republican ticket, "The Man Who Put Capone Behind Bars." *Delenda est Capone.* I didn't think Capone liked being compared to Carthage. In general, I thought, he wasn't easy with his lawyers. He was used to hiring lawyers to get a job done, to make a deal, to fix up the papers. He had ordered his lawyers to settle this case; they had made a deal with the feds, a year or two in jail, but Wilkerson kicked it over. If that had happened in gangland, it would have brought out the machine guns. Capone sat porcine, paranoid eyes slitted, uncomfortable, occasionally leaning forward with a steely expression. "Let's get this thing over," the expression said. "What am I paying you for?" I would not have liked being Ahearn or his cozy, old-shoe partner, Albert Fink, the man in the poorly fitting brown suit who did the dog's work, who knew the law and the citations, who smoothed Judge Wilkerson down after Ahearn's violent words. I didn't really like sitting so close to Capone. Sometimes when I was scribbling furiously I looked up and he would be staring at me, not a wisp of expression on his face but his eyes like bullets, registering the fact that I was writing things down. I didn't like that look and I didn't think I liked the thoughts that ran behind his dark brow and the drawn lids of his eyes. I didn't like the way he chewed gum, stick after stick of Juicy Fruit. I would not have liked being the thin, nervous accountant who had ratted, the man who kept the Capone books, the double books, and now had to go over the double-entry columns, line by line, under Capone's scrutiny, Ahearn jabbing at him again and again. I would not have gone home at night if I had been that bookkeeper.

I thought there wasn't a bigger story in the world than Al Capone, and I was on it, writing the day leads, but not under my

name. The leads bore the signature of Robert T. Loughran, who
had never written a story in his life. Loughran was a Chicago
police reporter, one of those you've seen in *The Front Page.* He
was UP's man at police headquarters. He had an open line to the
office. He picked up the phone and shouted: "Rewrite!" One of
us would scribble it down on yellow copy paper with a black copy
desk pencil. When it was a very hot story, I tucked the telephone
into my shoulder and batted out the bulletins directly on the
typewriter, turning Loughran's snorts and grunts into running
copy. It was always hot. Unless it was murder or a five-alarm
fire, Loughran didn't bother to call.

That was Chicago. That's what we sold the world on our wire.
Gangsters and Big Bill Thompson, always mayor or running for
mayor on a platform of "I'll bust King George in the snoot."
That was as close as Thompson got to Chicago's problems. The
city was broke. The country was broke. In Chicago alone, there
were five hundred thousand out of work. Western Electric closed
its huge West Side plant. That night my roommate Julian Bentley and I (we shared quarters at the Berkshire and saved a couple of dollars on rent) had three newly jobless Knox College
classmates of Julian's sleeping on the floor of our room.

I went out Halstead to the West Side to see my old friend
Reuben from Royalston Avenue. All of the West Side was unemployed. The West Side was the Jews, the Poles, the Bohemians,
the Italians. The city was spending seven million dollars a year
on relief, seven million dollars to help five hundred thousand
people, fifteen dollars a year per person. The city was bankrupt.
Reuben was now in Chicago with his father and mother and sister and brother. No work for his father, but Reuben got a few
odd jobs, drawing. His sister, Bessie, did a little clerking. Mr.
Rosen had nothing to say these days. Reuben was grim. "It is
very bad. It's going to get worse." What could I say? My mind
was filled with Capone, Machinegun Jack McGurn and boom-
boom Chicago. But I knew he was right. I didn't dare ask my
father how much he was making. I just sent the money home, ten
dollars some weeks, fifteen dollars some weeks. Julian did the
same. He came from a farm at Big Foot Prairie, Illinois, the
richest dairy country in the land. There was no market for the
milk. They milked the cows and poured the milk into the creek.
That was the worst, pouring out the milk. Tears came to Julian's

eyes when he told me about it. Julian's ten or fifteen dollars kept his father and mother and brother going.

"I'm changing my name," Reuben told me. "Why, for God's sake?" I asked. "Fascism is coming," he said. "Mussolini has taken over Italy. Next it will be Hitler in Germany. It won't be safe to be a Jew. I'm changing my name. I look Italian and I can pass as an Italian." He must have seen shock in my eyes. "No use to take any more chances," he told me. "It's hard enough without being a Jew. My father agrees."

One Saturday morning, I met Reuben at the lower level of Michigan Avenue, next to the Wrigley Building. There was to be a demonstration against the *Chicago Tribune,* against its support of Japanese aggression in China. It must have been the Mukden incident of 1931. We climbed the iron steps to Michigan Boulevard. A couple of thousand people were carrying banners and posters. There were lots of Chicago police, lots of them mounted on great black and chestnut horses. I fidgeted with my press card. Better to put it in my hat? Better not to? I kept my hand on it in my pocket just in case. I heard a mild pop—like a firecracker. How many times I would read and write: "There was this pop. Like a firecracker." And John F. Kennedy went down. Another firecracker and Martin Luther King went down. Another firecracker—President Reagan went down. Always it sounded like a firecracker. I don't know who fired this shot. I don't believe anyone was hit. I saw no revolver. But the mounted police went crazy. They surged into the crowd, horses bucking and rearing, nightsticks flailing just the way Mr. Rosen said the Cossacks had done in Russia, people falling and screaming. Reuben and I whipped down the stairs, across the cobbles of the lower level, and cut back to State Street, panting, out of breath. "Well," I said, "I guess I better get to the office and write the story." I was due on the desk at noon. "I guess I'll go home," Rub said. "I guess it's all over for now."

That was the first demonstration for both of us. Later the demonstrators would come out again and again and again, not thousands, but tens of thousands, hundreds of thousands. The target would not be the Japanese or the *Chicago Tribune;* it would be the White House, Mr. Hoover, the Capitol, the government. Ahead lay bonus marchers, Douglas MacArthur, sharecroppers, Iowa farmers, the unemployed, and every day I was thinking harder and harder. Of course the system was not working now, but something had to have been wrong for a long, long time, something functional. Certainly Mr. Hoover didn't have a clue, probably didn't even think anything was wrong. Every time he spoke, more people lost their jobs. Julian Bentley and I talked a lot. We came from Republican families, but that didn't seem to have any relevance anymore. More and more I found myself thinking the unthinkable—that there was truth in what the Non-partisan League had been saying, in the Farmer-Labor party program, in Bob La Follette's Progressive party, in Thorstein Veblen's tart words. The root of the trouble, I now began to believe, had to be in New York and in Washington—in the New York banks and Wall Street, in the long rule of conservative Republicans in Washington, in their interconnections and team-work—in a word, in the Interests. This, of course, was the line of Floyd B. Olson. Maybe, I thought, he had the answers.

Some Sunday afternoons I took the "L" to Hyde Park on the South Side, near the University of Chicago, where my cousins lived, two first cousins, Lucille and Florence, daughters of my long lost, mysteriously vanished uncle Wesley. Florence taught in the Chicago high schools. She had a job but was paid in scrip; not money; the schools were out of money. Grocers accepted scrip. That kept the family going—her grandparents, the You-manses, her sister, Lucille, and Lucille's husband and two infant children, Lucille's and Florence's mother, Clara, and her sister Ada. Clara and Ada were blind and almost deaf. Ada had a remarkable mind, was a leader in the international world of the blind; Clara seemed to do very little. She had been a pretty girl with a pretty face, played the piano well and enchanted Wesley until whatever happened happened. In our Victorian family such things were never explained. Only by chance did we find out the family secrets.

The flat belonged to the grandparents, the Youmanses—a long railroad flat, five or six rooms. The Youmanses were in their early eighties. I liked them very much. Lucille's husband, Harry, had lost his job and money in Detroit. There were nine people living in this flat, on one salary.

There was good talk at the Youmans table, talk of England and life there in the 1880s, brisk lectures by Ada on the international situation and the rising threat of Hitler, tart comments by Lucille about the antics of Chicago politicians and Mr. Hoover's doleful speeches. The children played and screeched. Florence's pay had to stretch a long way, but this was a warm and lively refuge.

My mother had a niece who lived in Chicago, and I was persuaded to visit Marguerite and her husband, Dwight. Marguerite was a simple woman, red-haired, freckled-faced, from the Pacific Northwest. Her husband was a dapper Dan, with pencil-thin black mustache, pomaded black hair, and rather long black sideburns, unusual for this period. There was a faint touch of Rudolph Valentino about him, an Iowa Valentino who had gone to an osteopathic school and seemed to have had a fairly profitable practice. I don't know why they were living in Chicago, but he was not at the moment practicing osteopathy. He was, in fact, superintendent of a small apartment building, for which he got a flat, rent-free. He made it clear that this was a temporary occupation, undertaken at his own initiative for reasons he did not make clear. He had a vaguely conspiratorial air, no humor, and possessed strong opinions on all questions, particularly political questions. He had no use for Mr. Hoover, no use for Mr. Roosevelt, no use, so far as I could understand, for any politicians I had ever heard of, with the exception of Father Coughlin, who he said "had some good ideas about silver." He was given to cryptic remarks and often raised his eyebrows to convey that he knew a great deal more than he was prepared to tell me.

Dwight was the first dedicated anti-Semite I ever encountered, a man who had read the Protocols of the Elders of Zion and believed them to be the literal truth. The Jewish conspiracy was behind everything, and especially behind the Depression. Jewish bankers controlled Washington and Wall Street and the world. I was not familiar with Nazi ideology, *Mein Kampf* and Julius Streicher's pornographic propaganda, but I later recognized the source of Dwight's philosophy. He warned my mother that the Jews had begun to distribute poisoned canned goods. The poisoned cans could be distinguished because they carried a small Star of David. Mother became quite alarmed, but was never able to find any cans so designated and finally decided it was just "one of Dwight's nutty ideas."

So it was, but it was only part of a pattern of such notions. I don't know where he picked up this drivel, though I know where it led him. In his Chicago days, he had talked about the dangers of the Jewish conspiracy, the need for vigilance (he showed me a rifle he kept in a closet). In 1936 he moved to the Pacific Northwest, and when World War II broke out, it was disclosed that he was a leading officer of the fascist Silver Shirts. He fled into the Oregon woods but was caught and spent a considerable time in prison, emerging at the end of the war, unrepentant and as filled with paranoia as ever. Dwight and Marguerite had an adopted son. I remember him playing on the floor of their North Side Chicago apartment, a tough, sturdy youngster with blue eyes and a mop of blond Nordic hair, very Nordic. He became an over-the-road trucker and was killed in a fiery crash of his rig.

One cold March Sunday, I took the electric train to North Chicago, Illinois, a small industrial town beyond Libertyville and Lake Forest. Not many on the train that morning. No one at the station, the wind at my back from Lake Michigan as I hiked through silent streets, shops closed, no traffic, snow half-plowed. I was making my way to another cousin, so distant I could not quite figure out the relationship. My aunt Sue had written me to look up cousin Emma Salisbury Faulkes and ask her about some family connections. Sue lived for genealogy and connections. The snowline was unbroken at the gray house where Emma Faulkes lived with her husband, George. The door had not been opened that day. They were farmers who had moved to this industrial town ten years earlier. They found North Chicago dirty and noisy. I thought it quiet as death and clean as Ivory soap that Sunday morning. I had written I'd be coming. No telephone. I knocked. After a long time, a gray woman—gray hair that once had been frizzed and auburn, gray calico dress, torn gray sweater, gray face, long gray bony hands—opened the door. It was Emma Faulkes, and she invited me in. I think she did, but I don't remember any voice from her gray lips. I walked into a bare kitchen, the floor covered with brown hexagonal-patterned linoleum curling at the sides. There were four brown-painted chairs with brown dime-store cardboard seats, and a kitchen table covered in worn oilcloth. There was a small coal stove for heating and a kerosene stove for cooking. I think there had been a fire in the coal stove earlier in the morning, but I may have been mistaken. It may have been the night before. George sat at the table. He was wearing heavy wool underwear, blue farmer's overalls with bib, and a worn sheepskin coat. His hands were in the pockets. On his feet were a pair of work shoes. He was as gray as Emma and as thin. My principal impression was the bones of their faces—heavy jaws, heavy cheekbones, foreheads carved with an adze. We sat at the table. I did not take off my coat. I could not imagine people existing in such cold. That was a dozen years before I went to Leningrad, in late January 1944, and saw how Leningrad had lived through nine hundred days of cold and hunger during the blockade. On that March day in 1931, my impression of Emma and George Faulkes was one of horror. This man and woman in their seventies had worked hard on a farm all their lives; ordinary people, ordinary farmers. It was not their fault that cataracts dimmed George's vision so he had to give up plowing and come to live in this frozen house in a frozen town in a society where all the heat had been turned off. It was not their fault and neither, by the standards of the times, was it the fault of anyone. Certainly Mr. Hoover did not see it as his fault. Certainly the state, the government, society did not feel any responsibility for what happened to Emma and George Faulkes.

We sat in the kitchen and talked. That is, Emma talked; I do not remember George opening his mouth. I had a list of questions Sue had given me. I ran through them, questions about people of whom I had never heard, most of them dead fifty or a hundred years. Emma Faulkes was painstaking in her answers. There was no suggestion of tea or coffee. In one corner of the kitchen stood an icebox, the old-fashioned wooden kind into which you put a twenty-five pound piece of ice. I had a feeling it was empty. I had a feeling that the shelves in the curtained cupboard were empty, that there was no more coal and no more kerosene, not a scrap of food in the house, and that Emma and George Faulkes were sitting at the oilcloth-covered table, their feet swollen, their bellies empty, sitting there because there wasn't a thing they could do. They would, I thought, sit at the table until they died, and it would not be a long wait. I closed my notebook, made some apologies, pulled myself together, shook their bony hands and walked back to the North Shore Electric as fast as I could. The wind from Lake Michigan blew direct in my face. Back in Chicago, I walked to the Berkshire Hotel and wrote a letter to my aunt. She replied: "It gives me the cold shivers to think that someday I may be vegetating just like that." It gave me the cold shivers too. She already had lost her job. She would never find another. She would never go on relief (principles). She would never get on WPA (politics). She would live with one relative or another, sometimes with Dorothy Canfield Fisher, poorer and poorer, renting out her one-room New York co-op for fifty dollars a month, her sole income, keeping a shred of spirit alive by hating Roosevelt, until a heart attack on a train leaving Minneapolis brought her life to an end.

I was lucky. I had a job. Newspapers were beginning to fail. The *Chicago Evening Post* went under, the *World,* my gospel, closed in New York. The *Transcript* died in Boston. UP laid on a ten percent pay cut and I went down to twenty-seven dollars a week. The parade of my friends never ceased, wandering east to west, west to east, anywhere there might be work. They rode the cattle trains free from the South St. Paul stockyards to Jersey City; all you had to do was lug a hundred pails of water twice a day for the cows. All the way out Halstead Street, the migrant workers sat on the curbs, thousands of them, no work, no hope. My uncle Andy's law firm blew up and he had no more receiverships, no more collections, nothing. He sat at his fumed-oak desk, played Napoleon solitaire and smoked his pipeful of Prince Albert. Then he went into the bathroom and reread *Barchester Towers.* Aunt Mary cried all day. No one asked her to make a dress, and if they did they couldn't pay for it. Their daughter's husband lost his job and died in a crash of his car. There was no money for the mortgage. It wasn't East Lynne, just everyday life in America, 1932.

I lay awake at night, a small coil of fear in my stomach, and listened to the "L," the trains going south, the trains going north. I listened to the echo of the trains bouncing off the buildings. MacKinlay Kantor had caught that sound in *El Goes South.* I lay awake and heard it, heard the train cutting past the open windows. God knows what you saw in those windows: men and women, white men and white women, black men and white women, women alone in the bedrooms, sitting on the beds, the wind from the "L" stirring the torn curtains, the iron beds, the men and women on the iron beds. I lay in my room at the Berkshire and heard the trains all night, the intervals greater and greater, and then, with graying dawn, the roar as they came near and the echo fading as they sped away, dragging all of Chicago's dreams, the sounds of the "L" and the sirens, the police cars roaring down Michigan, roaring down Clark, sirens trailing like aural banners. I lay in the Berkshire and thought of Chicago, sleeping Chicago, the flats where men and women sank into sleep, sleeping and sleeping and wishing there would be no tomorrow because tomorrow would be a worse today, a colder today, a hungrier today, more desperate. Yes, I knew now that Chicago was not boom-boom, not Capone. I knew it had the dark, sour stench of desperation. At this hour, there was no one in the city awake, all of Chicago was asleep, all but myself and the "L."

Bentley and I got out of the Berkshire. An end to the old actress and the young actress, to the pimps and their girls, to the Filipino bellhops and the Polish waitresses in the coffee shop, to the smell of Lysol in the corridors. We took an "English basement" on Elm Street with two friends, $75, four of us, only $18.75 each a month, half what we paid the Berkshire and we could cook our own meals, beans, hash, fried potatoes and ketchup. I began to spend mornings on the Oak Street beach. Coming home from the all-night shift at UP, a cup of coffee and over to the beach, no one there but myself and a very tanned girl with dark hair, handsome long nose, dark glasses, tight dark bathing suit. We lay near each other every morning and every morning I would swear I would pick her up but I never had the courage.

Roosevelt came to town and accepted the Democratic nomination. It was my first national political convention. I had never been so excited. I got no sleep for a week. I was a registered Republican, but FDR was my candidate. My Minnesota friend Gordon Roth made fun of me. He said FDR was just another politician and a blue-blooded New York aristocrat. What we needed in the country was a real revolution. Gordy was writing publicity for the Republican candidates in Minnesota, but I think he cast his vote in 1932 for Norman Thomas. Mine went to FDR.

FDR carried Chicago, carried Illinois, carried the country, but in Chicago there was a curious feeling that something else was happening, something that had to do with Capone and Mayor Anton J. Cermak, the Democrat who was elected over Big Bill Thompson. It was hard to put a finger on, but the gang war grew hotter and hotter and rumors began to circulate that Cermak and his police were siding with Roger ("The Terrible") Touhy in a war against Capone. By Christmas 1932, so Bob Loughran reported, Capone was ready to sue for peace. Loughran knew the gangs. He seldom came into the newsroom, just rasped a few words on the telephone.

One day in January of 1933, Roosevelt elected but still not in office (inauguration then was March 4), the Depression worse and worse, the country coming to a halt as it waited for the new President, Loughran slipped into the newsroom one morning. He was a rather small man with a red face and he walked very rapidly. Some days he covered miles and miles on his feet, but most days he sat in the pressroom at police headquarters, playing poker. He wore a gray felt hat just like Walter Winchell's and never removed it except in church or in courtrooms. He was in great excitement as he walked rapidly into the room, and pulled Gene Gillette—a tall, lanky man who looked like a professional basketball player, chief of the Chicago bureau—and myself into a corner away from the windows and away from the rewrite men, the wire filers and the machine operators.

Loughran had a whiskey voice although he never touched alcohol. Now he spoke in his husky whisper, an expression of anger, almost rage, on his face. "I'm going to tell you guys something," he said. "I don't wanna tell anyone, but I hafta. If either of you guys ever whispers a word, it's curtains, and not just for you, and I don't mean maybe and I'm not kiddin'. There is no kiddin' about this—that clear?" Gillette, a slow-speaking man from Iowa, looked seriously at Loughran, swallowed hard (he had a large Adam's apple) and said, "O.K. What's the pitch?" I just nodded; adrenaline had begun to flow in my veins. "You got it, Salisbury?" Loughran asked. You bet, I said. "Now," said Loughran, the temper that had flushed his face fading a bit, "here is the thing. There is nobody in this goddamn office I trust but you two guys and I don't always trust you but I gotta trust somebody. All the rest are a bunch of punks and if I can't trust you then the hell with it because this is just one helluva big story, the biggest goddamn story you'll ever get your asses into."

Loughran's whisper dropped lower and he pulled our heads closer to him, literally pulled them close. It wasn't easy to pull Gene's big handsome head down, but Loughran did it.

Now, said Loughran, if we work this right and there aren't any foul-ups from those assholes on the desk and those assholes that run the wires, little ol' UP is goin' to get the scoop of its lifetime. That is the way Bob Loughran talked.

What had happened, Bob said finally, was this. A source in

whom he had total confidence had tipped him that Tony Cermak, Mayor Cermak, was going to be bumped off. The execution would occur on a Saturday morning as the mayor walked up the steps of city hall. It had been set for that time and place out of "humanitarian" considerations. On Saturday morning, the streets would be clear, there would be almost no one about city hall, and the action could be carried out with little chance of killing anyone but the mayor. Bob's source was into the action to such an extent that he would tip Bob by telephone a few minutes before the gangsters headed for city hall, a margin of time sufficient for Bob to go to a phone box in a cigar store directly across from the city hall steps. Bob would hold a phone open. When the moment came, Gillette and myself must be in the UP office, ready to hold the line for his flash. If neither Gillette nor myself was in the office—no story. He would not trust it to the assholes on the desk. God knows what they would do with it. Only Gillette or Salisbury. No one else. We had to give our word. Not one mention to anyone. Not even to New York. Not now or ever. Eternal secrecy. He had promised his source and we must promise him. This was the Big Time. No Boy Scout stuff. Now, said Loughran, the only thing we don't know is which Saturday this will happen. So from now on, you guys must be in the shop every Saturday morning until I give you the signal. Gillette and I solemnly shook his hand and Loughran relaxed. There was even a whisper of a smile. Happy hunting, he said, and vanished.

I was tremendously excited. God! I said. Yes, said Gillette.

Both of us were on duty the next Saturday. Nothing happened. And the next. Nothing happened. And the third. No action. Loughran said not to worry. The affair was on. It took a little time. Don't get edgy.

That week, the bottom fell out of the country. Banks had been closing with extraordinary rapidity. Governors were declaring "bank holidays," arbitrarily closing all the banks in the state. More and more of the country was affected. Cries were rising for joint action by Hoover and Roosevelt. In Chicago the banks were still open, but everyone was rushing to get his money. In Michigan the windows slammed down; every bank in the state was closed in the middle of winter. The UP was covering Michigan like a house afire, but it had run out of cash for taxicabs, meals, needle beer, phone calls; there were no more nickels, dimes or quarters. No credit cards in those days. I was sent off to courier money to Detroit. I loaded my uncle's alligator bag with rolls of nickels, dimes, quarters, stacks of dollar bills, bought a $3.75 coach seat on the New York Central and headed for Detroit.

I didn't know what was happening to the country, but it looked as though the whole system was going down. We pulled through Gary, the steel mills hardly turning. The train sped over the flatlands of northern Indiana and southern Michigan, fertile, rich farming country, dotted with small and medium-sized industrial towns. I kept my eyes glued to the window as we approached Detroit. It was an environmentalist's delight. Not a trace of smoke from a factory chimney. The landscape gray and dead. The heart of America was not beating, the closer to Detroit the more evident, the River Rouge plants of Henry Ford quiet as a cemetery, the GM factories, the Chrysler plants, not a plume of smoke, not a wisp of steam. Dead. The heart of the system was dead. The system was dead. Along the banks of the Detroit River I began to see the shantytowns, thousands upon thousands of tin-can hutments, the kind we see today on the outskirts of Caracas or Rio or in Soweto—the industrial debris, the former workers standing mute and helpless around the iron pots and tins in which slumgullion was cooking or water bubbling, the fire to keep them warm. Thousands of men looking up at the train with a feeble glance.

Hell, I said to myself, it's finished. The U.S.A. is through. I suppose somehow someone will put the country together again, but it will never be the same. They have run it into the ground. "They," to my mind, was Wall Street, the Interests. What would happen? I had no notion. All I knew was that Detroit was dead, and if Detroit was dead the country was dead. Today Detroit dies and the country shrugs. In those days Detroit *was* America; Henry Ford was America; what was good for General Motors was good for America and no one doubted it. Even Lenin, so I had heard, tried to get Ford to come to Russia and show them how to organize their industry. Where did we turn now? It was hard to believe that Floyd B. Olson or anyone else could put Detroit back together again.

I sat in the New York Central coach and looked out. The campfires glowed amber in the dusk and threw into silhouette the hulks of the factories, dark and forlorn. It was, I wrote in my notebook, the apocalypse of the American dream. My feet resting on a gladstone bag full of dimes and quarters, I watched it, the swan song of the dinosaurs. I could not imagine the future.

I hauled my bag of change to the UP and next morning went down to city hall to talk to Detroit's radical young mayor, Frank Murphy, a new face, a new name, later to be sent to the Supreme Court by FDR. His office was out in the open, behind a heavy mahogany railing in the middle of a baroque city hall. While I waited, four or five men arrived. I knew they were important because of their dress. I have an image of morning trousers, spats and at least one gold-headed cane: large men, dignified— bankers. Murphy greeted them with a boyish smile, trying to make them comfortable, but they were beyond comfort. They had run the country off the rails and they did not know what to do. They had come to ask this young radical politician for help. I could not hear the conversation, but I could see their lips quiver and one broke into tears. Murphy shyly put his arm around the man's shoulders. What could he do but utter a few words of Irish blarney? Nothing could help and Murphy knew it, the bankers knew it; their banks were busted. Years later, when I tried to understand the hostility in Cleveland to Cyrus Eaton, I thought of that scene in Murphy's office. Cleveland had gone down like Detroit, but Eaton was the man who didn't go bust, the man who had enough left in his pockets to pick up the broken pieces. No wonder there were those in Cleveland who never forgave him. They said they hated him for his friendship for Khrushchev, but I reckoned it was because he had survived the Depression and they hadn't.

I talked to Murphy for a while that morning. He had a trace of the brogue and a warm heart. "I saw you with the bankers," I said. "Yes, the poor devils," he replied. "There's nothing I can do but help them keep their self-respect. Can you imagine what it takes for them to come to me, to Frank Murphy, that radical Democrat, and ask a favor, and they so flat broke they haven't even got a dime for the streetcar?" He smiled. "It's not so bad for us," he said, and now he was patting me on the shoulder. "We're young and we've got a life to make. But those men are finished."

I felt sorry for the bankers, but I felt more sorry for the debris of humanity along the Detroit River, broken, raped, abandoned. I went over and tried to talk with them. It didn't go very well, no better than it had talking with the men in the IWW hall in Minneapolis. Their eyes turned down. They had been driven

My grandfather's study at 107 Royalston Avenue, preserved
virtually unchanged until the house was sold in 1924.
(*Photo about 1890, by my father, Percy P. Salisbury*)

The house at 107 Royalston Avenue, Minneapolis, built by my
grandfather, where I lived during the first sixteen years of my life.
(*Photo about 1895, by Percy P. Salisbury*)

My mother, Georgiana E. Salisbury, taken by my father about 1905.

Myself, wearing Lord Fauntleroy suit, taken about 1912 by my father.

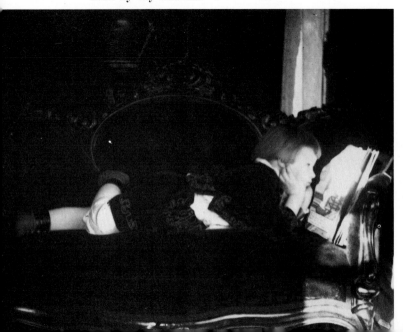

Percy P. Salisbury,
self-portrait, taken about 1900.

Percy P. Salisbury, wearing
Lord Fauntleroy suit, taken in
Mazomanie, Wisconsin, about 1872.

My son Michael, wearing
Lord Fauntleroy suit, taken at
Mamaroneck, New York,
1942, by myself.

My sister Janet and myself,
taken at 107 Royalston Avenue
by our father about 1912.

In the Arrowhead canoe country, Minnesota, 1928,
Judson Anderson at left.

In United Press newsroom,
New York City, World War II.

In North Africa,
November 1943.

Bidding farewell to the dacha at Saltykovka,
outside Moscow, in 1954. Dedya Petya at right.

Luncheon with poet Bella Akhmadulina, 1967.
My son Stephan, Bella, my stepdaughter, Ellen Rand.

With Nikita Khrushchev, New York, 1960.

With Charlotte in Taconic, taken by Inge Morath.

11 | Arcturus

Seven P.M., wake-up time for the night shift. Narcotized by the restless sleep of daylight hours, the room close, shades drawn, windows shut against street noises, I heard a knock on the door and Julian Bentley walked in, a leprechaun on his arm, an Irish minx, with dancing eyes, a smile to melt a miser's heart. "This is Mary Jane. How about a wake-up snort?" That was our ritual, Julian's and mine, a swig of gin straight from the bottle before we got out of bed, to prove that we were young men—very young men. I didn't need a wake-up shot. Those Irish eyes did it. I didn't care if Julian looked like Ronald Colman, his straight black hair, pencil mustache, sounded like Rudy Vallee (for years Julian was to be "The Voice of WLS, the Prairie Farmer Station," and Midwestern housewives in ten states fantasized to his rich tenor voice). He was a man of the world, at whose feet women swooned, and he hopelessly in love with his older cousin (and she with him); was carrying on an affair with a young woman whom he called a "congenital virgin," meaning that she suffered from vaginal spasms, sometimes extremely painful for her male partner; was constantly telephoned by a passionate vixen who worked and slept with an aging doctor, over forty, who could not satisfy her. Julian was a man, in a word, overwhelmed by feminine supplicants. Never mind. The moment that tiny woman danced into the room, I knew she was meant for me. I gulped my gin and heard myself say that if she would step outside for a moment, I would fling on my clothes and join her and Julian for dinner. Julian grinned. Mary was a friend of a friend and, he told me after we had escorted her home, he had been hoping I would take her off his hands. I did. Seven months later, on Saturday, April 1, 1933, Mary and I took the elevator to the clerk's office on the fourth floor of the Chicago City Hall and at 11 A.M. we were married. I put on her finger the platinum ring I had bought with my last twenty dollars at Peacock's jewelry store on State Street. Then we went to Marshall Field's for our three-dollar wedding breakfast and at 1 P.M. I walked down State Street to work. I did a twelve-hour shift on Saturdays, but this day I got a dispensation. I was let off at eight in the evening to join my bride in the fifteen-dollar-a-week room I had rented in a transient hotel on Division Street. A week later, we moved into a furnished basement apartment with a battleship-gray cement floor and regiments of cockroaches, one room, divided by a green scrim curtain, at 8 Walton Place, next door to the house where Jane Addams lived. Every morning we saw her helped down the steps by the chauffeur of her black Buick, which took her to Hull House. Our landlady's name was Tucker, and later that summer she let us have a flat on the second floor, with a bathroom across the hall. Across North Clark Street was the Newberry Library, which I began to haunt, digging up dope for freelance articles.

Mary was, as I say, a leprechaun. She possessed dancing eyes and dancing toes. She had danced for her father on the big kitchen table at family parties, danced and sung as a five-year-old in her starched lace petticoats, sung an endless repertoire, but not one Irish ballad. There wasn't a drop of Irish blood in Mary Jane Hollis. She was 100 percent Hungarian. Her father had been a miner at Harco No. 1 in the bloody coal fields of southern Illinois, near Galatia. Mary remembered how she had been hidden in the oven of the cast-iron stove during weekend shoot-outs. Before she was ten, both her parents died and a high school teacher from Evansville, Indiana, Mina Beers, improbably adopted her and raised her as a kind of living doll. Miss Beers, rigid, moralistic, hating sin, hating Catholics like sin (Mary's parents, of course, were good Hungarian Catholics), narrow, a spinster to her fingertips, led a double life. The roomer at her house, as Mary was not to discover until she left home, was in fact Miss Beers's husband, the marriage eternally to be concealed lest Miss Beers lose her teaching post (marriage was automatic grounds for discharge of a female teacher), her husband long unemployed, his glassblower's job lost in a strike which ruined the union and closed the glassworks.

My marriage bore the stamp of Depression. Mary had come to Chicago to learn stenotypy and get a job, but when she lost the job there was no other opening and she had to go back to Evansville. That blew up in a row with Miss Beers, and quickly Mary was back in Chicago, out of work, no prospects, no money. I had my twenty-seven dollars a week and was sending ten dollars home. The only way I could support Mary—and I wasn't at all sure of that—was to get married. But this presented a dilemma of conscience, because I loved Mary but I knew by now that my Irish lassie was not all spice and sparkle. She had a fiend of a temper and spent money like Saturday night in a mining camp. Still and all, in for a penny, in for a pound; maybe it would work, just maybe. I did love Mary. She did love me. Love laughed at locksmiths. Love laughed at the world. So we would defy the world and conquer it. My head dizzied with sugarplum dreams and formless nightmares, with clichés and qualms. I knew my mother would erupt in hysteria. Let her! Mary was what the family needed, a bright new spirit, sunshine on a gray landscape. Well, that is the way I thought, my mind whirling like that of all young men possessed by love, devoured by passion. Mary had grown up as a little golden princess, first of her father, then of Miss Beers, dressed in party clothes, hugged, kissed, then sent to bed without her supper or locked in a closet when her temper spilled over. But all this would vanish and only the sunbeams would remain, so I imagined. She would be my princess. Yes, I was a naive young man, but there was within me, too, an inward eye which watched with cold detachment. It asked questions. How will you go on sending money to your dad? How will Dad get on without that money? What about that quick temper? The cold voice rebuked me for leading an immature young woman onto a trail that could so easily end badly. But I brushed that aside. I could not conceive that I had embarked on a course that would spell tragedy, not small but great, for Mary, for myself, for us all, a savage wrecking of lives which need not have been.

I got off my shift at the Consumers Building about eight, sent a telegram to my father and mother, grabbed a streetcar to Division Street, and began my married life in a room with a folding bed. No one made a joke about its being April Fool's Day.

I can't say it was love on the dole. I worked like fury and got my three-dollar pay cut reversed. I worked days now. Each morning at 8 A.M. I relieved Steve Richards, a far, far distant cousin; like the Evanses, the Richards family hailed from Jackson County, Ohio, part of the big Welsh migration. Steve went to Jackson County every fall and brought back jars of crystal-pure moonshine, best in the world. He and I shared a dream of the north woods, and in the long night hours Steve's fancy carried him deep into the wilderness. In the morning I would find him swinging his hand around and around in circles, his eyes lost in the distance. "What are you doing, Steve?" "I'm just twirling my gun, deciding when to shoot." He had a friend who shared his wilderness dream. In the fall of '33, Steve quit and with his friend and his friend's wife took a cabin deep in the Northwest Angle on the Minnesota-Canada border, fifty miles from anyone. Late in January 1934, Steve made it out to International Falls on snowshoes and flew back to Chicago. "I had to get out," he said. "If I had stayed another night I would have killed him or he would have killed me or she would have killed us both." Close quarters.

I walked to work each morning, stopping at a greasy spoon for coffee, a fried egg and toast, fifteen cents. I watched the short-order cook work. If I lost my job, I would go to work as a short-order cook. I knew the drill. The only thing was remembering all the orders. I did our shopping. I bought loss leaders at the big stores. Lots of beans; Spanish rice, nine cents a can.

One Sunday afternoon our doorbell rang. A patriarchal man, sandy-haired, about my father's age, stood there, an old friend of Dad's, he said, he did business with the bag company. Dad had asked him to look us up. I had never heard of him. We made coffee. He stayed for lunch, spaghetti and meatballs. Terribly embarrassed when he got up to go. He had mislaid his wallet. Didn't have a cent on him. Could we let him have twenty dollars? Twenty dollars? I didn't know anyone who had twenty dollars. I had three dollars to last until Wednesday. He made it plain that the money would be returned twofold. I called a friend and borrowed ten dollars. The man left with shy apologies and I wrote Dad that night about his funny friend. Dad wrote back. Never heard of him. Very funny. A bunco artist. A few weeks later, the gentleman turned up in the Minneapolis workhouse. It was his standard gig: read the papers for out-of-town marriages, drop in on the newlyweds, con them for what the traffic would bear. Ten dollars up the creek. I had to get going!

I did. Nineteen thirty-three was the year of the Chicago World's Fair. Broke, the city found thirty million dollars to build a world's fair on the shore of Lake Michigan. It did not change the architectural climate of America like the fair of 1893, but it provided a kite's tail for FDR's New Deal. Somehow, for no good reason, it brought fun, frivolity, lightheartedness to the grim city of closed machinery plants, slack packing plants, the city of gangs and unemployed. It changed my life.

I wrote a story for the opening of the fair, May 27, 1933. Fifty years later, it still glistened in the minds of some readers, who had committed lines to memory and quoted them back to me decades after I batted them out on my old Remington Standard.

The story began with these words: "A silver beam of starlight stabbed out of the interstellar void tonight after a journey of forty years and by a miracle of science's making turned the Century of Progress Exposition into an iridescent pool of rainbow color."

The beam came from the star Arcturus, and the glint of that story turned my career with UP into a skyrocket. From that day I became one of UP's top writers, an Arcturus at twenty-five, a certified "young veteran." It was a dazzling summer, with its story after story about the World's Fair, the Pabst Blue Ribbon Pavilion, Sally Rand, a plain, straight girl from Greenwich Village, a nice girl; some of my Minnesota friends lived on the floor of her studio while they were hunting jobs in New York. A virtuous girl whose ostrich feather fans turned her into a sex object of objects for the rest of her life. Endless stories: a near catastrophe when Commodore Balbo flew in from Italy and I scooped the world by landing him seven minutes before his plane touched down, the seven longest minutes of my life; the flop of Commander Settle's balloon, a flight to the stratosphere which ended in the Burlington yards a mile and a half from Soldier Field. I ran the mile and a half, racing through the yards, stumbling over the ties, dodging switch engines, calling in the story from a freight yard hut lighted by a kerosene lantern. One story followed another, the Wynkoop case, a sensational trial of a hatchet-visaged female doctor who was convicted of killing her daughter-in-law. On my own now, not writing under Loughran's by-line, the story going to a thousand newspapers, signed by Harrison Salisbury (no E. in the signature yet). I brought visitor after visitor to the fair, everyone in the family, everyone we knew—we counted eighty-nine guests that summer—free passes for all of them, taking them through the grounds, living it up, passes to the fair restaurants, passes to the fair shows, no worry about money so long as the fair was on. Then I was sent to Banff in Alberta, Canada, a free pass on the Canadian Pacific, to cover the Institute of Pacific Relations, long before the institute was to become a McCarthy target.

Karl Bickel, UP's chief, had sent me there. He blazed through Chicago, ordered me to Banff and promised to keep me in mind for the Far East. Sugarplum dreams and guilt. Mary got pregnant and the abortion had to be done before I got back from Banff. I knew I should be by her side. I knew I had to turn down Banff. But I didn't. I used one hundred dollars of my expense money to pay for the operation and got Julian Bentley to take care of Mary. I said I couldn't finance it without the expense money. But that wasn't true. I could have got the money somehow. It was ambition that won out. Sugarplums. It would not be the last time.

On St. Valentine's Day, 1934, ambition paid off. Not China, not the Far East, but Washington, D.C., capital of the New Deal, in a blizzard that brought Christmas to the city in February. Washington eleven months into the New Deal and counting, Washington bubbling with every new idea in the world, Washington the dullest place I had ever been, nothing but politics—not a gangster, not a real story, just politics. Washington the city with the invisible Chinese wall, as Raymond Clapper, the Scripps columnist just going to work for Eugene Meyer and the *Washington Post,* told me: Washington where no one knew, no one cared, what was happening beyond the Chinese wall, Washington waking up from a hundred years of Southern slumber, Washington where Georgetown was suddenly chic for bright young lawyers from Harvard and New York. Washington— Hugh Johnson, Harold Ickes, Tommy Corcoran and Ben Cohen, Harry L. Hopkins, Mrs. Roosevelt, David Lilienthal, Steve Early, John L. Lewis, Frances Perkins. Washington, D.C., where it was dull, dull, dull.

Six months passed and Washington had become my story, focus of the world, more young men on the make than in any city since Caesar's Rome. The alphabetic agencies proliferated so fast I kept a checklist on my desk.

Washington. In the first years I was mostly an inside man, a writer, sometimes an editor, but I was caught up, we were all caught up, in the wine of the times. NRA, PWA, WPA—the initials seemed to be written with fire. CIO. Out of nowhere, John L. Lewis, the lumbering conservative, blazed up, a radical organ-

izer, to be memorialized by my new best friend, Cyrus L. Sulzberger, nephew of the *New York Times* publisher, hired by UP
after a breaking-in in Pittsburgh. Ed Leach of Scripps's *Pittsburgh Press* sent him to Lyle C. Wilson, UP's Washington chief,
an Oklahoma conservative, an Oklahoma reactionary, a black,
black Republican, ultimately, God save him, a McCarthyite, but
the best bureau chief, the warmest, kindest human being I knew.
Wilson set Cy loose on the labor beat. Every night when I came
in at 11 P.M. I found Cy telephoning around town, the brassiest,
boldest telephoning I ever heard: John L. Lewis at midnight,
Eleanor Roosevelt at 1 A.M., Madame Perkins, secretary of labor,
at 2 A.M. By 3 A.M. he would have hammered together an exclusive, as hot as any Capone story I had filed out of Chicago, a
wire-opener in this era which left the gangs behind, a startling
piece of New Deal intelligence, sharpened and carved out of Cy's
thickets of words by my sharp pencil and brisk typewriter as he
watched, howling and groaning, but relaxing to the cheers of
coast-to-coast play.

Washington. Almost a revolutionary city. Maybe a revolutionary city. One night Mary and I sat reading in our Georgetown
apartment, in a rickety red-brick house at 3512 P Street, when
missiles whammed through the window, one-two-three. "My
God!" Mary shouted. "The revolution!" It was Cy and his
friends, announcing their arrival with oranges through the vene-
tian blinds. But yes, revolution was in the air, a new order of
things.

Revolution. It came into our office. Heywood Broun led it, a
newspaper union was formed. No, not a union, a newspaper *guild,*
a significant difference, a union that was not a union, a brother-
hood of craftsmen, of artisans of talent, newspaper writers and
editors. Broun was the founder, but simultaneously the guild
was founded in Washington with a rush that swept up all of us
in UP—well, not quite all. Lyle Wilson held aloof although, he
said, he was sympathetic. One or two others held back. Everyone
else joined in a swirl, our purpose noble and sincere. We would
lift the quality of newspapers, the quality of reporting, the quality of editing; we would help the publishers do what we believed
they wished to do but had not been able to do because of competition. We would help them put a floor under wages which would
automatically, we believed, improve quality standards.

I remember sitting in the evening with the Washington found-

ers, most of them Scripps writers. Herb Little, Ruby Black, Lou
Heath, Tom Stokes, Ray Clapper, Harry Frantz, Bob Buck,
Mark Childs, Ken Crawford—who wasn't there? the whole town
swept up in a wave of enthusiasm. Of course, we said; it is natural. Some publishers have to put up resistance, pro forma. But
really they all will welcome us, and no one more than UP. UP
was the underdog. It had never been able to afford standard
wages because it operated on such thin margins. It wasn't rich,
like AP. But now we would put in the floor, AP and UP would
be even-steven, we would insist on professional standards, UP
would win a terrific advantage. It had the best men, and the best
men would flock to it once they were assured the same pay they
might get at AP. It was a lovely, youthful dream. Paradise come
to earth, the lion and the lamb lying down together. It was nonsense.

The dream, the great gift to UP, did not seem to be visible to
management in the person of Hugh Baillie. Baillie had taken
over as chief, replacing Karl Bickel, the international journalist,
a man of fawn gloves, fawn spats, fawn hat, continental dash;
Bickel knew the railway timetables of Europe by heart and how
you could get across Central Asia by plane from Ashkhabad to
Tashkent. He cultivated relations with Konstantin Oumansky,
chief of Tass, the official Soviet news agency, who later died in a
mysterious 1940 plane crash. Bickel knew Karl Radek, the virtuoso of Marxism, the German-Polish-Russian Communist whose
death in a Yakutsk concentration camp I would report years
later after a visit to that land of permafrost. Bickel knew everyone in Europe and Asia. He was the most sophisticated man I
had ever met. How I envied him! Could I ever wear spats?

Hugh Baillie, a rangy Scot who delighted in pipes and haggis,
wore his hair in a crew cut before a crew cut had become ideological, but his ideology prematurely matched his hair. A UP editor
assured his career for life by getting Hugh a window seat for the
coronation of Edward VII at the position where the Scots
Guards pipers broke out with "The Campbells Are Coming";
Baillie turned to his wife and said with joy: "Darling, they are
playing *our* song." To this sturdy Scotsman, the philosophy of
guild uplift of UP was not comprehensible. Hugh's idea was simple: Hire cheap, sell dear. He made a lot of money adhering to
this principle.

Baillie came out of Southern California. He had covered

sports and police for the *Los Angeles Record.* To Bickel, Moscow was a critical spot. He insisted on the best. In the late 1920s, he sent Eugene Lyons there. Lyons worked for Tass, and that was why Bickel sent him. He thought an intelligent Communist sympathizer best equipped to cover the emerging Soviet Russia. Stalin, his victory over Trotsky, Bukharin, Zinoviev, Kamenev, the ferocity, the vicious tactics, turned Lyons upside down. He came back from Moscow to denounce his former faith, in *Assignment to Utopia,* and to become a founding member of the tribe of ex-Communist-sympathizer anti-Communists.

Baillie first sent a fine young preacher's son and then a Los Angeles police reporter to Moscow. Neither one worked out and Baillie lost interest in Russia. He liked to step into the New York newsroom and send a wastebasket sailing through the air with a well-placed kick. "Christ, we've got to get action around here *somehow,* " he would exclaim. On other occasions he would lament that "I am up to my armpits in pygmies."

If Baillie did not understand the guild's program for helping to better the UP, neither did the Communist party. The party attempted to control the national organization through the New York guild, leading to years of warfare between the New York and Washington guilds. Down the drain disappeared my dreams of editorial betterment, journalistic ideals, evolution of a guild code of reporting, writing and editing.

For four years this conflict beached me, landed me on Baillie's blacklist—no raises, pay frozen at sixty dollars a week, no chance of getting off the desk, no promotions, no good stories. Well, not really no good stories. I was, after all, an Arcturus and I was turned loose again and again, Baillie or no Baillie; but no raises. That was definite. No promotions. That was definite. In Baillie's book, I was a Communist, a goddamn red. That was definite.

And naturally I would not back down. That was definite.

12 | Huey

It was four-fifteen in the morning, Monday, September 16, 1935, when the Curtiss Condor eased down through the fog and heavy rain and splashed to a landing at Spartanburg, South Carolina. The weather was shivery. I wished I had put on my vest before running for the plane in Washington. Now I pulled up my coat collar and made a dash for the cozy flying office with its big fieldstone fireplace. A radioman was huddled over his set. He pushed back his earphones as I came in. "He's dead," the man said. "The flash just came through. Died at 4:10 A.M."

I was flying with my fellow UP correspondent Harry Ferguson to Baton Rouge, Louisiana. Huey Long had been shot Sunday night in the state capitol. No one knew what might happen. Maybe a revolution.

"Christ!" I said to Fergy. "We've missed it."

"Don't be sure," Fergy said. "Maybe it's just beginning."

I didn't know Huey Long well, but I had covered him. He was pretty nearly the hottest story in Washington. I had reported his speeches and had jammed into the press gallery on nights when word raced around that Huey was starting another filibuster. He stood up in the chamber, a little bulky around the middle, where he had strapped a rubber bag going down his pant leg so he could urinate without leaving the Senate floor, a stack of clippings on his Senate desk, a Bible to read when he couldn't think of anything to say. He would move about, talking in his easy Louisiana drawl, face a little puffy and soft, like the faces of so many Southern men, always the gentleman on such occasions, playing to the galleries, tossing kisses to the ladies, nodding to his friends, reading recipes for turnip greens and corn pone, for catfish fries and chowder, putting on the best show in town, moving down long corridors of oratory that led to his thesis, "Every Man a King," lambasting the rich and the big utilities and big oil (he blackmailed them mercilessly for his campaign chest and the profit of his friends), not quite breaking with FDR but the threat there, making plain that next year, 1936, things might be different. The Roosevelt people were nervous. Huey was moving out beyond Louisiana and beginning to reach into those Northern industrial clusters with their stubborn core of unemployed, just as years later George Wallace was to move out of Alabama into blue-collar Indiana and Ohio.

I loved Huey's shenanigans, but what was he all about? What did he stand for? Wasn't he a catfish Mussolini? I wasn't wild about Roosevelt after two years in Washington, no idolater like the White House regulars, men like Ernest Lindley of *Newsweek* and Fred Storm of UP, who spent the weekends in Hyde Park, playing poker with Roosevelt in the little back cabin on Sunday evening, but I didn't think Huey was an alternative. There was a smell of gunpowder about him.

I knew Roosevelt's tricks. They were so obvious: dances for the press in the Blue Room, the little birthday notes, the Christmas parties; good fun, but there had to be a bill. The best thing about FDR, I thought, was his enemies—the Liberty League, the Du Ponts, John Raskob, Colonel McCormick. FDR had to be doing something right. I watched him at his press conferences. We all crowded in, the twenty or thirty of us, backed up against the desk in his office with the ship prints (never, never was it called the "oval" office; it was the President's office), and I, as an agency man, avoided the front row. I took a place close to the door, because when the conference ended it was a free-for-all by the AP man, the UP man, the INS man, across the lobby, around the dangerous corners of the Filipino water buffalo table, across the black-and-white linoleum tile to the pressroom (three phone booths for the agencies, half a dozen desks, a bulletin board, nothing more), to get in first with the dictation. (One afternoon, UP man Merriman Smith broke his shoulder in the scramble.) FDR put on a fine act, but it was an act.

Roosevelt was running scared on the left. It wasn't only Huey. It was the Reverend Father Coughlin and his radio spiel Sunday nights from Royal Oak, Michigan; it was Upton Sinclair in California; it was Dr. Townsend and his two hundred dollars a month for the elderly; and it was the Technocrats—God knows how they were going to save the country, but they had a great pitch. If Gillette wanted, it could make a lifetime razor blade and sell it for a quarter. But Gillette wanted to sell you for a dime a new one for every shave. The same disposability principle applied to

all of American industry, especially Detroit. Well, the Technocrats were right, I thought, but how would that get people jobs?
Charlatans, the whole batch, and Huey too.

There was one man to my taste, Minnesota's own Floyd B.
Olson. Floyd was coming on strong. Like Huey, he was seeking a
national constituency. He didn't talk "Every Man a King." He
went for the jugular. The system was rotten. He would wipe it
out and put socialism in its place. He was a radical, he said, and
he spelled it with a capital R. I had been looking forward to a
duel of giants, Huey and Floyd Olson in the U.S. Senate. That
blew up when Huey Long died as the old Condor came in to its
landing at Spartanburg, and now I sat in the warm Eastern Airlines flying office, waiting for the rain to stop so we could get
into the air again. I didn't know that Floyd Olson would be dead
before the year was finished, of cancer of the throat. FDR was
going to luck out.

It was nearly 6 A.M. before the weather cleared enough for
takeoff. We hopped along under the clouds and for the first time
I saw the South, eroded red-clay fields, the wreck of the earth. I
kept looking for cotton. I saw only gullied lands, so scarred they
made my heart sick. We had breakfast at the Atlanta airport and
took off in mud that blinded the cockpit windows. All the way to
Montgomery and Mobile I kept looking for cotton and didn't see
a dab. We followed the coast and then up Lake Pontchartrain to
the New Orleans airport, Shushan Airport, a crisscross of run-
ways where Eastern had once nearly lost a plane in the bog.

We got into a tiny red charter plane and flew up the Mississippi to Baton Rouge. I saw sugarcane for the first time and
then Huey Long's Louisiana capitol, a tall shaft lifted toward
the sky. A big man with a forty-five-caliber revolver on his hip
rode the car that carried us to town, but he swore he was just a
mail courier. Everywhere I saw men in plain clothes with heavy
guns sagging on their hips, big burly gents, red-necked, thick-
necked, thick-fisted, Long's State Bureau of Criminal Investigation. These were the men who gunned down Dr. Carl Weiss in the
capitol corridor after he shot Huey.

Alan Coogan was the UP man in Baton Rouge. He was wall-
eyed and smoked cigars continuously, one in each hand as he got
excited, three or four as he told stories, each cigar a character.
He was at the capitol Sunday night when Huey was strutting
about. Alan gave him a clipping from the *New York Daily News,* a

picture of Huey cheerleading LSU students. Huey rushed around the chamber like a kid, showing the clipping to the legislators. It was just after nine. Alan sat down at his desk in the front of the chamber. Huey had left the floor.

"Then I heard something in the corridor," Coogan said. "It sounded like firecrackers, but I knew it wasn't firecrackers, and a chill ran up my back." Firecrackers . . . Coogan showed me the small, dark brown stain on the corridor floor and the chips in the wall from the bullets the bodyguards had pumped into Weiss as he slumped on the floor.

Bodyguards were everywhere. I had never seen a revolution, but I wondered if this wasn't like the moment when Alexander II was blown up beside the Winter Canal in St. Petersburg. I watched the guards moving swiftly, eyes alert, hands on holsters, the crowds sullen. Sullen supporters of the Kingfish, their leader betrayed; sullen enemies of the Kingfish, their moment at hand; they could hardly wait to strike at the sansculottes. This was what I was here for—to cover the revolution, the civil war. It might break at any moment.

I. I. Femrite, the UP New Orleans manager, got a four-minute beat on Huey's death, but it could have cost his life. He slipped into the hospital, across a small lagoon from the capitol, where Huey lay dying. The place swarmed with gunmen. Femrite walked in with a Long official and sat down on a porch near Huey's room. No one asked questions; they took him for an official. When he saw the lights turned off in Huey's room, he strolled past the guards, slipped down a staircase to the basement, entered a vacant room, picked up the telephone, delivered his scoop and walked out a rear door. He didn't know that an AP man had tipped the guards, who were hunting him with drawn pistols.

I felt the tension as I entered the capitol. The national guard had been called out. The guardsmen clambered into the capitol at mess time, then went back to their barracks across the lawn. Huey's police sat at the door on folding chairs, cleaning the barrels of their guns; taking out the cartridges, tumbling them in their laps, then slugging them back into the chambers.

I worked the night trick. Clouds of mosquitoes clustered around the guards, clustered around me, clustered around the electric bulbs and the floodlights that bathed every approach like Very lights in no-man's-land. When I talked to civilians, they lowered their voices and looked over their shoulders. They expected the New Orleans crowd to take over. A coup d'etat. Then the people would come up out of the bayous. Civil war.

They brought Huey's coffin into the statehouse on Wednesday and thousands crowded in, come to see the man who promised to share the wealth, to make them rich, to bring an end to poverty. All that night, workmen dug a grave on the capitol lawn as I watched. They dug a narrow trench and lined it with concrete reinforced with steel rods. All night the crowd shuffled past Huey's coffin, the body lying in state, the face powdered and rouged like a chorus girl's. No one seemed to notice. Around five in the morning, as light was breaking in the east, they finished digging. Bells in a Catholic chapel sounded for morning mass. The workmen took their shovels and rattled away in trucks. Half a dozen, red clay on their shoes and overalls, climbed the capitol steps and took a last look at Huey.

There was a lot about the assassination that I didn't understand. But as I talked to the Louisiana newspapermen, I began to get a few things straight. The vitriol and paranoia hadn't been on one side. True, Huey had used every device to pressure his opposition. But the opposition, particularly the press, the *Times-Picayune* and the *States-Item,* had replied in kind. In this war, the pot called the kettle black. There was no truth. Truth got blown away by power and passion, the first casualty of conflict. In the escalation of rhetoric, someone was bound to take a shot at Caesar.

Saturday morning, Huey two days buried, I began to find out what had made Huey Long. It was hot and clear and we took the ferry across the river, a segregated ferry with segregated galleries for white folks and black folks, then up a bumpy bank to one of Huey's concrete highways and north at sixty miles an hour toward Alexandria, sixty miles an hour through swamp and bayou, a tangle of dark green, lonely country, wide ditches beside the concrete strip where steam shovels scooped up the clay for the roadbed, green water in the ditches and pink and blue flowers floating there. Spanish moss. A regiment could move a furlong off the road and vanish forever. I would not see country like this for thirty years, and then I would see it in Southeast Asia, in Vietnam, south of Hanoi. Cabins, dirt floors, nothing painted, one-room-and-a-shed covered with scarlet flowers, straggly long-horned cows, razorback hogs, skinny chickens, black children with distended bellies, men, black and white, plodding along highway shoulders on their mules. Huey gave them the best roads in the country, but no cars, no money for gas. Scrawny cotton patches, dirty cotton piled against sagging lean-tos, mules hauling wagons piled with cotton, three or four blacks or whites sitting on the load, tenant farmers, sharecroppers, taking a year's work to the gins, not for money, just credit it on the books for last year's fatback and grits, always a year behind, sometimes more.

There was no way out, I saw that now. These people, white or black, could live a hundred years in the swamps and not lift themselves up an inch. Then came Huey. He knew something was wrong and he gave them an idea there might be a way out. He didn't know the way, of course, but he began to open minds. We came to sugarcane country, miles of cane higher than a man's hand above his head, little clearings for the sugar centrals, here and there a school, bare, unpainted. Huey spent millions on roads and not much on schools, except for the fine new university and its football team. I was learning that roads were a gift of life. A man spent a lifetime within three miles of his cabin. The toll ferry stood guard. A dollar toll, a half-dollar toll. It might as well have been a million. When Huey built roads and bridges, he freed people who had lived like the untouchables in India. I had never seen such poverty. The poor of the cutover timber lands in northern Minnesota would have been middle-class citizens in Louisiana.

We drove through the Evangeline country, St. Landry parish, Opelousas, and on to Alexandria, where they hadn't liked Huey, more cars on the road now and more black-curtained buggies than I ever would see, men on horseback cantering beside the highway, pouring into town for the speaking, in a green grove of pecan trees, a sound truck on either side of the platform, each painted like a circus wagon, blazing "Every Man a King" and "Share the Wealth," decorated with golden crowns for the plain people, and on the platform a thirty-seven-year-old man who looked like a YMCA director. His name was Gerald L. K. Smith and he was preaching the death and resurrection of Huey Long. "His spirit will never die," he shouted, and the women yelled louder than the men. A few blacks listened with careful faces; a quiet woman let down her dress top and gave her baby suck.

These were the people from the countryside, from the piney woods, the red-clay hills. Smith proclaimed God is on our side, surely we cannot fail. A boy with khaki shirt and red face stood on a truck and sounded Taps. The crowd sang "Nearer My God to Thee" and we dashed to the Bentley House, rambling, wide-lobbied, with iron-grille elevators, across from the levee that held back the Red River, flowing higher than the town, up to Smith's room, jammed with men, Smith walking naked out of the shower, toweling himself, a big, pink-bodied, boyish preacher, toweling himself carefully and seriously. (Why do pols walk about naked, bare their bodies? Huey did it, soaking in a tub and talking for hours with reporters; Lyndon Johnson, naked in his White House pool or with pants down, on the john, calling his aides to come closer, talking, talking.) Gerald L. K. Smith, naked with a towel, deadly serious and determined to take over Huey's movement, determined to keep the movement national. It looked this afternoon as though Gerald L. K. was the new Huey. Pete Daniell of *The New York Times* and Allan Raymond of the *New York Herald Tribune,* old Huey reporters, a little drunk on hill country moonshine, confessed that tears came to their eyes as Gerald L. K. talked. "Of course it's horseshit," Allan said. "But goddammit, I cried." I thought I understood. But it was not going to work, and that was soon obvious. Gerald L. K. couldn't win the support of the Long machine. The Longs pulled together, the family and the servitors, and Smith wandered into a life of demagoguery which carried him deeper and deeper into anti-Semitism, proto-Nazism, hate-mongering, down into the sewer of national politics, one more young politician devoured by frustrated ambition.

That night we rode back through the moonlight, through the swamps, the swamp smell more and more bitter, stopping at a wooden shed, bare-bulb lights, Dr. Pepper on sale outside, white lightning inside, a phonograph going, kind of a dance hall, girls in red calico, in cotton-sack shifts, fourteen years old, sixteen years old, for sale for twenty-five cents in the bushes, angry young men, seventeen and eighteen, watching with hating eyes, fingering long-bladed knives, the girls sidling up. "C'mon in the bushes. Try me. Only a quawter." We four Northern newsmen backing, backing slowly toward the car, eyes on the girls, eyes on the boys, stumbling into the car and hurrying down the highway, frightened.

I had the taste of Louisiana now, I thought. Huey had been right but not tough enough; too easy on the predators; too sleazy with the money, but essentially, everlastingly right. He had taken too much for himself, but he had given the people something back and he had shaken them up. Of course Huey didn't know anything about economics except Robin Hood's steal from the rich and give to the poor, and of course he was a clown, but who else could have stirred the people? Now perhaps the education would go forward. I didn't think Long's survivors would divide the booty with the poor. Maybe they would support the university, the medical schools and the hospitals, the highways and the bridges. Maybe the seed would germinate, but I thought Huey's vision was dead unless Gerald L. K. gave it life, and that was not going to be.

I thought I had learned one thing—that a revolution was a serious business, a bloody business, suffering and killing and robbery and pillage and stealing and murder. It did not divide the booty equally. I did not think there was going to be a revolution in Louisiana. No revolution in the South. Anything real would take a lot longer and something, I didn't know what, that we didn't have. But I hadn't got the country straight yet. Oh, I knew what had happened in Big Foot Prairie and on the farms of the Middle West. I knew about Chicago's West Side. I knew the shantytowns on the Detroit River, and now I had seen Louisiana. It should fit together. Yes, it was economic. Yes, it was social. Yes, it was political. But to me it was like the pieces of the jigsaws we dumped on the dining room table in Minneapolis: the black women at the State Street bridge, the little Polish girls at the dime-a-dance hall, the two-bit girls on the Alexandria highway, Emma Faulkes and her husband in North Chicago, my dad on his feet eight hours a day in the factory, my friends who rode the rods and the cattle cars, looking for work, the bonus marchers and the gangsters in Chicago—all parts of a system on the blink. But how to put it together? I didn't think any of them— Roosevelt, Long, the Du Ponts, Floyd Olson, the Republicans, the Socialists or the Communists—knew how. Maybe John L. Lewis had some good ideas. The CIO was a blaze of hope, the steel workers, the auto workers, the coal miners, the textile unions. Things were moving. But my God, the distance to travel! I thought, as we rode back through the swamps toward Baton Rouge, of my old neighborhood, of the Oak Lake Addition in

Minneapolis, the pleasant Victorian house my grandfather built and the "slum" in which I had grown up. The slum seemed to me more and more like heaven. There had been more seeds of a brave new world in those cluttered immigrant Jewish kitchens than in all the bayous of Louisiana or the oratorical swamps of Washington.

Sunday afternoon, we went by train to New Orleans. I spent Sunday night in the French Quarter—Sazerac cocktails at the St. Charles, dinner at Arnaud's, a delicious octoroon sitting on a white piano, beaded skirt above her knees, chicory coffee and doughnuts in the French market, still a market then, at 5 A.M.— and rolled Coogan onto his early train for Baton Rouge. I caught the Eastern Airlines back to Washington and slept all the way.

13 | On the Eve

Michael was conceived at Nags Head, North Carolina, just as Chamberlain was flying to meet with Hitler at Munich, our vacation broken off, called back to Washington, listening to the radio all the way, sure war was at hand, thinking it might break out before I got back; Michael was born March 16, 1939, as Hitler was marching into Prague, our ears glued to the voices of Kaltenborn and Murrow. At birth he weighed three pounds four ounces, six weeks premature, a child conceived and born under the dark sign of war, a hospital incubator for a mother until the end of April, no formula suited, one mixture after the other, not goat's milk canned or fresh, crying and crying, protesting the cruelty of the world into which he had been thrust, the agony of war eloquent in his lungs. Betty Beal, wife of my UP friend John Beal, was nursing her baby, had milk to spare and saved Michael's life. Never had Mary and I felt more close, the frayed bonds knitted by the magic of Michael and the crisis of war. I have called myself a "child of war"; Michael was a true child of war, the omens plain. I expected war as I waited for Mary in the hospital on March 16. Each day brought war closer.

Mary and I and our new child were a family. Not so a year earlier, when Mary suffered a miscarriage and my mother rushed to Washington to "help out." Not for a moment had these two women accepted each other. One evening I came back to our Georgetown flat to find them quarreling. Mary cried that she could not stand "that woman" another moment; "that woman" cried that she would not listen to such language another moment, each demanding fealty unlimited, the claims of a mother on her son, of a wife on her husband. Finally, I shouted: "I can't stand either of you. I'm through." I slammed the door and scuttled down the narrow staircase to the street.

I walked the streets of Georgetown, hour by hour, my feet taking me in great quadrants, out Wisconsin Avenue to the National Cathedral, over to the Naval Observatory, back to the river. All I knew was that I could not go back to those women. I could not suffer their eyes, the hate, the spite, the meanness. I thought of

my father and how he had struggled and failed to cope with my
mother. Now it was my turn, and I could not think what to do. A
light rain began to fall, fresh and cool. My face felt hot; maybe I
had a fever, maybe I was catching pneumonia. I hoped so. I
would never go back to P Street. I had come to the end of the
road. I would be thirty years old in a few months, and I had
accomplished nothing—nothing in my personal life, nothing in
my professional life. I had not written the great American novel.
I was thirty, over the hill. I was locked in a dead-end job and a
dead-end marriage. I hated Mary. I hated my mother. I hated
UP. I hated myself. What could I do? Mary was not going to
change; she had been difficult when we were married and I had
known it and accepted it. There wasn't anything original about
my dilemma; it happened every day.

The other side of the case began to flood into my mind. I had
put everything I had into this life; I could not walk away and let
it go down the drain—my daring gesture to the world, my defi-
ance of my family, my bravado. No. I must make a go of it for
myself, if not for Mary. I could imagine the cat's grin on my
mother's face if I gave up. Anything but that. I had made my
bed and now must lie in it.

My feet turned back toward 3512 P Street. I didn't have any
other place to go. I must go back and face the two women. Oh,
how sorry I felt for myself. Back I went, climbing the stairs,
walking into the living room. There they were, the two of them,
sitting quietly, peacefully, faces bland and easy, as if it were the
most natural thing for me to spend the evening on the street, as
though I were a small boy and they knew that when I was tired I
would come back. "Would you like something to eat, dear?"
Mary asked. "Yes," Mother chimed in. "I've been keeping something warm for you on the stove." I looked at them as though
they were women from Mars, and went to bed. Neither ever mentioned that night.

I was, I know now, very stubborn not only about my marriage
but about everything. It was a good trait in a way. It got me into
many places where people wanted to keep me out; it was to get
me exclusive dispatches; it took me over hurdles; it pushed me
through doors. I would not take no for an answer. It was this
that kept me in Russia for five, nearly six years, long past the
time when a reasonable man would have given up and retreated

to New York. I stuck it out, telling myself that if I had the grit to hang on, I would be there when Stalin died, and that was the biggest story in the world. And I was there on March 5, 1953, when Stalin died, but in the words of a famous Victorian cartoon: "My, what a long rain." Yes, I got some big stories. I got into Hanoi during the Vietnam war and into every backwater Communist country on the map. I got interviews and page one exclusives where others might have failed. Only stubbornness kept me determined to write the story of Leningrad's nine hundred days of siege, though twenty-five years passed between the time I entered the ice-clad city and the day my book on it was published.

I know my stubbornness served me well, but I know, too, that it paid back many a bitter penny. This was true in my long feud with Hugh Baillie, the head of UP.

When Hugh Baillie put me on the blacklist, a sensible man would have got another job. I didn't. I was determined to overwhelm Baillie by my brilliance. I was going to show the son of a bitch. True, I did cast about for another spot, but with no great diligence. The only place I wanted to work was *The New York Times.* Ultimately, and again because of stubbornness, I got a job on the *Times,* but with a little common sense I would have got on the paper before rather than after World War II.

I didn't press too hard for the *Times* because I was writing my head off for magazines. I wrote for anyone who would take my copy, all the pieces under other names because UP had a rule against outside writing. Soon I was earning two or three times my frozen UP salary. I clung to UP because—well, because I loved it. It had spirit and I would never find its like—newsmen like Lyle C. Wilson, Mert Akers, Bill Lawrence, Joe Alex Morris, Julius Frandsen and Earl J. Johnson, UP's general news manager. A newspaperman's newsman, a professional, Johnson possessed the most sensitive touch I ever saw, a wizard out of Kansas. Most of the UP came from Kansas, Missouri, Nebraska, Illinois, Indiana, Ohio—lily white, not one black on the staff, few Jews, few Catholics, ambitious, devils for work, jealous, frustrated, on the make, excitable, enthusiastic, unmanageable. Johnson managed us, welded us into an unbeatable team. We worked together, we loved each other, we hated each other, we loved UP, we hated UP, we would die for EJJ. During World War II, I got to know a woman in England—well, let's be frank:

I fell in love with an American nurse in England, a member of a surgical team, and she told me what it was like, being on that team, each nurse, each doctor, part of the whole, so close, so knowing, so intimate, not a word was needed, the surgeon reaching for his scalpel at the precise moment a nurse was putting it into his hand, each part of the whole, senses so intermingled that when the operation was over no one needed to speak. At its best, UP was like that. We knew ourselves and we knew each other; we compensated for one another's weaknesses, the punchers pacing themselves to the rhythm of the rewrite man's typewriter, the rewrite man pacing himself to the dictation speed of the reporter. We did not exchange a word. That was Johnson's genius. If a word was needed, he always had it, cynical to the cynics, romantic to the romantics, sophisticated to the sophisticated. That kept me with UP, that and my pigheadedness. But I was earning my living outside UP, making it with my typewriter, every night, every weekend, the typewriter chattering, long hours in the Library of Congress at research, sometimes half a dozen articles a month, two or three items for "Periscope," the prediction and gossip page of *Newsweek*. I would write anything for anyone, but most of all I wrote for *Coronet* magazine, for Arnold Gingrich, David Smart, Bernard Geis, Barbara Brandt and Oscar Dystel —surefire, short, upbeat, bright, flashy, easy-to-read pieces. One month I had four in *Coronet,* each signed with a different name, but the name I used most of all was Michael Evans, and Gingrich and Geis and Dystel always called me Mike.

It was Arnold Gingrich who turned me toward Europe, and the approaching war. Spain had already captured my heart. Night after night, my friends and I sat around Washington emotionalizing about the war. We agonized over the Loyalist dispatches of Herbert R. Matthews in *The New York Times* and inveighed against the editors who gave equal play to those from the Franco side written by William Carney (we didn't know, of course, that rival pro-Republican and pro-Franco editors in the Times Building were acting under a Solomon's edict by managing editor Edwin L. James to measure Matthews and Carney with a ruler, playing the story by strict linear equity). Discussions grew more emotional when I came to New York and stayed in Greenwich Village with an old Minnesota friend, an early fellow traveler. Had I known of Stalin's sabotage, of the plotting by Soviet agents, particularly against the anarchists, had I known that as the Soviet generals and diplomats returned to Moscow they were, one by one, systematically put up against the wall in the basement of the Lubyanka, I would have—God, I don't know—I think I would have been ready to go to Moscow and give my life in an attempt on Stalin's.

Yet for all this, I did not know a single American who joined the International Brigade, nor did I meet one until years later. I was sitting at my desk in the *Times* one day in the mid-fifties when the city desk sent me racing down to the Communist *Daily Worker.* Internal Revenue agents were taking it over for nonpayment of taxes. When I got to 35 East 12th Street, I found half a dozen IRS agents in the cluttered *Worker* city room and several New York policemen looking a little uncomfortable. I asked Joe Clark, foreign editor of the *Worker,* whom I had known in Moscow, what was going on. Suddenly the *Worker* staff picked up their typewriters and began to chant: "They're suppressing the Free Press. Defend the Free Press!" One by one, still chanting, carrying typewriters and bundles of copy paper, they headed for the offices of the *Daily Freiheit,* the Yiddish-language Communist paper, one flight down, on the seventh floor.

Standing to one side, observing the scene, was a compact man with a military bearing, smoking a pipe. He was, I discovered, John Gates, editor of the *Worker,* who had been commissar of the International Brigade in Spain. He spoke in a quiet, confident voice, not a quiver of excitement, and I knew instantly that he had been a brave and good officer regardless of politics, intrigues, Soviet conspiracy or party line. Here in this shabby scene, a leftover from the Living Theater of the 1930s, I had finally set eyes on an American volunteer for Spain.

In a matter of months, Gates, Clark and most of the *Daily Worker* staff pulled out of the Communist party and set off on independent courses. They had been able to live with the Stalin purges of the 1930s, they had stomached the Nazi-Soviet pact, the Finnish winter war, the quarrels of World War II, the postwar strife, the postwar purges, the death of Stalin, but when Khrushchev finally began to dot the *i*'s and cross the *t*'s of Stalin's bestiality, his assault on millions of his countrymen, his persecution of foreign Communists and, above all, his anti-Semitism —this proved too much. They quit, Gates at their head, puffing quietly on his pipe, keeping his cool, keeping the troops in line, unflappable, still brave, capable of looking back, with frankness, not raising his voice, on the years in which he had been used. But how he must have burned within.

Of course, John Gates was only one of many. When I returned to Moscow in 1959, after being barred by Soviet authorities for five years, I met my wartime friend Ilya Ehrenburg, the Soviet writer, whom I had not been able to see in the long, cold period of 1949–54. He told me how he had returned to Moscow from Spain in 1937, having heard the rumors that something was going on, not really believing them, not really understanding what was happening until he went to the offices of *Izvestiya,* the newspaper for which he was writing, and walked down the corridor, office after office locked and vacant, names taken down from the doors, not one of his friends to be seen.

When I first went to Moscow, in wartime, I met some of the Spanish Loyalists who had found refuge in the Soviet Union in 1939, children without parents, wives without husbands, a few men, living in poverty and distress. They had been greeted with bouquets, but now Russia was at war and they were forgotten. These were the lucky ones, who had not been sent to death in Stalin's camps. I saw Dolores Ibarruri, La Pasionaria, the red flame of Spain, a tragic woman, with dark, lined face, sunken eyes in which I thought an ember of fire still glowed. Pasionaria was now playing a bit role in the morality plays of Soviet politics, a set speech at the International Women's Conference, a set speech at the Congress Against War, written for her by the hacks of agitprop, her son killed on the eastern front in World War II, a woman in whom the whole of Spain's tragedy was encompassed: God knows what thoughts lay behind those doomed eyes.

That was all to come, but the dark shadows of Stalin's evil had already fallen over the late 1930s. The purges in Moscow were in full swing and they raised fearsome questions. Yet my naiveté was intense. I remember one evening suggesting to a friend as we drank very cheap wine in a very cheap Village café that maybe the purge trials were just a different kind of "show," a double show, something like a Chinese shadow box.

Once, so I speculated, once the roles were played out at the former Noblemen's Club in Moscow, where the trials took place, the players, removing their masks, wiping off the greasepaint, congratulating each other on the skill of the performance, drank toasts to the success of the Revolution at a great Kremlin banquet in St. Andrew's Hall, Stalin and Bukharin downing a *rumka* of vodka, *do adna,* bottoms up, Zinoviev and Vishinsky drinking their mutual health in fine old brandy, Kamenev, Radek and the others jollying it up with Molotov and Kaganovich, all under the benign eye of old General Ulrich, the presiding judge. Yes, my friend agreed, that made sense. It was impossible to believe that all these old revolutionaries were traitors, that they were being sent to the wall. What silly children we were!

If the drama of Spain focused my attention on Europe, it was Arnold Gingrich who placed Spain in context for me, and made me see that war was inevitable, inescapable. I would, I think, have come to this conclusion myself, but Arnold wiped all doubt away.

Gingrich and David Smart, daring, bright young Chicago editors, had formed a partnership in the late 1920s and created an instantly successful magazine called *Apparel Arts,* designed to carry prestige advertising of the men's clothing industry. They parlayed this success into *Esquire,* the *Playboy* of its day but a more sophisticated *Playboy,* printing the fiction of Hemingway, Dos Passos, Steinbeck, Van Vechten, alongside sleek, satiny Vargas girls of improbable sexual dimensions. Then they launched *Coronet* ("Infinite Riches in Small Room"), on which I cut my free-lance teeth, and finally *Ken,* a skyrocket which blazed fiercely in the prewar sky, dedicated to arousing the world to the danger of Hitler and World War II. Into this project Gingrich poured all his knowledge of Europe—writers, political commentators, caricaturists. *Ken* was given a prepublication promotional budget of a million dollars, astronomical for its time, and soared into hundreds of thousands of circulation. Then it plummeted like a spent shell and vanished from the horizon. It died just as the peace-that-was-not-peace became the war-that-was-not-war, in September 1939.

I spent three years of my life—or more—in the last twelve months of *Ken*'s existence. Arnold had brought me in on it soon after the start, and flew me out to Chicago, putting me up in extravagant quarters at the Ambassador East, a few blocks north of my old home, the Berkshire. I was wined and dined and invited to David Smart's apartment on East Walton Street. This high living bedazzled me, not least Smart's apartment, a creation of black marble, cut crystal, polar-white rugs and very, very low lighting, and the beauty of his friend Gabrielle, very young, only seventeen or eighteen, I thought, pure blond, pure Aryan (to Smart's dark, olive complexion), accompanied by her mother.

Arnold and David wanted me to come to Chicago as editor. The skyrocket had already begun to sputter, they were beginning to cast about for safety nets, there was lots of money in it (by my Spartan standards), it was gulpingly attractive, and as Arnold pointed out, I would be in the front line in rousing the nation, rousing the sleeping doltish world of Chamberlain, Daladier, and the Midwestern isolationists, La Follette, Norris, Wheeler, Walsh, Shipstead and Lundeen (my heroes of agrarian revolt but now the villains of isolation), against the danger which would engulf us, he was certain, within a year.

It was tempting, God knows it was tempting to me, still in the box at UP. I was already putting in more hours per month for David Smart and Arnold Gingrich than I was for Hugh Baillie, and I loved it, I loved the idea. I wanted to strike my blow. I was filled with the guilt of Spain. This would help square my account. I had been educated by Gingrich to understand what was happening in Europe. Gingrich was a man whose friends were John Gunther, Red Lewis, Dorothy Thompson, William Shirer, the Mowrers, Genevieve Tabouis and Pertinax, the nom de plume of the famous French commentator André Giraud. Gingrich knew Ignazio Silone and Thomas Mann and everyone who had made it out of Germany. He knew the crowd at the Adlon bar, the Dôme, the Sélect, and in London he dined at Rules or the Café Royal. What held me back? It must have been common sense. I thought the risks were too great.

I knew that *Ken* was in trouble, had been in trouble almost from its blazing takeoff. It was too hot for the isolationist soil where David Smart and Arnold Gingrich had their economic roots. David had begun life as a producer of sleek four-color advertising brochures for Midwest apparel shops, Gingrich as advertising manager for Kuppenheimer Clothes. *Apparel Arts* lived on the advertising budgets of the big men's-clothing makers. The same firms were heavy users of *Esquire.* Many had come into *Ken*'s first issues. But *Ken* was too hot. It was violently anti-Hitler, violently anti-appeasement, violently against hypocrisy not only in Europe (where this was safe enough) but in the good old U.S.A., which the manufacturers loved so dearly. It was, some of them thought, too radical, even Red.

Many Midwestern industrialists in 1938 and 1939 were stolidly isolationist. What went on in Germany was Germany's business. Hitler, to their way of thinking, was authoritarian, not totalitarian; totalitarian was Russia. Did they think there was money to be made in Hitler's Germany? Quite likely. The strongest backing for the America First movement was centered in the Midwest, with General Robert E. Wood of Sears, Roebuck at its head. Henry Ford in Detroit was a staunch noninterventionist. Not a few banks and businessmen who hated Roosevelt opposed intervention simply because Roosevelt favored it.

Lightning began to strike. If *Ken* didn't pipe down, out came the ads from *Esquire* and *Apparel Arts* (they were already tumbling out of *Ken*). This was hardly a novel experience to me. I had learned at the University of Minnesota and in Minneapolis that publishing the truth was not the way to win popularity.

I think David Smart would have thrown in his hand quite early. *Ken* was costing him millions and threatened to cost millions more and even to destroy his publishing empire. Arnold was the opposite. *Ken* was his creation, the product of his apocalyptic vision of the world. He would not be put down. True, he had to rein in. He flipped *Ken*'s format away from coated-stock four-color quality presswork, he cut its pages and then, in a dramatic switch, turned it into a fortnightly, with a format remarkably like that employed today by *Time* and *Newsweek,* hitting again and again on his monotheme: Hitler is going to bring on World War II and Chamberlain and Daladier do not have the will to halt him. Issue after issue, week after week.

His virtuoso effort was conducted by a staff that consisted, at the end, of three or four people. There was Clark Kinnaird in Chicago, who put the magazine together. There was Claud Cockburn in London, owner and distributor of an extraordinary private newsletter, *The Week,* which he sold for a staggering subscription price, over two hundred dollars a year, a plain mimeographed sheet which contained more inside diplomatic information than the American embassy in London reported in a year. Cockburn, a Communist (sometimes he said he was a party member, other times he said he had been too busy to fill out a card), was iconoclastic, totally cynical about the world (how did that fit Communism?), a believer in no one and no doctrine so far as I could discover, certain that if man was given the slightest chance he would do himself in. Thin as a railbird and, as I discovered when I met him in wartime London, as badly dressed as any Great Russell Street intellectual, in baggy oxford grays, gray cardigan, dirty-collared shirt, rag tie, he left a cigarette burning in the corner of his mouth, hopelessly yellowed—no, browned—teeth, sunken cheeks. He wrote the most elegantly sardonic prose I have ever read. Cockburn, first cousin of the Waughs and father of the contemporary columnist Alex Cockburn, airmailed from London (with a small wireless update) what amounted to three or four print pages of diplomatic intelligence, marvelous materials. From Washington I contributed an equal quantity of gossip, guesses and persiflage. My quality was mediocre by Cockburn standards, but it filled the pages. That was it. That was *Ken* in its last stand. Remarkably good, but doomed despite Gingrich's indomitable spirit, his determination to hang on until war started—and vindicated him.

This endeavor was in full swing at the time Michael was born. It finally sputtered out in the summer of 1939, existing in its last six weeks as a kind of green-paper intelligence sheet. Gingrich to the end sported this quotation from Abraham Lincoln above the masthead: "Let the people know the truth and the country is safe."

That quotation might serve as *Ken*'s epitaph. It gave me one more lesson about the price of truth. It did not come cheap. It had cost David Smart several millions of dollars and we, the country, all of us, were the losers. I don't mean to suggest that *Ken* was the only voice trying to raise the alarm, trying to alert America to the danger of world war. Probably the finest group of foreign correspondents the United States ever possessed was dedicated to this purpose. But the lesson of *Ken* was chillingly similar to lessons I had been taught by Fred B. Snyder and by the *Minneapolis Journal:* the truth is no defense; the truth is dangerous; it upsets applecarts. In another era, the messenger bringing the bad but true news was beheaded. In our times, the punishments were more diverse.

14 | Going to War

I was a few months shy of thirty-one when World War II started; Michael was not quite six months old. My long feud with Hugh Baillie had been ended by mutual consent, and I was a certified star writer and reporter for UP (I continued to write extensively for *Coronet*). I had, I thought, a working grasp of Washington and national politics; I had been attending the national political conventions since 1932 and I knew the Senate well, particularly men like Nye and La Follette. George Norris had been my hero. I knew most of the political figures at close hand, although not intimately. I had become fond of Eleanor Roosevelt, an affection that would continue to the end of her life. I knew Lorena Hickok, the newswoman whose close friendship with Mrs. Roosevelt later caused a stir. I disliked Lorena intensely and had since I first encountered her in Minneapolis, working for the *Tribune,* a coarse, cigar-smoking, tough-talking reporter.

I spent a good deal of time at the State Department. I respected the crusty Cordell Hull, though I knew the secretary of state had little influence with FDR. Under the tutelage of Arnold Gingrich, I had lost some of my insularity.

Washington was a more comfortable, more commonsensical place than it is today. The security mania had not taken over. The only credential you needed to cover the White House was a plain white pasteboard issued by the Correspondents Association and signed by Stephen T. Early, FDR's press secretary. No plastic idents on a chain, no four-color laminated photos, no background checks, no metal detectors, no fingerprints, and you never even showed your card. There were no guards at the White House gates, just a friendly White House policeman at the pressroom door who knew everyone. In the New Deal years, I never saw him stop a single person. At the State Department, there were no credentials at all, no guards; anyone could enter and wander from floor to floor of that wonderful General Grant pile. The floors were marble parquet and there were beautiful mahogany slatted doors at each office so the breeze stirred up by the ceiling fans could circulate in summer. Sleepy black servitors sat outside the offices of the secretaries of state, war and navy (all three in the building then) and nodded to visitors.

A few years ago, I read a study of the Alger Hiss case which described how difficult it would have been for anyone on the outside to have got access to secret State Department documents. The author, a man named Epstein, mentioned guards, credentials, clearances. There were no such things. Corridor after corridor was lined with old wooden filing cabinets, no locks, stuffed with State Department documents. Anyone could stroll down the halls, stop, pull out a drawer and select what he wanted. Secretaries, clerks and minor officials did it all the time. War brought a little change to this; not much.

Nothing was more inevitable than the outbreak of World War II. By September 1, 1939, it had become totally unavoidable. But nothing was so amazing to me, to the country and to the world as the signing by Molotov and Ribbentrop of the Nazi-Soviet pact on August 24, 1939. True, rumors had circulated in Moscow, since shortly after the May 1 dismissal of Maksim M. Litvinov as Soviet foreign minister, that a deal with Germany might be possible. But they had been dismissed by all reputable commentators including *The New York Times*'s Walter Duranty. After the event, a dozen clues to what had been developing were quickly identified, but until August 24, nobody paid heed to them.

Forty years would pass before I would discover that the inside story of this event, the negotiations between Hitler and Stalin, had not been secret at all. The whole thing had been made known in meticulous detail to the governments of the United States, Great Britain, France and Italy, all this through the daring of a young German diplomat, Hans Von Herwarth, or Johnny, as he was known to my old friend Charles ("Chip") Bohlen, who told me much of the story and presented what he knew in his memoirs in 1973.

What Chip knew was that Johnny, an attaché of the German embassy in Moscow as Bohlen was an attaché of the American embassy, had briefed him, step by step, as the secret Nazi-Soviet diplomacy progressed. Bohlen did not learn until after the war that Johnny in 1939 was a member of an anti-Hitler underground desperately hoping to keep Hitler from starting a war. Nor did Bohlen know that Johnny had talked with anyone else. It was not until 1981 that Johnny revealed he had first tried to alert the Italians, hoping that Mussolini might halt Hitler. He tried agonizingly to convince the British and the French that unless they unfroze the glacial talks they were conducting with the Russians in Moscow, Hitler would leave them at the starting post.

None of these efforts succeeded. Mussolini was only mildly interested. London and Paris gave no sign they even read the dispatches instigated by Von Herwarth. Only in Washington were Bohlen's reports taken seriously. Late in the game, very late, Secretary Hull called in the British and the French to warn what was impending. There is nothing in the record to show that Hull influenced the Foreign Office or the Quai d'Orsay in the slightest. As Von Herwarth told me in 1981: "They lacked the imagination to perceive that a Nazi-Soviet pact was possible, and even had they foreseen this, they had nothing to offer the Russians"—that is, they were not prepared to conclude a genuine alliance. The fatally feckless course of Chamberlain and Daladier continued. What a sensation it would have been had *Ken* been able to expose what was really happening in Moscow during that summer of 1939. Not even Cockburn's long nose managed that, and I had no ability to pry out such materials, nor had any American correspondent. Neither Cordell Hull nor Franklin Roosevelt, both of whom understood the implications of the German-Soviet talks, gave thought of leaking the information to the press in order to compel the British and the French to derail the Hitler-Stalin talks. Such publicity would have delayed the outbreak of war or at least put the world on warning as to what lay ahead. Neither Hull nor Roosevelt acted, and Von Herwarth's courageous attempt to alert the West constituted, in the end, the first great intelligence disaster of World War II.

I asked Von Herwarth later why, in his view, no one followed up on the rumors of Soviet-German contacts which had circulated in Moscow during that pleasant summer of 1939. He had no answer. He could not understand it. He had risked his life by leaking the details, in the belief that any experienced diplomat would draw the obvious conclusions. They had not. The episode reinforced my belief in the eternal rightness of those words of

Abraham Lincoln that Gingrich had put on the masthead of *Ken*.

It was not and would not be leaks that would do us in, but suppression of the facts of what was happening in the world.

The war changed my life. Six months after the outbreak, I was transferred to New York to handle the cable and wireless reports from London, Paris, Berlin and Moscow. I got to New York just in time for the transformation of the "phony war" to the real war, to write of Hitler's invasion of Denmark and Norway, the Low Countries, the fall of France. I didn't have a moment's free breath. In the summer of 1940 came the political conventions, the nomination of Willkie at Philadelphia and Roosevelt for a third term at Chicago. I covered both, torn between my liking for Willkie and a sense that times were too dangerous to change leaders. Mary and I took a vacation in Minneapolis after FDR was nominated. It was a quiet interlude. Dad and Mike played together in the backyard, we took long drives in the Minnesota countryside, the harvest at full swing, the great red combines cutting golden wakes across the endless fields.

While we were in Minneapolis, we got a letter from a woman named Lucy, who with her husband had been looking after our house in Mamaroneck: "House has been searched by an unknown person." Nothing seemed to have been taken. She had called the police but apparently only my papers had been disturbed. The police wanted to know if I had left behind anything important, "especially Mr. Salisbury's papers concerning the war."

Of course, I had no important papers about the war, and when we found that our war bonds—$475 worth—and my insurance papers were intact, we stopped worrying. I talked to the police when I got home and they minimized the affair: probably just some high school kids who wanted to use the house for a party.

I dismissed the matter myself. The question about war papers lingered in my mind, but I thought that was a product of the growing hysteria. France had fallen. The battle of Britain was beginning. Soon we would be listening to Edward R. Murrow saying: "This—is London."

The Luftwaffe seemed all-powerful. Hitler had invented the blitzkrieg. Would he invade England? The world had suddenly grown dark and dangerous. I was working harder and harder. We bought a lovely old Federal house, at 303 North Barry Avenue in Mamaroneck, from Henry Steele Commager. He refused to make any profit, sold it for what he had paid, $7,500. "I don't believe in taking advantage of a hard-working young newspaperman." We put in a garden and played badminton with our next-door neighbors. I learned about suburbia and commuting. We had no car. Once again I felt restless and frustrated. Sometimes I missed my train and had a martini or two with a young magazine editor. I told her I wanted to be a war correspondent. I was sick of sitting at my desk and pounding out roundups and new leads all day, going home on the commuter train. She sympathized a lot.

Saturday, June 21, 1941, was a lovely early-summer day. We had invited Bernie Geis, the editor of *Coronet,* and his wife, Darlene, to spend the weekend. I worked late at UP and after dinner we sat on the back porch, drinking rum swizzles and talking about the war. I said that the Germans were going to attack Russia that weekend. Bernie was skeptical. I told him every report that had come in indicated the Germans were massed on the Soviet frontier, ready to invade. This was the word from London, from Washington, from Switzerland, from Sweden, from Tokyo, from Turkey and even from Berlin—if you read the dispatches carefully. The only place where the news seemed to be totally bland was Moscow.

"I just can't believe it," Bernie said. "Why would Hitler do that?"

"Well," I said, "he's always wanted to and now he's made up his mind on the *Drang nach Osten*—the drive to the east." I told Bernie that I had written flatly in my war lead—flatly without qualification—that the German assault would come this weekend.

"As a matter of fact," I said, looking at my wristwatch, "it's ten-thirty now. That's four-thirty A.M. Sunday in Moscow. I wouldn't be surprised if they were going across the border right now."

The telephone rang. "O.K., Bernie," I said, "there it is."

It was. The office was calling me to say the Nazis had attacked Russia all along the frontier. I dashed for the train. By the time I got home again, it was noon Sunday. The Germans were deep into Russia and had already destroyed most of the Soviet air force.

For the second time, a massive intelligence failure had occurred. Now, because Stalin stubbornly, insanely, had refused to credit the reports submitted to him, the world faced a catastrophe. Stalin had not believed the evidence of his own remarkable spy network in Berlin and Tokyo, he had disregarded warnings from Churchill, Roosevelt and even Mao Zedong (although, of course, we did not know this then). Thus the Soviet almost collapsed under the Nazi blitz and was saved only by the sacrifice of twenty to thirty million lives of her citizens.

The Nazi-Soviet pact had caught me by surprise. Not so the Nazi attack of June 22, 1941. I had seen the evidence mount up. For nearly three weeks I had been predicting the attack and on that Saturday afternoon of June 21 I had taken all the facts and put them before Earl Johnson. "I want to do something we have not done before," I said. "I want to write tonight without qualification—without any qualification—that the German war against Russia will begin this weekend." Johnson read the reports carefully. "O.K." he said finally. "But remember it's your ass if you're wrong." I grinned. I didn't have to remind him that it was his ass too.

The Western news agencies and newspapers were caught badly off base when war came to Moscow. Because of intense American partisanship for the Finns, they had pulled their correspondents out during the Russian winter war with Finland and hadn't sent them back. Even the news agencies had only bare-bones staffs. UP had Henry Shapiro and AP had Henry Cassidy. That was all.

I was appalled as Hitler's Wehrmacht swept into Russia. There seemed to be no stopping them. The military experts in Washington and London predicted it would be over in six weeks. Not until later was it revealed that Colonel Faymonville, long-time American military attaché in Moscow, alone among military specialists insisted from the start that regardless of losses, the Red Army would prevail. He was to pay a heavy penalty for being right, for betting on the Russians and not the Germans. In 1943, he was yanked out of Moscow, and finally he was drummed out of the army, because his colleagues considered him "pro-Soviet"—one more example of the fate of men who report an uncomfortable truth.

I could not believe Stalin had been caught by surprise. Of course, neither I nor anyone outside the Kremlin realized that he had fallen into a trauma, had run away to his dacha and locked himself within, convinced that "all that Lenin created for us had been lost forever," as Nikita Khrushchev was to reveal.

Of all this there was no hint in 1941. True, the Red Army was falling back; true, the Germans were advancing; but Stalin was receiving the emissaries of Churchill and Roosevelt—Harry L. Hopkins, W. Averell Harriman, Anthony Eden, Sir Stafford Cripps. He admitted his problems, but radiated confidence.

It was clear that Roosevelt and Churchill saw the war as a common cause. I knew that we were going in sooner rather than later. I knew that we were not going to permit Hitler to destroy England or possess Russia. Somehow I was convinced that the invasion of Russia had sealed Hitler's downfall. How did I convince myself of that? Well, Napoleon's example was the main thing. Another was my conviction that the United States would shift the balance.

Yet as I came in each morning to write the war leads and watched Hitler's armored forces race across the Ukraine (they claimed they inflicted two million casualties in taking Kiev), storm up to the gates of Leningrad (would the Russians be able to hold the northern capital?) and in early October drive to the suburbs of Moscow, I could not but wonder. Then toward the end of October 1941, it began to seem to me that the Nazis had been slowed; they had not taken Moscow as Goebbels had proclaimed they would; they had not broken into Leningrad. Maybe, just maybe, the tide was beginning to turn, and I reflected this feeling in my dispatches.

Saturday, December 6, was a beautiful springlike day, the grass still green on the Mamaroneck lawns, and when I went to work that morning I saw buds opening up on the lilacs. In the newsroom, December 6 was another day of crisis. We had become inured to weekend crisis because Hitler had made them a cliché. If something was going to happen, it happened on a weekend. Every dispatch that reached my desk from the Pacific spoke of imminent war: Japanese convoys, Japanese warships, ominous preparations. This was the word from Frank Hewlett in Manila, from Robert Bellaire in Tokyo, from Pepper Martin in Shanghai, from Dick Wilson in Hong Kong.

I had been watching closely the talks in Washington between Mr. Hull and the Japanese. It seemed clear that they had broken down. That the crisis was coming to a head I had no doubt.

As always, I wrote a general lead on Saturday night, wrapping up the war news. I said: "War in the Pacific seemed powder-close Saturday night." But I qualified this, raising the question of whether the Japanese would attack this weekend or a bit later.

There were two reasons for my qualification. The first was that the Japanese had permitted a freighter, the *Tatuta Maru,* to sail from Yokohama for the United States four days earlier. The second was that the dispatches from Moscow made clear that the Red Army had gone over to the offensive and was beginning to drive the Germans back—the first time the Germans had retreated since Hitler unleashed the Wehrmacht, September 1, 1939. I thought the Japanese might delay action until after January 1, 1942, in order to observe developments on the eastern front. I had convinced myself that war was to Japan's disadvantage and that Japan's civilian cabinet opposed war. Of course, I was right on both points, but I did not understand the strength of the militarists who actually ran Japan.

Sunday, December 7, the weather changed. Mary and I went to the Polo Grounds with our friends Nordau Schoenberg and his wife, to watch the big pro football game, the Brooklyn Dodgers versus the New York Giants. There was a huge crowd and a stiff cold wind. We left before the end of the game and went to Nordau's apartment for a drink. We turned on the radio as an announcer cut in with "additional details on the Japanese bombing of Pearl Harbor."

Nordau was deeply moved. I had a curious reaction. "Those poor little Japanese bastards," I said. "The suicide boys have got them in the soup. They are finished. They are through. They haven't got a chance."

By attacking Pearl Harbor, I said, the militarists had cast the die for war, and war with the United States meant defeat for Japan. That was true. But defeat was years away and would cost many lives.

I went into the office and heard how heavy the fleet losses were—though the figures were only a fraction of the real total.

I had no notion that the United States had broken the Japanese purple code and was able to follow the government's secret movements and decisions, but immediately after Pearl Harbor I began to hear from friends in Washington sensational reports about our real losses and the failure of the army and navy in Hawaii to maintain an alert. They had, I was told, lowered vigilance over the weekend of December 6–7; though the attacking

Japanese planes had been detected by radar or sonic devices, the signals had been ignored. The smell of a major intelligence breakdown was strong. Before December 1941 was out, I understood that while we had anticipated an attack by Japan that weekend, we had not imagined that it would strike Pearl Harbor. Southeast Asia, Hong Kong, Singapore, Manila, Indonesia—yes, all this was anticipated, but not Pearl Harbor. Even though MacArthur had been strongly reinforced with planes in anticipation of war, the Japanese had managed to destroy his air arm.

As would be revealed in due course, Pearl Harbor was the third intelligence disaster of the war. War, it would seem, almost by definition consists of intelligence failures; World War II would provide extraordinary evidence of this.

In the first week of January 1942, I went to Washington to handle the big war stories there, principally the battle of the Philippines, which MacArthur was fighting gallantly but obviously was doomed to lose. I handled reports of the battle in Malaysia, the rapidly deteriorating situation in Indonesia and the threat to Burma. I got the full story of the Pearl Harbor losses from Wallace Carroll, UP's London correspondent, who arrived in Washington after a journey around the world via Russia, Iran, India and the Pacific. He had much information about the incredibly careless conduct of the U.S. command in Hawaii. Naturally, none of this could be published.

I was dismayed by the lack of public understanding of war; the wild expectations of immediate victory; the ignorance of basic logistics. People could not see why we didn't just rush troops to Southeast Asia and shatter the Japanese. I found to my surprise that I had acquired some notion of war's reality from studying the Civil War during my Washington days. I had read and reread Douglas Southall Freeman's classic four-volume biography of Robert E. Lee, and G. F. Henderson's study of Stonewall Jackson. I had visited the battlefields at Gettysburg and Chancellorsville, walking over the terrain. This gave me some understanding of the importance of preparation and surprise. The side that was ready to strike possessed an extraordinary advantage, which could not quickly be overtaken by the other side. It might hold good for a year or two years; it might even cause defeat. I applied this principle to the Russians and concluded that not before late 1942 or 1943 would they be able to make up the damage inflicted by the initial Nazi attack. I put the same measure against the United States in the Pacific and inferred that it would take us equally long to begin to turn the tables against the Japanese.

I don't pretend that all my conclusions were farseeing. Many were not. Some were childish. Since I wrote them down, I can cite them against myself. I predicted in early January 1942 that Singapore would be lost by February 1, the Dutch islands by March 1. These were good guesses. I suggested that the next big battles would be in Burma (correct) and in Alaska and Australia (totally wrong). I thought the Germans would attack Cyprus and Malta, but that their main target would be Ireland (totally wrong). I thought that the Pacific east of Hawaii was gone. I thought the Nazis would drive deep into the Caucasus in the spring of 1942, aided by Turkey. The Germans went for Stalingrad and the Caucasus, lost both. I thought Rommel would cut the Suez. He tried and failed.

I was disturbed to find that my friends in army intelligence and in the State Department didn't seem to think much of the Soviet achievement in halting the Germans before Moscow and successfully counterattacking in December and January. The Red Army had driven back the Nazis fifty or sixty miles, the first land defeat Hitler had suffered since moving into the Rhineland in 1936. In Washington, this was attributed to General Winter, not the Red Army. I thought the Moscow victory plus the aid that we and the British would give Stalin marked a turn in the war. I was more right than the military intelligence people, but it would not be until the Russian counterblow at Stalingrad late in 1942 that the outcome of the war would be finally fixed.

I was depressed by Washington. The capital seemed overwhelmed in bureaucratic struggle. FDR was dominant over Congress and setting the pace, but the congressional isolationists still held powerful positions and were only biding their time. Already the shape of America First policy had begun to emerge—fight the Pacific war and leave the British and Russians to cope with Germany. I thought the isolationists' real objective was to arrange a peace between the West and Germany, permitting the Nazis to polish off Russia while we wiped up Japan.

The strongest impression I had—and this came in large measure from some of the air corps men whom I knew, men like General Carl ("Tooey") Spaatz, Colonel Henry Berlinger and others

—was what I called the "mass ignorance, stupidity and ineptness of the top American [military] staff." I thought this condition would prevail until the wear and tear of battle cleared out the deadwood. I didn't know much about General George C. Marshall, but what I did know spoke well for him. I formed a high regard for General MacArthur despite his loss of air force to the Japanese—it was a regard I retained throughout the war, intensified when late in 1944 I got to his command headquarters in New Guinea, met him and observed the extraordinary military machine he had welded together—in his own image.

For the generals in Washington, I am afraid, I had little but contempt. As I noted at the time: "[They] seem to have learned little or nothing from the war so far; [have] no comprehension of the significance of Pearl Harbor; are more inclined than ever to keep their heads down, do nothing (especially nothing new) to avoid presenting a moving target." It was, alas, a picture I would see many times during the war and after.

"It is almost impossible," I wrote, "to locate an offensive-minded, realistic, hard-boiled thinker in the army high command. To a suggestion that propaganda might be utilized as a military weapon, they throw up their arms in horror, exclaiming: 'Of course, we wouldn't think of using a Nazi method!' "

It was almost certainly Tooey Spaatz who gave me that vignette. The air corps in January 1942 was in revolt. They talked gloomily of the loss of the whole Pacific and the complete collapse of the British, even of heavy German air attacks on the U.S. coast if the drift of the early days was not quickly halted. The navy, of course, was in a state of shock.

I was back in New York at the end of February, determined that I would go abroad as a war correspondent. The UP had on January 21, 1942, applied for my credentials to go overseas. This didn't mean that I was going. The UP asked accreditation for a group of us, just to be prepared. But I was moving toward a resolution of my personal and professional life. I did not see how I could stay out of the war, feeling as I did about Hitler, believing as I did that the future of the world depended on the defeat of Nazi Germany and the Japanese. I was capable of great hypocrisy, that I knew, but I did not see how I could live with myself without taking a hand in the struggle of our time. There was a lot of old-fashioned American patriotism in my makeup.

TR and Blackjack Pershing had not been my youthful heroes for nothing. And, it should be added, patriotism was not a dirty word in 1941. Perhaps I should simply volunteer for the army. But this did not seem right to me. I might or might not be a good soldier. I knew I was a good reporter and could serve the war effort by reporting from the front. This was the story of my lifetime and I wanted a part of it.

There was building up once again a crisis in my personal life. Mary and I were not getting on. I had, or thought I had, fallen in love with another girl. I didn't know how this would work out, but I believed that if I threw myself into the war I could clarify my feelings; distance and total involvement in the fighting would give me perspective.

Mary was not warm to the idea of my going abroad as a foreign correspondent, but she was not hostile either. Many of my friends were preparing to go. The young woman who had captured my affections thought I should go. "Let's face it," she said. "You are a writer. The only place for a writer in these times is at the front."

It took six months for the details to be worked out, but by autumn 1942, UP had decided to send me to London. The situation in the London bureau was chaotic. A remarkable correspondent, Webb Miller, had headed London before and after the outbreak of war, but in the spring of 1940 he was killed when he fell from a British train during a blackout. Miller, a gifted, poetic writer who felt that the war would destroy the England (and Europe) he loved, had been deeply pessimistic about the future, and embodied much of his pessimism in a brilliant book, *There Is No Peace*. Miller drank a good deal but was not a man to lose control. The autopsy said he fell from the train as he stood between cars to relieve himself. I always thought it was suicide.

The bureau then had been placed in charge of a hard-hitting war correspondent, Edward W. Beattie, Jr., but Beattie had gone off to the front. The store was not being minded and Joe Alex Morris, UP foreign editor, was sent over to straighten things out. He and Earl Johnson finally decided I should go to London and take over the bureau.

So I found myself in December 1942 dashing about New York getting inoculations, loading up on vitamin pills and sulfa drugs, buying a money belt, into which the UP business office stuffed God knows how many beautiful white English ten-pound notes, each almost the size of a double damask dinner napkin, to help finance our London bureau. (No one told me that bringing in these black market notes was a violation of English wartime currency regulations, for which I might go to prison. When I got to London I turned them over to our startled English bookkeeper. He locked them away in a safe, almost afraid to touch them.) I picked up my war correspondent's credentials on December 14, got my plane ticket, had a multiple-martini luncheon at the old Ritz grill with the sympathetic young woman who had encouraged me to go abroad. My father, mother and sister Janet came east from Minneapolis for Christmas (my departure was scheduled for December 29). It was the last time I would see my father. I had a deep premonition of this. He looked thin and worn. I knew he shouldn't still be working at the factory, but there was no persuading him.

And then—nothing. I did not take off for England. I went out to the Marine Air Terminal at La Guardia to board the American Export clipper. All the formalities had been completed; my passport was to be handed to me at the plane. But it was not. The passport control office said it had been withdrawn. There was no explanation. I went back to New York. The UP raised hell. Lyle Wilson, my friend and UP's Washington manager, took up the matter with the formidable Ruth Shipley, for many years director of Passport and Emigration for the State Department. A couple of weeks later, the passport was issued. A bureaucratic mix-up, Wilson told me. "You've no idea how fouled up things can get," he said. "They had an order out to pick up Cy Sulzberger's passport if he tried to leave the country. He's gotten into a row with the British command in the Eastern Mediterranean. When you came along, somebody got the names confused." Well, the story didn't make much sense, but I caught the next available plane, a Pan-American clipper, and at 9:30 P.M. February 4 I arrived in London.

I don't know whether Lyle Wilson ever got the true story of why my passport was blocked. I didn't get it until some forty years later, when, applying for my FBI records under the Freedom of Information Act, I uncovered a twisted chain of events which led back to that late July of 1940 when our house at 714 Bradley Street in Mamaroneck was broken into and "searched," as the letter from Lucy had reported with such excitement. I still don't know if I have the whole story, so much has been suppressed in the documents the FBI turned over. But here is what I believe happened.

Someone, a neighbor lady, I believe (her name has been carefully blacked out in all the FBI documents), was possessed of a vivid imagination. She had, according to the Mamaroneck police, occasionally reported "things" to the police, who paid little attention to them. On this occasion, she seems to have told the police that I was a "code expert" for United Press and an "employee of the German government," and that I had attempted to recruit other individuals (possibly including herself) for "undercover work." She reported that I had installed hidden microphones in my living room and recording devices in the attic. My electric bills, she said, were astronomical.

We were absent from Mamaroneck for about a month, and it was during our absence that the gossip passed on her suspicions to the Mamaroneck police. I cannot entirely reconstruct what followed, but I think I have it worked out pretty well. On July 25, 1940, between 1 P.M. and 4:15 P.M., someone forced open the front door and searched the Bradley Street house. Lucy and her husband, keeping an eye on the house, were absent and had taken our two dogs with them, so she wrote at the time. When they returned, they found the door forced but nothing apparently taken. Only my desk had been disturbed and my papers scattered around.

They called the police, who investigated. The lock of a trunk in the basement had been forced, but there was no evidence of burglary.

Who made the search? Forty-two years after the event, I managed to track down Lucy. The occasion was still present in her memory. "Well, they were government men, weren't they?" she said. "And I think the police came too, didn't they?"

"Why do you suppose, Lucy, they wanted to search the house?" I asked.

"Well," she said, "I think somebody thought you were a spy."

There it was. Somebody did, all right. Regardless of who that somebody was and who conducted the first search or the second search, it is clear from the surviving documents that the Mamaroneck police did not take the matter seriously. When I got back in early August, they told me not to be concerned about the incident, and later they were to tell army intelligence that the lady who was the source of the rumor was unreliable, of "a very imaginative mind," her reputation in the community not of the best. They said she came from a family that they described as "known to be nefarious prevaricators." They thought the story was a figment of her imagination. They told the army they had taken the precaution of inspecting the Bradley Street house (presumably this was the search to which Lucy referred on July 25) from attic to cellar and found no recording devices, microphones or bugs. They checked our electrical bills and found they averaged about $5.50 a month, not high enough to pay for the elaborate equipment the lady said had been installed.

Looking back on the dusty reports, I think the Mamaroneck police did their work competently, efficiently and with intelligence. They never told me about the lady's allegations, but that seems fair enough—why create trouble?

Fair enough except for one circumstance. On September 10, 1940, a routine report of the incident was received by the FBI in New York City from the Mamaroneck police. An FBI agent went to Mamaroneck, visited police headquarters, got a rundown on the affair and on September 16 submitted a report to E. E. Conroy, special agent then in charge of the FBI's New York bureau. The New York office of the FBI gave no further attention to the allegations and a year later, on September 10, 1941, notified Washington that the matter had been placed on "deferred status."

I have not been able to retrieve from the FBI the full text of the agent's report, but the action of the New York office is commentary enough—obviously the FBI took the allegations no more seriously than did the Mamaroneck police.

Or did they? Once the agent's report of September 16, 1940, had been turned in, certain events inexorably followed.

The first occurred January 30, 1941, when B. E. Sackett, the special agent in charge of the FBI's New York office, forwarded to Mr. Hoover in Washington my name for inclusion in a list of "Persons for Custodial Detention: Internal Security." The grounds: "Pro German . . . Is a code expert for the United Press Association and stated he is in employ of German government." This memorandum was sent to Mr. Hoover in response to his telegram of June 15, 1940, requesting field bureaus to forward to him names of "Communist, Fascist, Nazi and other nationalistic background" to be placed on a master list of persons who would be "apprehended and interned immediately upon the outbreak of hostilities between the U.S. Government and the Government they serve, support or owe allegiance to."

Mr. Hoover's action was taken on his own initiative. He established his list in September 1939, without reference to any other branch of the government. When the existence of the lists was discovered by Attorney General Francis Biddle, on July 13, 1943, Mr. Hoover was ordered to dismantle them. This Mr. Hoover did not do. He simply changed the heading in his files. Instead of being listed for "Custodial Detention," the names were placed on a "Security Index."

The Security Index under various permutations was maintained by Mr. Hoover during all the years in which he headed the FBI—that is, until his death, on April 2, 1972.

Congress ordered the list (or lists, there now being several such) destroyed in 1971. But under new titles—"Administrative Index," or "ADEX," and "Reserve File"—they merrily persist to this day.

When United Press in January 1942 submitted my name to army public relations for accreditation as a war correspondent, the provost marshal in his routine check submitted my name to the FBI. On April 20, 1942, the FBI furnished the provost marshal the information that I was a code expert and an employee of the German government.

Because, perhaps, of the complexity of the federal bureaucracy, this report did not halt the wheels of army public relations. In due course, they accredited me to serve as a war correspondent.

There the matter rested until the eve of my departure for England, when, on December 19, 1942, Captain Wallace, the Visa and Passport officer of Military Intelligence, pulled out of the file the Mamaroneck report and sent it to the Passport Division of the State Department. The wheels of bureaucracy move slowly —so slowly that I almost took off for England before the security alarm was sounded. On December 21, still unaware of Captain Wallace's report, the redoubtable Ruth Shipley sent my passport file to Michael McDermott, the State Department's press chief—a good friend of mine and an even better friend of the UP's Washington bureau head, Lyle C. Wilson—for approval. McDermott signed it and sent it back to Mrs. Shipley, who received his O.K., according to the stamp on the letter on December 24.

Only after the Christmas holiday, as I was about to board the clipper at La Guardia, did the warning come through to hold me up.

I knew nothing of this, nothing of the blazing bureaucratic row which broke out between army intelligence, the provost marshal's office, army public relations, the State Department and the FBI over what manner of person I might be. I did not know that intelligence agents had been sent scurrying to interrogate the unflappable Mamaroneck police, who patiently led them through the case of the gossipy woman from the family of "nefarious prevaricators"; I did not know that the late police captain Louis Giancola had painstakingly drafted a two-page statement giving me the highest kind of references; I did not know that Captain Earle of military intelligence had submitted a comprehensive report clearing my record; nor that the FBI, when all this was over, would launch its own investigation and decide that it had done all the right things, a report carried out at the very top of the agency by none other than Mr. Hoover's right-hand man Louis B. Nichols, which he submitted to Mr. Hoover's other right-hand man, Clyde B. Tolson, a report which like all the others cleared my name but failed to mention that I had been put on the "Custodial Detention" list and that it was the raw, unverified bureau version of the Mamaroneck police report which had caused the whole imbroglio.

A tempest in a teapot for certain, an incident that happened long ago and had such trivial consequences that it does not seem worth mentioning. Except for two chilling facts: the placing of my name on a list for "Custodial Detention" and the possibility that to this day, so far as I have been able to ascertain, it may still be carried on one of the secret FBI lists.

One more thing not of trivial consequence. At intervals over forty years, one government agency or another has requested of the FBI a rundown on what their records show about me. Once, President Johnson gave a dinner party for Burma's leader Ne Win and his wife, Katie, who had lavishly entertained my wife and myself in Burma at a time when Americans were not welcome in that country. Our names went to the FBI for a routine check. Invariably the FBI résumés begin with the passport incident, invariably noting that I was "cleared," but of course the aura of the "charges" hung over my name and continued to do so for years and years and years without my being aware of it. I never knew that Lyndon and Ladybird Johnson had thought of inviting my wife and me to dinner; we would have been pleased to see Ne Win and Katie, and to have had a little chat with the Johnsons, although we were not exactly friends of his Vietnam policy. However, possibly because of that 1940 slander, or possibly for some other information contained in the FBI report, we never got an invitation.

I don't think anyone in the last four or five years has bothered to ask the FBI for a security check on me. But the last time one was run, in 1974, the "nefarious prevaricator" report still topped the résumé.

Not a pretty story. I have spent a good deal of my life behind the iron curtain, where the presence of police surveillance, wire-tapping, censorship and all the rest is the conventional business of the day. I hesitate to think of the thousands of miles I have been tailed in the years of travel I have undertaken in the Soviet Union. But it never occurred to me that all during this period I had, in the Russian expression, an American *khvost,* an invisible tail, planted on me secretly and irresponsibly by our own public servants the FBI.

15 | There Will Always Be an England

A cockney porter had me out from under the gloomy fretwork of Paddington Station before I knew it and into a taxi. It was nine-thirty of the night of February 4, 1943, and I had never seen anything like London in blackout, stars sparkling in the dark sky, around me the thousand fireflies of pedestrians' torches and in the street the Christmas wink of red and green traffic lights. And the quiet—a quiet so deep I heard every footstep, the soft civilian steps and the rasp of hobnail boots, whispers floating over the pavement and a cough that sounded like a revolver shot. I could not take my eyes from the cab window, straining to see the skeletal silhouette of the blitz as the taxi chuffed through unknown streets into the Strand, Fleet Street and up to No. 30 Bouverie, under the clock that marked the home of *News of the World*. Here United Press had quarters.

London in blackout made my heart ache. One evening in early spring, walking back from Haymarket and looking up to the gambrels of St. James's Street, the lead-and-copper gutterwork gleaming like molten emeralds, the chimney pots old as King Arthur and gray as carp, a low moon making a rather stagy appearance, I turned to my companion, a young woman, and said: "You know, after the war London must go on blackout every summer so people will not forget how this looks." It was a silly remark, because no one could forget the beauty of the London blackout any more than they forgot the beauty of the blitz, London burning against a velvet sky, remarkable coups d'oeil, the sensations heightened by the adrenaline of war.

Here I was in the heart of it. Forty-eight hours ago, I had taken off from New York in a flying boat, a kind of aerial yacht with white-jacketed mess boys, berths for the night, a lounge for gin rummy and cocktails, had made languorous pauses at green-and-sapphire Bermuda, tropical Horta, the Hotel Aziz in Lisbon, a haunt of spies and intrigue, the river Shannon, sunshine and showers and the smell of burning peat, blasted Bristol—and now London. I could not believe I had arrived in this extraordinary city at this extraordinary moment. The hunchbacked taxi with its tiny beam of light, its worn leather seats, its cricket of a driver, maneuvered through the crowds of Piccadilly, overtook an elephant that was, in fact, a two-decker bus and deposited me at the Park Lane, where a handsome man in silk hat, green uniform and gold braid took my bag and ushered me over Turkey red carpets to the reception desk, glowing with mahogany, steeped in quiet broken only by a distant hubbub which was, as I later learned, the sound of Canadian officers at their nightly drinking in the Park Lane's formal lounge.

London. It was, I thought, the Paris of World War II. Excitement throbbed through my body. *Everything* was new. I arrived at the office before eight in the morning. A boy was going to the Black-and-White across the street and a deskman asked what I'd like. A cup of coffee, I said. The youngster was back in no time with a steaming mug. I tasted it tentatively. Then I tasted again. It wasn't coffee nor did it seem to be tea; possibly it was some ersatz substitute. The boy obviously could no more understand my Midwest American than I his Bow bells tongue. I said to the English deskman: "I asked for coffee. I guess he misunderstood." The deskman had a word with the boy. "Well," he said with a quizzical smile, "he says that *is* coffee."

I had quite a few misunderstandings. I caught a double-deck bus in front of the Park Lane to Fleet Street, buying a tuppenny ticket. On the third day, a conductor gently explained that I should buy a thruppenny ticket. He wouldn't let me give him the extra penny. I was puzzled the first time a girl said, "Knock me up in the morning." I was surprised to learn you never ordered a single whisky in a pub, always a double, and a double was only half an American drink. And I didn't have to say Scotch. There wasn't any other kind, not even at the Savoy's American bar, so pastel gray and chic I kept looking to my shoes, fearing I was tracking mud over the pale carpet.

El Vino's was *the* Fleet Street pub, a place of dark woods, sherry casks, cobwebbed bottles (not many left on the racks in those days), gleaming brasswork and a cozy room to the back, with a round table and Queen Anne chairs, one of which bore a brass plate with the legend: "The incomparable Bob Davis, Friend of Man, sat here." In 1943, the name of Bob Davis was at the fringe of memory: a long-dead correspondent of the long-dead *New York Sun.* There was no brass plate in Bleeck's in New York to recall his existence. I was awed by the sentimentality of the English.

Aneurin Bevan was sitting in Bob Davis's chair the day I met him. I did not like him and never was to. I thought there was a vainglory to him that reminded me of Ernest Lundeen, the Farmer-Labor senator from Minnesota, who shared some of the same views of the world. But Lundeen was a sloppy man. He did not have a hard core. Probably I was wrong about Bevan; certainly no one at the table that day would have agreed with me— not Bevan's wife, the magnificent Jennie Lee, straight as a King's Lancer; not Michael Foot, the diffident, intelligent editor of the *Evening Standard,* who, improbably, would ultimately lead the Labor party; not Hilde Marchant, the gingery imp from Hull who had worked for Beaverbrook and was now the star of the *Daily Mirror.* One member of the band of brothers of the left, as I came to think of them, was not there that day. He was Frank Owen, whom Foot had succeeded as editor of the *Standard.* Owen was now in the tank corps. I think—but I am not sure—that Frank might have come closer to agreeing with me about Bevan.

This company, I quickly concluded, made up the next generation of England's leaders, the men and women on whom the future of the scepter'd isle would depend. It was they, more than anyone, who would determine whether, indeed, there would always be an England. While I later developed serious doubts about England's left, I at that moment believed in it. Even in my brief days in and en route to London, I had been struck by impressions that badly dented the idealized picture I had drawn of Churchill's England, bright and noble, organized for total warfare, ready to fight on the beaches and in the hills, prepared to sacrifice all for the cause of freedom. Already my eyes told me that the case was not so simple. True, I had arrived in London after the crisis had passed. Since June 1941, the war on the eastern front, the titanic battle of the Wehrmacht and the Red Army, had taken the Luftwaffe off the backs of the British. England's skies had become almost peaceful; no more fire raids devouring London, blasting Coventry, turning Hilde's port of Hull to ashes.

Even before I reached England I was vibrating to images of Europe's poverty: the earth-floored huts, barefoot peasants and scrawny cattle of the Azores; the rosy-cheeked ten-year-old bellboys at the luxurious Aziz; Irish peasants tilling stony fields. True, these were Europe's outposts, but they had given me a dimension by which to judge the social balance.

Now in London I was beginning to see the pinched faces of the English underclass, their thin bodies. I heard the hack of catarrh-raddled lungs, saw the chilblains, the acne, the snot of dwarfish children. And I saw something that shocked me more— the unmobilized manpower (as I believed it to be). There were the silk-hatted doormen at the Park Lane, the Dorchester, the Savoy. A healthy lad (not a maid) wearing white tie and tails brought me tea and *The Times* at 7 A.M. (I paid a one-pound bribe to get on the list for *The Times;* Lord knows whom the hall porter scratched off.) The Strand, Fleet Street, the City, were filled with morning-coated messengers; bank clerks rode in dark maroon phaetons, delivering bonds and stocks and titles and deeds from one Dickensian business house to another. The Law Courts and Lincoln's Inn Fields abounded with well-fed servitors. True, there were young women ticket takers and even a few women lorry drivers, but not many. The police were male. In the countryside, men of military age worked the fields. Fair enough, but they also held on as gatekeepers, butlers and gamekeepers. They drew the ale at country inns and spun the roulette wheels in the gambling hells of London. They were doormen at the ancient men's clubs along St. James's.

Of course, I did not know Mayfair; I did not know English society. But in the swirl into which I was quickly drawn, it seemed to me that countless wealthy men and women were leading lives totally divorced from the ordinary people. They filled the luncheon tables at the Ivy and they danced at the Savoy dining room, they gathered at the Connaught for tea and the Embassy after the theater. I tried to assure myself that perhaps the men had physical disabilities, but what of the pointless duties they were performing? I repeated to myself what I knew was the truth: that the British had sacrificed without stint while America dawdled in peace, while Detroit spun off automobiles for the most profitable year in its history—1941. I knew the British were brave, indomitable people. Yet there was something amiss, this nagging evidence that I saw all around me of something wrong, of an unfairness in the social order, privilege for the privileged, the continuing toil of a serving order.

I connected this with class. In spite of reading Veblen, I had not been personally aware of class in the United States.

But it was different in England. I found myself, because I was head of a large and important American news agency, propelled into the upper class. I dealt with cabinet ministers, ambassadors, the Astors, Lord Camrose, Lord Kemsley, Lord Beaverbrook, the great newspaper proprietors. I dealt with Sirs, with Mark Twain's belted knights. I came to know duchesses (but no dukes). London was, in a sense, just like Washington. These men had the power; they ran England. But there was something different about it. The cockney kids in the UP office whose talk I couldn't make out; the quiet English clerks and tape punchers; the English on the desks and in the back office—they were working class, they were, I suddenly realized, the proletariat of whom the Marxists spoke. They were locked into their class and there was nothing that would get them out. This was true of those clerks with the top hats and morning trousers. They were locked into their station in life and nothing, nothing would get them out of it.

I was fresh from the exhilaration of John L. Lewis, Walter Reuther, Philip Murray, Sidney Hillman, the CIO organizing drives, the sit-down strikes in Flint, the bloody battles in South Chicago, the struggles of Youngstown—the revolution that had swept American labor out of the stodgy cigar smoke of Samuel Gompers and William Green into the cresting wave of industrial unionism, organizing the unorganized, the National Labor Relations Act, the New Deal transformation, that had made the American labor movement the most dynamic social force in the world.

English labor as epitomized by Clement ("good old Clem") Attlee, Ernest ("good old Ernie") Bevin and Sir Stafford Cripps seemed to me archaic, trussed by the bonds of class, tradition and rote. No spark, no spunk. It had not used the war—as it could have—to press its demands, to trade high production and round-the-clock effort for political and social goals. It was, I thought, moribund. Churchill ran rings around Attlee. I thought Churchill a holy wonder; I thought his social views medieval.

But the bright band at the table in the rear of El Vino's was something else. I admitted to myself that my doubts about the moon-faced, tousle-haired Nye Bevan might, in part, reflect deep prejudice against my fellow Welsh. He was the member for Ebbw Vale, authentically Welsh, authentically a coal miner, brilliant, ambitious, with a rare gift for language and speech. I have puzzled for years over why I never felt attracted to him, never trusted him, always thought of him as Ernie Lundeen (as I wrote at the time) and not Floyd B. Olson, who remained for years my benchmark for pragmatic radicalism. I was to see a fair amount of Bevan at El Vino's, which was a favorite base for him, as Jennie Lee was to write in her memoir, and later at their home at 23 Cadogan Place. But the initial reaction never vanished. He made the hair bristle on the back of my neck.

Jennie Lee was pure delight. I loved her the moment I saw her and love her still. Her heart was right and her mind had no trouble following it. She laughed easily, but she was very serious, very much a fighter. There couldn't have been a better moment to meet her, for after a decade out of Parliament she was engaged in a gallant campaign to win a by-election in Bristol. Jennie was running as an Independent, not on the Labor ticket. Labor had ousted her for membership in the left-wing Independent Labor party. Nye could not openly support her candidacy in Bristol, but of course he was in her corner. Michael Foot and Hilde Marchant were campaigning for her. None of them expected Jennie to win, but her challenge was notice to Churchill and the Conservatives that they would not win postwar England without an all-out fight from the left. It carried a similar notice to the dozing dons of Labor—the Attlees, the Bevins and the rest. The left was throwing down the gauntlet for an England that would not repeat the experience of the years after World War I. They would not permit England to go back to sleep and allow a new fascism to rise. Nor would they repeat the tragedy of the 1920s—social sloth, industrial stagnation and, ultimately, the dole, in which half the country idled on a pittance of a few shillings a week. Jennie was sounding the clarion of the new England, a clarion that thrilled me. These were people who believed Churchill was deliberately delaying a second front in order to drain Russia's strength. They knew that there were those in England who still hoped that Hitler and Stalin would fight until each destroyed the other. They were not going to let the reactionaries get away with this.

I was wiped out by Hilde Marchant. She must have been twenty-five or twenty-six years old, with rusty blond hair, firestruck eyes of green, and so much verve in her small body she seemed not to walk but to bounce from step to step on springs, a whirlwind of energy, fierce opinions, anger and pity. She had been the chief feature reporter for the *Daily Express,* working for its great editor, Arthur Christianson, becoming his mistress, then leaving him in a fiery quarrel and joining the *Mirror,* the hottest paper in London, a tabloid guided by the erratic genius of Guy Bartholomew.

Hilde was the *Mirror*'s star, headlined, front-paged day after day. Jennie had come from a labor background in North Lamark in Scotland. Her grandfather had been with Keir Hardie, Bob Smillie and the others. Hilde came from Hull. She had the grit of that gray port ground into her being. Her temper flared like a torch. Once I rode from Fleet Street to Hyde Park Corner with her on the upper deck of a bus. She started talking about England's tormented coal mines, talking so fast I could hardly pick out the words as they poured from her mouth. But I got the point. It was a dying industry and if it died England might die with it. Every year it needed thirty thousand replacements for the rheumatic men who had given their lives to the pits. No more than eight thousand young men were following in the traces of their fathers. The industry would peter out if new machinery, safe, sanitary conditions, were not brought in—but was there an economic base to support rationalization of the pits? Hilde had just been in Wales and had done a sensational series on the miners, the old men of seventy-six and seventy-nine still in the pits, earning less per week than young girls in the munitions plants. She painted sad pictures of the working people of Hull; she told of the terror of the dole; of her efforts to pull herself, the daughter of a working-class family, up by her fingertips. I looked at her small hands and their tiny, ink-stained, nail-bitten fingers.

Hilde had been living with Bill Dickinson, my friend and right-hand man in the UP's London bureau, for a year when I first met her. She was riding the crest. She had her own five-minute spot on the BBC every evening after the nine o'clock news. She had a daily column in the *Mirror.* She wrote front-page features. She went to northern Ireland to explore the life of the Irish at war and to Scotland to explore bombed-out Glasgow. She wrote shilling pamphlets every few months on subjects like "Women at War." Her name was plastered on the sides of every *Mirror* truck. She was as widely known as any woman in wartime England. She made twice as much money as Bill and, improbably, they planned to be married, at the end of the war if not sooner. She loved Bill's flat Kansas City voice, his big, easy way of moving, even his homemade pot-baked beans, of which he was very proud. Hilde delighted in Americans. She thought they were enchantingly naive children. The first time she met Tom Wolf she danced up with a pert face and said, "Hello, old cock." He had just landed in London and had not heard the Briticism before. She saw his jaw drop, and looking him in the eye, said, "That's O.K. You can call me old cunt if you like."

When I met her in El Vino's, she was going down to Bristol almost every evening to campaign for Jennie Lee. She was a blazing orator. Many expected her to follow in Jennie's footsteps and herself stand for Parliament on the Labor ticket once the war was over. Bill, of course, dreamed of bringing her back to the U.S.A. He wrote pages to his family about this wondrous mite of a woman.

But it did not happen. Sometime, somehow, in the late autumn of 1943, the implausible romance of the girl from Hull and the romantic American came to an end abruptly. Bill left London and went to the Southwest Pacific, where he took over UP's coverage of General MacArthur. Hilde flung herself into her reportage, her pamphlets, her work. But she did not run for the House of Commons after the war and soon she began to drift. She was drinking now, and when I went to London and asked about her, people looked a bit uneasy, a bit guilty. They didn't know just what she was doing. By the 1960s, she had begun to haunt the pubs of Gray's Inn Road near the printing offices of *The Times*. A friend of mine was in El Vino's one night when a shabby old lady crept through the door and sidled up to the bar. "We thought she was a beggar," he told me, "and gave her a few shillings." It was only as she slipped away that he realized it was Hilde. One morning in 1970, the police found her on a bench on the Embankment, back of the Savoy Hotel. She was dead. I cannot bear to think of that bright imp snuffed out in the deadly wastelands of life.

Frank Owen was not at El Vino's on the day I met Jennie Lee, Aneurin Bevan, Michael Foot and Hilde Marchant. I met Frank late one April day in his Westminster Gardens flat. His wife was there, a long-stemmed American beauty, a real one, a statuesque blond showgirl, Grace Stewart McGillivray of Boston, who had come to London, and married Frank on the eve of the war. One night, a German bomb crashed through the glass skylight of the Savoy dining room and Gracie's face was badly cut. The scars were barely visible, but the wounds to her psyche did not heal and the blast of Frank's personality had already begun to unsettle her nerves.

Frank was asleep when I arrived at the flat. He had come up from his tank unit, training somewhere in the countryside, and was tired and dusty. He grinned, apologized and said he'd take a tub and wake up. Gracie drew the tub, Frank flung off his clothes and invited me to talk while he relaxed in the boiling water, a black Welshman, with black gleaming hair, his face, neck and shoulders red from the sun, and muscles that rippled across his chest—a physical man, all gristle and hairy body, his mind racing a mile a minute, deep blue eyes sparkling with profane comment about the bloody government, the bloody army, the bloody war, the bloody tanks. He was having the time of his life.

Owen was a Liberal, but he thought very much as did the Laborites Bevan, Lee, Foot and Marchant. Beaverbrook had picked him up as he picked up Foot, as he was forever picking up the brightest left-wing minds, and made him editor of the *Evening Standard.* The Beaver got a bit more than he counted on. Owen's *Standard* fought Munich and the Cliveden set. It fought Chamberlain. It fought Hitler and questioned the phony war. After Dunkirk, Owen, Foot and a man named Howard wrote an overnight pamphlet called "Guilty Men," which they signed "Cato." It excoriated Chamberlain and the appeasers. It swept England like a prairie fire and swept Churchill into office. It was the most powerful political jeremiad of the war.

The *Standard* supported Churchill before he came into power. It supported Russia after June 22, 1941. It backed the second front. To all this Beaverbrook agreed. But the bite of Owen's words was more than the government could take. When Owen was suddenly called up to the army and entered the tank corps, there was talk on Fleet Street. The government was getting a tiger off its back. Was the Beaver ducking too? It was a question that never got answered.

When I met Owen he was full of swagger, a muscular man with a daredevil's courage. You knew he would pick up any challenge thrown down. I was never satisfied with the words I chose to describe him, not then, not now. Words were poor instruments to capture his animal movement, the computer speed of his mind, the robustiousness of his style, the grin on his face. There was nothing he couldn't do. I thought if he had been given charge of the war, he would have run Hitler off the planet within a year. I wrote once that he was an Irishman who happened to be Welsh, a careless son of a bitch.

I had only to meet Frank Owen to pick him as the best man in England's future. Owen drove himself day after day after day, taking only an hour or two of sleep until he collapsed. There was no one on the left or the right (I thought) to compare with him, not Bevan, not Foot, not Morrison, certainly not Cripps or Bevin, not Attlee. I hadn't heard of Harold Wilson and would not meet him until he began to come into Moscow in the late forties and early fifties on timber-buying missions for some Scottish syndicate. He did not win my favor with his slippery statements and I quickly put him at the bottom of my list of English pols. In the end, I was by no means certain that Owen or anyone could pull off the postwar transformation England needed, but I was certain he would come closest. He inspired instant loyalty. His army chums swore by him from the day he donned his uniform. The *Evening Standard* staff loved him. I could believe that there were those on high who thought it better to dress him in the khaki of the tank corps than let him lead the editorial cry of the *Standard,* preparing for a left-wing takeover.

One night I sat in Jack's Club, a black market eating place favored by American journalists, a clothes closet of a place, tucked into No. 14 Orange Street, just behind the Haymarket. There were half a dozen of us—Ray Clapper, the Washington columnist and my old friend, Jack Knight, editor of the Akron paper and later head of Knight-Ridder newspapers, Walter Cronkite, who covered the Eighth Air Force and worked with me in UP, and a couple of others. We got to talking about Frank Owen. What would happen to him when the war was over? One of three things, we agreed: He would become prime minister, commissar of a revolutionary England—or a bum. Each fate was within his grasp.

Owen went to India. He served on Mountbatten's staff, fought in Burma, then came back to London. At the end of the war, he became editor of the right-wing *Daily Mail.* Somehow he had lost his edge. He was drinking heavily. The copybook romance with the long-stemmed American Gracie had foundered in alcohol and boredom. A succession of young Americans occupied Gracie's life; Frank slept around, a different bed almost every night. No longer was he the wonder of Fleet Street and the fear of Whitehall.

Owen, it began to become apparent, was a broken man. Had he broken himself or had Beaverbrook, that Machiavelli, spotted Owen's weakness, prized open the crack a bit and let nature take its course? What happened to Frank Owen? This is not just a personal question; it is a national question. How had his talents been destroyed; how could his country have been deprived of his remarkable energies? His friends did not understand it. It was easy to say, as many did, "It was the drink that did it." To be sure, the drink did. But Owen possessed the ability England needed above anything, that careless talent for inspiration, the courage that could have set the country on a new course. I do not think this is just my romantic image, the fancy of a young American hardly landed in London, inexperienced in the world. I go back to that conversation in Jack's Club and the fearful accuracy of our prediction—prime minister, commissar or bum.

Frank was never again to do anything memorable. He held on at the *Mail* for a while and when that blew up he wrote some potboilers. Beaverbrook came to the rescue and commissioned his biography; Owen turned out a piece of boiler plate, with some difficulty. Then amazingly it was all over; this lion of a man became a drooling hulk, his mind a gray swamp, his body wasting. Gracie died in 1968. I have always thought she should have died in the Savoy bombing. Her life had not been worth living since her face was cut. Frank lived until the summer of 1980, finally dying of cancer. Better he had been killed forty years before in Burma with Wingate and left his legend for young England to burn a candle to.

It was not easy to know and understand Michael Foot, and even now I am not certain that I do. At El Vino's I saw him thin, dark, shy and taciturn, as waves of talk swirled about him. It would have seemed outrageous to suggest that this young editor of the *Evening Standard* might head the British Labor party, one of the most formidable political forces of the Western world.

Surely I did not expect that to occur, but before I left England I recognized that he had greater qualities of leadership than I first imagined. But I still considered Owen the only man on the left capable of capturing the British masses.

One afternoon, Beaverbrook invited me to the Mayfair apartment to which he had removed after a fire at his house at Cherkley. Max Aitken was a gnomish man with a small boy's grin which gave many people the impression that at heart he was more

mischief-maker than menace. He invited me into his study, where
he was using a Dictaphone. Two secretaries walked in and out
with papers. Most of his messages were to his general manager, a
man named Robertson. "Robertson," he dictated, "I see that you
have not yet cut down on the advertising in the *Express*. Cut it
down. Immediately." He chatted a bit about John Cowles, the
publisher of the Minneapolis papers, and his brother Mike, publisher of *Look* magazine. Then another memo: "Mr. Robertson,
the advertising rates in the *Evening Standard* are too low. The
Evening Standard must be the most expensive advertising medium
in England. Come and see me about this. Tomorrow." I had
begun to ask him about his campaign to revive the authority of
the House of Lords (in which he sat) and his bitter battle for a
second front, when Michael Foot walked in, in horn-rimmed spectacles, gray cardigan sweater, looking like so many people in England, a little shabby. In an instant Beaverbrook was setting me
at Foot, encouraging me to ask sharp questions about the Labor
party and the left and what Foot thought would happen after the
war. I fell to it with a will. Afterward I felt that I had been
unfair, but I excused myself by saying that I wanted to strike
sparks. Foot was a Socialist and I pressed him on his ideas of
what the political temper of the country would be after the war.
Would it be 1918 all over again? Would there be another khaki
election? Beaverbrook intervened to say that he believed Britain
was fundamentally conservative and the United States was also
conservative. It was his view that Conservative power would be
retained after the war and go on and on. He called Hugh Baillie,
the head of United Press and my boss, a "bloody Tory." Wallace
Carroll, the former UP London chief, now with the Office of
War Information in London, was a "leftist." What, he said to
me, was I? I responded that I was a newspaperman who wanted
to know what made people tick. That was not a complete answer,
but I did not want to get into an ideological match with this
sharp-tongued man. Tiring of this pastime (never having let
Foot give me a fair answer about postwar England), Beaverbrook took some scrapbooks from his shelves and began to read
quotations from English statesmen of recent years, especially
embarrassing attacks by Churchill on Russia and Stalin. Beaverbrook said he had volumes on everyone, filled with deadly parlia-
mentary ammunition.

As Michael Foot watched, he took a copy of the day's *Evening*

Standard, spread it on the floor, pointing to headlines with his foot, criticizing the makeup and the placement of stories. It was, I realized, a show for my benefit and designed to chastise Foot, but the Beaver's criticisms were apt. This was a brilliant editor at work, and in each instance I thought he was right and Michael woefully agreed. It was not, he admitted, a particularly good paper. Another idea struck the Beaver. He turned to his Dictaphone: "Mr. Robertson, the *Daily Express* must have the best newspaper library in the world. I want you to see that this is done." Michael interjected that the *Standard* library did not possess several important series of government documents. Back to the Dictaphone: "Mr. Robertson, Mr. Foot informs me that the *Evening Standard* does not have such and such. Get them." (A day later, I saw a want ad in the *Standard* inquiring for the needed government volumes; Mr. Robertson was carrying out his instructions.)

Michael Foot and I lunched soon after this at the Cheshire Cheese. He had just read Wendell Willkie's *One World.* We found we had a mutual admiration for Willkie and similar views on many things. We talked about his hopes for England after the war and I began to realize better the mettle of which he was made. He was a newspaper editor largely by chance, by the chance of Frank Owen's being called up to the army, but he was a writer and a publicist born. He was a scholar from a scholarly family, one of five sons of Isaac Foot, a remarkable, largely self-educated solicitor in Plymouth, a sometime Liberal member of Parliament, an iconoclastic observer of life and an orator of such appeal that crowds turned out whether he spoke from stump or pulpit and whether they agreed with what he was saying or not. Four sons entered politics—Hugh (later elevated to the peerage as Lord Caradon), Dingle and Michael—who were sometimes called "left" Foot (Michael), "right" Foot (Hugh) and "center" Foot (Dingle)—and John, who never acquired a designation, not that these designations were necessarily accurate. Each Foot shared the iconoclasm of the father. Party whips were forever having trouble with them.

Within the year, Michael would leave Beaverbrook, leave the *Standard,* for the left-wing *Tribune,* established by Bevan, and at war's end he would enter the House of Commons, first winning at Devonport, and with Bevan's death in 1950 taking his place at Ebbw Vale.

Michael was no ordinary politician. He never lost his literary taste, his love for books, inculcated by his father. I thought that he was more comfortable with pen and typewriter than with the speaker's lectern, but he came to be as effective on the platform. I never thought Michael possessed the killer's instinct that seems characteristic of powerful politicians. He was a humane man, he respected his fellows, he did not employ the big lie or the little lie, as did so many rivals. Nor did he turn his back. There was some estrangement between himself and Beaverbrook after he left the *Standard*. But Foot never forgot what Beaverbrook had taught him about editing and, even more, about life. Beaverbrook had after all, as he said, been a second father to him. Toward the end of the Beaver's life there was a reconciliation and a second honeymoon of these two men whose personalities clashed so vigorously, whose views differed profoundly but who shared a warmth of human understanding.

After I had seen Foot and Owen together, I understood each much better. They complemented each other, they respected each other's strengths. I had been wrong to suppose that Foot's diffidence meant weakness. Each man had guts.

"Both of them," I wrote April 26, 1943, in my journal, "are the sort who would tell Beaverbrook or Churchill or anyone else where to get off in a real showdown. But Owen would do it with a string of bloody cuss words and Foot would say it very quietly, very firmly."

There was courage enough to go around within the "band of brothers," but this did not suffice to give any of them or the group (minus Owen) immediate postwar leadership in the Labor party. They tried, and certainly Bevan tried hardest, to reshape the party and its views, but they did not succeed, Bevan no more than Foot. As years passed, Foot slowly rose within the party, and with the death of Bevan he emerged as the spokesman for the left. But basically the old guard prevailed, just as I had feared, and none of the group at El Vino's could change its course, nor could they change the course of England. There was not the postwar renaissance that had to be if there was always to be an England capable of holding the substance of power and glory. In one form or another, Churchill's formula of England as a junior partner to the United States prevailed.

Steadily year by year, the figure of Foot loomed larger. His integrity, his courage, his intellect, lifted him toward the top of his quarrelsome, divided party. In the main, the Conservatives provided England with such leadership as it had. I did not believe the decline of England could be blamed upon the Conservatives. They did the best they knew how, but Labor languished in the flabby hands of the Bevins and the Wilsons, who did not possess the imagination to understand the breadth and depth of England's decay. They were wedded to preservation at any cost of the small trade union gains of the past; they quailed at the notion of extricating themselves from the bear hug of American economic and foreign policy.

Long before I left England in 1943, I had concluded that the chance for a real comeback was almost nil. I went back to London briefly in late 1945, and the sight of that great city, absent the exhilaration of war, grubby, tired and grim, tore my heart. I could see no signs of hope, nor could I hear them. The faces in the Strand and in the City were pallid; I saw dull eyes, heads down, coat collars turned up against the chill. Mayfair was frightened of the loss of capital; the East End feared the loss of jobs. No one could face the fact that the United States had become *the* world power and was taking England's markets and production away. Churchill's boast that he had not become the Queen's first minister in order to preside over the dissolution of empire had become a pitiful joke. England was losing, as I had understood it would (and not myself alone), India, the colonies, South Africa. Canada and Australia were cuddling up to Washington. China and the rich trade of the Yangtze and the treaty ports was going down the drain. Soon the fierce competition of Germany and of Japan would resume. (Mistakenly in 1943 I had thought that Russia also would assault England's markets with low-cost goods, but the Kremlin was as rigid and stupid as Attlee and Bevin.)

I saw by 1945 that my belief that Foot and Owen and Bevan and Lee and Marchant would put it all together was a lost vision. Even my deepest wishful thinking could not make that seem very likely. For the first time, as I flew home from the joyless London of 1945, I was beginning to understand that it was not holy writ —nowhere was it written large that there had always to be an England.

16 | Breaking In

London swept me off my feet, bombarded me with sensations. I was up at seven, into Bouverie Street before eight, stopping at Kardomah House in Fleet Street for ersatz coffee and ersatz scrambled eggs. Never had I known a place as cold as the United Press offices in the *News of the World* plant, a cement-floored factory building. The only heat came from what the English called "electric fires," feeble grilles mounted on the ceiling; there was no heat whatever in my bleak office. In my trenchcoat, I huddled over my typewriter, a tiny heater tucked in the knee space of the rolltop desk, and batted out my early-morning stories with frozen fingers. About nine o'clock, Miss Stronach, a sturdy Scotswoman who had been a secretary to young American correspondents all her life, strode in—no-nonsense shoes, head-to-toe Scottish wool: wool skirt, wool stockings, wool blouse, wool sweater and, I had no doubt, wool undies. "My, my!" she would say. "How stuffy it is in here." She would pull open the mullioned windows and stride away. The moment she left, I slammed the windows shut. In a moment she was back. "My!" she would say. "How curious! I thought I had opened the windows." And she'd throw them open again. This child's game might go on for an hour. I never said a word. I was scared to death of Miss Stronach. She put my letters into English English, freight yards changed to marshalling yards, gasoline to petrol, trucks to lorries, all the rest. When I asked her to correct them, she would say, "My! Didn't you say that? I thought you had. How curious!" I gave up.

Mornings I worked on the desk, editing, writing, making assignments, keeping up with the news. At lunch I set myself a fearsome task. I would lunch *every day* with someone of consequence: an English politician, a French diplomat, an American general, someone whom I did not know and whom I must know if I was to write intelligent and informed dispatches. I had to do this, I told myself, if I was to make a success of London. I was painfully, fiercely shy about meeting these people, but each day I told the little blond telephone operator to get me this one or that, to make an engagement, to book a table at the White House, L'Apéritif or Prunier, restaurants where the luncheon bill came to three or four pounds, astronomic by my New York standards. There, I had eaten every day at Volk's under the Third Avenue "L" at Forty-second Street, seventy-five cents for bratwurst, fifteen cents for a stein of beer, a ten-cent tip.

London was the fastest company I had ever seen, but I was going to keep up, if I died in the attempt. I had acquired a literary agent named Carol Hill before leaving New York and she put me onto an agent in London, an exceptionally pleasant man named A. D. Peters. He took me to lunch at the Savile Club in Brook Street and put me up there as a visiting member. I was so awed by curt English nods, grunts which passed for conversational gambits, the in-ness of the rituals, the coffee and port in the billiard room, that visiting the Savile was like running a gauntlet. Somehow I compelled myself to face it. Peters had chambers in Albany, a glorious birdcage of Victorian England, all pastels and blues and yellows, which he very much wanted to rent to me. Why I didn't take up his offer I cannot imagine. The Albany was (and is) the dream of my life. I went on living in my cubbyhole at the Park Lane instead.

I stood in total awe of the professionals of the Foreign Office with whom I dealt. How could a bumpkin from Minnesota cope with their Cambridge polish? Yet if I was to get under the surface of wartime London, there was no alternative. Only my fierce ambition enabled me to go through these torments. I understood that London was my great chance. I had given up a lot for it— Michael, my home, quite possibly my marriage. In her first cable after I arrived, Mary said she was going to divorce me. This threw me into a tailspin. I didn't know what it meant. Had she discovered my fling with the magazine editor? Was there another man? Was it hysteria? When she finally began to write to me, six or seven weeks after I got to London, there was a hard, bitter tone to her letters, but I never found out the cause and gradually the crisis seemed to fade away. For months, though, I tortured myself over what was happening at home. I had thought that going abroad would enable me to sort out my feelings. Instead, at one moment I wanted Mary and the next I could not bear the thought of her. I got more and more mixed up.

I was agonized by a conviction that I would never see my father again. I wrote, gently suggesting that he retire, but I knew this was only an exercise to spare my conscience. He would no more retire than would an old firehorse. When I thought of these things (and I did constantly), I knew that I should never have come to London. But the next moment I was telling myself how much I had riding on London. It was not just the war and wanting to be part of it. London was the road to my future, the path to making a name for myself, to propelling myself to fame and fortune. I could become a correspondent like John Gunther. I could write a new *Inside Europe*. Maybe a best-selling novel. I could get a job with the *Saturday Evening Post* or *Collier's*. There was no end to what London might do for me. But only by achieving these goals could I justify the gamble I was taking—and as I worried night after night, I was not certain that these prizes could make the game worth the candle.

There was one man with whom I seemed to get on well. This was John Winant, the idiosyncratic Republican governor of New Hampshire whom Roosevelt had drafted as his ambassador to the Court of St. James's to replace Joseph P. Kennedy. Winant was a Lincolnesque sort, with high cheekbones, black hair and saturnine skin. I usually saw him in late afternoon, when dusk had settled over the American embassy in Grosvenor Square. I would be met by Winant's secretary, Jake Beam, who later achieved diplomatic fame as ambassador to Yugoslavia, Poland and the Soviet Union. He was then a very young foreign service officer who gave the impression of being as frightened of his job as I was of mine. He would open the door to Winant's huge office and vanish. I would find Winant sitting behind his desk in the gloom, no lights lighted, the curtains drawn against London's blackout. I would greet the ambassador and sit down. He would give a slight nod, almost invisible in the murk. We would sit in dead silence until I broke it with a banality. Winant would not respond. Some afternoons, I sat in darkness and silence for fifteen minutes. Then, haltingly, Winant would begin to talk about whatever happened to be on his mind. One afternoon he told me every detail of his experience on December 7, 1941. He had been certain that the Japanese attack was coming. Having been with Churchill at Chequers the weekend of June 22, when the Germans attacked Russia, he decided to go to Chequers on December 7, getting there about noon. Churchill met him outside the house. "Do you think the Japanese are going to attack?" Churchill asked. "Yes," said Winant. Churchill paced back and forth. He seemed upset. Finally, he said: "If they attack you, we will declare war. If they attack us, you declare war." Winant was taken aback. "I'm sorry, Mr. Prime Minister," he said, "but I can't guarantee this. Only Congress can declare war." Churchill fell silent. "Well," he finally said, "let's go in and have lunch." After the meal, Churchill retired for a nap and Winant went walking in the country lanes with some young people. It gave him distraction from the tension over the news that might come at any minute.

Some time after Winant returned from his walk, the prime minister roused himself, got dressed, and they sat before a fire, having a drink. Churchill was grumpy. There were long silences (I could imagine that if Churchill wasn't making conversation, they must have been very long). Finally, Churchill rose and returned with a little radio that Harry Hopkins had brought over. They turned it on just as the news came up. It began with the report that Japan had attacked Pearl Harbor.

"Does that mean war?" Churchill asked. "Will the United States declare war?"

Winant said: "You can't declare war on a mere radio report. Let me call the President. The Germans know what's going on, so it doesn't matter even if they do listen in."

Churchill agreed and the call was put through almost immediately. Churchill listened on an extension as Roosevelt told what had happened. Then Winant said: "I've got someone with me who wants to speak with you." "Who's that?" FDR asked. "You'll find out when he speaks." Churchill talked with the President and by the time he was through they had the whole picture. Winant and Churchill stayed up until 5 A.M., December 8, getting everything set. Churchill gave instructions that Parliament should be called early so the declaration of war against Japan could be acted upon immediately. Roosevelt had said he was convening Congress at noon. Churchill thought it was an opportune moment to get Eire to join the war and decided to send Lord Cranborne over to talk with De Valera. Cranborne was dispatched, but could not budge the Irish prime minister.

I carefully noted Winant's remarks in my journal, but never wrote publicly about what he had said. Great argument has arisen among historians as to whether Roosevelt and Churchill colluded to instigate the Japanese attack in order to permit the

United States to join the war at England's side. This is possible, of course, and they surely would not have made the plainspoken Winant privy to such a scheme; he would not have gone along with it. Nor would Cordell Hull, for that matter. Winant's account seems to weigh against a Roosevelt-Churchill conspiracy or foreknowledge of what the Japanese were going to do. The fact that both Churchill and Winant expected the Japanese to attack that weekend is natural. The weight of public information pointed to a weekend attack. Churchill's remarks about "if they attack you" do not seem to prefigure knowledge of Pearl Harbor. An attack on Manila was commonly anticipated, along with attacks on Hong Kong, Singapore, Malaya and Indonesia. It is true that Churchill could hardly wait for the American declaration of war. But this impatience was characteristic of his personality. I do not think it bespeaks preknowledge. Though the Winant story is not conclusive, it tilts against collusion.

I should, of course, have questioned Winant more closely about the events of December 7. But it had not entered my mind that FDR might have deliberately goaded the Japanese into an act of war. While I knew the Americans were pressing the Japanese very hard, I had no foreboding that we were pushing so hard the Japanese would feel war their only alternative.

Usually Winant's talk was not of such moment. One day I asked him about the anti-American feeling in England, which was rising in direct ratio to the increasing number of American troops. The *Daily Mirror* had run a series on VD in England and the program the Americans had instituted to protect their troops from infection. I told Winant that Frank Owen had said that his tankmen were enraged. Feeling was so intense he was glad to get away. "Let them go back where they came from," his men were saying, "if they don't like our girls. There is more VD in the U.S.A. than there is here." Winant was wearily amused. He said it made him realize how young they all were.

In fact, the commerce of the GIs and the English prostitutes was omnipresent. The girls began to congregate in late afternoon in Leicester Square, with its big movie houses and long queues and many Americans. The throngs thickened as you approached Piccadilly Circus, where I had to shove my way through the bantering GIs and girls. This was called the "combat zone," and the prostitutes were nicknamed "Piccadilly commandos." They jammed the approaches to the big Red Cross Rainbow Corner

Club, the boys and girls shouting to each other. "Put on your knee pads, Yank," I heard one girl say. "You'll need all you've got if you come with me." Prices followed a rising scale, lowest at Leicester Square, a bit higher at Piccadilly, and highest for the girls who slowly sauntered up toward Hyde Park Corner, humming little tunes and murmuring, "Hello, dearie." An army prophylactic dispensary was strategically located just above Green Park station. One evening I counted twenty-one "better-class" whores between the Park Lane and the station. I had never seen anything like this, nor had the GIs. It had a curious effect. The mass of the girls somehow deprived them of sexuality. Piccadilly reminded me of a kind of grown-up kindergarten game. Yet sex hung in the London air like the fog, its scent permeating every corner, the earthy companion of war, stimulated, I thought, by an instinct of the race to make good the wholesale loss of life.

Most of my talk with Winant issued from the lumber room of wartime diplomacy: the problems with the French and the Poles, the conflict over strategy, Churchill's foot dragging on the second front. It did not take much sensibility to understand that Winant was a troubled man, a depressed man, but I could not measure the pervasiveness of the depression. He had been placed by Roosevelt in a most awkward position. FDR had dispatched Averell Harriman to London as his special "lend-lease" envoy, the man with whom he conducted his principal business with Churchill. But he had left Winant in place as U.S. ambassador. The important transactions flowed through Harriman's hands. It was Averell who spent the weekends at Chequers, it was Averell who sat over brandy with Churchill of a long evening at No. 10 Downing Street, it was Averell who got the urgent messages from Roosevelt.

In September 1943, I was discussing with Winant the coming three-way foreign ministers' talks with Russia, the preliminaries to the Teheran Conference. No date or place for the meeting, Winant said, had been set so far as he was aware. Eden and Molotov favored Moscow, but the United States had not made up its mind. The British had submitted an agenda for the meeting. What about the U.S. agenda? I asked. Winant said he did not know. He had not been filled in. I was appalled. It seemed to me an amazing breach in the conduct of foreign policy if the ambassador to our principal ally did not know what was going on. I determined to write a dispatch about this if I could squeeze it past the censor. (Of course, later on, in the Kissinger era, it became commonplace for important U.S. ambassadors to be totally bypassed. Often they had to depend on chance visitors from Washington or news correspondents for a clue to what was happening.)

I was much more sympathetic to Winant than to Harriman, whom I considered (at that time) a Johnny-come-lately, a rich dilettante whom Roosevelt by some whim had sent over to London. In this view I ran counter to my fellow correspondents, particularly those who had been in London for some time. They were attracted by Harriman's easy hospitality, his access to Churchill and Roosevelt, his style and, quite likely, his fortune. In a professional sense, they were right and I was wrong. They were much more likely to get a good story from Averell than from the dour Winant. Averell's daughter, Kathy, was in London, on the staff of *Newsweek* magazine, in which Harriman had a financial interest. A clique of correspondents was soon buzzing around the special envoy—Joe Evans of *Newsweek,* Geoffrey Parsons, Jr., of the *Herald Tribune,* Ed Murrow, Helen Kirkpatrick of the *Chicago Daily News,* Pete Daniell of *The New York Times.* They constituted a kind of elite and I didn't get along well with them, nor they with me. They thought I was too much of a scoop artist. All this was to matter very little. Soon Averell and I would be in Moscow, and our relationship would undergo a radical transformation. A few years later, Winant, back in New Hampshire, took his own life. I cannot say that it surprised me. The look of doom had sat too long on his shoulder.

Casting myself as a young apprentice (which I was), I consulted Frederick Kuh, the diplomatic correspondent of the *Chicago Sun* who had for years been United Press correspondent in Berlin, about how to cover the diplomatic world. He was the best diplomatic reporter in London since the prime of Claud Cockburn. There was no diplomat Kuh did not know, no Foreign Office man he had not dealt with. No one was better at worming out a tiny fact, employing each fragment to pry out another until he had a story clear and complete, his sources quite uncertain just what they had given him or how he had done it.

Kuh's skills were so great, his reports so often embarrassing to the Foreign Office, that a secret minute was sent to desk officers not to receive him without special permission. The day after the secret minute had been circulated, Kuh walked into the under secretary's office with a copy in his hand, demanding to know its meaning. That was the end of the minute and Kuh continued to scoop the world.

Fred's advice was brief. "Maisky is your man," he said. "He knows more than anyone else in London. If he'll see you, you've made a beginning." I started carefully. Before the ambassador himself, I decided first to meet the Soviet press attaché, Konstantin Zinchenko. I asked the UP operator to call him. His name had slipped my mind and I asked her to get it from the Soviet operator before putting me on the wire. A moment later she was back to me. "The operator says the press attaché isn't there," my girl said. "So I asked for his name and she said, 'What difference does it make?'"

Well . . . This was my introduction to a psychology I would come to know very well over the years. (Zinchenko, a rather elegant man with perfect English, ultimately became one of Trygve Lie's under secretaries at the United Nations. He vanished into the Soviet camps in 1951 and emerged only after Stalin's death.)

I saw Ivan Maisky for the first time May 17, 1943, and then every fortnight or so until his abrupt recall to Moscow in August. He was a Santa Claus of a man, a Russian Santa Claus, roly-poly, with twinkling eyes, neat spade beard, very good Bond Street clothes, looking, I thought, more like a Vienna colleague of Sigmund Freud than a Soviet diplomat. But Maisky had been a genuine revolutionary from boyhood, although not a Bolshevik. He had been a Menshevik and made the switch to Lenin's side only after November 7, 1917, a circumstance that haunted his career more than I could have imagined at the time. In 1943, he was one of a handful of senior Soviet diplomats who remained closely associated with Maksim Litvinov, who had been unceremoniously deposed as Soviet foreign minister on May 1, 1939. After Hitler's attack on Russia, Litvinov had been put back on the diplomatic front line and was serving as ambassador to Washington. When Maisky and Litvinov were simultaneously removed from their posts in August 1943, it was supposed to signal Stalin's anger at the delay in opening a second front. Actually, there probably were other motivations: both men were Jewish; both belonged to the revolutionary old guard; neither was the kind of man on whom Stalin wanted any dependence. Their recall stimulated speculation that Moscow might be considering a separate peace with Hitler—and that may have been precisely what Stalin intended.

I found Maisky an extraordinary guide to the complex diplomacy of London. He had been serving in his post for fourteen years and there was not much he didn't know. He was most discreet and almost excessively courteous. In fact, he sometimes deliberately let the conversation drift into nothingness, not responding to a question and keeping silent until I changed the subject. He was almost as disconcerting as Winant. It never occurred to me that Maisky might be fearful of his conversation's being recorded (by both the British and the Soviet secret police). However, I came to understand that not infrequently, Maisky's refusal to comment was in itself a comment. It was like something I later learned in Moscow—the important thing is not what *Pravda* says but what it doesn't say.

One day Maisky got to talking about the Finns. "What are we going to do about a people like that?" he asked. "There are only three million Finns and they think they should have Leningrad and the territory all around it."

It was the same, he insisted, with the Poles. The Polish question then was the hottest in London. "There are twenty million Poles," he said, "and two hundred million Russians, and we live next door to each other. How can the Poles justify the kind of demands they make on us? It's not reasonable." What Maisky was telling me was that Russia was a great power and it would not put up with postwar demands by small neighboring countries that it saw as unreasonable. Maisky's observations would serve me as an unfailing guide to understanding postwar Soviet diplomacy. It was as valid in 1982 as when Maisky spoke in the summer of 1943.

Each time I came to the gloomy embassy in Kensington Palace Gardens, I had to wait in a huge reception hall decorated with busts of Stalin and Lenin, dark brown busts. I decided that talking with Maisky was like talking with a tough algebra professor. He gave me the materials from which I could construct an answer to my questions, but I had to do the paperwork myself.

Once I got him to talking about the Comintern. Stalin had just announced its abolition as a gesture to his wartime capitalist allies. I suggested that this seemed like a hard swing to the right—

was the Soviet really giving up the cause of international revolution? Maisky squinted his small eyes. Wait and see, he said. Acts are what count, not words. I said I thought it curious that World War I had virtually killed the Second International and given rise to Lenin's Third International. Now World War II had killed the Third. Would it take another war to destroy a Fifth (I was delicately taking account of Trotsky's Fourth International). Another world war, said Maisky, will destroy more than an International. It will destroy everything.

That afternoon as I left the old pseudo-Gothic embassy building, I noticed that on the lawn Maisky's gardeners had planted geraniums in the shape of a red star. Perhaps, I thought, that is symbolic—they keep the red star but do it in geraniums instead of bayonets.

I had never dealt with a Soviet diplomat and I was astonished at Maisky's circumspection. Of course, I knew nothing about his relations with Stalin; I did not know that when the Germans attacked Russia in 1941, Maisky had been left for days with no instructions: not a word; no answer to his urgent cables; no one willing to respond; the Politburo in disarray because Stalin had locked himself into his dacha and would not come to the telephone.

When I went to Moscow in 1944, I occasionally met Maisky at receptions. Though he shook hands warmly enough, he never encouraged small talk. I tried to contact him when I returned to Moscow for the *Times* in 1949, but got no response. Nor would he speak when I saw him once at an official function. Late in February 1953, less than two weeks before Stalin's death (as I later learned), Maisky was arrested. He spent more than two years in solitary confinement and was finally released, all charges wiped out, in the summer of 1955. If Alexander Nekrich, Maisky's first graduate student and close friend, is to be believed, Maisky was the victim of two frame-ups, one superimposed upon the other. Stalin in the winter of 1953 was busily preparing a purge to end all purges. He planned to exile all Russia's Jews to Siberia and he planned to wipe out most of his old Politburo associates, including Molotov and Voroshilov. Both were to be categorized as long-term "British agents," and Maisky, as the former Soviet ambassador in London, would be cast as chief of a "London spy ring" under the control of Molotov. It would include not only Maisky but my old friend Konstantin Zinchenko, the press attaché, a man named Korzh, whom I knew in Moscow during the war, Ernst Genri, who headed *Soviet War News* in London, and several others.

Preparations for the "plot" had been under way for a long time. Zinchenko and several others had been arrested nearly two years earlier.

After Stalin died, persons like Maisky were almost automatically freed. But when Khrushchev and his associates arrested Stalin's police chief, Lavrenti P. Beria, at the end of June 1953, they asserted, rightly or wrongly, that Beria had intended to make Maisky foreign minister when he gained control of the Soviet state. It took some time to sort this all out, and in the process Molotov and Voroshilov lent a helping hand to Maisky.

Perhaps it was this support that caused Maisky, when I saw him in 1967, to speak warmly of Molotov as a "strong-minded man" who played a positive and independent role in Soviet foreign policy, in contrast to Stalin, for whom he had not a single good word.

When Maisky emerged from prison, he took up his career again as an academician, busied himself with his memoirs, taking some bold digs at Stalin and Stalin's Foreign Office, which appeared in the magazine *Novy Mir* but vanished in the published book. Maisky died in 1975 at the age of ninety-one. At our 1967 valedictory meeting, in his splendid apartment on Gorky Street, he had a bottle of Johnnie Walker Red Label on the table with Schweppes soda beside it, offered me a choice of Chesterfield or Kool cigarettes, and was disappointed to find I no longer smoked or drank. He had suffered a stroke, which slightly paralyzed his left side, but as he said, "Thank God, it has not affected my mind." He did not need to say a word for me to understand that this cozy meeting was his way of making up for his enforced coldness during the long, long Stalin years.

We spent a good deal of time that day talking about Stalin. He had, Maisky said, sent Stalin warning after warning from London of Hitler's impending attack. Stalin had ignored every message. "Stalin distrusted everyone," Maisky said. "The only man he trusted was Hitler."

I spent my afternoons cultivating men like Maisky and Winant. Then I would dash back to 30 Bouverie Street, check the wires, answer urgent messages, write a dispatch if one had formed in my mind and depart on a new round, first to El Vino's, on to the American bar at the Savoy to meet a visiting American, Ralph Ingersoll or Wendell Willkie, and at eight o'-clock to Jack's Club in Orange Street for drinks, a game of snooker and a black market steak.

Why it was called Jack's no one knew, but before the war it had been an English theatrical club, catering to the upper edges of the music hall or the middle range of the theater. War transformed it into an inner sanctum of the American press corps. Only a handful of actors remained, slipping in before the early curtain to consume a solitary double with Tracy, the bartender, a magisterial man who looked like the suspect butler in an Agatha Christie mystery. Sandy was proprietor of the establishment, a scruffy little man. He and his wife, Chris, who kept the books, lived in the Kentish countryside an hour from London. No one knew how they managed it, but Sandy had access to sides of beef, racks of lamb and, although he didn't like to mention it, excellent horse-meat steaks. You didn't order at Jack's Club, you ate what Sandy cooked and what Jan, the motherly, long-suffering waitress, put before you. Sandy and Chris were bantam cocks. They fought all evening about Sandy's girls. A dozen times an evening, Sandy slipped down the street to a small nightclub. A few minutes later, Chris would notice his absence, dash out of the club (it was a tiny dining room, a kitchen, and a downstairs room for snooker) and bring Sandy back, clutching him by the ear as she led him to the kitchen. Dinner at Sandy's consumed the evening. You ate when Sandy told you to. It was often nearly eleven before the meal was on your table.

Every news desk in London had Sandy's telephone number. If you were at Sandy's, there wasn't much chance you would be scooped. Your competitors were there too. One night a call came in for an INS man who wasn't there. Cronkite took the call and on a whim said: "He's not here. I think he's gone out to the airport to meet General Marshall." We all laughed. "That'll give them some bad moments," Walter said. Twenty minutes later, the telephone rang for another absent newsman. In ten minutes there was another call. Then a call to one of our number. His desk had heard that General Marshall was arriving. We had a big laugh. But when the telephone rang yet again, Walter said,

"You know, this isn't so funny. Maybe Marshall is coming to town." And he dutifully got on the telephone to check the false rumor he had himself started.

At midnight I would leave Jack's. Sometimes there would be a taxicab wandering through the blackout, a little blue light signaling its vacancy. More often I walked home to the Park Lane. Sometimes there would be a small air raid. The searchlights in Green Park, big as giant tubs, would spring into action, blue beams patterning the clouds, sometimes trapping a plane like a moth, the guns going and shrapnel carving the pavement with flashes of fire. I was not afraid of bombs, but we were all afraid of shrapnel. When it began to pepper the street, I sidled into the nearest doorway. One night I was walking home after an evening with Bevan and Jennie Lee at Cliveden Place. I became confused and found myself somewhere in the vastness of Hyde Park as an air raid started, no cover anywhere, and the massed guns began to go, shrapnel splashing the night with sparks. I was terrified. I started to run, for some reason keeping my head down as though bullets might crisscross the landscape. Suddenly I saw a little brick structure, God knows what it was, possibly a shed for garden tools. I took shelter under a canopy, plastering myself against the wall. Then I looked up, to see gunfire sparkling through the glass roof.

One evening when there was a fairly heavy attack, I was standing in the lobby of the officers' mess in South Audley Street, waiting for the raid to end. The great rocket guns in Hyde Park began to slam out and the crowd scurried to the shelter. I waited a bit and then with Bill Dickinson and Ellen, a Red Cross nurse of whom I was becoming very fond, walked down to Green Park tube station. The all-clear had just sounded and passersby were climbing up from the station shelter. Down on the platform I saw twenty or thirty old men and women, some in bunks, some sitting and gossiping, some getting undressed for bed. To them it was just a usual night. They lived at Green Park station. The moldy smell of their old bodies and damp bedclothes is still in my nostrils. Every underground station in London had its bombed-out residents. Until V-E Day the underground would be their home, and for some it would be their grave. One day a station cave-in killed more than a hundred people.

I found a solitary echo of Oak Lake in London. My aunt Sue asked me to call on Clara Derickson, one of the "Derickson girls" who had lived in the house across from 107 Royalston Avenue where I first met Reuben Rosen. Clara had been in Europe since before the First World War. One afternoon in mid-March, I strolled across Hyde Park, past the Serpentine, over to Bayswater Road and on to Pembridge, where in a not too heavily bombed, gone-to-seed neighborhood I found the flat where Clara lived with two companions, Miss Taylor and Mr. Rains. Miss Derickson, well into her eighties, told me how she and Miss Taylor and a friend had been caught in Italy at the outbreak of war and had some difficulty in getting out. It was only later that I realized she was talking of World War I. Conversation was difficult because she was almost totally deaf. She talked about the good times she and her sisters had had with Percy and Sue and the other young people who lived in Oak Lake, but mostly she talked about her cat. A very large bomb had exploded just down the block and she had asked the watchman if she might pick up firewood from the bombed houses and had brought many armloads home. Now it was all gone and they had nothing but green branches from a tree which had just been cut down. Mr. Rains was one of those of whom it is always said that he is a fine figure of a man: tall, straight, thin, good shoulders, a military bearing despite his eighty years and feebleness. He had toured America in the 1880s and told me about Daly's Theater on Fourteenth Street, Delmonico's, the old Waldorf. He had gone to the United States on a steamship with fourteen pieces of luggage and had never been back. I had brought a packet of tea, some chocolates, some biscuits and a few cans of fruit from the commissary. We had a nice tea and I noticed on the bookshelf a volume of Oscar Firkins's *Two Passengers for Chelsea*. Clara Derickson was deaf, Miss Taylor was blind and Mr. Rains was feeble, but the three had managed in the blitz and were coping not badly. Coping—perhaps, I thought, that was what this blessed London was best at. I wished I could cope as well.

17 | A London Diary

Early on the morning of February 27, 1943, three weeks after I arrived in London, I met Hal Leyshon and Jack Redding, public relations officers, and Colonel Gates, the chief army censor, and the four of us in a command car drove out into the English countryside, my first sight of the soft green fields, the hedges, the narrow roads, the sleepy sheep and fat red cows. Sprouts and cabbages thrust through the muddy earth, daffodils were beginning to show yellow faces; the sun tucked in and out of the clouds but was not quite as warm as it looked. We lost our way and stopped a dozen times to ask directions. Everyone was helpful. They told us just what to do: "Down the lane to the King and Keys, then first right, second left, you ca-a-an't miss." And so we would go until we asked the next person. The English had taken down all road signs when they thought the Germans were going to invade, and they had not put them back. We were headed for an Eighth Air Force base called Molesworth, from which shortly after dawn the UP's correspondent Walter Cronkite had taken off on a bombing mission over Germany, the first time correspondents had been permitted to go on a raid. It had been set up before I arrived in London. I was not happy about it, but a dozen elephants could not have kept Walter out of the B-17 Flying Fortress.

It took us so long that when we got to Molesworth the planes were back and the fliers just coming out of the interrogation room. Soon Walter appeared, looking serious. No wisecracks. I had never been so relieved. I was too new to England to understand the full danger, but I knew enough to be frightened to death for him. I had spent the evening before talking with two youngsters, a Royal Air Force lad from the Bronx and an Australian. Both had the DSC and the Bronx boy had the bar as well. I knew long before the end of the evening that they did not expect to survive. They had to kick each other into the planes and their only prayer was for bad weather. I don't know what the odds were on returning from a daylight bomb run over Germany, but they were not very good. Five of the seventy-six Flying Fortresses did not return that day; two of the seventeen Liberator B-24s were lost, one of them carrying Robert Post of *The New York Times.*

I clucked over Walter like a hen. He was the star of our staff and my close friend. Now he was wound up like a top. It was so cold in the windowless room where he was writing that he kept his coat on as he typed. I hovered about, trying not to interfere, trying to be of help. People kept coming in with reports about Post. It was definite that he was missing. I fed Walter some headline phrases, out of which he constructed a memorable lead: "I flew through hell today." Then I retreated to the lounge, where a handful of crew members lolled about, trying to read *Life* magazine, their attention span very short. A radio played quietly in the background. Blond English WAAFs strolled past in their blue uniforms. I remember two of them skipping down a corridor, arms around each other's waists, their faces innocent as choir girls', singing: "When the lights come on again all over the world." I spoke to a WAAF about the young fliers on the base. Her face became solemn. Oh, our lads, she said, there is nothing we can do for them but hold them very tight and tell them we love them and we know they will come back, but most of them won't. She began to cry and I felt like a fool. I wondered how many boys she had held in her arms and how empty those arms must feel when the flights limped back and the boys did not return. "Don't make friends with the kids," Walter had told me. "Don't get to know them too well. It's just too much when they are lost, and most of them, you know, will be."

It was very late when we left for London. Homer Bigart had even more trouble than Walter writing his story. (It was on one such occasion that Bigart said: "I hate to write, but I love punctuation.") It was a long ride back to London, ten of us in the command car built for four, everyone on edge. Gladwin Hill, the AP man and later my *New York Times* colleague, had a talking jag. Walter kept poking sarcasms at Gladwin, who never noticed, he like everyone in deep gloom over the loss of Post. Two parachutes had been seen, but no one believed either was Post's. We didn't get to Bouverie Street until 11:30 p.m. and started pouring the copy in to the censor. There was the inevitable snafu. AP's copy cleared briskly, Walter's was held up. We lost a lot of play, but his "Hell" headline swept the British press. Pete Daniell of the *Times* was on the phone, sore at me because I had told

New York that Post was missing before he could nerve himself to do it. Pete was clogged with guilt; felt he should have flown the assignment; feared people would say he pushed Post into it because he and Post didn't get along; to make things worse, Post's wife had just arrived in London, intending to stay with her husband for the duration. It was a mess.

More than a mess—it was a scandal, but it took me considerable time to understand the extent of it. The origins ran as deep as General William ("Billy") Mitchell's fight for an independent air force in the early 1920s. It involved some tricky politics between the RAF and the USAF as well.

I had heard a lot about the air corps in long evenings in Washington at Lyle Wilson's, listening to Tooey Spaatz and other air officers. They were true believers in air power and their convictions had been reinforced by Japanese bombings in China, Mussolini's in Ethiopia, Spain, and the Luftwaffe's success in the early phases of the war. Spaatz's first objective had been to win independence for the air corps. His second was to demonstrate that air power was supreme, stronger than all other military arms. He had the independent air force now and in England he and his men were building a strategic air force which they believed would win the war.

Germany's bombing of England had been primarily by night. The daylight air battles were designed to wipe out the British fighter command. The Germans lost that one—by a hair's breadth. German night bombing was quite successful. It was not, of course, accurate, but no bombing was. Though it did not knock out British industry, it laid waste workers' housing. It was a terror weapon, except that the English did not panic.

I didn't understand how air power worked until one Sunday when I took a bus with Ellen to Petticoat Lane to see the East Enders at the street fair, with its sparse remnants of the blitz: secondhand shoes with inch-thick soles, mangy furs, five-and-dime jewelry, clocks and watches (stolen), plaster dogs, musettes, a few flowers; there were men doing card tricks and lots of tarts, not out for business, just shopping for pleasure in tattered finery; and all around, the desert left by the bombers, a desert that encircled St. Paul's, the Liverpool Street station, the City and down Commercial Road to the East India docks. The docks were working, cranes overhead, lift machinery battered but operating, yet all around lay the rubble of the dockers' grimy barracks. I understood then why it was said that the East Enders had great respect for bombs. The East End no longer existed. God knows where the people lived; lots of them, of course, lived in the underground stations. We went into a pub which stood alone in a row of smashed tenements. It was filled with men, men with thin faces, chicken necks, pinched shoulders, nasal voices. They looked at us with sullen eyes. I didn't blame them. There was not enough beer to go around, let alone whisky or gin, without strangers barging in. We slipped away without a drink.

It was my first glimpse of successful bomb warfare. I understood now what Tooey Spaatz was talking about. This was what they wanted to do to Germany.

Had there been no RAF Bomber Command, no Air Marshal Harris, I believe the American Eighth Air Force would have established itself in England and embarked upon a merciless night campaign to savage the Germans, to wipe their cities off the earth. The air force insisted that the Norden bombsight made hitting a German target like shooting fish in a barrel. I remember how we parodied that phrase until the PR men stopped using it. (The same claim, of course, was made during the Vietnam war and trapped Lyndon Johnson into the contention that American bombs were destroying only "steel and concrete," a claim my Christmas trip to Hanoi in 1966 would demolish.)

But the RAF had preempted night bombing. It was doing very well at it, thank you, and would be glad to have the U.S. Air Force join in too. By no means had the Eighth Air Force been established to become an appendage of the RAF. That was not for the likes of General Ira C. Eaker, or a young cigar-chomping, tough-talking colonel named Curtis LeMay, or the others. The Eighth Air Force was a high-octane outfit. It was run by ambitious men and backed by an ambitious command in Washington. It had set up a large public relations staff—men from newspapers, publicity firms, advertising agencies—and made use of Hollywood celebrities. They were not attracted to the air force because they thought it was going to take directions from the English.

Although no one would admit it, that, I thought, was why someone had invented the daylight bombing doctrine. Later on, when the air force grew so large that it could saturate the German defenses and fly almost at will through German skies, starting fire storms at places like Hamburg and Dresden, daylight bombing became something different. Under such conditions, daylight bombing was an effective military weapon, particularly for destroying cities and civilians. It was necessarily imperfect, but it followed the well-trodden tradition of Attila the Hun and prefigured Hiroshima.

On February 27, 1943, the Eighth Air Force was flying its third daylight mission over Germany. The target was Bremen, but because of poor weather, the planes were diverted to Wilhelmshaven, which undoubtedly was why losses were so low. The total force of ninety-three planes mustered that day was just about maximum capability, a long way from the numbers needed for saturation. The day's toll of seven planes lost was trivial; missions frequently lost a third of their planes, sometimes half of them or more, and in the case of the terrible Regensburg disaster, all but one. These were not what a military man would call "acceptable" losses. Again and again the bombing had to be halted or slowed in order to build up the backlog of planes. To fly in the Eighth Air Force in those days was to hold a ticket to a funeral. Your own.

The command tried to justify daylight bombing in every possible way—by exaggerating results, by lying about losses, by long-winded theories of how the day-and-night pressures produced by round-the-clock British and American bombing were driving the Germans to the brink. I thought there was a lot of mush in the theory and I could tell by talking to generals like Eaker and air marshals like Harris what the real competitive issues were between the British and the Americans. They were the issues that had compelled my hero, Blackjack Pershing, to insist on an independent American command in World War I despite the pressures and blandishments of Marshal Foch and Lord Haig.

Not until I got to Russia and saw war on the eastern front did I learn what was really wrong with the U.S. strategic bombing "theory." There was no such thing as strategic bombing in the East. The Germans had given it up almost immediately after the start of war, June 22, 1941, and the Russians never tried it, except for a few splashy morale raids on Berlin. Neither side could afford it. The results were too skimpy. They were too busy fighting the real war on land, a struggle of men and guns and tanks.

Air power was used as it should be used, as long-range artillery and close-support artillery. The Germans at Stalingrad didn't bomb the internal railroad systems of Russia or plaster the steel mills of Magnitogorsk. They pulverized the broken factory buildings in which the Russian troops had taken shelter and tried to smash pontoon bridges, a few yards away across the Volga, by which the Russians got their ammo and grits. When the Red Army turned the tables and broke the Nazi armored strength at Kursk-Orel in the summer of 1943, they didn't strike at the supply routes far behind the fighting zone; they plastered the German tanks with every bomb they could drop.

Of course, in 1943 we had no second front. Our land battles were in Africa, Sicily and Italy. But the air force had little interest in joint operations and had never learned to collaborate intimately with ground forces. Many remarkable air-infantry operations, particularly use of helicopters as mobile fire platforms and for quick movement of troops, were developed in Vietnam, but the air force's heart still was locked into strategic bombers, B-52s whose powers were irrelevant in the jungle.

The glimmering of this that I got on the eastern front was confirmed by the U.S. strategic bombing survey at the end of World War II, which spotlighted the military uselessness of much of the spectacular strategic operations of the Eighth, the Fifteenth and other air forces. But the lesson was never accepted by the heirs of Billy Mitchell.

The important thing, as the Eighth Air Force saw it in 1943, was to establish a presence, to prove a doctrine, to stake out a position in public consciousness. If this cost the lives of many fine young men and inflicted no really serious damage on Germany's fighting capability, that was too bad. War was war and people were bound to be killed.

And they were killed. Bob Post was killed. There was nothing special about his death except that he happened to be a newspaperman and the first one to be killed on an air mission, flying, of course, in total violation of the Geneva conventions. All the correspondents spent three or four days in indoctrination. They were instructed in how to handle a machine gun. They were combatants and automatically lost their civilian status. All this was part of the campaign begun so long ago by Billy Mitchell, one more building block in the relentless drive to establish public belief in the invincibility of air power.

Years later, Homer Bigart was musing over the operation. He thought it was total luck that it had not come off more badly. He wondered how many of his colleagues had shot their machine guns. None had had more than three hours' practice, just enough to learn how to point the gun and pull the trigger. "I used mine," Homer said. "I just hope I didn't shoot down one of our planes. I saw one of the B-24 Liberators go down. Wouldn't it be awful if it was one of us who shot down the B-24 with Bob Post in it?"

Freddie Chapman was killed sometime on May 4, 1943, when the plane in which he was flying with General Andrews, the U.S. commander in England, was lost on a flight over the North Atlantic en route to Iceland. Freddie was a lieutenant colonel, just promoted from major, General Andrews's personal aide, a boy from Alabama full of "Thank you, ma'am"'s and "Yes, sir"'s, whom I had known in Washington. He arrived with General Andrews from Cairo to take up the London post and we met the next day, each thinking it a lucky omen. In no time, I was on first-name terms with the general. By accident, I had an inside track on U.S. military operations from England. Freddie watched over his general like an adoring son, and the general, a gruff, tough, exquisitely professional old-army man, treated Fred like his boy. They lived at the Dorchester, but Fred had found the general a big English house in Hampstead. The general could hardly wait to get into it. First, he thought he would make an inspection trip to Iceland, where his old friend General Bonesteel was commander. I wanted to go along, but at the last moment I couldn't break away from the office. I had been writing in my journal and had dropped off to sleep when the telephone rang. It was 12:30 A.M., May 5, and the office was calling to tell me General Andrews had been lost on a flight to Iceland. I phoned the Dorchester to see if by chance Fred had missed the plane, but no luck. I got dressed, went to Bouverie Street and wrote the story. It was the first time in the war I had lost someone close. I could hear Fred's slow, slow drawl wondering whether his mama and his papa had heard that he had made lieutenant colonel. He didn't think anyone in his little hometown had ever risen so high in the army.

I began to wobble; London was too much. I ran about town all day. I was up half the night. I was drinking too much. I began to

sleep with girls, sometimes because I was fond of them, sometimes because we found ourselves together at the end of an evening. Entries began to appear in my journal: "Terribly sloshed
last night"; "Must cut out these evenings and get to work." Once
I noted a remark by Jeff Parsons: "How much whiskey in the
world can a man drink?" To which I had replied: "We're finding
out."

I had to change this pattern. I went down to the country to
spend a weekend with Constance Spry. She lived in a rambling
brick house with stone floors, possibly two hundred years old, in
Kent; it was twenty miles southeast of London, about five miles
from Orpington station. She had just enough gasoline on the ration to get to the station once a week.

I'd never met a woman like Mrs. Spry. She must have been
sixty years old and had been part of that sophisticated, almost
precious set which dominated English social life in the late twenties and thirties, something like Fleur and her friends in the last
of Galsworthy's Forsyte novels, a member of the crowd that ed-
died around the Duke and Duchess of Windsor. With a difference. Constance Spry was as energetic, as talented a woman as I
had ever met. She reminded me of my aunt Mary (as unsophis-
ticated a woman as lived) because she was so chipper in the face
of adversity, so warm, so human. She had won international recognition for growing flowers, for arranging them, the Cecil Bea-
ton of her profession—had set up a shop in South Audley Street
and another on Park Avenue, had commuted between Southampton and New York on the *Berengaria*. When England went to war
in 1939, Constance Spry threw her energy into traveling the
country from Lands End to John o'Groat's, she and her friend
Rosemary Hume, teaching recalcitrant British housewives how
to cook, how to cook without boiling the last vitamins out of their
Brussels sprouts, their cabbages, their potatoes. She hymned the
virtues of greens, of cucumbers, of coleslaw and raw cabbage.
She taught that lettuce was edible, that tomatoes could be grown
in backyards, that life was possible without roast beef and York-
shire pudding.

I went down to her quiet household, she in a pink calico apron,
living in the kitchen with its copper and tiles, serving on the
kitchen table, a Brussels lace tablecloth over the old boards, ancient silver and five-and-dime utility china. Her greenhouses
were filled now with tomatoes and corn, but she had acres of
flowers. We picked sixty bunches of roses and I can't guess how

many other flowers, to be brought up to London early Monday morning by horse and cart. She had no coupons to send them by truck, and the railroads wouldn't accept "nonessential" freight.

I lay in the sun, pulled weeds in the rose garden, played with the four-year-old son of a gardener, taking "trips" to London in the cart, inspected the cross goose that chased him, admired a flock of yellow chicks and petted a rabbit which he looked forward to eating at next Christmas dinner.

In the evening I sat by a gray-stone fireplace and talked with Shed, Constance's husband, recuperating from a ghastly heart attack, a onetime India civil servant, about the Civil War, his hobby and mine, about Douglas Southall Freeman's Lee and what a guide it was to the real nature of war, Henderson's Jackson and Carl Sandburg's Lincoln, which he was then reading.

The weekend at Constance Spry's transported me a long way from the complexities that were pulling my life apart, but on Monday morning I was back in the midst of them.

One evening I dined in London with Storm Jameson and her husband, Guy Chapman, and lost my heart to the two of them. Margaret (Storm's true name) was rather small, quiet, very intelligent, and possessed a fiery spark that lighted up her whole being. I described Guy then as a cherubic man with a puckish sense of humor who talked very openly and freely, with lots of laughter, lacking the reserve I had seen in so many English. But I don't remember him that way, probably because later images were superimposed on that first one. I remember him as wry, ironic and, ultimately, tragic. That evening Guy and Margaret talked a lot about Wales, where he was teaching in an army school. He had plunged into World War II supposing he would find again the golden days of World War I, a comradeship of men and duty and danger in the hell of Flanders, about which he wrote his classic account, *A Passionate Prodigality;* but 1940 was not 1914 and the past is quicksilver that can never be held in the hand. In our postwar meetings, this was starkly apparent. For many complicated reasons, Guy and Margaret were turning inward on themselves, a relationship so close, so total, I have never seen another like it.

Margaret was looking that first night, as was Guy, toward the future, toward the England that would emerge with the peace, and neither of them liked the face of what they saw coming; nor that of Europe. They dreamed of an island where they could loll in the sun and read and talk and write, but certainly they did not find it. Nor did Guy achieve his ambition of living again in his beloved France. He was a scholar of France, a great one, but so dedicated, so precise, he could hardly bear to turn in a manuscript to the printer.

They hated the Wales in which they were condemned by the war to live, a narrow, secular people, clannish, tight, raw, uncomfortable, and living was harsh, a primitive inn with scant food and abominable cooking.

Margaret was already one of England's finest novelists, with a spare, strong prose and a relentless honesty which was her strength. The tragedy of her life was Guy's death. He left her alone in a world that only the two had shared. She never got used to it. For reasons of their own, they had never had a home, always living in rented quarters, moving from pitch to pillar, she winding up at Cambridge in the late years and abhorring it, she said, although I think she got a warming comfort from her fierce refusal to accept the banality of life.

I had breakfast with Ellen one Sunday at the South Audley Street mess (once it had housed London's Bachelor Club). We walked in Rotten Row, not many horsemen out, and the barrage balloons cuddled close to the ground. I thought it was because of the wind, but Ellen said an ATS girl had told her it cost too much to let them go up unless there was a good chance of a raid. The Serpentine was alive with flowers, ducks and geese swimming by, so peaceful and appealing we decided to go to the country. We caught a train to High Wycombe, a Westchester kind of town, then clambered onto the second deck of a great red London bus and were off down country lanes. We alighted at a crossroads and rambled into a rather unattractive Gypsy camp inhabited by what looked like extremely businesslike Gypsies, Romany without romance. Over fields and muddy paths, we found ourselves at the Crown. I thought it must date back to Richard the Lionhearted, a stout, half-timbered building with low ceilings, paneled walls, hunting prints, pewter mugs and a fireplace with deep corner seats, harness brasses and a slow oaken log burning. I could have stayed forever. At midnight we were back in London, chilly, tired and rested. How pleasant it would be, I thought, to wander over England with Ellen, how easy I felt with her and she, I knew, with me. But I closed my mind to these thoughts because Ellen was the friend of a friend and this kind of thinking was not loyal.

There was no peace in London. Hugh Baillie, the evil genius of my UP career (as I saw him), was headed for England. He had not been to London since the start of the war. The news filled me with apprehension. Baillie must have the best. He must stay in the best suite at the Savoy. He must meet Churchill and Eden, the air marshals, the U.S. brass. He must go to Parliament (where I had been only once). He must see the countryside (which I hardly knew). I must take him to dinner every night at the best restaurants and he must be seated at the best tables. There wasn't much on at the theater, but he must have the best seats at the best shows. The UP bureau must impress him with its get-up-and-go. We must have exclusive stories every day. I must be suave, sophisticated, tough. I must show him I had entrée to the highest circles, that there was nothing I couldn't do, no one I couldn't see. I must come up with a world-beating story. Maybe more than one.

When these thoughts raced through my mind I felt I was bouncing off the ceiling. My God! It was all I could do to keep my head above water—and now Baillie. I could handle the American military all right and the Eighth Air Force, I was confident of that, but what about the English, the Foreign Office, Churchill, his mean-spirited aide, Brendan Bracken, and those restaurants so chic my knees wobbled as I encountered the maître d'hôtel, and how could I wangle the suite at the Savoy?

I was beginning to worry about money. Mary was crisscrossing the United States, moving every two or three weeks. She had rented out the Mamaroneck house, moved to Washington, gone to Minneapolis, left for Florida, and now was back in Minnesota. It cost a fortune. I counted up how much I owed one night—it was more than a hundred dollars, and I didn't dare draw more from the office. I stayed home three nights that week, ate cold Spam and soda crackers, and held my living expenses to eighteen shillings a day. If I could do that for two weeks, I might square my accounts.

I met Baillie at Paddington Station and hired a car to drive him to the Savoy. He behaved exactly as I had on my first night, his head out the window all the way to the hotel. He loved his suite. He should have—it was delicate blue and white, with graceful curved windows looking out on the Embankment and the Thames. He didn't want a drink, he didn't want anything to eat, he just wanted to get rid of me and get out on the street and see London, *his* London. He didn't want anyone sharing that first impression. I hadn't understood that Baillie loved the city as only a colonial Scotsman could love it. Before his visit was over, he had walked my legs off. He took me to the City and showed me where the Great Fire had halted. He showed me how the German bombs hit almost exactly the same area. We walked it street by street and he told of the buildings that had been turned to dust. He took me to Westminster Abbey and led me past the graves of the mighty and the poets. He knew every one. We went to St. Paul's and he marveled at the great bomb that had fallen through the sacristy and been defused. He inspected the ruins of the Wren churches, ate at the Cheshire Cheese, and we went up to Hyde Park to look at the antiaircraft installations and the searchlights by night. He attended Commons and heard Churchill. He spent two days with Walter Cronkite at Eighth Air Force bases and would have flown a mission if General Eaker had let him. He thought the spirit of the fliers was like that of a University of Southern California football team before the big game. He talked to General Devers, who had replaced General Andrews, he met Eden and Air Marshals Harris and Peck. He dined with Beaverbrook and Lord Astor and all the rest. He came with me to Sandy's, had late drinks at the Savoy, he loved the UP bureau, never had met such correspondents, never been so thrilled, he even loved me, gave me a raise and promised to promote me to the post of European News Manager. I was walking on air. My worries vanished.

But Baillie had a protégé named Virgil Pinkley, a Southern Californian like himself, a salesman who was doubling in brass on the news side in North Africa. Virgil had won a place in Baillie's heart by the simple trick of putting in the hands of the desk each Saturday during football season two telegrams. One said: "Congrats, we won again!" The other read: "Tough luck, we'll lick 'em next time." The desk waited until the USC score came in, then dispatched the appropriate sentiment. Whatever Baillie's mood, win or lose, Pinkley had it covered. Virgil flew up, took Baillie back to Algiers, and was named General European Manager. When Baillie told me he was going to promote me, I had written a sad note in my journal: "I hope he does but he might forget. Really." Well, he did forget and I found myself working for Virgil. I didn't handle that very well, but there was no way I could. We were strange dogs, sniffing and growling at each other.

One Sunday in September, I called Ellen and invited her to spend the day with me. I had hardly seen her all summer. My life had become too complicated and I thought I should put some distance between us. We took the train to Maidenhead, rented a canoe and started up the Thames. It was a winy autumn day, and we relaxed beside each other and let the canoe move very gently. There were many swans sailing, majestic and white. I had never seen a swan except in a park. Now they floated up to the canoe, looking at us with great curiosity, arching their necks. I took some peppermints from my pocket and tossed them to the swans. They turned out to be peppermint freaks. I switched to chewing gum. They liked gum too. It was an enchantment—the river, the swans, the countryside and the girl beside me. My worries floated off into the white clouds that lazily passed overhead. We fell in love that day. We spent the next weekend together in her flat in Weymouth Mews. There was a rather sharp air raid, the guns awakening us, heavy gunfire, the drone of the planes overhead, searchlights. We watched it, holding each other, and went back to sleep before the all clear. I should have been in seventh heaven. I was. But I wasn't. I was more filled with guilt than ever. Ellen was my friend's girl (well, I knew that had faded). I was betraying Mary (well, I had done that before). I was betraying Ellen, because there was no chance of a future together (well, we had talked about that; we each knew it). What else? There was my gnawing ambition. This was no time to fall in love. I should be clearing up my life, not bringing in something new and overwhelming. (Since when had logic and reason held back the heart?) I didn't know what to do, so I began spending every possible moment with her.

Something happened a week later that I could not have imagined. I was invited to lunch with the directors of *The Times* of London—the paper that long ago my mother had hoped I might be editor of. I've no notion why Lord Astor sent the invitation, but to me it had a solemn, almost sacred import. To be sure, I was ill at ease in the faded red-brick building across from the

Times offices in Old Victoria Street, just down from Blackfriars Bridge, but no matter. I was there in the house that had been for so many years the home of the Walters family, publishers of *The Times*. Here was John Walters himself, old and spare, and Lord Astor, tall, handsome, with a shy smile and a severe limp, who apologized that only five of the directors could be present. Nothing happened at this luncheon. Nothing of significance was said. No matter. I was served by two old butlers whom I had often seen around London at formal affairs. The food was excellent, a tomato puree of real tomatoes, not from a tin, a very good chicken which had been allowed to run and peck a bit, peach Melba, Stilton cheese, port and cigars. I have always been sorry I didn't take a cigar. Most of the directors wore proper morning clothes with waistcoats, pin-striped trousers and gates-ajar collars. I was very aware of my Bond's suit (walk a flight–save ten dollars) and my scruffy shoes. A proper coal fire burned in the grate and after the port and some small talk with Colonel Astor about the postwar problem of newsprint, we broke up. Later, writing a schoolboy's account of the occasion to my uncle Andrew, who had read *The Times* of London all his years, I bathed again in the aura of the occasion. I might be in sixty-nine kinds of trouble, but I had been taken into the bosom of the Old Thunderer. It was something to cherish through a lifetime.

Luncheon at *The Times* did nothing to dispel my problems. They stood impacted, impossible of resolution, when on October 12 a cable arrived from Earl Johnson in New York. He ordered me to leave London immediately, proceed to North Africa, reorganize the UP's coverage there (left in a mess by Pinkley), go east to Cairo, to Moscow, to New Delhi, and await instructions. Perhaps I would return to London, perhaps I would go on to Chungking. I did not have to read the cable twice to understand that Johnson had come to my rescue. He had saved me by sending me into orbit. I only realized how desperate I had become when the surge of excitement hit my brain. Johnson had given me an open-ended invitation to cover the war all over the world; no one had had such an opportunity. My imagination took off, my blood tingled. I was not doomed to purgatory in my beloved London. I had been cut loose just as the express train thundered down the tracks. No one could stop me now. I was on my way.

So I thought in one grand rush. Then bittersweet flooded my

heart. My new love! What of her! Had I found her just to lose her? But wasn't it always thus? When the hero pledged his love he must go forth and slay the dragon. This nonsensical Arthurian imagery actually flashed through my head. I had been right and so had Ellen to understand that there could be no future for us. This was war. Now I began to feel like Hemingway. Farewell, Catherine! I had army orders to fly from Prestwick in Scotland to Marrakesh in Morocco. I booked a compartment on the *Flying Scotsman* and at 8:40 P.M. on the evening of October 23, 1943, my love and I left London, holding each other all through the night. At 6:40 A.M. (we were always so precise during the war with our travel notes), the train arrived at Prestwick, the air chilly, fog creeping about, heather hidden, the sun not yet up. We stood on the platform and kissed an endless farewell. Then I caught the army bus for the air base, leaving Ellen standing at the station, looking back as long as I could at this woman with chestnut hair, red cheeks, pert nose, brown eyes and my heart in her hands, standing alone in her dark blue uniform.

18 | Russia!

I spent my first night in Russia in the old, old city of Astrakhan, at the head of the Caspian Sea. It was January 13, 1944, and I had been waiting since before Christmas in Teheran for the weather to clear so that a Soviet DC-3 could fly over the sixteen-thousand-foot Elburz Mountains and into Russia. My North African experience had been fleeting. True, I had met General Eisenhower, a frosty, rather unpleasant meeting. He called me in a couple of days after I arrived in Algiers, to warn me to mind my conduct. Anyone who cut corners or violated rules was consigned to a slow boat back to the U.S.A. I think the lecture was instigated by my AP competitor Ed Kennedy, a tough agency man who later won ignominy when he violated a pledge to Eisenhower and secretly transmitted to AP word of the war's end, on May 7, 1945. I was not taken by Eisenhower nor by his headquarters, ridden by cliques and rich with intrigue. The war had moved up to Italy and Ike was marking time for the shift to England and preparations for the landing in France on June 6, 1944. I never got to know Eisenhower, but I did get to know his brother Milton, whom I liked and respected. I believe we will always be in Eisenhower's debt for his farewell address, with its warning against the military-industrial complex. The language was written by Milton, but it was Dwight Eisenhower who understood the danger, spoke the words and left it as his legacy to the American people.

I took off from Teheran for the Soviet Union, my mind imprinted with images of poverty and disease. Algiers, Tunisia, Cairo and Persia, the contrast of incredible riches and horror: dirty little girls of eight or nine being offered for twenty-five cents by their eleven-year-old brothers; the stores of Cairo filled with symbols of American good living—Campbell's soup, Quaker oats, Del Monte peaches, seventy-five cents for Heinz tomato juice, an astronomical dollar a pound for Maxwell House coffee, everywhere English woolens, Paris jewelry, perfume, furs, silks, a selection that I thought could not be had in New York, and the streets stinking of human excrement. But Teheran—Teheran had to be the worst: beautiful German-built apartment houses, but no sewers, no water system; a ditch beside the asphalt streets carrying mountain-pure water, contaminated every few feet by defecating humans and horses; women washing clothes; women drawing water to drink; a naked seven-year-old with one testicle the size of a walnut, the other big as a coconut; a pubescent girl with green pus dripping from a blind eye. I saw the shah, a nervous youngster, wondering whether the British, the Russians and the Americans would let him keep the Peacock Throne or dump him as they had his terrifying old father.

One day I sat beside the fieldstone fireplace in the U.S. officers' club at Camp Amirabad, aromatic pine logs filling the room with their scent, eating pistachio nuts and sipping vodka and tonic and wondering whether there was a way in which these wretched people could be rescued. No one had an idea. "It's too much," one thoughtful major observed. "We can't get a hold on it. The only ones who can help are the Russians. They are closer to the gooks [yes, we called them gooks]. I think we ought to turn Persia over to the Russians. Maybe they can do it." There was no one around the fireplace—all of us in uniform—who disagreed. We thought that with the end of war, everyone would turn to resolving the world's ills. It would be like the early New Deal days—only on a world scale, the Russians, ourselves and possibly the British. We didn't think the French would take a hand.

Now I was flying over the blue Caspian Sea in our Russian DC-3, first stop Baku. We had some American oil engineers with us and they thought Baku was just like Galveston, Texas, a sprawling town, derricks, refineries and oil tanks scattered over a sandy spit. After a bite to eat and a customs inspection (an apologetic clerk took some lemons away from two English correspondents who had been vacationing in Palestine, then relented and gave them back), we took off and were flying between two thousand and three thousand feet—Russian pilots in those days never took much altitude—when we hit a downdraft. It was like dropping through a hole in the sky. The water rushed up at us and I thought we were going in. But with a tremendous groan the plane stabilized just above the waves and the pilot fought it onward and gradually gained a fair altitude. At midafternoon we bounded down on the dark, cold, windy Astrakhan field.

No stop had been planned at Astrakhan, no arrangements had been made. We were taken to a dismal little hotel with heat only on the third floor, where, thankfully, we were harbored. I dumped my musette on the blue-painted iron bed and rushed for the street. I was in *Russia!* The most exciting place in the world. I couldn't wait to get out, bundled up in an Alpine army parka I had bought at the U.S. Army store in Cairo, and a beaver cap that I had had made in Teheran at a cost of fifteen dollars. Russia—it was too much to believe. When I got my instructions from New York to go to Moscow and run the bureau while Henry Shapiro took a brief vacation, I hadn't quite taken it in. I had to get a visa, and put in my application in Algiers. To my amazement, the visa was waiting for me in Teheran two days before Christmas. Of course, I couldn't read what it said. I didn't know a letter of Cyrillic. The only Russian I knew was half a dozen words I had been given by a girl in Cairo named Zette, whose parents had fled to Sofia at the time of the Revolution. My vocabulary consisted of: *da* (yes), *nyet* (no), *mozhno* (may I), *spasibo* (thank you), *puzhalista* (please) and *ya vas lublu* (I love you). She acknowledged that I didn't really need the last expression. "Russian girls are very realistic," she said. "But it will amuse them if you say 'I love you.'"

The first thing I did on the cold, windy streets of Astrakhan was to look at people's feet. They all wore shoes or felt boots, except for one woman, rather elderly, who wore a pair of rubbers over three pair of stockings. I had remembered the first dispatch of my friend Cy Sulzberger when he got into Russia in late summer 1941. It started out: "The Russians have shoes." A curious fact to report, with the Germans pounding toward Moscow, but a significant one. What Cy meant was that despite Hitler's attack and the terrible losses, Russia was still able to feed and clothe itself. If the Russians wore shoes they were capable of fighting. This was big news. Astrakhan was down-at-the-heels, but the kids looked healthy, well-fed, red-cheeked, warmly dressed. They had just got out of school for the day and tagged after us, fascinated by the sight of foreigners. There were few trucks, no passenger cars, no troikas. But I saw one smart-looking Russian officer driving a spanking mare in a droshky and thought of *Anna Karenina.* Crossing a bridge to get back to the hotel, I encountered a blind musician, a pale young man with upturned collar, playing a violin with wool-gloved fingers. Passersby were dropping kopecks and ruble notes into the fur hat at his feet. My first day in Russia, my first beggar. I saw two more, women begging at a factory gate, as I walked around Astrakhan like a prospecting miner. Every little speck was gold.

At the hotel there was chaos. We had no money to pay for our rooms or meals. Our Intourist tickets were good only in Baku or Stalingrad. The hotel manager talked to one official after another. After an hour she got permission to feed us. It was my first lesson in Russian bureaucracy. The manager said she'd had the same problem with the Archbishop of York. He'd sent her the rubles from Moscow. She had entertained Anthony Eden too, but he paid cash. She liked him a lot. She fed us black bread and tea and a slab of tough beef, some vodka and watery beer. I was running a fever and slipped off to aspirin and bed under a pile of blankets, but not before I had heard her tell about the Germans. They were very strong, the strongest people in Europe, and the Russians were not nearly so cultured, not nearly so advanced. But, she said, "We are very cunning people. The Germans will not be so strong again." I thought about that as I sweated my fever away. She had screwed up her face and her eyes squinted a Mongol squint. I was too ignorant to know that Astrakhan was an old Tatar city, one of their last strongholds (as well as the birthplace of Lenin's father, Ilya Ulyanov, from whom Lenin derived a measure of Tatar blood), and I did not recognize in her remarks an echo of the peasant tradition—to appear ignorant, blockheaded, stupid, but in the end to use cunning to overcome educated, cultivated, cultured people.

I pondered that night about those beggars. How did they fit into the workers' paradise? And our landlady's preoccupation with money—what about that? Certainly there was a lot to learn in the Soviet Union. No sign thus far of the new Soviet Man or the humanistic society of which, I had been told, Lenin dreamed.

Between the fever and the excitement of arriving in Russia, I did not sleep for hours. I had never felt so far from London and New York. In the two months since Prestwick, I had been cut off, no word from Mary, none from Ellen. I had been working like spit. I knew I had made a hit at Cairo, handling the Teheran Conference story; this was the kind of professional job at which I was a master. Now I stood on the doorstep of a new world. Tomorrow I would be in Moscow—the Kremlin, Stalin, the Red Army. Headlines danced in my mind. Every kind of person had come to Russia: correspondents with red stars in their eyes, romantics hunting the Revolution, seekers of utopia, believers, scoundrels, men on the make. I thought I had a big advantage. I was not going to Moscow with a bagful of illusions. I was a hard-headed newsman. That was what I thought, and it was pretty true, pretty true. But not entirely true. I had infinite regard for the Red Army and the Russian people. I had seen those banners in London's East End: "They gave us Quiet Nights." Or just little signs in windows saying: "Quiet Nights." A lot of emotion rode in that. I distrusted Stalin, feared him, but I respected him. So far as I knew, he had done a brilliant job of fighting Hitler. He was a tough, hard dictator, of that I was certain, but he had had the guts to stand up to the Nazi armies (how little I really knew!). Already the Russian bureaucracy was rubbing me the wrong way. But what I could not then comprehend was the real depth of my ignorance, not only about Stalin and Communist Russia, but about the eternal Russia that had existed long before the Romanovs and would persist long after the Soviets. What I knew that night, huddled under my mountain of blankets, sweat turning me into a soggy mass, was that I had started on a new path. I did not know where it would lead or what it would bring, but I had finally cut loose. I was on my own. I felt very much as I had that frosty January morning thirteen years before when I had stalked up Michigan Boulevard. Russia was the big one and I was going to make it my own.

It was my fifth day in Moscow and I was at Spaso House, the merchant's palace that George F. Kennan had acquired in 1933 as a residence for the American ambassador, when a telephone call came from the Foreign Office: A trip had been set up for the correspondents to visit Katyn Forest. The name Katyn rings soundless in minds that today react instantly to the name Auschwitz, but it is one that is not forgotten in Poland. Katyn is a pleasant wooded region not far from Smolensk, where in a place called Goat's Hill some thousands of Polish officers, possibly 4,500, possibly more, were killed in 1940 or 1941, each with a pistol bullet in the head. The officers had surrendered after the brief hostilities that followed the Nazi-Soviet partition of Poland in September 1939. They had been placed in internment camps in Russia and then brought to Katyn. The Germans announced the discovery of mass graves and bodies April 13, 1943, and put the blame on the Russians with a propaganda flourish overseen by Goebbels. Forensic specialists, academicians of various countries,

an international commission of inquiry, foreign journalists, were
hurried to the scene, graves were opened, bodies exhumed, autopsies performed, letters and newspaper clippings presented, to
suggest that the men had been killed in April and May of 1940—
that is, when still in custody of the Russians. The sensation was
tremendous. In occupied Poland, the German version was generally accepted. Families of the officers, it was said, had not heard
from them since spring 1940. Relations with the Poles and the
Russians, always stormy, became impossible. Moscow broke diplomatic contact with the Polish government-in-exile in London.
The Soviets maintained that the Germans had committed the
atrocity.

Kathy Harriman was in Moscow with her father, now ambassador to Moscow. She had a job with the Office of War Information and acted as her father's hostess, bringing life and gaiety to
a banal scene. She turned the embassy ballroom into a badminton
court and found a cache of old Hollywood films in the Spaso
attic. They were so brittle they broke a dozen times during a
showing, but we ran them just the same.

Kathy was present when the Katyn announcement was made
and said she'd like to go along. The Russians promptly invited
her and John Melby, a young embassy attaché. They laid on a
special train—international wagon-lits, a mahogany-paneled dining car, quantities of caviar, champagne, butter, white bread,
smoked salmon, cake, beef Stroganov, cutlets Kiev—and we were
off to look into one of the war's great tragedies.

The Russians had recaptured Smolensk in September 1943 and
now they were about to explode their own propaganda bomb. The
Western correspondents were invited as part of the stage setting.
I don't think the participation of Kathy Harriman and John
Melby was calculated U.S. policy. I think it was spur-of-the-
moment impulse, but it is true that Averell Harriman was fed up
with the "London" Poles and when we came back from Katyn he
told me he had been convinced for a long time that the Poles had
fallen for a German atrocity story and what we had seen
strengthened his conviction.

I am deeply grateful to the Soviet press department for arranging this expedition. It was (and remains) a vivid lesson in
Soviet methodology. There was the embarrassing extravagance of
the train, outfitted with snowy linen, perfumed soap, down
quilts, white-jacketed waiters, luxury fit for the Czar. In fact, it

may have been one of the Czar's special trains. To sit in the dining car, tables laden with bottles, crystal and silver, plates heaped with *zakuski,* and look through lace curtains at wooden freight trains where wounded Red Army men, heads in bloody bandages, arms in splints, legs amputated, gazed from the next track, shivering around potbellied stoves, was almost too much. As Dick Lauterbach, the *Time* correspondent, said, turning away from the stare of the young soldiers, many of them not more than fifteen or sixteen: "Comes the revolution . . ." What he meant was that once the war was over, there would *be* a revolution, times would change, the young veterans would come back determined to end the inequality, the suffering, the terror, the ugliness of Russian life. That seemed plausible to me. How could they fail, no matter what repressions the regime imposed? As we now know from the examples of Solzhenitsyn and others, that was what Stalin feared; that was why SMERSH, the front-line secret police, ferreted the young Solzhenitsyns out of the army and sent them to prison camps long before war ended; that was why Red Army men released from starvation and torture in Nazi POW camps were sent straight to Stalin's camps in Siberia; no intermediate halts; that was why the end of the war signaled new and sharper repressions. Stalin had never seen the eyes of the young Russian soldiers. He had never visited the front, from first day to last. But he knew what to fear. "When these boys come back from the front there are going to be lots of things different here," I wrote in my journal. I was right but, alas, the more things changed, the more they became the same.

I think we all wanted to believe that the Germans had done Katyn. Whatever their idiosyncrasies, the Russians were our allies. We hated the Nazis. Atrocities were what the Nazis were all about. What more natural than to kill the Polish officers, blame it on the Russians and sow trouble? But the Russian expedition got off on the wrong foot and never changed. I didn't like the fact that the inquiry was being conducted by a "Commission to Investigate the German Atrocities at Katyn Forest." That established the verdict in advance. Perhaps the Nazis did it, but I wanted to hear the evidence and make up my mind. The Russians couldn't understand what we were talking about. Of course the Germans did it. Why would we be having this hearing? That was a topsy-turvy world to me. The man was convicted before the evidence was presented. Some of my colleagues told me that Rus-

sian law was based on the Code Napoleon. First a thorough inquiry was conducted, and unless the man was guilty, he was not
put on trial. I didn't buy that.

When we got to Smolensk we drove out to the forest, out a
well-laid road through a pine woods and new-fallen snow. At
Katyn there were log fires everywhere, tents, doctors in white
smocks and surgical caps, nurses, Red Army men with shovels
and entrenching instruments. It took some time to see the bodies,
neatly stacked like cordwood, hundred after hundred of them in
precise, rectangular excavations in the sandy soil. It was hard to
believe that these were bodies, that they had been men, that this
was not some kind of outdoor festival in the north woods of Minnesota.

But it was real enough and we went from tent to tent, watching the surgeons perform autopsies, trepanning skulls with fine-
tooth medical saws, cutting open stomachs and depositing the
contents in flasks of yellow and blue fluid, an anatomical labora-
tory suddenly transported into a snowdrift. The sweet cheesy
stench and the sight of the carcasses were too much for some of
my colleagues, Henry Cassidy of the AP for one, but Kathy
seemed unaffected. So was I. There was something about the
mass of bodies that deprived them of humanity.

I was struck by the neatness of it all. Every man executed
exactly in the same way, a pistol bullet fired close up at the base
of the skull. Almost all the men wore their army greatcoats and
had been buried with their boots on. This did not impress me. I
was too new to Russia. But it struck my colleagues. "I can't believe the Russians would bury those boots and that warm clothing," Alex Werth said. After I had seen Russians scavenging on
the battlefields, I was inclined to agree.

The evidence of the commission was poor and its presentation
worse. The witnesses were a dreary lot. After much argument,
the correspondents were given the right to ask questions through
the commission. I did not please my hosts by my insistence on
finding out the prior and present status of the witnesses. (It
seemed apparent to me that they had been arrested, were prisoners and probably headed back to prison—potent incentives for
them to tell the story as their captors wanted them to tell it.)
When I asked the quisling deputy burgomaster of Smolensk if he
had been arrested and whether he was now in prison, the commis-

sion refused to put my question. Finally, the novelist Alexei Tolstoy, a relative of Leo Tolstoy and a member of the commission, said that the man had indeed been arrested but that he was presently at liberty and was going to Moscow. Not much of an answer. The commission was ill at ease with our sharp inquiries. Finally, they called the thing off at midnight and we were hustled back to our train luxe for our fifth banquet of the day. We stayed up until 4 A.M., arguing and drinking. I told Apollon Petrov, a Chinese-archaeological specialist, who for some reason was deputy chief of the Press Department, that Russia would get better American public support if it let U.S. war correspondents go to the front. "Mr. Salisbury," he told me soberly, "if the Red Army's victories have not won American support, I don't think your stories will help." One of our colleagues was a newspaperman who represented something called the "Free Polish Press." He had looked pale and ill all day and when we got back to the train went straight to his berth. Small wonder. He had once been a Polish officer.

We had embarked on the trip expecting that the Russians would have an airtight case. The evidence had been poor and the presentation sloppy. "Our verdict," I wrote in my journal, "was: A lot of Poles have been killed by revolver shots in the back of the head. They have been dead for some time. We wished we knew who killed them." In other words, the old Scots judgment: "Guilt not proven." That was the tenor of the dispatches we filed. The censors killed all skeptical remarks and deleted references to the caviar.

The tragic evidence of Katyn has been pawed over time and again, almost entirely by "London" Poles and others antagonistic to the postwar Polish regimes and to the Soviets. The Soviet government made a halfhearted effort to submit the case to the Nuremberg War Crimes Tribunal but never pushed it, and no indictment was returned. Forty years after it happened, Katyn remains in limbo, but few, indeed, are the Poles who do not believe it was Stalin's secret police who committed the crime. Once, Stalin let drop a remark in talk with the Poles which convinced some that the execution had been carried out by accident, by chance, by misinterpretation by Beria of a casual remark Stalin had made. That seems nonsense. Nor is there support for another report, that Nikita Khrushchev at the time of the Twentieth Party Congress contemplated making public the evidence about

Katyn but was dissuaded because the consequences on Polish-Russian relations would be so catastrophic.

The truth is that at any moment the Polish government wants to establish and make public the facts about Katyn, it has the means to do so. The same is true of the Soviet government. Had the Germans committed the massacre, the sober bookkeeping evidence, the orders, the statistics, the whole dreary business, would long since have turned up, no matter how cleverly it had been hidden. Yet some things nag—the burial of the overcoats and boots and one bit of evidence never publicized: The bullets the Poles were shot with were German bullets fired from German pistols. But, it is said, the Russians bought a shipment of these handguns from the German firm of Gustav Genschow & Co. in 1929. Who knows? Until someday an impartial commission gives the final verdict, Katyn will remain dark, bloody and tragic as it was in the January days of 1944 when I first saw it.

By the time I returned from Smolensk, I knew that the task of understanding and interpreting Russia was going to be more difficult than I could have imagined.

I went to the Foreign Office one afternoon and met Max Litvinov for the first time. He was one of my heroes. Since the days when he stood up in the League of Nations in the 1930s and thundered "Peace is indivisible," I had seen him as a champion against fascism. Henry Shapiro, the UP's permanent Moscow correspondent, took me to the Foreign Office, housed in a warren of old buildings off Lubyanka Square, across a narrow street from the vast headquarters building of the GPU, the secret police, and its enormous Lubyanka Prison. I did not then know it, but the whole area around the Foreign Office was honeycombed with police institutions and, as it later would emerge, the Foreign Office itself for practical purposes had been in the hands of the police since May 1, 1939. To see Litvinov, we did not use the main entrance of the Foreign Office; instead we entered by an obscure side entrance. I never figured out the significance of that; there was an armed guard at this entrance just as at the main one. But each time I called on Litvinov, he had instructed me to use this entrance. It was the same with his other foreign visitors. We liked to think there was something conspiratorial about it. Litvinov had been on the shelf since his recall from Washington to Moscow in August 1943. Now I sat down with him in a little office somewhere behind the back stairs of the ministry and he talked long and frankly, just as "twinkling, beaming, rotund," to quote my journal, as I had always imagined him. "It was nice," I noted, "to meet a Western mind again." When I brought up the diplomatic problems of the day (there was a great flap on over rumors of separate British peace talks), he smiled wearily and said that if we got the main question of collective security resolved, the smaller problems would fall into place. Then he led the conversation away from politics into a tale about the twelve-day trip he had taken from Washington to Moscow via Montana on his flight back to the Soviet Union. A plane-ferrying route via Montana, Alaska and Siberia was then functioning.

I wasn't certain of the validity of his thesis that if the basic relationship could be resolved, the little things would fit into context. I think he was saying that if America and Russia and Britain could construct a solid postwar structure, small problems would not fester so badly.

I saw Litvinov possibly a dozen times before leaving Moscow. Never without profit. Always his talk was civilized, penetrating. Always he managed to distance himself from the pompous rigidity of Soviet diplomacy, giving me an insight into what lay behind it. Sometimes he just shrugged his shoulders and cast his eyes upward as if imploring heaven as his witness that he understood it no better than myself (perhaps he was just drawing my attention to hidden microphones). He never ducked a question; never found a subject too sensitive. He was the only Soviet official I was to meet whom I found unfailingly decent. I knew then that he was a man of courage, but I had no understanding of his real situation. That would not come until long after his death. He visited the American embassy often, attending receptions, dinners, movies. Whatever the company, whether in the presence of Molotov or not, Litvinov consistently spoke with me and the other correspondents, not just diplomatic froufrou, always talk of substance.

When many years later Ivan Maisky told me that Litvinov had slept every night of his life from the mid-1930s onward with a pistol under his pillow (later, Pavel Litvinov told me his grandfather had shown him the gun), that he had confided to Maisky that if they came to arrest him he would shoot himself, I was not surprised. This was in Litvinov's character. Perhaps that is why the knock never came.* When I returned to Moscow in 1949, I wrote letters and made calls to men in official positions whom I had known during the war. Only Litvinov replied. I had sent him a letter suggesting that he write for *The New York Times* a brief memoir of FDR on the fifth anniversary of his death, in April 1950. I promptly got a note back, thanking me for the suggestion, assuring me that were it not for "indisposition," he would be happy to do as I suggested.

Not quite two years later, on January 2, 1952, *Pravda* published a five-line notice on its back page that Litvinov had died December 31, 1951. I was shocked. Not by the news—Litvinov had lived beyond his life expectancy in the Stalin epoch—but by the shamelessly obscure notice of the death of one of the great men of the twentieth century, the greatest diplomat of the Soviet era. It was a shabby thing. In my outrage I called the dean of the diplomatic corps, Ambassador Yves Chataingeux of France, to see if the corps had been invited to the funeral. He had not even heard Litvinov was dead. I called the Foreign Office and discovered the funeral was being conducted at that moment. I threw on my coat and raced over to the old building on the Kuznetsky Most, entering the drafty reception room at the moment the cortege was emerging, Andrei Gromyko at its head, and in his train, deputy ministers Zorin and Gusev (who had replaced Maisky in London), Litvinov's wife, Ivy Low, who had dreamed of conducting a postwar salon in Moscow, and Litvinov's son and daughter. His grandson Pavel, who, carrying on the family's tradition of courage, would become a dissident and ultimately settle in the United States, was not there. He was off on a ski trip with his high school class. I was the only foreigner present. What an insult, I thought, to Russia's history this seamy ceremony was. A nation that had no respect for its history could only be a state with no respect for itself.

I did not know in 1944 the reality of Litvinov's position; nor did I in 1951. It was not until his former secretary, Yevgeny Gnedin, published his memoirs in samizdat, that is, in the underground literature which circulates in the Soviet, that some concept of what happened to Litvinov could be established. Lit-

*Nikita Khrushchev revealed that plans had been made by the secret police to kill Litvinov by running him down with a truck, but they were never carried out. (*Khrushchev Remembers,* 1970, p. 262.)

vinov's removal from his post as foreign minister on May 1, 1939, and his replacement by Vyacheslav Molotov, was no mere shift of jobs. It was a takeover of the Foreign Office by the secret police and the opening of an attempt to concoct a case for the arrest and execution of Litvinov. Gnedin was head of the Press Department at the time, probably the man closest to Litvinov on the Foreign Office staff. Like every Litvinov associate, he was summoned to the Foreign Office on the evening of May 2. He didn't even know that Litvinov had lost his job. He had seen him the day before in Red Square, standing with the Soviet leaders at the May Day parade. That evening he was questioned by Molotov, Beria, Malenkov, and V. G. Dekanozov, a police associate of Beria's who had been named number two to Molotov in the Foreign Office. The questioning went on in the presence of Litvinov.

They were laying the foundation for the case against him. Every man in the Foreign Office, Gnedin among them, who had an association with Litvinov (and many who did not) was arrested. Some committed suicide. Others, including Gnedin, were tortured. Gnedin was interrogated by Semyon Kobulov, Beria's number two in the secret police (who was executed with Beria in 1953). Twice Gnedin was taken to Beria's office, where Kobulov and Beria alternately beat him, knocked him to the floor and kicked him almost into insensibility. Gnedin refused to confess that he was a spy, that Litvinov was a traitor, and finally he was shipped off to the Sukhanov isolator, the most terrible of Stalin's prisons. Later, he was sent into "eternal exile." The effort to concoct a case against Litvinov was still in progress at the time Hitler attacked Russia. It was suspended (but probably not dropped) in order that Stalin might send Litvinov back to the United States to stir up sympathy for Russia. I would guess that the case being fabricated by Stalin at the time of his death in 1953 against Molotov, in which Maisky was arrested, was descended from the Litvinov case; had Litvinov lived, had he not died at the end of 1951, he would have been given a central role in Stalin's grandiose 1953 extravaganza, probably cast as Molotov's "secret agent" in plotting with the United States, just as Maisky had been assigned the role of Molotov's "secret agent" in liaison with the British.

19 | To Leningrad

Three people drank tea with me around a low table in Room 346 of the Metropol Hotel, the UP's office, on the afternoon I arrived in Moscow. A gloomy cave, Room 346 contained two or three tables piled with newspapers; a built-in cabinet full of tea things, canned goods, little hoards of sugar, husks of black bread and snippets of cheese (to be put on the floor for the mice so they wouldn't enter the cupboard); a built-in sofa upholstered in faded brocade; bookshelves spilling over with books and clippings; a two-burner hot plate; a crystal chandelier; and a small sleeping nook and bathroom behind a heavy green portiere. Windows looked into the courtyard, where women in cotton-padded jackets chopped wood for the Metropol furnaces all day. Room 346 was the crossroads of the hotel, where people came in and out all day and all evening.

One of the three at the table was Henry Shapiro of UP, a chubby little man with broad forehead, Stalinesque mustache and a Rumanian accent. A onetime student in Moscow University's law faculty, he had supported himself for a while as a tourist guide. He had come with his parents to New York at an early age and graduated from Harvard. He was, in his way, a brilliant man, but his Byzantine mind, which often aided him in dealings with the Russians, sometimes affected his relations with his colleagues.

Seated beside Henry was Ludmilla Nikitina, his wife, with her ash-blond hair, pure white skin, almost skeletal face (she was remarkably thin). She was wearing a gray crêpe de chine dress whose low-cut bodice displayed her white bosom, of which she was rightfully proud. Ludmilla worked for UP as a translator and also acted as a correspondent for Religious News Service. She had graduated from the Gorky Institute of World Literature, and as I later came to understand, she had solid roots in the *kupechestvo,* the Moscow merchant class, so brilliantly satirized in the plays of Ostrovsky.

Beside Ludmilla sat Olga Florentievna Khludova, a striking young woman who, I was to discover, liked to caricature herself

as a gaunt borzoi. She was thin enough to make this plausible
and there was an air of the aristocrat about her. Before the Revolution, the Khludovs had been one of the great entrepreneurial
families that arose in nineteenth-century Moscow. They were
closely connected with the Morozovs, an enormously wealthy textile and banking family. Saava Morozov financed Stanislavski's
Moscow Art Theater, collected French and Russian avant-garde
art and subsidized Lenin and his Bolsheviks with hundreds of
thousands of rubles, before finally he drew a circle around his
heart with an indelible pencil and put a bullet through it. He left
an insurance policy to Maxim Gorky's wife to help the revolutionaries.

Naturally, I knew nothing of this on that January day. I did
know that Olga Florentievna possessed a sharp wit, spoke English not very well and worked for UP as a courier—taking telegrams to the Foreign Office, running errands, standing in
queues for permits. She and Ludmilla practically lived in 346,
although Ludmilla was often absent at her parents' home, caring
for her three-year-old daughter, Arisha (Irena). Olga lived with
her mother, a medical worker at the big Stalin auto works. She
painted with great sensitivity, aquarelles and small oils, and occasionally drew caricatures for Moscow magazines. Professionally she was an animator, a great admirer of Walt Disney. Her
studio, the Russian equivalent of Disney's, was shut down because of the war.

I was attracted to Olga the moment I saw her green eyes, *châ-
tain* (the Russians used the French word for "auburn") hair,
freckled face and the lilt of her head. She smoked cigarettes in a
long amber holder and, as I was to learn, wore most of the time a
simple brown jersey dress with a lace collar. Her proudest possession was a brown caracul *shuba,* a warm winter coat with a
hood. She made a very stylish appearance, with her long stride
and erect carriage.

On *Maslenitsa,* Shrove Tuesday, Ike Patch and Fred Barg-
horn, young officers at the embassy, had a blini party in their
apartment at the chancellery on the Mokhovaya, across Manezhny Square from the Kremlin. The building had been built
for artists and the young Americans had a studio with a twenty-
four-foot ceiling. There was a good deal of vodka and marvelous
blini, caviar and *smetana,* thanks to Pasha, their housekeeper,
who spent her life trying to make Ike wear his galoshes so that

he wouldn't catch cold. At midevening, Olga decided to leave and I offered to escort her back to the Metropol. We came out onto the Mokhovaya into a swirl of snow, snow everywhere—in the air, under foot, in our faces—and skipped past the National Hotel, crossed Gorky Street, where scores of *dvorniki,* women with long-handled witches' brooms, were at work, and as we passed the Gosplan Building, we turned to each other and kissed and went down the street, our lips still together, kissing and kissing, past the Hall of Columns, where the purge trials were held, past the big Sverdlov Square metro station, across the asphalt desert in front of the Bolshoi Theater, past the Maly Theater corner, across to the Metropol, only pulling apart as we approached the hotel entrance with its sheep-jacketed militiaman. Into the hotel we went, side by side, across the lobby, past the drowsing "angels," the plainclothes police, up in the wheezing iron-cage elevator to the third floor, got the key to Room 346 from the sleepy woman *dezhurnaya*—floor attendant—entered 346, locked the door, and were in each other's arms without, I think, saying a single word.

Nothing like this had ever happened to me. I woke up next morning not knowing what to think. I was entranced with Olga. More than that I could not say. I made no attempt at trying to fit the evening into logic. It had happened. What would follow I had no idea, but when next I saw Olga, she would hardly speak to me, her eyes smoldering. Somehow I had offended her. It was totally mysterious. I held my peace, hoping that time would give an answer. Days raced by. Every moment I was absorbing sensations, walking through Red Square (much bigger than I had thought), enjoying the children skating on the frozen Moskva River (I thought of Mike at home), meeting diplomats (much less formal than London), watching Stalin at the Supreme Soviet (not nearly so tall as I had imagined), visiting the markets (pitiful collections of potatoes, onions and carrots). I found it hard to get an echo of the feeling I had had in the distant days at 107 Royalston Avenue; there was nothing in the Communist Young Pioneers to remind me of the boy soldiers whom I imagined to have defended the Winter Palace. No spark of that enthusiasm which burned in Nathan Rosen's eyes as he told me about the Revolution. It was impossible for me to envision Moscow as the beacon of revolutionaries from all over the world. I saw the stone in the Kremlin wall with John Reed's name on it, marking the urn where the ashes of the author of *Ten Days That Shook the World* had been placed. I had never read *Ten Days,* although Reed was on my litany. And I saw the stone bearing the name of William ("Big Bill") Haywood, the IWW who had jumped bond in Los Angeles during his trial for dynamiting the *Los Angeles Times* and taken refuge in Russia. The IWW had not and never would lose my romantic interest. I had heard of another IWW, Bill Shatov, who had helped run Siberia and build the Turk-Sib railroad, but when I asked, no one seemed to know what had become of him. He had, of course, been shot.

One afternoon I met Ilya Ehrenburg, the author and war correspondent, a man with a mop of gray hair like Einstein's, a fine English jacket, a fawn-colored French pullover, a Gauloise dripping ash over his sweater; he possessed contempt for Americans, total belief that the only good German was a dead German, and a prayerful dedication to Paris, where he had spent more of his life than in Moscow.

On a Saturday in February, I found myself with Olga on a train bound for Zagorsk. The Troitsa monastery, seat of the Orthodox Church, was there, a complex of fortress churches where Russia's fighting monks under St. Sergius had beaten off attacks by invading Polish Catholic knights.

We were spending the weekend at Zagorsk, six of us who had formed what whimsically we called the Anglo-American-Russian Walking Club. Olga and Ludmilla were the Russian members, myself and Ike Patch the Americans, and George Bolsover and Pat Kirkpatrick the English. It was just an excuse to get ourselves out in the country on weekends, and Olga was its founding spirit. Russians don't walk for pleasure any more than Americans do. But Olga had been brought up under strong English influence. Her father, an engineer, educated abroad, had taught his daughter to like fresh air, cold baths, dogs, riding horses, walking in country lanes, tweeds, plain shoes, shooting a gun, fly fishing, and what he called "being a gentleman." No matter that his mother was a personal friend of Lenin; that the family had given the Bolsheviks aid and that Lenin suffered the old grandmother to scold him for not taking proper care of tropical plants in the orangery of the family estate, which he confiscated: Olga's father had been arrested.

This was part of the substance of the young woman with whom

I was riding that day to Zagorsk, a cold, overcast day with snow spilling into the air. The train was filled with peasant women in *valenki*—felt boots—black coats and black shawls, clutching their *avoski,* their string shopping bags (the nickname means "perhaps"), into which they had jammed whatever they had found in the Moscow markets—mostly onions on this day. Olga and I brought the provisions and would get our quarters in the dirty little Zagorsk hotel ready for the others, who were catching the next train.

Hardly a word was exchanged in the two-hour ride. We sat side by side, she reading a Russian book, its back protected by a paper wrapper, her eyes, I thought, angry, face cold, body rigid. Thinking of the night we had been together, I scraped a patch in the frosted window to stare at the Russian countryside—groves of birches, ghostly against the snow, clumps of pine, small log huts, whole villages of log huts—and in the train the smell of *makhorka,* the peasant's strong tobacco, and of wood smoke and wet wool.

Finally, we arrived at Zagorsk. It was only midafternoon, but already getting on for dusk. The hotel manager showed us to the rooms we had reserved, one for the men, one for the women. They were small, three iron beds in each and a big tile Russian stove. In our coats and mittens, we sat on a bed. We could see our breaths. It was about twenty degrees outside and seemed colder within, the stove just beginning to heat up. Olga sat stiff as a kitchen chair. I longed to put my arms around her, but instead tried to make conversation, talking about winters in Minnesota when I was growing up. Olga had nothing to say. Gradually it warmed up a bit and Olga began worrying about our friends. It was full dark now. They should have arrived. Perhaps they had missed the train. I began to hope they had. Olga threw back the hood of her *shuba.* She didn't look angry anymore. Our eyes met and then switched away. Her face was rosy, almost like the blush of a young girl. I was embarrassed too. I knew what we both wanted—that our friends should miss the train. But they didn't. They arrived with shouts and hugs and a draft of cold air. The moment was gone.

Next day we explored the icy old monastery, the churches with their bulbous domes, resounding to the deep chant of the priests, the scent of incense in the frozen air, a tiny glint of candles burning at the altars, peasant women's devout faces haloed by the candles, peasant carts and horses with wooden yokes clattering to the market. This, I knew, must be the deep heart of Russia. We went outside and threw snowballs. Diamonds sparkled in Olga's hair, in Olga's eyes. We rode the train back to Moscow, the train jammed, standing all the way, crushed to each other. Three youngsters had an accordion, they sang *chastushki,* street songs, improvising the verses as they sang, ribald words, the crowd laughing, teasing the boys, Olga and I very close. I put my arm around her. She did not push it away.

Later Olga told me that when she awakened on the morning after *Maslenitsa* she was outraged at what had happened. She had been angry at me from the first afternoon, when, asking a question and not knowing her name, I said, "You, I mean you," and pointed a finger at her. I was, it was clear, another rude, vulgar American, and the morning after *Maslenitsa* this feeling came back very strong. She had got a little tipsy that night and this vulgarian had taken advantage of her, as he would of any whorish Russian girl. He had wanted a quick bounce and that was what she was—another Metropol girl, going to bed for a warm bath, a piece of soap, a little butter. She hated herself and she hated me. She remembered what her father had told her. He had talked to her as frankly as Chesterfield to his son. He told her what men were like; what they thought of women; just an object for their sex; a thing. Women, he had said, played the men's game. They played "the flirt," they led men on, then let men use them. He taught her never to blame a man in her personal relations; she would get what she deserved, no more, no less.

On the evening of February 6, I boarded a train for Leningrad with a dozen correspondents. The nine-hundred-day siege had ended. For the first time we would visit the city where so many had died to keep the Germans from their northern capital. I would, and already I think I knew this, fall in love with the city of Peter and be forever humbled by its people, awed by its beauty and bravery.

We had no fancy train to take us to Leningrad, nothing laid on like the Katyn trip, just a regular train following a very circuitous route. Though Leningrad was free once more, its rail connections were still tenuous. Almost forty years have passed since the cold morning when we debarked at the Nicholas (now, to be sure, the October) station in Leningrad, almost a three-day journey, roundabout through Vologda, moving slower and slower over new-laid tracks as we neared the city. I don't think I have forgotten a detail, standing at a window watching the endless snow, the birches and pines, and saying to the man standing next to me, "That looks like northern Minnesota," and learning that we were both Minnesotans, both graduates of the university. He was Homer Smith, a black who had come to Russia during the Depression as a "postal expert" (having been a clerk in the Minneapolis post office). Now he wished he hadn't. Like all exotic foreigners in Russia, he had been abandoned with the coming of war and was surviving largely through help from the foreign correspondents. His brother and sister were officers in the U.S. Army. His choice of the workers' paradise had proved a bad gamble.

I cannot go back over it all again. I have written so much about Leningrad in *The 900 Days,* which is dedicated to her people. Each of those I met in the winter of 1944 has etched a place in my heart. But a few things must be said. Leningrad was not only a living monument to heroism, to the tradition of "Pyotr," as they called the city in memory of Peter, who founded it. It was not only the little girl at the Kirov works who went out with her friend one afternoon a week to check her parents and her friend's parents to see who was living, who was dead, to put a body on a child's sled and drag it to the mountain that climbed higher and higher near the gates of the Nevskaya Lavra. Nor the girls and boys with their dogs and mine detectors in the frosty twilight, slowly crisscrossing the frozen fields beyond the Czar's palace at Peterhof, never knowing when the next mine would blast away their legs or lives; the sudden blast and the column of smoke when they touched off a mine, and the explosions I heard in the distance.

Beneath this facade of courage ran a deadly current of Kremlin politics, more dangerous even than German tanks and bombs. Of this I only occasionally caught a glimpse, as through a door left accidentally ajar, a whiff of the terror that had swept the city after the assassination of Sergei Kirov on December 1, 1934, which set off Stalin's great purges. I knew then (and, of course, much more in later times) that there was something rotten about the Kirov case; just what, I could not say. I caught it in the nuances of remarks, cautious, oblique. *The people did not want to talk about it.* I had been in Russia only a few days, but I already knew that if Russians did not want to talk about Trotsky, for instance, or the Kirov case, something frightening lay behind it.

In Leningrad I saw that Kirov was honored. His name had been given to the great Putilov steel works, owned by a Russian Carnegie named Aleksei Putilov, a friend of the Morozovs and the Khludovs. But no one would talk about the "Kirov case," the purge trials, Zinoviev, Kamenev, Bukharin and the rest of the executed old Bolsheviks or the thousands of Leningraders who had been arrested, shot or exiled. This held no reality for me, I could not grasp what terror meant, until a few months later when in Central Asia, in Tashkent, I met a young Russian composer named Aleksei Kozlovsky and his wife, Galya Geras, an American who had been brought to Russia by her parents, her father having been an important revolutionary before 1917. Galya whispered the story to me during a performance of *Uleg Bek,* an opera she and her husband had written. In 1937, Kozlovsky had been exiled from Leningrad to Central Asia and she had come with him. He had done nothing. By chance he had been in the same high school class with three "Trotskyite" schoolboys. The schoolmates were shot. All that happened to Kozlovsky and his wife was that they were totally cut off from Western culture (she had not spoken a word of English for nearly eight years) and compelled to live in a mud-floored Central Asian house, where they composed "national" operas for the glory of Uzbek culture. What had happened to the Kozlovskys had happened to tens, perhaps hundreds, of thousands of Leningraders.

The terror lay deep under the city. Hitler was not the only enemy. There sat in the Kremlin the most dangerous man of all, Stalin. It would be many, many years before I pieced together the details of this peril. No one outside the tight circle of the Kremlin and the Leningrad leadership knew exactly what had happened in 1934 and the years after. No one outside this circle (and not all within it) knew the inner story of the siege, of Stalin's faithless conduct of the Leningrad defense, the feud between Andrei Zhdanov, Kirov's successor as Leningrad party leader, and his Politburo rivals, Georgi Malenkov and Lavrenti Beria. I was ultimately to learn that Stalin's tactics had almost opened Leningrad to the Germans; that he ordered the city mined and was prepared to blow it up and abandon it to the Germans, halted in this, it would later appear, only by the herculean efforts of Marshal Georgi K. Zhukov, who took command at the critical moment.

Neither I nor any of the correspondents could judge the political standing of Andrei Zhdanov in 1944. We saw his picture everywhere; many, many pictures of Zhdanov, only a few of Stalin. I never saw this kind of iconography anywhere else at any time in Stalin's Russia. Did this mean that in Leningrad Zhdanov was popular and Stalin not? We tried to see Zhdanov but got nowhere. On our last day we met the number three man. Mayor Pyotr Popkov, tired, worn, only forty-one, an engineer who had been at his post all through the siege, cautious and tough, very careful about a question that is still in dispute today, the number of deaths in Leningrad from starvation, cold, disease. Some Leningraders told us they thought the toll might be as high as 2,000,000 (for years the official Russian total was 632,253, but careful official Leningrad calculations now place it above 1,200,-000). Popkov was only willing to discuss the small, almost inconsequential casualties of civilians killed and wounded by bombs and shells—a total of 5,000 killed, 15,000 wounded. He was uncommunicative on how many adults and children had been evacuated. It later became clear that hundreds of thousands of lives were lost in this badly managed, criminally tardy operation; many children were sent to places in the path of the Nazi advance.

Popkov had a right to be wary. When I returned to Russia in 1949, stopping first in Leningrad, I asked to see him. I thought my mention of his name had impressed the hotel manager at the Astoria, but I did not see Popkov. What I did not know and the manager did was that this dedicated, hard-working veteran of the Leningrad siege had been arrested a few days earlier in the so-called Leningrad Affair, which wiped out almost every surviving associate of Zhdanov, dead of a heart attack a year or so earlier. To mention Popkov's name in the Astoria was like asking about black spots on a man's face in a city of the plague.

When I got back to Moscow in February 1944, I wrote a story about the future role of Leningrad. Pointing out that Lenin had moved the Soviet capital "temporarily" to Moscow in March 1919 because of the danger of German occupation of what was then Petrograd, I said it seemed not unlikely that Leningrad might be reinstated as capital of Russia. Its palaces and imperial

avenues were almost intact despite the siege—they were too grandiose and solid to be wiped out by Nazi bombs. My article was an
open plea that Leningrad again be Russia's capital. It was not
passed by the censor, nor were similar stories by my colleagues.
My article, I confess, was more an expression of my feelings than
anything else. True, some Leningraders had spoken of the idea,
but no officials, except an architect or two working on plans for
postwar Leningrad. I am not certain that one of us did not toast
Leningrad as the once and future capital of Russia at a great
banquet of the Leningrad intelligentsia given in the Hall of
Scientists. There were so many toasts that night that after the
seventeenth or eighteenth, the listing kept by one of our number
became unreadable. Finally, his pencil simply ran off the page.

There was a good deal of talk among us along these lines and
we were, of course, all *foreigners* and all, by definition of the
GPU or the OGPU or the KGB or whatever the secret police
chanced to call itself at the moment, *shpioni,* spies.

Thus I suppose it was logical that one charge in the Leningrad
Affair—invented by Beria and his underlings—should have been
a conspiracy of the Leningrad leadership with "foreign agents"
to transfer the capital of Russia from Moscow to Leningrad and,
of course, to overthrow Stalin and set up a new regime. It was all
quite logical to a mind as twisted and conscienceless as that of
Stalin.

It would be totally wrong to suggest that in February 1944 I
had any suspicion of currents so dark, so deep, so dangerous. At
that time I could still refer to Stalin as a great builder in the
tradition of Peter the Great. But I did come away from Leningrad with a conviction that there were secrets beneath the tragic
city, beyond my ability to probe.

It is also true, as I wrote in my journal, that "I fell in love
with Leningrad." It is a love that has endured a lifetime. I
vowed that someday I would write the epic of the city and finally, in 1969, *The 900 Days: The Siege of Leningrad* was published.

After *The 900 Days* came out, after it had become a best-seller
in America and in every country in which it was published, the
Soviet government wheeled out their greatest general, the man
whose ruthless determination saved Leningrad from the Nazis,
Marshal Zhukov, and signed his name to a full-page article in

Pravda attacking me and *The 900 Days* for "vilifying" Leningrad and carrying out anti-Soviet propaganda. I have never met anyone from Leningrad who took this view. Again and again, Leningraders have thanked me for writing the story of their city, for telling the truth about the horror, the sacrifice, the terror, the mistakes, the intrigues that marked their struggle. To this day there has not been published in the Soviet Union an honest or complete account of the siege. Not one. Oh, of course there have been dozens of books, particularly since *The 900 Days,* including a collection of dramatic eyewitness accounts published by my good friend Daniel Granin, the Leningrad author. But what difficulty he had getting out his book; what obstacles were put in its way; what a small edition; how much censorship!

The tragedy and glory of Leningrad sticks like a bone in Moscow's throat, in the throat of the party leaders. Not even Khrushchev could get up his courage to publish the truth about the Kirov case, about Leningrad or the Leningrad Affair. It was too shameful, too black, too odious. But Leningrad will endure. It may never again be Russia's capital, but the full story of the wounds inflicted upon it by Stalin, his henchmen and his survivors will, in the end, see light.

20 | The "Stalin Case"

I was celebrating George Washington's birthday at Ike
Patch's apartment with Bill Lawrence of *The New York Times,*
Jim Fleming of CBS, Dick Lauterbach of *Time* and some others,
when I got a call to come to the Foreign Office immediately.
Something important. I looked at my watch. It was near 9 P.M.
Could it be? Like every correspondent in Moscow, I had written
a letter to Stalin asking for an interview. He hadn't seen a correspondent for years, although he had met with Ralph Ingersoll,
the editor of *PM,* who had come to Russia for FDR.

An interview with Stalin—it seemed too good to be true, but I
could think of no other reason for a Foreign Office call at this
hour. I slipped into my coat, telling no one where I was off to.
Bill spotted me leaving. He never missed a thing. "Where are
you going, Gospodin Salisbury?" he said. "Got a scoop?" Oh,
sure, I said, and hurried to the street. It was a five-minute walk
to the Narkomindel. Good God, I thought, suppose it is Stalin; I
haven't even got a list of questions. I began to think frantically:
Was he satisfied with the Teheran results? Did he expect a second front? What was the meaning of the rash of jabs at London
and Washington in the press? Had something gone sour? Was he
afraid of a separate peace? The questions tumbled through my
mind as I hustled up Kuznetsky Most between the snowbanks. I
showed my red *propusk,* my pass, to the guard at the ministry
entrance and hurried into the Press Department.

There was an air of excitement in the dingy chambers. The
press director's door was closed. Subordinates hurried in and
out. I was told to wait. I crossed my fingers. This looked like
something big. Soon Nina Brint appeared, a small, brown-eyed
Georgian girl, barely twenty-one, bright (all 5's, the equivalent
of A's, in her studies, we had heard), the best English-speaker in
the Press Department, a favorite with the correspondents. "I
will escort you," she said. My hopes took a drop. If she was escorting me, the best I could hope for was Molotov. "Where are
we going?" I asked, as we threaded the corridors. Nina did not
reply. We went up two staircases, down a third, up another, and

arrived at a door guarded by a soldier. Nina nodded slightly and we were ushered into an office, where, standing at a long table of polished Karelian birch, I saw the rather solid figure of Vladimir G. Dekanozov, Vice-Commissar of Foreign Affairs—broad forehead, dark hair, cruel face—resplendent in his new-issue Foreign Office uniform of finely tailored gray cloth, with gold-braided shoulder boards that showed he held the equivalent rank of a colonel general. He nodded, gave me the coolest and briefest of handshakes, waved me to the table, pointedly rejected my offer of a Chesterfield and picked out a Moskva from the paper box on the table. I was not going to see Stalin, that was certain. Nor was I going to see Molotov, and from Dekanozov's manner, it did not seem that he was going to hand me a great scoop.

In a severe voice, speaking from notes penciled in red on a white pad, he told me that United Press had slandered the head of the Soviet state in a dispatch carried from London, and that unless United Press promptly apologized, we "would not have the possibility of having a correspondent in Moscow." That meant me.

The UP, he told me, had transmitted on St. Valentine's Day, 1944, a dispatch which asserted that at Churchill's birthday party in Teheran, Marshal Timoshenko made "a careless speech" and Stalin had struck him "in order to silence him." The yarn was attributed to "a neutral diplomat."

Having delivered his ultimatum, Dekanozov rose and began to pace back and forth, in a signal that the interview was over. Nina Brint was so nervous I was afraid she would cry. (In fact, as it developed, she was so upset that she had failed to translate the critical fact that Dekanozov was demanding a public not a private apology.) I was not going to leave the room until I had put in a few words. When Dekanozov reluctantly sat down, I told him I had never heard of the story, it was obviously false, I had personally handled the Teheran communiqué. I knew Timoshenko was not even there, and if UP had carried such a story, they would, of course, make good the damage in any possible way. "We would like to think this," Dekanozov replied, "but . . ." His voice trailed off.

I sent off to Hugh Baillie and Earl Johnson a report on what had happened and expressed my conviction that they would promptly make amends. Within twenty-four hours, they were showering apologies down on Stalin and Dekanozov and submit-

ting the draft of a public declaration they proposed to make. On
February 25, I found myself again at the Foreign Office. A
young attaché named Timofayev anxiously asked, "Is it going to
be all right?" "Yes, indeed," I said, "it is going to be O.K." "On
both sides?" he persisted. "Yes," I said, "on both sides." He was
greatly relieved.

I showed Dekanozov the proposed retraction and apology. He
offered three small changes and it was carried on the UP wires
two days later. The question, I thought, had been settled expedi-
tiously, and I believed with some credit to UP. Dekanozov had
told me that the Press Department was upset by the matter, sym-
pathized with me, but as he said, "business is business." Ralph
Parker, then acting as a special correspondent for *The New York
Times,* had been off on a special trip to the Korshun battlefield
in the Ukraine. He heard from his escorting officer that I had
been expelled and the UP bureau closed. I think the Foreign Office originally planned simply to throw me and UP out.

On the evening of February 29 (it was leap year), my phone
rang and once again Dekanozov wanted to see me. I was fed up
when I got to the Foreign Office. I had no more dreams of meeting Stalin. In fact, I was beginning to think the happiest solution might be to lose "the possibility," as the Russians put it, of
being a correspondent in Moscow. I later came to realize that I
was being given a sublime lesson in Kremlin tactics, though I did
not exactly relish the experience.

This time Dekanozov was not cold; he was hot. The apology we
had made was not an apology. We had not said plainly that our
report "was a lie." We were trying to evade responsibility. If we
sincerely wanted to correct this matter (and maintain a correspondent in Moscow), we must carry a declaration which he
handed to me. It was headed: "Denial by the United Press
Agency." It repeated the London story, said it was unfounded in
fact; was an invention; a lie; that UP had sent its apologies to the
Soviet government and taken steps so that nothing like this
would ever happen again. The statement concluded: "The present
denial is made public by the United Press because of the unsatis-
factoriness of the statement it published on February 27 on this
question."

Dekanozov was reading from red-penciled notes. This time I
was sufficiently informed to understand that Stalin used a red
pencil. From consultation with Averell Harriman and the Brit-

ish ambassador, Sir Archibald Clark Kerr, I was beginning to suspect that Stalin himself was behind the affair. Perhaps he had drafted the statement Dekanozov had just read. I concluded that I would be polite, yet there was nothing to lose by frankness. Dekanozov had dealt badly with me and he knew it. I had asked him, first, to specify the language that would be satisfactory and he had approved our draft with the changes we had made. If anyone was at fault, he was. I told him we would do all we could to make the amends his government wanted; that we had already done what he had said was proper and the clumsy language of the dictated "apology" betrayed to everyone that these were not UP's words but Moscow's; that to anyone who had read the original apology, the new statement would only raise more questions than it answered. Dekanozov did not budge. He had his orders—print the new statement or get out.

I was not happy to cable New York that once again we were in trouble, or more properly that we had not, as I had thought, extricated ourselves from trouble. Nor was I surprised that New York did not immediately respond. We had been put into a ridiculous situation, but I was sure there would be no Soviet backdown. Saturday afternoon I went to Spaso House to see a Fred Astaire movie. There was a newsreel of the fighting in the Pacific. I wished I were there. After the movie I took a slow walk back to the Metropol through the slush of the Arbat, the narrow shopping street just beyond Spaso, jammed with people. It was the route Stalin took when leaving the Kremlin for his villa on the outskirts of town. Not a few times, I had watched his convoy of black limousines speed down the street, militiamen suddenly slapping their nightsticks across their chests in salute and all the traffic lights going red.

Saturday night. Not likely that New York would do anything about the Stalin story over the weekend. Maybe the Russians would. Maybe I would be packing my bags. Hardly had I got to the hotel than the telephone rang. It was Vera, the long-suffering Press Department secretary. Could I come to the Press Department at six-thirty? Yes, I sighed. Certainly. What was it this time? She seemed embarrassed. "I was told to tell you to come at six-thirty," she said. "Mr. Palgunov"—head of the Press Department, a man whom Cy Sulzberger had christened a "mechanized cockroach"—"will see you."

When I got to the Press Department, it was obvious that a

new and perhaps final act was about to unfold. Saava Dangulov appeared, a press official of whom I was fond, a small, warm-hearted Georgian whose English was very defective. He was to escort me to whatever it was I was being escorted to.

Off we went. After two or three turns in the maze of the Nar-komindel, I saw we were not going to Dekanozov. God, I said to myself, not Vishinsky! He was, as I thought, number one in the Foreign Office next to Molotov. I wanted no part of that foren-sic gentleman who had won notoriety as the prosecutor at the purge trials. Suddenly we emerged from dim passages into a well-lighted antechamber. Four uniformed soldiers stood at at-tention with bayoneted rifles. Hardly given time to take in the scene, I was whisked into a side room and told to wait. I sat in a stiff black leather chair at a stiff black table and felt like a schoolboy waiting to see the principal. I had smoked one ciga-rette and was lighting another, when a pleasant blond Foreign Office man led me to the corridor. "Mr. Molotov will see you now," he said. Well, I thought, they are really doing this up with ribbons. We went into a big office, thirty or forty feet long, where an official in Foreign Office gray stood tall and lanky be-side a table. It was a man we called "the other Pavlov" to distin-guish him from the small, nervous Sergei P. Pavlov, Stalin's in-terpreter. In a moment, a little man in black suit, gates-ajar collar, pince-nez, entered with a curious ball-and-toe gait and shook hands with me. It was Molotov and he looked and acted like the rather elderly head of an English public school, precise in his movements, his dress and his words, not an emotion color-ing his dead-white face, not a nerve that seemed to have a nerve ending.

He asked me, in Russian, if I spoke Russian. I did not and responded, *"Ya na panamiya russki."*

"Nyet," he said. *"Ya ni ponimayu parusski."*

He *was* a schoolmaster. Somehow that gave me hope. If he was going to chop off my head, I didn't think he would bother to correct my syntax.

We sat down and Molotov read me a thin-lipped lecture. He repeated his points several times, speaking very slowly as though talking to a simpleminded pupil in the back row.

When he had finished, he had said not one word that had not already been spoken to me by Dekanozov. Having decided that I might as well be shot for a wolf as a sheep, I made no bones about putting the blame where it belonged—on Dekanozov and the Foreign Office. We had done what was requested, quickly, courteously and exactly. Now they said that we should start all over again. All right, I had no doubt we would do as they wanted, but they should know that the results were not likely to win American friends. They would be stirring up a matter long settled and forgotten. I suggested the trouble might have arisen because of differences in American and Russian usages. We had published an apology and a correction of the type conventionally carried by the U.S. press. The wording he proposed was, perhaps, conventional in Russia, but it would puzzle and even antagonize U.S. readers. However, if they insisted, I was sure we could comply.

He then said we didn't have to publish the apology as Dekanozov dictated it—we could use our own language. And turning the discussion to general terms, he wanted to know how the Soviet Union could protect itself in the future from slander and libel—should they have recourse to the American courts? I didn't think this idea would fly, but I did not say so to Mr. Molotov. I told him the Soviet government was free to use all the facilities of American law to defend its rights, though I hoped this was not necessary.

After an hour of talk, I was dismissed. I felt that somehow I was not going to be expelled. Somehow we would come up with a solution. And I was now confident that the man behind all this was the Generalissimo. On Molotov's table there had been a telltale sheet of paper with notes in red pencil.

That weekend, UP carried the Dekanozov text. It was put on the national wires between 2 and 3 A.M., Sunday morning. I never saw a U.S. paper that carried it, but the text was delivered to Mr. Molotov and at 10:30 on Tuesday, March 7, I had a call from "the goon," as we sometimes called Palgunov. "Mr. Molotov considers the incident now closed."

For years, the Stalin affair was incomprehensible to me. Oh, I knew how it had arisen. A fine, patient, rather humorless UP man named Sam Hales from Oklahoma had been told the story by a Spanish diplomat in London. The diplomat said that during the Churchill dinner, Timoshenko had started to make a drunken speech. Stalin had quietly risen from his place, picked up a bottle, come behind Timoshenko and bopped him, causing him to shut up and collapse into his chair. Stalin went back to his place and said to Churchill, "I don't believe you have this trouble with your Field Marshal Montgomery." The story added: Field Marshal Montgomery neither drinks, smokes nor swears.

It was an amusing item. It got widespread play.

I knew the sensitivity of the Russians to suggestions of lack of culture. I could understand that Stalin could get mad at the insult (as it seemed to him). I could also understand that the incident fitted the pattern of Soviet prickliness which had developed in this winter of 1944. There had been a succession of things: *Pravda* printing a "rumor" from Cairo that the British were negotiating with Ribbentrop; Moscow telling off the *London Daily Telegraph* for a supposed slight; a gratuitous attack on a *Life* article that Wendell Willkie had written fifteen months earlier. Both Harriman and Clark Kerr had been needling the Russians about the Soviet press. So it could be a case of tit for tat, but it didn't quite feel that way. I still don't know the answer; it may even have been some premonitory reflex of the coming Polish quarrels.

It never entered my mind that there was a factual basis for the Stalin story. But there was. It was years before this came to light. My curiosity was first aroused in 1969, when I saw a paragraph in Harold Nicolson's *The War Years: 1939–1945*. Nicolson wrote of an exchange between Churchill and Stalin at Teheran which arose because "Timoshenko got dead drunk." "Do your generals drink so much?" Nicolson quoted Stalin as asking Churchill. "No," replied Winston, "but then it may be because they are not such good generals." Nicolson's editors footnoted that Churchill mentioned no such incident, but that Anthony Eden in *The Reckoning* told of a Kremlin banquet of December 20, 1941, at which Timoshenko had too much to drink and Stalin seemed a bit embarrassed. "Do your generals ever get drunk?" Eden quoted Stalin as saying. Eden remembered replying: "They don't often get the chance." That set me on the trail and I uncovered more recollections of the evening. Lord Cadogan, permanent under secretary of the Foreign Office, was seated next to Stalin that night. He recalled that Timoshenko got "rather tight" and that Marshal Voroshilov became uproarious and then "ominously silent." An aide-de-camp tried to get Voroshilov to his feet and he sprawled into Stalin's lap. Sir John Russell, then a very young foreign service officer, remembered Timoshenko becoming a "slobbering, hiccupping drunk and making a long, loud, incomprehensible speech." At one point, Russell told me, he and Voroshilov indulged in Indian wrestling, elbows on the table, clasped fists. Voroshilov licked him easily. Russell's friend Sir Frank Roberts, another junior participant, recollected an extraordinary amount of drinking, even for the Kremlin. He had no specific image of Timoshenko, but in the Indian wrestling, as he remembered, Voroshilov and Russell wound up on the floor and Voroshilov was removed "for repairs."

Had I possessed these delicious details, I would have put up a stauncher defense of the UP's dispatch—erroneous, to be sure, in some details though not alien to the spirit of the Kremlin banquets. Svetlana Alliluyeva, Stalin's daughter, and Nikita Khrushchev have given us vivid pictures of Stalin rendering his companions of the Politburo falling-down drunk, putting tomatoes on their chairs, compelling Khrushchev to dance the peasant *gopak*, slyly sipping white wine and carrying on private and deadly conversations in Georgian with Beria, conversations none of his colleagues could understand but which all of them rightfully feared. Stalin's anger over the story, it finally became clear, stemmed from the fact not that it was "a lie," as Dekanozov and Molotov said so often, but that it was too close to the truth. While the details were a bit skewed, it described precisely the kind of drunken brawling that went on in the Kremlin night after night. Once again, it was the truth—or a slight distortion of the truth—that had caused the trouble.

Sometimes it is better not to know all the facts about the person with whom you are dealing. If I had known who Dekanozov was, I would have been scared stiff. I did not know in February 1944 that he was a senior officer of the Soviet secret police. I did not know he had been inserted into the Foreign Office in May 1939 when Litvinov was ousted. His true role has never been exposed; not by Khrushchev in 1956, not by samizdat or the Soviet dissidents. Before May 1, 1939, Dekanozov was one of Beria's top police aides. Like Beria, he was a Georgian, and he had come up to Moscow with Beria when Stalin ousted Yezhov and installed Beria in his place as chief of police operations in 1938. Dekanozov entered the Foreign Office as number two to Molotov. His initial function was to direct a purge, the practical task of cleaning out men loyal to or associated with Litvinov and preparing the case that Stalin proposed to bring against his foreign minister. But this was not his only function. He occupied a special role in Soviet 1940–41 relations with Germany. Soviet diplomats who had handled the early contacts were, for the most part, weeded out and sent to prison camps or shot. Dekanozov was Beria's (and Stalin's) watchdog. He was sent to Berlin as ambassador after Molotov's frosty negotiations with Ribbentrop in November 1940, which should have given Stalin a clear signal that all was not well with his pact with Hitler. Dekanozov accompanied Molotov to Berlin for the talks and was sent back as ambassador because Stalin and Beria felt they could fully trust him.

Stalin formed the opinion that Hitler was a cautious man, but that his generals might stage a provocation designed to compel Hitler to attack Russia. At all costs, Stalin wanted to delay an attack until the spring of 1942. Dekanozov's instructions were to beware of provocations. The Berlin embassy had excellent information on the German preparations for attack. Dekanozov forwarded the information to Moscow, and in every case suggested it was part of a provocation.

On the weekend of the Nazi attack, June 21–22, 1941, so Moscow gossip had it, Dekanozov left the Soviet embassy on Unter den Linden and went to the country with his mistress. It was nearly twenty-four hours before he could be located. When he got back to Moscow late in July 1941, he feared Stalin might shoot him. He was summoned to appear before the Politburo. "Ah," said Stalin, "so here you are, Dekanozov—a real Russian man." He was forgiven and free to pursue his deadly career.

The story is apocryphal. Dekanozov was present in the embassy all day June 21, as a young aide, Valentin Berezhkov, tried again and again to get through to Ribbentrop, whom Molotov had ordered Dekanozov to see. Not until nearly 4 A.M., June 22, did Ribbentrop receive Dekanozov—to announce that Germany had gone to war against the Soviet Union. There was one element in the Moscow tale that was true. Dekanozov was with his mistress that weekend, as he had been ever since coming to Berlin. He had not brought his wife to Berlin. But his secretary accompanied him, his wife's sister—his mistress.

Dekanozov came back into the Foreign Office after Berlin. He was number two to Andrei Vishinsky, whose whole career was associated with the police. It is clear that from May 1, 1939, onward, the police apparatus dominated the foreign ministry—and would continue to do so until Stalin's death.

The full role, importance and evil of Dekanozov became apparent only after Stalin's death, when he was arrested and shot along with Beria and other high officers of the KGB.

I saw a lot of Averell Harriman during the "Stalin case" and I quickly learned that my London evaluation of him as a dilettante was wrong. He had a good mind, he was stubborn (I liked stubbornness), and his principal weakness at this point lay in the peremptory instructions given him by Roosevelt. I dropped by to consult Harriman almost every morning at Spaso House. He spent the first hours of his day working in his bedroom, the curtains drawn (they might as well be drawn, it was so dark in Moscow in February), night lamps burning beside his big bed, attending to urgent business in his dark silk dressing gown and red Morocco slippers. He had a fine young aide, Robert P. Meiklejohn, who had worked for him before he entered the government. Meiklejohn had been commissioned a navy lieutenant on coming to Moscow with Averell. I did not envy him. Averell could be testy at that early-morning hour (but never to me). Meiklejohn brought in the overnight cables, the news bulletin, anything he thought the ambassador should attend to. I would walk into this scene at 8 A.M. or even earlier and tell Averell what had happened in the Stalin affair, and we would discuss what to do next. He didn't want any overt involvement, yet he wanted to know exactly what was happening. We both felt it was an important barometer. Behind the maneuvers of Dekanozov and ultimately Molotov, something else seemed to be happening—we didn't know just what.

It must have been at the first of these meetings that Averell asked me to undertake a special mission. The Red Army Day reception was being held that evening, February 23. He wanted the correspondents to be on their best behavior because of the bottle-bopping story and because of something else. At the big reception on the November 7 holiday, the Russians had picked on Sir Archibald Clark Kerr as their target for the night. The civilized and experienced Clark Kerr was more than capable of handling himself, but he went down under the fierce assault of Russian toasts. Molotov himself had to be helped from the floor and taken to the emergency sobering-up station which was a feature of Soviet festivities at that time. He had his stomach pumped out, was injected with caffeine and sent back to the party an hour and a half later, very pale but able to navigate. The first aid facilities were not offered to foreign guests. Clark Kerr was carried home before midnight.

Harriman was certain that an American would be the objective of the Red Army festivities. He wanted me to warn my fellow correspondents of the danger, to encourage them to imbibe lightly. He said he possessed a case of Scotch whisky, just flown in from England. If the correspondents stayed on their good behavior, we would gather at Spaso House Saturday and privately drink to our hearts' delight.

Though I thought I already had enough on my hands, I agreed with reluctance to undertake the mission. I knew my colleagues, and I didn't think they would like Averell's message. They didn't. "Uncle Ed" Angly, the lively correspondent of the *Chicago Sun,* who had left his revered *Herald Tribune* because Mrs. Helen Reid thought him too old to cover the war, burst into wrath. No pin-stripe diplomat was going to regulate his drinking habits. Bill Lawrence simply said, Fuck him. David Nichol of the *Chicago Daily News* worried that the Russians would think we were not being polite. (It was true that the Russians believed you drank to get drunk and that it was a friendly act of hospitality to drink a man under the table.) Dick Lauterbach thought it wasn't a bad idea; he preferred whiskey to vodka. After a lot of banter, the correspondents agreed to watch it.

I didn't attend the party. At midafternoon, the Press Office called to tell me that in view of "events," my invitation was "not valid." I had to sit in my Metropol room and wait for a report from my colleagues. It came soon enough. Averell himself had been selected as the target. Molotov and Mikoyan toasted with him and then a group of wide-shouldered marshals and generals encircled him, each proposing an individual toast *do adna,* bottoms up. Averell found himself drinking five *rumki* of vodka to each one drunk by his hosts. The effects began to be felt. When the ambassador's plight was detected, staff members, the military attaché, General Deane, and Kathy Harriman sought to rescue him. But it was too late. He waved them off with an airy assertion that he was "aw right." By the time the rescue squad

broke through, their hero was past hope. As Lauterbach wrote in
Time magazine: "As the evening wore on, the Union Pacific's
headlights grew dimmer and dimmer."

Saturday night came and went. We never saw that case of
whisky.

Harriman's hope of avoiding involvement in the "Stalin case"
had a special foundation. He had been sent to Moscow in October
1943 with categorical instructions from FDR: Get along with the
Russians. He was to get them what they wanted, give them what
they needed; quit wrangling (as Averell's predecessor, Admiral
Standley, had been doing). No more bartering for concessions.
All out for the Russian war effort. Anyone who wasn't aboard
that mission could be shipped home. There were quite a few career diplomats—Freddie Reinhardt, Eddie Page, Maxwell
Hamilton, Tommy Thompson and others—who did not share
these ideas, but to Harriman an order was an order. He knew
what Roosevelt wanted. He knew that the U.S. embassy before he
came had spent more time fighting old wars with the Soviet than
helping win the present one. His instruction was to bring an end
to this. For this reason, he had no intention of becoming involved
in UP's difficulties.

Later on, much later, there would be a great deal said by Averell and by others about his excellent judgment and tactics in
dealing with the Russians. He became known as a man who took
their measure at a time when others did not. I accept a lot of
that, dating it, however, to a slightly later period. Not until
George Kennan arrived in Moscow in the summer of 1944 did I
notice any extraordinary perceptions by Harriman. Kennan
knew the Russians as no one else in my generation. He was appalled at what was going on. Of course, he wanted the Russians
to win the war, but he did not think it served our purposes or
theirs to spoon-feed Stalin. There should, Kennan said, be some
measure. The Russians should understand that we observe the
norms of international intercourse. We would make certain that
a free flow of supplies reached their side, but we wanted reci-
procity. Kennan would not have stood aside from the "Stalin
case" (and many others that arose in this period). He would have
laid it on the line. We were in the war together and precisely for
that reason we should observe standards of respect, fair play and
common sense in dealing with each other.

Harriman was jealous of his own access to Stalin. He had that access as he should have had, as he had had with Churchill. While Stalin was not totally dependent on the United States, the U.S. could make his task more difficult or less difficult. Stalin was a realist and he understood this. So of course Harriman had access. I was not certain that Harriman realized the leverage he possessed—a leverage that inevitably diminished, the closer the Red Army came to winning the war. Harriman didn't like others coming in and seeing Stalin. He felt Stalin could use them to whipsaw Harriman's diplomacy. There was something in that, but it was also the classic bureaucratic response: control access and you control all. After Kennan's arrival, Harriman proved himself a good learner. He had a long memory and, as it turned out, a long career, and he grew with the years.

I don't want to sound critical of Harriman. He was very good to me (except for not paying taxi fares; he never carried money in his pocket). I grew to like him and admire him, especially for the way he stuck to his last. He had grit and persistence. He believed in serving his country, and there are few men who have more earned their country's gratitude. He was not a terribly good politician, yet he was a good governor of New York. If he felt he could do a good job, he didn't mind working for men for whom he had less than complete admiration. That he demonstrated to John F. Kennedy's amazement. I happened to be with Averell on the April evening in 1960 when the results were coming in of the West Virginia primary between Kennedy and Hubert Humphrey. We had done a radio show and Averell invited me back to his house (he was living in New York then) to listen to the returns. As Kennedy's overwhelming victory over Humphrey began to pile up, Averell turned to his wife, Marie. "It's just shocking," he said. "You know what they have done. They have just used their money to buy their way. They simply bought that election."

The greatest tribute to Harriman was the fact that in his later years he became the elder statesman of America. He was respected by every President, by both parties, and not least by the Russians, who, I think, he finally came to understand as well as any public figure in America.

I expect I got more sophisticated advice on the "Stalin case" from Sir Archibald Clark Kerr than I did from Averell. Clark

Kerr was the only man I ever knew who wrote with a quill pen and took snuff, the eighteenth-century kind out of a little silver box, not the Copenhagen snoose of my Minnesota childhood. He trimmed the quills for his pens himself, kept them in a shot glass on his desk and dusted his letters with sand to dry the rich black ink. His letters are as splendid as works of Chinese calligraphy, written on stiff white paper. I think they will endure for five hundred years, difficult to read, but no matter. He had been in Chungking before Moscow and I never knew a correspondent in China who had not been his friend. That was true in Moscow too. He was the kind of man who put chicken huts in the backyard of his embassy and dug himself a vegetable plot outside his study, often coming in with his spade in one hand and his shirt slung over a shoulder to greet a Soviet diplomat dressed in his newest uniform. The Russians could not make him out. They finally decided he was one of the "mad Englishmen" of whom they had read in Turgenev, eccentrics who possessed extraordinary power and fabulous wealth—a duke, no doubt, masquerading under one of his lesser titles.

To correspondents like Lawrence, Lauterbach, Nichol, John Hersey (when he arrived), Edgar Snow (when he arrived), myself and a few others, he was Moscow's saving grace, a totally cultivated man who loved good talk, good drink and good food (this last the most difficult to find in wartime Moscow). We ran to him with our problems, our questions, our enigmas. He could not solve them, but he often convinced us they didn't matter that much. He told ribald stories about his Russian colleagues, his English colleagues, his American colleagues (he and Averell were not exactly chums), and about himself. He was married to one of the most beautiful women in the world, Maria Teresa Diaz Salas, a Chilean with Devonshire-cream skin and a figure that flowed into (and out of) gowns by Chanel and Schiaparelli. Naturally, she would not accompany him to Chungking or Moscow. She was twenty years younger than Archie, then sixty. He made brief, harassed trips to London or New York or Palm Beach for a glimpse of her. It was a quixotic arrangement which I never understood and I think it inflicted extraordinary pain on him. I thought Clark Kerr had absolute pitch so far as diplomatic judgment was concerned. I do not mean that he always understood the Kremlin. No one did. But he knew precisely what would happen within certain givens—the British response, the American, the Russian. I don't think, for instance, that he for a moment thought England or the United States would ever have a real hand in postwar Poland. He didn't mind fighting for a U.S.-British influence. He enjoyed sticking banderillas into Stalin's hide. But he knew what he was doing. He did not make the cheap mistake of confusing rhetoric with diplomacy.

Clark Kerr told me one of the most important things anyone has ever told me. We were at the founding conference of the United Nations in San Francisco in the spring of 1945. It was a wild affair, things constantly getting out of hand. Molotov had come in because Truman had got up such a head of steam there was no telling what Soviet-American postwar relations were going to be. Like almost everyone, I was bubbling with hope. We were laying the foundation of a new world. Never mind the static. No more war, no more Hitlers. Archie and I spent an evening together. We had a good dinner in one of the San Francisco restaurants which were never so good as they were in that spring of 1945—probably Charles Fashion's on O'Farrell Street. After dinner we walked through the San Francisco streets, one of my joys, talking about the world. He told me then that he would be leaving Moscow soon.

I was aghast. I knew that Averell would not be staying long either. "But," I said, "this is just the time you are needed most in Moscow. You have been all through the war. You know the people. You know what has gone on and who said what."

Archie smiled the gentle smile he reserved for sophomores.

"That's just it," he said. "It's time for a change. The war is over. Policy is going to change. We don't want anyone in Moscow who remembers what was said and done. That would just be an embarrassment."

I was silent for a long time, then I let out my breath.

"Archie," I said, "is it all going to come apart—is that the way it is going to be?"

"Yes," he said, "that's the way it's going to be."

He came to Washington in 1946 as ambassador. He was Lord Inverchapel now, happy in his honors, happy in being with his American friends. His marriage to Maria Teresa had been dissolved and we thought that would help. It didn't. The British ambassador in Washington must be a PR man, an operator, not a shrewd gentleman who writes with a quill pen and takes snuff.

We had formed an Archie Clark Kerr fan club to cheer him on, but we could see Washington was doomed for Archie. Lord Inverchapel stayed a couple of years and that was it. Back to Scotland, retirement and, I am afraid, unhappiness. He died in 1951.

I often think of our walk in San Francisco and what he said, particularly as the scholars argue about how and when the cold war got started.

21 | The Metropol

I had no special qualifications for covering Russia, none. I didn't know the language, I didn't know the history, I didn't know the culture, and I knew little more about the Revolution than I had heard from Nathan Rosen in that upstairs flat of the old Derickson house on Royalston Avenue. True, I was a good journeyman reporter, but on specifics I was blank. I had taken a course at the university in the Sociology of Revolution, given by a man named Pitirim Sorokin. Sorokin was an émigré with an accent so thick I could hardly make out what he was talking about. Principally, he seemed to be telling the story of his escape through Siberia, hiding in ditches from Red Army cavalrymen. I had no idea that he had been a leading member of the Kerensky government nor that he would go on to a distinguished career at Harvard. I had read *War and Peace* and I loved *The Cherry Orchard,* but I didn't suppose they had much connection with the Russia of 1944. I knew Walter Duranty's *I Write as I Please* and Eugene Lyons's *Assignment to Utopia.* I knew a bit about Lyons because he had been a UP man in Moscow and I had been impressed with tales about the hoard of art he was said to have brought back from Moscow, enough to start a gallery or found a fortune. He had made a good thing out of Moscow and written a best-seller.

Lyons had left as a monument a co-op flat on Furmanov Street in the Arbat, which he acquired for UP in 1933. Though the Moscow Soviet long since had taken over the building, Henry Shapiro had the flat; he couldn't live there because the pipes froze and burst during the winter of 1941–42, when he and the other foreigners were evacuated to Kuibyshev as the Nazis advanced on Moscow. It now stood, ceilings fallen, holes gouged in the walls, furniture damaged, uninhabitable, and so it would remain until it was reoccupied, unhappily, by Walter and Betsy Cronkite in the winter of 1945–46, when the snow in Furmanov Street reached up to their second-floor windows. That was the winter Virgil Pinkley in London refused to authorize a car for Walter (every other correspondent in Moscow had one). Pinkley's factotum, Clifford Day, suggested to Walter that "perhaps you should get a bicycle; many of the men in London find them quite useful." Walter cabled: "Get me out of here." I was UP's foreign editor and I did. Soon he left UP for greener fields.

The Moscow assignment before the war had gone, for the most part, to men who acquired towering reputations, like Duranty or Lyons or Louis Fischer or Max Eastman or William Chamberlain or the *Berliner Tageblatt* man, Paul Scheffer, or eccentrics like the incomparable Malcolm Muggeridge or the improbable Alfred Cholerton of the *Daily Mail,* whose beard found its way into every Moscow book of the time, sometimes described as purple, sometimes as white, yellow, salt-and-pepper, pink, red and even mauve (there were some who attempted to correlate the color of the beard with the politics of the author). These correspondents were men of ideological orientation, strongly pro or strongly con, or as often happened, strongly pro at the start and strongly con at the finish. They were men of political opinion, dedicated to the causes of the left and the right. They took militant positions on Lenin, Trotsky, Bukharin, Radek and Stalin, whom some knew quite well in the early days.

Our crowd wasn't like that at all. We had a few whose roots went back a way. Maurice Hindus of the *Herald Tribune* had been born in Russia, in the Jewish Pale of Settlement, and his dream was to return to his native village in Belorussia once it had been liberated, a dream I believe he never fulfilled. Maurice had electric hair, like Jascha Heifetz. He could talk for hours about Mother Russia. He believed in the Russian peasant and black bread and the Russian potato. He bought potatoes and black bread in the market, boiled the potatoes on his electric hot plate and ate them with *smetana*. Perfect food! Maurice bubbled enthusiasm for Russia, for the peasant, for the potato, for the future, for the past. He had been coming to Russia for years, then going back to the United States and lecturing at colleges and women's clubs. College girls and clubwomen swooned over him.

Alexander Werth carried on a bit of the old tradition too. Born in St. Petersburg, the son of a Jewish industrial family, he had lived most of his life in Paris. He reported for *The Sunday Times* of London, a languid, Chekhovian man who could spend all day in his big Metropol Room 393 (which I inherited in 1949), playing Chopin on a Bechter grand, lost in dreams of Pushkin and Lermontov, fiercely jealous about Leningrad (his city, he felt), impractical, often currying favor with the Soviet officials. After the war he abandoned Moscow and his Moscow companion, a Scotswoman named Marjorie Shaw. Marjorie was ill, out of a job, penniless, despondent. The Press Department in their only act of kindness I ever knew cared for Marjorie, saw that she got medical treatment and helped her return to Scotland.

We had no other links to the tradition of Moscow correspondents and we did not need them. We were not there to cover the Romanov past, the glories of Tchaikovsky and Tolstoy, Turgenev, the Revolution, Communism, nor even the horrors of Stalin, the purges, the camps or the police. We were there to cover the Red Army. At one of my first meetings with Palgunov, he told me: "We do not recognize the institution of war correspondents." By which he meant we could not go to the front and be assigned to an army headquarters as we could with other fighting forces.

For as long as I was in Russia, I railed against these restrictions, and so did my companions. We got nowhere. But in fact, we were given extraordinary facilities for seeing the Red Army and occasionally, in spite of every precaution of the Press Department, we encountered guns being fired in anger.

Under restrictions I considered unconscionable, I traveled almost constantly—to Smolensk, Leningrad, Kolomna, Kharkov, Dnepropetrovsk, Odessa, Kalinin, Zaporozhye, Simferopol, Yalta, Poltava, the Urals, Siberia and Central Asia. Not too bad for a stay of seven and a half months. I saw places no one had seen for generations and would not see for more generations. It was like having Pandora's box opened for your pleasure. Yet I was not pleased at this access. I was outraged. Like Oliver Twist, I kept shouting: "More!" I wanted to stay at the front. My visits were usually limited to four or five days or a week. I demanded to go to the actual lines of fire. I was escorted by young men and women who were more concerned about my not getting killed than not getting a big story. I made my views known to every Soviet official with whom I came in contact. So did my colleagues of the A group, as I thought of us.

None of the A group were experts on the Soviet Union, none of us, so far as I knew, were ideologues. (I have always thought that it was my own fierce antagonism toward ideologues and ideological orientation which caused cold war men like Eastman,

Lyons and assorted ex-Communist anti-Communists to lambaste me so fiercely. They lived in an ABC world. If you weren't dedicated to the destruction of the Kremlin, you must be defending it. News reporting and facts didn't interest them.

Well, we didn't come up against much of this kindergarten logic in 1944, except from the Russian side. If we were fighting the war together, the Russians said, why do you insist on putting in those "bad things"—i.e., references to secret police, arrests, shabby treatment, Soviet mistakes, ruthless diplomacy, the Katyn case, persecution of the Poles . . . The list was endless.

I thought of myself, just as my best friend Bill Lawrence thought of himself, as a hard-hitting, two-fisted, call-them-as-they-come reporter. Bill and I were all for the Red Army, all for winning the war, all for beating the Germans; we did not, however, think this gave the Russians a right to pretend, for instance, that their Supreme Soviet was a parliament; that they had freedom of politics or press or any right to lay a censorship on us. We fought them every step of the way, and my experience with the "Stalin case" hardened my conviction that the Soviet government (as distinguished from the Russian people) was two-faced, lying, cheating, impossible. I made no effort to conceal my thoughts, although I did not always insist on calling a spade a goddamn shovel, as did Bill. I was working with journalists whom I respected, admired, men who were my professional peers. No more the inferiority qualms of London. Russia was a story I could handle. Bill Lawrence had been my friend since the morning he walked into the Washington UP office in 1935, fresh from covering the auto workers' sit-in at Flint, the only reporter inside the plant, whiling away his time like the workers, making blackjacks. He came into Washington on an American Airlines pass and announced he couldn't decide which assignment he would take over—the Senate or the labor run. Bill, I think, was twenty-three. Lyle Wilson sent him back to Detroit. "You need more seasoning, young man," Lyle said. Three weeks later, he brought him back and put him on the labor beat. Now Arthur Krock had given Bill a job on the *Times.* I had seen him off in London for his Moscow assignment, one hundred pounds overweight, sweating in his air force sheep-lined leather flying suit (it was a lovely late September day), Arctic flight boots, pockets stuffed with whisky, cartons of cigarettes and black-market-steak sandwiches from Jack's Club. Sandy was under the impression there was no food in Russia and he did his best to supply Bill for the duration. Lawrence drank more than any two of us. One night in Leningrad, we carried him back from a banquet, got him upright in the Astoria's revolving door, caught him as he fell out the other side, and then, I am afraid, dragged him up two flights of stairs, his head bumping on every tread. He survived that and he even survived a drinking contest with "Mike" Kalugin, the party boss of Novosibirsk, *katushas* (vodka with a champagne float, in a champagne glass) *do adna*. Kalugin collapsed after his fourth. The triumphant Lawrence downed a fifth and fateful glass. Kalugin was restored by the local resuscitation squad. Lawrence was out for the evening.

Lawrence was the best hard-news reporter I ever met, a bear of a man, lusty, the darling of the Katinkas. He never missed a deadline and he got more scoops than anyone I knew, and that includes Scotty Reston. He was tough, arrogant, overbearing, tender, and as sentimental as a puppy. AP had fired him because at the age of nineteen, covering the Nebraska Young Democratic Convention in Lincoln, Lawrence got so excited he took the floor and made a speech. AP said reporters must not participate in stories they cover. UP thought it was a great stunt and hired him. Bill hated Communism but he loved the Russians. He fired the *Times* string correspondent in Moscow, Ralph Parker.

Parker had been taken on by Cy Sulzberger. For years, Parker had been the London *Times* man in Eastern Europe. He had covered Prague and the Nazi takeover at the time George Kennan was in the U.S. legation there, and then had gone to Yugoslavia. His wife was killed by a Nazi bomb during the fall of Belgrade, and Ralph narrowly escaped with his life. The London *Times* sent him into Russia on one of the dangerous Murmansk convoys. Once in Moscow, he acquired a vivid Russian woman named Valentina as his translator. Valentina had married an American black named Scott, who took refuge in the Soviet Union during the Depression. She had two girls by him, one a lovely youngster who wound up in the Bolshoi corps de ballet. In no time, Parker had flipped from Tory to Soviet sympathizer. He continued with the London *Times* until the end of the war, then switched to the *London Daily Worker* and stayed in Moscow for the rest of his life. When I arrived in 1949, I found him nervous, depressed and, I thought, on the edge of a breakdown. He was in the process of selling off his library and tried to persuade me to hire Valentina as my translator. One morning very, very early, one of my friends saw him coming down Lubyanka Hill. I don't know whether he was coming from the Foreign Office or the KGB across the street. He was white as plaster. My friend took care not to be seen, but Ralph's eyes were so glazed he would hardly have recognized Stalin himself. A day or two later, I was at dinner with him, Valentina acting like a fiend. At one point she stood up on her chair, walked down the dinner table, jumped off and vanished. Ralph had been trying to get a visa to attend a peace meeting in Glasgow. But actually, he said, he wanted to get to England because his mother was dying. My impression was that he wished, at any cost, to get out of Russia. He had applied, vainly, for an exit-and-reentry permit. Now he couldn't even get an exit visa. He had had a lot to drink that night and kept turning to me: "Don't you think *The New York Times* should publish a story about the fact that the *Daily Worker*'s correspondent can't leave Russia? Don't you think that's a news story?" I thought it was, and thought, too, that it would finally fix the cart of this tormented man caught between —what was he caught between? Had he really gone over to Communism? Was he really a dedicated party agent or did this all spring from the emotion of the war, the tragedy of his wife's death, and a fatal infatuation with Valentina, who was gradually turning into a witch. I couldn't decide then and I can't now. A few months later, Ralph published a shoddy anti-U.S., anti-British book which purported to expose the machinations of the British and American embassies—Harriman, Walter Bedell Smith, Clark Kerr and all the rest. Ralph had paid his dues; he became much more relaxed. One of the targets of the book was the English military attaché, General George ("Pop") Hill, with whom Parker had been very close in the war days. Hill, red-faced, bow-legged, head bald as a stone, had survived adventures as a British agent in Russia in 1917, and came back in World War II in the same role. I was never entirely convinced that Parker, like many before him, was not linked to MI6 as well as to the KGB. If so, small wonder at his concern in the spring of 1949.

A complicated man, Parker. He died in 1970, never at ease in the twilight land he inhabited. In the end, I felt very sorry for him, but during the war I despised him.

I hadn't known Dick Lauterbach before Moscow. He was tall, dark, handsome, a Dartmouth man, spoke some Russian, and reported for the Luce publications. He was twenty-eight years old and brilliant. I envied him. He had all the tickets, all the things I didn't have. He wrote well and he took pictures. Picture-taking in Russia was a high-risk occupation. You never knew when you might be arrested. We were standing in a great square in Odessa one morning, Dick photographing passing people, when we saw, a quarter mile away, a cavalry patrol headed for us at full gallop. "Christ!" Lauterbach cried. "We're in trouble. Those guys have seen me taking pictures." He tried to get his camera back into its case, but the horsemen bore down too fast and clattered up with a sweep of gravel. They carried carbines and sabers. In an instant, one was off his horse and striding toward us. He threw us a salute and said: "*Pozhalista*, please, take our pictures?"

Dick had come to Moscow via Vladivostok and the East, he had traveled in Russia in 1935 and had a better background than any of us. We were devoted to him—Bill, myself, Jim Fleming, David Nichol, Paul Winterton of BBC, Ed Angly, Alec Kendrick of the *Philadelphia Inquirer*—all of us, like him, members of the A group. When correspondents are thrust together on a running story like the Russian assignment, a bonding process occurs instinctively among those with a similar approach to the news. I mention this because later on I think it was claimed that Dick held opinions to the left of ours. Nothing like that was apparent in 1944. After the war, he spent a year as a Nieman fellow at Harvard, traveled to the Far East for *Life,* wrote a book, and then went to work for *PM* and its successor, the *Star.* Each of these papers slid more and more to the left, as did the *Star's* heir, the *Compass.* Dick did not join the *Compass.* He had some notion of starting a "penny press," whatever that might have been. Nothing came of it.

I think that of the eighteen of us who ended up in the Metropol in 1944, Dick was the one with the most talent, the most promise. I knew nothing of his background, but I thought he had the world before him—family, children, a super job, the kind of cool intelligence, judgment and enthusiasm that should take him anywhere. Like all of us, Dick had problems which he shut away. He worried about Tina, his wife, who was, I understood, a handful, too much drink, too much temperament. That sounded familiar. I thought of Dick as the scion (I still don't quite know what "scion" means) of a well-to-do New York family, with money, social position, prestige. Well, I guess that wasn't quite true. His father had lost his money in the Depression; and it never occurred to me that Dick was Jewish. When we got back to New York, I realized there was something seriously wrong in his family life; much worse, I thought, than in mine, though when I went a few times to their house, on East Eighteenth Street, that was not evident. I considered them a very New York family with very New York problems.

Dick and Tina had traveled together to Russia in 1935. She was still at Smith and Smith girls were not allowed to marry before graduation. So they married secretly in Moscow, very romantic, and only a few knew it. I guess, from what friends have said, that Tina at some point joined the party; I can't see Dick as a party man, though. He was radical, but he possessed an iconoclastic mind; with his sharp wit, he was a better critic than claque. I can't see him following a party line, whether it was Communist or capitalist. He liked too much to disagree. That was one of his attractions.

When I got my FBI files, I noticed with irony the entry: "in correspondence in fall of 1949 with Richard Lauterbach." I had written precisely one letter from Moscow to Dick, in October. Uncle Edgar was watching.

What is important is not Dick's politics but Dick's life. It slowly turned into tragedy. He and Tina had moved off into a kind of no-man's-land before I ever saw the two together. He stood by her because he didn't believe she could make it alone— and what would become of the children? Not an original dilemma, but a tragic one.

One Sunday evening in early September 1953, Dick rode back from Amagansett, where he had spent the weekend with Tina and the children. His life was locked in a vise. There was no way of resolving his marriage, he had come to a cul-de-sac in his career. He had left *Life,* he had left the *Star,* he was engaged on a biography of Charles Chaplin and he didn't know whether it would work out. His handsome face was drawn. His best friend drove him into the city, full of worry about Dick. There seemed to be no exit from the cordillera into which life had driven him. Four days later, Dick was dead. Thirty-six years old, three children, three books, creator of beautiful reportage, just coming into his full powers. His friend, who had been at his hospital bedside when he died, at 2 A.M., got to his office later that morning. His secretary said a woman had been calling. She would not give her name, but asked him to come up the street to a hotel, where she would be waiting in the lobby. The friend hurried to the hotel. A woman rose and approached him. "I know you," she said, "but you don't know me." It was the woman with whom Dick had been totally and hopelessly in love, a woman of whose existence his best friend had no idea.

I was in Moscow when I heard that Dick had died, and I was desolate because I had not seen him before I left New York. It would have made no difference to him, but it made a lot to me. "I just can't imagine Dick dying and in such a way," I wrote a friend. Polio, so they said. I think "of an impossible life" would have been a better verdict.

Life at the Metropol was a little like living in a prison run by the Mad Hatter. We had adjoining rooms, we ate together, traveled together, drank together, we suffered together and fought together, we knew who slept with whom and who didn't and when the partners changed.

I used to say that you could put a blindfold on me and set me down anywhere in the Metropol and I could say where I was by sniffing—which floor, which corridor, which room. I knew the rank humanoid smell of the fifth-floor dormitory, the scent of the raspberry-tinted wax put to the floors by the polishers (they did it with soft rags tied around their old carpet slippers), the wood smoke of the courtyard, the doggy odor of food being cooked by the Uzbek couple on the third floor, the vodka fumes seeping around the locked door of the Japanese consul, the gaseous cabbage cooking on the fourth-floor back corridor, the acid polish applied to the brass rails of the second-floor skywell, the rancid grease of the elevator shaft. The Metropol was a museum of smells and I knew each one.

It was the same with the inmates. We knew each other well—too well. We all knew that Jerome Davis, the tall, elderly correspondent for some obscure U.S. agency, a man who had first come to Petrograd in 1917 with a YMCA prisoner-of-war mission, was so stingy he charged his secretary for the bread and butter he saved from his Metropol meals. The rest of us gave our surplus food to our secretaries and couriers, who got only a No. 3 ration, bare subsistence. Everyone knew that Jerome had collected German wine bottles on the Leningrad battlefield and brought them back to Moscow, where he made his secretary sell them in the black market at ten rubles apiece. We knew he had got for nothing from a church rector the German-occupation marks he sold to GIs at Poltava for a dollar a bill.

I knew all about the life of Natalie Petrovna Rene, because she told me, dropping in of an afternoon for a glass of tea in Room 346. Tall, terribly thin, fortyish, very Russian, she worked for Hearst's International News Service. Mr. Hearst was forever being attacked by the Soviet press. "How does it affect my position?" she would ask tragically. Not at all, I would reply. After a particularly vicious attack by a magazine called *War and the Working Class,* she came into Room 346 late in the afternoon. It was already dark. She announced: "I have spent the afternoon in the cemetery. It is very quiet there and very beautiful and very sad. I always feel much better when I come home from the cemetery." She had been a young secretary to Eugene Lyons in November 1930, when one day he asked her to telephone Stalin and say he wanted an interview. It couldn't be done, yet, she told me, she telephoned Stalin's office, and the next day Lyons got his interview—the first Stalin ever gave to an American newsman. Now Natalie was filled with worry. Her husband had vanished at the front in the first weeks of war. She thought he was dead. Her mother thought he was alive. Natalie was living with another man. But suppose Rene was alive? As it turned out at the end of the war, he was, but everyone was civilized, Rene got a divorce, Natalie married her lover. That didn't end it, though. Soon the new husband was arrested and shot. Natalie turned her back on love, threw herself into what had been her hobby—the study of ballet—and became Russia's leading balletomane.

We knew each other's lives. When Raymond Arthur Davies, a particularly obnoxious Communist correspondent for some Canadian paper, cooked up a scheme, we knew about it. He put ads in Canadian papers promising to make inquiries about families in the U.S.S.R.; send a dollar, enclose your address, the names and addresses of your relatives. Who knows how many dollars he collected before turning the names over to the International Red Cross, to handle as they saw fit? If Mike Handler, my UP colleague, knocked Henry Shapiro down and threatened to choke him to death (because Handler believed Henry had tipped the authorities to the name of the girl with whom he was having an affair), we knew every detail. If Harold King of Reuters, a bull terrier of a man, got into a brawl with Shapiro and tore down the only map from the wall of the Foreign Office pressroom, we knew and enjoyed it. As we did Harold Hooper's goodhearted effort to get Henry and Harold back on speaking terms. Harold was King's assistant and he thought it hurt our image with the Russians. "At least you could preserve the amenities," said Hooper. Finally, King and Shapiro agreed to resume speaking. "Nothing more than hello," King insisted. One evening the two met at the Press Department to handle the evening communiqué and, as arranged, nodded and murmured a polite "Good evening." Next morning at breakfast, Hooper eagerly inquired how it went. It had gone all right, King growled. Then an idea struck him. "By God!" he said. "I'm on speaking terms with Shapiro." He grabbed the telephone, called Shapiro's number and said, "O.K., Shapiro—now that I'm on speaking terms with you, I just want to tell you what a son of a bitch you are."

Everyone knew that Eddy Gilmore, the AP correspondent, lived barricaded in his fifth-floor room and would not emerge for fear someone might steal Tamara, the beautiful fifteen-year-old (well, I guess she was seventeen by this time) whom he had taken away from an English tobacco buyer, knocking the man to the ground and carrying Tamara up to his chambers like a knight of yore. And why shouldn't he protect this Dresden doll—hadn't he got Wendell Willkie to intervene with Stalin himself when the Moscow police sent Tamara back to chop wood at her grandmother's log hut, fifty miles outside Moscow? True, Eddy couldn't marry Tamara, because his wife in Washington refused to divorce him. Eddy lived behind his barricade in the corner room, on guard. I can't prove that Eddy would have killed anyone who tried to take Tamara, but I think he would. The barricade was no ordinary one. It was built of canned goods, bags of flour, of sugar, of powdered milk, and other comestibles. Once a month, a shipment of foodstuffs was trucked over from the U.S. military mission for the correspondents. It went straight to Eddy's room and he presided over its division. A lot of us gave up our shares so that the families—Gilmore's and Shapiro's and a few others—got a more ample supply. Not until Stalin died were Eddy and Tamara able to sanctify their love with marriage and was Eddy able, at long last, to bring his bride back to his hometown of Selma, Alabama. Tamara died a few years ago and the papers said she had been a Bolshoi ballerina. Ballerina she wasn't, but Russia never produced a more exquisite fifteen-year-old.

It was in the Metropol, in the UP's Room 346, that I met Konstantin Simonov. His was one of the few Russian names I knew, already famous around the world for his novel *Days and Nights,* the story of the battle of Stalingrad, an instant and huge best-seller. (There would not be another Russian best-seller in the U.S.A. until Pasternak's *Doctor Zhivago* in 1958.) Simonov seemed, somehow, not terribly Russian. He was handsome, almost like a movie star, with a serious, rather businesslike expression. He smoked a briar pipe and had a drink of Scotch. I don't know where the Scotch came from, but Simonov was lucky. The next day, a Red Army general dropped in who was crazy about what he called *Amerikanskoe vino.* He drank it by the glass. After his visit, the bottle was empty.

It was an incredibly busy period for Simonov, as I later learned from his wartime diary. He had been continuously at the front and he was just back from the trial in Kharkov of German war criminals, a trial attended by many of the American correspondents. He was spending two or three weeks in Moscow, turning out a movie script of *Days and Nights,* then returning to the front. I was excited. I told Simonov I had seen his play *The Russians* in London and liked it (although not wildly), and I had just seen it at the Moscow Art Theater, where I thought it was better acted. In London, one of the two Nazi officers was played as a well-meaning weakling manipulated by his comrade, who was bent on raping and murdering a young Russian army girl who was his prisoner. In the Art Theater version both officers were black as the devil. I don't think I got my point over; Simonov spoke no English, I no Russian, and he had other things on his mind. Half a dozen correspondents dropped in to say hello. Ludmilla had known him since before the war, when both were students at the Gorky Institute, he a year ahead of her. She and Olga worshiped him. They thought, as did most Russian women, that his poem "Zhdi Menya," "Await Me," was a talisman. Written in the first terrible weeks of the war, the verse simply says, "Await me—and I shall return," a prayer by a soldier that his girl be faithful, and if she is he will come back to her, he will live. And the same pledge by her. In the early war, when millions were dying, Simonov's lines gave faith that all was not lost, that there was hope the loved one would not die. Russia lived by that poem, lived by it until the turn at Stalingrad in December 1942, and then went on living by it because the men and women of Russia went on dying every day until the last day of the war.

This slim, reserved young man—he was twenty-eight when I met him—had contributed as much to the war as anyone, far more than many of Stalin's generals, the cronies and the putrescent police generals.

I did not know all this the day we met, a sunny February day at the Metropol, but I learned a lot from Ludmilla.

Konstantin Simonov, a serious man in 1944, a serious man all his life, had worked so hard at the Gorky Institute, Ludmilla said, that she and her friends called him *zhelezny zad*—ironbottom. He sat down at his desk and wrote, wrote, wrote for hours. He did this until he died, at sixty-two. I saw him half a dozen times, I suppose, in 1944, but only once on one of our front trips. He moved in higher circles. He was on intimate terms with Red Army marshals and generals, had been before the war and would be after it. Stepson of a czarist colonel, Simonov always seemed a soldier in his bearing. His first battle experience had come before the start of World War II. In summer 1939, the Japanese attacked the Mongolian frontier at Khalkhin Gol and a major engagement built up. Stalin sent General (later to be Marshal) Georgi Zhukov out to teach the Japanese a lesson. He did, inflicting a smashing defeat that kept them off the Russians' backs during the desperate years that followed. Young Simonov, known for his poetry and a play or two (Stalin had said of Simonov's first love poems that they should be printed in his-and-hers editions), was sent to cover the fighting. It was a dress rehearsal for what was to come.

Simonov was at the front from the first days of war to the last. God knows how many tens of thousands of words he wrote, every one of them loyal, true to the government, true to the party line; not slavish potboilers, however, they always painted the soldier's life accurately, honestly, precise in technical detail. Countless times, his own life was at risk—in patrols behind the German lines, gunboat expeditions through Arctic ice, the trenches of Stalingrad. He lived as a Red Army man, and if he was the most famous war correspondent of his time, the Ernest Hemingway of the eastern front, if his dispatches were published in New York and London and Chicago, if his articles appeared in

Collier's and the *Sunday Pictorial,* you could not have guessed it
by his conduct. I don't know how many Stalin Prizes he won
(and Lenin Prizes when they changed the name after Stalin's
death), including one for a very bad anti-American play which I
saw at the peak of the cold war. (I think, perhaps, he regretted it
later. He would have been the last person to claim he had made
no mistakes.) I would agree with those in Russia who said at the
end of his life that he was an honorable man. After his trip to the
United States in 1946, I saw nothing of him for many years.
When I went back to Russia in 1949, he, like every political and
literary figure I knew, would have no contact with me. I was
poison, branded, like all U.S. correspondents, as a spy by the Soviet government. The penalty for contact with a spy was prison
or execution.

Simonov had become a favorite of Stalin's during the war.
After the war he was still a favorite. Yet in the despicable campaign against Jews (the so-called drive against cosmopolitanism)
his name does not appear. He must have had some part in it—
after all, he was a secretary of the Writers' Union—but I don't
think he signed any denunciations and he did not sign any lists. I
know that he made the best amends he could. He earned millions
of rubles (and not a few dollars) in royalties and prizes. No
writer in need ever left him empty-handed. He helped many
when they could get no work in the last Stalin years. Not a word
about this ever escaped his lips. He was generous, compassionate
and private. That is not said of many Soviet literary figures. An
honorable man—to be so judged in Russia is rare. In recent
years, some have written bitterly about him. I do not agree with
those who have accused Simonov of being a trimmer, a lackey for
Stalin, a careerist, a panderer. He was a brave soldier. He risked
his life for his country again and again. It is true that he did not
denounce Stalin during Stalin's lifetime; who did? He did not
speak out—so far as I know—against the arrest of the members
of the Jewish Anti-Fascist Committee and their execution in
1952; who did? He was not sent to camp and he was not executed.
I cannot condemn him for escaping this fate. There was a mea-
surable difference between Simonov and such a man as Aleksandr Fadayev, another secretary of the Writers' Union, who
did name names and sign lists and who after Stalin's death took
his life in remorse. Simonov was a Soviet citizen who lived
through one of the darkest ages of his country. It is easy for

those who did not experience the Russia of those days to hurl stones and epithets, and even easier, perhaps, for those who did. Those who survive are not always kindly toward their fellow survivors. The fate of a man in Stalin's Russia was a complicated one and I think Konstantin Simonov's conduct speaks for itself.

After Stalin's death, Simonov became editor of *Novy Mir,* the finest literary journal in Moscow. He launched the post-Stalin literary renaissance, publishing Dudintsev's *Not by Bread Alone.*

He might be called a premature anti-Stalinist, and his liberal course cost him his editorship. He abandoned Moscow, went to Central Asia, and on his return devoted himself to writing about the war, the central theme of his time.

In these years I saw Simonov occasionally, but we were not close. I did something that lies on my conscience. I borrowed his externals, his face and his wartime poems, and gave them to a disreputable character named Smirnoff in my Leningrad novel, *The Northern Palmyra Affair.* Simonov read the novel and said to a friend: "Why did Salisbury do that to me? I never did anything bad to him." He was right. It was my laziness, not any antagonism, that caused me to steal his dress and mannerisms.

In the 1970s, we began to correspond. We wrote about what was on our minds, a good deal about the war and Russia. We worried about the peace and the future and relations between our countries. I had not been able to get a visa to Russia for many years, but in the summer of 1979 I was going back with a group of writers. We looked forward to a reunion, but a few days before my arrival, Simonov died of a heart condition. His wife—his third wife, that is—Larisa Zhadova, his beautiful daughter, Alexandra, and his son by his second wife, Alyosha, had not yet returned from the funeral. Simonov had been cremated and they took his ashes to the great battlefield at Mogilev, the first battle of the German assault on Moscow, which Simonov covered, a battle fought on the site of Czar Nicholas II's headquarters in World War I, not far from Borodino, the battle of the Napoleonic war. There his ashes were scattered over the soil, so steeped with Russian blood. I could not think of a ceremony more right for this man who wrote with a gun strapped at his side. I considered it apt that he should have died soon after the publication of his wartime diary, *Razni Dni Voiny,* "The Days of the War." These were excerpts with his commentary. He had refused for years to publish it because he could get no assurance that it would be printed with his observations on the traitorous scandals at the early stages of the war. Again and again Simonov declared he would only publish the bitter with the heroic, the criminal with the glorious. Permission was always refused.

In the end, Simonov did not win his battle for unconditional publication, yet he came close enough to leave no doubt of what he saw, what happened and what he thought. He was confident, I believe, that in time to come the uncut pages would see light.

In 1967, he put down on paper his appraisal of Stalin and the duty of the writer and the historian to his country. His views were incorporated in an article which he called "The Lessons of History and the Conscience of the Writer." It was directed to writers of both fiction and nonfiction and was accepted for publication in the October issue of the historical journal *Voprosi Istorii*. He called on writers, "with all the blood in their hearts," to write the truth, nothing but the truth, about Stalin's crimes, to face the facts of the deadly blows struck at the Red Army by the purges, by the murder of Defense Minister Marshal Tukachevsky, the Soviet general staff and most of the Red Army's officered corps on the eve of the war. He analyzed the climate created by Stalin's conduct and how it affected public opinion and the surviving military leadership, and paid tribute to the army and the people for fighting on to victory under such a heavy burden. He gave writers the task of recording the story of Russia, regardless of consequence, for, as he said, failure to heed history is to make oneself prisoner of its tragedies. This was the testament of the man who had been called Stalin's favorite.

In that most hoary of Russian traditions, Simonov's courageous words were suppressed by the censors. *Voprosi Istorii* was forbidden to print them. They have survived thanks only to samizdat, preserved in those badly inked copies for the benefit of future generations of Russian patriots.

22 | Death in the Family

By June I had practically settled into Moscow for the duration, London drifting off toward the horizon. I was still London manager for UP, but I didn't think I would ever return. I had heard nothing from Ellen since I left her in the Scottish fog, and little from the United States. There was no word of Shapiro's return. I had become part of the Metropol world and half the time I was away with the Red Army. I crossed the Ukraine and crossed it again. I had never seen mud so deep, no bottom at all, thousands of German trucks, tanks, gun mounts, troop carriers lost in the *chernozöm,* the famous black soil. But the Red Army was moving—on foot, on horseback, in carts, in *telyagas,* peasant wagons, by old buggies pulled by horses, mules, donkeys, cows, oxen, an occasional camel and many snorting farm tractors—a helter-skelter movement, relentlessly westward. Nothing would stop them, and I thought the quickest way to Berlin was to stick with the Russians.

We went to the Crimea, the Germans finally driven out, corpses bobbing on the rock shore of the slim peninsula where the last stand was made, and over the stony land the Limburger stench of putrescent bodies; heavy, it got into your clothes, it clogged your throat, it hung in the air like plague. Here I inhaled the essence of war. I saw the pig-bellied bodies, eyes starting out of rotting heads, flaxen hair like wigs on a Kewpie doll, and the smell of piss-clotted uniforms, pants cruddy with excrement, with the pale worms of intestines, dirt, slime, paper, paper everywhere, brown-stained toilet paper, brown-stained newspapers with their Gothic print, broken bottles, jagged edges sparkling in the sun, rusty cans, the sleek white wood of ammo boxes, coppered coils of machine gun bullets, unmailed postcards, photos of girls stained with blood, here a splintered bone, the flesh torn like cotton rags, orders, commands, penalties, sentences (a sergeant sentenced to be shot; he had been apprehended trying to copulate with the captain's mare on the village street), surrender leaflets, bits of green grass and dandelions, stinking fish floating in the gentle waves beside corpses gas-filled, buttons burst from faded green uniforms.

The Crimea did it. I had seen the winter corpses at Katyn, at Leningrad, in the Ukraine. Death in winter is clean. The bodies freeze in rigid forms. There is little stench. Except for the horses. The horses were the worst, winter or summer. They blew up like titanic counterfeits, the eyes still alive with terror. Snow quickly covered the winter dead. Now in the Crimea the dead were omnipresent.

German prisoners with dead eyes stumbled among the corpses, carting them off to endless trenches under the tommy guns of sullen Red Army men. I could not tell whether either Russians or Germans knew what they were doing. The Germans moved like sleepwalkers. The hardest thing, they told us, was the moment of surrender. Unless you were in a big group, a hundred or a thousand, you didn't have a chance. The Soviet tommy gunners just mowed you down. The Nazis had been waiting for the boats to take them off, the boats that never came.

This was war and now I understood it. War was the garbage heap of humanity. It was shit and piss and gas from the rump; terror and bowels that ran without control. Here Hitler's Aryan man died, a worse death than any he devised in the ovens of Auschwitz, anus open, spewing out his gut until a Red tommy gunner ended it with a lazy sweep of his chattering weapon.

When I came back to Moscow, I went on long walks with Olga. It was the only way we could be alone. She told me about her father and his dreams of the Revolution and how the arrests had begun. He hadn't been a Bolshevik, but he backed them. He was a good engineer. Then they came for him. He was held in prison awhile and finally exiled to Kazakhstan. He died there before the war started, no medical treatment for his heart attack. Olga was her father's daughter and she had never got on with her mother. It was hard enough living with her mother, and harder when there were seven families sharing six rooms, including old ladies who had lost their minds and wandered about at night. Olga liked to tease me about being an American, the way I walked with long, swinging strides. She said she could always tell Americans, they walked so freely, heads up as though they could go anywhere and do anything. Russians, she said, walked with heads down, shoulders hunched, slow steps as though they were carrying roped burdens.

We spent an afternoon at Zvenigorod, a village beyond Moscow where scientists lived. One of them was Peter Kapitsa, a physicist. I knew his name because Bob Musel in our London bureau was a nut on heavy water. He was sure scientists somewhere—Germany, Russia or the United States—were going to split the atom and create a terrible weapon. Kapitsa, he said, was a man to watch. He had been a physicist at Cambridge University and then had gone back to his homeland. Olga pointed out his simple, log-built dacha, but we didn't glimpse him—already, perhaps, busy on Russia's A-bomb. A peasant woman invited us into her kitchen with its brick scrubbed floor and gave us milk and *tvorg,* cottage cheese. We walked in every park in Moscow and found out-of-the-way corners where we could embrace. I began to understand a bit about Russian life. We visited a Russian sculptor named Vera Mukhina, a strong, serene woman whom Olga admired. She created remarkable *cris de coeur* against war, which she draped in canvas when her distinguished clients—members of the government, academicians, generals—sat for their busts. She had done Stalin and Lenin and the symbolic figure for the Soviet exhibition at the 1939 New York World's Fair. There was nothing, I thought, of Russia's agony which this woman had not endured. I did not understand how she could live, an official sculptor glorifying the men who were creating a world she hated. I had not seen enough to know how many Russians lived two lives, the external life of obeisance and the internal life of revolt. I didn't care for Mukhina's son, a member of what was called Moscow's "golden youth." He collected gold coins and U.S. dollar bills, the bigger the better. God knows what he was accumulating money for. When I came to write *The Northern Palmyra Affair,* I remembered Vera Mukhina and gave some of her character to my heroine, Irena Galina.

Olga told me how she had grown up, hunting and fishing with her father whenever she could. She still belonged to a hunting club and took me to a store near the corner of Neglinnaya and Petrovskaya. Even though the war was on, the store had beautiful chased shotguns and hunting rifles, fishing rods and lures, on its shelves. The warm chestnut stocks and the filigreed engraving reminded me of my father's gun. Only members of the hunters' clubs could buy these lovely things. We dreamed of going to the mountains for trout (I had never caught any trout in my life), knowing we never would.

Sometimes Olga talked about her days in school. The teachers were terrified of their pupils, who might denounce them to the party. Many students in the art classes never learned to draw, understood nothing about anatomy and had hardly heard of perspective. They were too busy going on "practical field trips," where boys and girls could get off alone together.

Constantly Olga worried about her brother, Mitya—Dmitri—now nineteen, handsome like his father, with a fresh grin, a high school boy who had lied about his age and volunteered for the Red Army at sixteen. "It is spring," he had written. "The sun is burning hot and the birds are singing. Don't worry about me. I swear to you that everything will be all right and we will meet in Moscow."

That was April. Now it was June. Every day Olga (and her mother) lived an age. So far, Mitya had only been lightly wounded. He was in the artillery, fighting on the Belorussian front. Everyone knew the war was nearly over, but everyone knew that the casualties went on and on. Wounds were not the only peril. An NKVD officer wanted to recruit Mitya to the secret police. They needed fine, brave youngsters like him, he said. Mitya had to avoid recruitment without offending the officer. Otherwise he might be sent to a *strafny* (punishment) battalion. The *strafny* battalions moved ahead of the troops to draw the German fire, enabling the regulars to avoid machine gun nests and artillery. The *strafny* men were made to walk the minefields, exploding the mines with their own bodies. When I told Olga about the youngsters blowing up mines on the Leningrad front, she asked immediately whether I had seen any machine gunners to their rear.

I promised Olga that when I left Moscow she could have my Arctic parka and my fur-lined boots for Mitya.

I had come to Moscow for three weeks, a month at most. I could leave at any time. Mike Handler could carry on perfectly well. But I didn't want to go. I hated the Russian bureaucrats, I hated the Foreign Office, I hated the censorship, the police, the meanness, the whole system. I thought the Red Army was a miracle. This was *the* war and this was *my* story, and I was in it for as long as I could stay in. And I didn't want to leave Olga.

I knew, all of us knew, that the Russians and the Americans were building bomber bases in the Ukraine for shuttle operations. Soon my old friends of the air force, those still alive, would be coming over from England and Italy, bombing Germany on the way, landing in the Ukraine, loading up and bombing again on the way back. It would double the weight of the air war and, it was hoped, persuade the Russians to give us bases in eastern Siberia, to finish off Tokyo. The American air arm was now a tremendous weapon, two hundred or three hundred planes to a mission; soon it would be a thousand or two thousand. There was no way the Germans could halt them. The epoch of Dresden and Hamburg was at hand. I could hardly wait for the U.S. planes.

And something else was up. Eric Johnston, an old friend of Bill's and mine, head of the U.S. Chamber of Commerce, was coming to Moscow. He had been promised a tour of areas in the Urals and Siberia no one had seen. Lawrence and I and Lauterbach, Eric promised, would go with him. We would have stories that would set the world on end—so I thought.

We had talked with General Deane, head of the Military Mission, privately, and everything was set, he thought, for the American group to cover the shuttle operation. I got a call at about 1:30 A.M., June 1, from the Press Department. We were leaving for Poltava at nine in the morning. I called Bill. He had heard nothing. I called Lauterbach and Nichol. Neither had had a call. Something had gone sour. Only six Americans, it turned out, had been told they could go. We staged a revolt against the Press Department, and all the correspondents, the A group, the B group, even those we called the Gastronom correspondents, the ones who had press cards just so they'd get rations, stood firm. We all went or no one. I never saw the Russians so angry. I was delighted as a child. Off we went to Poltava, all of us, in the glorious spring weather, the Ukraine a garden of blossoms, apple, peach and cherry, flowers everywhere, crackerjack American bases, jolly Russian girls, cheerful GIs, cheerful Red Army men, a joy, a model of what the two countries could do when they tried. Three separate air bases had been built in four months. Harriman flew down. So did Kathy, General Deane, a bunch of Russian generals. There was a concert and dancing that evening, GIs dancing with Russian girls, even GIs dancing with Russian boys.

We spent the next morning talking to GIs. The army had picked them with care. Many spoke Russian. You could not have assembled a better bunch of young Americans.

At about two in the afternoon, the Forts came in, flying against high cumulus clouds building up in a vast blue sky. Almost as soon as we saw the planes we heard their roar. They passed overhead and there was a spit of rain when the first touched down. The formation moved in lazy circles as the ships came in, one by one, with mechanical precision.

"I don't know when I have been so proud to be an American as at that moment," I wrote in my journal. It was true, it was very heaven, the American flag in the light breeze, the great silver Forts, the precision, the American fliers. The next morning we flew over the countryside at chimney level, from one base to another, talking to Americans and Russians. The air was so fragrant, the GIs couldn't get over it. "Russia!" one said. "Nobody ever told us it was pretty." I couldn't remember when I had been so happy—not since the war started, not since I had come abroad, not since I had got to Russia. Everything was coming out right.

On the evening of June 5, I was sitting on my bunk in the railroad car which was our barracks, typing out hometown stories about GIs, when Tex McCrary walked in. I had known Tex in New York when he was writing editorials for the *Mirror*. Now he was PR for General Eaker and he had just come back from a quick run up to Moscow. He handed me a note from Mike Handler. Mike reported that a cable from New York had come in. It said that Dad had had a stroke and his condition would be uncertain for twenty-four hours. I sat on my bed and tried to take it in. Mike didn't say when it had happened. I was thousands of miles from Minneapolis and there wasn't even a communications base. I couldn't send a cable until I got back to Moscow. I sat on the bunk and closed my eyes and saw Dad at Christmas, 1942, playing with Mike. Dad was so worn and frail. He had walked out of 303 North Barry Avenue and I felt I would not see him again. I put my arm around his shoulders and said that he must, just must, take things easy so that he would be there when I came back. What a fatuous remark! Finally, I climbed into my bunk, lay down and after a while slept. We had to be up at five in the morning for the B-17s' takeoff. I felt lousy when I woke, but I made it. The takeoff was just as smooth as the landing. I had some coffee and came back to the railroad car, took out my Remette and wrote a V-mailer to Dad and one to Mary. I didn't know anything about Dad's condition, but I knew, I positively knew, that if he was alive when my letter got there, he would not die. I would write every day. As soon as I got to Moscow, I would find out how to get to Minneapolis. I could keep him alive and I would keep him alive. It depended on how many days it took for the V-mail to get from this miserable base in south Russia, halfway around the world, to Minneapolis.

I was sitting at my typewriter when Jerome Davis came in. Of all people in the world, he was the last I wanted to see at this moment. Jerome was panting. "Say, boys," he said, "I've got some big news for you. The second front has opened. They're landing in France." I glared at him, hardly taking in what he said until he repeated it. He didn't have a detail. Christ, I thought, I wonder whether it's true. I didn't trust Jerome to get things straight. This time I was wrong. The Allies had landed in Normandy. We heard it on a whispery BBC broadcast. "Funny," I wrote in my journal. "So that was it. I didn't feel very elated." I went over and talked to a Russian girl who was chopping wood. David Nichol told her about it in halting Russian. She looked up. She was a fine husky blond girl with muscles that made my arms look like chicken wings. "You heard it on the radio?" she asked. We nodded. *"Khorosho"*—O.K.—she said, and went on chopping wood. It was like that. The second front had started and Dad was dying and I was a long way off. I picked up my V-mailers and took them to the post office. Later that day, we flew back to Moscow. There was a lot of shouting around town, but I didn't go out on the street. Some of the boys went over to the Moskva Hotel to celebrate. I didn't. I sat and talked with Handler awhile. Could I get back to the States? How to go to Minneapolis? He showed me the cable about Dad. It was dated June 3. Nothing happened the next day. No news. Eric Johnston, in from Washington, was full of bubbles about his trip, about taking us along, about seeing Stalin. He went off to the theater and we had dinner with Averell and Kathy and talked until 12:30 A.M., very relaxed. Next day the cable came. Dad had died about the time Jerome Davis was telling us we had landed in France.

The days that followed were full of talk and intrigue connected with Johnston, his meeting with Stalin and the great tour. Johnston had got in June 1, expecting to see Stalin and start immediately on his trip. This did not happen. Delay followed delay. He was the guest of Mikoyan, who approved our going on the trip, but the Press Department said no. Johnston went to Leningrad and all hell broke loose. Some correspondents went with Johnston, some with a separate trip arranged by the Press Department; all returned in a rage. They had hoped to visit the Finnish front but didn't. The Press Department talked about going back to Leningrad on a third trip. I had one peaceful weekend. I went for a cruise on the Moscow-Volga canal with Eric. We lay on a sandy beach in the sun and got tanned. We had a picnic lunch, spent the night on board the boat and didn't get back to Moscow until Monday morning. I was still in a state of shock. I blamed myself for abandoning Dad, for leaving the country, for going off to the war. I was plunged into guilt. I had left Dad, I had left Mary, I had left Mike, I had left Ellen in London, and what was going to happen next? I would leave Olga in Moscow. My mind whirled like a top.

I went to bed a bit early one night in my dumpy little Room 264, on the courtyard, next door to the Chinese Central News Agency correspondent. I lived on the same corridor as General Ulrich, the judge in the purge trials. God knows what he was doing in these days with no purges going on (so far as I knew). Olga had pointed him out to me in a whisper. He was a man of medium height and medium age, with cat's eyes, a cat's smile. Though he had a bland Russian bureaucrat's face, a face that was shaved every day in the Metropol Hotel barbershop, behind that blandness there was something else, the ghost of a cat's grin, a cat that knew things it would never tell. He smelled of eau de cologne, something like the Florida Water my father used, and there was a touch of talc on his jowls. He carried a neat black leather briefcase, a bureaucrat's briefcase, not a schoolteacher's. It showed no wear. I often thought about the papers he brought home to his hotel suite, down the corridor on the Theater Square side (Sverdlov Square, as they called it now). His room was at the corner, very convenient. He could see the Hall of Columns, where he had presided over the trials of the greatest men of Russia, just across the square, and by looking up the hill he could see Dzerzhinsky Square, where stood the Lubyanka, with its basements in which the men had met their end. General Ulrich was a neat man, careful in his clothing, precise in his timing. You could set your watch by his departures and arrivals. I never saw anyone chat with him. I never saw him ask the *dezhurnaya* for his key. I never heard the maids mention his name. He passed through the corridors and was gone, leaving no trace except, at least in my mind, a hint of evil and a vague scent of cologne.

On this particular night I had gone early to bed. I could not get my father's gray face out of my mind nor the guilt out of my heart. I lay there, windows closed (it was mid-June but chilly), curtains drawn around my bed in kind of a great womb, a silk puff, a comforter, pulled up as I read—what, I do not know—my thoughts far away, fluttering to Minneapolis, to Mamaroneck, to London and back to Moscow, ranging over the building blocks of my life that I had piled up so carelessly, one on one. Finally, I fell asleep. I awoke quickly. I had gone to sleep with a cigarette in my hand and it had dropped to the puff and begun to smolder. (I smoked a lot in those days, a cigarette before I got out of bed in the morning, a cigarette before going to sleep.) I leaped from bed and flung the puff into the bathroom adjacent to my bed with its velour draperies. I threw some water on the bed where the cigarette had burned through a sheet to the mattress. I shook the puff, put some water on it. No sparks. I left it in the corner, pulled a blanket over the mattress and went back to bed. I don't know how long I slept this time, but when I woke there was smoke in my nostrils and flames leaping up the drapery, too fierce to fight. I threw on my trench coat, dashed out of the room and raced around the corner and across the second floor to the *dezhurnaya,* asleep, head on arms. I shook her. I didn't know the Russian word. "Fire! Fire!" I cried in English. She blinked. I grabbed her by the arm and ran back to the room. She took the door handle and pulled it. The fire was locked in the room! I thought I would go mad. I had no Russian, she no English. I ran up to the third floor and awakened Olga. By the time she got to the scene, the woman had come to her senses and roused someone; the fire was put out.

In the morning, I could hardly bear to inspect my room. Everything had been destroyed, I was certain. But when I went back to 264, I found that nothing of mine had been damaged except a few shirts. The bed was a wreck, a mirror stand had been burned, the draperies ruined, and two rugs damaged. That was it. The contents of box number one, which I had shipped up from Teheran filled with vodka and toilet paper, the contents of box number two, filled with canned tomatoes, grapefruit juice, cigarettes and a lonely bottle of Angostura bitters—all was intact.

I had been lucky. I was more a wreck than was the room. Olga had got me through the night by making tea, joking about my appearance—my hair standing straight up, the terror in my eyes—and holding me tight. I was not consoled. Everything, I now concluded, was coming apart.

23 | On the Road

After melodramatic scenes, a personal plea to Stalin by Eric Johnston (against Averell's advice: "It's the sort of thing I wouldn't do; they're good boys, but sometimes they push the Russians too hard"), we got word at a midnight press conference at Spaso House that despite a flat no from the Foreign Office, Stalin said we could make the dream trip with Johnston. Sometimes I got fed up with Eric. A small, dapper man who bounced through life like a tennis ball, perpetually campaigning, dashing to play volleyball with a bunch of NKVD men, making us sing a woeful "Three Blind Mice" because the Russians had entertained us with a haunting "Stenka Razin," a cut-up high school kid with girls (but perpetually frightened the Russians would slip a lusty *blondinka* into his bed)—all these things got on my nerves, yet he was probably the only man with the gall to ask Stalin to let us go with him. Of course, Eric had his own reasons. The trip was part of a long-range buildup, looking to a postwar Republican presidential candidacy.

So at 6 A.M. of a breathtaking June morning (only in the north are there such June mornings), we found ourselves standing outside the Metropol waiting for a car to take us to the airport. A babushka with a white scarf over her gray hair and a white apron over her black skirt was hosing down the sidewalk. We were in the way. She gave us an angry squirt of her hose and we were off.

Yes, the trip was as fabulous as I had imagined. We saw two industrial centers in the Urals, Magnitogorsk, the iron and steel city which had been thrown up in the early thirties by young Komsomols, including sympathizers from the United States— among them Edmund Stevens, our colleague in Moscow for the *Christian Science Monitor*—and Sverdlovsk, a steel and machinery complex. Under its earlier name of Ekaterinburg, the city had entered history as the scene of the Bolshevik murder of Nicholas II and his family. We were not taken to Ipatiev House, where the execution was carried out. Eric thought it wouldn't be tactful. We saw Novosibirsk and Omsk in Siberia, Alma-Ata, Tashkent and Samarkand in Central Asia. Our journey imprinted on

me an understanding of Russia's space, her variety, her contra-
dictory nature, and the perversity of the system, which gave me
a benchmark by which to measure all the other Russias I would
see. I felt as though I had pulled back a curtain and scrambled
into a world I did not know existed, one that had little to do with
what I saw in Moscow or on our trips to the front. It was not so
much the specifics and the facts I collected (many of them striking); it was the degree of deviation between the real Russia and
the facades of Moscow. I began to sense how much of old Russia
lay hardly hidden under the new Communist dress which Lenin
and Stalin had hastily and carelessly tailored. It was a lesson to
last a lifetime.

And there were the mysteries. We traveled in two planes. Ours
carried the four correspondents, caviar, vodka and other rare
comestibles from Moscow, china, silver and table linen and a
waiter—all from the National Hotel. The other carried Johnston;
his aide, Joyce O'Hara; the embassy agricultural attaché; William L. White, a writer who had attached himself to Johnston in
Washington; Mikhail Nestorov, head of the Soviet Chamber of
Commerce; a man named Kirilov from the Foreign Office, and
an interpreter.

After the stop at Magnitogorsk, we boarded our plane on another glorious spring morning. I recorded what happened in my
journal: "June 26 11:15 A.M. left Magnitogorsk for Chelyabinsk.
Arrived 12:50 P.M. Thought it was Chelyabinsk. Then found out
it was Sverdlovsk." Nobody had bothered to tell us; nobody said
why.

At Omsk, it was announced that we would not be going to
Tomsk; "the schedule was too heavy." Tomsk was the old Siberian capital, which so far as I know has not been visited by a
Westerner for fifty years. It was a thriving city in the seventeenth century and boasts one of Russia's oldest universities.
Our last stop was to be Samarkand, Kublai Khan's capital in the
fourteenth century. When we got to Tashkent, Samarkand was
scratched. The airport was too small for our planes. After two
days of argument, Samarkand was put back on the itinerary. We
went by train.

I suppose the changes related to security. The trip had been
laid on for Johnston. The addition of four pushy correspondents
changed the mix. We were apt to stick our noses into things
Johnston wouldn't notice.

Behind the scenes, something else was going on, some intrigue which never quite came to the surface. Johnston had been invited because he was a backer of aid to Russia. He supported a proposal Roosevelt was toying with for a six-billion-dollar postwar lend-lease package to help the Soviet Union get back on its feet. Stalin needed that six billion. He made no bones about this. He told Johnston that the U.S. would have a bad depression after the war. How much would be required in Soviet orders to keep American factories going? Eric said he didn't know whether there would be a bad depression or a mild one. Well, Stalin said, he thought that American businessmen ought to get together and figure out how many orders they wanted from Moscow to avoid a depression. Why are you doing this? Eric asked. Well, Stalin said, you have helped us and we want to help you. It was his way of stating a quid pro quo for the six billion.

But perhaps it wasn't that simple. Perhaps there were those, and Stalin may have been one of them, who were not sure that they wanted the postwar aid or that the United States was prepared to give the help without attaching conditions Moscow wouldn't accept. The Soviet press had been irritable since Teheran, querulous and nit-picking. In spite of the second front and the Poltava bases, an undercurrent of tension persisted. Johnston had had to wait nearly three weeks to see Stalin.

At Omsk, two "reporters" had shown up, claiming to represent Tass and Moscow Radio. They questioned Johnston about what kind of long-term credits Russia could expect and what, after all, a long-term credit was. (Eric said it was up to twenty-five years.) Their questions made me think someone was nervous— maybe Stalin, maybe someone who didn't want the Soviets to rely too much on the United States.

Then came the incident at Novosibirsk. The central figure in this was party boss Mikhail Kalugin, the man Bill Lawrence had drunk under the table. Kalugin said he was forty-four years old, but he looked a rock-muscled thirty-two. He possessed enormous energy, claimed to have fought in the civil war and said he had learned to slash White Guard officers through to the ass with his saber. That was the best way, he said, almost frightening Bob Magidoff to death by adding that he knew very well Bob had been a White Guard officer. (Bob was an émigré from the Jewish Pale of Settlement.)

After we had been in Novosibirsk a couple of days, Kalugin came into Eric's suite in the party dacha we occupied on the bank of the river Ob. Saying he had a memento for Eric of his stay in Novosibirsk, he tossed on the plush-covered table a large white envelope. Inside, Eric found a series of smaller white envelopes. He opened one and out rippled a handful of diamonds. He opened another and it was full of rubies. Another held emeralds. And so on. There turned out to be, I think, fifty-four gems, precious and semiprecious.

Eric told Kalugin it was too much—he couldn't take the jewels. Mike affected to be insulted. "I sized you up," he said imperiously. "I figured out that this gift was about what you should have. I have all the wealth of Siberia at my command." He refused to take back the stones. Eric could throw them in the river or dump them in the ocean, but he mustn't return them.

Eric made several efforts to give back the jewels, but each time Kalugin flew into a tantrum. Finally, the morning we left, Johnston tried a zany gambit Bill White had thought up. Eric appealed to Kalugin on the grounds of party discipline. He said he knew Kalugin would obey any order the party gave him. Kalugin agreed. Eric said he, too, was a member of a party, the Republican party, and under its discipline, he was forbidden to accept the gift. Kalugin was deeply moved. He yielded to this argument but said he would keep the jewels until Johnston returned to Siberia. Party lines sometimes changed. Perhaps someday Eric could take the gift. And he would not be the loser. The jewels would grow in value with the years.

While this charade was being played out, Kalugin delivered an ominous toast directed at "false friends," those who seem to be friendly but betray their friendship. The Russians, he said, knew how to deal with such traitors. They rose up in righteous wrath to strike down anyone guilty of treachery. Johnston thought this was the stick that went with the carrot of the jewels.

Perhaps it was all part of Stalin's game. Though he had done well at Teheran, it would not have been in his nature to accept such results at face value. If Roosevelt (and Churchill) had been so accommodating—what was their real game? Wasn't this a moment for more caution, more suspicion than ever? I think that lay at the root of the charade.

No one among the diplomats—not Harriman, not Clark Kerr, nor even American specialists like George Kennan and Tommy Thompson—appreciated the density of Stalin's suspiciousness, the genuine paranoia that was there. It didn't show in their talks with him. He was all business, often very tough, sometimes amiable, always on top of the subject, always in control. Everyone knew he had shot the generals, the Old Bolsheviks, confined millions to prison, but of the men dealing with him, not Churchill, not Eden, not Harry Hopkins, not Roosevelt, not one had been able to take the full measure of Stalin's derangement. No hint of this appeared in the World War II memoirs, or in my conversations with Harriman and the others who dealt with Stalin constantly. Not even Kennan, with his exquisite insight into Russian psychology, grasped it.

I think Kalugin was a man following orders from Moscow. He was not the princely viceroy of a neo-Cossack Siberian empire, as he portrayed himself and as, I confess, I half thought at the time.

The jewels left behind nagging questions. Where did Kalugin get them? I do not believe he had a stash in the party safe in Novosibirsk. That would not be the Russian way of doing things. The gems must have come with us on our plane, along with the caviar and the National Hotel waiter, and handed over to Kalugin with his briefing by one of our escorts, possibly Novikov, the Foreign Office man.

Two Americans had visited Novosibirsk before Johnston. One was Donald Nelson, head of the War Production Board. The other was Vice-President Henry Wallace, whose party had left the city only thirty-six hours before we arrived. In fact, I saw them take down Wallace's name and put up Johnston's on the door of the principal suite at the dacha. What about Nelson and Wallace? Did Kalugin offer them a selection of "all the wealth of Siberia"? Did they turn him down? There is no way of finding out; now both are long dead. One more thing: As Kalugin left the plane, having said goodbye, I saw him slip a white envelope into Johnston's pocket. I wonder what was in it.

There is the conventional Russian footnote. Kalugin seemed to me the most impressive Soviet boss I had met. He had Novosibirsk at his fingertips. He spent more time shaking hands with grease-covered workers and pretty girls in the factories than in escorting Johnston. He was a tough, loyal, energetic, imaginative party man. He was arrested soon after the war and released only after Stalin's death, and he died a broken man in September 1956. God knows what "plot" was made up about him—foreign espionage, stealing Siberian jewels, smuggling them out by Americans?

From beginning to end of our Siberian odyssey, Dick Lauterbach suffered from diarrhea. When our plane took off from Novosibirsk for Alma-Ata, a great basket of the sweetest, reddest, ripest strawberries I had ever seen had been put aboard, carefully done up in a damask napkin. Lauterbach had to use the plane's facilities. He came back shuddering, and said: "This is Russia. A basket of the most beautiful strawberries in the world and the can hasn't been cleaned since the trip started."

We got back to Moscow in midevening of July 9, the city still bright in the long days of the summer solstice. We had traveled something over ten thousand kilometers. It had been, I noted in my journal, "the greatest reporting trip which had ever been in the Soviet Union." That was a brag. I added more realistically: "We had seen a lot of Russia. I think we know a good bit more about it."

That was it. I did know a good bit. The journey had been difficult—eighteen-hour and twenty-hour days, on the move, taking notes until my wrist ached, absorbing impressions until my brain ached, vodka banquets every night—but it had been good. It had taken my mind away from my father's death and the shock of the fire in Room 264.

I went up to the office and found Olga pale and silent. She threw herself into my arms and silently began to cry. I knew what it had to be—her brother. He had been wounded. Her mother had just got the gray card. I held her and told her I loved her. What more could I do? I tried to tell her it was not such a bad thing. Mitya was wounded. He was not at the front. He would be in the hospital for a long time. He would not go back to the war. By the time he was recovered, the war would be over. Olga didn't say anything. She looked at me like—well, I thought her eyes looked like those of a doe that has been shot and is slowly bleeding to death. That was how my imagination ran. We sat for a long, long time and said nothing, just holding each other. I was so tired I could hardly sit up. Finally, Olga sent me off. "Oh, yes," she said. "There was a cable. Henry is due back next week."

I don't know how we got through the next two or three weeks. Olga was a ghost. She thought of nothing but Mitya. There had been a note from his commander saying that the wound was serious and that Mitya had been taken to a base hospital. I tried to convince Olga that now he would get better treatment. She sent packages of food. I gave her my vitamins, my sulfa drugs and chocolate. I tried to get some penicillin sent up from the Persian Gulf Command. Yes, I knew this was done for my conscience and Olga's too. But doing something, anything, is important when the reality is more than you can bear.

Henry came back and I began making arrangements to leave. Moscow was coming to an end. I had the miserable business of settling with the hotel about the fire. They submitted a bill for 19,315 rubles, almost four thousand dollars at the official rate of five rubles to the dollar. And the Foreign Office notified me that I must pay the charges before they would permit me to leave.

I didn't have four thousand dollars. I told the hotel they were trying to drive me to bankruptcy. Finally, I turned the whole thing over to Henry. He knew these people; somehow he had to get it fixed. I had promised to give my parka and my boots to Olga for Mitya. It was a terrible moment. How was I going to raise the money for the Metropol? And Mitya had taken a turn for the worse. I was half mad. So was Olga. We sat in a dark corner of the Metropol and talked and talked. At last, we made a kind of child's agreement on what to do. Olga would buy the boots at the black market price (God knows how). She would sell my parka and my civilian suit in the black market and I would keep the rubles. I would give her my woolen socks, shirts and underwear for Mitya. I would give her the enormous case of toilet paper I had lugged up from Teheran for my fellow correspondents (the shortage had been relieved before I arrived). She would sell it, we hoped, for enough to pay for the boots several times over, not as toilet paper but for rolling cigarettes. (*Pravda* sold for three rubles a copy for this purpose.) She could make millions. We both laughed.

One hot, dusty August afternoon, Olga and I slipped away from the Metropol. We took the metro to the Arbat and walked through the old streets and up Ulitsa Furmanova to the flat Eugene Lyons had acquired for UP. It was just as I had seen it in winter—ceilings sagging, walls broken, furniture in dust wrappers. We made a little nest for ourselves in a bedroom, and shutting out the disarray of the flat and of our minds, the war, the sorrow, the foolishnesses of fate, time, circumstance, place, spent an afternoon within a world of our own creation. We had known from the start that something like this lay ahead, but as the months passed we had forgotten what was going to happen. I had begun to talk of coming back to Moscow when the war was over. Henry was restive; I knew that he had been thinking of returning to America (he did so in 1945). It was not entirely illusory to talk of returning, yet it was hardly realistic. This day, we put every thought of the future and of the past out of our minds and lived for two or three hours in a present in which only the two of us existed. At the end of the afternoon, we locked the door behind us and went back to the Metropol.

On the night before I was to leave Moscow, I sat all evening in Room 346 with Olga, holding her cold hand in quiet, desperate rage. I did not have the money to pay the Metropol bill. Henry was downstairs negotiating with the manager. From time to time he would come back and report that they would not budge. I would say, well, then I can't leave. This game of idiots went on until sometime after midnight, when Henry finally came upstairs with a new bill. The hotel graciously had agreed to pay "half" the costs. With some money Henry lent me, I managed to pay this bill. It was too late to go to bed. My plane left at 5:45 A.M. I had to be at the airport by 3:30. That meant leaving the hotel at 2:30 A.M. Olga would not come to the airport. I left her at the hotel, almost unable to talk, crazy with worry over her brother and anguish at my leaving. I do not remember going out of the hotel, getting to the airport. The last thing I told Olga was that I would come back to her. Did I believe that? Today it is hard to think that I did. It had to be wishful, romantic, fuzzy thinking of the kind that was characteristic of me. I always seemed to be leaving a girl, going on to some other place, creating the impression that I was coming back and believing that I was. But inside, some nodule of realism told me I wouldn't. I was addicted, I now know, to half-true, half-hopeful illusions that glistened like bubbles and were about as durable. Did Olga believe me? Yes. She had fallen in love in spite of good sense and her father's precepts, in spite of her humor, her cynicism toward men. She believed it. There was nothing else to believe in.

I did not know nor did Olga on that night that Mitya was dead, that he had died a month earlier. Not for many months would I hear of this and that Olga had gone to the Caucasus to try to patch her life together. I did not know how she had thrown her life up for grabs; I did not know the truth of her agony. Perhaps I still do not.

It was not a happy flight. I was sick with shame, burning with sorrow and overcome with a malaise I had never experienced before. My destination was Teheran, then New Delhi, beyond that, Chungking. It was a long, demanding journey. Travel arrangements were catch-as-catch-can. I had not felt well since coming back from the Johnston trip. One night I had gone to bed early because I felt so tired, yet I could not sleep. My heart seemed to be pounding like an express engine. I got up and walked about. That felt better, but when I lay down, the pounding came back. I decided I must be having a heart attack. I got to sleep about three-thirty. The next night it was the same. I feared I had smoked so much it had affected my heart. I was so nervous I could hardly sit in a room. I had to get up and walk around, to be on the move. On the plane to Teheran, strapped in my bucket seat, I felt the symptoms again, and the next day, at Camp Amirabad, I determined to find out what was wrong. There was a hundred-foot swimming pool at the camp, fed by icy mountain water. I decided to plunge in. If there was something wrong with my heart—well, let it stop. If not, the hell with it all; I would pay no more attention. I dove into the pool, swam a fast breast stroke to the end and back. I felt fine. I came up out of the ice water shaking my head, and began to consider my symptoms.

I remembered that just before I had left the States for London, I had been ill. When I was about to leave London for Algiers, I had come down with a high fever. I remembered that when I was a Boy Scout in summer camp, I had hated the idea of an overnight hike and came down with "appendicitis," which vanished after my tentmates had left. There was no use trying to kid myself. It was my mind, not my body. Then I picked up a *Reader's Digest* in the officers' lounge and read an article about "fliers' fear," suffered by wartime pilots. Sometimes it was called "anxiety neurosis." That was me. I felt much better.

I managed to oversleep and missed my flight to Abadan. When I got to Karachi the next day, I found myself directed into a transit barracks the size of a football field, maybe a thousand men, waiting for orders, waiting for transportation. I was supposed to go on directly to New Delhi, but my priority did not come through. I spent forty-eight hours as comatose as the other thousand comatose men, lying in a bunk, dozing, doing nothing, not reading, not writing, my mind filled with baroque thoughts. I might spend weeks or months in this anonymous place where I knew no one and no one knew me. I had drifted into a backwater of war. The camp was a Sargasso sea in which men broken on one front, assigned to another, drifted from horror to horror; men who had lost touch with reality, with themselves, with life, drowsed in their bunks for weeks. After a day, I began to pull myself together. I met several officers from Merrill's Marauders, who were being sent home the slow way. They talked of the bloody disasters in Burma. One captain had been on Guadalcanal and told about the "mercy" killings of Japanese. He knew a man who had chopped off a hundred heads. I thought probably he was that man. My journal notes: "They were swell kids, all of them." I was losing touch, trembling on the edge of this human swamp. I got up, went to the office, got my travel orders and flew to New Delhi. There was news for me. Joe Alex Morris, my friend and superior, was leaving UP to become managing editor of *Collier's*. I was to return to New York immediately and take over his job; at last, a real promotion.

There was no way I could go on to Chungking. I had tried in Moscow to fly the back-door route that led through Alma-Ata, Urumchi, Lanzhou and on to Chungking. But the Press Department took special joy in denying a favor to an American correspondent for whom they had no love. General Robert E. Wood flew into India just then on an inspection mission for General H. A. ("Hap") Arnold, chief of the air force. Wood had a C-54 at his disposal and it had the range—barely—to fly from India to Australia. If I could hitch a ride with him, I could come home via the South Pacific, see MacArthur and the war against the Japanese. General Wood had no one flying with him except a couple of aides. He was delighted to have my company.

I spent my time in New Delhi with the UP's Darrell Berrigan, a bright, attractive man who seemed to have his hand in everything. He had an air-conditioned flat in a brand-new Delhi building, luxury I had not seen for ages, and he let me stay with him. Pat Moran, the AP man who later won a Pulitzer, lived in the next suite. No one in India, I thought, did a better job than Berry. He seemed to know everyone, especially the OSS men and women—and there were lots of them, enterprising, eager, daring young people dedicated to the most outlandish and dangerous plans for operations behind the Japanese lines in Burma, Siam and Indochina. Berrigan was part of this gang. I envied his easy manners, his good looks and, perhaps most of all, the adoring young women who were in and out of his apartment, night and day. I had never seen a man with more attractive women in his life.

This is why I have never believed the stories of Darrell's death. He stayed on in India for UP after the war, then left to start a newspaper in Bangkok. I thought he had lost his mind. There already were two or three English-language papers in Bangkok. How another could make it was beyond me. A bit later I understood that it was not Berrigan's paper, it was a CIA cover. I remembered Berry's intimate relations with the OSS. He had been part of it, and many of them were still there, still up to their daring schemes in Southeast Asia and along the border of Communist China.

One day in 1965, a news item reported the death of Darrell Berrigan. He had been murdered, it was said, in a back alley of Bangkok. Police believed, because of the condition of his clothing, that he was killed in a homosexual encounter. Instantly there flashed into my mind the image of the gorgeous young things who had floated into Darrell's stylish flat during those New Delhi days and nights. It did not add up. Nothing about it did. Berrigan had lived long enough in the East not to be caught like that, even if, as seemed unlikely to me, he had bisexual tendencies. No, I said then, and no, I say again, Berrigan did not die in a homosexual setup. Murder, yes, but it had something to do with his role in the CIA, just as, I believe, the "disappearance" in March 1967 of James Thompson, the famous Thai silk entrepreneur, a wartime OSS man and, I am convinced, a peacetime CIA operator, was not the case of this extraordinary sophisticate going out for a walk in the woods and getting lost. He, too, was murdered. Nor would it surprise me if the two deaths were connected and if, in some fashion, the hand of the Royal House of Thai was involved. These are chapters that will probably go unwritten (and unresearchable under present secrecy rules) for many years. I made a small pass at digging into the Thompson case for his family in Chicago, but quickly realized that one would have to invest two or three years, with no guarantee of success—especially since the agency insisted that Thompson had no connection with it and that his death was not related to the CIA.

I flew across the Indian Ocean with General Wood. He won a few dollars from me at gin rummy, and we landed in the remarkably named Potshot, Australia. I went up to Brisbane, where I met Bill Dickinson, flew to Hollandia when MacArthur moved his headquarters to New Guinea, had a pleasant meeting with MacArthur and island-hopped my way to Honolulu, flying over an atoll or two where Japanese took perfunctory shots at us. Admiral Nimitz invited me to talk to his staff about the war in Russia. It seemed so far away, I wondered if I had ever been there. It had been getting farther and farther away as I traveled. Even in Teheran, the U.S. officers were chafing to go home. It was all over, they said. Yes, they would stay on if the Russians came in for the final phase against Japan. In India, forget it—except for the bright lads and lasses of the OSS. I spent a long afternoon in Calcutta with Davidas Gandhi, Mohandas's son, a dark, angry man who could not wait for the war to end to launch anew the struggle against the British. He hated the war. In Australia, the Aussies were coming home by the thousands. Anzio and the U.S. bombing of their men had been the last straw. MacArthur—that was different. That was real war, and so was the navy's, but the barbed wire on Waikiki seemed like a stage prop. It didn't feel much like Stalingrad.

I got back to New York on September 23. Mary was still in Minneapolis. She and Mike flew in a couple of days later. I went out to La Guardia to meet them. It was a great thrill. I couldn't get over Mike, but in the taxi to the New York hotel where we would stay until we could go back into the Mamaroneck house on October 1, I knew that I had made a terrible mistake. It wasn't going to work.

24 | Home Again

There was a splash of publicity when I got back to New York. The UP sent me out to make speeches, capitalizing on my around-the-world assignment, "visiting every fighting front." Though not quite true, it had a ring to it.

I didn't mind this. I had got a big break and I was going to make the most of it. I dashed out magazine articles, no longer "Michael Evans" for *Coronet,* but signed and sometimes cover pieces for the *Saturday Evening Post, Collier's, The New York Times Magazine, Liberty.* I began to review books for the *Times.* I appeared on CBS and NBC talk shows. Famous people called me up and asked my advice. Walter Lippmann invited me to lunch.

Everyone wanted to know about Russia. This was the hot question.

It was the question on my mind as well. I came away from Russia with mixed feelings. I wanted to believe that the Soviet Union and the United States would work together in the postwar world. I wanted to believe that when peace came, Stalin would relax and offer some relief to the Russian people, who had given their lives to win the war and broken their backs for twenty-five years, trying to build Soviet society.

I had assumed at first, without thinking much about it, that the end of the war would brighten the horizon in Russia; there would be no more censorship (naturally, I gave this priority); no more heavy-handed police; no more fear and regimentation. It seemed to me that "when the boys came home," they would see that this happened. That shows how little I understood the Stalinist state, and by the time I left Moscow, I wasn't so sure I was right. I spent a long evening talking with Henry, Ludmilla, Olga, Alec Werth and, I think, Ehrenburg. It was just after Henry returned from America. We were talking about what would happen when the war ended. I said immediately: "Better times for everyone." Not at all, responded Ludmilla. Henry agreed. So did Ehrenburg (if memory serves). Alec played Hamlet, as always. Only Olga had a hope for brighter days. The rest said no, it would be the other way. There was so much to be done; the country must be rebuilt. It would be the hardest time Russia had ever had. Didn't I know that in the Ukraine, they hadn't been able to sow the crops—no men to help with the plowing, no horses, no cows, no seed for the planting. In many places, women harnessed themselves to wooden plows and dragged them through the heavy black soil. The villages were destroyed. No thatch for the roofs. No men, just young boys, war cripples and grandfathers. If a man did turn up, the women would not let him sleep only with his wife or sweetheart. It was share and share alike, and would be for years to come. I hadn't put this together, my thoughts being concentrated on industry, on restoring the Dneprostroi dam and power station, getting the coal mines of the Donbas back to work. Basic Russia had passed me by.

Ludmilla was almost contemptuous. "How can you talk about easier times?" she said. "It is bound to be worse." Ehrenburg, I believe, raised the question of help from the United States. He wasn't sure American aid and friendship would endure. He thought there were already signs of U.S. hostility. Ehrenburg always distrusted the United States, so I discounted what he said. But I could see that the others had a real point.

I found few in the United States who had a concept of the destruction in Russia. I did not possess words to bring to my readers what it meant when Stalingrad was turned into rubble fields, with a few tin pipes sticking up from cellars and dugouts. No one in New York understood when I told them I had not met a Russian man or woman who had not lost a wife, a son, a mother, a loved one, in the war. They had no measure by which to understand and I was not skillful enough to find a way to carry it home.

I was surprised—though I suppose I should not have been—to find there were Americans who didn't mind what happened to Russia, didn't care how the Russians suffered, who had no interest in helping and who, in some cases, simply said that once we had finished the Nazis, we would have to "take care of" the Russians. I knew that no people had given more lives than the Russians. I had no liking for Stalin or his government, but I was appalled at the barbarous idea of an unprovoked attack on the Russians. I didn't think these people, at their cocktail parties and dinners, had any measure of the Red Army. Russia might be half destroyed, but the Red Army was not one I would lightly challenge. That was the kind of dinner I had begun to be invited to. I was "that bright young man just back from Russia." People wanted to meet me. I quickly found they didn't so much want to listen as to tell me what they thought they knew.

Soon after Hiroshima, in early October 1945, the weather very fine, I was invited to a great estate in Greenwich, Connecticut. My host was an enormously wealthy member of a family that had been engaged in mining and metallurgical enterprises for three generations. The guests included several other entrepreneurs and the head of a large advertising agency. I had been asked so that they could get a firsthand report on the Soviet Union—what did Stalin intend to do and what about the Red Army?

I had to confess that I did not know Stalin's plans, but judging from the devastation of his country, he must give priority to restoring the industry of the Ukraine and the Donbas, getting agriculture going and rebuilding the great cities—Minsk, Kharkov, Stalingrad, Kiev, Kursk, Leningrad and many, many more.

I was listened to with some impatience. I was not telling them what they wanted to hear. What about Stalin's plans for conquering Europe and the world? I expressed doubt that this held a high spot on his agenda. After lunch, we sat in the warm October sunshine on a brick-floored terrace and continued our talk.

My host said that regardless of casualties and damage, Russia was out to take over the world. Europe was weak and defenseless. We already were dismantling our army. The danger was growing day by day. We must prepare to halt Stalin before he had conquered Europe and Asia and began to knock at the doors of America itself.

Nothing I said had the slightest impact and I finally got fed up.

"Look," I said, "if you believe that Stalin is preparing to attack the United States, then this talk about building up our strength to resist him is meaningless. The thing to do is to attack right now before he gets any stronger. We have the atom bomb and he doesn't. The only prudent course—if you believe, as I think you do, that war is inevitable—is to drop the bomb. Forget the preliminaries. We have the edge. We can wipe out Russia right now. Later on, perhaps we can't. It is criminal to delay—if what you think is true."

My rough talk had an effect. My host was seized with a coughing fit. He had swallowed his drink the wrong way. One of the guests congratulated me. "That's the way to talk," he said.

"We've got the drop on them and we have got to take 'em now. Get 'em while they are weak and we are strong. It's the chance of a lifetime."

I agreed. "If you think Russia is simply gearing up to wipe us out, why wait?" I repeated.

Somehow the talk slithered to an untidy end. I sensed that while my host liked to pound the table and talk tough, the prospect of annihilating Russia now did not, somehow, appeal to him.

I suppose that this kind of talk—and I heard many variants of it—was a logical extension and distortion of Henry Luce's doctrine of the American Century. I heard a lot about that too.

What was happening was that we had moved toward that change in direction, toward confrontation, of which Archie Clark Kerr spoke in San Francisco.

The opening shot, publicly at least, had been fired from a rather uncertain musket, that of Bill White, my erstwhile companion on the Eric Johnston trip. *Reader's Digest* had published two articles by Bill (brought out as a book called *Report on the Russians* in 1945). Bill presented his record of the Johnston excursion, decorated with what his companions on the trip, including myself, felt were mean, ungracious, even vicious remarks about the Russians. Well, that was Bill's business. I thought it bad taste, but that was his privilege. However, there was something else. Bill told a number of stories and reported on various seamy matters, described concentration camps and political repressions which he said he learned about in the course of the trip.

That stuck in my craw because these things had not happened. Bill was at our side all through the trip. His book hit the bestseller list (there was a good market for this kind of thing) and touched off a god-awful wrangle. Prominent writers who should have known better called on the publisher to suppress the book in the interest of good relations with our wartime allies (a similar appeal had caused Harper & Brothers to suspend publication of Trotsky's biography of Stalin from 1941 to 1945); and an elaborate pamphlet was made up by the National Council for Soviet Friendship, challenging Bill. Behind a lot of this could be perceived the hand of the U.S. Communist party and its sycophants. The correspondents in Moscow were dragged in. The Friendship Council called on them to sign a petition denouncing the book (none of them had seen it, let alone read it). Eric Johnston was highly embarrassed. Two of our colleagues on the trip, Dick Lauterbach and Bob Magidoff, signed the Moscow correspondents' declaration. Lawrence and I did not; neither of us had much taste for petition tactics. We were sore as hell at Bill, though. If that stuff he reported had been going on, a reader could legitimately ask why Salisbury, Lawrence and the others hadn't mentioned it. We had been there with Bill; we knew these things hadn't happened; Bill knew that we knew it—why did he do it?

Well, I don't know why he did it. I guess he didn't like the Soviet Union very much. Finally, one of White's letters, larded with nasty remarks about his fellow writers, got under Lawrence's skin. He was in La Paz, Bolivia, on some obscure mission, but he fired off a letter to the *Saturday Review,* which had become a forum for "l'affaire White." White slammed back with sarcasm about Bill's attitude to Communism, and I decided to jump into the fight. I wrote a letter, very brief, very bitter. I listed all the well-known Whites, about eight of them: Bill's father, William Allen White of the *Emporia* (Kansas) *Gazette,* Frank White of Time-Life, another Bill White who then covered the Senate for UP, and so on. I said that among this company there was only one black White. That effectively severed my personal relations with Bill for many years.

Apparently, what Bill had done was to use the Johnston trip as a clothesline on which to hang various yarns, some of which may have been true, which he had picked up, even before he left New York.

It was a shoddy business, but not without significance.

A year later, Bill wrote in the *Saturday Review* that had he held up his report for a few months, there would not have been the explosion of indignation. I am afraid he was right. He was swimming with the tide, but had got a little ahead of it.

Archie Clark Kerr's words in San Francisco didn't entirely sink in. I understood what he was saying, knew that if Archie spoke, it had to be true. Trusting his diplomatic judgment totally, I felt he would not have made the remark had he not wanted me to understand what lay ahead.

I was not enthused by the San Francisco proceedings, but as I wrote a friend on May 3, five days before V-E Day: "It is a fairly tough and realistic meeting in which the Big Three know where the chips lie and are lining it out pretty much as they think it should be."

I thought there had been a dangerous deterioration in relations between the Russians and the West. "Most of the fault, I feel, and I think I can judge it pretty accurately," I wrote, "lies with the Russians. Some with us but much more with them." I thought that a lot of trouble arose from the long efforts of the West to isolate Russia, but that the near-range frictions came from the Russian side. I was certain that the Soviet would come into the war against Japan, but "actually, we don't particularly need them."

With all that, I didn't entirely absorb Archie's statement until that night in February 1946 at Fulton, Missouri, when Winston Churchill rang down the iron curtain.

I had awaited his address with trepidation. I could not think of a reason why Churchill would come to Missouri to speak platitudes. He wanted a platform and he was going to say something important. That could only be the switch Archie had signaled nearly a year earlier. After Fulton, I got the point.

My central preoccupation now was my book. I had never written a book and Carol Hill had got me a contract with Macmillan. The idea scared me. I went down to St. Petersburg, Florida, to get the writing under way. Mary and Mike played on Sunset beach and I sat in the damp cottage day after day, batting away at my typewriter. It didn't go as fast as I had expected. By April I was back in New York. One afternoon I went to Rockefeller Center to meet my UP friend Jack Beal, now working for *Time* magazine. He came late, in a great hurry. "Roosevelt has died, Harrison," he said. "I've got to go right back to the shop." So did I and then down to Washington to write the story and up to Hyde Park for the burial in the rose garden. I got to the Roosevelt estate so early there was no one there, no one in the long, bare gatehouse. I walked over to the rose garden, where the grave had already been dug, made some notes and came back. Now I had a companion, a tall, lanky, ill-jointed man with a rugged face and straggly black hair. It was Joe Ball. I had broken Joe in on the rewrite desk of the *Minneapolis Journal,* doing obits and traffic accidents, when his father sent him down from Crookston, Minnesota, to get a job. His father had known the Joneses, who published the paper. Joe was a big farm lad and when he hunched over the typewriter (I don't think he had ever seen one before), I thought he was going to smash it apart, stabbing at it with two fingers like pistons. The whole desk shook. I had forgotten that Joe, by then a political reporter on the *St. Paul Pioneer Press,* had most improbably been named U.S. senator from Minnesota. He hadn't noticed me and I watched as he prowled back and forth in the bleak hall in black suit and black string tie, his hands clasped behind him, his shoulders slightly bent, a solemn, no, a *grave* expression on his face. I got it. Joe was playing the role of Lincoln. I walked up behind him and said, "Hi, Joe, how you doing?" He was so startled the Lincoln look flew from his face. But he hastily put it back in place and shook hands gravely. "This is a sad day for the nation," Joe said. "Sure is," I said, and stopped teasing him, because people had begun to arrive and I had work to do.

The rose garden filled up, the dignitaries arrived: the foreign diplomats, the senators, the congressmen, the men and women of the New Deal; Eleanor Roosevelt with a widow's veil tucked in her hat, strong and handsome, her face compassionate as always; the children: Anna, the best of the lot, so like her mother; James and John, looking like pallbearers; Franklin, Jr., handsome, close to tears; and Elliott. My mind went back to an evening in London when he sat on the dance floor of the Embassy nightclub and gave imitations of his father and then—God save him—of his mother. That had been in 1943, when Elliott's photoreconnaissance squadron was based in North Africa and his plane often came up to England on "the whisky run," as the men called it. Now it was time for the last salute and the playing of taps. I wrote my story and caught the train back to New York.

Roosevelt had been President since I first voted, the only President I had known and sometimes it seemed the only President we had ever had. I had seen him at too close a range in Washington to be an idolator, and idolatry was not my nature. I thought I knew his faults and foibles pretty well and I had a sharp distaste for his political trickery. But he was or had been my hero, especially in the early days. His coming had begun an epoch, and if I had first mistaken the New Deal for a revolution, that was understandable. I believed now that what he had done was to carry out a counterrevolution, and carry it out with such deftness that the country he saved, the men of great wealth, the enormous corporate interests, Wall Street and the rest, did not realize what he was up to. (But Floyd B. Olson and Huey Long caught on very early in the game.)

I thought as the New York Central train roared along that magnificent stretch of track beside the Hudson that Roosevelt had done better than I or anyone could have imagined. He had saved the country and he had saved the world. A certain amount of adolescent tricks are permissible in the achievement of that end. I remembered the days in March or April of 1933, after the inauguration, after the banks began to reopen, when I walked down State Street and saw the bright new NRA banners blowing in the Chicago wind from Marshall Field's, from Carson Pirie Scott, from every one of the great stores. What a thrill! What did they mean? Well, let's face it, nothing tangible, just a magician's stunt to tell us that hope had returned and the country was going forward again. Now FDR was dead and we had Truman. I didn't know about him.

The war ended for me, the European war, in San Francisco with a dull thud. The news was broken by Ed Kennedy of AP. No one else could get it. To a competitive UP man like myself, the disaster of an AP exclusive on the war's end overshadowed the event itself. All day I called one diplomat after another, looking for confirmation—or better yet, denial. No luck. At the end of this day I left the opera house and walked down to Market Street. It was six in the evening and the street was filled with a ragged bunch of celebrators, many men in trim whites, street girls, foreign merchant sailors, young draftees, a few soldiers, high school kids, the ragtag of the city. Somehow the crowd offended me. It wasn't the *people*. I didn't see many men and women in dungarees, no one who looked as though he or she had just come off the assembly line. No rich men and women from Nob Hill or estates in Marin county. No blacks. I walked four blocks up and four blocks back and then headed for my room at the St. Francis. It wasn't much like the day my father and my sister and my mother and I joined the crowd on Nicollet Avenue on November 7, 1918, when we celebrated the end of that war, four days prematurely, the "false armistice," reported by UP and its go-go young president, Roy W. Howard. It seemed as though war's end brought out the lowest common denominator in the news agencies. I went to bed that night lonely and depressed. What, after all, had been achieved? Yes, Hitler was defeated.

The Nazis had fallen. Soon Japan would come crumbling down. But what were we going to put in their place? There was the chilling implication of Clark Kerr's words. I thought the UN conference was hammering out a good platform, but there was not going to be much room for dreams and ideals. And when I looked back on my own life of the previous five years, I could see that I had made progress as a writer, as a journalist, I was moving ahead in my career. But what wreckage lay behind!

My manuscript was wrapped up by early July, designated for publication at the end of the year. But wartime production and paper difficulties kept Macmillan from bringing it out until June 1946. In a sense, that was good. I got into it some feel of the deterioration in relations, the first signs of the "cold war," a term that was not yet in general use. (Not one review of *Russia on the Way* used it; none of them mentioned Churchill's "iron curtain.")

I was proud of *Russia on the Way,* but ashamed of letting Dick Lauterbach beat me to the book stalls. While I was dashing about and basking in my new glory, he had been hard at work, even before he left Moscow. His *These Are the Russians,* covering much the same ground, beat *Russia on the Way* by six full months. My book was not a great commercial success, but despite well-founded comments about my ignorance of Russian spelling and transliteration (I blush when I read the book today) and my lack of knowledge of Russian history (then almost total), the reviewers gave me high marks for impartiality, objectivity and my effort to dig out the facts. I still admire my reporting. It was good, solid, accurate, lots of detail, fresh, and the writing is not bad, if I may say so. But so far as political analysis is concerned, well, la, me, as my aunt Mary would have said.

A lot of it isn't worth the paper I wrote it on. I understood that the Soviet Union and the United States were in for a long, long period of quarreling, but I did not foresee the polarization nor its depth. I kissed off Poland and the Balkans ("To America this means nothing"). I thought the Dardanelles and the Iranian province of Azerbaijan meant a lot to the British, little to us.

But I did get some things right. I thought that the most likely point of friction was the Far East and I pointed out in that very early day something no one else was saying—Moscow's curious lack of interest, even its disinterest, in the fate, fortune and future of the Chinese Communists. I correctly suggested that Russia's principal concern in the Far East was security along the China border and the return of everything she had lost in the 1905 defeat by Japan and since—the ports, the bases, the railroads, the special sphere in Manchuria.

So I give myself a few pluses. I probably got some of my ideas on China from Clark Kerr and some from Edgar Snow, the author of *Red Star over China.*

I find nothing for which to apologize in my closing lines:

"I do not think that Russia and the United States will ever wage war. I cannot conceive of either country attacking the other. Should this happen in the atomic age nothing else would matter very much. Obviously there would be no victor in such a conflict. In all probability after such a conflict there would be no world."

It wasn't going to work. That was what I had said to myself on that homecoming taxi ride from La Guardia with Mary and Mike. Yet I did not accept it. I had come home to a new job, finally moving up the ladder, I had been batting around the world like a pinball, chasing will-o'-the-wisps, tearing my life into bits and pieces, mortgaging my heart like a real estate speculator. It was, I told myself, time to end that and settle down. Of course I could make it work, Mary and I and the most wonderful boy in the world. No, it was not as I had dreamed, but what marriage was a dream? I was just getting acquainted with Mike. I played with him by the hour; we lived in the backyard, had swings and a treehouse and rope ladders. There was so much that was good: the house, friends next door, I was writing my head off, soon I would move out of UP; everything I had wanted was beginning to seem possible. All I needed was patience at home. I must not expect too much. This sounded sensible until I got into bed and began to think.

I had heard the Russians talk about how difficult it was to learn to live. I wasn't even trying to learn. I was always putting ambition, the main chance and my own satisfaction ahead of anything else, while assuring myself I was doing the opposite.

One thing seemed certain. I never would touch foot on Russian soil again. It had been an exciting assignment and I had profited professionally, but I had taken all the Russian bureaucracy, all the propaganda, I could take. That chapter was closed and would stay closed.

The chapter of my life in England was closed too. Ellen had married an RAF pilot who was now flying in civil aviation and living in Devon, a quiet life, not altogether happy, but a refuge and a breathing space from the years of the war.

If the past seemed to be a book that was closed, the present was filled with half-started chapters, scratched-out pages, torn-out sheets, false starts. Mary and I knew that our life was going badly, but we would not address the question. We quarreled, God knows we quarreled, about everything—about the fact that I missed my train coming home after work (as I more and more did; the same old thing); about the way she threw money around; about her temper. We could quarrel about an ant in a sidewalk crack. None of the quarrels made any sense. They did not touch the simple reality that after a couple of years apart, two people who had not been getting along well weren't getting along any better. We were drinking too much. We decided to have another child and we hoped, both of us, that this would be the magic that would change the future. I don't think that is a good reason for bringing children into the world, but Stephan made up for a lot of things even if our marriage was on the rocks before he entered the family on March 20, 1947. He arrived precisely on the dot, no drama, and was as sunny a child as ever was born. It was the Ides of March again, but no Hitler, no war on the horizon, the world peaceful enough, except for atom bombs, Berlin and the cold war.

I had come back to New York to nail my name to the journalistic pinnacle. Instead I plunged ahead, eyes open, into a dilemma that would cause everyone connected with me grief and anguish. I was realistic enough to say this to myself, yet I didn't have the guts to make a decision. Ellen had returned to the U.S. to get a divorce. She settled in New York and we began seeing each other again.

Mary knew that something was very wrong, but not exactly what. I knew everything and understood nothing. I came home at night, Mary and I would quarrel, and I would retreat to my study and sit at my typewriter. I wasn't turning out copy the way I had been. I was losing the high momentum I had brought back with me in 1944, but I did keep hammering away on one thing—*The New York Times*. I began to cultivate its foreign editors, Ted Bernstein and Manny Freedman, and I got to know Lester Markel, the Sunday editor, who was always in the market for new "interpreters" of Russia. When I left UP, I knew where I was going—to the *Times*.

I hadn't lost interest in Russia. At San Francisco, I had talked to Molotov, a sly smile on his face as though we shared a secret, which in fact we did. When Andrei Gromyko came to the UN at Lake Success, I tried to carry on negotiations for United Press. UP was syndicating memoirs of the great figures of the war and they thought I might get Stalin, Molotov, Marshal Zhukov, Marshal Timoshenko, Litvinov. I had a long, serious talk with Gromyko. It was impossible to have anything other than a serious talk with him. He was interested in what I had to say, but it had to go back to Moscow, and Moscow never replied. Gromyko was very young. When he had been sent to Washington to replace Litvinov in 1943, he was only twenty-nine or thirty, the youngest of the wartime diplomats (and so he has survived them all, except Harriman and Molotov). Gromyko's public reputation at the UN was bad. He was always saying *nyet*. In private, he was respected as a hard-working and intelligent diplomat, whose greatest problem was the short string on which Moscow kept him. I liked him. He was straight, all business, no chuffing about, with occasionally a very dry humor. I liked him a lot better than Dekanozov or Vishinsky.

I was keeping my hand in. When Simonov and Ehrenburg came to the United States, I escorted them on some of their visits, arranged for a big luncheon with UP executives and tried to figure out their purpose. Ehrenburg was more friendly than I had ever seen him. He had abandoned his superciliousness toward Americans (he quickly regained it when he began to write about the U.S.). It seemed as though Simonov and Ehrenburg had been sent over to gather materials for fresh anti-American propaganda; that was all that appeared under their names in the Soviet press. But it may not have been the whole story. This was an uncertain time. The cold war was getting under way, but there were undercurrents in the other direction. How it would come out was not as plain as it looks in retrospect. The pair went south to study "the Negro question"; they went to Hollywood. They visited the Ford plant in Detroit and saw the Chicago stockyards. They talked to many American writers, almost all of whom were friendly to Russia if not to Stalin. Their companion was old General Galaktionov, who had been a *Red Star* editor during the war. He didn't speak a word of English, and most of what happened passed him by. He was dour and unsmiling, but years later, when I talked to Simonov—Simonov knew him very well—he said the old general had greatly enjoyed himself. He had never expected to have such an experience in his life. America was a wonderland. Perhaps Simonov and Ehrenburg were supposed to be sampling American intellectual opinion, trying to judge whether it would line up for or against the Soviet Union. If so, they must have submitted a pretty muddled report. The divisions were so manifold, no one could have figured it out.

I wrote magazine articles about Soviet policy and analyzed for UP what was happening in the Kremlin. I was trying to live up to my reputation as "that young man who knows a lot about Russia."

I liked to hear that phrase, but I didn't really believe it until I met Sir Bernard Pares. The greatest of British specialists on Russia, Sir Bernard had gone there just after the Russo-Japanese War and become a page on the floor of the Duma Nicholas II established when he thought the 1905 revolution might cost him his throne. Pares was now in his seventies, a chickadee of a man, who loved to talk. He had read *Russia on the Way* and liked it. His enthusiasm for my book told me that I must be on the right track. Pares had got to know the Russian leaders before World War I. He and an American scholar named Samuel Harper, from the University of Chicago, teamed up. They wanted to know what made Russia tick, and no one before 1917 or after had a better chance than this unlikely pair. If there had been an MI6 in World War I, Pares would have been its leading agent, along with Bruce Lockhart. Had Lloyd George paid heed to the advice Pares brought to London, the story of postwar Russia would have been far different. Pares believed devoutly in the cooperative movement in Siberia, then flowing with milk, butter and cheese, the richest dairyland in the world. If Pares had been able to promote his co-ops, the Communists, I think, would not have had a chance. How I envied Pares his experience!

After the war, the Bolsheviks put Pares on the blacklist. He knew too much. Lenin didn't want him poking around. Nor did Trotsky. Pares knew them and everyone else worth knowing. He knew Rasputin, Prince Usupov, who killed Rasputin, the Czarina, the children, the Czar, the Dowager Empress. He spent his time writing *The Fall of the Russian Monarchy,* the classic on the Czar's fall, and the best one-volume history of Russia anyone has ever done.

Now Pares was teaching in New York and he made me a kind of protégé. He would spend evenings telling me about the Czar, about the Revolution, the Constituent Assembly, the SRs, about Lenin, whom he rather liked but never trusted ("too much Tartar blood"), tales of Rasputin's orgies. He put a spell on me. He had gone back to Moscow just before World War II. They put him up at the Metropol, where he had stayed when Rasputin used to brawl with his fine ladies in a room off the balcony of the great dining room, sometimes leaning over the railing and taking down his trousers to expose his private parts to the diners. One night when Pares was in the restaurant, a drunken officer took a pistol and shot holes in the ceiling.

On his first night back in Russia, Pares was invited to the Bolshoi Theater to see *Swan Lake.* He gasped when he was taken to his seat. It was in the same box he had occupied the last time he had been in the Bolshoi, on the afternoon of July 4, 1918, when Marya Spiridonovna got up and announced that her SRs were overthrowing the Bolshevik government. They almost did, too, taking the Lubyanka and plunging Lenin into panic. His seat in the box, Pares said, could not have been an accident. Someone remembered.

Pares insisted that I return to Russia. He saw me as he had seen himself in the years before 1910, young, energetic, curious, a person who poked his nose into things he shouldn't and asked naughty questions. I said it didn't make sense. I didn't even know the Cyrillic alphabet. No problem, Pares insisted. You can learn the alphabet and the whole language in the morning while you shave. Just as he had done. He went to the chest of drawers in his shabby hotel room, pulled forth a shirt, yanked out the gray cardboard, wet his pencil with his tongue and wrote the Cyrillic alphabet for me, neatly in a clear hand. He gave me some simple grammatical forms, the pronunciations of the letters ("It couldn't be more simple, my boy, it's all phonetic. Nothing like our silly English tongue"), and told me to start learning the next morning. I didn't, but there would come a day not very far when I would prop the cardboard beside my mirror and follow his advice. If I lived a hundred years, I would not know Russia as Pares did. He knew *people*—politicians, aristocrats, peasants, revolutionaries, scholars, officials. He had crisscrossed Russia in a way that made my travels look like a package tour. For all the tyranny of the Czar, there had been elbow room. The government was lazy, the civil servants slept more, and you could always apply, as Lenin once said when he was trying to get a marriage license, "palm oil," a judicious bribe. It was a lot more fun in Pares's day.

I owe a debt to Sir Bernard. He was the man who put a spark in my mind about Russia as a profession. Though I didn't really believe what he said, it flattered my ego and in the end I belatedly put Russia into the center of my life. A few years ago, I dedicated my history of the Russian Revolution, *Black Night, White Snow,* to Sir Bernard, because he was the man who taught me to go back into the Russian past. By examining the past I could begin to understand the present, and if I understood the present I might have a clue to the future. It was the best advice anyone could give, and I have been trying to follow it ever since.

25 | A New Beginning

In the months after Stephan's birth, I found myself lurching through heavy seas. The conflict between my marriage and my love for Ellen was tearing me apart and, along with it, everyone around me. I turned to the psychiatrists. My doctor was a straightforward, no-nonsense kind of man. He said: "Make up your mind. What do you want? You are destroying everyone around you." I made up my mind, left Mamaroneck and moved to New York. But the guilt was too much. I began to wobble more and more, as jittery as a burned cat, so nervous I could no longer bang out the seventy-five-word-a-minute lead stories that were my hallmark. I sat at my typewriter staring into space, unable to get a word on paper. Sometimes I couldn't even sit on the chair. I felt myself flying apart. I persuaded my sister Janet to come to New York and get a job—something she had been wanting to do for years—my motive being to have someone to fall back on if I couldn't handle the exploding fragments of my life. I had always been a take-hold, take-over person, and the idea that I couldn't keep my life together frightened me.

I couldn't figure where this was leading. I had rubbed everyone's nerves raw. I knew that Earl Johnson was beginning to worry about my lessening control at UP. I saw no way to pay Mary alimony, support the children and marry Ellen, and I couldn't concentrate enough to continue my free-lance articles. What I wrote was apt to be turned back.

Finally, I realized I had to take leave and get some psychiatric help. What had hit me, although I did not realize it, was my old friend from Russia, "fliers' fear." It was totally debilitating. There was nothing to do but let nature and time slowly restore my nerves to their normal elasticity. It could not be rushed. I was unable to concentrate my mind and will the symptoms away. A giant vise had grabbed my body and held it rigid and captive, no longer obedient to my control.

Sometimes, late at night, it occurred to me that I was being paid my just deserts for the selfishness that had led me to leave Michael and my father behind, to fall in love with Ellen and leave her behind, to fall in love with Olga and leave her behind. As I began to get a little perspective on myself, I saw how sick and childish that was. No one benefited from this collapse. No one. I was just piling disaster on disaster. Not until late spring of 1948 did I begin gradually to pull out of it. And the first sign of health came when once again I sat down at my typewriter. I went back to free-lancing, hard at first but slowly acquiring momentum. None of my problems had been solved. All of them had grown worse. But if I could use my typewriter, if I could write —well, there was hope.

I was not yet able to go back to UP, and Earl Johnson began to hint that possibly I should find something not so demanding, not so full of constant tension. So I got a job with *The New York Times* and went to Moscow.

Of course, it was not so simple. It was not simple at all. It was tough, tough going and I was very lucky.

Since coming back to New York in late 1944, I had been cultivating the *Times*. Two of my closest personal friends were C. L. Sulzberger, chief *Times* correspondent in Europe and technically the director of the *Times* foreign staff, and William H. Lawrence, the chief political correspondent in Washington. Both used their influence in my behalf, but the man who gave me the job, somewhat to his surprise, was Edwin L. ("Jimmy") James, the managing editor.

I had been dropping in on James for a couple of years. In the summer and fall of 1948, I began to see him more often. There was nothing easier than getting an appointment with Mr. James. But there was nothing more difficult than getting him to talk business—that is, to talk about putting me on his staff. Mr. James was a raconteur and had served in Paris for many years. A small, debonair man who talked with a rasping, nasal voice, he was much more interested in betting on the races than in tomorrow's front page. The classic story about Mr. James concerned the time federal agents seeking to break up a ring of bookies zeroed in on his office in the belief he was king of the bookies, not one of their most generous clients.

Mr. James liked an audience, and as long as I was willing to sit in a brown leather chair across the desk and listen, he was willing to have my company. An hour would go by, and when I began to shift about a bit, thinking I had outstayed my time, he would say, "Well, let's see, Salisbury, there's nothing doing on any assignment right now. Just keep in touch."

I would leave Mr. James and stop by for a word with an old friend, Turner Catledge, the assistant managing editor, who was fated to sit outside Mr. James's office for nearly seven years, waiting to succeed him. Turner would grin and say, "Well, anything doing?" And I would reply, "Not yet." "Well," he would say, "don't give up, Salisbury." And I didn't.

I had told Mr. James that I was ready to take any foreign post the *Times* had open with the exception of Moscow. I had no desire to return there. Western Europe, the Far East, the Middle East, Africa—anything else would be fine. Mr. James said he understood my feelings about Moscow. The *Times* didn't even have a correspondent there at the moment, Drew Middleton having been refused a reentry visa in mid-1947.

Cy Sulzberger had hopes of getting me sent to Cairo, but when I met with Mr. James at Thanksgiving time, he said there was nothing doing in Cairo (I did not then understand that Cy and Mr. James were at swords' points about assignments).

Mr. James volunteered that he had finally closed the *Times*'s Moscow office because he had given up hope of getting a man into the Soviet Union.

My UP salary was coming to an end in January. I was doing a fair amount of free-lancing. I had been offered the editorship of the new *Reporter* magazine and a position under Otto Fuerbringer at *Time* magazine, but I wanted that *New York Times* job. In early December, I bit the bullet and told Mr. James that if the *Times* wanted to send me to Moscow, I would try to help get a Soviet visa, although I could guarantee no result. Mr. James leaped at the offer. I tried to see Ambassador Panyushkin in Washington, but had to settle for the counselor of the embassy, a man named Zotov, who promised to forward the proposal to Moscow. I wrote Cy Sulzberger about the idea and got back a rather unpleasant letter. He was still plugging me for the Middle East.

On Sunday, December 26, 1948, *The New York Times Magazine* featured an article I had written for Lester Markel, *"Russia Tightens the Iron Curtain on Ideas."* I wrote of the increasing pressure of the Soviet censorship. Nationalism and xenophobia held the dominant position in Soviet criticism. I recalled the purges of the 1930s and said Russia was now suffering from the "internal repercussions of the Cold War." The ordinary Soviet citizen was barred from all contact with foreigners. "The intellectuals are being whipped into line," I said, and intimidated against independent thought. "After 30 years of Marxist indoctrination and party propaganda the Kremlin still finds it necessary to launch a 'thought purge.' "

It was a tough, uncompromising article. When I read it over on that cold, snowy Sunday after Christmas, I smiled a little grimly. "Well," I said to Ellen, "if I should by any chance get a visa for Russia, no one will ever be able to say I tried to soft-soap my way into Moscow." (Of course, they did nonetheless.)

On any scale of rationality, this article blew what prospects I might have had of getting a Soviet visa. You don't spit in a man's eye and expect him to invite you into his house.

On page three of the editorial section of the *Times* that same Sunday, I found a two-column headline which read:

A CHRISTMAS LETTER
TO MARSHAL STALIN.

It was a column by Mr. James in the form of an open letter to Stalin, proposing that he give a visa to allow the *Times* to send a correspondent to Moscow. Mr. James assured the Marshal of the interest of the *Times* in presenting the Soviet side of the controversies dividing our countries.

"There is too little exchange of information," James wrote. "It is our feeling that if the two peoples could know more about each other the task of their leaders, on both sides, would be infinitely easier in keeping the peace and bringing about prosperity from which both would benefit.

"This newspaper would like to help in the better understanding.

"The *Times,*" he continued, "is unable to maintain a news bureau in Moscow, as it does in London, Paris, Rome and the other great capitals of the world. We think we could help toward that better understanding."

I did not think James was apt to influence the hard-bitten men of the Kremlin. In fact, I thought it was a screwball gambit. However, on January 6, 1949, *eleven days* after Mr. James's "letter to Stalin" was published, the telephones in Washington and New York began to jangle. There was a call from the Soviet embassy to James Reston in the Washington bureau, and hardly had Scotty hung up than another Soviet diplomat was calling Arthur Krock, the chief Washington correspondent. Mr. Panyushkin's secretary called Mr. James. They called everyone but me. When Mr. James finally got me on the wire to tell me the news, I simply couldn't believe it.

"It looks to me," James said, his twang so strong it was almost a snarl, "as though you have gotten yourself a job, young fellow."

So I had. Four and a half years after leaving Moscow, hoping never, never to return, I was going back. I was happy. I had my job on *The New York Times,* a lifetime ambition achieved. It came after the worst year of my life. There had been moments in the spring of 1948 when I wondered whether I would ever hold a correspondent's job again. No, I didn't look forward with enthusiasm to going to Moscow. I knew it would be worse than I had experienced in wartime, and that had been bad enough. I had summed up some of the handicaps in my December 26 article. But I was to find there were a lot more—and they were not all in Moscow.

The *Times* job left my personal life fragmented. The question of a divorce hung fire, impacted by Mary's anger. Never, she said, never. Stephan was too small to be affected, but Michael was a very unhappy little boy. The *Sturm und Drang* of 1948 had taken a deep toll of Ellen. I proposed that she come to Moscow with me or join me as soon as I had scouted out the territory. She was most reluctant to go and I was equally reluctant to leave without her. I was not going to run off yet another time from the woman of my love. But none of our talk had any real effect. The impasse would have to be worked out from a distance and by time. I was, I suppose, buoyed by my escape from disaster. I had no doubt that Stalin himself had responded to Mr. James's plea and approved my visa. There was no other way to account for this swift action. Surely with that kind of momentum, I could handle my other problems.

I got my visa from the Soviet embassy on January 18, 1949, a month to the day from my application, and on January 23, with considerable fanfare, the *Times* announced that I would be going to Moscow as their correspondent. An editorial said: "Mr. Salisbury's instructions are those given to all *Times* reporters in all fields—to get and present the news fully, accurately and without bias. He will be subject to the restriction imposed by the Russian Government . . . but he will do the best he can to give our readers a truthful and impartial picture of what is taking place on his beat. We hope he can contribute to a better and more friendly understanding between the two countries."

These words faithfully expressed the sentiments of Arthur Hays Sulzberger, the publisher of the *Times,* who regarded the Moscow post as one of special importance. The *Times* had had a succession of notable men in Russia—my friend Bill Lawrence, the quondam *Times* drama critic Brooks Atkinson, and earlier, the great Walter Duranty. To the *Times,* the Moscow post possessed unusual significance, and never in history had it been given to a man who, like myself, had just walked in from the street.

Sulzberger was conscious of this even if I was not, and he made it his business to get acquainted with his new Moscow man. Arthur Sulzberger and his remarkable wife, Iphigene, had themselves visited the Soviet Union in 1929, a journey that left a bad taste in Sulzberger's mouth. He counted himself on the liberal side, but he did not care for the Soviet state. He was a fastidious man and the filth, disorder, smells, bedbugs, the lack of decent food, housing and services, had a strong impact on him, as I came to realize when, on my return from Moscow in 1954, he gave me the report he had written of his trip. He commented, as I would always do, on the transition from the "flies, dirt and disorder" of Russia to the spotless town of Helsinki once you crossed the Soviet frontier. But in fairness, he confessed that confronted with the ills of Russia under the Czar, he, too, would have been a Bolshevik in November 1917.

Sulzberger performed a notable service for me. He personally escorted me from his own fourteenth-floor office suite through the whole Times Building down to the sub-subbasement presses. He was proud of the *Times* and proud of its plant and I could not have had a more knowledgeable and thoughtful introduction to the mysteries of the remarkable newspaper to which my fate and fortune would become attached. He spent many hours telling me of the newspaper's traditions, its goals, its principles, its aspirations, and what it expected of its correspondents. He introduced me to his editors and laid the basis of a personal relationship which would endure through his life. He was a modest man, so modest that many people believed him when he uttered his throwaway lines about having got his job by marrying the boss's daughter. That was true in a way, but he held his job because he had intelligence, responsibility and a keen eye for the future. He gave shape to the contemporary *Times* and positioned it in such a manner that when his son, Arthur Ochs Sulzberger, finally and unexpectedly became publisher after the untimely death of his brother-in-law Orvil Dryfoos, young Arthur, or "Punch," as he was universally called, moved it up to almost impregnable heights.

All that I knew about the *Times* before I went to Moscow I learned from Arthur Hays Sulzberger. It left me deep in his debt. He even offered me a bit of advice about the CIA. He said that I might be approached by a government intelligence agency. If that should happen, what I might decide to do was my own responsibility. But he left plain his hope that I would steer clear of such commitments. He need not have worried. No one ever approached me and I had no trouble in steering clear. I suppose there must have been a CIA station chief in Moscow during my years, but his profile was so low that even in that incestuous atmosphere I never had a clue to his identity.

As I plucked at the raveled edges of my life in preparation for Moscow, I found there was little I could do, so ulcerated were relations with Mary.

Ellen and I talked—and didn't talk—about Moscow. She would not come with me. I had to accept that. I said she must come by June. She was not certain about this. She was undergoing psychotherapy herself, was very uncomfortable, upset, distressed, working full time as a psychiatric nurse and, I know now, very skeptical of a future for herself and me. She concealed that because she thought it would be too distressing to me.

Twice I had tea with Sir Bernard Pares. I confessed to him my doubts about going to Russia, but he would have none of them. "You must go," he insisted. "They are not offering this visa just for amusement. It has some meaning. Everything in Russia has a meaning. You must go and find out what it is."

I remembered the admonition I had from Archibald Clark Kerr in 1944: "Don't forget, everything in Russia is political. Everything." Sir Bernard took the same view. He would not listen to my objections. I must find out why the Russians had given me the visa. If I would study his cardboard Cyrillic chart (already I had put it beside my bathroom mirror), I would be talking Russian in no time. Sir Bernard's ideas were romantic, but no more romantic than those of a much younger Russian specialist, who told me there was no reason not to take Ellen. "You can take rooms with a Russian family," he said, "and live like the Russians. You will learn the language and you'll learn Russia too. Don't pay attention to all this cold war talk." Well, he was really out of touch. I urged Sir Bernard to come to Moscow and show me the city. Though he promised, I don't think either of us thought he would. Before the end of my first year in the Soviet Union, he had died.

I had long talks with Lester Markel, the *Times* Sunday editor, about articles from Russia. One would be on censorship, another on what it was like to live in Russia, another on how a Russian got a job, and one on a typical day in a Russian school. Lester was enthusiastic about my assignment. I had already written half a dozen articles for him on it, and as many important book reviews. The only editor on the *Times* whom I felt I knew well, he was a strong supporter of my work.

One day I had a call from Walter Duranty, *the* Walter Duranty, the man whose *I Write as I Please* had been a model for me in the 1930s. Duranty had left the *Times* on the eve of World War II and hadn't been in Russia for more than ten years. I was flattered when he called and invited me to lunch at the Algonquin. I had never been in the Algonquin. We lunched in the Rose Room. Everyone seemed to know him, a little man with a limp and a cane and an air. No one would ever mistake him for Harrison Salisbury. He reminded me of the Foreign Office types with whom I lunched in London during the war. But this time there was nothing to make me uncomfortable. Walter had two martinis and talked in a charming and proprietary way about Russia. He was off Russia, off Stalin, didn't like the way they had treated him and didn't know whether he'd ever go back. It was up to Stalin, really, he said; Stalin knew Walter's conditions. Either he had a free hand, travel where he wanted, no censorship, or he wouldn't come. He had seen enough of Russia. He didn't have to go back. He'd inquired a time or two and got no encouragement, so he would let them sit awhile. Eventually they would come around. It did not take me long to realize that Duranty was not in touch with today's Russia. I thought he knew damn well he

was never going back. Better for his ego to say they had to come
to him.

About the *Times* he was a bit ambiguous. He was not fond of
Mr. James, that was clear, and he seemed equivocal about Arthur
Sulzberger. Mr. Ochs and his managing editors, Van Anda and
Birchall, he spoke of with warmth. For years, Duranty had been
devoting himself to lecturing, platform appearances with his old
friend H. R. ("Red") Knickerbocker, once a foreign correspondent of the *New York Post,* debating about Russia, Duranty pro,
Knickerbocker anti. They had fabulous times debating Red
Russia and lots to drink. But Knickerbocker had lost his life in a
plane crash in the Far East and Duranty (although I did not
know this) had fallen into hard times. His lectures were not
going well, he hadn't found a new doubles partner, the McCarthy
era was beginning, the novels he was writing were trivial and the
market for articles had vanished. Even his wizardry with women
had faded.

None of this was apparent from his manner. The point of our
luncheon, I found, was a mission. He had a son in Russia by his
common-law wife, Katya. It had been years since he had seen the
boy, and in fact he had long since stopped contributing to the
support of the boy and Katya. About this, of course, he was silent. Katya, he said, had been "a very bad girl." She had not
written him about his son. Would I call on her and send him a
report? She was still living in the flat which Duranty had obtained from the Soviets twenty years before, her tenancy secured
by renting the flat to the American embassy, she keeping quarters in it for herself. He gave me the address and I promised to
visit Katya. I was surprised that he didn't send a present or a
letter with me.

When I got to Moscow I looked up Katya. The flat was occupied by an American sergeant, head of the motor pool, and his
wife. They had no idea who "the old Russian witch" was who
lived in the room off the kitchen. The name Duranty meant nothing to them. I met Katya. She had been a beauty in the 1920s,
but time had been unkind. Her face was wrinkled, her shoulders
stooped, her eyes squinted, she looked like any other Moscow babushka. I told her who I was and that I brought greetings from
Walter. "Why doesn't he write?" she said. I had no answer.
Their son, she said, was doing his army service. He was eighteen

years old and in good health. If Walter was interested, he could write a letter to his son. He hadn't for years. She was bitter and hostile and, so it seemed to me, with some reason. I left as soon as I could. I wrote Walter and said I would go back again, but I never did.

Before I left New York, I put in an evening or two on the foreign desk, watching how copy was handled, and got some instructions on filing procedures. I had a long, quiet lunch at Sardi's with Emanuel Freedman, the new foreign editor, a serious, solemn man who dressed very well, in English suits. He had spent some time in London at the end of the war and Clifton Daniel once told me he had chanced to open Manny's closet and found there twenty suits, each hung neatly in the best of press and each with a pair of shoes to match. Manny and I agreed on one matter of importance: what to do if Stalin died. We assumed that censorship would be total. I was to file a cable addressed to the chief auditor of the *Times,* containing Freedman's name. It would read: "Must ask you increase expense allowance as of _____ [the date of Stalin's death]." I carefully noted the text of the message in an old notebook, along with my shopping list.

I sailed on February 18, 1949, on the *Gripsholm,* of the Swedish-American line, for Göteborg, a ten-day trip. We had a party in my cabin before I sailed—Ellen and a friend of hers and two old friends of mine, Gene Gillette of UP and Bill Lawrence. Bill brought a bottle of champagne and everyone drank but me. I had gone on the wagon in preparation for Moscow. I vividly remembered the endless *do adna* toasts of wartime. Moscow would be rugged enough without vodka. This was one of the few smart things I have done in a rather sloppy life. Another occurred in 1951 when, suffering in my Metropol Hotel room for the fourth time that winter with the flu, lying in bed smoking cigarette after cigarette, I reached for another, then drew back my arm, saying: "Salisbury, who is running your life, cigarettes or you?" I never smoked again—although I had such withdrawal symptoms (I was a three-pack-a-day man) that I wasn't sure I would survive.

The morning of the sailing, I telephoned Michael at his school and told him I was leaving. It wasn't a very good goodbye. Nor was it a good goodbye for Ellen. I stood at the railing as the *Gripsholm* pulled out into the Hudson, and watched her figure grow smaller and smaller and smaller until I couldn't see it anymore.

The *Gripsholm* was my first ocean liner. It wasn't full—not many midwinter passengers for Scandinavia. It was a smooth trip. No Atlantic storms. I had never had so much to eat, every hour smorgasbord, bouillon, smoked salmon, hot chocolate, great platters of sweets and fruits, two or three breakfasts, enormous luncheons, teas, dinners, midnight snacks. I swam in butter and sugar all the way across the Atlantic. My cabin was cozy, the ocean lovely, the sky blue. I had a pile of books about Russia. I began reading *Anna Karenina.* I floated out of the world of actuality into some Swedish heaven-on-earth.

On the third day out, I picked up the ship's news bulletin. It reported that Anna Louise Strong, an American correspondent, had been arrested in Moscow as an agent of the CIA, held for a week in the Lubyanka, then escorted across the frontier and expelled from the Soviet Union. Good God! I said to myself. If Anna Louise is being expelled as a CIA agent, what is going to happen to me?

26 | Back to Moscow

It was evening, full dark, a raw evening, the temperature a bit above freezing, when the train from Helsinki reached Leningrad on March 7, 1949, myself burning with anticipation of seeing the city again, fuming at delays, coming in to the old Finland Station where Lenin arrived from abroad on April 17, 1917, and took command of the Russian Revolution.

I had fretted all day. I had routed my return to Russia through Helsinki so that I could go first to that Leningrad I had seen with such awe and, yes, reverence at the end of the blockade in February 1944. Five years had passed. I wanted to enter Russia by way of Leningrad and I wanted to write my first dispatch under that dateline, reciting again the heroism of the city and its people, telling of their return to peace. I thought the spirit of Leningrad was the best in Russia, the best in the world, and I wanted to start my assignment on that note. I wished to find the girl worker at the Kirov plant again, to talk to the architects about their dreams for the northern capital, to meet with Mayor Popkov and see how it was all coming out. I knew that I would not find Andrei Zhdanov there. Leningrad's enigmatic and somewhat mysterious wartime leader had died a few months earlier, on August 31, 1948.

The train had made a mule's progress from Helsinki, start and stop, start and stop. We had left about midnight after a big Sunday dinner at the American legation, at which the American minister, Avra M. Warren, presided over a gargantuan roast of beef and a small tub of fresh horseradish, the first of the season, the roots dug from the new-thawed soil and ground for the market stalls by white-aproned Finnish farmwives. The horseradish was so strong it blasted out my sinuses and brought tears to my eyes. The minister ladled it up and got so red I thought he might burst.

He and his wife and an American diplomatic courier joined me on the train.

The first delay came when the train approached the Porkkala area south of Helsinki, which the Russians had taken over at the end of the war as a fortified zone. The train halted and heavy wooden "muzzles" were fitted over each window, doors were locked and Red Army soldiers with fixed bayonets stood between the cars. "What are they concealing?" I asked. "Nothing," said the minister. "Absolutely nothing." He explained that occasionally there were cracks in the "muzzles" and diplomats could see out. "We've looked and looked," he said, "and no one has ever seen anything. We think the muzzles are to keep us from finding out that the fortified zone is actually not fortified."

When we had passed through the zone, the train halted again. The wooden shutters came down, then the train was searched and the guards got off. We proceeded very slowly until we reached the Finnish border town of Viipuri. Here Lenin's fellow Bolsheviks had met his train on the night of April 17 and escorted him to Petrograd. The Finnish border control stamped my passport, inspected the train and finally we eased across the border into Russia. It was already past lunchtime and my hopes of an afternoon stroll on the Nevsky Prospekt had gone glimmering.

We halted longer than ever, for customs examination. Everything in the baggage car, including my big trunk loaded with clothing and supplies, electric hot plates, accouterments for the office, had to be hauled into the customs shed. I had twenty or thirty books in my trunk, the *Columbia Encyclopedia,* the *World Almanac,* the *Statesman's Yearbook,* a Rand McNally atlas, Pares's *History of Russia,* Deutcher's *Stalin,* and on top of the heap, Trotsky's *Stalin* and Orwell's *1984.* I knew that Trotsky's name was anathema in Stalin's Russia—but I wanted to see the reaction. I did not know whether Orwell was well enough known to cause his book to be seized. It was, I confess, a minor provocation on my part.

A thin, dour young man came to inspect my trunk. He had only a few words of English and was taken aback by the pile of books. Why did I have so many? I told him in pidgin English that I was a journalist, these were my professional reference works. He stared at the books so fiercely I thought he would have pitched them into a bonfire if one had been nearby. Though he could not read English, he knew that books, particularly foreign books, were dangerous. He stacked the books to one side, painstakingly inspecting the rest of my stuff. Then he sighed deeply, looked at me angrily, said, *"Minut,"* and left, to return with a tired, worn woman whose age I could not guess. She spoke

English and I knew she must have been through the Leningrad blockade. With a sad smile, she said, "You are a correspondent?" Yes, I replied, I was on my way to Moscow for *The New York Times.* "I was in Leningrad during the war," I told her. "I came there when the blockade was lifted." "Oh," she said, "you know our city." I said that I admired Leningrad more than I could say. "I lived through the blockade," she said, "my daughter and I. We survived. My little girl was eleven years old. She had bright blond hair. I watched it turn gray." I shook my head; what could I say to such a woman? "We have seen war," she went on, "we people of Leningrad want peace. We do not want war with America." I bowed silently and when I wrote my first dispatch from Moscow, I quoted her words. She spoke briefly to the customs man. "I must apologize," she said to me. "My comrade is not a very cultured man. He did not understand. I told him that you must have these books for your work. I am sorry if you have been inconvenienced."

No one, not the little man, not the survivor of Leningrad, had given Trotsky or Orwell a glance. My juvenile stratagem had been a failure.

Finally, we got going again. I was glad that I had telegraphed ahead and asked for reservations at the Astoria. I would need a couple of days to see the city again. We were hustled through the Finland Station so fast I caught only a glimpse of the historic armored car from which Lenin made his first speech on the evening of April 17, 1917. The throngs of people, crowds in the station, crowds in the streets, hurrying along under the dim streetlamps, overwhelmed me, the evening bustle of a Russian city, workers, men and women, doing last-minute shopping before going home to dinner.

There had been no crowds in Leningrad in January 1944. There were hardly 500,000 people left of the 3,300,000 who lived there when the war started, June 22, 1941. Now the life of the city seemed normal. Streetcars plowed along, men and women clinging to their sides. There were lots of trucks, a few civilian cars, and many jeeps and command cars still painted army khaki. That was all I could see in the quick passage from the Finland Station, over the Neva to St. Isaac's Square and the Astoria.

It was 6 P.M. when we straggled into the hotel. The Intourist girl told me I was booked to leave on the Red Arrow at 11 P.M.

that night. But, I said, didn't you receive my telegram that I would stay over two days? She stared blankly at me and reiterated that I was leaving on the Red Arrow. My latent anger at Soviet bureaucracy boiled up; I had been back in the Astoria less than five minutes. I went to the manager, who was equally unmovable. I had an idea. "You know," I said, "I was here during the war and met Mayor Popkov. He is my friend. I don't think he will like it if he hears that I was not permitted to stay and pay him a call." I saw the manager flinch. Ha! I said to myself, it is the same the world over. If you know the right people . . . I went ahead. "Get me Mayor Popkov on the telephone, please. I will speak to him about this." The manager seemed to tremble at my words. He broke off the conversation and disappeared. I was pleased. Obviously, he had gone to consult higher authority. In fact, he never appeared again. Nor did I talk to Mayor Popkov. We had a hasty meal, then went off to the Mariinsky Theater, where I watched the first two acts of *Swan Lake*. I had not been so embarrassed in my life. Warren, his wife, myself and the courier went to the theater together. By the rules of his job, the courier was not permitted to leave his mail sack of diplomatic correspondence behind. It was, in fact, locked to his wrist. He tried, gently, to dissuade the minister from including him in the party, but the minister was in an expansive mood. "Of course you're coming, man," he declaimed. So off to the Kirov we went with an Intourist guide, a nice young woman who did not exactly understand what lay ahead. When we got to the theater, in we went, courier, bag and all. Naturally, the ushers halted the courier and insisted that he check his bag at the *gvarderobe*—in Russian theaters, everything must be checked. Not a hat or a coat may be worn into the hall, not a *sumka* (shopping bag) or a parcel can be carried to your seat. To do so is *nekulturny,* and whatever else it may be, the Russian theater is *kulturny.* I tried to divorce myself from my companions as the minister bullied his way past the ushers and propelled the unhappy courier and his bag down the aisle, front and center to front row seats. The ushers and the house manager fluttered like sparrows, but finally flung up their hands in disgust. When it was time to leave, I slunk away. What was worst was that the minister and his wife saw nothing wrong with all this. They acted as though they were dealing with the natives of some remote British colony in the day of Queen Victoria. God, I said to myself, let's hope *Krokodil* (the Russian satirical journal) doesn't get hold of this one. They'll murder us.

I checked into the Metropol about noon on March 8. I did not think the omens were good. Leningrad left a bad taste in my mouth and I was worried about the Anna Louise affair. Nor was she the only correspondent who had been expelled. Bob Magidoff, the NBC man who had been with us on Eric Johnston's trip, had been thrown out a few weeks earlier, also branded as an American spy. Bob had come back to the United States, but in the paranoia of the day, he was not hailed as a hero. When he went to Detroit for a speech, the Neanderthals of the auto industry called him a "Commie" because he didn't preach war against the Soviet Union. This kind of blind-siding, as I would learn, was not uncommon in the cold war.

I found the American news colony much diminished, only seven in all, including myself, Eddy Gilmore and Tom Whitney of AP, Henry Shapiro of UP, Joe Newman of the *Herald Tribune,* Ed Stevens of the *Christian Science Monitor,* and Andrew Steiger, who represented U.S. News and the English Exchange Telegraph agency. There was one English correspondent, Don Dallas of Reuters. It was a far cry from the hustle and bustle of wartime.

The Metropol was more grim than ever. Jack Margolis, the London cockney who had managed the hotel since before the war, was gone, his place taken by a Russian woman who called herself Mrs. Grey, an assiduous student of English. At any hour she could be seen at her desk beside the staircase, poring over grammars and exercise books. I don't know where she got her English name. She could not tell me what had happened to Jack, but I later found that he had vanished into the prison camp system.

I had been assigned Room 393. Alec Werth's grand piano was gone, but the room was furnished in the same heavy mahogany, with an enormous bed backed by a carved headboard, a pier glass that reached to the high ceiling, a wardrobe big enough to hide a pony, break-back chairs upholstered in faded brocade that dated to Rasputin's days, a desk of fumed oak filling the space between the window and the French doors which gave onto the courtyard, a settee, a worn and dusty Oriental rug which covered most of the parquet floor (replaced two years later by a blue-and-taupe

Chinese rug about three inches thick, part of a shipment that swamped the Metropol management one day) and a handsome round mahogany table, which had belonged to Cholerton and been left in the care of a succession of correspondents since his departure before the war.

Room 393 boasted an elaborate chandelier fitted with a dim light bulb. When I sat beside Cholerton's table and peered at the shadowy corners of the room, I could see Rasputin's ghost mocking me with obscene gestures. The Metropol had been built just after 1900 (it seemed much older) and was decorated with mosaics by Golovin, which had so deteriorated I was hardly aware of their presence. Before World War I, nothing was more chic than the Metropol. The discreet rooms off the balcony of the dining room were the rendezvous of the city's millionaires and their most expensive ladies. After the Revolution it became Dom Sovetov (House of Soviets) No. 2 and here were held meetings of the Soviet Executive Committee, including that which approved the execution of the Czar and his family.

It did not take long to confirm my forebodings about Moscow. The U.S. embassy was in a state of siege. The atmosphere had grown poisonous in the last days of Ambassador Walter Bedell Smith. There had been two security scandals: a young woman of Slavic origin named Annabelle Bucar, who had been in the information section, had defected to the Russians (she fell in love with a tenor at the Operetta Theater) and published a small book "exposing" the nefarious deeds of the Americans, their spying, their anti-Soviet plots; and a young man in the code room had recently gone over to the Soviet side. No embassy staff member or member's wife was to walk the streets of Moscow alone. In the hysteria, few poked their noses out of their flats. No ambassador had been named to replace Smith, and Foy Kohler, the able chargé d'affaires, was running a very tight ship. Correspondents, I quickly discovered, were not entirely trusted by the embassy. After all, they lived in the "outer" (Russian) world. Other embassies were not much better. The British were trying to shelter a dozen Russian women who had married Britishers during the war. The husbands had been compelled to return to England and the Russians wouldn't give the wives visas to get out. Originally there had been a hundred cases. One by one, the women vanished. Now many of the remaining dozen were living in the embassy to avoid being picked up by the NKVD (as the Russian police were called at that moment). A British subject was living in the embassy basement, a man accused by the Russians of having transmitted venereal disease to a Russian woman. He would go on living in that basement until Stalin's death, the British unwilling to have him go to prison on a false charge. An American sailor was being held in prison in Odessa, serving out a five-year sentence for a minor brawl. The French had given refuge to several elderly gentlewomen who had come to Russia before the Revolution as governesses, and were now unable to get exit visas. The disappearance of maids, cooks, chauffeurs, clerks or, in the case of correspondents, couriers and translators was a daily event. These hapless people were provided to the foreigners by an agency of the NKVD. After they had worked a year or two, the police considered them "turned," arrested them and sent them to prison camp.

Well, I had known it was going to be bad. I had talked with Magidoff before leaving New York. I had tried to extrapolate from my wartime experience. But not until I set foot in the Metropol did I realize how bad it was—and even then I didn't know the worst things. These took years to put together.

It didn't take long to get the feel of the Anna Louise Strong case. I heard—in whispers—that her old friend Mikhail Borodin had been arrested too, as well as the full staff of the *Moscow Daily News,* on which they had long collaborated. The *Moscow Daily News* itself was closed down.

I quickly learned why I had not met Mayor Popkov in Leningrad. There had been a lot of changes in Leningrad since the death of Zhdanov. Popkov was now officially described as "no longer in Leningrad." Just where he was and what he was doing I could not find out.

These facts came to light within a week of my arrival in Moscow, when the dismissal from his government and political positions of N. A. Voznesensky, a Politburo member, head of State Planning, a member of the "Leningrad group," was revealed. Along with him went Popkov, A. A. Kuznetsov and others close to Zhdanov. Not even now is the full story of the Leningrad Affair known. In his "secret speech" of 1956, Nikita Khrushchev referred to the "affair" and said that Kuznetsov, Popkov, and Voznesensky had lost their lives. He provided no details. In later speeches in Leningrad in the summer of 1957, Khrushchev and

Marshal Georgi K. Zhukov said Malenkov had been afraid to come to Leningrad because he was responsible for the Leningrad atrocity. Malenkov and Zhdanov had been bitter rivals to succeed Stalin. In 1946, by means not yet known, Zhdanov drove Malenkov out of the Politburo and out of Moscow, but within a year he made a comeback and the rivalry intensified. It did not last long. Zhdanov died, so it was announced, of a heart attack on August 31, 1948. He had been suffering from heart disease for some time. Stalin's daughter, Svetlana, knew Zhdanov and his family well. She liked Zhdanov and respected Zhdanov's closest associate, A. A. Kuznetsov. In the last year of Zhdanov's life, knowing Zhdanov's heart was bad, knowing the critical strain on him, Stalin deliberately taunted and reviled him, increasing the pressure. It was at this time, Svetlana once told me, that the Leningrad Affair was building up, fed by reports from Malenkov and Beria, then in alliance. How Stalin could have believed anything bad about these men, Svetlana could not understand.

She felt that her father's conduct hastened Zhdanov's death. Stalin may have gone further. When the "Doctors' Plot" was announced, on January 13, 1953, Zhdanov was listed as a victim of the conspiracy of Kremlin doctors. All his life, Stalin had demonstrated a tendency toward medical murder, first displayed in 1925 when he insisted that M. V. Frunze, the war commissar, submit to an operation that he did not wish and did not need. The operation cost Frunze his life. In the mid-thirties, Stalin blamed "criminal doctors" for the death of Maxim Gorky and others whose deaths he himself hastened if not arranged.

In fact, Stalin's conduct with Zhdanov had a parallel in his attitude toward Lenin during Lenin's illness in 1922 and 1923. Lenin suffered a series of strokes and was increasingly incapacitated. His doctors insisted that he carry only a light work load and that, above all, he be spared stress or strain or emotional upset, which might cause a sudden rise in blood pressure. Stalin was well aware of these medical strictures, yet he deliberately upset Lenin, opposing Lenin's projects in and out of the Politburo and behaving in a rude and vulgar manner with Lenin's wife, Krupskaya. This caused Lenin to flare up in angry outbursts—just the response the doctors wished to spare him. Whether Stalin acted as he did with the intention of imperiling the lives of Lenin and Zhdanov cannot, of course, be determined; the effect was the same.

Without question, Stalin was responsible for the deaths of Kuznetsov, briefly sent to the Far East and then executed in 1949, and Popkov, who may already have been shot when I was trying to telephone him from the Astoria in March 1949 (small wonder the hotel manager hid). Voznesensky was not executed until 1950. No one has ever explained the delay.

Svetlana married Yuri Zhdanov in 1949, only months after his father's death. Stalin had been encouraging this match for a couple of years. Andrei Zhdanov was the man who, it then seemed, Stalin had picked as his successor. The marriage of his daughter to the son of the heir apparent was a way of securing the succession. Stalin's daughter would stand at the side of the new emperor, Stalin's grandson could inherit the throne. Stalin's first son, Yakov, whom he hated, had died in World War II. His second son, Vasily, whom he despised, was drinking himself to death. But through the Zhdanov alliance the dynasty could be secured. Dream stuff? I do not think so. Hardly had Zhdanov died and the ascendency of Malenkov (and Beria) been ensured, than Stalin changed his tune and tried, in vain, to dissuade Svetlana from marrying Yuri. When Svetlana did not get along within the Zhdanov family (Yuri came under severe political pressure after his father's death), Stalin rudely told his daughter he had warned she would not be happy with the Zhdanovs.

Not since Ivan the Terrible had such fear and intrigue gripped the Kremlin. No wonder I found the air in Moscow exuded evil.

In *The 900 Days,* published twenty years after the Leningrad Affair, I managed to collect some details of that shadowy plot, but the fact that neither Khrushchev nor anyone since has dared to make public the full record bears witness to its horror. It stands as a monument to the limitless terror political rivalry inspires in the Soviet Union.

Indeed, the political wounds of the affair and the siege were still so fresh and so deep in 1969 that my account of the heroism of Leningrad evoked a violent propaganda attack upon the book and myself. But the people of Leningrad who read smuggled copies of the book were unanimous in their praise and embarrassing in their gratitude that I had erected at least a small monument to their pain and courage.

I knew enough in my first weeks in Moscow to realize that

something was badly wrong in Russia. Something was wrong wherever I turned—Leningrad, Anna Louise Strong, Borodin, the Jews. I had stumbled into one of Stalin's worst paroxysms. Anti-Semitism, camouflaged under the title of a drive against "cosmopolitanism," was raging like the plague. The Czar's Black Hundreds and *Okhotnoryadsy,* the masters of the pogrom, would have felt at home reading the names of the victims and looking at the "Semitic" noses in the cartoons. To understand why this was going on was another matter, and I am not sure that I do even now.

On March 13, I sat down at my typewriter in my new office in Room 317 of the Metropol, looking out over the asphalt of Theater Square and across to the Moskva Hotel and the tumbledown pile that housed Moscow's animated-film theater. I began to tap out my first copy for *The New York Times.* I wrote about the mood I had found in Russia. It was, I said, "a preoccupied land, preoccupied lest new war break out while the scars of the old are not yet healed." This was my most important impression, that a palpable fear of war colored almost every phase of Russian life, and lay behind the terror. Moscow itself had not been damaged by World War II, but most of European Russia had been devastated. Leningrad bore deep scars. Its outskirts were a vast ruin. The same was true of the other great cities—Kiev, Kharkov, Stalingrad, Minsk. When you realized the totality of destruction, I wrote, you understood more easily why fear of what would happen if new war came was so vivid in people's minds.

I submitted this dispatch to the censorship. They held it for many hours, then returned it with all these conclusions deleted. It was up to me whether to send it forward in this dilapidated form. Finally I affixed a limp kind of lead to it and it ran in the *Times,* referring to "physical and psychological changes" and the preoccupation of the Soviet press with "organizing an international front to protect world peace." I then sketched a picture of what Russia looked like and quoted the Leningrad customs woman on war and peace. But my main conclusions the censor had simply obliterated.

That same day I filed a second dispatch, describing the atmosphere of suspicion and terror that had been created in Moscow by the deterioration of relations between the United States and the Soviet Union.

I called this "a painful and difficult" subject, but insisted that the readers of the *Times* must know the conditions under which the newly reestablished bureau of the newspaper was operating.

All foreigners, and particularly Americans, I said, were subject to harsh restrictions, including a prohibition on direct contact with officials of the Soviet government except as arranged by the Foreign Office. This regulation was backed by a draconian state secrets act. Travel was tightly restricted, some roads leading out of Moscow were closed at the city limits. Many regions of the country were closed entirely to travel. All dispatches were subjected to a rigid censorship.

"There is what might be termed a psychological hazard," I wrote, "arising from repeated suggestions by the Soviet press that the chief function of many foreign correspondents is spying and espionage. In the case of Americans this hazard had been extended to the physical sphere by the expulsion of two correspondents—Anna Louise Strong and Robert Magidoff—within the past year. Both Miss Strong and Magidoff were charged with intelligence operations."

Normal everyday contact between American correspondents and Soviet citizens had become nonexistent.

The result, I observed, was that most American reports were mere rewrites of the Soviet press.

My dispatch was held for two weeks and then killed in its entirety by the censors. I was to learn that no mention of censorship and no negative comments were ever passed.

In my first letter to Mr. James, on March 28, 1949 (sent through the diplomatic pouch), I told him that the censorship was "substantially worse than I have ever seen it." I pointed out that almost everything that did not appear in the Soviet press, as well as much that did, was deleted. Conclusions, analysis, speculation, was cut. So were biographical details, identification of individuals, and comparisons. "Threats to peace" were passed, but "threats of war" were not.

"All dispatches enamating from Moscow—*mine* as well as those of the news agencies," I wrote, "are automatically biased. They definitely misrepresent the news and distort it to fit the frequently incomprehensible Soviet propaganda line. These dispatches are printed in the *Times* with no indication to the reader that they have been tampered with."

This, I said, "adds up to a fraud on the American public—a dangerous one under present conditions and a dismal one under the best of circumstances."

I recommended that the *Times* place labels on all my dispatches (and others from Moscow): "Passed by Soviet Censor." Warning that this might bring reprisals, I told Mr. James this was a risk which must be run.

I am sorry that for no reason which was ever made plain to me, Mr. James, Arthur Hays Sulzberger and *The New York Times* in general, individually, collectively and repeatedly refused to follow my recommendation. I know now, having examined the internal files of the *Times,* that Sulzberger on at least two occasions proposed that the *Times* place a "Passed by Censorship" slug on my dispatches as I had requested. His recommendations were not adopted, nor was any explanation ever offered to me, except a suggestion that there were many censorships and if Moscow was slugged, all would have to be. Since the only other permanent censorship (it still exists) of importance was the Israeli military censorship, this did not seem a valid reason, nor does it now. The matter became moot when the Soviet finally abolished censorship in 1961, but it was not a moot question in 1949 and it became less so as the cold war deepened, with serious consequences to readers of the *Times,* to myself and to the paper.

I sent through the diplomatic pouch or by other private means every scrap of my censored copy, along with a commentary on the significance of the cuts. I made weekly recommendations for handling these materials, often proposing that stories be written locally in New York. Sometimes this was done, including an excellent article on "cosmopolitanism" by Harry Schwartz, then a Syracuse University professor free-lancing for the *Times.* The story used my material and carried his name. Taken all in all, however, my efforts had little effect on the executives of the *Times* or the deskmen. They either did not read the record of censorship (or the excellent analyses made of my materials by Will Lissner, a longtime *Times* specialist in Communist affairs) or did not grasp its significance. Nor did the editors seem to understand the distortions they were presenting to the American public. To be certain, my dispatches had great value—if they were read in the appropriate context. But to present them raw, with no reminder that they had been processed by Soviet censors, was a disservice. To this day I cannot understand what was in the minds of men like James and Catledge and the foreign editor, Manny Freedman. Again and again and again I wrote to them. They sat like bumps on a log and did nothing. When my reports began to be publicly criticized, they flopped around like hens in a chicken coop, forgetting all my warnings, and in some cases even suspecting I was a purveyor of party propaganda. It was a sorry show.

Within a week of my arrival at the Metropol, I began to wonder if I might be in over my head. There was no way in which I could evaluate what was happening behind Kremlin walls. But the currents were deep, swift and terrifying. I did not have to understand the Leningrad Affair, cosmopolitanism or Anna Louise Strong to sense that I had landed in a Moscow that was filled with fear. I had in my usual frenetic way dashed off letters or made telephone calls to everyone whom I had met in Moscow during the war. I did not reach anyone, and when I began to bump into people I knew on the street, they looked right through me. Quickly enough I understood that this was only sensible. Contact with an American "spy" was fatal. But understanding did not make my job any easier. The old bureau had been wiped out. There was no secretary, no translator, no chauffeur, no car. I didn't even have letterheads or stationery. Costs were higher than anyone had anticipated, and I was stuck with a living allowance of one hundred dollars a month and an expense account too low for survival. I wanted to bring Ellen to Moscow, but we would have to live, I saw, in the faded splendor of Alec Werth's old room. No doubt, as Eddy Gilmore said, they had popped me into Werth's room to save the expense of bugging another room. Well, I didn't give a damn about bugs. I wasn't going to be saying or doing anything that I wanted to conceal. But I was disturbed by the costs, the fortress mentality and the terror-tinted atmosphere. Could I bring Ellen to this kind of Moscow? What would it do to her or to us? And how would she occupy herself in Moscow? Certainly not playing house in Room 393.

"It is hard to convey the atmosphere of the foreign colony here," I wrote her on March 15, a week after arriving. "I should say, however, that it is the sort of thing that Oechsner and Beattie and Shirer are more familiar with than you and I. Or Howard Smith, for example. You might want to reread that last book of his." All these men had been correspondents in Hitler's Berlin.

I hadn't been in Moscow a month before she wrote to say that she was not coming in June, that she was not ready to make up her mind about coming at all. I was stricken; I cabled, I telephoned, I wrote letters like a madman. After a while, she fell in love with someone else. Then, I think, she fell out of love. Strand by strand, our relationship simply unraveled. It was ending, but it took me a long, long time to believe that.

The *Times* thought I was doing very well, censorship or no censorship. I got glowing letters from Manny Freedman and Arthur Hays Sulzberger and Cy Sulzberger, and I would have been even more pleased if I had been able then to read the analyses by Will Lissner. He started as a skeptic but soon became as powerful a champion as I could have, understanding the problems of my daily struggle with the censorship, the nuances of my writing, the implications of the censor's cuts even better than I did myself. It was a remarkable service and stood me in good stead when, as soon would occur, I badly needed confidence within the good gray portals of the Times Building at 229 West 43rd Street.

And, as I have found by consulting the journal I kept of my observations, my grasp of what was going on in Moscow was far better than I thought at the time. I correctly understood that Voznesensky and the other victims of the Leningrad Affair were adherents of Zhdanov; that Zhdanov and Malenkov had been rivals for power; that with the death of Zhdanov, Malenkov was purging the Zhdanov men. (I did not, of course, know that they were being shot.) I knew a great deal more about the cosmopolitanism drive than I could report—the extent of victims, the closing of Jewish theaters, newspapers and cultural institutions, and the dissolution of the Jewish Anti-Fascist Committee. (I did not then know of the murder of the famous Jewish director S. M. Mikhoels in 1948, nor that the members of the Anti-Fascist Committee would, in due course, be arrested and most of them shot.) I had made the correct connection between the arrest of Anna Louise Strong, the closing of the *Moscow Daily News* and the vanishing of Mikhail Borodin. And again, although no one was paying heed, I noted that: "The Kremlin is still very unsure of the situation in China. [China] gets very scanty reference in the press and even statements by the Chinese, laudatory of Russia and the Soviet leadership, are handled most gingerly. My opinion is that the Kremlin has its fingers crossed on its Chinese friends and will keep them that way for some time."

One thing I couldn't figure out. If it had been Stalin who was in such a hurry to see that I got a visa, why wasn't he letting me report what was happening in Moscow? This was a question to which I never would get an answer.

27 | Olga

The lobby of the Metropol was a cavern of gloom, marbleized pillars, faded frescoes, shadows and deep leather chairs in whose depths slumped the "angels," as the Russians called them, the "YMCA boys," as the Americans said—in a word, the *shpiks,* the plainclothes agents whose duty it was to follow the handful of foreigners who still resided in the hotel, to keep an eye out, particularly, for meetings with Russians. The *shpiks* were shabby young men in their twenties or early thirties, and their thin faces bore hangdog expressions. They looked away when you glanced at them, as though trained not to lock eyes with a "client."

After Stalin's death, when I began to travel unattended except, sometimes, by swarms of these insect-men, I discovered a great tease. I would point my camera and watch them run for cover behind posts, around corners and even, on one occasion, under a park bench. A trivial occupation, it gave me mild pleasure, something like lazily scratching a fleabite.

The *shpiks* were bred or trained to type. They wore a particular kind of gray water-resistant topcoat in spring, fall and early summer, velour hats and sturdy shoes. One May Day, standing in the Red Square section reserved for diplomats, correspondents and the lowest order of foreign guests, I spotted thirty or forty *shpiks,* each with a new purple or green velour hat, each with new yellow shoes with thick soles and each with a new gray topcoat, May Day presents from the ministry.

It was no trick to pick out these gentlemen. I seldom bothered, but occasionally out of boredom I made a sudden turn into a doorway or a shop or around a corner, then reversed my direction and bumped into the poor *shpik,* hurrying to get me back in sight. I sometimes spoke to them. That always embarrassed them. Admiral Alan Kirk, an easy-mannered and sensible navy man, came to Moscow in June 1949 as ambassador. Two carloads of plainclothesmen followed him wherever he went. He made it his practice to speak to these men (other ambassadors pretended they didn't exist). The men gradually began to behave more like human beings. Once when Kirk's car broke down on the way to the foreign ministry, he insisted on their giving him a ride so he would not be late. When he went on a trip to Lake Baikal in Siberia, the plainclothesmen took him out on the lake for a row.

I made no effort to conceal my movements. They could not have been more conventional: trips to the American embassy, visits to other foreign missions, the Bolshoi, the Conservatory of Music, the Art Theater, the movies. I saw two or three Russian plays a week—my substitute for the Russian life from which I was excluded. I had to put up with an overdose of anti-American propaganda—half the theaters were playing spy melodramas which featured American villains (U.S. diplomats or the CIA or both). These productions often boasted what the Russians took to be "realistic" Broadway sets, phonographs playing American jazz, American "spies" in dark glasses, women in sexy "American" gowns, American cigarettes and whiskey. I quickly understood that part of their appeal was the forbidden allure of American life, just as Leonid Utesov, conductor of the All-Russian State Jazz Orchestra, now rechristened the All-Russian State Vaudeville Orchestra, kept alive by playing excerpts of "cannibalistic, anti-humane American jazz" and then giving a lecture on how terrible it was.

I think the professional shadowers found me poor game. There never could be much doubt what I was up to. The *dezhurnaya* on the floor always knew whether I was in my room or not and who was with me. The tap on my telephone kept them up to the minute on who I talked with. The bug in the room would inform them of conversations there. I acquired a courier, a middle-aged Russian lady named Lydia, who did my shopping and took my cables to the telegraph office. She reported on that. I had a chauffeur, Vasily, good-natured, inefficient and strongly addicted to vodka, whose pride was a *cherv,* or tapeworm, that had been removed from his intestine. It measured, he swore, several meters in length. Vasily, of course, reported where he drove me.

I began to study Russian with a tutor from Burobin, the agency of the Foreign Office (or more properly, the police) that provided services and employees to foreigners. I quickly got rid of my first tutor, a pleasant young woman, a recent graduate from the language school; her interest was not in teaching Russian, but in practicing her English with a live American. I got another, who thought her mission was to indoctrinate me in the glories of Communism. I turned her back and finally hired an elderly woman who had been teaching Russian to two generations of American embassy people. She was quite satisfied with her English and had long since given up propagating Communism. She was pedantic, but she began to bang some Russian into my skull. All these ladies were available to report on my movements, as was a translator I got after a period in which Ludmilla Shapiro helped me out.

With this array, there wasn't much the plainclothesmen didn't know about me. I avoided casual contact with Russians. If someone stopped me on the street to ask directions, I would respond if the inquirer was a peasant who couldn't tell a foreigner from a Muscovite. But if I was sitting on a park bench and a stranger tried to pick a conversation, I took to my heels. If someone, as is the Russian custom, took a vacant seat at my table in a restaurant and opened up a conversation, I would turn a deaf ear. I went on the principle that anyone who spoke to me was either ignorant and didn't realize the danger he could get into, or an agent provocateur. Either way, I wanted nothing to do with him.

Once a nice man sat down at my table in the Metropol café and insisted on conversing. He said he was a doctor from Tashkent, in for a medical meeting. He wanted me to join him in a visit to the museums, the theater, or at least for dinner. I refused these propositions. Finally, he asked to have breakfast with me. I was too ashamed to say no, but got a colleague to join me the next morning. We had a pleasant breakfast. The man invited both of us to do some sightseeing or go to the theater, but we refused. What a naive provocation, I told my friend; how in hell did the NKVD expect us to fall for that? How, indeed. About two years later, Stalin having died, I was waiting at the Tashkent airport to fly to Samarkand. A plane came in, the passengers debarked and there was my doctor, delighted to see me. He had been exactly what he said he was—an innocent visitor from Central Asia. But the paranoia prevailing in Moscow had infected me along with everyone else.

I had one habit that must have bothered the secret agents. I walked the streets of Moscow, by the hour and by the day. Cut off from Russians, lacking the normal contacts of life, I hit on the idea of getting to understand Moscow by continuous observation. I didn't know what it would tell me, but I was sure I would learn more than I could from the cast-iron newspapers, the propagandist drivel, the communiqués, *Pravda* editorials and diplomatic gossip.

Almost every day I took a walk, I got to know the Arbat quarter of the city as well as I had known the Oak Lake Addition in Minneapolis. I knew the houses, knew who had lived in them (an excellent book by Sytin on the streets of old Moscow had just come out, and it gave me open sesame to the city). I loved the *kitai gorod,* the Chinese city, just behind the Metropol, and the honeycomb of medieval streets back of GUM on Red Square, now largely obliterated by construction of the hideous Hotel Rossiya. Here in Razin Street stood the original small stone house of the Romanovs, long a museum but closed and dilapidated during those late Stalin years. Sometimes I dreamed about the old streets behind Red Square, the massive buildings that had survived Napoleon's fire in 1812, the underground cut-stone chambers that (I was certain) connected the Kremlin cellars with these old palaces and with the embankments of the Moskva River just beyond. I knew all about the Neglinnaya, the river that once flowed through the heart of Moscow, and gave its name to a crooked shopping street. Once a moat, now the Neglinnaya flowed underground beside the Alexandrovka Gardens along the Kremlin walls. God knows where, I thought, this maze of tunnels led, but I was certain there were secret doors and secret exits and that Stalin and his men could walk for miles under Moscow and emerge somewhere in the Arbat, or slip under the Moskva River and wind up in Zarechye, once the quarter of the boyars beyond the river.

I got to know the Moscow streets, the Moscow crowds, the traffic patterns, the shopping habits. I spent hours in the Mostorg, once the proud department store of the Scottish firm of Muir and Merrilees. In those days GUM, with its gray-stone arcade across Red Square from the Kremlin, was devoted to government offices. Stalin had decided it constituted a security risk—he thought someone might wander into this Alexander III pile with a high-powered rifle and put a bullet into his office. So the department store was closed, the goods packed, and offices, clerks, red tape and paperwork moved in. No need for the old store anyway. It reminded people of the days when you could get anything you wanted in GUM. Better close it and stop the remembering. (One of the first acts of the heirs of Stalin was to renovate GUM and reopen it as Russia's premier department store.)

I shopped the stores—the food stores, the bookstores and particularly the jewelry stores—making my way among the generals' wives hulked over the gold, diamond and precious-stone counters. I got to know every gem in the collections and particularly the huge emerald that glistened in a store on the Stoleshnikov for several years. It was priced at 144,000 rubles. I don't know how to calculate a price like that in the dollars of the early 1950s, probably $20,000 to $25,000. As Scott Fitzgerald might have said, it was an emerald as big as the Metropol. Month after month, I watched the wives of party bosses stare at this bauble with greedy eyes. It was still there a year and a half after Stalin died. But finally it vanished. I often wondered whether the buxom lady into whose bosom it fell—it had to be a buxom lady —dared to display such an example of conspicuous expenditure in the workers' state.

The jewelry stores were barometers of cash flow, price and exchange values. When rumors of price changes or currency revaluation swept Moscow, the jewelry stores and commission shops thronged with buyers. The response was always the same: Buy anything—particularly those little pellets of gold your dentist was supposed to use in fashioning your new gold molars. The Muscovites were never wrong. They knew that any change would be for the worse. Sometimes the government simply confiscated the people's savings or arbitrarily decreed that today's ruble represented ten of yesterday's. The only protection was *things.* Any old bric-a-brac you bought in the commission store was better than rubles in your pocket or in a savings bank.

I could plot the rise and fall of the economy by shortages and surpluses in the stores—an abundance, say, of expensive clocks and a shortage of pots and pans meant more metal going into guns, less for the consumer. If sausage began to disappear, I knew the harvest was bad and Moscow was stocking up for a hard winter. If there was nothing for sale at the women's underwear counter, if every woman in Moscow was hunting frantically for bras to contain her robust bosom, I knew the cotton crop in Uzbekistan had failed again.

I could follow the fluctuations of foreign trade. When oranges from Israel (Russia still had relations with Israel in those days) appeared in the stores at five dollars an orange and sold out overnight, I knew Anastas Mikoyan had scored another coup. He was paying Tel Aviv only a half cent apiece for them. When I found more sidewalk vodka stands on the streets than white-aproned country girls selling *morozhenie* (ice cream), I knew that the dairy industry was doing badly and the government was pouring vodka into the trade system to increase its revenues (and cater to chronic Russian alcoholism).

Oh, there was no end to what I could learn by keeping my eyes and ears open on the Moscow streets. As I grew to know more and more Russian, I could understand what the women were saying in the queues. They were always careful. You never heard the name Stalin. But I got the meaning.

One day, after Stalin had died, I was walking up Gorky Street. I sensed something had changed but I couldn't spot what it was. I halted and simply stood still for two or three minutes looking at the street and the passing crowds. Suddenly it came to me: no uniforms! For years every other man on the street wore a uniform, not necessarily an army uniform—a railroad worker's uniform, a miner's uniform, a river transport uniform, a communications ministry uniform. Overnight they had vanished. As the men passed in their gray overcoats, I could see threads dangling where epaulets had been ripped off, new buttons sewed on. It was a symbolic part of the new post-Stalin era.

Of course, I don't pretend that I could penetrate the secrets of the Kremlin by a tour of Moscow streets and stores. But I learned a lot, just as I learned a lot by going to the theater and finding that Ostrovsky's plays about the Moscow *kupechestvo* of the mid-1800s outdrew the anti-American productions of Nikolai Virta. Often the theater made good stories; the plays conveyed points the censors would not let me make directly. And often the censors told me more than they understood by what they killed. When an absurdly offensive play about President Truman was staged under the title *The Mad Haberdasher,* the censor would not even let me transmit its title. The line between domestic and foreign propaganda was drawn very nicely in experiences like this. As the year wore on, I became more and more surefooted in my judgments, and looking back now at my journal, I will match my observations against anyone's of that era. I can't say as much for my dispatches, because their quality (and quantity) was so rigidly controlled by the censors. Even here, however, I developed indirect means of getting my points across. Unfortunately, when I wrote obliquely enough to slip my thought past the censor, it usually slipped past the drowsing copyreader in New York, and like as not, I would receive an inquiry asking me to clarify the very point I had couched in Aesopian language to evade censorship.

Once I spoke of conditions in Siberia as resembling those to be found at Leavenworth, having in mind, of course, the famous penitentiary. I was delighted when the censor passed the comparison (as they rarely did)—then New York promptly asked what I meant by comparing Siberia to Leavenworth. On another occasion (this was after Stalin's death), livestock production was announced in actual numbers, as it had not been in decades. They showed that Russia's livestock census for the first time since the Revolution exceeded that of the last czarist year, 1916. Naturally, the Soviets did not make this comparison; I established it through my own statistical tables. I knew I could never get so direct and damaging a revelation past the censorship, so I couched my dispatch in flattering language, saying that there had been a splendid improvement in livestock figures. Lower down I buried the fact that "this even exceeded that for the year 1916 under the czars." To my joy, the censor let my story through. To my dismay, I got a message from New York rebuking me. What did I mean hailing Soviet livestock production when it barely exceeded that of 1916?

I was, as I said, totally sealed off from the Russian populace. I saw none of my old friends. I cultivated no new friends. I had no casual acquaintances. I associated only with Russians supplied to me by Burobin—a translator, a courier, a chauffeur, a cook (two or three single American embassy men who lived in the Metropol joined with me in an informal mess). That was it.

Except for Olga. Extraordinarily, we had met again and occasionally, with conspiratorial precautions John Le Carré might have envied, we began to see each other. We understood the total danger and unwisdom of such encounters. Olga was courageous, almost a daredevil, this being the tradition bequeathed by her father. But she had no intention of exposing herself or me. I was even more cautious on her behalf. She could be arrested and sent to Siberia. The most that could happen to me, I thought, was an effort to "turn" me by threatening reprisals against Olga. Or I might be expelled. We talked about these perils and decided for the same reason, I think, to risk them. It was not a flaming up of old passions. We felt warm and close and affectionate, but had no illusion that we had a future. Each of us was lonely, isolated, trapped in the great Soviet prison society. Olga had only one close friend. She was alienated from her mother and her stepsister. I had no close friends (although soon two would emerge). I did not admit in words that my relationship with Ellen was at an end, but inside I understood that this was so.

We felt very, very close or we would not have dared the risks. We never communicated except by public telephone, and we telephoned hardly at all. We set the time for our next rendezvous before separating. We met only at one place—the room in a communal flat that Olga shared with her mother, the lion's den being the safest place of all. Olga's mother still worked at the automobile factory, round-the-clock forty-eight-hour shifts. We met only when she was on duty. Each occupant of the communal flat had his own doorbell ring. Olga's was three longs. She always answered the door—greeting me in Russian, I mumbling quietly (I could not speak Russian yet)—and led me to her room, only two steps from the door. She locked the door and we were in each other's arms. It was an old building with thick walls. Once inside, we were free for the evening, a little nook of our own in the heart of Hades.

Of course, I first had to make my way to the flat without observation. It was located in a rabbit warren of streets, eight or ten blocks from a metro stop. I would leave the Metropol at the supper-hour rush and head for the metro station as if going to the embassy, wearing my gray caracul hat and an inconspicuous overcoat. I did not stand out except for my height. I would board the subway, ride a few stops, standing close to the entrance, then get off just as the doors were closing, swiftly glancing back and forth to see if anyone got off after I did. No one ever did. I would then board the next train at the very last, making certain that no one standing on the platform got in after me. Having repeated the maneuver several times, I felt (and was) secure. No one could now be tailing me. I would proceed to a metro stop near Olga's and walk through the streets, turning corners and doubling back. There was little foot traffic and I could easily spot anyone following me. No one did. A militiaman had a post at a corner not far from the entrance to Olga's building. Olga and her mother felt sorry for him. He had three children, was an ordinary policeman, not a *shpik,* worked long hours, standing through the cold in winter, got a tiny salary and had a hard time. The Khludovas often gave him tea and something to eat. I saw this man several times, but never got close enough for him to take note of me. Never did I encounter anyone on the dark stairs (no lights; no heat; smell of cabbage and mold).

We had a bite to eat—more than a bite, for Olga made these occasions special. I was so stupid she had to explain to me she didn't have money to get meat or fish. I brought her a dozen presents, but never anything practical. Stacks of paperback detective stories, which she loved. Once I brought George Orwell's *1984.* "What are you trying to do to me, Harrison?" she said in horror. "My God," I said, "I didn't think. I'll take it away." She looked at it a minute. "No," she said. "The hell with them. I'll read it," and read it she did, and next time we talked about *1984* for hours. She thought Orwell gave too much credit to the party. "They just can't organize that well," she said. "He's thinking of Germans, not Russians." She was right. Neither of us knew that Orwell's inspiration had come from a remarkable book by the Russian author Zamyatin, called *We.*

What did we talk about? What didn't we talk about! No matter the fear that hung in the room, that never left my mind (nor, I am certain, Olga's): there were no barriers to our conversation. I told her how I had mucked up my life, bit by bit, all the way from leaving Moscow in August 1944 to coming back in 1949. "I never thought I'd see you again," I said. "I *knew* I'd never see you again," Olga told me.

She told me what had happened after I left Moscow and after her brother died. She could hardly remember the autumn of 1944. She had lost all sense of reality. Sometime in November or December she had left Moscow and gone to the Caucasus, winding up in Tbilisi, living in a "wild" room, a room rented privately, a hovel. She had nothing to do there, no friends, no money, no desire to live. She drifted day by day, sitting in sidewalk cafés, drinking with Georgians, wandering into the mountains, spending days in the vineyards, carried along like a chip in the surf. How long this went on she could not say. Probably until the summer of 1945. The war was over. She met a young Georgian. He seemed to have an important job; she never knew exactly what, but he was very busy and he needed someone to travel between Tbilisi and Moscow, a courier, a messenger. She was glad to do it. It meant nothing to her, but he said it would pay well and all she had to do was sit in a plane, come to Moscow, deliver some papers, wait a few days, get another packet and go back to Georgia. "I was simply drifting," Olga said. "I thought I could paint in Georgia. But I didn't. I sat in the cafés, I drank wine, I read books. I wouldn't kill myself, but if I had fallen into the river or slipped on a cliff, I would not have struggled. I didn't have anything to live for."

She thought the Georgian "businessman" was amusing. He was like a child. He was serious about his business, but the rest of the time he sat drinking in the cafés, sang songs, and had a good time. He was handsome and girls liked him. He told jokes and made Olga laugh. It was the first time she had laughed in months.

I don't know how many trips Olga made. When she found she was getting fifteen hundred rubles a trip, she knew something must be wrong, yet she paid no attention until it occurred to her that the portfolios she was carrying were too heavy for papers. They had all been heavy. She had even made a remark to her friend. "What do you have in here, Saava? It is heavy as lead." She remembered his sharp look and his quick reply: "Well, you know, nothing is more heavy than paper." But that wasn't true. The portfolio was much too heavy. Sitting on the plane, she fumbled with the bag and the catch sprang open. She reached inside and found a packet wrapped in heavy paper and tied with cord. The knot was sealed with red wax. She held it a moment and dropped it back into the bag with trembling hands. It had to be gold! It all fell into place—the unbusinesslike businessman, the courier trips, the ridiculously high pay. Dear God, she said to herself, let me get this out of my hands. Smuggling gold—she could be shot. She got to the Moscow airport, handed over the packet, and that was the end. She knew she ought to go to the police, but she did not dare. Who would believe she had been so stupid? She had been an idiot. She had risked her life without knowing she was risking it. But this experience shocked her out of her despair. She settled in Moscow and went back to her old job in the animation studio. She accepted her brother's death. Nothing would bring him back. I had vanished into America. She would never see me again. She had good times with her friends in the studio. None of them had any money, but when someone needed a bribe to get a room, all chipped in, one for all and all for one. It was a silly life, but they laughed a lot. They saw foreign films at the closed showings of the State Film Committee. Eric Johnston's organization still shipped in pictures, even though Moscow never bought them. The only foreign pictures being shown publicly were old American films seized in Berlin in 1945, particularly Johnny Weissmuller Tarzan pictures. A youngster Olga knew had seen Tarzan sixteen times, very good for the film houses, which were dying on the vine. No one could make a profit on Stalin's propaganda pictures.

Olga told me a secret. Her studio was located in the tulip-bulb church that stood at the doorstep of Spaso House, residence of the American ambassador. There in Spas na Peske, Savior on the Sands, the film animators worked in little cubicles carved out of the church walls. Outside romped the neighborhood children, some Russian, some American, ignorant of the chamber of magic behind the old church tower.

Olga's stories took me into the private corner of Moscow that she inhabited—the problems of the studio, underpaid, over-worked, perpetually behind "plan," sometimes harangued by party agitators, sometimes called upon to fulfill dangerous as-signments, like the time when on twenty-four hours notice they had to paint posters and banners to hail the visit of an Arab chief of state. No one knew why the order came so late; no one knew why it landed on this obscure collective. All night they painted and at dawn lugged their wet canvases to the city hall on Gorky Street, knowing that if they had one letter, one comma, one detail of Stalin's portrait wrong, they would lose their jobs and be sent to Siberia.

Olga had thought a great deal about her life since the days in the Caucasus. She did not expect to fall in love again. She did not expect a romantic marriage. Yes, she might have an affair now and then, but she did not expect 1944 to be repeated. She had not expected anything like that before we met and she did not expect it again. Her life was in a holding pattern. Though she drew comfort from our meetings, she knew they could not continue long. She knew Russian life and its cruelty. Loving her work, she yet did not believe that she could be a great artist. It was a matter of talent and temperament. She possessed talent, but unless she was willing to pander, curry favor, she could not succeed, and sycophancy was not for her. She had too quick an eye for cant. She would break out laughing in the wrong places. What to do?

Well, there was a very nice, very decent, very dull academician who was paying court to her. He had a solid reputation, a fine income, a beautiful apartment filled with objects of art. He was a great collector of—I forget what, possibly Napoleonic medallions; something small and solid like that. He had a cook and a maid, a dacha in the country, went to the best Black Sea resorts, occasionally visited Budapest and Bucharest. True, he was twenty years older, had a comfortable paunch, wasn't very exciting. But, Olga said, he was a good man. It was a tempting prospect; his wife had died, he was lonely, he was very much in love with her. Then Olga would laugh. Imagine, she would say, pouring tea in my salon for the ladies of the academy while the academicians with their black beards and solemn faces discuss whatever it is that academicians discuss. Imagine her, Olga, the tomboy, the madcap, the satirist who couldn't take a stuffed shirt seriously, marrying an academician. What a joke! When he wanted to make love to her—what about his pointed beard and his nice round paunch? She would double up with laughter and remember the bawdy stories her father had told her of the old Russia, of the time of *Domostroi,* the rules for regulation of Russian households and the management of Russian women, to be beaten regularly for their own good, and of Russian men—what a race! Her father had told her about the old estate owners stalking through their houses, and if they found a woman on hands and knees, skirts tucked up, scrubbing the floor, they would be astride her in a minute, the woman bucking and swaying and screaming howls of pleasure as the *barin* thrust away at her, the whole thing over in a couple of minutes. The Russians! She would almost spit out the word, the Russians painted by Kustodiev, the Russian baths and the huge-thighed women and the big-bellied men lazily enjoying each other, and the peasant orgies at the summer solstice, the whole village copulating on the green or in the church. Russians! She would peal with laughter.

I told Olga what had happened to me, of going back to my family, the failure of that experiment, the reappearance in my life of Ellen, the trauma, the violence, the upheaval, and now, it seemed, my life was changing again. We talked to each other like the veterans of many campaigns, talked about the wounds to our hearts, the ones we had inflicted and those inflicted on us. It brought us very close, and always Olga talked with her own cool, clear irony, her amusement at herself and at me.

She made fun of her academician. But I knew that life as the wife of an academician had an appeal. She had had too much of adventure and tragedy. It was a safe and comfortable harbor. It would be so easy to marry him, it would solve so many problems, and he would be so grateful, so proud of her, so delighted to show her off. She was a Khludov. He knew what the Khludovs were, and the other academicians knew as well. So did their wives. It would put Olga in the highest level of Moscow society, and there *was* a Moscow society, even after fifty years of the Bolsheviks, even under Stalin, and in this society, to be the wife of an academician and to be a Khludov and to possess a grandmother who had lectured Lenin about her orangery and to be a connection of the Morozovs—well, it mattered. She laughed, but it mattered.

Olga and I shared our evenings with Macbeth, her black Great Dane. If Olga had a passion at this moment, it was for Beth, as she called this monstrous, heavy, charming dog, as big as Olga, as big as myself. Owners flew their bitches from Odessa and Siberia to be bred to Beth. When Moscow's streets swarmed with robbers after the post-Stalin amnesty, Olga walked fearlessly late at night, sometimes startling conveys of muggers, who would flee the great dog, hurling mother oaths at Beth and Olga. When Olga left her room, she put her valuables under the mat on which Beth lay. They were safer than in a bank vault.

Dogs were a passion which Olga's father had bequeathed to her. She was secretary of the dog section of DOSAAF, the civil defense organization, a piece of bureaucratic chummery, a way of making it ideologically possible to go on raising dogs. In Russia, dogs had not been the companions of proletarian and peasant. Dogs were the property of the wealthy, the de-Russified nobility, breeders of borzois, the canine symbol of a wastrel aristocracy. There was no niche in Marxist theory for borzois. So naturally one was made, under the comfortable wing of the military; cronies of Stalin like Budenny and Voroshilov kept the bloodlines alive by giving dogs pseudo-military status. During the war they were drafted into the Red Army. One German shepherd named Gero (Hero), who belonged to an old actress, was called up for duty, deserted and came back home. Gero was arrested and ordered shot—the wartime penalty for deserters. Thanks to a general who had been the lover of the actress in her youth, Gero got a reprieve and was ordered to guard the actress's home for the duration.

The dog section held shows and trials on Sundays in Red Army Park. Sometimes I wandered in and watched the show, Olga busy recording the results. We met openly but distantly in these surroundings, seeing no peril in such an un-Soviet byway.

Olga had created a life almost outside the clichés of Soviet existence. Nothing could have been less worldly than her studio with its curious passengers on the good ship *Bolshevik* or the breeders of borzois and Orlov horses, happily preserving the bloodlines under the powerful patronage of Budenny and Voroshilov.

I don't know how long our life in this quiet eddy went on; about a year and a half, I would think. Then we had a scare, a serious one, and agreed we must not see each other again. I left Moscow late in 1954. One day in New York, I was browsing in a Russian bookstore when I spotted a book by Olga about snorkeling in the Black Sea. It had a grainy picture of her in diving suit. In the winter of 1967, I happened to be in Moscow and went to the Art Theater to see *Uncle Vanya*. I was waiting for the curtain to go up when I saw Olga enter with a young man, the same tall, long-legged woman with green eyes, high-held head, freckled cheeks. I intercepted her at intermission. "My God," she said, "it's you." "It is," I said. She put her hand on my wrist and looked into my eyes. "What do you see?" I asked. "Oh, Harrison," she said, "you haven't changed very much." I smiled. "I'm married," she said. "So am I," I said. "He's a very nice man," she said. "He loves me very much and we are happy together. I've taken up deep-sea diving." "I know," I said. I told about finding her book. The young man, a visitor from Hungary or Rumania, stood to one side. "You know," she said, "I think I should tell you this. I got into a good deal of trouble about seeing you. They called me in and wanted me to report and work for them. I wouldn't, but they bothered me for quite a while." "I'm sorry," I said. "I didn't know that. I haven't been good for you." "No," she agreed, "you haven't. And yet . . ." She let the phrase hang. "I've taken up a whole new career. We couldn't have children and my husband didn't want me to work after we got married. So I began scuba diving." The intermission bell rang. "Are you happy in your marriage?" Olga asked hastily. "Yes, I am," I said. "And I'm glad you are happy in yours."

She smiled. "So that's the way all good stories end," she said, "with both the characters happily married." We grinned at each other and she went back to her seat.

We never met again. Ludmilla Shapiro told me of Olga's death of cancer in 1975.

28 | The Other World

I never thought of it that way at the time—the other world, I mean. Then it was a hodgepodge of impressions, of stories, of anecdotes, the bits and pieces of Russian life, sometimes told me by Olga, sometimes by Ludmilla, sometimes by others; no headlines, not in *Pravda,* not in *The New York Times,* no news—fragments that floated past my ken and lodged there like bright pebbles in a mountain brook. Years later, I realized that here was a collage of the real Russia, not the cardboard facade the cold war had built.

In this other Russia, there was flesh and blood. In this Russia, people bled and cried. They laughed, they joked, they suffered. They were ridden by ills and plagued by superstition. They were, in a measure, still the "dark people" whom naive revolutionaries of the nineteenth century hoped to enlighten; the object of the "Going to the People" movement, which sought to teach the muzhiks the way to liberty; the peasants whom the Narodnaya Volya, the People's Will, sought to liberate by killing the Czar and the Czar's despots; the hordes that made Lenin's revolution and that he and his Europeanized commissars feared and despised.

I loved this Russia, but it was a long time before I understood that it was the real thing, that I was getting a glimpse beyond the starched pinafore with which Communism sought to conceal the Russian figure and hide the manacles Stalin had fettered to her wrists and ankles. It was a long time before I understood that Lenin and Stalin had failed, that Russians were still Russians and always would be Russians, whether ruled by a "little father," the Czar, so distant and so high; by a Mongol-eyed intellectual who possessed a Victorian dream of a "better life"; or by a stone-hearted novitiate who fed their bodies by the million into the meat grinder of his paranoia.

In this world, old Russia lapped at the end of Moscow's pavement, and sometimes crept right into the city. I had been struck that brick and mortar and steel halted at Moscow's limits, running water, steam heat, electricity dissolved into wooden huts, hand-drawn wells, mud paths and kerosene lamps.

It was not just these tangibles. Only the summer before, three Moscow boys from good—that is, middle-class—families went camping in the forest a hundred kilometers from Moscow, near a *dremotnii,* a drowsy village that lived as it had for centuries: everyone knew everyone, everyone was related to everyone, doors not locked, no locks on doors. Suddenly came a wave of petty thefts—clothes vanished from a line, a chicken from a yard, an ax from beside a door. The villagers met at evening. They were of a mind as to the thieves. They armed themselves with clubs, descended on the camp of the youngsters and methodically beat them to death. The story was the talk of Moscow. Muscovites did not venture into the backcountry of the Upper Volga or the Oka, the land of the "dark people."

Nor was Moscow life as pale and pasty as the pages of *Pravda* painted it. There was the case of two young medical students, a boy and a girl, lovers. The boy abandoned the girl for another. His sweetheart persuaded him to spend one last night together. She plied him with vodka laced with morphine. The next thing the young man knew, he awakened in terrible pain. His sweetheart had taken a pair of surgical scissors and relieved him of his testicles. She got an eight-year prison term and said it was worth it.

And I heard of the seventeen-year-old and his chums who celebrated November 7 with vodka. They went to visit a friend and on the stairs made a lot of noise. A man asked them to be quiet. The boy whipped out a "Finnish" knife (they were always called Finnish knives when used in a crime) and killed the man. A lawyer tried to get the boy off. He was a good student, had never before been in trouble, had never before been drunk. The court was not moved. The boy got eight years at corrective labor.

A man in his early twenties came back from the camps after a three-year sentence for belonging to a gang of burglars. He got so light a term because of his youth. He returned to his old apartment and began to live with a young woman, not exactly a prostitute, but promiscuous. He promptly joined a new gang of thieves and within three months was again in jail. This time he got eleven years and the woman three. Everyone in the seven-room communal apartment had known what was going on. The couple had stolen money from most of them. Not one lifted a finger. They hadn't reported it to the police. Better not to get involved.

Better not to get involved. This was the law of Moscow. I had heard it first in wartime. Hurrying to the Foreign Office one cold morning, I saw a woman, a babushka, lying on a snowdrift, unconscious or dead. No one halted. No one gave more than a glance. I asked Olga about that. People don't want to get involved, she said. If they stop, if the police come along, they will be questioned, maybe even blamed. Better not to notice. This was life behind the dingy walls of Moscow, the gray buildings I passed and repassed as I walked the streets, people with their heads down, leading their lives as they could amid crime and squalor and passion and violence.

I learned of miracles as well as crime. There was the story of the Virgin Mary in the Nemetsky *kladbyshy,* the old German cemetery. A member of a respected Moscow family went to the cemetery one winter Sunday to look to the family plot. He found a queue of people there. Drops of water were falling from the chin of the Virgin's statue in the family plot and people were gathering the water in tin cups and glass jars, leaving contributions of two or three rubles. An attendant suggested he put an iron fence around the statue and collect ten to twenty rubles from each visitor. They would go partners on the receipts. The man said no. The next Sunday he came back, to find the Virgin gone. Notes of thanks were still pinned to the pedestal: "Thank you for returning my husband," "Thank you for giving back my health," "Thank you for making Ivan love me." A priest from the patriarchy, the attendant said, had got into a dispute with the cemetery administration over jurisdiction of the miracle-working figure and the patriarchy had carted the Virgin off to Zagorsk. It was, I thought, the kind of dispute that could have arisen in the time of Ivan the Terrible.

Cemeteries, I would learn, were politically sensitive institutions. As would have been true under Peter the Great, cemeteries had a table of rank. At the top was Lenin's mausoleum and there, naturally, Stalin, too, would be placed (only to be removed by Khrushchev). Next in status was the Kremlin wall. Here were buried early revolutionaries and later political and military leaders. Feuds and political fissures might be opened up by whether or not a man was buried in the wall, as would be the case when Khrushchev and Mikoyan were denied a place by the Kremlin. Next in rank was Novodeviche, resting place of great artists, poets and leaders who missed the wall.

There was a category for lesser mortals, headed by the Nemetsky *kladbyshy,* the Vvedenie cemetery, originally established for foreign residents. To get a plot here cost a bribe of hundreds of rubles. The cemetery was full, but for "palm oil" an old plot would be dug up, the skeleton thrown out and a new grave provided. The pressure for burial space was so great that churchyards of villages around Moscow were being invaded by families who did not want to put the ashes of their loved ones into a kind of concrete mortuary filing system. Moscow suffered chronic lack of housing for the dead as well as the living.

In this city of frustration, a yearning for miracles seemed natural, even inevitable, a yearning for solutions of the unsolvable.

Moscow talked of the sixteen-year-old who had worked wonders, so it was said, and then died. Muscovites flocked to his grave, gathered sand from it, put spoonfuls into little sachets and wore them for good luck on a string around their necks, like asafetida. The fad grew and grew. Finally, the authorities circulated a rumor that the teenager was just a gangster killed in a street brawl. That brought this "miracle" to an end.

I heard of another miracle—that of the washerwoman of Rostov who had refused to go with her husband to the cathedral for services on Easter eve. Instead she did her washing, saying she would rather earn five rubles than bother with church. Two days later, a crowd began to grow outside her house. It was said she couldn't stop washing. She washed all Easter eve, all Easter day, all Easter night, all Easter Monday, and was still at it. Thousands had gathered by the time the police arrived. They found the door guarded by two strong youths. Inside, the woman was angry. There was, she said, no truth to the story. She hadn't done any washing on Easter eve. She hadn't done any since. She hadn't done any for two months. She had had to hire the two young men to keep the people from breaking down her door. The police went back to the crowd, selected a dozen fervent "believers," brought them into the house and let them talk to the woman; the crowd gradually dispersed.

I learned about Gypsies. I had seen few in Moscow, although I knew that once they had been Russia's favorite entertainers; "going to the Gypsies" had cost many a nobleman his fortune and even his life. After the Revolution, enthusiastic idealists worried about them. They didn't fit into the new system, they

344 | A JOURNEY FOR OUR TIMES

had no fixed residence, no jobs, no role in society. They were what they were—Gypsies, moving freely about the country, living by their wits, by tricks, by stealing. One comrade had an idea. Give them a house in Moscow for the winter. They would be glad to escape the cold. Leave them alone. By spring they could be organized into Soviet life. So a fine house was provided and the Gypsies entered it with delight. Spring came. The comrades asked the Gypsies how they had fared. Wonderfully, they said, a warm house, no cold winds. The comrades beamed. The plan was working. Then they entered the house. They found a shambles— furniture gone, floors ripped up, woodwork pulled off. There had been campfires everywhere and the fires fed with the furniture. Next morning, the Gypsies loaded their wagons and vanished.

There were few Gypsy fortune-tellers left in Moscow, the Gypsy theater was on the decline, only one Gypsy orchestra still was playing, on a boat tied up at the Khimki river station, and the Yar, the famous restaurant where they had sung and danced, had been turned into the Aero Engineers Club. Later I would see Gypsies roaming Siberia, particularly backwater towns like Barnaul, and along the Volga on almost every wharf. Probably they had been harried out of Moscow by the police.

Fortune-telling was a pastime of young Moscow women as it had been in the time of Pushkin. On Orthodox New Year's Eve, not Western New Year's, Olga and her studio friends told fortunes in the traditional way. They put a diamond ring into a glass of water, set candles to each side and peered in the glass until they saw the image of their husband. Then they dropped wax from the candles into cold water. The shape of the wax foretold their future. They spun a saucer on a paper marked with the alphabet to find the initials of their love-to-be.

Olga did not think of herself as superstitious. These were games to while away the time. And yet—her father had given her his gold cuff links just before he was arrested and sent away to labor camp, never to return. Never wear them, he told Olga, and she didn't. But she had them made into a ring, and not long after she began wearing the ring, her brother Mitya died of his wounds at the front. She gave the ring to a friend and told her never to wear it. The friend had the ring made into a pair of earrings. She wore them for the first time and the next day learned that her mother had terminal cancer. The friend put them away.

After a while she gave them to a woman whom she did not know well. She told this woman not to wear them. What had happened to this woman Olga did not know. She did not want to know.

There was a wry quality to Moscow jokes and gradually I came to realize how much the jokes told me about these people, their fears, their hates, their frustrations, the illusions they cherished because only illusions made life possible. Never—never—did I hear a joke about Stalin. His name was not mentioned. Nothing could have been more dangerous and I understood this although at that time I had not heard how the poet Mandelshtam had been sent to his death in exile for making a joke about the dictator. Aleksandr Solzhenitsyn still languished in labor camp, the world and I unaware that his reference to Stalin in a letter to a fellow officer at the front had sent him into the Gulag. I had not heard of these cases; but I knew the terror possessed by Stalin's name. I had been at Dynamo Stadium one Sunday for the football, European football, Dynamo versus Spartak, a big game. After the game, in the throng making its way to the metro, I spotted a drunken fan staggering down the passageway, miraculously cleared, no one around him. As I approached, I understood why. He was shouting at the top of his voice about Stalin—I don't know what, I didn't understand Russian then, but I understood the crowd. They were moving away as fast as they could. They didn't want even to *hear* someone shouting about Stalin, whatever the shouts.

So there was no reference to Stalin in Moscow's jokes. Not until Khrushchev came to power did I hear jokes about the country's leader. The jokes about Khrushchev were evidence of the distance that had been traveled since March 5, 1953.

There was in Moscow's jokes a strong element of fantasy, of nostalgia—laced with unselfconscious racism. The emphasis was on Georgian "toasts," Armenian riddles and anti-Semitic jokes.

A Georgian toast: A young man is walking beside a stream when a frog asks him to pick it up. The young man objects. The frog insists and says the man will not be sorry. He picks up the frog and when he gets home the frog asks to be placed on the bed. He objects, but the frog tells him he will not be sorry and he obeys. Now the frog asks him to undress and come to bed. He objects, but the frog says he will not be sorry, so he obeys. "Now," says the frog, "kiss me." He objects, but finally complies, and the frog turns into a beautiful woman. At this point his wife walks in. So . . . let's drink a toast to wives who *believe* the stories their husbands tell.

An Armenian riddle: What is it that is long and green and hangs in my living room—and squeaks. Answer: A herring. It is green because I painted it green. It hangs in my living room because I put it there. It is long because it is a herring. And it squeaks—so you won't guess what it is.

A Jewish joke: A Jewish boy falls through the ice. A Russian jumps in and saves him. The boy's father appears and says: "You saved my boy?" "Yes." "You dove in three times to bring him up?" "Yes." "Then why didn't you bring up his cap?"

So long as I stayed in Russia, I was to hear anti-Semitic jokes, and never did I find a Russian who thought they were anti-Semitic. Indeed, more than once when I chided a Russian for indulging in anti-Semitism I got the angry response: "There is no anti-Semitism in Russia. We have a law against it!"

In the time of Catherine the Great, her minister and lover, Count Potemkin, had once built a string of modern and prosperous villages across the Ukraine, which he displayed to the empress on a royal progress to demonstrate to her the success of her agricultural program. I did not then know that Stalin's ministers were playing Potemkin, creating an illusion of happy, prosperous rural life in films which they showed him at a time when people in the Ukraine were starving, and instances of cannibalism were not unknown (as would be revealed by Khrushchev).

I did hear the simple tale of what had happened in Olga's film studio when a Rumanian delegation came to visit. The staff was assembled the day before and told to wear their best clothes, the girls to have their hair done and use their best makeup. New curtains were put up, potted plants brought in and the rooms tidied. There wasn't time to repaint the walls, but posters were plastered over the worst cracks and stains. The best-looking girls were put into one workroom, where it was hoped the Rumanians would halt. On no account were workers to hold private conversation with the visitors. They were to reply to questions only in generalities, no technical information; all talking through interpreters.

The day went well except that one girl in her excitement got into a conversation in French with a Rumanian who kept asking what was the matter, why was no one willing to talk with them, why couldn't they sit down and discuss how to make animated films? Could she perhaps go out for supper and a bit of fun? The girl was embarrassed. The interpreter was looking daggers. Somehow she managed to decline the dinner date. When the visitors left, she was summoned by the party secretary, dressed down and made to give a full account of her conversation.

This other world was not the world of the Kremlin, not the world of the Sovietologists, not the world of the cold warriors in Moscow and Washington. It was the private world of Russia, which went on regardless of who occupied the Kremlin—bending here, yielding there, compromising in another place, but as eternal as the Volga, *Volga matushka,* Volga the mother, as the Russians called it. I did not know the value of my impressions, but as time passed, and particularly after I had begun to live in and explore and understand Saltykovka, a village near Moscow where soon I was to acquire a dacha, I began to grasp some strands of the Russian fabric, strands in a pattern which would be elaborated as the years passed, as I exposed myself to Russian life, to the breadth and depth of this continental country, a process, still in progress, that reached its apogee in the remarkable years of 1953 and 1954, when, after Stalin's death, I was able to crisscross the entire land, penetrating into its heart, as had rarely been possible since the days of Sir Bernard Pares (though it was far more limited in access than the Russia seen in the 1880s by the first George Kennan, the distinguished early relative of our contemporary George Kennan).

I did not think of it at the time, but as years passed I realized that it was this cross-grained knowledge of Russia—of its people, its geography, its folklore, its literature, its past and the projection of that past into the present and into the future—that I came to possess and that would form the fundament of my so-called expertise about the country. It was this that often sharply distinguished my judgments, appreciations and attitudes from those of what are called Sovietologists or Soviet specialists.

For the most part (I don't want to generalize too widely), these specialists approached the Soviet Union from a contemporary and ideological position. They had (at least some of them) studied Marxism, whatever that is, and the "philosophy" of the Soviet government, its political jargon and all that.

In the period of which I write, one of the best of this order of specialist was in Moscow as counselor, I believe, of the U.S. embassy, a pleasant and thoughtful man named George Morgan, who wrote a rather famous article for *Foreign Affairs* under the name Historicus. George approached Russia via Marx, Engels, Lenin and Stalin. His posture was not unlike that of John Foster Dulles, who used to boast of keeping a copy of Stalin's *Problems of Leninism* on his desk, as though that were a key to what was happening in Moscow. I must confess that I have never read *Problems of Leninism* and never expect to. Dulles treated it as a kind of *Mein Kampf* (although I'll wager dollars to doughnuts he never read it). From the beginning I was skeptical of there being any "key" to Soviet policy. I remember George Morgan and others of that time who liked to talk about the "operational code" of the Soviet. I recall endless discussions, particularly with American military men, who believed there was a "blueprint" of Soviet intentions, or at least a list of Soviet priorities. "How high a priority do they place on [let us say] Norway?" an attaché would ask me. I didn't know how to answer that question. I still don't. It seemed to me then, as it does now, that Soviet policy was affected by "targets of opportunity," sudden chances which arose out of unpredicted or unpredictable events. I could not see any long-range, cool, coldly calculated schemes or plans.

Maybe that reflected my Minnesota turn of mind, which saw the world in more anarchical terms, which didn't perceive "order" anywhere and particularly not in Russia. When I traveled down the byways of Russian life, when I saw how people twisted, turned, squeezed and shoved to attain their goals, and when it occurred to me (as I think it should to everyone) that in this "planned" society no one ever knew what was going to happen next, I began to rely less and less on "codes," "doctrine," textbook quotations, and more and more on reality. I still do.

And so, I suppose, what I call my commonsense approach, deeply rooted in Russian soil and souls, has set me apart, time and again, from those who I tend to think have tried to bend Russian reality to fit some political concept, either ours or theirs.

I confess to evenhandedness in this. I have always had a hard time trying to understand the principles of the Republican party, to which I belong. To me it seems to range from the wild radicalism of a La Follette or a Borah to the wild conservatism of a contemporary Jesse Helms. There can't be much meaning to a platform that supports such disparate figures. Nor can there be much of a monolith in a Communist world that ranges from the medieval obscurantism of an Enver Hoxha to the (relative) liberalism of a Yugoslavia.

I guess what I found in this other world and in Saltykovka, preserved, as it were, in amber, was that Russia Sir Bernard Pares had known. I had to extrapolate a good deal. I could not in the Stalin days travel widely. I could not know many Russians. I had to use my wits, my eyes, my ears, and often my nose to tell which way the wind was blowing and whence it came. I could not neglect *Pravda,* but there, too, I understood that it was more important, in most instances, to know what *Pravda* was not saying than what it was saying. My first big lesson in this was China. From 1944 onward, I had noticed again and again that *Pravda* did not behave toward Mao Zedong as though he was Russia's man, its warm, close and valiant ally. I was too timid to draw conclusions, but beginning in 1949, I watched the vibrations of Russia and China and found that, by my measurement, there was something wrong—continuously. They were not in sync. Sometimes that might be reflected in what was said. But more often it was in what was left unsaid. In this, instinct may have played some part. But comparing my judgment with those whom I regarded (and still regard) as ideologically influenced specialists, I believe my lack of Marxist pedantry served me well. I could see the forest for the trees. Just because Marxism dictated that all Communists *must* be allies did not, in my view, *make* them so. If, historically, Russia and China had been consistent enemies and rivals—well, that element must be given its weight. The same was true in other areas.

I read a lot of Russian history—*Russian* history, not *Soviet* history—in those long evenings in the Metropol. This told me how closely Stalin fitted the historical pattern of the eternal Russian drive for warm water (Constantinople, the Persian Gulf), in the passion for dominating the Balkans (shared with Nicholas I and Alexander III), in a wish for Far Eastern dominance (shared with Nicholas II), in a consciousness of British (now Indian) rivalry in Central Asia, in a love-hate relationship with Germany (shared with a hierarchy of czarist rulers and foreign ministers).

I thought that told me a lot more about Soviet foreign policy than the Communist Manifesto. I still do.

29 | A KGB Plot

I celebrated my first New Year's Eve in Russia—December 31, 1949, a fine New Year's, the ground covered with snow that squeaked under my heels—at a party at Spaso House, where Ambassador Kirk and his wife, Lydia, brought gaiety to the self-imprisoned embassy staff, music and dancing and paper hats and noisemakers and champagne at midnight.

I didn't stay long after the champagne. Walking out past the fur-capped militiamen at the gate, I wished them *"S novem godem, s novem schastii."* They saluted and went on stamping their feet and swinging their arms. I headed for the Metropol, a half hour's walk in the frosty air. Moscow was a nine o'clock town, but not on New Year's. On New Year's there were lights in apartment windows, bands of vodka-happy strollers, arms linked, singing as they walked down the middle of the streets, quarreling queues trying to force their way into the restaurants, and a special police detail at the Metropol to keep out the drunks.

Moscow was jolly if not happy. I was neither jolly nor happy. I was an observer not a participant in the festivities. Moscow, I thought, had grown more grim since my arrival. The band of foreign correspondents had dwindled until I was the only one left who represented a newspaper. Joe Newman of the *Herald Tribune* had left in June, Ed Stevens of the *Christian Science Monitor* soon thereafter. I had spent Christmas seeing off Don Dallas of Reuters and his wife, Frankie. Reuters was closing its bureau and putting its affairs in the hands of a stringer, Andy Steiger, who had been working for Exchange Telegraph, by this time defunct.

Something sinister occurred during the holiday week. A woman named Tatiana Sofiano had been acting as a secretary-translator for foreign correspondents since before the war. An intelligent, efficient, well-informed woman, she had worked most recently for Don Dallas and as a string correspondent for *Time* magazine. One of Sof's assets was a voluminous clipping file, the only one of consequence maintained by a correspondent in Moscow. Everything going back to before World War II was in it. I often took advantage of her patience in looking things up. Sof had got a new position with the Academy of Sciences, which was starting a series of reference journals and could utilize her excellent knowledge of English. It was a fine job and she was lucky to get it. I was eager to acquire her files and made a deal to buy them for the *Times* for two thousand dollars in cash. On Christmas weekend, I lugged most of the cartons up to my room and then interrupted my chores to go out to lunch. When I came back, Sof was there, her face gray, the envelope in which I had given her the greenbacks in her hand. She thrust it at me. "I have to have them back," she said in a choked voice. "I can't sell them to you."

I saw the agony in her eyes. She did not have to say a word. I knew what had happened. The police, the KGB. She had been told to get the papers back—or else. "Of course," I said. "I understand, Sof." "I have to have them right now," she said in a voice from which all hope had drained. "O.K.," I said. I worked most of the afternoon, putting the papers back. How had it happened? I wondered. How had it happened that an old dog like Sofiano, so sophisticated, so experienced (for years she had to have been reporting to the police), had made this dangerous, possibly fatal error? Who could ever say? Maybe Sof got greedy. She knew she could not keep the files in her new job, saw a chance to sell them to me, and got caught.

Whatever the details, the fear of God had been put into her. She did not know whether she was going to get out of trouble or go to the camps. A young man helped me move the files. Sof said he was her nephew, come to help her clear out her office. I thought he was there to see that she complied with the ultimatum. When the job was done I left her. I could not look at her eyes. By Monday morning, her room was cleared and she was gone. Months later, I saw her at a concert. She did not speak, but she raised her eyebrows a fraction. I understood that, somehow, it had come out all right.

The last Russian working for the foreign press vanished at about this time, Natalie Petrovna Rene, improbably still at the Metropol, still accredited to Hearst. One day Natalie was standing at the curb in the Arbat waiting to cross, when a truck knocked her down, breaking her leg and injuring her spine. For weeks she lay in bed in her cubbyhole room with its hundreds (or thousands) of books about ballet in tottering piles that reached the ceiling and filled the space under the bed. I could see the fear in her eyes when I dropped in and she told me, over and over, the story of her accident. How could that truckdriver have been so careless—he had driven right up onto the sidewalk. He was drunk, I said. No, Natalie said pensively, no, he was not drunk. He had sped away and the police had never found him. Very curious. I am sure he was not drunk, she would repeat. I realized one afternoon that Natalie thought her accident was not an accident. But who could have wanted to injure this Chekhovian woman with her passion for Ulanova and cemeteries? It made no sense to my Midwestern mind. It just showed the paranoia that affected people who lived too long in the Metropol. I had seen this often enough. A pleasant young man, a student of Russian, had arrived in October to join the embassy staff. He was put into the Metropol and joined the little mess I had set up in Room 393 with two other embassy bachelors. It was a pleasant group. Our cook was a peasant girl, Nadya, provided by Burobin. Within her limited repertoire, Nadya cooked not badly. Once, inspecting the table, I noticed a dirty plate. Nadya was appalled. She picked it up, spat on it lightly, polished it with her elbow and put it back, apologizing all the time.

Fred, the new attaché, had been warned again and again before leaving Washington of the dangers of entrapment. Now almost every day he reported a suspicious circumstance—a midnight telephone call from a woman, strange knockings at his door, someone following him on the street. He apologized for his fears, but they grew deeper. We tried to reassure him. Nothing helped. Before New Year's he had been shipped back to the United States, close to breakdown, there to spend some months returning to normal. Nor was this unusual. Almost every month, someone at the embassy was sent back home, and there were others who should have been; one attaché used to spend his evenings "talking to the ceiling." He would retire to his bedroom after dinner and lie in bed shouting obscenities to the ceiling, where, he was certain, the microphones were concealed. Hearing loud voices, his friends sometimes hammered at the door. Reluctantly he would admit them. "I've been giving them hell tonight," he would say. "Wait till Stalin gets this report." Somehow he was permitted to stay out his full term.

I was hardly surprised at what I considered to be Natalie's paranoia (I had no idea that her husband had been arrested and shot by Stalin, and that she feared the same fate). One afternoon when I dropped in to cheer her up—the doctors thought she might be bedridden for a year—she told me in her shrill, wavering voice that she was giving up being a correspondent. It was too hard. Her health was never going to be good again. Every time the Moscow papers mentioned Hearst, she shivered. She was going to make a career writing about ballet. That was, she said, her real interest in life. And so one day she, too, vanished from the Metropol.

No one could fail to observe these signs. The walls were slowly closing in. Yet somehow I didn't think of this as affecting my own life. In part this was due to preoccupation with my complicated personal affairs. Michael had now gone to live with my mother and sister in Minneapolis, a great relief, but I was upset by the sudden move. Mary now seemed to be talking seriously about a divorce, which was a positive development. However, Ellen was spinning beyond my periphery. I was beginning to think of a quick trip to the U.S.A. to try to put my affairs in some order.

At the same time, I felt that I finally was able to write with confidence about Soviet developments; my study of the Russian language was moving forward; and the quality of my dispatches had improved. Not that this was necessarily apparent to New York. The censorship was harsh and in January 1950 it would kill outright thirteen of my stories—about half my output—and alas, five stories that reached New York were cut to snippets by the desk.

I did not know—and it was as well that I did not—that there had arisen at 229 West 43rd Street deepening concern for my personal safety.

The source of this was Will Lissner and his continuing analysis of my dispatches and the censorship. He had spent years studying Soviet propaganda, Soviet economy and Communist tactics. As a man with a right-wing socialist background, he had engaged in endless battles with the American party going back to the 1920s.

He feared that I was recklessly antagonizing the Soviet authorities by the boldness of my reporting and by the sharpness of my complaints. As early as April 2, 1949 (when I had been writing from Moscow only two weeks), Lissner warned the *Times* editors that my "reporting zeal" might lead the Russians to expel me and attempt to besmirch my reputation by creating a scandal and possibly involving me with a woman.

Lissner warned that the closest precautions must be taken to prevent knowledge spreading of the secret reports I was sending back from Moscow. He cautioned the editors to keep my reports (and his analyses) under lock and key; they should be read only by editors who had a specific need to know. He recalled past instances in which Communists on the *Times* staff had rifled desks and searched wastepaper baskets for sensitive materials.

I frequently passed on information designed to be used by Lissner or Harry Schwartz, the erstwhile professorial consultant, in writing stories about Soviet developments. Lissner warned that the source of this information should not be revealed to Schwartz or anyone else.

Lissner worried (as I did) about internal security on the *Times*. My concern had been aroused when I received in the open mails in Moscow a letter from Freedman that had been intended for the diplomatic pouch. The envelope was marked: "OK for pouch." As Lissner said: "We ask enough in asking Salisbury to try to do an honest job of reporting; we should not ask him to put himself at the mercy of careless idiots."

By November, Lissner became convinced that I was in real peril. He believed I had placed myself in a "very dangerous" category by calling the attention of Soviet authorities to my independence and my bitterness against Soviet authority. He felt I might be thrown out of Moscow and that I had made personal enemies in the Foreign Office and in Glavlit, the office of censorship. "In a feudal society like Communist Russia's," he commented, "that may easily lead to reprisal." Lissner feared not only for my personal safety but that the *Times* might lose its foothold in Moscow. He felt I must stay on, my dispatches having proved sound, my private reports having been especially valuable (he held a low opinion of the agency men then in Moscow). His sense was that a big new purge trial could be in the making and that I should make every effort to hang on in order to cover it—every effort short of compromising my reporting or the position of *The New York Times*. He felt that the *Times* should, on its part, be equally circumspect. Looking back, I must say that his intuitions and warnings proved exemplary. Unfortunately, his cautionary words were not understood or not taken seriously by the editors. As I was later to discover, my confidential communications were not held private. They became known to an ever-widening circle inside and outside the *Times,* including the CIA. Considering the extent of these leakages (of which I am now aware), I cannot be sure that the existence of my materials and at least some of their content did not become known to the KGB.

Ten weeks after Lissner had delivered his strongest warning to my New York colleagues, a decree reestablishing the death penalty (it had been "abolished" in May 1947) was published in *Izvestiya* on January 13, 1950. I attempted to file a dispatch pointing out that the new penalty would be applied only to "traitors to the motherland, spies and subversive diversionists," whereas in 1947 the government had announced that the "cause of peace" and the "unity of the state" was so great that the death penalty was no longer needed. Every word I filed was killed (almost every word came straight from the pages of *Izvestiya* and a lengthy 1947 declaration by Andrei Vishinsky). Not a line got through. I wrote in my journal that it was obvious some new "show" trials were in prospect.

"A much more sinister possibility," I wrote, "is that they have in mind some nice little proceedings involving one of those American spies (i.e., correspondents)—of whom by their definition there are five still left in Moscow. Since I am potential meat for this stew I most surely trust that this is not what the Kremlin cooks have in mind. But stranger things have happened in this strange country."

I do not think I took this prospect too seriously, but it did dance across my mind. This was a time when "spy" trials and purge trials were sweeping Eastern Europe—Laszlo Rajk in Hungary, Slansky in Prague, Traicho Kostov in Bulgaria, one after another. Spies, trials, purges—these were the commonplace of the day. In Moscow there was fear and terror and rumors. No wonder that speculation about a Moscow trial had reached Lissner.

The idea of a foreign correspondent being caught up in the whirlwind was not alien to my thinking. I knew it had been in the minds of Stevens and Dallas. I knew it played a role in the retirement of Sofiano and of Rene. Later on, in 1953, the possibility of a correspondent playing a central role in the new super-purge Stalin was preparing would be on my mind day by day.

In this winter of 1950, I thought it was only a daydream, not to be taken seriously. Had I known that someone across the ocean, someone in the heart of that block-long city room of *The New York Times,* had heard a report that I had become a target of the KGB and might be arrested, shot or killed in an "accident," I would have been totally unbelieving—as unbelieving as I was when Gay Talese in *The Kingdom and the Power* quoted Lissner as saying just that.

When I read that passage I went to Gay immediately. "Did Lissner tell you that?" I asked. "Of course," said Gay. "You don't think I made it up?"

Of course I didn't, but I was dumbfounded. I went to Lissner. Certainly it was true, Will said; hadn't he ever told me about it? He could not tell me, nearly twenty-five years later, from whom he got the tip. It might have been a man named A. J. Gordon, long since dead, a kind of a gumshoe who for years was on the *Times* payroll, engaged in undercover inquiries (I had a very low opinion of Gordon's investigative abilities, but I knew him only at the end of his life). Gordon had a brother who owned or operated a Times Square movie house that played Soviet films. Somehow Gordon was reputed to have excellent "inside" connections with the Communist party. The word, Lissner said, might have come from him, it might have come from one of a dozen shadowy contacts, but it was solid information, Lissner felt, and it fitted his own (as I thought) melodramatic image of my derring-do in Moscow. He had written a memo to Arthur Hays Sulzberger and warned everyone to be very, very careful not to put Salisbury on the spot. When the cable desk didn't hear from me for several days, he had gone to the *Times* morgue, got out the clips and composed an obituary to have ready in case the KGB gunned me down.

Even then I did not take Will's story as literal fact. He had retained no copy of his memorandum, nor could I find it in a search of Mr. Sulzberger's files. I did find all Lissner's reports on my dispatches neatly preserved. I read them with intense interest and deepening respect for Lissner's insight and judgment. He had a far better grasp of Moscow than Manny Freedman on the foreign desk, Ted Bernstein in the bullpen, or Mr. James. Lissner had understood exactly what I was up to—and up against.

But no memorandum on the KGB attempt was preserved in any folder I could locate. Nor when I went to the advance obituaries file could I locate the one Lissner remembered doing.

What had happened to Lissner's memo? What had happened to the advance obit? Had they existed or were they the product of that creeping growth to which stories are subject in our minds as the years pass. I had seen this process in so many of my colleagues when I worked on *Without Fear or Favor,* my study of the *Times,* published in 1980. Instinct told me that Lissner's tale had grown. The alarm and concern he had expressed on paper, the fear of scandal, of provocation and expulsion, somehow now were remembered as possible murder.

I had been, I was willing to concede, in real danger in the winter of 1953, but not in this early period of 1950. Lissner wasn't quite sure of the date, but his monitoring of my correspondence ceased when I came back briefly to the United States in late spring 1950 and he undertook a lengthy assignment in Central America. I thought this fixed the winter of 1949–50 as the time of his alarm.

I may have been wrong in my judgment of Lissner's tip.

Years passed. On a mild evening in March 1977, I sat at a table in the Bella Vista restaurant in Arlington, Virginia, a flashy, not very stylish Italian place with exceedingly dim lighting and a view across the Potomac of Washington, the dome of the Capitol lighted, the Washington Monument and Lincoln Memorial visible. I was having dinner with a man who called himself George (or Yuri) Nosenko and a mutual friend who had spent many years in the CIA. Nosenko, a bulky man with a craggy Russian face, looked a bit like a beat-up heavyweight boxer, a man who had spent too many years in preliminary fights.

So far as I know (and so far as he said), we had never seen each other before, and until about a year earlier I had been only vaguely aware of his existence. He was a defector from the KGB who had turned himself over to the CIA in Geneva in February 1964. I suppose there was a splash about his defection; it escaped my attention. I had heard of him more recently because of the surfacing of a long-standing controversy within the intelligence community over whether he was possibly a Soviet plant, sent to the CIA to convince the United States that the KGB had no connection with Lee Harvey Oswald and President Kennedy's assassination.

On the evening of March 24, 1977, I was aware of nothing

more than the vague outlines of this complex dispute. All I knew about Nosenko was that some months earlier, I had seen a paragraph in an AP news story that quoted him as saying there had been a plot against me by the KGB. The story spoke of a Soviet attempt to drug me and get me out of Moscow. It was vague, I couldn't see that it made much sense, and my instinct was not to believe it—any more than I had believed the Lissner report when Talese published it.

Nonetheless, I had set about to find out what Nosenko knew, a task easier said than done. Nosenko was in what I guess the intelligence people would call "deep cover." He was still on the CIA payroll as a "consultant," I was amazed to learn (I was even more amazed to learn that he was employed by the CIA to give lectures to its staff, but that is another matter), and the agency was extremely wary of putting him in touch with anyone from the press or anyone at all.

After eight months of on-and-off efforts, this dinner had been arranged. I was not, I confess, much taken by Nosenko, who looked and acted exactly like a KGB officer, not of the first rank, the kind of man I had seen a thousand times in Moscow and with Soviet groups abroad. He might well have been one of the burly security guards who came over with Nikita Khrushchev on his trips to the U.S.A. in 1959 or 1960, or one of the plainclothes policemen I saw at every Moscow football game (football was their passion). He had big ears, big jaw, big nose, big strong voice. His ears, in fact, were very big, as big as I've ever seen. And he had a big appetite. Like many Russians, he waited to see what I ordered, then ordered the same. I ordered fettuccine Alfredo. He ordered fettuccine Alfredo. It was sticky, not very good. I didn't finish mine. He finished his long before I gave up.

Nosenko came on strong, very friendly, out to make points with me, obvious ones, the kind that put my guard up. He said he had read my novel *The Gates of Hell* (which opens with a scene depicting Yuri Andropov, chief of the KGB): how could anyone who was not a Russian understand so well what Russians think? For years he had wanted to meet me. There was no one in Russia who did not know my name.

I did not connect him immediately with the late minister of shipbuilding, Ivan I. Nosenko, who was, he said, his father. George had been born in the shipbuilding port of Nikolaev on the

Black Sea. His father had been an ordinary worker, but his
mother's grandfather was of the aristocracy or had some connection with the court; possibly he worked for the Czar. His mother,
he said, had taught his father manners and "smoothed" him out.
George had studied at the Institute for International Relations
and then went into naval intelligence, working in the Far East
and the Baltic. He was in Moscow in 1953, and soon after Stalin's death, he was transferred to the KGB and put in charge of
a section that oversaw foreign correspondents. This was, he said,
in the spring of 1953.

The main tasks of his section, if I understood him, concerned
the American embassy, but his own initial task was the correspondents. Bulky files were turned over by his predecessor and
he read them for background.

Among those files, of course, was one on myself. "A big, fat
file," he said. As he read back into it, he said, he got a shock. He
found that a proposal had been made "to Stalin" that I be given
a drug that would induce paralysis. It would not cause death and
the paralysis would wear off after, maybe, eight months, but it
would be severe and serious enough to cause my departure from
Moscow. After careful consideration, permission to activate the
plan was refused. It was found, he said, that the drug was too
risky. They could not be certain that paralysis would be temporary; indeed, medical specialists said that it could well be fatal.

I felt a few goose pimples crawl up the back of my neck as he
shoveled in the fettuccine and talked in everyday fashion about
the KGB's plan. But this was not my only response. Why had
the KGB wanted to take such extreme measures? What was it
that I had been doing?

Well, Nosenko said, the plan was devised because my dispatches were regarded as "too dangerous"; they revealed that I
had much too intimate a knowledge of government policy; I must
have extremely good sources high up in the government, even in
the Kremlin itself. There had been an intensive effort to find out
who was supplying me with these important materials, but no
connection could be found. The only remedy, it was decided, was
to eliminate me.

I asked if he recalled any specific dispatches that had been so
upsetting. He could not recall any details. He knew that high
policy was involved and he thought, also, that I had demonstrated too intimate a knowledge of high-level personnel changes.

Why, I said, granting that they wanted to get rid of me, could they not simply fake a car accident and run me down as they had the Jewish theatrical director Mikhoels in Minsk (or, although I did not mention this, as they may well have tried to run down Natalie Petrovna Rene in the Arbat).

No, he said, outright murder was not authorized in this case (whatever that meant). Paralysis was O.K., if it could be guaranteed. I confessed that this didn't seem plausible. They had other alternatives—they could simply announce that I had violated the rules and expel me; they could confect a case like that against Anna Louise Strong or Bob Magidoff and throw me out.

He agreed this could have been done. But this was not what was done.

Well, I said, is it your idea that they wanted all foreign correspondents to leave Moscow? I had developed this feeling strongly in the winter of 1949-50, when so many of my colleagues had left, and in fact, Eddy Gilmore and I had gone to the Foreign Office to discuss this question. Gromyko did not see us, but the head of the Press Department did. When we put this idea to him, he strongly denied it. We told him that whether they wanted it or not, they were achieving the same result by making conditions so difficult—the impossible censorship, restrictions on normal reporting, constant harassment by the bureaucracy. For a few weeks after our meeting, conditions improved a little. I got to visit a Soviet school—a project I had been waiting eight months for.

Nosenko said, yes, they wanted everyone to leave except the "good correspondents," that is, the ones they could rely on and control. He mentioned two or three, but the fact was (as he did not seem to know) only one of them was in Moscow at the time.

Though he had not convinced me, it seemed plausible that *something* had been put on foot by the KGB. When had this drug proposal been made? Nosenko was uncertain. It had been a couple of years before his assignment—probably in 1951 or 1952, maybe as early as 1950. He no longer could be certain. It was a detail in a mass of materials which he had ingested very quickly. What had struck him was the unusual concept, the high concern expressed about the accuracy of my reporting and the likelihood that I had a source within the Kremlin.

There was no way that I could dig beyond these impressions, gathered twenty-two years before. What I could do was talk to

Nosenko about the correspondents and see how his recollections matched mine. He knew the names of the other correspondents in Moscow in the spring of 1953, when he came into the KGB—Eddy Gilmore, Eddy's wife, Tamara, Henry Shapiro, Ludmilla, Tom Whitney, Tom's wife, Yulya Zapolskaya, and Andy Steiger. He didn't seem to remember that Steiger had a Russian wife, named Shura. He recalled the string correspondent of Agence France-Presse, Jean Noe, who was married to a woman whose father had been the leader of the Red Army orchestra, but he appeared not to have known Jean Champinois, a leftist French correspondent who had been in Moscow since before World War II. He tried to cover his nonrecognition, but didn't quite.

As we talked, I found that he was much more familiar with the later generation of correspondents than with those of the Stalin period—not unnaturally, since he had not worked in Moscow then. He didn't seem to realize he had lost all his original "charges"—Gilmore, Shapiro, Whitney and Steiger—except for myself within a few months of taking over his job. All left Moscow in the summer of 1953, when the post-Stalin regime authorized visas for Russian wives to depart with their husbands. Nor did he seem to know of or be interested in my extraordinary travels through the Soviet Union in 1953 and 1954, which, I should have thought, would have been a prime responsibility for a man charged with oversight of correspondents.

I asked if there had been any attempt to influence correspondents in their reporting. No, he said, the KGB was not interested in that. But it did help "cooperative correspondents" by arranging with the Foreign Office to see that they got news announcements perhaps fifteen minutes ahead of the others. He mentioned two who had been given this advantage. Though I had known about this favoritism by the Foreign Office for many years, I had not connected it with the police (nor did I on his say-so). Favors given and received by the Foreign Office didn't require intervention by the KGB.

Perhaps he sensed that I was dubious about his credentials, because he suddenly told me that I had had a maid named Masha, who was "tall, thin and dark-haired." I couldn't recall having ever had a maid of any kind. And, he said, I had had a chauffeur named Sokolov, a young man in his thirties. I had had two chauffeurs in Moscow; neither answered his description, neither was called Sokolov.

Nosenko said his connection with the U.S. correspondents came to an end in 1955. He returned to this job again in 1960, continuing on to 1962. In the interval, I gathered, he was in a section that dealt with tourists, which was how he had gained some connection with Oswald during the period of his defection to the Soviet Union.

I asked Nosenko about a KGB campaign that I thought might have a connection with the abortive attempt to paralyze me. During the upsurge in American contacts with Moscow in 1959, there had been a rash of knockout-drop attacks on Americans, correspondents and embassy personnel. The tactic was always the same: A young man or woman would pick an acquaintance with the American, they would go to a restaurant, have a few drinks, order dinner. The victim would suddenly feel ill and lose consciousness. He or she would awaken in early morning in a drunk tank or in bed with a sex partner, photographs having been taken. A crude blackmail attempt would be presented. The embassy simply flew these victims out of Moscow. Some correspondents toughed it out, telling their offices what had happened and ignoring the blackmail. It was my impression that these incidents were carried out by recruits from the Young Communist organization which had a close link with the security agencies.

To my amusement, Nosenko strongly defended the knockout drops. I said I didn't think they produced targets of any value and the scandals were counterproductive. Very naive, I said. Not at all, he insisted; I simply didn't know the ones who had cooperated with the KGB rather than tell the embassy.

I didn't follow this up. I had never seen or heard of real results from knockout drops. It was the tactic used on sailors, enlisted men, clerks and the like. Petty stuff.

I asked Nosenko specific questions about several Moscow colleagues who were rumored to have associations with Soviet intelligence (or suspected of being "doubles," encouraged by U.S. agencies to maintain contacts with the Russians). His replies faithfully followed my own (and the conventional) suspicions.

The evening came to an end and left me very uneasy. I had no doubt that Nosenko had been connected with surveillance of correspondents. He did not know as much about me and correspondents of the Stalin period as he might. But he knew enough. Had he made up the story of the plot against me? Probably not. Probably some harebrained scheme was considered and I thought I could pinpoint the occasion.

In the spring of 1951, I made my most extensive trip of the Stalin period, a ten-day visit to Tbilisi and Georgia. I spent three months getting permission. My Russian was now good enough so that I was operating on my own and I proposed traveling by myself. Suddenly a young man in the Press Department told me he was planning to take his vacation in Georgia—perhaps we might go together. I was delighted. He was pleasant enough, spoke a little English and we had never had harsh words. We agreed on arrangements, departure time, train, itinerary. I must confess that my friends Tom and Juli Whitney expressed concern about this plan, Juli in particular. She said it "didn't smell right." Two days before we were to leave, I was told by the Press Department that my friend had already left for Georgia. We would not, after all, be going together. No explanations, nothing. I was furious. Tom and Juli became even more concerned. Juli was convinced that some provocation was afoot. I believed it was merely one more example of hostility and bureaucratic confusion. I made the trip to Tbilisi in a compartment occupied by three Red Army officers. There were no foreigners on the train, plenty of opportunity for skulduggery. I reached Georgia safely enough, although somewhat worn by the constant drinking of my companions, who had casks and goatskin bags of Georgian wine and turned the trip into a long Georgian feast. Because Juli had felt so strongly that an unknown danger hovered over me, I sent back to Moscow several messages by diplomats whom I encountered. Each reported "so far so good." Soon the warm air, sunshine and Mediterranean atmosphere drove thoughts of plots from my mind. I never saw the Press Department man and turned my attention to such pursuits as digging out of the state library in Tbilisi some romantic old revolutionary poems of Stalin (which the censors refused to let me transmit). The *Times* played my stories in gingerly fashion and Prince T. K. Bagration, a Georgian nobleman, the tombs of whose ancestors I had seen at the ancient cathedral of Mtskhet, wrote an angry complaint that I had seen nothing but police agents in Georgia. I now prepared to go on an even longer trip, to Siberia, but this did not come off. Cy Sulzberger wanted me to go, but Mr. James thought I should go on no more trips—reporting from Russia was getting too controversial. So I didn't go until after Stalin died.

Reflecting on Nosenko's story, I think Juli Whitney's suspicions about the Georgian trip were probably sound. The trip could have been set up to stage the provocation, administering the paralyzing drug far from Moscow with my friendly Foreign Office aide on hand to handle the messy details. If Nosenko was right, contrary instructions caused the scenario to be canceled. The Georgian gambit is hypothesis. But it represented the only occasion in nearly six years in Moscow when anyone from the Foreign Office volunteered to spend time in my company. I thought little of it at the time. In retrospect, I wonder.

30 | Scoop

February 1950 was the month when the long and enigmatic discussions between Stalin and Mao Zedong, begun in early December 1949, finally bore their fruit, a skinflint pact of friendship and mutual aid.

I thought there was something fishy about the treaty. It provided that Moscow would give the Chinese $300 million in loans, not grants, over a five-year period—that is, $60 million a year. Peanuts! And while it professed to restore Chinese sovereignty over all Manchuria, it kept the bases and the railroads in Russian hands. Moreover, the treaty imposed on China joint-stock companies in which Moscow held the controlling 51 percent, not much different from the comprador deals of the nineteenth century. It came as no surprise to me when Nikita Khrushchev revealed in 1956 that Mao would have packed up and turned his face to Washington—if the U.S. had not been even more hostile.

Ambassador Kirk, a canny navy man who had served in China, recommended in November 1949 (along with other U.S. diplomats) that President Truman grant Communist China diplomatic recognition. Truman was not averse, but he felt he had to wait until he got his budget through the Republican Senate.

Kirk had told me his views on China privately. Truman had taken an informal poll of his best diplomats and there was general agreement on going forward with normalization as soon as possible. It seemed clear to me that Russia and China were far from chummy.

I was, thus, more than a little surprised when Cy Sulzberger broke an exclusive story from Paris a few days after the signing of the Sino-Soviet treaty, claiming that it contained secret protocols under which Mao had placed his armed forces at Stalin's command and turned over the Manchurian ports to the Soviet navy. The Kremlin, Cy asserted, now directed a one-billion-man Communist mass extending from the Elbe to the Yellow Sea, a terrifying threat to the U.S. and the world. The *Times,* naturally, gave this chilling intelligence smash play. I was in no position to challenge Cy's story. He had better sources than I, including, as I later understood, access to high U.S. intelligence officials. I had no sources whatever, only my wits. Nonetheless, I didn't think Cy's story was right and I wrote him, tactfully expressing doubts.

I had found it totally impossible to cover the Mao-Stalin talks in any conventional journalistic sense. I never saw Mao, despite many efforts. I even barged into the Chinese embassy, much to their embarrassment. The closest I came was one evening when the Chinese rented the dining room of the Metropol to give Stalin a reception. Even though Mao and Stalin were under my roof, as it were, even though I could hear the murmur of the multitude from the lobby door, I didn't catch a glimpse of the distinguished principals. When I went around to the side entrance of the Metropol, the security men chased me away. For weeks I couldn't even be sure Mao was still in Russia, let alone what course the negotiations were taking.

Finally, desperate from lack of information, I took to filing stories about the talks anyway. I just made them up. I reported that Mao was out touring the countryside. That was killed. (I deduced that he was not touring the Soviet Union.) I said the talks concerned trade and security matters. That was passed, but with none of the details I had incorporated (hoping to get some guidance from the censor's cuts). I managed in this way to establish that the talks were continuing; that Mao and Stalin were participating in them; that they were reviewing a whole range of issues; that there was sensitivity about the length of the meeting (all references to "protracted" talks were deleted). In many subtle ways I detected uneasiness. Ordinarily, negotiations in Moscow were totally ceremonial; the chief of state arrived, had his picture taken, attended a Kremlin banquet, paid a few calls, signed the treaty and went back home.

I was impressed by the nuances that could be adduced by careful phrasing and rephrasing of my submissions to the censors. (My fail-safe was that if the censor's treatment was unclear, I did not have to transmit the story.) I decided to try this kind of three-corner billiards on the question of U.S.-Soviet relations. Here I had more materials with which to work. I had a sense that the Soviet Union was ready for a new try at diplomacy with the United States. Moscow had hit a dead end with the Berlin blockade; relations with China were sticky; President Truman's decision to proceed with the H-bomb had plunged the nuclear

questions into a new era. Ambassador Kirk was going back home
for a month and we talked the situation over. He had been kept
on a short leash since his arrival. With nothing to talk to the
Russians about, he and Mrs. Kirk had spent their time trying to
improve the glacial morale at the embassy. Now he, too, thought
the Russians might be ready to talk.

I decided to test this thesis, banking my shots against the censor. I wrote a general story, a sober piece quoting "some diplomatic quarters" (that is, Admiral Kirk and myself), who felt
that the Soviet Union was now ready to join with the United
States in an effort to solve outstanding problems, including the
issue of atomic controls.

I pointed out that there had been "no Soviet statements" to
this effect; outlined the differences in positions of the two countries; and cited Soviet declarations that indicated that the differences were not irreconcilable.

I put the dispatch into censorship and waited. It was held up
about thirty hours and then passed without a single word being
cut. This was significant. If I was flying a kite, it was a kite the
Russians wanted flown. For whatever reason, they elected to tell
the world they were not averse to talking with the United States.

The *Times* gave the story good play. I then added a twist to my
tactics. I sent a letter to Generalissimo Stalin, posing a series of
questions on the nuclear arms race, the H-bomb, the possibilities
of a joint effort by the U.S. and the Soviet Union to tackle those
problems and achieve a general political settlement. I waited a
few days to allow time for this to reach Stalin's attention (and be
answered directly if, as sometimes happened, he wished). I got no
reply from the Kremlin. I then read carefully through the current periodicals and spotted in *Soviet State and Law* an article
discussing a declaration by Stalin, of a couple of years earlier,
that the peaceful settlement of disputes between the United
States and the Soviet Union was not only possible but absolutely
essential.

I turned up a series of declarations in various contexts which
provided possible answers to the questions I had put to Stalin.
Incorporating these in four separate dispatches, I filed them one
a day, and sent two further questionnaires to the Generalissimo.

My stories went into the censorship on February 13. Just before midnight of the eighteenth, I got a call from the censor's
office—most unusual—to tell me they had cleared my materials

and they were ready for transmission. I bundled into my sheepskin and hurried through the snow-choked streets to the Central Telegraph Office on Gorky Street, a fast ten-minute walk. To my astonishment, I found my dispatches bore only a few nominal cuts.

This made it clear that the Soviet Union was, in fact, inviting an American response, as I hastened to advise New York (and the State Department) through private channels.

As in so many examples—past and yet to come—no tangible result emerged from this exercise. A month or so passed and the clouds closed in once more; the censors resumed their arbitrary slashing of my copy and I prepared to go back for a short visit to the United States. But I had learned something that I would employ in the future—the use of the censorship against itself as a device for testing my evaluation of Soviet policy. For a long time to come, there would be diplomats, American and others, who were certain I had a secret, high-level source in the Foreign Office if not the Kremlin. It is possible, I must admit, that there may have been some in the KGB who also arrived at this totally mistaken view.

I flew to New York in late May, paused briefly to consult the editors of the *Times,* then went to Minneapolis and picked up Michael, now a robust eleven-year-old. We proceeded to Pyramid Lake Ranch in Nevada, where I would spend the obligatory six weeks and then get a divorce. The long matrimonial battle had ended. The ranch was a joy for Mike and me. We rode every morning over the desert and up mountain trails. Neither of us had ridden before, but Mike took to it like a cowboy and galloped circles around me. We swam in the somewhat saline lake in the afternoon and occasionally drove sixty miles into Reno, where I got acquainted with slot machines and roulette. No other guest at the ranch was male, a strange society of women waiting for their decrees, many deeply unhappy, all disoriented. Some years later, Marilyn Monroe's movie *The Misfits,* which Arthur Miller wrote for her, was filmed at this ranch.

I felt disconnected from the world. Russia was in another solar system. New York had vanished. Ellen was going her own way. Somehow none of this mattered. Mike and I rode out on the desert as the sun was coming up and we caught the magical perfume of the flowers and grass awakening in its rays. I had never seen people like the ranchers. One morning a woman drove calmly into the sheriff's office, the body of her husband trussed to the roof of her station wagon like a deer. "Lock me up," she told the sheriff. "I shot the son of a bitch last night. He got drunk once too often." They locked her up for an hour and then she went back to running the ranch. It was a man's world, where a husband could get a divorce by asking for it. A neighboring rancher had had eight legal wives and no one knew how many by common law. Every day a great station wagon, the springs down to the axles, paused at the ranch to fill up with gas. It was a well-known entertainer, on his way up the desert track, where forty miles into the foothills he had a hideaway. Each day he loaded his station wagon with canned goods, preserved hams, corned beef, flour and sugar to help him survive the atom war he thought might erupt at any time.

I was still waiting out my divorce when, totally improbably as it seemed to me, war broke out in Korea. I knew we were in for a long, hard haul and that the freeze in Moscow would get worse and worse.

The place for me was Russia, but some things could not be speeded up. I would not be back in the United States, I felt certain, for a long time. It had taken me six months to persuade the *Times* to let me come home, so fearful were they that if I left I could not get back in. Now I had my return visa in hand and I hurried to get my affairs in order. Mary was selling the house in Mamaroneck; I arranged to have my things put in storage; I made elaborate plans to bring Michael with me to Moscow. To my despair, at the last moment, passports ready, cabin reserved on the *Queen Mary,* Mary refused to let him go. I finally sailed for England in mid-August.

The Korean War had touched off a spiral of war hysteria and anti-Russian emotion. I had been to Washington and found people holding their breaths in fear Russia would intervene. Many felt we were at the edge of nuclear confrontation. The greatest fear was of a Soviet attack on Europe. I had gained confidence in my ability to extrapolate from personal observation. War against the U.S. was no small matter. If the Russians were preparing to take advantage of our preoccupation in the East to strike a sudden blow in the West, there was no way they could hide their preparations along the main railroads.

I made my plans accordingly. I stopped briefly in London,

consulted my colleagues in Paris and booked myself first class on the *Orient Express*. I was, I confess, excited—not just because I knew I had the makings of a great scoop, but because I had grown up on E. Phillips Oppenheim: *Le Train Bleu* for romance, the *Orient* for international hugger-mugger. I got on it at midevening, and looked in every direction for the whirl of a black lace skirt, a whiff of exotic perfume, a gentleman in spats and white gloves, the bulge of a pistol in his pocket. The train was almost empty. The iron curtain had descended on classic espionage. In my trench coat, I looked more a spy than did anyone else. There were four or five paunchy Germans who dropped off at points in Bavaria and then I was alone with a young mother and her six-month-old baby all the way to Prague. I had not been in Germany since the war. When the border police knocked at my compartment and asked rudely, I thought, for my passport, I found to my surprise that I deeply resented complying with this simple request by a German. Not until 1966 would I compel myself to visit Japan; the wounds of the war had left deep scars.

From the moment of daylight, my eyes were glued to the window as we rolled across into Czechoslovakia. I saw no troop trains (I hardly expected that), no signs of new construction, no hustle or bustle—just the lazy provincial pace, hardly anything to jot down in my notebook. Well, I conceded, I had passed through most of Czechoslovakia at night. Armies could have been waiting and I would not have seen them. There were no military on the station platforms, none on the train, no Russians, no truck convoys crawling over the hills.

I stopped over in Warsaw a couple of days and found no war fever there. The *Times* man, Ed Morrow, took me around town. I don't know how long Ed had spent in Warsaw, but it had been too long. He had fallen into the disease, so easy to acquire behind the curtain, of playing games with the security detail that had been staked out to keep an eye on him. He had got so deep into ducking and dodging them that he hardly had thought for anything else. Warsaw's air bore the scent of fear. It looked to me as though the Poles were on shorter rations than Moscow, but Ed said there had been no recent changes. A brief flurry of hoarding occurred when the Korean War broke out, but things had quieted down. No sign of troop movements, no new security precautions, no rumors of anything doing in the East, no signs of Russian alert. I thought the testimony of this worried man bore some weight. If anyone was on the lookout for Communist moves, it was Ed. We talked to people in the embassy; no sign of war preparations, and the embassy had reported this to Washington.

I boarded the *Kuriersky Express* in Warsaw with anticipation. The route of the *Kuriersky* across Poland, to the border city of Brest and on to Moscow, was the main invasion route from west to east (as followed by Hitler and Napoleon) or from east to west as followed by the Red Army in its drive to Berlin. Baranovichi, Minsk, Orsha, Smolensk, Vyazma, Mozhaisk—a roll call of the critical battles of 1941. Here, if anywhere, I would find evidence if the Red Army was mobilizing to strike Europe.

We spent a day at Brest, where the train halted, the carriages were changed to the wide Russian gauge, we went through customs. Again the customs man couldn't read English, so my books and luggage were sealed and sent on to Moscow. I was left only *Vie de Bohème* to read. I persuaded the customs officer that it was merely the story of an opera and because it was in French (apparently he did not think French so subversive as English) he let me keep it. I suffered from both lack of reading material and lack of rubles. I had forgotten that I could change no money. I spent the days on a diet of excellent pâté de foie gras which Cy Sulzberger had given me in Paris, some Nescafé and three worm-eaten apples.

During the long halt at Brest, I strolled about the town. It was a major junction. Here if anywhere I should find supplies moving up—guns, munitions, rations, flatcars with weapons concealed under tarpaulins. I had seen the Russian railroads in war. I knew what they looked like, I knew the jams on the sidings, the swarms of troops that collected at every transit point. I found none of that. True, there was a large bustling freightyard. True, there were lots of military, but as far as I could see, as many were coming back from Germany and Poland as going in. The freight traffic was civilian traffic—cars of grain, flatcars of timber, machinery, gondolas of coal. I didn't see a gun except for the rifles and sidearms of the border guards; there were plenty of them. There was the normal range of foodstuffs in the stores and trainside stalls. Something unusual might be going on in Russia—but not here.

It took two and a half days to get to Moscow from Warsaw, and I was all eyes. By the time I arrived in Moscow, however, I

had pretty much come to a conclusion. In the entire journey, I
had seen not a single piece of artillery, not a tank, not an antiaircraft gun, not an antitank gun, not a troop train, not a food
queue. To be sure, people were buying bread from the train's dining car at station stops, but I had never seen a train in Russia
where that didn't happen. In those days, there wasn't a place in
Russia where white bread was not in short supply except Moscow
—and even Moscow sometimes ran out.

I believed I had a first-class, even sensational, political and
military story. So far as at least one "reasonably quick observer" (as I was to call myself in my dispatches) was concerned,
Russia was not getting ready to jump Europe. She might be preparing something big in the Far East, yet I was dubious of that.
From what I knew of the Soviet economy, a prospective major
military move in the Far East would have shown up in shortages
in the civilian sector as far west as Brest—and probably Warsaw. I determined to explore Moscow thoroughly for further evidence to confirm or upset my hypothesis.

By September 13, I had scoured the city. I could find no sign
in the department stores, the food markets, the supply depots,
the hardware stores or the drugstores of unusual shortages or
hoarding. I heard no rumors, or underground gossip, suggesting
the Russians feared they were about to launch an attack. (Soviets were fearful of American attacks.) No unusual call-ups had
been uncovered by the U.S. military. The consensus of the diplomatic colony was that the Russians were keeping their heads
down, more concerned with being dragged into war against their
will than with broadening the conflict by their own design. The
city was a scene of unusual construction and reconstruction. New
skyscrapers were going up, new efforts were being made to put
the city's dilapidated housing into repair. I had seen much the
same from the train. I had seen, too, that many concrete bridges
demolished during the war had not yet been replaced or repaired.

This did not add up to a picture of Moscow buckling on its
sword and girding for battle, and so far as I could ascertain, no
one in the American embassy, diplomatic or military, believed
they were.

I sat down on September 13 and over the next three days wrote
seven or eight detailed, factual articles reporting precisely what
I had seen coming into Russia and what was evident within the

country itself. As I said: "Naturally one correspondent's rail-road car window view is not conclusive but it is recorded here for what value it may have and in a reasoned effort to present a strictly objective account. In view of the present state of world nerves it seems that this is a fact worth recording and possibly even underlining."

I contrasted my present observations with those I had made in Russia-at-war in 1944. I suggested that the program of recon-struction in Moscow was inconsistent with a scenario that would involve the Soviet Union in war with the U.S.A. I laced my copy with warnings that I was aware that the impressions I was offer-ing might conflict sharply with many that the readers held of a trigger-happy Russia that at any moment might lunge into Ger-many or strike at the American forces in Korea.

Each dispatch was held a day or two in censorship—indicating that it received high-level attention—and then released with fairly trivial cuts, among them, oddly, the description of a dog show at Sokolniki Park (I had seen Olga there). The censor de-leted my account of Soviet troop transit traffic in Brest, and cut an important passage dealing with Muscovites' concern that the Korean War might spread and involve Russia in general hostili-ties.

I thought then and think now, having reread my copy closely, that it was factual reporting of a competent level and that it pre-sented invaluable information for U.S. policymakers and the public. It was conservatively written, loaded with caveats, and it offered a true, realistic and clear picture of a major component in the world situation.

But this was not how it was perceived in New York. First there was an ominous quiet, then a fire storm of inquiries, ques-tions, suggestions for revision, more and more requests, delays, and as I was to become aware, the whole thing began to spill over into the public eye, with the *Daily Worker* and Communist spokesmen charging that the *Times* was suppressing an impor-tant series of articles by its Moscow correspondent.

The stories arrived in New York at a moment when Arthur Sulzberger was in Europe and General Adler, the business ma-nanger, a staunch patriot, an army man who had never been pleased with my appointment, was in charge. Mr. James was also away. Turner Catledge was sitting in as his deputy. Lester Markel, who had long been a supporter of mine and would be again, now joined General Adler in what I can only describe as a vicious attack on the series and upon me as a Communist dupe. I suspect Lester's motivations lay in his unrealistic ambition to succeed Mr. James and, also, in some problems he was beginning to have over allegations of Communists on his Sunday staff. But that does not show in the record.

Catledge was instructed by Adler to obtain from me a remarkable amount of information, most of which had little or nothing to do with my articles—inserts, elaborations, statistics, new facts galore. Somewhat to my amazement, I got most of this material and cleared almost all of it through the censorship, except, of course, for prices. The censor never cleared prices.

Adler and Markel apparently thought the articles were Communist propaganda. I can only suppose they did not actually read them. And there was another spoon in the stew, as my later research revealed—that of Irving Brown, who was then the AFL-CIO representative in Europe, very active in anti-Communist doings and later to be described by *The New York Times* as having CIA connections. I've no notion how he got involved, but he did and he stimulated Markel very handily.

Matters had reached a point at which Adler and Markel were demanding that I be recalled from Moscow. When Arthur Sulzberger returned to New York, he was handed a revised and much condensed version of the series, put together by Freedman, which, alas, eliminated a great deal of my factual observations of the state of Soviet military preparedness.

Sulzberger promptly ordered publication of the condensed version, with an editor's note of the type I had been campaigning for from the day I reached Moscow. It pointed out that the dispatches had passed through Soviet censorship and warned the reader that some materials requested by the editors could not be transmitted through censorship.

By this time, considerable hubbub—*shum,* as the Russians would say—had been generated. The stories were promptly seized upon by party spokesmen as a demonstration of a Soviet "desire for peace," which was not the point at all. I had no notion whether the Soviet leaders wanted war or peace. I thought, actually, that they had no objection to war if war served their interests. In this case, apparently, they had decided it did not. It was therefore important for U.S. policymakers to know that they could go forward in the Far East without much worry of a Soviet counterblow in the West. If anyone got this point from the mangled articles, I never encountered him.

The row did not die down easily. Years later, I discovered through an FOIA action that poor old Major General R. W. Grow, military attaché in Moscow at the time, had sent the Defense Department a complaint about my report. He thought my stating that there did not appear to be a war scare in Moscow or signs of panic buying was "extremely dangerous" and inclined "to lull the American people to a false sense of security." His superior in the Pentagon, General Bolling, agreed, and wrote back that he thought the article was a "handout from the Soviet Ministry of Enlightenment."

La, me, here we are again! I didn't know about all this. I didn't know about the row in the top levels of the *Times,* which went on until Arthur Hays Sulzberger put it bluntly to Markel: did he really want Salisbury fired? Markel backed down a bit untidily. I didn't know that General Grow, who within the year would suffer the humiliating disaster of losing his diary in Germany and having it published by the Communists, one juicy, silly passage after another, regarded me as a dangerous "pink." I went on thinking of him as one more gruff, decent military man, produced like sausage from a machine, an American Colonel Blimp, not very well equipped to handle the simple task of observing facts and putting them together in a coherent picture.

I didn't know all this, but I knew enough to recognize that what I thought had been a reporting coup had been turned into a disaster by some rather ignorant cooks. For a long time to come, I could observe in the responses of my editors a touchiness, a reserve, a—well, let's face it—a lack of confidence which held them back from giving my dispatches the play and attention they deserved.

Gradually I began to understand what had happened. Once again I had violated the rules. I had reported an important but unpalatable truth. What I had said about the Soviet Union and its war preparations did not fit the cliché of the day. The fact that what I said gave us a free hand (but for Mao and the People's Liberation Army) in the Far East, that we could go forward with little fear of a European threat, made no difference. The Russia I depicted did not fit the popular image, and without consideration of what I was really saying, a large gob of smear was thrown in my direction. The bearer of unpleasant news was getting his deserts. Once I figured this out, I felt somewhat better. But I remained sore and frustrated. I still am.

31 | Saltychikhi

The sulky young woman sitting beside the window in Room 225 of the Metropol Hotel was reading a book and eating a tangerine, pulling back the peel, breaking off sections, one by one, and putting them into her mouth. She did not look up when I entered and I did not speak to her, a slender, dark-haired girl with narrow shoulders, gray-green eyes, high cheekbones, thin face. She must be, I thought, Juli Zapolskaya, the Russian wife of Tom Whitney, who sat across the desk from her. I had heard a good deal about Juli—that she was temperamental, brilliant, a musical genius, unpredictable, *dangerous,* an enfant terrible who might pounce at any moment. "Be careful," I was told. She did not speak; neither did I, nor did Tom introduce us. He was a thin, bespectacled, studious man with a close-cropped Prussian haircut, an extraordinary Soviet specialist who had been recruited by the OSS and sent to the American embassy to work for Averell Harriman not long after I arrived in Moscow in 1944. We had not met in that time. I was a war correspondent, totally interested in the Red Army; he was an economist, extrapolating from thin data the status of Soviet steel production. His only other interest was Juli, whom he met a few weeks after arriving.

Now Tom was working for the Associated Press, a tenuous foothold which enabled him to stay in Moscow with Juli, his appointment at the embassy having expired. Had he left Moscow, Juli would have gone straight to a labor camp, as had the other women whose wartime husbands had been compelled to leave them behind.

Tom and I gossiped about the news of the day, then Juli suddenly spoke: "Want some?" She held out a segment of the tangerine. I took it in surprise and she returned to her book, scowling as if she was very angry, though I couldn't imagine why. A moment later, I went back to my office. There were, of course, more meetings. In the narrow circle of Stalin's Moscow, we all knew each other. More and more, I found myself making my way to the narrow *pereulok* behind the Vakhtangov Theater where

Tom and Juli had a flat in a Russian building, no other foreigners—a cluttered Moscow flat, paint peeling, staircase defaced, steps crumbling. One day in spring, a concrete balcony fell off the fifth floor, narrowly missing a babushka sunning a baby in the muddy courtyard.

As time passed, my life came to center on these two people: the American from Toledo, as typical a product of the Midwest as myself, or more so, from a real estate family, Methodists, teetotalers, his father (like Tom) an Amherst graduate; and the Russian girl whose name was redolent of all the Russias, Zapolskaya —beyond the fields, or the outer meadows. Nothing was more Russian than the *polye,* the meadows: fragrant hay, women in white kerchiefs, men in embroidered shirts, the flashing blades of the scythes, haycocks in the summer afternoons, wagons slowly making their way to the ancient barns, the Russia of history, of the smell of black bread, of sweat and *makhorka,* and over the *polye* the perfume of the flowers of the fields and of the strong-muscled women.

Juli was not a strong-muscled woman; strong-willed, yes, sinewy, a supple figure and a mind that would have given the devil pause, Russian to the tips of her long fingers, which rippled over the keys of her piano and composed without effort. "Play me a summer afternoon," I once said, and the summer afternoon—golden shafts of sunlight, long shadows, green lawns and playing children—sounded in my ears. "Play an empty corridor," and the corridor opened, with Kafka-gray walls, no windows, straight, endless in time, endless in space, and the piano drifting into silence. Tom would be sitting nearby at his worktable, fingering his slide rule, calculating with sharp-pointed pencils, calculating the uncalculable, the statistics of Gosplan, the State Plan, prying from them the evidence the planners thought they had concealed, of underfulfillment of critical industries, magical feats of math which he tossed in the air like bright spinning balls but could never pass through the censorship. In fact, he did not bother to submit them; they would only have alerted the security men, revealed to them that their disinformation could be reconstituted into vital facts and figures.

Often there was present the third member of this family group, Juli's mother, gray-haired, worn, puttering over the gas range, cooking a *skilerada,* a frying pan, of sausage and sliced potatoes, of eggs and onions, or sometimes, joy, *gribye,* mush-

rooms we had just picked in the Moscow forests, *podsosniki,*
poddubniki, podbereyozovki—under-the-pine-trees, under-the-oak-
trees, under-the-birch-trees—succulent mushrooms, impregnated
with the taste of the Russian forest, the scent of the Russian soil,
simmered for an instant in sweet Russian butter.

On a spring day, the frost hardly out of the ground, the mud
deep beside the road, Tom and Juli and I (and more and more it
was becoming Tom-and-Juli-and-I) drove out the Chaussée Entusiastov—the Highway of the Enthusiasts, which led to Siberia
—past two chemical works, across a long bridge over the railroad
yards, past a NKVD military camp behind blue-painted fences
marked with red stars, along a road under reconstruction, to the
textile town of Balashikha, turned right on the Ryazan chaussée,
crossed a small bridge and drove into the village of Saltykovka.

My heart sank: the gray skies, the rain, the mud of spring, the
leafless trees, grass just greening after the winter, small log
houses, unpainted, untended, behind unpainted wooden fences,
the car slithering almost into the ditches, scrawny chickens, a
few fierce geese, a goat, pine trees, tall and straight and lonely. I
thought of Lake Minnetonka in Minnesota, where I spent childhood summers, and the old, plaster-caulked, snug log cabin of
"Grandma" Moore, where we stayed—not much like these raw
huts, mud, mud, mud, gray skies, gray women in dark coats,
skirts hiked up out of the mud. Oh, Lord, I thought, this is
Russia—God save me from it!

We pulled up before a brown-stained wooden house, with a
small front porch, an open deck above, an attached outhouse, a
third of a hectare, a little less than an acre of land, in a row of
four identical dachas, worn by wind and winter. This was it, the
man from Burobin said, this was the dacha Burobin was willing
to rent, the ground floor—living room and bedroom and kitchen
—to Tom and Juli, the single attic room with balcony and outdoor staircase to me. I thought it was awful. I was ready to turn
back immediately. Juli thought it heaven.

Saltykovka . . . Years later I stumbled on a book by a woman
from Odessa who came to Saltykovka in the late 1920s. She first
saw it on a dark autumn day. Never had she felt so forlorn: no
sidewalks, no bridges over the little streams, mud so deep she lost
a galosh and stood like a stork, not wanting to plunge her foot
back into the muck, a twenty-minute walk from railroad station

to dacha, an attic room so narrow she could hardly turn around, no shops, a single co-op which sold vodka and "coffee" made from ground roasted carrots, not much more, the worst place she had ever seen, so alien to her sunny Odessa. She burst into tears. But when summer finally came, she fell in love with it, a village of ponds, streams, birch and pine forests, fresh air, neither the noise nor the dust of Moscow. When she had to leave, she threw herself on the narrow mattress, hugged it, kissed it and cried all over again.

Saltykovka would change my life, but of this I saw no sign on that murky April day, no sign as we spattered back to Moscow through the drizzle, endlessly waiting to pass the truck-clogged detours of the Chaussée Entusiastov.

We rented the dacha, but I had hardly a glimpse of it for many months. I went to the United States and by the time I returned it was September, summer over, just a quick taste of sleeping on a mattress on my attic floor, smelling cut pine, reading myself to sleep by candlelight, listening to roosters crow in the thin autumn dawn, breathing the heavy scent of the last hay as the sun fingered its first beams on the rough wood walls, letting down the bucket in the common well, winding up the heavy rope, lugging two balanced pails back to the dacha and sloshing icy water over my shoulders, walking a mile to the peasant market on Sunday, women with bags of sunflower seeds, bags of potatoes, bags of onions, heaps of turnips, strings of garlic, pots of *smetana,* buckets of milk, a butcher with ragged scraps of meat, God knows from which part of which animal, a Chinaman —well, probably he was a Mongol—selling buns like the hot cross buns I ate as a child in Minneapolis. I got a taste of this, and it was my first taste of Russia.

In the next eighteen months, day by day, week by week, I vanished into Russia. I did not notice this. No one else knew it. Surely *The New York Times* did not perceive it. In part it was Saltykovka, in part Tom and Juli, mostly Juli.

By the spring of 1951, Soviet Moscow had closed in on me. I was the only newspaper correspondent left. My ability to originate stories had steadily been curtailed. The censorship was turning my dispatches into a cold plate of gruel—no originality, no color, no depth. Looking back over my file of stories to the *Times* from my return from Georgia in late spring 1951 to August

1952, I find only a few that provided any special insight. If you had taken all my dispatches and wrapped garbage in them, you would have lost very little. Part of this came from my deep depression over the row about my post-Korea dispatches (even though I did not know the inside story) and the chorus of critical letters published by the *Times*. I again urged New York to protect its readers and its correspondent by putting the "Passed by censor" label on my stories; again my proposal was rejected. I asked that the Letters to the Editor column pay heed to the content of the letters they were publishing (often from a tight group of anti-Communists associated with McCarthy); not infrequently they deliberately misrepresented what I had reported; repeatedly they complained of the omission of facts removed by the censor. Late in 1951, Charles Merz, editor of the editorial page, promised to consult with the foreign desk before printing tendentious letters. I felt frustrated, angry, uncertain how to break the vicious circle.

My response was to spend more time in Saltykovka. I burrowed into this cubbyhole of Russian life, hardly affected by revolution and the modern world. It was not a conscious decision, nor did I perceive that I had against all odds penetrated every security barrier of Stalin's apparatus and walked right into the heart of Russia.

In the eighteenth century (and possibly before that), Saltykovka had been an appanage of the Saltykovs, a rich and powerful noble family. Within Saltykovka had been perpetrated the most infamous of the atrocities of Russian serfdom, acts which resounded over the long years of the revolutionary movements against Nicholas I, Alexander II, Alexander III and Nicholas II. The central figure of this cause célèbre was the Countess Darya Ivanovna Saltykova, a brutal sadist whose name reverberated still in Russia's catalogue of infamy. So I was told by Juli and this was the story believed by the villagers. In reality, as I learned much later, the murders occurred not at Saltykovka but at another small village in the Moscow area, and I can find no evidence that our Saltykovka was actually connected with the unspeakable countess. The name Saltykov is a common one and it was borne by not a few families of the nobility. When I lived in Saltykovka, though, I believed it was the scene of the crimes of the bloody countess. She was formally charged with 139 murders and probably committed many more, unspeakable crimes, almost all against serfs who were her personal property. On the death of her husband, Saltykova, twenty-five years old, inherited six hundred souls, as they were called—that is, heads of serf families attached to estates in the Moscow region. Most of those whom Saltykova put to death were killed by torture, often by her own hand, almost all of them women, not infrequently girls of eleven or twelve. She accused them of doing the washing badly or not scrubbing the floors. She would begin a victim's punishment by beating her with a rolling pin. Then she called her grooms and footmen and ordered them to beat the culprit with birches, knouts and leather straps. Saltykova would stand by, crying: "Beat her to death! Beat her to death!" And the grooms would beat the girl to death. In "special cases," Saltykova burned the hair from her victims' heads, drenched them in boiling water, tore off their ears with red-hot pincers, threw girls to their deaths from towers, starved and tortured them. After a six-year investigation, Saltykova was sentenced to death in 1768, but Catherine II reprieved her and put her into an underground cell for the rest of her life, thirty-three years, during which time she gave birth to a daughter sired by one of her guards. She was formally deprived of her name, yet, in the twisted form *saltychikhi,* it lives in the Russian language to this day, a synonym of "torturer."

I thought often in those days of this witch, this *saltychikhi,* whose story had been told and retold in the endless struggles of the young radicals of the nineteenth century, trying to free Russia from the dark tyranny of the Czar, whose power brooked no more limit than that of the *saltychikhi* over her serfs; and in the declamations, the poems, the legends the revolutionaries told the people, calling on them to throw off their shackles and erect a new system dedicated to liberty, justice and enlightenment. Decade after decade they gave their lives, wearing out their bodies, dying in prisons, swinging from the Czar's gibbets. A young woman raped by a guard in the Peter and Paul Fortress burned herself to death in the flames of a kerosene lamp for the sake of revolution. There was nothing they did not do: they blew themselves up making bombs; died in attacks on the Czar; wasted to death of tuberculosis in garrets; spent their blood like wine, generation after generation. To what end?

Now I found myself in Saltykovka, whose name was a symbol of what Russia's revolutionaries had struggled against, and twenty miles away in Moscow sat a man in the Kremlin whose crimes made those of the *saltychikhi* seem like a schoolgirl's prank. Where she had done to death, say, 139 souls, most of them women, for not doing the washing properly, the man in the Kremlin didn't bother with excuses. He simply killed and killed and killed.

This was beyond my comprehension as I sat outside the dacha on a late summer day, my nostrils filled with the narcotic scent of the nicotiana blossoms, the heavy perfume of clover, the sensuous odor of ripened grain, the village drowsing, a murmur of three women chatting at the well, the lazy sound of a hammer as a soldier, jacket off, army shirt off, only his khaki breeches and his purple undershirt clinging to his sweat-drenched body, set into place another two-by-four in the slowly rising dacha of his commander, the general.

This was, in a sense, a village in hiding, hiding from the restless *saltychikhi* of the Kremlin. Years ago, I had learned, Saltykovka had some relationship to the State Planning Committee. State Plan workers got dachas here; gradually, in those mysterious ways by which Russians bend and twist the planned society to make it more and more a facsimile of Old Russia, they became permanent residents. Such were the Balakiryovs, next door. I never knew how many members the family possessed; at least three worked in Moscow. They kept their heads down, did their chores, had no close friends, lived by the rules, went to party meetings, avoided advancement, special assignments, good work and bad work, stayed in the middle and survived. They boarded the electric train at the Kursk Station each evening and headed for Saltykovka. They walked the mile and a half to their dacha. Here they grew potatoes and onions, tended three goats and carefully bent back the picket fence occasionally to let the goats and chickens browse in our garden. They were quiet mice, very watchful for Kremlin cats. They kept their barriers up, never speaking unless it was essential (as when Tom complained about their goats).

The pleasant colonel across the way, who had lost his arm at the front, kept his head down too. He was half retired, still had a desk job in some military institution, but gradually he was building his home in the country, first a shack, then year by year the framework of what would someday be a snug little brick house,

all the work done by him. I watched him work, admired his industry and valued his care. He had no friends in Saltykovka. He
never spoke to me. He never spoke to his Russian neighbors, kept
a distance; it was safer that way. The village was filled with people who were making themselves invisible to Moscow, to their
neighbors. Mostly they were middle-class, white-collar, but not
all were. There were peasants too, and they displayed a different
spirit, were freer in manner, hostile to their neighbors the re-
fugees from Moscow, hostile to foreigners like myself, Tom and
Juli. There was only one other foreign family in Saltykovka, a
Hungarian diplomat, his wife, mother-in-law and two children.
But they spent only a month and then left.

Natasha was a peasant. I suppose she was twenty-five or
twenty-six, not unattractive except for her small round eyes;
blond, energetic, mean-spirited, she was the mother of two or
three dirty children by a thin, sour-faced militiaman, tubercular,
cowed by Natasha's vigor. She and her family lived about 150
yards from the dacha, in a building that looked like a tar-paper
chicken house and was called the "barracks." Natasha did the
"black work" at the dacha, the chores, the scrubbing, the washing of linen, sweeping (not much), dusting (not at all). In summer, she went barefoot, wore a cheap figured-cotton dress, sort
of a sack, nothing else, not even a kerchief. In winter she wore
rubber boots, dark wool skirt, dark sweater, worn wool coat, and
heavy wool scarf over her head and shoulders. The chance to
make a little money was a break for Natasha, but she never displayed any pleasure in it. She never smiled at us. I think she
hated us with the classic peasant hatred for the overclass or possibly the classic peasant hatred for the foreigner, perhaps both.
Our presence made all the neighbors uneasy. Foreigners brought
unpleasantness—the police, the secret police, Moscow, trouble.
Natasha was one of the few who benefited from our presence. Of
course, she reported on us to the police and she must have earned
a bit that way.

Natasha did not like us and I don't know that she liked anyone. Certainly not Dedya Petya. Dedya Petya looked the legendary figure of the Russian man of the forest, tall, straight, with a
face that had been carved by an ax. I could see him walking out
of a Russian *skazka,* a fairy tale, or across the stage of the Bolshoi in Prokofiev's *The Stone Flower.* Dedya Petya would come
around the fence at the dacha, his gray Russian blouse tucked in

a broad leather belt, his threadbare neat, clean blue drill trousers tucked into polished black boots, ax in hand, grasped close to the blade, a postcard Russian Ded Moroz, Grandfather Frost, a graybeard with hesitant, respectful, dignified mien. He bowed slightly before speaking and he spoke with a deep, melodious voice, slowly, clearly, choosing his words. He was a retired railroad man and the sight of him melted my heart. A watchman for the dacha trust now, he kept an eye on our dacha and the others nearby that belonged to the trust. He lived in the "barracks" with his ailing wife. I always asked politely about Maria Petrovna and he would pause and with a serious face tell me that unfortunately she was no better; or unfortunately she was somewhat worse; or unfortunately she was very poorly. This was true and within the year his wife died of what I suppose must have been cancer.

Nothing was more unpleasant about Natasha than her bullying of Dedya Petya. She called him an old fool, said he was a liar and threatened to write up a report on him, that is, to denounce him to the police. He patiently stood his ground, although he confessed to Juli his fear that Natasha would do him harm. I don't know whether she did or not; he did not live long after his wife died.

The local overseer of the Saltykovka dachas had two great interests, hay and trees. He claimed the right to the hay of the dachas, which involved him in violent rows with dachniki who sought to cut the hay for their own purposes. When a new dacha was built, one tall straight pine provided the lumber. The trees were under Dedya Petya's custody. His duty was to protect them from local residents and vagrant woodcutters. This led to a terrible incident, the kind that cuts to the soul. An argument arose over cutting down a tree. The overseer wanted it cut. Dedya Petya said he must have permission from Moscow. The overseer struck Dedya Petya in the face, not a strong blow, but the indignity devastated Dedya Petya. Never had such a thing happened. To think that a Soviet citizen, a party member, could act like this! He never got over it.

His last months were darkened by another event, which he took as a reflection on his vigilance. One winter's night in 1952, a man broke into our dacha and stole a bottle of vodka and a nickel-plated samovar. Dedya Petya discovered the break-in on his morning rounds; the dacha door was open, the samovar gone and a trail of footsteps in the deep snow led across to the "street." There, as I saw later that day, the steps zigged and zagged for half a mile to a shed, where Dedya Petya and a militiaman found the culprit asleep, lulled by the vodka, clutching the samovar to his breast. It was a petty crime, there was no loss other than a half liter of vodka, but Dedya Petya was shaken. No matter that we did not blame him. He blamed himself. His task was to protect the property and he had failed.

And there was the Saltykovka lady who had a sister in Chicago. She and her husband owned a fine dacha somewhat closer to the station than ours. I passed it on every walk to and from the railroad. It possessed a glassed-in porch, neatly caulked windows, fine fruit trees, berry bushes, a garden with tomatoes and vegetables—an "excellent economy," as the Russians would say. I had seen the woman and her husband many times but naturally never spoke, not in those days. Nearly fifteen years later, I paid a sentimental visit to Saltykovka. As I was returning along Dachnaya Street, I crossed a little stream and started up the hill, when I saw the lady of the dacha outside her house, wearing a very good dress, a city dress, a city hat, carrying a white handbag. She hadn't been dressed like that when I passed her on coming from the station. As I approached, she smiled. "Excuse me for speaking," she said, "but I see you have come back to our Saltykovka. You have been away a long time." Yes, I said, it had been a good many years. I had come back to see how Saltykovka had changed. She nodded her head; the houses were better, some had been enlarged. I agreed. "Excuse me," she said, "but I know you are a foreigner—are you an American, by any chance?" Yes, I admitted, I was an American. "I thought so," she said. "I often saw you in the old days and I thought you were American." She paused, considering what she was about to do, and took the leap. "You know, I have a sister who lives in America. I wonder if you know her, by any chance. She lives in Chicago." The woman gave me her sister's name and address. She had not heard from her for a long time. I promised to try to find her when I went back to the United States. The woman thanked me with great emotion and I walked on toward the station. I felt a strong emotion too. I thought of her during all those years, seeing me pass back and forth, back and forth, a hundred times, two hundred times, each time remembering her sister, wanting to speak, not daring, never daring to make that simple move because the consequences could be fatal, but the hope and the desire still lay on her heart. Then finally I vanished. She did not see me for a year, five years, almost fifteen years. Then on this June day she had seen me striding down Dachnaya Street. She must have made up her mind instantly. She must have rushed inside, slipped on her best dress, got out her white summer bag, put on some makeup, put on her hat, the one she thought was so chic, which she had got from a saleswoman who kept it under the counter in a shop on Gorky Street. She had come out into her yard and watched for my return. When she saw me coming, she sauntered to the gate and stood there waiting for the big moment in her life, properly dressed to encounter the American, ready to put to him the question that might at long last restore contact with her sister. What had she hoped from that meeting? Well, I think she had hoped it might open the way to a new life; to her escape from Dachnaya Street. Pleasant as was Dachnaya Street in comparison with many streets I saw (and many I was not permitted to see), it was still an unpaved nineteenth-century street in a country run by the heirs of the man beside whom the Countess Saltykova was only an amateur in the practice of Russian bestiality.

What happened to me in those long, quiet, frustrated, motionless months in Saltykovka was a simple thing. I learned Russia, Russia as I would never forget it. One day, Juli and I set off for a walk; we did not know where, and it made no difference. We walked down grassy Dachnaya Street to the path bordering the creek and east across the Ryazan chaussée and continued on the footpath. After the Ryazan chaussée we never saw another road. We followed one footpath after another, some slippery with mud, some sandy lanes that wandered for miles in and out of potato fields, grain fields and little forests of birch and pine. This was ancient Russia, the Russia people of Moscow never saw, the Russia of peasants and farmers. We passed a little dam and millpond that provided water for a gristmill; we found ourselves in the courtyard of a dairy farm; we crossed pasture after pasture, and each herd of cows, each herd of goats, was guarded by a girl or an old man with a long crooked stick who had walked straight out of the time of Catherine II. We halted under an oak tree, ate black bread and cheese, then walked until we came on a flat saucerlike lake set in sandy shores. Poking through the aspens, we saw across the lake six imposing houses—not dachas, real houses, with cement pillars, iron gates and stone steps. Juli turned quickly in the path by which we had come, and silently retreated a couple of hundred yards, maybe a quarter mile, before she spoke. "We must hurry away from here," she said. "I don't know who lives in those houses, but they must be generals. Or more important people. It would not be good if they found us here." We got back to the dacha in late afternoon, sunburned, a little weary, and I, at least, very happy. I felt that I could have walked to the ends of Russia on those footpaths, and have found myself in any century I wanted to choose. I could have stumbled upon the town where Chekhov's Three Sisters lived; I could have found the Cherry Orchard and old Firs listening to the chop-chop-chop of the woodcutters as they cut down the trees; I could have emerged on Levin's estate at Pokrovskaye in the pages of *Anna Karenina* or met Pushkin, seated at a round table in a small pergola beside a reedy meadow stream. Or I might have found a band of peasants grasping their scythes and sickles, leaving the *lug,* the little gulf of meadowland, where they were cutting hay and rushing as a maddened mob to set torch to the barns of the *barin.* The path, I felt, led back through Russian history, and who could say whether, following it, I would ever return to the mid twentieth century.

There was in Saltykovka, as I learned, a whole life that had nothing to do with Marx or *Pravda.* Nothing was done in Saltykovka according to Moscow's rules. If, as it happened, we wanted our dacha painted, we did not go to the landlord, the Moscow dacha trust. We spotted a dacha in the village being painted and asked the man if he would paint ours. He and his friend would negotiate on a price (they furnishing the paint) and then we provided two liters of vodka to "seal" the deal. Where did the paint come from? The local factory where they worked. They smuggled the paint past the gatekeeper. They painted the dacha in the long summer evenings, one of them continuously drunk. How he held his job I couldn't guess, but after a while in Saltykovka I understood. The painter did not violate Stalin's strict laws under which he might have been sent to Siberia for chronic absence from work. He went to work each day, then crawled into a closet and slept until closing time. God knows how

many workers were doing the same. Vodka made the wheels go
round. There were a dozen vodka stands in Saltykovka, but only
one shop where you could buy bread, and often there was no
bread on its shelves. The only thing we got from the dacha trust
in three years was some blue and amber glass to decorate the
windows we put into the porch. This request was so totally Russian (it was, of course, Juli's idea), it captured the fancy of the
dacha trust man and he got from the Ministry of Railways half a
dozen squares of signal glass. The blue and amber lights were
much admired by our neighbors. I think they saw them as evidence that the foreigners were becoming Russified.

It was hard to find examples of either "collectivity" or "comradeship," those basic theoretic attributes of Soviet life, in Saltykovka; here it was every man for himself. The "new Soviet
man," as far as I could see, was remarkably like the old Russian
man. This thought came to me when I observed the "battle of the
well." The village well was located about two hundred feet down
Dachnaya Street from our dacha and served about twenty families. It was beside a substantial two-story dacha, surrounded by
a wooden wall. The owner had a closely planted orchard, with
raspberry and gooseberry bushes growing between the fruit
trees. I think the owner was a former official of the dacha trust.
He had a private gate in his fence beside the well. One morning,
the residents of Dachnaya Street awoke to find that the owner's
fence had pounced during the night and enclosed the well—
snatch, and it was gone. This was a matter of importance to our
community. There was another well, but it was a block away, and
those residents were not eager to share it.

Tom and I fired off letters to the dacha trust and to Burobin.
In this emergency we had a few words with our neighbors. We
thought we could join them in a complaint to the village soviet.
In general, they seemed to believe a complaint would do no good
because the well-grabber had higher rank and greater influence.
They had no desire to be associated with a foreigner in any way.
After two or three days, they found their own means of dealing
with the crisis. Women began to gather in the evening outside
the fence that now enclosed the well. They cursed the well-thief
and talked of what they were going to do. Some said they would
break down the fence and put a dead cat into the well. One spoke
of a dead horse, another of kerosene. One told of neighbors who

planned to tear down the fence and chop down the fruit trees.
Another urged her neighbors to set fire to the dacha the next
time there was a high wind. It would be easy. Just toss flaming
rags over the fence and the house would be gone before firefight-
ers could arrive. This kind of talk went on for two evenings, carried on in loud voices until nearly eleven o'clock. The next morning, the fence had been taken down. Word spread through the
village that the owner had had second thoughts. Though he still
claimed the well was his property, he had decided to "compro-
mise" and let the others use it.

The roads at our end of Saltykovka were unpaved grassy lanes
and those from the Ryazan chaussée were not passable in spring
or fall or after a rain. We complained. Nothing happened. Then
we gave a picnic for Ambassador and Mrs. Kirk. Other diplomats visited us. Their cars got stuck and so did those of the police.

This, I thought, should produce action. It did. One morning we
found that ditches had been dug rather awkwardly across the
access lane and we heard that the village soviet was meeting to
consider the state of the roads. I was delighted. I thought that
the villagers were taking this opportunity to get a much needed
improvement. No more mud. No longer would they lose their
galoshes in the depths. I could not have been more wrong. The
"drainage" ditches had been dug in the hope that our cars could
not get by them. The village soviet had indeed met to consider a
request by the Foreign Office for improvement of the roads. The
question as the soviet saw it was that in spite of bad roads, there
was already one foreign household in the village. Now other foreigners, important foreigners, ambassadors and the like, were
coming. If the roads were improved, more foreigners would come
and, who knows, high officials from Moscow. No, they decided.
By no means would they improve the roads. The worse they got,
the more chance that no more foreigners would come and those
who lived in Saltykovka would go away and the village could be
left in peace.

Comfort and efficiency had little to do with the logic that decided questions in the Russian countryside, as in the case of the
Ryazan chaussée. The chaussée passed over a small bridge across
a stream which flowed out of a pleasant lake with a sandy bottom
—not too big, very shallow, too shallow for fish, but pleasant for
swimming in summertime. Not a few Muscovites came out on

Sundays. There was a small dam in the stream and a little summer restaurant called the Vodopad, the Waterfall, which sold vodka, soda pop, cheese and salami sandwiches. There were a few outdoor tables beside the dam.

Two men with a barrel of tar began work on the Ryazan chaussée the year we rented the dacha. They were laying tar over the cobblestones. As long as I knew Saltykovka, that work went forward at a pace of possibly a third of a mile a year. I don't know how two men could work so slowly. (They had only one barrel of tar; it took two or three hours each day to heat it with a small wood fire and then begin to spread it over the stones.) Gradually they approached the bridge. One day a truck appeared and dumped some logs and stringers beside the road. I thought the authorities were going to repair the bridge, but they had decided to delay work until the vacationers went home. I was wrong. A year passed, then at the height of the *next* summer, the dam was opened, water poured out of the lake and left a stinking hole. Still nothing happened, except that by the following summer the Vodopad was closed. Whether Saltykovka residents complained I do not know, but the work had not begun by the time I finally left Russia, in autumn 1954. Five years later, I found a new bridge, identical with the old one, finally in place, but the Ryazan chaussée was still being tarred. The bridge builders, I could only assume, worked on a schedule known to themselves alone, and the layers of tar had turned a summer's occupation into a lifetime job. Here was presented the inflexible rule of life in the real Russia—self-interest comes first, it overrides all other considerations.

32 | Juli

Night after night, Tom would shout to Juli: "Come on to bed,
Juli, it's one o'clock. Let Harrison go home." And an hour later:
"Juli, it's two o'clock. Come to bed." And at three she would still
be talking, the two of us in the kitchen under the naked light
bulb, myself leaning against the wall and Juli, crouched on a
kitchen stool, hands forming a rest for her chin, talking, talking,
talking, "clarifying our relations," as she said, her words for
that most Russian of conventions, talk *po dusham*—talk from the
soul—laying bare the deepest of feelings, beliefs, the roots of behavior. Never before nor afterward did I have such talks, talks
that sometimes left my spirit raw or reeling, but in the end, I
know, ripped from my consciousness layer after layer of hypocrisy.

Juli was an outrageous experience for a Midwesterner like myself, as she had been for Tom. She was the essence of the feminine, in part *intelligent*, in the Russian sense of that word—educated, sophisticated, socially conscious—in part earthy Russian
woman, and in part Juli. Mother Russia, I believe, is a literal
eponym. Russia is female and the female principle is dominant
over the male. I do not believe this is true in the United States.
This is not a matter of economic or constitutional rights; it is
physical, cultural and historical.

The biography of Juli's family was so conventional (in contemporary terms) that it might serve as a prototype for two or three
Russian generations. One grandfather was, I think, a small merchant, the other a lawyer or manufacturer. Her father, Aleksandr Zapolsky, went to Belgium, a favorite place for Russian
students, before World War I. Estella Khokhlovkina followed
him there. They had met and fallen in love in Moscow. Her family tried to stop her, but they married and studied economics at
the University of Liège, both taking their degrees; a thousand,
two thousand, young Russians did the same thing every year.
Were Tolstoy writing today, he might say all Soviet families are
the same; all non-Soviet families are different, each in its own
way. They did not know they would become a Soviet family, or

perhaps they would have settled in France. They read and spoke
French and German freely, English less well. Juli's mother was
devoted to France through her whole life; she read French literature, Balzac, Zola, Stendhal, Flaubert, Maupassant. She adored
Colette, and when I got her a dozen Colette novels from Paris,
she was happy for the several weeks it took to read them.

As it happened, the Zapolskys loved Moscow and returned to
Russia not long before 1914 ended the world into which they had
been born. Aleksandr Zapolsky became a respected, successful
economist, specializing in standardization. The Revolution had
little effect on their lives; of course, Moscow almost starved for
two or three years and they lost a couple of rooms from their
comfortable six-room apartment on the Arbat, but work and life
went ahead. Though they were apolitical, like most Russians of
their age and class they had deep sympathy for the early ideals
of the Revolution.

Not until 1928 did a flash of lightning illuminate what lay
ahead. Aleksandr was arrested in an obscure prepurge trial. No
one remembers this trial anymore, a petty affair beside those
Stalin staged in the 1930s, but Zapolsky's arrest wasn't child's
play. He was held under interrogation for eight months. Again
and again the interrogator tried to make him confess he was a
saboteur, a wrecker, that he had connections with the "Labor Opposition" (whatever that was), with the Mensheviks, with foreign
governments. Juli's father was a strong, vigorous, independent,
free-speaking man. He had never had party connections. The in-
vestigator finally gave up and Zapolsky went back to his job,
vindicated. (In those days you could be arrested and vindicated.
Later on, this was not possible; arrest was equivalent to conviction.)

Three or four years later, he met his interrogator on the street.
The man was pale and thin, his lungs racked with consumption.
He apologized to Zapolsky. "There wasn't any case against you,"
he said. "We didn't have any evidence. I was trying to make you
confess so I could get a promotion. I know you cannot forgive
me, but I want you to know I am sorry." A few weeks later, the
man died.

Juli was nine years old when her father was arrested, a shadow
that passed lightly over her childhood because her father made
fun of it; refused to take it seriously. He was a handsome, sharp-
tongued man, and Juli worshiped him with the total commitment

of a child; this was the rock on which her life was founded. One afternoon she was walking with her father on Gogolevsky Boulevard. He had a woman on his other arm, not her mother. The lady and her father were chatting gaily, but this did not bother Juli. Her hand was warmly held within her father's and he squeezed it every few steps. She was wearing her light blue sailor's blouse with the embroidered red anchors at the corners of the square collar, her straw hat with its Italian-striped band, her white half socks and black patent leather shoes. Her chestnut hair streamed down her back, and she knew she was the most beautiful girl in the world. Seeing a plate-glass window, she dropped her father's hand and dashed for a quick glimpse of herself, then dashed back and without looking up grasped his hand again. Now she perceived that the hand she was clutching was cold; her father's was warm. This hand was dry; her father's was moist. This one was white; her father's was tanned. She raised her eyes and saw a strange man looking down. Her father was walking a few paces ahead, she saw, lazily moving forward, one arm around the waist of his companion, the other playfully tilting back her chin, and as Juli ran forward, he lightly kissed the lady and they laughed as though there were no one else in the world. Juli ran right past her father—who was still talking with the woman, whom she later found was his lover—and darted around a corner. "Lucia," he called, "Lucia." That was her family nickname. But she did not come. She ran home as fast as she could. Nothing in her life, she said, was so shattering. In that moment she knew that she was not first, not all-embraced by her father's love. He had put another ahead of her. She went on loving him, but she never trusted him, never forgave him, even when he vanished into Stalin's camps and quickly died in the midst of the war in 1943. All those years, her father had gone ahead with his career. He had published articles and books. He was valued in the ministry. He had risen to the top level of the Russian Bureau of Standards. Not an echo of the affair of 1928 had touched him, not even in the late 1930s, when his brother-in-law lost his job as director of the champagne factory in Gorky and was never heard from again; when like everyone, the Zapolskys went to bed each night wondering whether there would be a knock at the door before dawn. They came through so safely that Juli thought nothing of it. Then in 1943, Russia deep in war, her father was arrested. It was like every other arrest. They came at night. They searched the apartment. Her father dressed and was taken away. Weeks later, Juli went to a little window in a decaying building at the top of Kuznetsky Most. Her father, the man said, had been sentenced to ten years for "subversive conversation"; he could receive parcels and had the "right of correspondence" (that meant he had not been shot out of hand). Within six months he was dead. Aleksandr had made scathing comments about the work of one of his friends. The offended man wrote a denunciation. A few months later, the friend, too, was seized and he, too, died in Siberia.

Juli did not forgive her father for what she considered his betrayal of her as a little girl. But she felt deep sympathy for him. She respected his frankness, his insistence on speaking out even when it might cost him his life. Somehow, she vowed, she would avenge his death. This thin-shouldered, artistic, egocentric, polymorphous woman possessed among other personalities that of knight in armor, defender of the Zapolsky name. When she was dying of cancer fifteen years later, nothing tortured her more than the thought that she was the last of the Zapolskys and she was dying without having made of her life a beacon by which the family name would be remembered.

The burden of family honor had not been part of her early heritage. She was a child of the Civil War, born in 1919, growing up in the confusion of the 1920s. She was not the firstborn; there had been another girl, an infant who died soon after birth. Juli made up stories about her "older sister." She imagined that she had been spirited away, that one day they would meet on the Svetnoy Boulevard. Juli would be sitting on a park bench, reading Pushkin (in Russian romance, it had to be Pushkin). She would be reading *Eugene Onegin* and look up. Beside her would sit another girl, just a bit older, blond where Juli was dark, a little rounder, but with eyes like Juli's, a hungry mouth like Juli's, a mind like Juli's. She, too, would be reading *Onegin*. They would look into each other's eyes and know that they were sisters, long-lost sisters.

There were a thousand variants of this dream, but always they would look into each other's eyes—and know. "To look into eyes" —this Juli was prepared to do for hours. This was very Russian. Russian men and women are more bold, more direct, than I was accustomed to. When Juli met someone who interested her, she looked long and hard and straight into his eyes until he finally shifted them. It was not only on first meeting that she looked so directly, so penetratingly. "To look into eyes" was a ritual that was closely related to "clarifying relations"; indeed, it was part of that exercise. "Looking into eyes" could be very dangerous. Many a man was sent to death in the Lubyanka because Stalin complained: "He won't look me in the eyes. There is something shifty about him, something suspicious." Russians believe that the eyes are the mirror of the soul. Surely Juli believed that. Many years later, when I was trying to put the essence of Juli into words, I wrote down "the mirror of the soul." That, I felt, was Juli—the mirror of my soul and of the souls of the others who came close to her. We looked into her eyes and saw reflected there the image of our inner self.

If Juli's "sister" was fantasy, not so her brother, Viktor. Younger by three years, Viktor was handsome, bold, saucy, with a quick tongue like his father's, Viktor's edged with humor where his father's was edged with acid. No one was more close than Viktor and Juli in their growing-up years. Juli envied him his handsome, easy way with girls; they fell to his touch. It was so much harder for a woman, she thought; why could she not be her brother? Boys had all the luck.

Viktor was nineteen when the Germans attacked Russia, on June 22, 1941. He lied about his age, volunteered, and by July was off to the front, that terrible July when all the fronts fell apart. His unit was pushed forward, half trained, half armed, pushed into combat around Smolensk, and in late summer he was reported missing—his was one of the many armies surrounded by the Nazis as they hurried on toward Moscow.

Viktor and some comrades became separated from their command. A peasant woman took him into her bed, fed him, concealed him, pampered him for his youth and his handsomeness, and finally helped him make his way back through the forest to the broken lines, the Russian forces, now falling toward Moscow itself. It was an act of courage and daring, typical of this bold youngster. He was given leave to come back to Moscow for two days to see his family. This must have been in early September, before the battle of Moscow began, before the whole city began packing up, swarming to the railroad stations, the streets filled with rumors that the Nazis were about to break in, the chimneys

of the Lubyanka belching smoke as the KGB burned its files, the
government spreading stories that the Jews were panicking and
taking all the seats in the evacuation trains, paying in gold—the
worst moment of the war. Somehow this handsome Russian boy
with his cocky air and his cocky tongue came back home. The
Zapolskys were still there, had not been evacuated to the Urals,
never were. Then he returned to the front and his death—death
by order of a commander, jealous because his girl preferred the
young hero to her older lover. The officer sent Viktor into a penalty battalion (that was where most Red Army men brave and
clever enough to escape encirclement wound up), having raised
the suspicion that Viktor had been enlisted as a Nazi spy. Each
day, Viktor was assigned to the most dangerous post on the pe-
rimeter. He was placed in the squads that moved ahead of the
main unit and attracted German fire. He was sent on mine demo-
lition teams. He was posted in the rear guard of the retreat. It
did not take long to kill him.

There was just time for Viktor to get word back through
friends: a last cry of help. Aleksandr Zapolsky tried to get permission to go to the front, but failed. Juli's mother, Estella, was
frozen in terror. And Juli? Her guilt was so intense I could not
decide what was real and what imagined. She felt that she could
have saved her brother and did not; that she could have persuaded a certain general to intervene but did not. She could have
slept with the general; he was crazy to sleep with her, would
have done anything for her; why hadn't she done it? It would
have meant nothing to her and her brother would be alive. She
had joined an entertainment unit, singing for the troops. Every
night they were at a new headquarters. There was wild excitement, the danger, the thrill, the men who fought over her, as
she sang her songs from the back of a truck, played a piano
in the commander's billet; up all night, traveling all day, every
day a new place, every night someone new to sleep with, if she
wanted; everyone begging for her. Yes, she said, she had been
carried away. She was crazy. She could not believe what was
happening to her brother and—though it was no excuse—she
thought they would all be dead. She did not see how they could
halt the Nazis; the lines were broken, they were dropping back to
Moscow, the Germans almost on its limits, breaking into the suburbs, everyone in the city digging tank traps and trenches, old
men and women dying, shovel in hand. Yes, it was crazy, insane,

but she could have saved her brother.

I don't know whether that was true or the product of the blind and total faith she had built within herself, a faith that had replaced her belief in her father. She thought she could do anything she wanted and she had not saved her brother. The guilt grew by the year. When she finally came to leave Moscow in 1953, she could hardly bear it because she had never gone to Smolensk to find her brother's grave. It did no good to say she could never have found it. She rejected the idea that all she had in evidence of Viktor's death was a letter from his friends and a gray piece of cardboard from the Ministry of Defense. She could see him as he lay dying, so young, so brave, not ready to die, never having really lived, dying as foolishly as only a boy can die for no reason except his bravery and his bright spirit. The look in his eyes, so hurt, so sad, because he had believed until the last moment that his sister would come to his rescue. This was pure melodrama, but what we believe is what we believe, melodrama or not. The worst indictment Juli brought against herself was that she was alive; her brother was not.

When Juli left Russia, she gave me a last command: If ever I got to Smolensk (and I must try very hard to get to Smolensk), I should find her brother's grave. It was there. She knew it was there. Alas, I never fulfilled her wish.

I believe that at the core of Juli's guilt was the perception of her selfishness. She was a woman of unlimited generosity, but she was so intensely focused upon herself that many things in life simply passed her by. And it is fair to say that she could be cruel, never for the sake of cruelty but in pursuit of ends which she believed justified such means. She was a person of extremes, extreme in her demands, extreme in her gifts.

There was in Juli's ritual something that she called "touching." This was long before the cult of "touching" arose in American "consciousness-raising sessions." "Touching" did not mean bodily embraces; it was confined to the fingers—the tips of the forefingers, for instance, the contact of the thumbs or, possibly, of several fingers.

It was sensation that mattered, on the principle that the lighter the contact, the more intense the sensation if you concentrated on feeling the infinitesimal touch of fingertip with fingertip, blocking out all other impressions: noise, sight (by closing the eyes), smell—every sensory input except this butterfly contact. She believed, I think, that with a partner as sensitive as herself, a gossamer touch could be as rich as that of any erogenous zone. There were variations, such as "holding hands," in which we grasped hands, not closely, no muscular pressure, and let the sensations flow freely, from one to the other. This might be combined with "looking into eyes."

The ultimate sensation required the most intense concentration. We sat apart, on opposite sides of the room, looking at each other, drawing in the essence of the other with each breath until the *feeling* became as powerful as, more powerful than, any physical contact or sexual response. I know this sounds quirky. It is. But with concentration, it produced a kind of mutual hypnosis. Looking back on these rites, I concluded that they held something in common with Buddhist practices. Juli was insatiable in her exploration of the human mind and the human response, and never more excited than when embarking on an adventure into the unknown. It was her extraordinary openness to the terra incognita of the heart that so attracted me.

There were limits, of course, to Juli's capability for adventure, although I do not think she recognized them. Flirtation in the classic, eighteenth-century sense was dear to Juli as it was to many Russian women. In fact, her whole cabinet of "clarification," of "eyes," of "touching," could be fitted within this concept.

The role of the flirt is formalized in Russian literature and is to this day assumed and played with virtuosity by Russian women. Juli was a master of the art: the long, lingering look, the cast-down eyes, the over-the-shoulder glance, the enticing gait, the lowering of eyes and sweep of long lashes, the whirl of a skirt, even the drop of a handkerchief—every nuance of the coquette, played as an art, a sport, an amusement, and sometimes as a very serious thing.

In flirting she picked her partners with skill for the particular value to be derived. I am not sure that this was true in her earlier years. She embarked, for example, on a grandiose flirtation with a much older man at a time when she was only eighteen, already no doubt an entrancing woman, talented, witty, bold, amorous. The object of her flirt was a writer in his early sixties, rather well known, with a wife, a mistress and much experience

with women. I think his eminence flattered her. She was delighted with such an admirer, delighted that she could extract
from him presents and favors—not for the sake of the favors but
for the power she could indulge. As she told the story, she played
her admirer like a trout. She was not unwilling to go to bed with
him after she had made him jump through the hoops and climb
the obstacles that she had invented. In fact, she was curious to
know what kind of lover he might be, for he had had affairs with
some famous women. The truth, as she confessed to me much
later, was that sex had never been a great experience for her.
What she enjoyed was the chase, the game, the intrigue, the emotions. She enjoyed using her body to attract men and her mind to
engage them. In this lay her feeling of power, of conquest, of
magic.

She toyed with her older lover with great pleasure. He gave
her flowers and even jewels; took her to the theater; to concerts;
to fine restaurants; fulfilled her every whim (and she had a vivid
imagination). Finally, she agreed to a rendezvous. He had become her slave; it was fair that he get his reward. She went to his
apartment one afternoon. She permitted him to caress her, his
passion growing; he became more and more excited, she prolong-
ing the preliminaries. Suddenly he fell at her feet unconscious,
and lay there gasping. Did she run for help? Not for a moment
did she think of that. She ran for her life, out of his flat as fast
as she could, running in fear, in guilt, she ran until she was home
and then threw herself on her bed, choking back the sobs lest her
mother guess what she had done—she was certain she had killed
a man. Fearful, she was not by any degree sorrowful, but angry,
angry beyond measure, at the man, at his weakness, at the awful
thing he had done in dying at her feet. (As it turned out, he had
not died; had not had a stroke; regained consciousness; went on
living. They never saw each other again.) Juli told the story with
no remorse, no self-criticism. She was still angry at *what the man
had done to her.*

Coquetry was Juli's amusement (and more than amusement),
but music was her profession. She was no amateur. She had
graduated from the Gnessen Music School and had plunged into
what had every sign of becoming a brilliant career in operetta,
musical comedy and light music. This did not entirely please her
parents. Her mother was a fine pianist—musical talent ran in

her family—and had hoped for a classical career for Juli. Leonid Utesov, whose remarkable jazz band was the talk of Moscow, had a connection with the family. In no time, Juli was composing songs for his productions, scores for operettas, ballads. Almost everything she touched was gold.

The cold war froze Juli into silence. Her music, strongly akin to American jazz, was denounced, its playing forbidden within a year of Moscow's victory parade in June 1945. Her music—and all other Western popular music—was swept off the boards by Stalin and his ideological hatchet man, Zhdanov. Juli herself was put under ban; she was married to a foreigner. So she was shunned, her music withdrawn from the repertoire, her collaborators warned against her, the offices of the popular music registry closed to her.

This was why she had turned inward, occupying herself for hours, days, weeks, months, years with intense introspection in a narrow circle in which the only Russian was her mother. It was a tragic existence. What for myself, for example, became an exotic experience, a kind of psychic treasure hunt, was the wellspring of her life. Only in Stalinist Russia, where almost every outlet for free creation, for poetry, for the joy of music, had been stifled, could such an unnatural existence have been imagined.

Had I not been frustrated in my professional life, at a dead end in my personal life, my children far away and almost beyond my influence, Ellen vanished into whatever world had swallowed her up, and had I not been galvanically attracted to Juli's dynamism, the long, complex relationship which I have sketched only in outline could never have emerged. We had time on our hands, inquisitive minds, a taste for adventure and, I think, a great deal of patience, although I must give Tom and Juli's mother credit for even greater patience. Our endless soul-searching was, I know, a bore to others. Tom fled to his books; Juli's mother said little, but I saw many a look of impatience cross her face.

There is no way in which I can repay my debt to Juli for holding up, as I have said, a mirror to my soul (or what passes for the soul of a cranky, skeptical Minnesotan). From our earliest meetings, she would say: "Don't tell lies, Harrison. You are such a liar. Stop it." This kind of remark was incomprehensible to me. Yes, I told lies on occasion, white lies, as I saw it; social lies. I got out of unwelcome dinners by saying that I was already engaged. I told girls I loved them when I wanted to sleep with them, knowing, of course, that it was sex and not love. I made flattering remarks to persons from whom I sought favors—an interview, let us say—complimenting a man on his keen powers of analysis when, as a matter of fact, I thought he was a horse's ass. This was the normal grist of life, done so often and so naturally that I was not aware of what I said or did. Someone once said that the trouble with the Russians is that they lack the oil of hypocrisy. Certainly this was true of Juli. Russians spoke their minds in a way few Americans did; they said unpleasant things, unpleasantly, often things that did not have to be said.

It was my lack of this frankness that underlay what Juli called my "lying." I never came to the point of total agreement with her. I believed then and do today that there are things best left unsaid; times when the shading of raw truth is better. But what I learned from her, I hope, was to be frank with myself; to bring to an end the fuzzy double-think that had turned my personal life into such a jungle. It was an exercise in self-examination and self-analysis which has served me for the rest of my life. Though it did not keep me out of tangles, it taught me to face up to fundamentals; to look at myself and the world more squarely.

I do not want to imply that Juli was a master of technique so far as her own life was concerned. Her life was painful, difficult and, in the end, tragic. But this was not because she failed to see and understand what she was doing (for the most part); it was because in spite of clear eyes, keen mind and generous heart, she plunged ahead, aware of dangers, aware of obstacles, but with total confidence in her ability to overcome.

33 | George Frost Kennan

A tall, lean, balding man came up to me one afternoon as I was painting the porch at Saltykovka. *"Y vas nyet svobodnaya komnata ili mezonik?"* he asked. *"Konechno,"* I replied, *"delya vas—vse."* He was the new ambassador, George Kennan, and he was asking if we had a room to rent or maybe an attic, and I was saying, "Of course—for you." It was the same question he had asked when he first came to Russia in 1933 and rambled about the country near Moscow, inquiring at a house for a night's lodging. In those days he had been a third secretary, advance man for the new American embassy, relations having been reestablished after talks between FDR and Maksim Litvinov.

Now Kennan had come to Moscow as ambassador, but a gulf lay between those experiences of a young man, trained for nearly six years in Russian studies, and of this veteran of the diplomatic service, a man of world reputation, author of the extraordinary "Long Telegram" of February 22, 1946, and the "X" article in *Foreign Affairs* in 1947, which fixed the parameters of postwar U.S.-Soviet postures.

I had long awaited this moment. If I had got my original impetus toward Russia from Sir Bernard Pares, I would now sit quite literally at the feet of Kennan, who was henceforward to be my guide, my inspiration, my mentor on Russia.

We talked awhile under the pillar-straight pines, George, Juli and Tom rattling away in Russian, I scrambling to keep up with the conversation. The dachniki strolled past at lazy intervals. It was a sunny day, the air heavy with the scent of spring flowers, an afternoon of peace and quiet. George's family, Annelise and the children, had not yet followed him to Moscow. He was at once nostalgic, a little lonely, romantic and at ease, at least for a moment, deep in that Russia to which he had long ago lost his heart.

As shadows lengthened, we went indoors and lighted our fireplace. The Russian mason had never built one before; in fact, he had never heard of a fireplace. It smoked badly, but it was our joy. The first night we lighted it, Juli burst into tears. "What on earth is wrong, Juli?" Tom asked. She answered, "Here we are, sitting by the fireplace we all dreamed of. We're so happy. I'm crying because we'll never be so happy again."

On this evening, Juli was happy. We sat on the floor around the fireplace and George played his guitar, as he had when he had roamed Podmoskovskoye, the Moscow region, in the early days. He played Russian songs, "Stenka Razin" and "Polyuska Pole" and Juli sang. Then he played his favorite, "A-tisket, a-tasket, a green and yellow basket," and we all sang, smoke in our eyes, hearts overflowing.

We gave George a key to the dacha so he could retreat there whether or not any of us were around, and I arranged my *mezonik* so there was a place for him to stay overnight (which I don't believe he did). He loved to stroll through Saltykovka, listening to the Saltykovka sounds—the talk of the dachniki, an accordion playing in the distance, the sharp smack of ax on wood, the thin whistle of the railroad in the distance. Once on Sunday he went to the market, but this was too much. Everywhere George went, he was accompanied by at least four plainclothesmen. When he drove to Saltykovka, two cars of *shpiks* came with him. A stroll through the village became a parade. It was better to sit under the pines and read Chekhov. For years he entertained the ambition of writing about Chekhov.

George Kennan's return to Russia in 1952 was at once a sentimental journey and a diplomatic mission to which he brought a mystical sense of purpose. Kennan had from an early time (and increasingly with the years) possessed a sense of identification with his relative the first George Kennan. This Kennan—not George's father or uncle, as commonly supposed, but a cousin of his grandfather—was a journalist, a publicist, an agitator, a man of passion who almost by chance committed his life to the cause of a new Russia. He had traveled widely, ranging the country from the ends of Siberia to the salons of St. Petersburg. He had written the single most influential American work about Russia, *Siberia and the Exile System,* published originally in *Century* magazine in 1888–89 and then as a book. The most incisive inquiry into the Russian prison system of the period, it was a work whose worldwide impact can only be compared to that of Aleksandr Solzhenitsyn's *The Gulag Archipelago.* It produced enormous sentiment in the United States and Europe against the

Czar, and within Russia itself gave impetus to the movement for reform and revolution.

Ambassador George Frost Kennan saw himself as his namesake's successor, perceiving parallels between his life and his predecessor's at every turn. But in fact the differences were profound. The second George Kennan came to Russia by way of Germany. He spent six months there at the age of eight, went to school and learned the language. His father spoke beautiful German and George was drenched in pre-1914 German culture. He came from Milwaukee, that city then almost more German than Germany. The summer before he entered the foreign service, he went again to Germany, wandering over the countryside, reading Goethe and Spengler in the original, speaking not a word of English. Then he returned to Washington and tackled the trade of diplomacy. When he embarked on his study of Russia, he went back to the Germany of the Third Reich and then to Tallin and Riga, cities strongly under the influence of the Teutonic knights who pushed eastward along the Baltic coast and melded into the Russia of Peter.

It seemed to me in the days when I was getting to know George Kennan that he was more powerfully shaped than he realized by German tradition, more a Lothar absorbing the wonders of Russian life than the Yankee at the court of Alexander III that the first George Kennan was. The earlier George had been a pragmatic, shirtsleeves kind of man (he started life as a Morse telegrapher), but there was in both Kennans a cranky, against-the-grain quality. Kennan seldom accepted anyone's conclusions without testing them. All his life he would be a loner, more comfortable speaking from his own pulpit than joining a chorus. I, having grown up in Minnesota, could see the particularity of this Wisconsin man, born four years earlier, who reflected the independent populist tradition from which I came.

Kennan was a severe judge of Soviet conduct, sometimes an unfair judge, but he was an equally severe judge of American conduct. He insisted that foreign policy could not be carried out on a basis of moral assessments; it must be founded on pragmatic self-interest instead of pontifications about good or evil. But he himself was a stern moralist and nothing disturbed him more in the 1960s than what he saw as the dissolution of moral quality in American youth. He was outraged by the decline in diplomatic ethics and conduct. In a sense, he became a living icon of tradition, wearing fine English-tailored suits with full vests, and, as my father had, a magnificent old gold watch chain. He abhorred the platitudinous rhetoric of John Foster Dulles and could not abide the sloppy solecisms of a Carter or a Reagan. He often stood alone for what he believed, and in this I am drawn to compare him with Charles Lindbergh. They differed profoundly, Lindbergh an isolationist and an America Firster, Kennan an internationalist, but there was in each a standard of values that put his country before any other consideration. If Lindbergh might more properly be described as an international isolationist, perhaps it would not stretch the truth to call Kennan an isolationist internationalist. In each there was a whiff of that climate which produced the La Follettes and the Farmer-Laborites.

Kennan was masterly in the arts of persuasion and skilled in bureaucracy. He might and often did inveigh against the system. He was an open, ardent elitist and once said that in the impossible event of his becoming secretary of state, he would establish a personal foreign service of two hundred specialists, and handle foreign policy through them. He would let the traditional establishment with its thousands of civil servants stay in place, churning out paper. But he would operate through his elite corps. What he was talking about was remarkably like the apparatus that was to grow up around the National Security Council of Henry Kissinger. Though the two men possessed totally different personalities, Kissinger's individualistic style of work was not too different from Kennan's. Neither man possessed much patience with mediocrity; each possessed total self-confidence in judgmental matters. But Kennan was more tolerant of subordinates, and lacked Kissinger's hot paranoia. Both were better working for a President or secretary of state with a coherent grasp of the world than in a position of naked responsibility. The comparison is in a sense unfair to both men. Kissinger's role models were Metternich and Machiavelli; Kennan's philosophy derived in some measure from Heine and Goethe. He was more deeply influenced by Spengler's gloomy doctrine than he realized, and while he loved Chekhov, I always felt there was more Dostoyevsky in his soul. The Yankee strain which Kennan highly valued, his love of Jefferson and Adams, had been diluted by his long immersion in German culture.

Kennan was antibureaucratic, but he knew how to use the bureaucracy to push his views. In politics he was not strong (nor was Kissinger, for that matter). Knowing what *should* be done, Kennan was not always realistic in what *could* be done. The practical politics that led Acheson and Truman to put the Marshall Plan through Congress by raising the Communist scare was anathema to George. In the Kennedy years, as ambassador to Belgrade, he knew what U.S. policy should be in support of Tito, but the catch-as-catch-can politics of Jack Kennedy drove him up the wall. When he left the State Department in 1953, he toyed with running for Congress from Pennsylvania, as unlikely a babe in the woods in eat-'em alive politics as could be imagined. His very act of listening to such a proposal was a measure of his distance from political reality. There was nothing Congress or the country needed more than Kennan in office; in precinct terms, nothing was less realistic.

Not much of this was evident to me as we sat before the fireplace, George contemplatively strumming his guitar, his mind lost in distant recall. I quickly perceived that he had devoted profound thought to the situation in Russia before he somewhat reluctantly undertook his assignment.

He had believed, as did I, that the chances the Kremlin would give *agrément* were slim. Kennan was identified in the public mind and in that of the Kremlin as the author of the philosophy of the cold war, laid down in his Long Telegram and the "X" article. This declaration (the article was simply a popular restatement of the Long Telegram) analyzed the sources of Soviet conduct, detailed postwar Soviet expansionism and proposed an American policy of "containment" which would erect a dike around the Soviet frontiers, to the end that every Soviet outward push would meet the hard rock of American resistance. It was on the basis of Kennan's theory that Dulles would create a network of anti-Soviet alliances which established a deadline that Soviet aggression would not be permitted to cross.

The "X" article in later years was to involve Kennan in deep controversy. He felt that it had been mistakenly interpreted and militarized, first by Truman and later by Dulles. What he proposed was that by a resolute stand we would discourage the Kremlin and bring it into diplomatic negotiations, not armed conflict. But of course, that was not the way the "X" philosophy was perceived by Washington and Moscow. It was taken as a blueprint for an armed standoff and the diplomatic solution explicitly stipulated by Kennan was overlooked by both sides. (And by revisionist historians who insisted that Kennan had merely offered a euphemism for militarization of foreign policy.)

I was so convinced that Kennan would not be accepted by Moscow that I wrote a long dispatch to this effect on December 26, 1951, drawing liberally on a *Pravda* article which characterized him as directing subversive activities against the Soviet Union. My dispatch was held in the censorship and finally released with almost every aspersion against Kennan removed. Within twelve hours, the Foreign Office informed the State Department that Kennan's appointment had been approved. Once again the censorship had provided a striking clue to Soviet policy, and by killing my adverse speculation it spared me an embarrassing error.

I don't know what conclusions Kennan drew from the Russian acceptance of him as ambassador, but he could hardly interpret it as a negative sign. He had not been in a hurry to assume his post. He wanted time for thought. The number of original thinkers in the world at any moment is small. Kennan is the only one with whom I have ever been close. An original thinker is, to me, someone who turns a problem about in his mind and emerges, not with ideas previously advanced, not with adaptations of or variations on old ideas, but with *totally new thoughts.* Kennan had formed the habit of periodically withdrawing to think and to write. This required a cover device. His was simple. He "came down with the flu," went to bed, put a pad of yellow foolscap on his knees, gazed out the window, thought, scribbled a bit, and began to dictate to his secretary. Thus he had composed his Long Telegram; thus he had written his dispatches about the Moscow purge trials of the 1930s; thus he had drafted his ideas for George Marshall when he, as secretary of state, put in Kennan as chief of policy and planning. Kennan did not call a committee meeting and emerge with a lot of "consensus" ideas; he locked himself in his bedroom and thought. It was a unique process in our bureaucratic days.

Before coming to Moscow in May, Kennan had formulated his general theses. He had not told anyone in Washington about this; at least, I do not think he had. (There is no hint of it in his memoirs.) I think that he first spoke of his ideas as he sat in a canvas chair under the pines at Saltykovka. He believed that his "containment" theory had succeeded. The outward expansion of Soviet power had been halted all around the periphery, and most notably at Berlin when the U.S. broke the blockade, and in Germany, where the Western powers were moving to consolidate their NATO alliance with Bonn. (Kennan was not very happy about bringing Germany into NATO.) It had been halted in Korea, where the U.S. had finally stabilized the situation on the 38th parallel, where the North-South division would remain for the next thirty years.

Stalin, George said, was no fool. Neither were the men of the Politburo. They might be difficult, dangerous, hostile, but they were, at root, pragmatic, shrewd men. If a policy did not bring results, if it brought defeat after defeat, sooner or later that policy would be changed; sooner or later someone at the Kremlin table would raise the question. Since Kennan assumed that the Kremlin put pragmatism ahead of everything—ahead of precedent, ideology, consistency—he believed that Moscow could change instantly from total antagonism to a willingness to meet and resolve mutual problems, with no embarrassment, no backward glances, no problem in answering questions, just a shift of the gears.

But American policy was now dug in so hard, American opinion had so crystallized, that diplomacy was almost paralyzed. Kennan did not believe that when the Soviets switched signals this would, necessarily, be understood by Washington. It was vital, he felt, that someone like himself be on hand to catch the first hint and be ready to capitalize on the change. In fact, he was prepared, like a good obstetrician coping with a difficult birth, to use the forceps a bit.

He had cleared with the Department one small gambit on which he set great store, a lowering of the decibel level of propaganda. He persuaded the Voice of America to refrain from attacking Stalin; he went to the Luce people in New York and asked them to bear with him for a bit by easing up on stories about Russia. If both sides stopped lambasting each other, a climate for negotiations might be created. He understood this was difficult. He was by no means certain the individualistic American press and radio, not to mention the still-undercover CIA enterprises Radio Liberty and Radio Free Europe, could be kept in line (they couldn't). He didn't get far. He talked to the Foreign Office but got no encouragement, and in fact he became outraged at the level and character of what he came to call the "hate America" campaign. I confess I was so inured (as I am sure the Soviet public was) that I hadn't even noticed it. One day George arrived at the dacha worked up at some posters he had seen. They hadn't even registered with me. They showed Soviet planes shooting down U.S. planes trying to cross the Soviet borders. George issued a public denunciation and refused to attend the Soviet Aviation Day show. In his rage he even accepted the naive statement of our air attaché that the Russians had put a dummy on the reviewing stand in place of Stalin. Some dummy! I was there, and Stalin had looked very snappy in his white summer uniform, talking and joking with his Politburo and his generals.

I did not know, nor was there a hint of it in George's talk, that he had been put on the shortest of reins by President Truman and Dean Acheson. They had, he revealed in his memoirs, given him no policy instructions. He had no functions whatever to carry out in Moscow, except that he must not negotiate or talk about Germany, Korea and nuclear weapons—the three key issues of the day. No wonder he felt frustrated. No wonder we missed an opportunity to resolve the German issue in our favor.

Truman and Acheson were hell-bent to obtain what they called the "contract"—the agreement that was to tie Germany into NATO; to remove Germany, once and for all, from neutrality; to line it up on the U.S. side. It was because of this that Kennan's hands were tied and lips sealed. He disagreed with the Truman-Acheson policy, but had to accept it.

That is why, I should imagine, Kennan failed to respond when I took up with him an intriguing bit of gossip. I had heard it, I believe, from Ralph Parker. It concerned Wilhelm Pieck and Otto Grotewohl, the East German leaders. They had been called to Moscow secretly during the winter and told that Moscow was preparing to sacrifice them and the East German regime in the struggle with the West over Germany. At all costs, Moscow wanted to block the Western effort to tie Bonn into its defense system and was prepared, if necessary, to consent to the reunification of Germany and the end of the Communist regime in the East. Of course, it was more complex than that, but this was the essence. It was news so sensational—if true—that I was totally enjoined against using it in any form, nor would the censors have passed it. I did, however, put it to Kennan as a hypothetical question. I got no response from him and, thinking that it was most likely not true, put it in the back of my mind. But I did not forget it as I observed the frantic offers Moscow began to make in an effort to halt the rapid progress of the "contract."

Suddenly the rumor was published in midsummer 1952 in newspaper reports from Washington. Pietro Nenni, the Italian left-wing Socialist, had been talking with Stalin. He was quoted as saying Stalin had abandoned all hope of a German settlement. The previous winter, the report said, Moscow had been prepared to give up East Germany and accept reunification.

So here it was—indirect confirmation of what I had heard months earlier. The Italian ambassador, Di Stefano, had talked to Nenni and that was the source of the report. Di Stefano told Kennan and Kennan told the State Department and someone leaked it to Joe Alsop. Nenni said Pieck and Grotewohl had told him they had been put on notice during the winter that Moscow might abandon them for the sake of an overall settlement. Now Stalin had given up on this tactic.

Of course, there was no way of being certain these reports were true. But they matched the hysteria of Soviet policy (and confirmed Kennan's estimate that up against the stone wall of containment, the Russians would change stance and negotiate). I wish Kennan and I had known each other better in those times and had been able to talk more frankly. In his memoirs, Kennan paints a woeful picture of a Washington totally frozen against any negotiations. Yet his Saltykovka talks reflected a note of almost mystical optimism. He seemed to believe that change would come in Soviet policy, that it was dialectically certain, and that when the moment came, he would be there to take advantage of it. I must confess I didn't believe a word of this scenario.

Kennan was an optimist and a romantic (he could also be deeply, almost physically gloomy in a Spenglerian sense, and realistic as a surgeon). His optimistic, romantic side was uppermost in his decision to take the Soviet post. He came to Moscow with an empty diplomatic knapsack and a few almost pathetic bits of paraphernalia. One was his guitar. He did not know exactly how he might put that to use, but somehow he saw himself playing his Russian songs as a way to winning someone's confidence—finding a totally irregular and undiplomatic route that would put him in touch with the men of the Kremlin. He had his old friendship with Tom and Juli, and I think he imagined that they (and perhaps I) might be in touch with some Russians to whom we could lead him and that this would be the first step. He had one other string to his bow. Before the war, he had been stationed in Prague and had got acquainted with a young intellectual Englishman, correspondent of *The Times* of London— Ralph Parker, not yet in his Communist phase, his wife still alive, a proper and serious and well-informed young man. Ralph had had to get out of Prague quickly when the Germans moved into Poland in 1939, and he left behind with George some of his possessions, or at least one possession—a painting. Kennan had kept it for him. Now Ralph was a medium of Soviet propaganda. In his book about the British and U.S. embassies, he had portrayed Kennan slanderously, saying he came from a rich family, had attended a military academy, and was "the most influential agent of the American warmongers." Never mind. This might even be to the good. Kennan had the picture with him and wanted to give it back to Parker and use him, I think, as a bridge to the Soviets, someone with whom he could talk off the record, totally informally. Parker could pass him on to a designated Russian, an unofficial channel, and words would begin to flow up and down the chain. Perhaps he thought that Tom and Juli might put him in touch with Parker. If so, he was disappointed. Juli would never have become mixed up in anything like that. Her sense of possible peril was too acute. Nor was I eager. Nothing came of Kennan's idea.

Or perhaps something did. It was not known to me then, but on a Saturday in early July, Kennan had a visitor at the embassy, a hysterical young man who dashed past the guards and identified himself as the son of V. S. Abakumov, Lavrenti Beria's right-hand man. He said his father had been purged and that he and several friends would, if given guns and support, be prepared to carry out the assassination of the top Soviet leaders. Kennan, who describes the episode in his memoirs, was appalled. He did not believe a word the young man said, refused his appeal for help in getting away from the embassy and sent him out into the hands of the police. He considered it the crudest of provocations and felt that Stalin himself, having learned Kennan wanted to talk with a Soviet citizen, sent him this queer duck. I believe Kennan acted in the only way he could; he had to get the young man out of the embassy as quickly as possible; he could have nothing to do with him.

But time and my broad acquaintance with Soviet citizenry, particularly young people, over the last thirty years suggests to me that it was totally possible that the man was, as he said, Abakumov's son and that he had come in naiveté to the U.S. embassy, expecting to be greeted with open arms.

George's visits to the dacha became less frequent with summer. His family was now in Moscow and the diplomatic routine began to catch him up. His mood was changing. His nostalgic pleasure in being in Moscow and the secret conviction that a basic Soviet change was at hand may have faded in the harsh cold war reality. This was particularly sad for Juli. She had greeted George with the adoration of a Juliet. Yes, both Juliet and Romeo were as much overage for their roles as were the three actresses at the Art Theater who persisted in playing in *The Three Sisters,* but no one who saw Juli's face light up and her eyes glow in George's presence could mistake the feeling. George was to her, I think, a character out of not Chekhov but Turgenev, sophisticated, wise, urbane, gifted with a philosophy and emotion close to the Russian heart. He was Russian but not Russian, American but a special kind of American. She could talk to him all day and all night, no bounds to the talk—this on Juli's side. It was or would have been much the same, I think, for George except for his feelings for his country and his wife. He understood Russia well enough to understand talk *po dusham.* The time for that was past for him. He was an extraordinarily happily married man, and strongly as he was drawn to this most Russian of relationships, he was not prepared to venture on an excursion down that path. The other consideration, one he felt strongly, he advanced to Juli in simple but, I thought, eloquent terms. He had long since, he said, made a decision of principle; he had placed himself at the service of his country, and this service came ahead of personal desires and inclinations. His life, in a sense, was no longer at his disposal; it was at his country's. This declaration, so similar to that of a priest's in dedicating himself to the service of God, might have sounded presumptuous in another man. But from the lips of the serious and solemn Kennan, one could only respect it. This Juli did. She smiled at him, she gave him her most tender looks, but she made no effort by the arts of her coquetry to woo him from his resolve.

One more act remained to be played out in the drama of Kennan in Russia. He left Moscow on the early morning of September 19, 1952, for a meeting of American diplomats in London. I was at Vnukovo airport to see him off. He was in a silent, withdrawn mood. Kennan's forays into the West had been plagued by unpleasant incidents. Each time, there had been stories and articles (some accurate, some not) attributing to him opinions calculated to embarrass him with the Russians. The tendency of these stories was to suggest that Kennan's private views about the Soviets were much sharper than those he expressed publicly. This would have been of little consequence had he not been engaged in a campaign to lift the norms of Soviet-U.S. diplomatic behavior. He felt certain that the Russians would assume he was putting out these reports—in a word, that he was a hypocrite and not seriously concerned with improving the diplomatic tone.

Kennan was upset at this; complained bitterly to the State Department; felt someone in Washington was deliberately trying to undercut him. He was uncomfortable in his relations with the Department and this apparent evidence of backbiting disturbed him greatly.

He had talked to me about the problem, but there was little I could advise. On the afternoon before he left, he called in Gilmore, Shapiro, Whitney and myself. He told us of his concern over these leaks, said he would say absolutely nothing while on this trip abroad; if he had something on his mind, he would call us in when he returned.

Meantime, he asked, what could he do with the press? What questions were likely to be asked? What did we think? He would try to develop noncommittal answers which would not offend the Russians.

The discussion went on a long time, more than an hour. Though a bit eerie, it was probably productive. I saw no reason why George couldn't protect himself with reporters; as for department leaks—that was another problem, only too closely related, I felt, to the McCarthyite influence, which even before the advent of John Foster Dulles had appeared within the Department.

In the morning, Kennan took off for London. There was a refueling stop at Tempelhof Airdrome in Berlin, and there Kennan, in answer to a question by reporters, compared conditions of diplomatic life in Moscow to those of Berlin under Hitler. He went on to London, the statement was carried around the world, and when I saw it I knew that Kennan's days in Moscow had come to an end.

How could it have happened? How could so distinguished, so experienced a diplomat, a man so full of foreboding lest any statement by him be misinterpreted—how could he have broken so much crockery? I do not know to this day. I have spoken of it to Kennan. For years he was reluctant to talk about it. I had heard that when he returned to Spaso House after talking to us, he found that one of the Russian employees, a pleasant woman who had worked for several years as a maid, had vanished (as did all Russian employees sooner or later) and that he was deeply upset. Later I heard that his two-year-old boy, romping on the Spaso lawn, had begun to play patacake with a Russian child through the fence at the lawn's edge. As Kennan watched, security guards sent the Russian youngster scurrying up the street. I could understand that either or both of these incidents would have touched Kennan's feelings. It was not until his memoirs were published in 1973 that he revealed that before he left on his trip, U.S. security agents had detected a Soviet bug in the wood-and-plaster great seal of the United States in the ambassador's study. Kennan was disturbed by this, although there was no evidence that anything of value had been picked up by the Russians.

So there is no question that Kennan was in a grim mood that morning of September 19. What happened, then, at Tempelhof? He never contended that he was speaking off the record, although he has suggested that he might have been. In the months after the incident, I took pains to question my colleagues in Berlin. Three reporters had met Kennan at the airport, as well as a representative of HICOG, the U.S. command. The newsmen represented AP, UP and *Stars and Stripes*. Each said the remarks were not placed off the record. The HICOG man confirmed this. Kennan had made similar statements off the record and his statements, of course, were true. Why, though, after the care he had manifested in talking with us the day before, did he throw caution to the winds? The human mind is a complex organ and George Kennan is a complex man. One of the things he began to say immediately after the incident was that there was no role for an ambassador in Moscow under prevailing conditions, no need to replace him. Had that conviction already formed in his mind, did some subliminal impulse impel the conduct that would certainly remove him from Moscow?

There is something even more tantalizing. In that conversation in which Pietro Nenni told Di Stefano about Stalin's views of Germany, Nenni also questioned Di Stefano about Kennan—what manner of man was he, what were his convictions, did he indeed represent the views of Truman and Acheson, could he be trusted? Di Stefano had known Kennan since before World War II, when they both had been young attachés in Moscow. He told Nenni that Kennan was one of the best diplomats he had ever known, totally worthy of trust, that there was no one more professional in conduct, more reliable.

Nenni was most interested in the answer, but made no effort to contact Kennan. Di Stefano told me he would not be surprised if Nenni was simply passing on a question asked by Stalin. If this is true, and it can well be so, it more correctly reflects Stalin's attitude than the enigmatic affair of the young man who called himself the son of Abakumov. It suggests that Stalin was considering taking Kennan up on the private, secret, semiofficial explorations he had proposed. It is further evidence that Kennan's feeling that Russia was nearing the time for a change in policy was not a mystical hunch. Kennan, I believe, left Russia at a moment when his intuition was about to be proved true, a moment when the secret pace of events had already been accelerating for some months and would go on accelerating until March 5, 1953, when Stalin would be pronounced dead.

After that, it would pick up more speed, but by this time Kennan was already being rusticated, John Foster Dulles having told him there was no place in the State Department where his unique talents might be of use.

Kennan retained his abhorrence of the Soviet's police methods and their leaden propaganda. He had no sympathy for Khrushchev, but found Brezhnev's foreign policy advisers surprisingly subtle and sophisticated. The more deeply he plunged into his historical studies of Russia and the Soviet Union, the more strongly he emerged as a backer of diplomacy as the only method of resolving U.S.-Soviet differences and the less patient he became with advocates of force. The raw interference of the mili-

tary in diplomacy, their emergence as shapers rather than servants of policy, weighed heavily on his mind. He began to speak
out for a diplomacy of realism as the only means of assuring the
world's survival, by ending the U.S.-Soviet arms race and halting the buildup of nuclear armaments. His personal relationship
with the Soviets underwent a gradual evolution; he and they
began more clearly to understand each other. Kennan threw his
prestige and energy into the establishment of an Institute for
Soviet Studies, attached to the Smithsonian Institution. It was
named for George Kennan the first, but inevitably would become
a living monument to George Kennan the second.

As Kennan reached his seventies, a feeling began to grow in
many quarters that his life might well be crowned with the award
of the Nobel Prize for Peace, an honor that would have seemed
unthinkable in the days when we sat under the pines of Saltykovka and argued about Stalin.

34 | The Plot

I cannot and will not pretend that I had a premonition in those golden weeks of late August 1952 that the Stalin era was rushing toward its end.

My life was lazy—long conversations under the tall pines at Saltykovka, casual bargaining with the babushka who sold icons in the market (she hid them under her long black skirts), hoeing the rows of spindly corn in the garden (the dachniki thought Tom and I had lost our minds), fierce games of *gorodki,* a kind of Russian tenpins, dips in a muddy pond. I described in a letter to my mother the lovely flowers we were growing—dahlias, gladioli, larkspur, asters, marigolds, zinnias, petunias, phlox, nicotiana. I said: "I don't believe anyone in Russia has a nicer dacha. It is a joy and a pleasure to live here."

A joy and a pleasure. I wrote those lines August 11, 1952. The next day, the twelfth, in the basements of the Lubyanka, Stalin did to death twenty-four members of the Jewish Anti-Fascist Committee, which had rallied world Jewry to the Soviet cause in World War II. They had been arrested during the cosmopolitanism campaign of 1948–49 and were secretly placed on trial July 11–18, 1952. Not one hint of that crime would become public until Stalin had been dead nearly three years. Sent to death that quiet August was my old friend Solomon Lozovsky, wartime Soviet press spokesman, whose fiery words and flaming spirit had made Russian surrender seem unthinkable in the terrible days of 1941 and 1942, and with him died a score of poets and writers and artists, Perets Markish, Itzik Fefer, David Bergelson and the rest. Of those put on trial, only Lena Shtern, a physicist, survived. She was given life imprisonment and lived to be released after Stalin's death.

By this 1952 summer, I thought that I had a good grasp on Russia. I had the language down pretty well; living in Saltykovka, wandering over the countryside, talking with Tom and Juli, engaging George Kennan in long discussions; I had learned how Russians behaved, their ordinary lives and attitudes, I had read Tolstoy, had seen Chekhov at the Art Theater (although its

Chekhov repertoire was sadly diminished in these last Stalin years), had got acquainted with Ostrovsky and Gogol. I felt the rhythm of Russian life; I knew the terror; I knew about the camps; the thought of the police seldom left my mind. I had become, I felt, competent in my profession as a specialist in Soviet affairs. Of course, I did not put myself in Kennan's class. No one, in my view, could touch him. I did not have Tom Whitney's expertise in economics, but I was willing to match my judgment against that of anyone in Moscow, and I had long since learned the weaknesses of the offshore specialists, in Washington, London and Bonn.

The quality of the Moscow diplomatic corps was not high. Expertise at the American embassy after Kennan's forced withdrawal was thin. The U.S. chargé was Elim O'Shaughnessy, a marvelously genial man (despite his ulcers), but Moscow was only a way stop for him. The extraordinary skills of the Israelis would soon be lost. They had staffed their mission with Russian-born, Russian-speaking diplomats. They had unrivaled access to friends, relatives, coreligionists—one reason, I thought, why Stalin developed such paranoia about them. When Golda Meir (then Myerson) arrived in 1948 to establish the mission, a two-block-long line of Jews waiting to shake her hand formed outside the Metropol Hotel. That exhibition in central Moscow within sight of the Lubyanka hit Stalin's anti-Semitic nerve and may have touched off the cosmopolitanism drive. In an indirect way, it may have caused Stalin to decree the deaths of the members of the Jewish Anti-Fascist Committee.

The British had a competent embassy under Sir Alvery Gasgoigne, but the brilliant wartime and postwar Russicists like Edward Crankshaw, Arthur Birse and Tom Brebner were long since gone. The French, as so often, were witty but not well informed. There were a few others—the Finns knew a lot but kept their mouths shut, and my friend Sigurd Ekelund of the Norwegian embassy was first-class. Ambassador Rolf Sohlman, of Sweden, who remained in Moscow for many years, never knew as much as he thought he knew.

The United States under the forced draft of the cold war had begun to pour money into Soviet studies and, with the aid of the Russian Research Center at Harvard and the Russian Institute at Columbia, eventually would produce a cadre of specialists second to none. But this was early on. The new Soviet specialists were skewed by the intensity of the cold war and handicapped by nonaccess to the Soviet Union. Their judgments were conditioned by contact with successive waves of Russian emigration: the tremendous outflow (largely Jewish) before 1914; the outpouring after the Bolshevik Revolution—the so-called Whites, that is, the upper and middle classes; and the political enemies of the Bolsheviks, notably the Mensheviks, the Socialist Revolutionaries and the Kadets. And now there had been a new wave, that of Russians displaced by the war, many by way of Germany. This Russian mass was naturally (and rightfully) violently antagonistic to the Soviet regime. In the context of the times, it is small wonder that American expertise tended to be sharply affected.

In this period, unfortunately, popular attitudes which failed to make a distinction between the Russian people and the Soviet apparatus took root, a tendency that would continue into the future and deeply disturb such a man as Aleksandr Solzhenitsyn, as strong an anti-Bolshevik and as strong a Russian patriot as could be found.

I wished in this summer of 1952 that Sir Bernard Pares had been living. I could imagine him sitting under the pines at Saltykovka in a canvas chair, George Kennan in another, myself, Juli and Tom beside them—what conversation! And weak and ungrammatical as was my Russian, I would not have held back from taking part. I thought Pares would not be ashamed of his disciple. I had accumulated a store of information about the Bolsheviks and their terrible master, Stalin. I did not think I could easily be fooled now and in this I was correct, except on one count—Stalin's paranoia, the totality of his crooked vision of the world and his mania that his closest collaborators were engaged in a conspiracy against him. (Later I would ask myself: Was this entirely paranoia? Hadn't at this late date at least some of them begun to *wish* to conspire even if they did not possess the courage?) The vastness of Stalin's suspicions lay beyond my imagination. There was too much hard grit in my mind; I had absorbed too much Midwestern skepticism, down-to-earthism, call it what you will. I could not envision a world leader so psychopathic, even when I used Hitler as a model.

So if someone had come up to me (as the young man did to Kennan) and told me that tomorrow, on August 12, Stalin would wipe from the earth the flower of Russian Jewish intelligentsia and that he had been twisting their limbs, torturing their bodies and flogging their spirits for nearly four years, I would, I am afraid, have thought that my informant was a victim of plotitis, which I understood to be a very common disease in Russia, dating back beyond Ivan the Terrible into the earliest days of the Mongol invasions.

Nothing as cosmic as the end of Stalin and his era was on my mind in those splendid August days. Yet I had begun to feel that *something* was in the air—just what, I could not say. In February I had written Manny Freedman, suggesting a revision of the code message I was to send if Stalin died. I had no reason to believe that his death was near, although a spate of stories in the Soviet press about the longevity of Georgians made me think that someone had Stalin's age on his mind (Stalin was then seventy-two). The stories reported that in the Georgian mountains, one not infrequently came upon men in good health at the age of 130 or even 140. I did not think Stalin was likely to live so long; neither did I think his death was at hand; but I wanted to be certain that if I sent a code message, it would not get lost in the paper traffic. The *Times* boasted of handling a million words of copy a day. The danger, I told Manny, was that "the messages are so innocuous that they are apt to be ignored by anyone who is not on the alert."

There is nothing in my dispatches or in my correspondence to suggest that in August there was any rise in my anxiety level. I was writing Cy Sulzberger that "news-wise we are really in the dog days." I told a friend that "everything is peaceful and quiet." I was leading "as uncomplicated an existence as you could find."

In another letter I wrote: "The countryside is lovely in its late summer aspects. The harvest is pouring in. The new buildings are going up. The new dams are functioning and, in general, everything has a rather mid-New Deal aspect."

There were, I must say, a few puzzles in my mind. One was the indication—which I would not confirm until November—that Abakumov no longer was serving as interior minister, that is, as the man in charge of the police. He had, as a matter of fact, been dismissed the previous November, 1951, but until the young "Abakumov" appeared at the U.S. embassy in July, this had been only a vague rumor. Official confirmation that he had been replaced by Semyon D. Ignatiev was still being held up by the censors at the time of Stalin's death.

Any question about the police—the most sensitive apparatus in the Soviet Union—attracted my attention. I didn't know what the rumors meant, but I kept them in mind.

I was very interested in the situation in Georgia, the bailiwick of both Stalin and Beria. In April 1952, a purge of the Georgian political and police leadership had been carried out at a plenary meeting of the Georgian Party Committee. Beria himself was present. This made it an event worthy of study. Moreover, the news did not appear in the Tbilisi newspaper until the end of May; and the censors killed my story out of hand. A couple of days later, *Pravda* ran an editorial commentary about the episode; I filed my story again and this time it went through. New York gave it only a few paragraphs, but I could not blame them. The censor had deleted almost all meaning from the dispatch. To me, however, whatever Beria did was significant. And the curious, finicky conduct of the censors told me that there was special sensitivity to the Georgian events.

But none of this indicated what was really happening, who was behind it, and what roles Beria and Stalin were playing.

Though I knew that some funny business was afoot, I missed the point entirely. I thought Beria had fired Abakumov and was shaking up Georgia. It did not occur to me that *Stalin* had fired Abakumov, *Stalin* was shaking up Georgia and shaking up Beria in the process. I knew that Beria had lasted a good deal longer than either of his police predecessors, Genrykh Yagoda and Nikolai Yezhov, but my conviction that the Stalin regime had reached a kind of plateau of internal political balance blinded me to a realization that by Stalin's timetable, the moment for replacing Beria was at hand; too often had Stalin used Beria to settle his political accounts (as in dealing with the powerful Army marshals, like Georgi K. Zhukov, at the end of World War II). Unless Stalin now dealt with Beria, Beria would deal with Stalin.

Nothing as cataclysmic as the end of Stalin can happen without premonitory signs; the great sphinx does not suddenly topple from its pedestal and shatter in a thousand pieces. There must be preliminary tremors. So there were in this case, but I did not read them correctly nor, I believe, did anyone else except the handful of men who were called Stalin's "closest comrades in arms."

The benign and comfortable Saltykovka days came to an end on August 17, 1952. That evening, we got the announcement of the arrival of a Chinese delegation, headed by Premier Zhou Enlai. They were to negotiate with Stalin and Molotov. The reason for this negotiation I never discovered, and soon it got lost in the cascade of events that spewed forth, one after the other. From that evening until Stalin's death (and for a long time after), there was no peace, no quiet, no rest; just story after story, headline after headline, a mounting crescendo and something else—terror.

At first it was the pounding of the news bulletins, stories breaking like waves on a barrier reef. Hardly had Stalin begun to negotiate with Zhou than we got the announcement that the party would meet in its Nineteenth Congress, the first since 1939, in October. The Politburo, the core of Soviet power since the days of Lenin, was to be abolished and replaced by a Presidium, whatever that might be. The next day, a new five-year plan for industry and agriculture was announced. The next day, Moscow proposed a four-power conference on Germany. Day after day, the *Times* played my dispatches on page one. There was a huge spread on plans for a gigantic power system; there were tough declarations about party discipline and tougher ones on "vigilance." There would be more and more articles about vigilance as autumn wore on. The run of news was so swift I had no time for contemplation. Hardly a moment to mourn George Kennan's vanishment. No more dacha. No more vegetable garden. No more talks *po dusham.* As event tumbled after event, I began to feel that I must prepare for even bigger news. The conventional cable facilities no longer sufficed. My old UP communications instinct broke through the surface and I wrote the *Times* bureau in London to arrange to dictate my late-breaking dispatches by telephone. Clifton Daniel was in charge and he promptly advised me that London had a man on duty every night until 3 A.M., Moscow time, who could, in a pinch, take my dictation. I felt reassured. Whatever was coming, I would be able to handle it. I tried to figure out what lay ahead. Not a new purge —of that I felt pretty certain. "The break with the 'purge' technique," I wrote in my journal, "is, I think, final." The party membership had been fairly well overhauled since the war. Deadwood had been cleared away. What lay ahead, I thought, was not a tempest at the national level but more localized storms, like that in Georgia. I was still watching Georgia closely, still not understanding that the "cleanup" was directed against rather than by Beria. The volume of my transmissions to New York was extraordinary. In the first fifteen days of October, during and after the Nineteenth Party Congress, I spent sixteen thousand rubles—full-value, four-to-the-dollar rubles—on tolls to New York. Ordinarily I didn't spend that much in four months.

I might not yet be seeing Stalin's forest for the trees, but I was understanding, reporting and accurately analyzing most of what happened at the Nineteenth Congress. I perceived that it provided a backdrop for the full emergence of Malenkov as Stalin's designated successor. He was given every opportunity to star, and took it. I also understood quite clearly that the purpose Stalin had in mind in creating the big new Presidium of twenty-five members and eleven candidate members was to dilute the Politburo and, in a sense, unhinge the status of all the old leaders. I understood something else: Stalin himself overshadowed the congress, yet made only one cameo appearance at the very end, a fleeting moment with throwaway lines. It was a gesture of contempt and of total power, as if he was tossing the congress a glove to fight over as a symbol of his dominance.

There was another fact, and I took notice of it in my journal. Malenkov *seemed* to dominate the proceedings, but did he really?

In mid-November I wrote: "People are apt to overlook Khrushchev. I wouldn't do that. After all, he is the Moscow party boss. That is the biggest single boss position in the country and I don't know of a party position where you are more likely to shine—if you really have ability—than Moscow. And Khrushchev obviously still had his finger firmly on the Ukrainian pulse. I think he ranks much higher than he seems to. . . . In general, it is fairly clear that should Stalin die in the present period, Molotov would succeed him as head of state, Malenkov as head of the party, and the actual power would be held in varying degrees by Molotov, Malenkov, Beria, Bulganin, Voroshilov and, quite possibly, Khrushchev."

And at the same time—and for the first time—I began to speculate on the possibility that Beria was dropping from the inner circle. One of the prime devices in analysis of Kremlin politics was the display of the portraits—that is, the order in which they were arrayed around the central figure of Stalin in published photographs and wall displays. For years, the order had been: Stalin, Molotov, Malenkov, Beria. Now, at a stroke, Beria dropped two positions. The displays on November 7 arranged the pictures in this order: Stalin, Molotov, Malenkov, Voroshilov, Bulganin, Beria. As I noted, unless Stalin was merely "exercising his jovial humor," that meant a tip of fortune away from Beria.

Though I toyed with the possibility that this phenomenon was linked in some way with the events in Georgia, I failed to draw what seems to me now the obvious conclusion that Georgia was being taken away from Beria. I hadn't yet pinned down the Abakumov-Ignatiev shift firmly enough to put it into the equation.

But I was tightening my belt for what looked more and more like a new tempo. There were only five American correspondents in Moscow now. No English whatever. We had coalesced into two harshly competitive groups: the AP's Gilmore and Whitney, with whom I aligned myself, plus Andy Steiger, the Reuters stringer, and on the other side, Henry Shapiro of UP, and Jean Noe, stringer for Agence France-Presse. The principal papers, *Pravda* and *Izvestiya,* were delivered to the Metropol at 8 or 9 A.M., and that was when the news agencies customarily had filed their stories. Because 8 A.M. was midnight in New York, too late for the *Times* except for the biggest news, I usually wrote and transmitted my stories in the afternoon or early evening, for use in the next day's paper. This gave me time to evaluate a development and write, I hoped, with more depth and interpretation than the split-second transmissions of the agencies.

Now, due largely to the enterprise of Tom Whitney, we were getting the papers the moment they became available at the *ekspeditsiya,* the special dispatch booths at the newspaper plants. Late papers invariably meant a big story. Each team assigned a man in rotation to be at the Central Telegraph Office a bit after midnight. He would wait until the papers came, then telephone his colleagues if there was big news. If the papers were delayed after 3 A.M., he would phone and we would all come down to be on hand for a big story. There was no problem in picking up *Izvestiya.* Its plant was in the center of town and the *ekspeditsiya* was just off Gorky Street. *Pravda* was another matter and rather scary. The plant was located near the Dynamo metro station, well out (in those days) on the Leningrad chaussée. The *ekspeditsiya* was at the back of the plant, in a compound patrolled at night by soldiers with rifles. As time ran on and tension built up in Moscow, going to the *Pravda* plant at 3 A.M. on a dark winter night with trigger-happy soldiers in an unlighted courtyard did not appeal to me.

But these exercises were important. We got the papers hours ahead of ordinary delivery. It made the difference, so far as I was concerned, between getting my story into the morning paper or losing it to an agency report. There was a seven- or eight-hour time differential (depending on the season) between Moscow and New York. If I got *Pravda* at 4 A.M., it was still only 8 or 9 P.M. in New York—plenty of time to make the second edition if the censor did not delay the story and if the telephone line to London came through promptly. Even if *Pravda* was delayed until 8 A.M., I could with luck catch the final edition in New York. This was meaningless for ordinary stories, but more and more we were dealing with front-page, lead-the-paper news. Night after night, I found myself sitting in the Central Telegraph Office, a big modern building on Gorky Street. The pressroom was located to the rear off a side street, a tiny mezzanine with four telephone booths, a table and a counter behind which worked two women— a telegraph clerk, who accepted our copy and delivered it to a closed rear room, where it was censored, and a telephone operator, who sat at an old-fashioned switchboard with telephone jacks and headphones. She placed our international telephone calls to London, Paris, New York or wherever. Sometimes Mongolian students descended on the cubbyhole to telephone their parents in Ulan Bator—they shouted so loud I thought they hardly needed a telephone line. This bandbox came to be my second home. Tom and I alternated on the watch. There were always two of us there, one from each rival syndicate, often not on speaking terms, stealing sly looks, wondering if the opposition was onto any special bits of information. In this close confrontation I came to realize that there were favors granted by the Press Department, that not all was a matter of equity or enterprise. On more than one occasion, my "opposition" would suddenly appear on the scene, tipped off, presumably by the Press Department, that something was about to happen.

Later it would seem to me that November 1952 was a brooding, oppressive time, a period of hush in which I could hear the rustle of unfamiliar noises in the background, hints of disturbing events. It was quiet, compared to the tensions of October; routine saber-rattling by Marshal Timoshenko on November 7, retrospective rumbling in the press about the evil George Kennan, new men put in to run two ideological journals—nothing dramatic, but an undercurrent of unease produced by the enigmatic Nineteenth Party Congress.

Not until December 1 did my apprehension begin to take a more tangible form. On that day, the Kiev newspaper reported under the simple headline "Chronicle" that a military tribunal had decreed the death by shooting of three individuals, all bearing Jewish names, as "enemies of the people," guilty of "counterrevolutionary wrecking." In my years in Moscow, I had never seen or heard of such an event. The "crime" for which the men were tried was fraud and peculation. Invocation of the death penalty and a military court in a petty commercial case, the phrase "counterrevolutionary wrecking" and the label "enemies of the people" instantly linked the event in every Russian's mind with the 1930s purges. It was as "enemies of the people" that Stalin sent millions of innocent Soviet citizens to the labor camps and it was as "counterrevolutionary wreckers" that he destroyed the Old Bolsheviks and his closest comrades.

The message was unmistakable. I immediately referred back to an address made by "General" Aleksandr Poskrebyshev, Stalin's chef de cabinet, at the party congress, in which he called for vigilance and inveighed against "wreckers." This man bore a reputation as ugly as his name (which contained the root of the vulgar Russian word for afterbirth). He carried out Stalin's most evil bidding. But in the weeks before Stalin's death, he himself was arrested. Later I would meet a woman, Galina Serebryakova, an Old Bolshevik who spent many years in Stalin's camps and lost two famous Bolshevik husbands, successively, Georgi Sokolnikov and G. P. Serebryakov, to Stalin's purges. She met Poskrebyshev in the Kremlin hospital in 1962. He did not die until 1966. He was, she said, not only unrepentant but actually proud of the crimes he had carried out at Stalin's behest. His memory was infallible. He fulfilled every order Stalin gave him without a tremor. Stalin executed Poskrebyshev's wife. He did not blink an eye. He had a story he liked to tell about Beria. He had asked Beria once whether a certain Bolshevik was "sitting" (the Russian phrase for being in prison). No, no, said Beria, he's not sitting any longer; he's lying flat on the floor. Poskrebyshev, telling the story, laughed uproariously. Serebryakova asked about a friend who she knew had died in prison. Had she possibly been poisoned? Poskrebyshev asked the date of the death. It was 1937 or 1938. She must have been shot, he said; "we didn't start using poison until 1940 or thereabouts."

Through December the arrest of persons in the trade networks, many bearing Jewish names, went forward. Many arrests were in the Ukraine. There were more changes in the ideological organs. *Pravda* got a new editor and a new round of criticism broke out on the economic front. My feeling of unease was not relieved when, unexpectedly, Stalin responded to a series of questions cabled to him by Scotty Reston, the *Times* correspondent in Washington. Stalin, responding to Eisenhower's election, seemed to be offering to act as mediator between the U.S. and Korea, and encouraging the idea of a meeting between himself and Ike. Nothing came of either initiative and Reston took some vicious criticism (including, I'm sorry to say, some from top *Times* editors) for having made himself available to "Soviet propaganda."

I met New Year, 1953, with some trepidation. I wanted very much to get back to the United States. I was worried about Mike and Stephan. Mary had finally come to rest in Evanston, Illinois, but reports on the boys were not reassuring and Moscow was becoming a strain. I saw no early end to Stalin and was beginning to wonder whether I could last him out. I had had a fine run of news, my standing with the paper had radically improved, I had published two good articles in the *Times Magazine* at year's end and felt that I had regained the confidence that had been lost by the Korean episode. But I did not know how much longer I could take Moscow, particularly a Moscow which on that cold New Year's midnight, swept by wind, the temperature well below zero, seemed to be acquiring an undefined aura of menace. I wrote my mother and my sister that I surely hoped to get back in 1953, though I could not yet be certain when. My uncertainty arose from a sense that I had lost track of Russia's direction. I could feel a hand on the tiller, but I did not know from what compass the helmsman was taking his course.

January 13, 1953, was an ordinary winter's morning at the Hotel Metropol. I was still living in Room 393. When I opened *Pravda* at about 8 A.M., I found in the middle of the back page, under the one word "Chronicle," a ten-inch announcement, which even today causes a chill to run up my spine.

It said that a group of nine doctors, all but three of them

Jews, had been arrested on a charge of plotting against the lives of high party, government and army leaders. They were linked through Zionist organizations with the U.S. and British intelligence and had carried out their activities by the negligence of Soviet security organs.

Here it was. I did not need one more detail. Here was the sketch for a purge to end all purges. Every Russian citizen who read the "Chronicle" knew exactly what it meant. Now I knew why gooseflesh had crawled on my skin during these winter nights as I tried to figure out what was going on behind the scenes. This announcement gave the whole scenario. I could name the defendants: the doctors, of course (and they were the most distinguished in the country, all connected with the Kremlin hospital, personal physicians to the Politburo); the security chiefs (that meant Beria and Abakumov); Jews (and this meant Lazar M. Kaganovich in the Politburo); members of the trade system, and this meant Anastas Mikoyan, whose Politburo rating had slipped badly; and Aleksei Kosygin, who had slipped even more. What about Nikita Khrushchev, whose ties to the Ukraine were so strong? Many, many arrests were taking place in the Ukraine. And would there not be a spot reserved for "foreign agents," representatives of the U.S. and British intelligence? I could see George Kennan being cast, in absentia, as the mastermind of the plot; he had been portrayed repeatedly since the Nineteenth Party Congress as the director of the international cold war against Moscow. Would it not be convenient to name someone still in Moscow as a link between Kennan and the other plotters —for instance, a foreign correspondent, or even better, two foreign correspondents who set up a "nest" in Saltykovka where Kennan could hatch his evil doings?

It sounds absurd today. In fact, it was absurd. But that did not mean that such ideas did not pass through the mind of the master of the Grand Guignol. There was nothing he was not capable of. He compelled his new son-in-law, Yuri Zhdanov, who had recently married his daughter, Svetlana, to attack ideological weaknesses among scientists. Zhdanov's father, the late Andrei Zhdanov, who had died August 31, 1947, was one of the alleged victims of the "Doctors' Plot."

As days went past, the horizons of the "plot" rapidly broadened. Rumors flew through Moscow. A man named L. D. Gurevich was arrested. I didn't know him, but the other correspondents did. He had worked for Tass, once had wide connections with foreign correspondents, acted, for a time, as kind of a go-between. Now he was "exposed" as an "ex-Trotskyite and intelligence agent." My old friend Palgunov of the Foreign Office and Tass had vanished. Madame Molotov had been arrested, it was gossiped, and banished to Siberia. She was Jewish and had been the best friend of Stalin's wife, Nadezda, who killed herself in 1933. There had been arrests in the universities in Moscow and Leningrad and in the Academy of Sciences. There were rumors about many Soviet diplomats. My old friend Maisky was repeatedly criticized, along with others of long standing, most of them Jewish. Central Committee members had been arrested.

The question was not who was in trouble—but who was not. I could hardly believe my own conclusions as I added up the potential defendants at the show trial to come. Not many members of the Politburo would escape. Could Stalin really be thinking of doing away with everyone—Molotov, Beria, Mikoyan, Kaganovich, possibly Voroshilov? (Khrushchev later revealed that this was exactly what Stalin had in mind.) Certainly Malenkov and Bulganin would not be in the cast—still, there were rumors.

And the Jews. The net was being cast very wide. On February 12, 1953, Moscow broke diplomatic relations with Israel and the long-harassed Israelis left the country.

Three times in February, Stalin went out of his way to meet with foreigners, Argentine Ambassador Bravo, Indian Ambassador Menon and the Indian peace leader Dr. Kitchlew. Each spoke of Stalin's "excellent health," his lively mind, his keen grasp of the issues. Only later did Menon tell me that Stalin had doodled on a pad with a red pencil. He was drawing pictures of wolves, many, many wolves. Stalin spoke of wolves, as well. He said Russian peasants knew how to deal with them—they killed them. Menon had thought the remark curious and I thought it even more curious.

Tom and I talked one day. Would there be a correspondent as a defendant in the upcoming trial? We both believed the chances were good that there would be. Tom thought he was a strong possibility. He was married to a Russian woman; he was close to George Kennan; he had come to Moscow with the OSS, that is, as an intelligence agent, and the Russians knew this. His reasoning was too good for comfort. I thought I was an equally promising candidate. I represented *The New York Times,* which every day was castigated by *Pravda.* I had a long, long record of conflict and hostility with the Russians, going back to World War II days. (Had I known of the Nosenko revelations, I would have considered myself the number one candidate.)

What to do? Should we pick up and ship out? That was easy for me: I knew the *Times* would agree if I told them the situation; I had no entanglements. For my four American colleagues, however, to leave would send their wives straight into concentration camps and maybe the wives would end up as defendants or witnesses at the forthcoming trial.

That was the kind of talk we had, riding in the blue Chevrolet of which Juli was so proud. We didn't want to talk indoors for fear of hidden microphones, nor did we want further to alarm Juli. There was no one at the U.S. embassy to whom we could turn for guidance or comfort. We knew the situation better than they did; there were no Kennans, no Kirks, no Harrimans, no Archie Clark Kerrs on the horizon in the winter of 1953. We were on our own. It was not difficult for me to make up my mind. I was frightened with good reason, I thought. But I would not have left Moscow if Turner Catledge had ordered me to. I was on the verge of the biggest story I had ever heard of. Of course I would stay. That was why I had come. I would take my chances on where I would find myself—in the dock or in the press box.

35 | Stalin

February is the longest month of the Russian calendar, its dark days bereft of sun, with cold winds, gray skies, falling snow day after day, the women in gray quilted jackets and gray shawls sweeping the streets with witches' brooms, the Metropol's corridors dimmer and dimmer, ghosts in the corners—a time when life congeals and hope vanishes. Russian winter sets in by late October. In December and January, the sun rises feebly after nine in the morning and its yellow wafer is fading at two in the afternoon. By February, I would wonder whether I could survive the two long months of winter still ahead. I understood now the peasant rhythms and the northern drunkenness, sleeping on the brick stove winter long, the frenzy of spring, the orgies of the midsummer solstice.

The rhythm of Russian life was compelled by endless winter, savage spring, fierce summer, brief fall, and this rhythm had been imposed on industrial Russia: the factories "storming" to meet their rigid production quotas, the somnolent pace in winter, molasses in spring, more lively in summer and madness as the year neared an end.

February was the low point, and February 1953 was not only low but foreboding. At the end of January, Juli's mother had died after a few days in hospital, a time of total grief and guilt for Juli, who spent every moment at the bedside, listening to the nurses gossip of the Doctors' Plot and whisper their own evil fantasies, the hospital alive with letter writing, denunciations pouring into the Kremlin.

Estella Khokhlovkina was buried in Vvedenie cemetery in a plot off a snow-banked *allée,* obtained by bribing the cemetery administration. I don't know what Tom paid—one thousand rubles, three thousand rubles, whatever was the going rate. Estella Khokhlovkina, at last at peace, lay briefly on an iron table in her wood coffin in a room with a cement floor in the basement of the Third Moscow *Krematoria.* I suppose a dozen people gathered there—a few relatives whom I did not know, edgy because of the foreigners, and motherly Maria Ivanovna, cook for the Whitneys and later for me. Outside the room, three women squabbled over the dress, the shift, the shoes, the stockings, they removed from the corpse of a friend, which lay on a trolley about to be wheeled to the crematorium furnace.

We rode in a small blue bus to Vvedenie; Tom, myself and two cemetery workers carried the coffin to the graveside. God knows whose bones had been disinterred to make a place for Estella Khokhlovkina. We stood a moment. Juli cast the first handful of frozen earth and the gravediggers began to fill the hole, the temperature at twenty-five degrees below zero, centigrade. Maria Ivanovna had brought a little bottle of vodka so the women could wipe their faces and the tears would not freeze on their cheeks. Then we went back to the apartment. Maria Ivanovna had prepared the traditional funeral *kutiya,* a dish of boiled rice and raisins. One more Russian soul had been laid to rest.

We waited. Slowly the days of February slipped off the calendar. On the streets, the black beetles who are the people of Moscow in winter padded past in their *valenki,* the slap of felt boots slurring into a soft murmur. I sat inside the Metropol and tried to understand what was happening, the ripple of arrests in every paper, the growing silence of the Metropol maids. No longer did they gossip around the desk of the *dezhurnaya.* Now they slithered along the corridors, eyes averted, faces closed. Did they know something? Or was it the fear of working with foreigners, any one of whom might be a *shpion,* a spy, or a *diversant?* Even a maid who cared for a *shpion's* room might find herself labeled an enemy of the people. The corridors of the Metropol, always so dark, now seemed hardly lighted. I pulled tight the heavy wine-colored draperies at my windows and tried to shut out Russia, but it seeped in through every crevice. I was afraid. I think all Moscow was afraid.

Toward the end of February, General Sokolovsky, a hero of World War II, replaced General Shtemenko, an obscure time-server, as chief of the General Staff. It wasn't announced. We found it out when Sokolovsky signed the invitations for the Red Army Day reception. Was this good news or bad? No one knew. Lev Mekhlis, a Jew and an old crony of Stalin's, a man whose intrigues had cost the Red Army heavily in the war, died, as the obituary said, "at his fighting post," whatever that meant. The leading pallbearer was Lazar M. Kaganovich, the only Jew in the

Politburo. The Jews burying the Jews? Perhaps. Stalin's son Vasily lost his job as commander of the Moscow Air Force, but the censor would not let me transmit the news. Minister of Health Smirnov lost his job; probably, I thought, he was being tagged in the Doctors' Plot. A brief obituary of General Kosynkin was published on February 17. He suffered an "untimely death." I had never heard of him. He turned out to have been Stalin's Kremlin commandant. These were little pieces of a big mosaic. I didn't know how to put them together.

My mood was touchy. I was nervous. I wrote sarcastic letters.

To Burobin (I had been trying to get an apartment for a year): "Is this a fair example of Soviet efficiency or does it reflect a general absence of adequate housing facilities in Moscow?"

To the Press Department (about Burobin): "Do you suppose there is anything your department can do to cause these Rip Van Winkles to bestir themselves?"

To Chief Censor Omelchenko: "What does a censor do with a cable which he or she passes verbatim after one hour and forty-five minutes—sit staring at it for one hour and forty-five minutes? Or does he or she sit drinking tea and reading light literature until the spirit moves him or her to bother with doing a small amount of work? Yours in some asperity, Harrison E. Salisbury."

I went out to Saltykovka. It was an hour's walk through deep snow from the station to the dacha, which stood peacefully in the grove of tall pines. Straight columns of blue smoke rose from the chimneys of neighboring dachas. I lighted a little fire and huddled over it, warming my frosted hands and ears, then walked back to the station. That night I wrote a friend: "I only wish the world was as quiet and peaceful as the countryside around Moscow now appears. Everything is covered in a deep blanket of white snow. There is a strong frost, close to 30 degrees below, centigrade, and the sky is that pale winter blue. The air is crisp and horses' and humans' mouths are quickly covered with hoarfrost. The countryside is sleeping quietly, the peasants are busy with their winter chores, the youngsters' skates are ringing on the village ponds and the forests stand dark green and silent and a little frightening. It looks and is a simple, comfortable world.

"But, unfortunately, I do not think we can consider this countryside exactly a symbol of the state of affairs in these perilous days."

Tom and I had established a new routine for night duty—one week on, one week off. It was my week on, the week of March 1. I spent the early evening of March 3 monitoring the dictation-speed Tass transmission. Tass sent its news to the small country papers all over Russia by radio dictation, the same thing I had done for UP in my early days at St. Paul, by telephone. The Tass reader, usually a woman, intoned the items slowly, spelling out every name *("M kak Maria, O kak Olga, S kak Sara, K kak Kostya, V kak Viktor, A kak Andrei—Moskva").* Once in a while, Tass dictation carried an important item before regular Tass. I listened with half an ear while combing the fifteen or sixteen provincial papers to which I subscribed. I was looking for clues, haunted by what was happening behind Stalin's curtains.

I found nothing in the papers, heard nothing on Tass dictation. I picked up my portable typewriter and made my way to the telegraph office. *Pravda,* upset at our prowling about the back courtyard, was now delivering the paper to the telegraph office. So was *Izvestiya.* I was uneasy as I opened my typewriter and settled down for the usual wait. Thanks to Clifton Daniel, I could dictate my stories to London until 3 A.M. The trouble was that hot Moscow news was breaking more and more often after 3 A.M. After that hour, since London had no one to take my messages, I had to use urgent cable service, urgent in name only. Night after night my stories arrived in New York hours too late. Since early February, I had been urging New York to arrange for all-night dictation. I truly felt there was something apocalyptic in the Moscow atmosphere. I could smell it. I felt it in the metallic taste of fear under my tongue. Somehow I had not been able to convey this feeling to New York. I had in my pocket a cablegram I had just received from Freedman, and it bore his phlegmatic touch: "Salisbury dubious about setting up London Paris dictation posts simply for late breaks Moscow but still awaiting results of cost inquiry. Freedman." Manny had sent that telegram at 12:57 P.M., March 3; I got it at 1 A.M., March 4—about seven hours transmission time.

How could I stir Manny out of his routine, his concern about costs, and make him understand that I was sitting on a charge of dynamite?

As so often in the long hours after midnight, I began to think about Russia. I had been living in Moscow for four years now, plus the better part of a year during the war—five years in all, give or take a few months. Every day I was learning how little I knew about this complicated country.

What was it that we were waiting for—what was it that frightened us so much? Simply that no one knew what the tyrant ruler would do next. "Watch out!" Eddy Gilmore had said. "The old man has reached for the bottle again." That was it. We were waiting for 1934, 1935, 1936, 1937, 1938, for the purges to happen again, the time when the Revolution was turned inside out, when the heroes were declared villains and darkness fell at noon. When Koestler's book first came out, I didn't read it. I could not abide the disputes of the sectarians, the worshipers and the skeptics. To me, they were all of the same pattern. I despised them. I think there was a little xenophobia in that, a feeling, basically, that they were a bunch of foreigners. Not until I came to Moscow in 1949 did I read *Darkness at Noon* and become powerfully moved at Koestler's insight.

These were the kind of thoughts that flowed through my mind as I drowsed at Entrance 11 of the Central Telegraph Office in the hours after midnight on March 4, 1953. I looked at my watch. It was two-thirty. No sign of the papers. The "opposition," Jean Noe, was across the room, his head on the table in the cradle of his arms, fast asleep. A dark, good-looking Frenchman who had come to Moscow as a soccer player and stayed on to coach the Russians, he had wound up as a correspondent for Agence France-Presse. So far as I could see, the only one awake in the telegraph office besides myself was Clerk Vassileva, the woman who took the telegrams, her face just visible through the little opening in the frosted glass.

At three-thirty, the papers still hadn't come, and I telephoned the *Izvestiya ekspeditsiya*. The woman had heard nothing. At four, the papers still had not arrived. I called again. No sign. I began to get jittery. Jean Noe had awakened and called someone. He did not go back to sleep. I called *Izvestiya* again. The woman said the papers were late. Well, that I knew. At five, I called Tass. No, they had heard nothing, but the man spoke in a way that

gave me an idea something might be up. Should I call Tom? I
decided to wait a few more minutes. Jean Noe was stirring about.
He had the same problem as I, but we did not speak. It was not
considered appropriate. We spoke when we met, a rather stiff
greeting but nothing more. I called the *Izvestiya* woman again.
The papers are going to be very late, she said. That was it. Something must be up. A little before six, I called Tom. "Better come
down," I said. "The papers are very late. Something must be
breaking."

A little before 8 A.M. we got the news. Stalin had suffered a
cerebral hemorrhage. He was unconscious and partially paralyzed. His condition was critical. The attack had occurred, the
announcement said, Sunday evening, March 1–2, "in his quarters
in Moscow," that is, the Kremlin. It was now Wednesday morning. The news had been held up more than forty-eight hours. It
was obvious that the chances of Stalin's surviving the attack
were slim. The medical bulletin was signed by ten physicians,
headed by the new minister of health, A. F. Tretyakov.

Even now, as I pounded out my bulletins, sending them on at
"urgent" rate (the London dictation facilities long since closed),
I thought of the Doctors' Plot. Stalin had arrested the men who
had looked after his life for so many years; now that life lay in
the hands of new and unknown physicians. Was this just an
ironic twist?

In this moment, I was filled with relief. The story I had been
dreading had been an announcement about the Doctors' Plot,
some new and terrifying revelation, an arrest of Politburo members or even of a correspondent, an announcement that the trial
was about to open. Something of that kind. Now Stalin himself
had been stricken. This had to be good news, although there remained the inescapable thought: Who might be charged with
guilt in the death of Stalin?

The next two days run together in my mind. I *knew* Stalin was
going to die. I knew that every word, every impression I could
record would be part of history. I was in constant motion. I traveled Moscow from Khimki to Sokolniki. I talked to the Americans, the British and the French. I broke my rules and talked to
Russians. They were very reserved. They did not know whether
Stalin's illness was good or bad, and they were not going to discuss it with a foreigner. Occasional official bulletins were issued.
Not very revealing. They showed that Stalin was alive, his condi-

tion grave, but little more. I had no more transmission problems. I could dictate anywhere I wanted—London, Paris, New York. Later I got a plaintive letter from Freedman, congratulating me on the coverage, on my insistence on better transmission facilities, apologizing for not setting them up more quickly and wondering how I had got "advance warning" on the big news. I could not bring myself to tell him that all I had had was a hunch based on the stories I had been sending him.

I went to the Central Synagogue and listened with pitying ears as Chief Rabbi Schliffer called on the congregation to pray for "our dear leader and teacher Josef Vissarionovich Stalin." He decreed a day of fasting and prayer. I went to the great Yelikhovsky Cathedral and there the Russian Orthodox patriarch Aleksei led the congregation in solemn prayer for Stalin. "All the Russian people and all people everywhere pray to God for the health of the sick one," he intoned. Acolytes held aloft the Bible in its golden case, and the patriarch, in gown of gold and purple, carrying his golden rod, passed through the multitude of kneeling believers. Hundreds of candles burned before the altars, young men and women joined with their elders in crossing themselves. Shudders ran down my back as I watched the people sink to their knees, chanting prayers for the man who had desecrated Orthodox churches by the hundred and unleashed an anti-Semitic terror second only to Hitler's. Back at the Metropol, I carefully read a volume of Walter Duranty's dispatches for his account of Lenin's last days, in January 1924. This, I felt, would be a guide to the ceremonials of 1953.

As I sat at my desk, my eye caught the carbon copy of a letter I had written a few days earlier, the last of scores to Stalin, small bets on the lottery of Letters to Stalin. Occasionally he responded to these, but never had he replied to one of mine. I had sent this letter the previous Thursday, inquiring if he wished to reply to a declaration by Eisenhower that he was ready "to travel halfway around the world" if a meeting with Stalin would serve the cause of peace and freedom. I had asked Stalin if he was willing to meet Ike, and if so, where. I had given the letter to my chauffeur to put in the Kremlin post box, that is, to hand to the sentry at the Troitsky Gate. At this moment, I thought, my letter lies on Stalin's desk, maybe at the top of the pile. It would have been put there Friday or Saturday. Perhaps he even read it before being stricken and set it aside, intending to return to it on

Monday. I decided to write a little story about the letter and Stalin's method of responding to correspondents. I wrote another story, a reminiscence of my trip to Tbilisi in 1951, of Stalin's early literary career, his romantic poems. I quoted my favorite:

The rosebud is opening
And all around are bluebells;
The iris, too, has awakened
And all nod their heads
In the breeze.
The lark flies high in the sky,
Chirping and singing.
The nightingale with feeling and quiet voice sings:
"May my dear country flourish,
May you wed and be happy, my dear land of Iberia,
May you wed yourselves to your studies
And to your youth and your homeland."

Good God, I thought, as I typed the lines. What had happened to this naive young poet in the years between nineteen and seventy-three; what had turned Dzhugashvili into the Stalin who had made a slaughterhouse of his country; what savage gods had possessed this Georgian youngster with his dark face, burning eyes and romantic spirit?

I typed the words out, picked up my dispatches, went over to the Central Telegraph Office and turned them in for censorship. Neither dispatch was ever cleared.

There were a few signs that Moscow was passing through a moment of high drama. More people than usual clustered around the pasted-up newspapers on the hoardings; queues gathered at the kiosks; the maids at the Metropol talked in little groups, quietly, not a word for foreign ears.

I spent the night at the telegraph office, waiting for the papers, but they had no more news. After two or three hours' sleep, I began my rounds on Thursday, March 5. Stalin had been ill, officially, since Sunday night, three and a half days. The crisis could not go on much longer. I was beginning to think that the measures to save his life were as much to prepare people for his death as to change his condition. Why had there been the long wait from Sunday night, when he was said to have suffered his attack, until 8 A.M. Wednesday, when the public announcement was made? My guess was that Stalin's "closest comrades in arms" were waiting to see how the illness was going to come out. If there was to be even a partial recovery, why say anything? Stalin would not thank his comrades for taking such authority. (I didn't know then that a few months before, he had told them that without him they could not survive. "You are blind like newborn kittens," he had said.) So they had waited, not twenty-four hours, but another twenty-four hours. When they put out that announcement at 8 A.M. Wednesday morning, *they knew what the end would be.* Stalin was dying and they wanted the country to know that and they were not now afraid that he would recover and send them to the Lubyanka cellars.

In the back of my mind was the thought that until this apparently fortuitous event, the Lubyanka cellars were where most of these good comrades had been headed.

All day March 5, I scurried about town—and waited. Members of the diplomatic corps this day went to the Foreign Office to express their sympathy over Stalin's illness. But not Jake Beam, my old friend from London, once Winant's secretary, now chargé d'affaires in Moscow. Charles Bohlen, another old friend, had been nominated as ambassador, filling the vacancy left by George Kennan. Bohlen had been given Soviet *agrément* but had not yet been confirmed by the Senate. In the interim, Beam was in charge. He was unable to join his colleagues because he had no instructions from Washington and did not dare act on his own. It appeared that John Foster Dulles was not certain whether we should act like gentlemen or make a cheap political display by omitting this conventional gesture. Dulles was a great one for meaningless rudeness. A bit later, he demonstratively refused to shake Premier Zhou Enlai's hand at Geneva.

I had my attention fixed on the Kremlin, where I presumed from the communiqués that Stalin lay dying. Not until Khrushchev's "secret speech" in February 1956 was it confirmed that Stalin died not in the Kremlin but at his country villa at Kuntsevo, called Blizhny—"the near one," to distinguish it from other, more distant villas. The fact was that for several years, Stalin had lived at Kuntsevo, commuting to the Kremlin in the swift motor convoys that I so often saw speeding along the Arbat.

We got a bulletin on Stalin Thursday afternoon. His condition was said to be markedly worse. Believing he would die before the night was out, I was determined to get a beat on the story. I decided to establish headquarters in the telegraph office and stay there until Stalin died. These were the days before transistor radios. I had a big Hallicrafters shortwave receiver (once these remarkable machines were the trademarks of CIA station chiefs). Mine was battleship gray (I had got it from a departing naval officer) and was the size and shape of a steel filing drawer. It must have weighed forty pounds. About 7 P.M., I lugged this monster to the telegraph office and set up shop. None of my colleagues had arrived. I was alone and a bit nervous about bringing in my set. No one had done this before. I hadn't been there ten minutes when two uniformed soldiers carrying bayoneted rifles appeared. Oh, Lord, I thought, I'm going to be put under arrest on the night of Stalin's death! They were grim, tough-looking. They demanded to know what kind of a machine I had there. I told them it was a radio receiver. Probably they had been told by my bête noire, Clerk Vassileva, that it was a transmitter. They ordered me to get it out immediately. Radio sets were *vospreshiate,* forbidden. I removed it with alacrity. Fortunately, my car was outside. I gave the set to my chauffeur, Dimitry Grigorievich. He would be my listening post. I tuned the set to Tass dictation speed and told him to listen for news about Stalin. If he heard something, he was to come quietly, I emphasized, quietly, into the office and whisper in my ear. I was not going to risk my scoop for anything.

I went back to the cubicle. My colleagues began to gather. We glared at each other like angry dogs. There was a new bulletin on Stalin at 8:45 P.M. He was sinking rapidly. I got that off to London, then went for a quick auto tour around the Kremlin. There were many cars in the Red Square parking area; lights gleamed from the government buildings. The flag flew at full mast over the dome of the central palace. Lots of bustle. Later I wondered about this; that trip of mine around the Kremlin occurred just twenty minutes before Stalin's official death.

Back at the telegraph office, I wrote dispatches for use in the event of Stalin's death. I listened to the midnight news broadcast. Nothing. Then I drove around the Kremlin again. Some cars were still parked outside. But many offices now were dark. At the telegraph office, I telephoned London with some of my early copy and at 3:30 A.M. I again toured central Moscow. Everything was quiet; one government limousine drove into the

Kremlin garage under the Moskva River bridge. There were three long black government limousines parked outside the Moscow City Soviet building, just a block up the street from the telegraph office. I got back to the telegraph office at five minutes to four.

A few seconds after four o'clock, my chauffeur slipped into the office and whispered in my ear. I quietly rose, my prepared cables on Stalin's death in hand, and gave them to the telegraph clerk. I also handed her my code message: "Freedman final expense account mailed last night regards Salisbury."

Before I could get back to my typewriter, bedlam burst loose. The agency men filed their flashes, shouted for telephone connections to London and dashed into telephone booths to await their calls. I had asked the operator to get me both London and Paris, but I was relying on Paris. There were only two lines normally to London and the operator automatically gave priority to the agency men. The shouting and excitement (and my code message) all went for nothing. The censors refused to pass any copy whatever. The telephone operator sat with hands folded, paying no attention to the shouting. Within a few minutes, a sleepy electrician in overalls appeared. As I watched, he ripped off the back of the telephone switchboard and yanked out the main cable. Moscow was broadcasting news of Stalin's death in a score of languages. But the Moscow correspondents could not transmit a word. I slipped outside to a pay telephone booth, put a ten-kopeck piece in the slot and called Jake Beam, waking him up at Spaso House. "He died at 9:50 P.M. last night, Jake," I said. "Thanks," Jake replied, and hung up.

I stood by until 5:30 A.M., then I went out for the fourth time that evening and toured the center of the city. All was normal. The red stars glimmered like jewels in the Kremlin towers, the Spassky bell tower chimed the hours, the traffic police in their warm uniform greatcoats and sheepskin collars stood at their posts under the brilliant lights of the central squares. The lights flashed green-amber-red, green-amber-red. There was no traffic. It was a chilly night. The streets were clean of snow, except for a light dusting earlier in the evening. Just as I returned to the telegraph office, I saw a small convoy of trucks coming down Gorky Street. I wrote more copy, turned it in and sent angry notes to the censor, demanding its release. Nothing happened.

The greatest story in the world—we had it in our hands but might as well have been manacled to the cellar walls of the Lubyanka. I almost died of frustration. The other correspondents alternately shouted, faces red, at the impassive women clerks or slumped into despondency.

One more time I walked out of the telegraph office. The golden hands of the clock in the Spassky tower had moved to six o'clock. Moscow was stirring. Buses were running. Traffic was moving. People had begun to appear. I drove down Gorky Street, around the Kremlin and through the big squares. More and more convoys of trucks were entering the heart of Moscow, mustard-green troop trucks, with soldiers sitting cross-armed in rows, twenty-two to a truck, blue-and-red-capped NKVD troops, the special troops of the Ministry of Internal Affairs, whose camps ringed Moscow in the little villages just beyond the city limits. The convoys crisscrossed the central squares. I was momentarily puzzled and wondered if a coup d'etat might be under way. I did not pursue my thought. I was hurrying back to the telegraph office to see whether the censorship was still sitting on the story. Just before eight o'clock, the dam broke, our copy cleared, telephone calls came through. While my colleagues fought over the London lines, Paris came up and I was dictating my dispatches just after midnight in New York. The story moved forward crisply and clearly. I had written in laconic terms. I did not want to give the censor any excuse for holding it up.

By the time I emerged from the telegraph office, the city was bustling. The *dvorniki,* the building porters, were putting up black rosettes and draping the buildings in red, placing black-bordered red flags in the stanchions. At the Hall of Columns, the old Noblemen's Club, workmen were stringing red and black bunting and hoisting into place an enormous gilt-framed portrait of Stalin. Here Stalin's body would lie at rest for the formal mourning, displayed in the beautiful old hall, with its white columns and crystal chandeliers, where the nobility had danced their quadrilles. Here, one by one, Stalin had brought the Old Bolsheviks—Kamenev, Zinoviev, Bukharin, Radek and the rest—put them on trial and then sent them up Lubyanka Hill to meet their end with a bullet from a Nagan pistol in the head. How apt, I thought, that Stalin would lie in rest in this hall. One way or the other, they all met their end in this glittering Romanov souvenir. The Revolution had been in power for thirty-five years and it had not yet created its own settings for the rituals of life and death.

I walked up past the Lenin Museum, once the City Duma, and entered Red Square through the opening left by the destruction of the Iberian Chapel. On the wall was now inscribed: "Religion is the opiate of the masses." I wondered. In Red Square I saw a sight I had never before seen in Moscow. A crowd of two or three thousand people stood in a cigar-shaped body opposite the Spassky Gate. They were waiting for Stalin's body to be brought out, presuming, as I did, that he had died there. Never had I seen a crowd like this collect of its own volition in Russia. In fact, it was against the law. Freedom of assembly was not among the rights guaranteed by the Stalin constitution.

I joined the throng and found it a startling experience, Stalin dead only a few hours and already people assembling on their own—no orders, no agitprop. They stood passively, not speaking, waiting. Here and there an old peasant woman sobbed a bit, the conventional symbol of mourning.

As I waited, I tried to sense the mood of the crowd. Was this a harbinger? I was not prepared to make a judgment. I did not think the people could yet absorb the fact of Stalin's death, of his absence from their life. In this I was right. Many older people went to their graves never having emerged from Stalin's penumbra. He was a true tyrant, and even in death he held the people in his granite grip.

Now the security troops were everywhere. They were moving in from all sides. Gorky Street was thick with them and traffic was trickling to an end. The autobuses halted. Truck and passenger cars disappeared. Tanks emerged at the head of Gorky Street. I could hear the rumble of their motors. No regular army troops could be seen. Just the blue-and-red-capped security men. I began to see what they were doing. They were placing a collar around the throat of Moscow, gradually moving in closer and closer, shutting off the circulation of traffic and blocking the streets with barricades of trucks and tanks. Now they began to enter Red Square, just a thin line at first, halting people from entering, then slowly but irresistibly—no force, no commands—simply advancing and pressing the crowd back, back out of the square.

I retreated into Sverdlovsk Square, past the metro station, toward the Metropol. I understood now what was happening.

Using the operational plan for traditional lying-in-state ceremonies, the NKVD was sealing off the center of the city. I had been through this many times on the occasion of other state funerals. The Metropol was within these lines and from my office I had a view of the Hall of Columns, the Moskva Hotel, past the Lenin Museum and the State Historical Museum toward the Kremlin itself.

My car happened to be within this inner circle, parked beside the Metropol. By dint of brass and patience, I was able to drive from the Metropol through Pushkin Street almost to the back entrance of the telegraph office. I did not have to run back and forth, dodge under trucks and tanks, argue with soldiers and officers, to get through the barricade, one more proof of the rule that if you are resolute, if you act with authority, gall and blarney, you can whisk through almost any security barricade.

Again and again I moved within the heart of the heart of the Moscow security zone. I sauntered into Red Square, the square sealed off, not a person there except a work detail chiseling Stalin's name above the Lenin Mausoleum in preparation for his interment there the next day, guards and soldiers all over the place. I walked up to the tomb as though I was conducting an inspection for the Central Committee, observed what was going on and walked out without a challenge by a guard. It never entered their heads that anyone would dare enter this sanctuary without authority. It was much the same when I left the Metropol early Sunday morning and made my way by foot through one barricade after another, walking with an air of authority past the soldiers huddling around their bonfires, and found that not only were Red Square and the center in the hands of security troops, but the whole inner ring, the "White Stone City," and beyond that the "garden ring" of boulevards. I walked to the Kursk railroad station, intending to take the electric train to Saltikovka and see what was happening in the countryside. I found some angry Muscovites reading a hand-lettered notice. Regular train service was running *out* of Moscow. But no trains were coming *into* Moscow. I knew that tens of thousands of Russians had clambered aboard trains to attend Lenin's funeral. This was not going to be permitted for Stalin's funeral. *No one could enter the city.* Moscow and all access to it was in control of the security forces. It suddenly struck me that Moscow was held by Lavrenti P. Beria. These were his troops, his tanks, his trucks, his guns. He held the Kremlin within his power. I was astonished. No one else knew this, I felt sure, no foreigner, none of the U.S. military attachés who spent so much time assiduously counting telegraph poles on the rail lines. They had not had the gumption or the imagination to get out into Moscow and have a look at what was happening. (When I first gave a detailed report of all this in my articles in the *Times* in the autumn of 1954, after leaving my Moscow post, the State Department and the military were amazed and, characteristically, inclined to dismiss my report as of no significance.) Alas, I could find no way of reporting this development. The censors killed every attempt, even when I praised the efficient "traffic" control of the police, the skill with which they avoided jams in the heart of the city and the special measures they had taken to handle the hundreds of thousands of mourners who were moving past Stalin's bier in the Hall of Columns, twelve abreast, day and night, in a column that I estimated would number in the millions. (I did not know then but was not surprised to learn years later from the poet Yevgeny Yevtushenko, who had witnessed it, that in an inner courtyard through which these lines snaked, something went wrong. Before the police could halt the inexorable advance of the column, twenty or thirty people had been crushed, simply squeezed down and trampled to death—not so bad a scandal as that which attended the coronation of Czar Nicholas II, when hundreds died in the throng assembled in Khodinka fields to receive the beer mugs and scarves that were the Czar's coronation gifts to his people, but the same kind of tragedy, the product of careless planning, poor police work and an unconcern for human lives.

From the first announcement of Stalin's illness, editorials stressed "vigilance," warned against "panic and disarray." I saw no signs of "panic." The theme of vigilance echoed that which had resounded so loudly as the drums beat over the Doctors' Plot. So far as I or anyone knew, the affair of the Kremlin physicians was still on the agenda. The scenario might take a few new turns, but there was no sign it had been junked, and in fact there soon appeared in the kiosks a new red-jacketed pamphlet, called "Vigilance," which cited the Doctors' Plot as the basis for today's need of vigilance.

On the surface, power seemed to have flowed smoothly to the

triumvirate of Malenkov, Beria and Molotov. Bulganin and Voroshilov were prominent, Khrushchev in the shadows. One new player turned up—Marshal Georgi K. Zhukov. He emerged from rustication as commander of troops in Odessa. Magically he was back in Moscow, deputy defense minister beside Marshal Vasilevsky, and in one of the pictures at Stalin's bier, Zhukov, Sokolovsky and Timoshenko peered out from behind Malenkov, Beria, Molotov and Company, as though they were the men who were manipulating the whole show. This picture was designed to send a message. The military, and Zhukov in particular, had played a role in the March events and would go on playing a role.

Stalin was buried on the morning of Monday, March 9, in Red Square. Three men spoke—Malenkov, Beria and Molotov. Malenkov, a middle-aged fat boy, was surprisingly appealing. He spoke beautiful, cultured Russian, his words were mild, he seemed to be promising a new, intelligent regime. Beria was ingratiating and condescending to his companions. After all, he held them in the grip of his security troops. Molotov impressed me most. His voice broke repeatedly, his face was white as paper. I jotted in my notebook: "Such sorrow in his voice!" Molotov alone of those present conveyed to me a feeling of loss. His words, as always, were dull metal. There was no poet in Molotov. I knew that his wife was in Stalin's camps. I did not know she had been in prison since 1949, that Molotov since then had been barred from Stalin's inner circle, excluded from the midnight drinking parties at Blizhny. I suspected that Stalin had marked Molotov as a target of his forthcoming phantasmagoria. Molotov knew all that. Yet his voice broke again and again, and he was close to tears as he spoke of his tyrant master—Molotov, whose nickname had been *kameny zad,* stone bottom.

At 11:50 A.M., Molotov concluded. The Red Army band of three hundred struck up Chopin's "Funeral March." The leaders, Malenkov, Beria, Molotov and the rest, descended from atop the mausoleum. The black and red coffin of Stalin rested at the portals of the tomb. There was a moment of silence. Then the hands of the Spassky clock pointed straight up. The tower bells pealed and the steel salute guns of the Kremlin sounded in counterpoint. Malenkov, Molotov, Beria and the others lifted the coffin of Stalin and carried it inside. Every factory whistle in Moscow screamed. The toll of bells halted at twelve, but the guns slammed on to thirty. The factory whistles fell silent. All over Russia, every moving vehicle halted—every train, every tram, every truck. There was total silence. As I watched, a single sparrow left the Kremlin wall and swooped over the mausoleum. Then the voice of General Sinitsin, commander of the Moscow garrison, thundered out, echoing against the gray walls of the still shuttered merchants' arcade across the square. The thousands of troops began to mark time, their leather boots raising a surf of sound. The band struck up Glinka's "Hail to the Czar" (comfortably retitled "Hail to the Russian People"). The red flag over the domed Kremlin palace slowly rose to full mast.

Notebook in hand, red press pass and passport clutched in the other, I slipped out of the stand beside Lenin's tomb, into the square jammed with marching troops, shoulder to shoulder, and running beside and against their stream of movement, I began to race to the Central Telegraph Office. I ran head up, eyes on the alert for any obstacle, moving on the flank of the troops, darting around their officers, past the State Historical Museum, out of the square, across the endless expanse of Manezhny Square, wider than three football fields, past the Moskva Hotel, shouldering my way through denser and denser concentrations of troops, on to the north side of the square, up to the great barricade of trucks that blocked the throat of Gorky Street at the National Hotel, then under the greasy truck bodies, scrambling up and over the next truck barricade, to the startled shouts of the lounging troops, down the far side, plunging like a football back through the knots of soldiers, stumbling now and panting like a hound. I raced up the incline of Gorky Street, past the shuttered vegetable shop, the shuttered antiquarian bookstore, the theater, on toward the telegraph office, encountering a truck barricade nearly three trucks high. I squirmed through and over it and staggered into Entrance 11, up the narrow flight of steps into the now deserted press cubicle, calling to the operator to put me through to London, the line coming up miraculously fast, and still panting, I told London to advise New York instantly: Stalin was buried; release my advance dispatch and new copy was coming. New York was holding the final edition until 6 A.M. for Stalin's funeral.

And so Stalin was buried in the mausoleum beside Lenin. He was dead, his era ended. Something new lay ahead. Next morning as I walked back to the Metropol in the hours before dawn, having filed my last dispatches about Stalin's funeral and the new epoch, I passed the Hall of Columns. Men were up on ladders, working under the ghostly blue of a carbon arc floodlight, taking down the sixty-foot portrait of Stalin. It slipped as it came down, and canted into the street at an oblique angle.

"Careful there," one shouted.

"Nichevo," another said. "Never mind. They'll not be needing this one again."

36 | Stalin's Legacy

When Stalin died, the world began to change so fast it made my head spin. It changed so fast that even today, after thirty years, many people still cannot believe it. When they think of Russia they think of Stalin. The mark that his devil's genius imprinted on the face of Russia is deep as or deeper than that of Lenin and of the Bolshevik coup which I celebrated on that November afternoon in 1917 on Royalston Avenue.

Scrub as they will, Stalin's successors cannot erase the stains; in part, because they have never been totally frank, totally honest, and that, in turn, at least in the early days, stemmed from the fact that every one of them had dipped his hands in the blood. Stalin made them all sign the execution lists.

Stalin's tyranny came to be worse than any Russia had known, but, as I noted in my journal of July 6, 1953, he was in the tradition of Ivan the Terrible, Peter the Great (for all his progressive reforms), Catherine the Great (for all hers), and of Nicholas I, Iron Nicholas, who said on his deathbed: "My successor [his liberal son, Alexander II] must do as he pleases, but for myself, I cannot change." I think I got this emphasis right. Stalin was the colossus of evil, but he presided over a land that long had been ruled by evil colossi.

No one in the United States, and particularly no one in the State Department of John Foster Dulles, seemed to believe that Stalin was dead. I think Dulles refused to accept Stalin's death in a political sense because if he did so he would lose his raison d'être. His career was dedicated to a single purpose: the destruction of Stalin and Stalin's Communism. Dulles had become possessed by a single-minded devotion to this end. For this Calvinist, Stalinism had replaced popery, and his mind was not capable of absorbing the fact that change in Moscow was possible. Only in 1959, when he was dying of cancer, did this frosty didact mellow a bit. He had an almost sentimental meeting with Anastas Mikoyan, who had come to America as advance man for Nikita Khrushchev. Of course, Dulles did not admit that he had ever been wrong, but he managed to convey to the shrewd Armenian that at long last he had withdrawn his anathema and given his blessing to the prospect of détente.

In this spring of 1953, Stalin's name had vanished. Before March 5, it often appeared one hundred fifty or two hundred times on page one of *Pravda*. From April 1, it was gone. I found it only once or twice a week, usually as one half of the adjective "Leninist-Stalinist." What soon would be known as the "cult of Stalin" had come to a screaming halt. Only three weeks after Stalin's death, his heirs were telling the world that Russia had embarked on a new course which in every way was to be as different as possible from Stalin's. They called in the British and Americans and told them they didn't have to move out of their embassies. The British said thank you, we had never planned to move; the Americans, with bureaucratic flaccidity, said they preferred to abandon their watchpost overlooking the Kremlin and move into the new quarters being built for them on Garden Boulevard, originally designed for KGB personnel and complete with built-in bugging systems, which would not be fully eradicated for years. The Foreign Office told the Americans, the British and the French that they could have exit visas long denied—for Russian wives of American correspondents (Juli Whitney among them); for elderly French governesses; for George Bundock, the prisoner in the basement of the British embassy; for dispossessed Greek businessmen, and for many others. The Press Department invited me in to talk about changes in the censorship and issued visas for a dozen visiting American newsmen. Travel restrictions were lifted. I was free to go at will almost anywhere, except for border areas and some Urals and Siberian industrial centers. (But the forty-kilometer limit on travel out of Moscow was retained.) The Korean armistice was signed; the Russians proposed talks with the West on a dozen impacted questions.

The Doctors' Plot was thrown out the window by mid-April and amnesty granted to tens of thousands of prisoners in the labor camps (but no politicals). The ex-cons descended on Moscow like vultures. Cavalry patrols had to be put on the streets, with orders to shoot at sight. I was up every night, dictating hot stories to London until 5 or 6 A.M., running back and forth through dark Moscow streets (at long last I moved out of the Metropol into an apartment on the Sadovaya Samotechnaya); the descent of the convicts was no esoteric matter for me. I was glad to see the cavalry patrols as I raced to the telegraph office.

It was a time of extraordinary excitement, of fulfillment. The agonizing years of 1949, 1950, 1951, 1952 had been, I now realized, a preparation, giving me the background, the intimate familiarity with Moscow, that enabled me to handle this avalanche of news. I wrote to Cy Sulzberger in early April, employing the metaphor that Ilya Ehrenburg later would attach to the epoch in his book *Rasputitsa,* "The Thaw":

"It resembles most, I think, the upper Mississippi River as I knew it as a boy when spring would come. The upper river was used for timber operations and all winter the logs would accumulate in the woods and the tributaries and in the river itself. Then spring would suddenly come, fast as it does in that northern latitude, and the ice would begin to move out with explosive roars that could be heard for miles. First the ice would break up and then the logs would start moving in a twisting tangled mass, end over end, downstream into the constantly clearer water, a dangerous, exciting and spectacular performance.

"Something like that *seems* to be happening. When a giant has been tied hand and foot for as many years as this country has and suddenly starts to awaken—the results are bound to be sensational."

It was not only John Foster Dulles who could not recognize what was happening. The Russian people could not. They did not dance in the streets. They were very cautious. But they did begin for the first time since the early revolutionary days to *stroll* in Red Square. They wandered around like sightseers from the moon. They clustered at the mausoleum with its newly chiseled letters: "Lenin/Stalin"; they watched the honor guard march out of the Spassky Gate with high goose steps, boots ringing on the granite paving, to stand duty at the tomb; they listened to the peal of the Spassky chimes, they gawked at St. Basil's, and when spring grew stronger, young people, arms around each other's waists, walked beside the Kremlin wall. Overnight Red Square had lost its threat and become a people's promenade.

But all this was tentative. Not until Beria's arrest did the Russians whom I knew and talked to (and this gradually became possible) begin hesitantly to toy with the idea that change was not only possible but was happening here and now.

On Saturday evening, June 27, 1953, I made my nightly pil-
grimage to the telegraph office. As usual, the papers were late.
Not until 5 A.M., Sunday, June 28, did a sleepy woman messenger
bring them in. At first I saw no reason for their lateness. The
news was trivial. That evening, the government had gone in a
body to the Bolshoi Theater to see a performance of the new
opera *The Decembrists.* That was hardly newsworthy. True, the
Decembrists, the young officers who had revolted in the 1820s,
had been a slightly sensitive subject in Stalin's day. He didn't
care for talk of revolution; he had told Zhdanov in 1934 that he
saw no need for publishing anything more about the Narodny
Voltsy, the fighting arm of the Socialist Revolutionaries. He
thought publicity about revolutionary plots and assassination
might put ideas into people's heads. Certainly an opera about the
Dekabristi was nothing to delay the newspapers by several hours.
My eye ran idly through the names of those who attended the
performance. Then I read the list again and sat down at my typewriter. This had been no casual social event. All the members of
government were there—except Beria. This was big news. Beria
was out! I had no doubt of it. But how to get the news through
the censor? I used my customary low-key approach. I simply reported the opera premiere and the members of government who
attended, adding one line—that Beria was absent. Then I sent
the item again. Each time, the censor deleted the line about
Beria. It was 6:30 Sunday morning in Moscow when I dictated
this little bombshell (minus the Beria line) to London—10:30
P.M. Saturday night in New York.

I thought of the block-long city room on Forty-third Street.
Saturday night, editors eager to be off, substitutes sitting in. It
was too much to expect that anyone would understand my Kremlin social note without my finger pointing to Beria's absence. I
would try again Sunday afternoon. That might draw some attention. But I had no luck. Sunday and every day thereafter, the
censor stopped all items about the Bolshoi performance; not a
snippet about Beria was allowed to pass. This was the same as
confirming the rumor. Moscow boomed with talk: Beria had been
arrested. High KGB officers had been seen rushing to their
apartments, stripping off their uniforms and vanishing. Some
people swore they had seen black smoke issuing from the inciner-
ators of the Lubyanka. Several young American embassy men
had seen tanks moving along the Garden Boulevard on the Sat-

urday of the Bolshoi performance. They swung into Kachalov
Street, where Beria lived in a three-story house set back a bit
from the street, surrounded by a high wall painted dullish green.
What that may have been about I still don't know.

No one was more interested in the Beria affair than Charles
("Chip") Bohlen. He had come into Moscow April 11 after a
nasty ordeal at the hands of the McCarthyites, who tried in the
Senate to block his confirmation as ambassador to Moscow.

It was a dirty piece of business and a good deal rougher than
Chip later would present it in his memoirs. Bohlen, like Kennan,
was one of the original band of State Department men trained in
the 1920s for ultimate service in Moscow. It would have been
hard to find men more different in temperament yet so equally
dedicated to the cause of understanding Russia than Kennan and
Bohlen. There was no one with whom I would rather have spent
an evening than Bohlen, with his stream of wild, woolly, witty
stories about the high and mighty, the frailties of a de Gaulle, an
Eisenhower, a Churchill. Yet he was a man with deep devotion to
the diplomacy of Roosevelt, George Marshall, Averell Harriman
and the great professionals. Moscow was his habitat as a specialist, but Paris was the city of his dreams. Nothing was more fitting than that he should have concluded his career under
Kennedy in Paris.

Eisenhower wanted Bohlen in Moscow. Dulles did too, up to a
point—the point of going against Joe McCarthy and the far-
right Republicans. Bohlen was nominated for Moscow, but the
enthusiasm displayed by Dulles in defending him was tepid. One
victim of the fight was Charles Thayer, Chip's brother-in-law, as
shrewd and witty a man as graced the foreign service, another of
those who had been in on the creation of the American embassy
in Moscow. Thayer resigned from the service rather than put his
family through the strain and stain of a lurid security hearing.
Chip fought his own case against McCarthy and a so-called security specialist called Scott McLeod, whom Dulles had brought
into the Department. Though Bohlen won a 10-0 vote of confidence in the Senate Foreign Relations Committee and a 74-13
affirmation in the Senate, he was bruised, shaken and spooked.
He got to Moscow at the precise moment that Kennan had predicted—the moment when basic Soviet policy would change—but

Bohlen hardly dared report this to the McCarthy-haunted State Department.

There were urgent questions to tackle: What had happened to Stalin? Had he died a natural death? Had his comrades killed him? What did this mean in policy terms? Into whose hands was power flowing? Were there real changes or just face-lifting? Dulles kept hoping for the outbreak of civil war or a bloody battle among the Kremlin survivors. He had given Bohlen no real brief. Like Kirk and Kennan, Bohlen was not supposed to *do* anything, no negotiations; just find out what the bastards are doing over there.

I used to wander into Bohlen's office in the new U.S. embassy building on Chaikovsky Boulevard in the morning and find him, feet up on his desk, reading the Moscow papers (there were eight dailies, virtual carbon copies of each other). He didn't have a strong staff. But he didn't need one. He was his own staff. He delighted in arguing with the four or five U.S. correspondents and playing poker with them on Sunday nights. Not much of the flavor of this got back to Washington.

"I made up my mind," he told me one morning. "I'm not going to give those bastards a line to hang me on. If I have something to say, I'll go back and tell it to Dulles and Ike face to face."

It was just too dangerous, he said, to put things down on paper. There were people in the Department scanning every line he wrote, looking for something on which to bring charges against him. I couldn't believe it was that bad in Washington. "It is," he said, clamping his jaws with that stubborn look he had, anger in his very blue eyes. Possibly Chip was a little paranoid, but his reactions bore the flavor of the times. Dulles had dismissed Kennan. He had taken Bohlen for Moscow because Ike wanted him. Ike liked Chip's stories, liked to play golf with him, liked to drink with him. None of this qualified Bohlen in Dulles's opinion. Dulles didn't like stories, golf or drink. He would tolerate Bohlen in Moscow; once he got there, however, Dulles would not do one more thing for him.

Chip thought he could work through it. He would fly back to Washington frequently, put it to Dulles directly, and then go over to the White House for a cozy session and give Ike the feel of things. It didn't turn out that way. Chip didn't get back to Washington that often, and when he did, he seldom had more than thirty minutes with Dulles. He didn't have a good talk with Eisenhower during four years in Moscow. If he saw the President, it was just a five- or ten-minute chat: how is the family, don't let the bastards get you down; nothing of substance. Sometimes Ike didn't even see him. He seemed to have no interest in the tales Bohlen wanted to tell about the new crowd in Moscow. Though not surprised at Dulles, Bohlen was shocked and bitter at Ike. Only a little of this comes through in his memoirs, but he let his hair down at dinners we had each time he came back to Washington. We—a few of his old friends among the correspondents—would spend the evening listening to his stories and ask him what was going to happen next—just the kind of evening he should have had with Dulles and Ike. He got some of his feelings about Foster off his chest on those occasions. Gradually, of course, he loosened up in his reporting to the Department and made some guarded recommendations; even so, relations with Dulles stayed bristly. After Eisenhower's victory in 1956, Dulles tried to squeeze Bohlen out of the foreign service. He brought his Moscow assignment to an end and could find no other suitable one for him. Post after post went to other men. Bohlen was on the verge of forced retirement. Some of his friends, myself included, thought he should quit. At the last possible date, Dulles offered Bohlen Siberia—that is, Manila. A post less suited to his talents could not have been imagined, yet he took it, more to protect his pension than for any other reason. I wrote him in Manila, telling him that since there was nothing to do there, why didn't he spend his time writing his memoirs? I could think of no man who had been present on more historic occasions and privy to such inside knowledge. Not until he finally wrote his memoirs, too many years later, when he was struggling with the cancer that took his life, did I learn that when Bohlen was relieved in Moscow, Dulles said he was doing it "knowing of your desire to take up writing as a profession." Bohlen was not a good writer. A great reporter, a raconteur par excellence, he did not like the discipline of writing. He preferred the social scene and, alas, his memoirs blur the sharp edges of Dulles's shabby conduct. Nor does Bohlen's account of the Moscow days catch the bold, boisterous zest with which he watched Stalin's pupils struggling to free themselves—and Russia—from the python coils in which Stalin had entangled them.

Bohlen did not get very far in resolving the events that led to Stalin's death. No one did until Khrushchev made his "secret speech" in 1956, but I was able to solve most of the mysteries about the Doctors' Plot and, in a sense, that was the Rosetta stone to other mysteries.

Once Stalin had died, I could see that Beria had been his number one target and that Beria's position had been almost destroyed by March 5. In the weeks after Stalin's death, Beria was everywhere—first in Georgia, then in Belorussia, the Ukraine, Central Asia. Everywhere, he put new security chiefs into office, new provincial bosses. He was getting rid of men his enemies had appointed and doing his own empire building. In Georgia, all those whose installation he had overseen in the spring of 1951 were arrested and Beria intimates like Dekanozov appointed.

When Beria was arrested, in June 1953, it was apparent that the rest of the leadership was acting to prevent his taking over the country. I was certain that the sudden eruption of rioting in East Berlin bore a relationship to Beria's fall and speculated on it at the time, although I could not quite figure out the connection. Finally, in a long rambling speech on March 8, 1963, Khrushchev confirmed the connection. Beria and Malenkov, he said, had proposed the liquidation of the German Communist regime. In an analysis for the *Times,* I said that the 1953 proposal was identical with that which Stalin had put forward in his conversations with Pieck and Grotewohl in the winter of 1952.

I think the evidence is strong that Malenkov and Beria, like Stalin before them, were prepared to abandon East Germany as the price for resolution of the conflict with the West. Like Stalin, they felt that reunification was a small price to pay for ending the cold war. The evidence, I believe, strongly supports the view that *twice* within eighteen months in 1953–54, Moscow was ready to give up on Germany and let their fellow Communists sink or swim in a unified Federal Republic, no doubt hoping that once the dust had settled, the German Communists might make a comeback.

Beria may have been in East Germany at the time of the Berlin riots. Khrushchev said that Beria was absent from Moscow in late June and that he returned only after he had twice been invited to attend a Politburo meeting that would deal with urgent "personnel questions." The "personnel" involved was, of course, himself.

Did Khrushchev, Malenkov and the others shoot Beria out of hand? Dozens of rumors arose after his arrest, stories of how he had come to the Kremlin not knowing what was happening, had been denounced and then, as he tried to leave the room, shot down. Some said Khrushchev pulled the trigger, others that it was Marshal Zhukov or some army men. The stories were melodramatic and gory, Beria dying on the Kremlin floor, his diseased blood staining the Kremlin carpet.

I did not believe those tales then and I do not now. Obviously, the army stood by in case Beria tried to rally his security troops, but I did not think Beria had been rubbed out gangster-style. My conviction was strengthened by an odd incident at the November 7, 1953, holiday reception at Spiridonovka House. For the first time since World War II, the Soviet leaders met on friendly terms with the Americans. Toasts were drunk. Bohlen offered one to peace "and justice." Marshal Zhukov rose in his turn. He said he wanted to support the toast of the American ambassador to "justice." This seemed to displease Molotov, and Mikoyan said sharply, "Offer a toast of your own." Bohlen thought he understood what underlay the marshal's words. Beria and his gang had been arrested at the end of June. It was now November. Five months had passed and their fate had not been resolved. In his memoirs, Bohlen said he didn't know what Zhukov meant, but at the time he had no doubt. Within a few weeks, on Christmas Eve, it was announced that Beria and his associates, including Dekanozov, had been tried, convicted and shot. A bit later, a similar announcement was made regarding Beria's associates in Georgia. In all, four and possibly more trials of the security chiefs were held—that of Beria and his top aides in Moscow; that of the Georgian apparatus in Tbilisi; that of Abakumov and others in Leningrad in December 1954, where they were charged with guilt in the Leningrad Affair (in 1957, Khrushchev and Marshal Zhukov in public addresses in Leningrad blamed Malenkov as well as Beria for this); and that, in Baku, of another group of Beria adherents, who were shot.

Though closed, these trials were not perfunctory. Witnesses were called to testify. The survivors of Beria's victims came forward to offer their personal accusations. Only after such dramatic spectacles was the verdict pronounced and the accused handed over for execution. The judge who headed the court that tried Beria was Marshal Konev, a symbol of the army's role.

Beria, I have been told, fell to his knees before Konev and begged for his life. His plea was spurned and he was dragged in a state of collapse to the execution chamber. Five days after the Christmas announcement of Beria's execution, a two-paragraph item in *Pravda* reported that a statue to Zhukov was being erected in his birthplace, the village of Strelkovka in Kaluga province. "Justice" had been done.

But what of Stalin's death? Had this been accomplished by Beria? Was it natural? Had there been earlier attempts on Stalin's life? Was this why he was paranoid about the Kremlin doctors?

I was convinced from the beginning that there had been no Doctors' Plot; that it was a contrivance. The new leadership was quick enough to overturn the allegations and announce the innocence of the doctors.

But what lay beyond that? I had demonstrated to my own satisfaction before Stalin's death that all or almost all of the Politburo was to be wiped out. If I could put this together, surely the intended victims could. Had they stood by like "blind kittens" or had they taken matters into their hands?

Here there would be no answer until Khrushchev's "secret speech." Back in the United States when the Twentieth Party Congress met in February 1956, I heard rumors that "something big" was going to happen.

Before the congress met, there had been a gathering of historians in Moscow to discuss the revision of Soviet history in order to rehabilitate the victims of the purges and correct Stalin's distortions of the record. At the congress, the tempo of criticism quickened. Mikoyan made a public attack and offered a roll call of Stalin's victims. Khrushchev spoke in the same vein. By the time the session ended, on February 24, I had written a series of interpretive articles: "Soviet History Purge," "Collective Leadership," "The Decline of Stalin" and "End of the Stalin Cult." Though I had been away from Moscow for fifteen months, I had sources in Washington and elsewhere and I could telephone Moscow direct with considerable freedom.

The end of the Twentieth Party Congress did not halt the rumors. It stimulated them. Chip Bohlen heard in Moscow on March 10 that Khrushchev had made a secret speech at the end of the congress. Ralph Parker was the source of his information.

Bohlen was unable to get official confirmation, but soon reports were circulating widely in Moscow. In New York, I heard of the speech on March 14 or 15 and broke the story on page one of the *Times* on March 16, under the headline: "Secret Khrushchev Talk on Stalin 'Phobia' Related." I had almost all the main points: the talk had been given February 24–25 over a period of several hours, at a closed session from which foreign delegates were excluded; Khrushchev called Stalin "not himself" and said he was subject to phobias about the treachery of his associates; Khrushchev declared the case against the Red Army commander, Marshal Tukachevsky, and other high commanders a falsification; he said Russia had been on the verge of disaster in 1941 due to Stalin's military mistakes; that Stalin kept members of the Politburo in ignorance of many of his acts; that older members of the Politburo were threatened with extermination; that Nikolai A. Voznesensky and most of the Leningrad leadership had been executed in the Leningrad Affair of 1949–50. Day by day, I was able to reveal more and more details of the speech, including the fact that it had touched off violent rioting in Georgia, Stalin's homeland.

There was no major segment of the "secret speech" that I was not able to report in the ensuing weeks—Khrushchev's distribution of Lenin's 1923 "Testament" warning the party against Stalin, details of Stalin's plots against the Jews, his scheme to exile them to Siberia, his case against the Jewish Anti-Fascist Committee, the charge that the Leningrad leaders plotted to bring Russia's capital back to Leningrad, and the rest.

The materials flowed in almost more rapidly than I could publish them—from diplomatic and government contacts, from returning travelers to Moscow. Sometimes Welles Hangen, then the *Times* correspondent in Moscow, was able to confirm a report that I had heard in New York, although he was not permitted to transmit it himself. It was an extraordinary period and it seemed to me that the whole inner history of thirty years of Bolshevism was tumbling into my hands.

I was trying, of course, to obtain the text of the "secret speech." I called friends in the State Department, besieged the CIA, foreign embassies and contacts in Europe—to no avail. Sydney Gruson, then a *Times* correspondent in Eastern Europe, shuttling between Warsaw and Prague, tried in both capitals.

He almost got a copy in Warsaw. Welles Hangen tried his best in Moscow. No luck.

Khrushchev disclosed in his memoirs in 1970 that copies of his speech were given to Eastern European Communist leaders and to a few other important Communist parties. Boleslaw Bierut, the Polish Communist chief, died in Moscow at the end of the Twentieth Party Congress. Khrushchev said that in the confusion attending his death, the Poles made copies of the speech and this was how the CIA got the text.

Whether Khrushchev's version is accurate or not, the CIA did, in fact, obtain the speech sometime in May and the clues indicate Warsaw as the source, although the agency has never disclosed this. It is known that a member of the French embassy in Warsaw was shown a copy by a Polish Foreign Office man and permitted to read it and take notes. The summary included many direct quotations. It was sent to the Quai d'Orsay, which leaked it to *France-Soir* and then to Cy Sulzberger. Cy wrote three columns on the speech and sent them to the *Times* for use beginning June 4.

Unknown to myself or Cy, a row had broken out within the CIA and the State Department over what to do with the Khrushchev text. James Angleton, the famous CIA counterespionage chief, strongly opposed putting it out. He wanted to use it to sow dissension and confusion among Communist ranks. He also wanted to "improve" it a bit. Curiously enough, Bohlen, when a copy was transmitted to Moscow for his consideration, also opposed its release. Frank Wisner, the legendary CIA operator who ultimately committed suicide and who had a hand in getting the copy, took the same view: no publication.

The decision to publish, as I learned much later, was made against the advice of these specialists by Allen Dulles, chief of the CIA, and his brother, Foster. Ray Cline, then a young CIA specialist, told me he was with the CIA director on Saturday afternoon, June 2, when Allen made the decision to go public. He simply telephoned Foster and the deed was done. The next call was to *The New York Times*. I got to Washington that weekend and wrote a preview of the text for the Monday paper, June 4. I said the State Department would be making Khrushchev's speech public the next day. On Tuesday, June 5, the text, four pages of Khrushchev and another of stories, was published by the *Times* and the lid was off. The State Department insinuated that the text came from Belgrade. The CIA text probably came from the same Polish Foreign Office man who let the French diplomat sneak a look at it. Moscow never released the text, but Khrushchev made only a perfunctory denial of its accuracy. The world, Communist and non-Communist, accepted it for what it was—genuine with the possible deletion of a few extremely sensitive passages, most of which filtered out in the next few months.

Khrushchev's action was an event of world consequence. He designed it to bring an end once and for all to Stalin and Stalinism, and to solidify his position as Russia's leader. He failed in his objectives and eventually, it could be said, instead of Khrushchev laying the ghost of Stalin, the ghost laid Khrushchev, playing a major role in his downfall.

So how, after all, did Stalin die? I do not believe Stalin was fatally poisoned by his colleagues. He was so afraid of poison he always made one of them eat the shashlik or taste the chicken tabak before he did. I do not believe they shot him. After all, Svetlana was present during his last thirty-six hours. But they did act—all of them—in a peculiar way during his last days and I think the possibility that a drug may have been given Stalin cannot be excluded.

Many of the men who had been important in his entourage had vanished not long before he died. One was his personal bodyguard, Vlasik. Another was his ghastly personal secretary, Poskrebyshev. In 1953, I envisioned him hovering over Stalin and manipulating the strings of the plot against the Politburo. I know now that he did not possess the courage to play an important role and that Stalin, about two months before his death, decided he was a security risk. If Stalin had not died, Poskrebyshev probably would have been shot.

The commandant of the Kremlin had died suddenly. The Georgian household servants whom Beria had installed had been replaced. The doctors who looked after Stalin for many years had been arrested in the Doctors' Plot. Vasily Stalin had been banished from his father's circle. Svetlana hardly saw her father. He hadn't permitted Molotov in his private circle since 1949. He had decided that Voroshilov, his drinking companion since the days in 1919 at Tsaritsyn (later Stalingrad; now Volgograd), had been for years a "British spy." Mikoyan was on the blacklist. None of the new members of the Presidium, elected in October 1952, were permitted in the charmed circle, now shrunken to Malenkov, Beria, Bulganin, Khrushchev and, occasionally, Ignatiev, the new security chief.

Stalin had mixed all the cards at the Nineteenth Party Congress in October. No one could figure how this new devil's device might work out. Stalin had done something else that was not known publicly. Twice he proposed to the Central Committee that he resign. He gave up the title General Secretary, which he had held since 1922, and assumed the simple title Secretary. What was this about? It sounds as though he was preparing for an orderly transition, but if so, nothing of the kind occurred. If he left a will or designated a successor, it has never come to light.

Did the quartet of Malenkov, Beria, Khrushchev and Bulganin speed Stalin out of the world? After Khrushchev's "secret speech," melodramatic tales circulated: of Voroshilov speaking up, hurling his party card on the table before Stalin; of Kaganovich and Molotov turning on their master; of the whole Politburo in rebellion against Stalin's plan to purge all Russia's Jews and send them to Siberia. (It later was said that plans were so far advanced that Ilya Ehrenburg had been picked to deliver a petition to Stalin *begging him* to permit Russia's Jews to emigrate to Siberia, to protect them against the just anger of the noble Russian people at their crimes!)

Several variants of Stalin's last hours were offered by Khrushchev, and I have come to believe that a stormy confrontation may have played a role in Stalin's death.

Khrushchev never varied from one element in his story: the four—that is, himself, Malenkov, Beria and Bulganin—spent Saturday evening and the early hours of February 28–March 1 with Stalin. They saw a movie at the Kremlin, then went to the Blizhny dacha and drank until five or six Sunday morning. He said Stalin was in good health, good spirits and quite drunk. Khrushchev expected a call from Stalin early Sunday evening, inviting him back to Blizhny. This was the usual custom. Stalin, particularly since he had sent so many servitors away and had killed so many of his former friends and most of his family, was a lonely man. His Politburo group had to keep him company. The Sunday call never came. Khrushchev (probably worried) ate dinner at home. Late in the evening (Khrushchev was already in bed), Malenkov telephoned and said the security detail at

Blizhny was worried about Stalin. He hadn't called for his dinner, as he usually did, about 11 P.M. Malenkov had telephoned Beria and Bulganin and proposed that they meet at the villa as soon as possible.

By the time the four assembled, the security men had sent an elderly servant, Matryona Petrovna, into Stalin's room. She found him asleep on the floor. The guards went in, lifted him up and put him on the couch on which he slept, in the same room where he worked, ate and held his drinking parties.

It must have been 1 A.M. or later when this occurred. Khrushchev phrases the episode delicately. They didn't think it was "suitable" to make their presence known when Stalin was in "such an unpresentable condition." By which I suppose he meant that Stalin was still drunk and should not be disturbed. They went back to their homes. A few hours later, they were hurrying back to the villa. The guards had sent Matryona Petrovna in again. Stalin was still sleeping soundly, but it was an "unusual kind of sleep"—the sleep of death, as it turned out.

They assembled some doctors, who found Stalin semiparalyzed, in a coma, apparently having suffered a stroke. They called in Voroshilov and Kaganovich, both in the "bureau" of the Presidium but no longer on Stalin's drinking list. Khrushchev gives no time for this, but it must have been early morning, Monday, March 2. He offers no further instructive details on Stalin's illness. Stalin's daughter, Svetlana, and her brother, Vasily, were summoned to the dacha sometime on Monday, perhaps in early afternoon. Svetlana stayed through to the end, at 9:50 P.M., March 5, and remained. Vasily, an alcoholic, arrived drunk, got drunker, accused everyone of killing his father and wandered off to the servants' quarters.

By the time Svetlana got to the dacha, Mikoyan and many other high officials had arrived. Molotov had not. He was not permitted into Stalin's presence in the last hours.

A few minutes after Stalin died, the leaders left Blizhny, Beria at their head, and made for the Central Committee Building in Staraya Ploshad, diagonally across from the Lubyanka, where the Central Committee was awaiting the news. (It never occurred to me that Stalin was not in the Kremlin. No wonder I saw so few signs of anything unusual going on in Moscow; I didn't know where to look.)

This touches one of the mysteries of Stalin's death: why the communiqués said he was stricken at his residence "in Moscow," which was generally interpreted to mean the Kremlin. I think security had something to do with this, security and the legend that Stalin lived and worked in the Kremlin, just as Lenin had done. I once read a story in a Moscow magazine about Stalin's Kremlin living quarters being redecorated in his absence with a lot of museum furniture and how angry Stalin got when he discovered what had been done. He had them moved out and his simple old table, desk and couch brought back. As if anyone in Russia would dare change a doormat in Stalin's quarters without his orders!

Then there was the business of the delay in public announcement of the illness. I think my original suspicion was right. They made no announcement until they were certain Stalin was going to die. They could not afford to have him regain consciousness and wipe them out for acting without his sanction.

But I am not so sure about the curious conduct on Sunday evening, the guards calling in the quartet after midnight or whatever time it was. True, they had been drinking with Stalin until five or six the morning before. True, it probably was not unusual for Stalin to get heavily intoxicated and sleep it off. But for the quartet to come to the villa, have the guards put the unconscious Stalin back on his couch, go away, and then return considerably later in Monday morning's early hours seems peculiar.

Did they think, as Khrushchev suggests, that the old man was just drunk again? Or did they hope something more serious was wrong and that if they let him go a few more hours they might be rid of him for all time? In fact, did they *know* something more serious was wrong?

Was the Saturday evening before as jolly, as benign, as Khrushchev suggested in his memoirs, or had some great row finally broken out? They knew, according to one of Khrushchev's accounts, that the doctors' case would come to trial in mid-March. The doctors had been under arrest—as well as many more potential defendants—since long before the Nineteenth Party Congress in October. Were they prepared to let events move forward and engulf their other old comrades and two or three of the inner circle? Of the four men in the inner circle, three—Malenkov, Beria and Khrushchev—were as crafty, as skilled, as resourceful figures as could be found in Russia. Each had been on the thin edge of disaster and death at Stalin's hands. Bulganin was a heavy drinker, a lightweight, not in their class. Did Malenkov, Beria and Khrushchev march down the path nearer and nearer to the end without trying for the big casino? I think not. And I know that my suspicions are shared by some who were close to Stalin's last Politburo. I believe—and I am not alone in this—that one or all of them on that weekend of February 28–March 1, when Stalin began his long sleep at the Blizhny dacha, played something more than a spectator's role. I never expect to adduce explicit proof. But I keep thinking of that powerful drug which, according to Nosenko, the KGB wanted to give me, the one Stalin is said to have refused to approve because there was no guarantee that it could not be lethal, the drug that induced paralysis which was supposed to be temporary, lasting perhaps a few months, and then disappearing. A small dose of this, slipped into Stalin's glass sometime as the hours were nearing 5 A.M., when his guard was relaxed and he did not think to have one of the quartet sip first, would have settled the Kremlin accounts. I think it could have, may have, in fact probably did.

37 | Russia Re-Viewed

I didn't give up my Moscow assignment until September 1954, when Clifton Daniel, my wartime friend in London, later to be managing editor of *The New York Times,* flew in to replace me, having taken a crash course in Russian at Columbia University.

I had come back to New York in autumn 1953, at what I had expected would be the conclusion of my Moscow assignment. I found that the *Times* had no one ready for Moscow and Arthur Sulzberger persuaded me to return for a few more months. I hated the idea, but he turned out to be right. It was during this brief interlude in the U.S.A. that I met Iphigene Sulzberger, daughter of Adolph S. Ochs, wife of Arthur Sulzberger, and for the first time got to know this remarkable woman who would become a friend and an object of boundless admiration for the rest of my life.

The new Russia proved to be a cakewalk for me, with page one stories almost every day. I traveled to the remote depths of the country—Siberian hellholes like Birobidzhan (the "Jewish Autonomous Region," where Stalin's anti-Semitism had left deep wounds); Yakutsk within the Arctic Circle, where I saw the wooden stockades of the labor camp (still active) where Karl Radek perished; the big military city of Chita and beautiful Lake Baikal.

Where didn't I go in 1953 and 1954? Down the Volga, a trip into the nineteenth century, with Russians in linen dusters, carrying binoculars and guidebooks and viewing the "sights," when they were not playing whist like characters out of Chekhov; Lenin's home town of Simbirsk, so shabby my steamboat companions talked of writing to the Central Committee: muddy cobblestone streets, droshkies, peeling paint, flies, Lenin's old house on the bluffs as dingy as when his father was a traveling school inspector in the 1870s.

I must have taken a couple of thousand photographs. These were virgin lands I was exploring; no foreigner had been in many of these places for a generation or more. The *Times* did something it had never before done. It ran double-truck—two-page—

layouts of my photographs of Siberia and again of Central Asia. The *Times Magazine* published articles and picture spreads, splashy stuff after my years as a hermit correspondent. I was arrested, reprimanded or held in custody by the police so many times for taking pictures I lost track of the count, less and less often in Moscow but more and more frequently in the remote countryside. Once I was arrested in a stony mountain village on the back road from Alma-Ata to Frunze, capital of Kirgizia. I didn't even know the name of the place and it must have been four thousand miles from Moscow, close to the Chinese frontier. Two Georgian students were traveling on the bus (a truck with wooden planks for seats) and they obtained my release. "How did you do it?" I asked. One of them smiled: "We told them you were an important foreigner. And I happened to mention that my father is an official in the Interior Ministry."

One Sunday I rang the great iron bell that signaled the start of trotting races at the track in Barnaul, a backwater town in western Siberia, and I spent Troitsa, Trinity Sunday, in a Siberian village where every man, woman and child over the age of twelve was staggering or falling-down drunk. I sometimes found a dozen plainclothes *shpiks* following me, as in Khabarovsk, capital of the still flourishing slave empire of the "industrial" department of the Interior Ministry, located on the Amur River across from China.

In Moscow, the new Kremlin leaders were beginning to make themselves known, attending diplomatic receptions, mixing with foreigners. I grew familiar with the sight and sound of Malenkov, Khrushchev, Mikoyan, Bulganin, Kaganovich, Voroshilov and the others who for years had been just a frieze atop Lenin's tomb at the Red Square celebrations.

For journalistic purposes I had all of Russia as my exclusive fief. There were few correspondents in Moscow, most of them agency men tied to the city, all of them new. I was the only old hand. It was like being a kid in a toyshop. There were so many good stories I could hardly go to bed at night.

During my brief stay in New York in 1953, I had signed a contract with Harper's for a book, and I had it half written before I got back to New York in September 1954. I had sent back, too, the start of a series of fourteen articles for the *Times*. The title, "Russia Re-Viewed," was suggested by Arthur Sulzberger, who took a personal hand in editing and promoting my series. I got a room at the Algonquin and finished my articles on the old Remington portable I had carried since 1942, when UP issued it to me. I had never given it back and I'm still writing on it.

I remember coming out of the Algonquin one evening and seeing a *Times* truck rumble by. On its sides were plastered broadsheets promoting "Russia Re-Viewed," starting Sunday, September 19, 1954. There was a huge photograph of me in my caracul hat. I was so excited I could hardly see straight. I'd made it!

It is difficult to recapture today the excitement the series caused. Into it I poured the enormous backlog of information that had piled up during the ice jam of the Stalin censorship. I didn't have it all, but—until Khrushchev's "secret speech"—it would be the best thing going on what had been happening in Stalin's Russia. Sometimes people would ask why I had not written these stories at the time they happened, sneaked them somehow past the censorship. The answer was simple. I knew a great deal now about what had been going on in Russia during Stalin's last years, but until he died, it had been impossible to put the puzzle together. Even today, nearly thirty years later, some of the pieces are still missing. Russia had taught me to beware of instant headlines. The truth, whatever it might be, was as elusive as *Rashomon* had demonstrated. For example, I did not know about the Leningrad Affair when I came through Leningrad in 1949; even in 1954 I didn't have all the details. I knew the Jews were being persecuted in 1948–49, but not until after Stalin died was I able to achieve a degree of comprehension. Only in 1954 was I able to fit the Beria case more or less together. And the same with many others. Sensation after sensation spilled out in the *Times*. The paper sold tens of thousands of extra copies. I became an instant celebrity, in demand for TV and for appearances everywhere you could think of. I was dead sure that I would win the Pulitzer Prize for my series, and on May 2, 1955, I was not disappointed.

My articles were not ideological. I did not make a deep analysis of the Soviet system, of Stalinism, of Communist theory or the philosophical issues that divided East and West. What I provided was hard-rock observations of reality as I had seen it in Russia from the Neva to the Amur, from the Lena to the Volga, a detailed reconstruction of Stalin's terror, an overview of Russia's real life—the drunkenness, the *poshlost* (banality), the bureaucracy, and the famine of goods, services and ideas after nearly forty years of Bolshevism—a firsthand and an intimate glimpse of the new leaders, the new policies, the extent to which they were, and were not, breaking from their Stalinist roots. I introduced Malenkov, Khrushchev and the others to American readers.

I presented, in a word, an update on the Soviet Union such as had not been read in the United States since the 1930s, one that was unique in many respects because my travels were unique, as was the degree to which I penetrated the surface of Russia in the months after March 1953.

Surprisingly, I had more critics than ever. Max Eastman and the old anti-Stalinists were very much in business, as were the big guns of the McCarthy camp. They did not like my reports. They did not believe anything had changed in Russia with the death of Stalin; in fact, the whole idea of change went contrary to their philosophy. Nor did they really like the fact that Harrison Salisbury was presenting this indictment of the Stalinist system. Long since, they had labeled me a "Red." Now I turned out to be what I had always been, a hard-nosed reporter presenting chapter and verse on a Soviet Union they no longer knew. They didn't want to challenge my facts, but they didn't like me any better for stating them. They said, All right, now you are saying how bad things are in Moscow; how come you didn't report this when you were there? Well, of course, they knew the answer well enough: the censorship. But they were not going to give credit to a correspondent whom they had been putting through the meat grinder of their prejudices for four or five years.

It was for me one more lesson in the dangers of telling the truth. Not only was the truth a volatile thing, but the truth depended on who spoke it and when and where it was spoken. These critics didn't really want the truth. They wanted to go on dealing in the shopworn prejudices and propaganda that had been their stock-in-trade for so many years, ever since they had lost their youthful idealism.

Nor was the truth more acceptable to another vocal chorus that was raised against me: the Communists at home and abroad. The morning my first article appeared, I sat down at my old wooden desk, one of the hundreds of fine oaken desks that then graced the city room, and found rolled into my typewriter a piece of copy paper left by one of my colleagues on the third floor. It said: "Judas Iscariot." I got quite a lot of those, all anonymous.

The Communist *Daily Worker* began a series by Joe Clark, who had been their correspondent in Moscow during part of the time I was there. The Clarks and their two small children lived on the third floor of the Metropol and I knew them well. Joe's series was headlined: "I Saw Salisbury See Russia." There were fourteen articles in his series, each designed to rebut one of my *Times* articles. They were republished by many other Communist newspapers and splashed in the Soviet press. Years later, when I got some of my FBI files under the Freedom of Information Act, I was amused to find that Joe's articles in the *Daily Worker* were repeatedly cited as "favorable mention" of my series. Another FBI official, obviously not acquainted with the first, proposed that the stories be mailed anonymously to known Communists as part of the FBI disinformation program designed to undermine the Communist movement.

Disillusion, as later would become apparent, existed even then and Clark himself was among the disillusioned. He left the Communist party not long after Khrushchev's "secret speech" had confirmed much of what I had previously reported. Clark's doubts, carefully shielded from a "capitalist" journalist like myself, had been present in the very Metropol days of which he wrote in "I Saw Salisbury See Russia." Later he was to describe to me an evening when the *Worker*'s foreign editor, the late Joe Starobin, was passing through Moscow on his way to Indochina in 1952. It was a weekend and typically the Clarks' plumbing didn't work. The two Joes spent half the evening on their backs on the bathroom tiles with a greasy plumber's candle, a flashlight, a screwdriver and a wrench, trying to fix the broken toilet. As they labored away, smashing their fingers, cursing the shoddy Russian workmanship, they asked each other questions: Why didn't *anything* in Russia work? Why was the bureaucracy so impossible? Where had the Revolution gone? What was the Soviet state really about? It was a dialogue in whispers against the flushing of the toilet. Only there did they feel safe in confiding in each other their dawning conviction that something was very, very wrong with the Communist utopia. Later I heard Ruth Clark's tale of terror of the bureaucracy, straight out of Kafka. For months she had lived in the Metropol without a *vid na*

zhitelsvo, the domestic residence permit required of all foreigners. Why hadn't she got one? She never knew, but it meant that
while her husband had the status of a high representative of a
foreign Communist party, she was a nonperson, subject at any
moment to arrest. Once, new to the city, she went shopping in the
Stoleshnikov, a few blocks from the Metropol. Suddenly she had
to go to the bathroom. But where? She knew no Russian. What
to do? She did the natural thing, inquired of a policeman. He
immediately asked for her *dokumenti.* In confusion, fearing she
might be arrested, she muttered something, slipped into the
crowd, somehow made her way back to the Metropol and collapsed. If this was the way she and her husband were treated,
imagine how they treated ordinary people! To which Joe added a
footnote. They were packed up for their return to New York. He
paid a farewell call on a Central Committee official in charge of
party liaison. They talked a bit. Then the man pointed to his
desk. Joe saw a stack of new hundred-dollar bills. It looked a
foot high. Maybe it was. "Please," said the Russian, "take what
you need." Somehow Joe managed to mumble that he was O.K.,
no need for anything. "Go ahead," the man said. Joe again
refused and said goodbye, the Russian miffed that his "generosity" had been rebuffed.

American in Russia was published February 14, 1955. I was not
running the risk of anyone getting ahead of me on the story of
the end of Stalin and the dawn of a new era. The book drew
warm reviews and hit the best-seller list. There was still a little
criticism from émigré Russian figures, Mensheviks, old SRs, mo-
narchists and some of the ex-Communist anti-Communists, but
the impact of my revelations made it difficult for them to continue their guerrilla war. I went lecturing coast to coast, and on
my second evening in a little town in northwest Connecticut, I
met a clear-eyed young woman who would in a few years change
my life. It was a fleeting encounter, but its consequences would
be profound. Her name was Charlotte Young Rand. No one I had
met before had spoken with such cool and perfect honesty, the
words tart and fresh, in a light but unmistakable Boston accent,
the opinions warm, no qualifications. I had never before found a
woman who would stand up to the devil (or Henry Kissinger)
and tell the truth to his face. The grace of her movements was
like that of a young birch. I did not know that over the years our

paths would come closer and closer; that one day we would marry. I did not know this, but her burnished image and the silver bell of her laughter would never leave me.

I now began to get reacquainted with Michael, an outstanding cadet at the Howe Military School in Indiana, and for the first time had some fun with my seven-year-old, Stephan, possessed of a disarming smile and a direct, to-the-point manner. I went back to Minneapolis and saw my mother, now seventy-eight, and my sister, who had helped me through the rough days before I went to Moscow in 1949. I plunged back into American life with an enthusiasm fueled by years in the paranoid wastes of Russia. Long experience abroad strengthened the conviction I had never lost that in the United States, and particularly in the Middle West, existed a society and a philosophy stronger, more free, more capable of nourishing humanity, more vital, energetic, skeptical, challenging than any other.

Russia did not vanish from my life. Before 1955 was out, Clifton Daniel had to give up Moscow because of ill health and the *Times* tried to send me back for a quick stay, no more than a year. This did not work. No matter that Khrushchev and his comrades were rapidly moving toward an exposé of Stalin's crimes that would make my exposé look like a Sunday school tract; my entrée to Moscow had been busted by "Russia Re-Viewed," *American in Russia* and articles I wrote for the *Times,* the *Saturday Evening Post, Reader's Digest, The New York Times Magazine* and other periodicals. I was, in Soviet eyes, a premature anti-Stalinist. It would become permissible to criticize Stalin, but only after Moscow gave the signal. The head of the Press Department announced publicly that the Foreign Office would not give me a visa to replace Clifton Daniel and that I would never again be allowed to set foot on Soviet soil. My name had been placed at the top of the permanent blacklist. There it would stay, through thick and thin, for the rest of my life.

Blacklist or not, I did get back to Moscow—but I was five years in the process and never again would I have anything but a hostile relationship with the Press Department and the Foreign Office. Though I became a friend, or at least a "respected American," to two leading members of the Politburo, you could count on the fingers of one hand the civil words I would ever hear from the Foreign Office.

I got back to Moscow in 1959, on the initiative of Anastas I. Mikoyan. I liked Mikoyan, having seen a good bit of him in Moscow. He arrived in the U.S.A. in the first week of January 1959, for a "vacation" as the guest of his friend Mikhail A. Menshikov, the Soviet ambassador to Washington. Of course, Mikoyan's trip was no vacation. It was a practice run, a preliminary to the exchange of trips later in 1959 that sent Vice-President Nixon to Moscow in July and brought Nikita Khrushchev to the United States in September. It was, in a word, an important diplomatic initiative, the first great move after Stalin's death to bring about an easing in tensions between the United States and Moscow.

Anastas Mikoyan was a small, dark, handsome Armenian who had been a revolutionary from boyhood. Born in 1895, he had been a member of the Soviet government for thirty-eight years. He had the quick-witted, outgoing temperament of so many Armenians and knew the United States well, or so he thought, having spent six months in the country in 1936, during which he examined the American consumer industry and brought back and introduced into Russia such products as cornflakes (never a success), tomato juice (eventually quite popular), mechanical bakeries (enormously successful in the U.S.S.R., still delivering fresh-baked bread twice a day to the bread stores of Moscow), Eskimo Pies and the Automat restaurant. On the basis of his firsthand knowledge of 1936, he was regarded as the Politburo's "Americanist," he told me. He hadn't wanted to come in 1959 because his impressions of 1936 were so pleasant and he thought cold war America would be frightful. He was to find out how wrong and out of date he was. Khrushchev joked about Mikoyan's forthcoming trip at the 1958 New Year's Eve party at the Kremlin. He wondered whether he would ever come back from America. "What business do you want to go into?" Khrushchev asked. "I can't tell you now," Mikoyan said. "I have to go there first and take a look." Khrushchev said that if Mikoyan decided to stay, the government would send him money so that he would not make statements against the Soviet Union. Llewellyn ("Tommy") Thompson, the American ambassador, interjected that if Mikoyan stayed in the U.S., he would become a millionaire. "That's what we have always said about him," Khrushchev replied.

This was persiflage. Mikoyan possessed enough talents to make a success anywhere, in almost any career. But the one he chose, that of revolutionary, was possibly the most difficult of all. One day, on a plane flying from Los Angeles to Washington, he talked with me about his early days in Baku and how his life had been accidentally spared when the "twenty-six Baku commissars" were executed in the Civil War. Mikoyan was a commissar, he was arrested and jailed with his comrades, but by accident his name was not on the list. He was spared, the others died, including two or three who were not commissars.

Dangerous as that had been, it was no more perilous than his position in the last years of Stalin. I don't know what put Mikoyan on Stalin's death list; most likely it was the fact that he knew too much. Mikoyan had come up out of the Caucasus and possessed every detail of the murky feuds that surrounded Stalin's early years. He probably knew whether, as some Georgians alleged, Stalin had in his youth been a police spy and informer. He knew Stalin's crimes in the purge years very well. His closest friend in the hierarchy was Sergo Ordzhonikidze, who shot himself in the 1930s in a vain protest against Stalin's course. Mikoyan knew the Alliluyev family, the family of Stalin's second wife, Nadezhda, mother of Svetlana. (Mikoyan was kind and attentive to Svetlana after her father's death.) Mikoyan knew why Nadezhda had killed herself, the circumstances of the tragedy on New Year's Eve 1932, of Stalin's vulgarity to Nadezhda and her efforts to sway him from his brutal course. All this was enough, indeed far more than enough, for Stalin to target Mikoyan for execution. Mikoyan had been in charge of supplies in World War II. He knew all of Stalin's blunders. He knew how foodstuffs and supplies were shipped *out* of Leningrad in the summer of 1941, as the Nazis approached and the siege of the city, which would take 1,500,000 lives, neared. There wasn't much Mikoyan did not know, and after World War II, like his old colleague Maksim Litvinov, Mikoyan began to carry a pistol wherever he went and placed it under his pillow at night. He would put a bullet through his head before they could take him to the Lubyanka cellars.

Mikoyan's case began to come to a head, as did those of the other senior members of the Politburo, at the time of the Nineteenth Party Congress in October 1952. At the plenary session of the Central Committee, held October 16, after the congress, Mikoyan, Molotov and the rest (except Kosygin) were elected to the new Presidium, which took the place of the Politburo. But at this very plenary, Stalin declared that Molotov and Mikoyan were British spies. He had also decided that Voroshilov was a British spy. Nonetheless, all three were elected to the Presidium.

The handwriting was on the wall. Beginning in December or perhaps a bit earlier, Stalin forbade Mikoyan and Molotov to attend the intimate sessions he had with the old Politburo members at his dacha at Blizhny. No longer were they invited to the midnight suppers or the Kremlin movies. For a while, Mikoyan and Molotov kept on attending the movies, tipped off by their comrades when they would be held. But Stalin put a halt to that.

Not a word of this, of course, did Mikoyan confide to anyone. No one close to him had any idea how critical the situation was. All they knew was that Mikoyan no longer smiled. He went about with a grave, almost haunted look on his face.

Mikoyan endured that as he had the Baku slaughter, and went on to play a leading role in exposing Stalin's crimes. Of course, he was not free of the stain. All of them shared the blame in one way or another. But no one proved more diligent than Mikoyan in setting matters straight. He stood at Khrushchev's side in the post-Stalin battles: the struggle against Beria and the police (one thing, he said, they decided as soon as Stalin was dead—never to let any one man control the police again); the destalinization, in which Mikoyan struck the first blows, even before Khrushchev's "secret speech"; the fight against Molotov, Malenkov and the others who tried to overthrow Khrushchev in 1957. This estimate of his role with Khrushchev was confirmed to me by Khrushchev himself, who repeatedly spoke of how "Anastas and I decided," "Anastas and I agree on," etc. Mikoyan was the only man in the Politburo to whom Khrushchev gave unqualified respect and support. This would not, however, help either of them at the time of Khrushchev's ultimate downfall, and Mikoyan's quick eclipse.

Mikoyan was eased out of the Politburo after Khrushchev's fall. This surprised many foreigners, including myself. I knew that Mikoyan was not admired by Mikhail A. Suslov and the men whom I dubbed the "right-wingers" of the Politburo. But Mikoyan had been with Khrushchev at Sochi on the Black Sea in the October days when the leadership crisis developed. I thought he was there as a Judas goat, to keep down Khrushchev's suspicions about the plot to remove him. The affair was more complicated than that, as I later learned. Khrushchev had, in fact, heard rumors of an intrigue against him and summoned Semi-chastny, the ex-Komsomol leader whom he had put in as head of the KGB. When Semichastny got to Sochi, Khrushchev began to swear at him. "You're just a piece of shit!" Khrushchev shouted. "Don't forget it! I made you. I put you in that post. You were nothing before I picked you up." Then he switched the subject. "What's going on in Moscow? They're cooking up something there."

Semichastny swore that nothing was happening in Moscow. Everything was quiet. Khrushchev finally sent Semichastny away. He caught the plane back to Moscow and joined the Suslov plot (if he had not already been in on the plans). Later Khrush-chev was to blame himself, saying that had he not thrown out Ivan Serov as security chief, the plot would never have suc-ceeded. Serov had been an aide to Beria. Khrushchev believed Serov would have been totally loyal to him. Semichastny was just a piece of shit.

Mikoyan, like Khrushchev, may have suspected something was afoot. I know from personal inquiry that Mikoyan did persuade Khrushchev to return to Moscow and face the Politburo and the Central Committee. He urged that whatever the Central Commit-tee decided, Khrushchev abide by its decision. But Mikoyan was not a member of the plot that removed Khrushchev and replaced him with the triumvirite Brezhnev-Kosygin-Podgorny. That op-eration was engineered by Suslov, who remained the éminence grise of the regime from 1964 until he died, in January 1982.

The fall of Khrushchev was a heavy blow to Mikoyan. A few months before, Khrushchev had decided to turn the Supreme So-viet, Russia's pseudoparliament, into a real congress, with real debates on the issues. He said he had seen enough of democratic parliaments to understand the value of free debate. In all the years of the Supreme Soviet's existence, only one negative vote had been cast—by a delegate from the country, who begged that delegates be permitted a night off to go to the theater. He was voted down, 1,256 to 1.

Brezhnev was the Politburo member charged with responsibil-ity for the Supreme Soviet. Khrushchev contemptuously said Brezhnev didn't have the ability to carry out the reform. "The only persons who could do that are myself and Anastas, and I'm too busy." He assigned the task to Mikoyan. Brezhnev never for-got the slight. Once he got power, he soon shuffled Mikoyan off

the stage. When he died, in 1978, Mikoyan was buried in Novodeviche cemetery, not in the Kremlin wall, which should have been
his last resting place under protocol. This was Brezhnev's doing.

The Mikoyan family is one of the great dynasties of the Soviet
state. Anastas's brother, Artem, was a leading aircraft designer.
Of Anastas's five sons, one was killed in World War II, three
went into the air service, and Sergo, named for Mikoyan's friend
Ordzhonikidze, became a specialist in Latin America. Sergo's
first wife, who died in the late 1950s, was the daughter of A. A.
Kuznetsov, the Leningrad party leader and Politburo member,
shot by Stalin in 1949 in the Leningrad Affair. Family roots in
the Kremlin are often as intertwined as those of Boston.

I sat with Mikoyan on January 20, 1959, in a parlor car of the
Pennsylvania Railroad, riding from Washington to New York.
We had been together night and day for the fortnight of his "vacation" in the U.S.A., traveling from New York to Washington,
to Cleveland and Detroit, to Chicago, San Francisco, Los Angeles, and back to Washington. Mikoyan stared out the car window at the New Jersey boglands and industrial slums, gray and
dirty in the January thaw. The air was soggy with rain. He sat
there, a little Chaplinesque man with pince-nez, looking with un-
seeing eyes at the landscape. In his hands rested the thumbed
copy of *Innostranaya Literatura,* "Foreign Literature," the magazine he had carried all over the United States, with hardly a
chance to read it. The mask of the public figure had dropped and
he seemed very small, very alone, old and tired. The spark was
absent from his eyes. I thought he was running back through the
years of struggle, of achievement, of danger. I could not help
recalling the remark he had made to Van Cliburn, who had
played at the reception at the Soviet embassy in Washington the
evening before. "You know," he said, "I never wanted to be a
revolutionary, really. What I wanted to be was a ballet dancer."
And I remembered the phrases he had used one day on the plane
about the "school of the Revolution." "My son," he said (Sergo
was with him), "has gone through higher education. He is an
educated man. They sometimes call me educated. But I am not,
really. I went to the school of the Revolution. I never went to
higher schools. My parents thought that I was a talented child
and that is why I was sent to the seminary [of the Armenian
Orthodox church]. Our children have advantages that we did not

have, and yet sometimes I think they are not as strong as we are."

Now Mikoyan was on the final stage of his American trip, an incredible trip, truly, an old Bolshevik taking to the hustings in America to try and change the course of U.S.-Soviet relations. He had seen the country and its riches. He was not the kind to fool himself. He knew we had the power. Once he had said with a tinge of bitterness that, of course, we had not had the war. His country had had the terrible suffering of World War I, World War II, a civil war and intervention. This was why it was still so far behind.

But he knew, too, that this was not the whole story. Now he was going back to Khrushchev. He was not going to report a failure, but so much remained to be done.

America had surprised him. When he last saw it, it was still crawling, battered and broken, up from the depths of depression. Now it was profligate and rich. He could never have believed it would be so rich, so powerful, so productive, that the American people would work so hard, would be so happy, that the capitalists themselves would be so socially minded. This he had not been prepared for. It was, he thought, something new under the sun. Marx had made no provision for this in his theories.

Mikoyan had discovered something else—the healthy virtues of the free press. He had never seen reporters like those of us who covered his trip, by his side every moment, from 6 A.M. constitutionals to late walks in the grounds of the Ambassador Hotel in Los Angeles, the streets of San Francisco or snowy Rock Creek Park in Washington. He was impressed. There wasn't a Soviet reporter with us when we started. But by the time we got to Chicago, Tass and *Pravda* men were calling up American reporters and asking where we were going and how to catch up.

Mikoyan didn't like some of the excesses of the American press, but he was quick to admit its virtues. You had a choice of reports. And he agreed that the Soviet leadership (and I am sure he included himself in this) had often been deluded and misled by the propaganda of *Pravda* and *Izvestiya*.

As I sat with him in the parlor car to New York, I asked him if he had found my reporting factual and objective. He had. I said I had been trying for five years to get back to Moscow to

have a new look. Could he help me? Of course, he said. He seemed
bewildered that there could be any question about this. And in
fact, in April the visa came through, slick as a whistle, and back
I went to Moscow, to get acquainted with Khrushchev.

I had been back less than twenty-four hours when I ran into
Mikoyan at a diplomatic reception at the Japanese embassy. I
thanked him for clearing the way for my return. He said he had
been informed by the Press Department that I had written some
"bad stories" about Russia. I asked him if he had any complaint
about my coverage of his trip to the United States. None at all,
he said. Well, I replied, that is the way I cover Russia. At that
moment, I heard a loud voice saying, "Beware, Mr. Mikoyan. Be
on guard. You are talking to the notorious American correspondent who has written so many lies about the Soviet Union."
Mikoyan and I saw a man named Mikhail Kharlamov limping
toward us. He had been wounded during the war and was now
head of the Press Department. He came up and began to bluster
ahead in the same vein. Finally, Mikoyan cut him short. "I know
Mr. Salisbury," he said. "I am familiar with his reporting in the
United States. I have a high opinion of his work and that of the
other American correspondents. They are hard-working and like
to see things at first hand."

Kharlamov fell silent. It was a nice send-off from Mikoyan,
but it put the Press Department's back up against me, like a
concrete wall.

38 | Nikita Sergeevich Khrushchev

There is no way in which I can pin down Nikita Sergeevich Khrushchev on paper. Try as I will, the moment I type the words, he bursts off the pages and plunges into life, hands flying, jaws working, little pig eyes darting, snub nose poking into everything, a bundle of curiosity as insatiable as the Monkey King in the Chinese fairy tale. Khrushchev looked like a butterball on short legs, but I never encountered such compact energy in human form. He was not very tall, probably five feet five. None of the men in Stalin's Politburo were tall. Stalin was short. Tall men made him nervous. Khrushchev was fond of referring to himself as a barefoot boy from Kalinovka in the Kursk *gubernia* on the northern fringe of the Ukraine.

I spent an hour sunning myself in the quiet courtyard outside the Presidium offices in the Kremlin on the morning of July 26, 1959, while Richard M. Nixon, then Vice-President, paid a ceremonial call on Khrushchev. It was supposed to last fifteen minutes. When Nixon emerged, he looked pale and shaken. A year passed before I learned what had happened. Khrushchev didn't like Nixon, never had, never would. He was tolerating Nixon's trip to Russia because he wanted to make a return trip to the U.S.A.

In the ceremonial meeting, Khrushchev offered a few observations about the hardships of his youth. Nixon replied in kind. He had been a poor boy too. He had often gone barefoot. Khrushchev said he was not only a barefoot boy; he had a job cleaning the *govno,* the horse shit, out of the stables. That's nothing, responded Nixon, I had to clean horse shit too. Well, said Khrushchev, I shoveled cow shit and that was worse. Nixon said he had done the same thing. Well, said Khrushchev, I've had the worst job of all. I had to shovel human shit. Nixon couldn't top that.

Later I heard Khrushchev in a argument with Spiros Skouras, chief of MGM studios, at a banquet in Los Angeles. Skouras told how he had been a shepherd boy in Greece, so poor he could not even afford shoes. Now he was head of a vast film industry. His

studio employed five thousand—or whatever the figure was—
workers. He had reached the top.

Khrushchev paid tribute to Skouras, then turned to his own
career. Also a barefoot shepherd boy, he had not had to leave his
own country. Right there in Russia, he had risen to head a whole
nation, with 230,000,000 people.

I spent a lot of time with Khrushchev. I got to know him as I
did the American politicians I covered in Washington or on presidential campaigns, and in much the same way—on the road,
traveling with him, getting up in the morning before he did and
sticking to him until he went to bed, at midnight or later. On a
campaign you see a man in constantly shifting crises, unexpected
encounters. After two or three weeks, you know each other
pretty well. Perhaps I got to know Adlai Stevenson or Richard
Nixon or Jack Kennedy better than I did Khrushchev. But I am
not so sure.

Khrushchev would have been a successful politician in the
United States had he been born here, just as Mikoyan would
have been a successful businessman. I think Khrushchev would
in fact have been a better politician in the United States. He
reminded me of Huey Long. When I knew Huey, he was twenty
years younger than Khrushchev. Both men had the same shoe-
button noses, round faces and ovoid shapes. Both were born rab-
ble-rousers, born actors. Khrushchev mustered tears in the corners of his little eyes when he was denied permission to go to
Disneyland, and you could see the fuses of nuclear rockets spark-
ing when he was angered by the mayor of Los Angeles. Put him
on the barnyard trail in Iowa and he was unbeatable. He had the
common touch. He didn't need media consultants to tell him how
to behave in Roswell Garst's corn fields. He was pure corn himself.

I was with Khrushchev on the afternoon when he visited the
American exhibition in Sokolniki Park in Moscow in August
1959 as the guest of Richard Nixon. Khrushchev was on guard.
When Nixon took him to a TV studio to demonstrate color video-
tape with instant replay, Khrushchev was sure Nixon wanted to
use the tape for some nasty stunt back in the U.S.A. When Donald Kendall, head of Pepsi-Cola, tried to get Khrushchev to taste
his product, he refused (although Mikoyan and the rest of the
Politburo accepted). When Nixon escorted Khrushchev into the
American Home exhibition, Khrushchev was determined to waltz

right through, to demonstrate his contempt for American "propaganda." Nixon tried to lure him to the model kitchen, but Khrushchev wasn't buying it. "We've got all that in our kitchens," he said. "I've got everything in my home that you have there." But then his eye caught a glimpse of the shiny new garbage disposal, the food blender, Lord knows what, and he was lost. His legs steered him over for a closer look and the famous "kitchen debate" was on—a debate that almost elected Nixon President in 1960 and made the reputation of Bill Safire, the PR man for the exhibit, who kindly lifted up the rope and let me sit on the kitchen floor at the feet of the champions of American Capitalism and Soviet Communism, enabling me to record almost all they said for posterity. It was a fine scoop and I've been in Safire's debt ever since.

I saw Khrushchev's curiosity lead him into a tour of the beautiful IBM building in San Jose, California, as the guest of Thomas J. Watson, Jr., who had no notion he was doing something revolutionary. The IBM facility was a fine example of a modern technological plant, an endless succession of cinder-block halls, one blending into another on a single level. Khrushchev started at the executive suite and moved into the general office section, along the assembly lines, into the shipping department, the warehouses, all the same building, all the walls pastel greens or pastel purples or pastel blues, all wall-to-wall carpeting, the same gentle piped-over background music, no lines of division, you couldn't tell whether you were in the director's office or the assembly line by the shape, contour and ambience of the structure, the same casually dressed men and women whether they were vice-presidents or on-line workers. Halfway through the tour, I caught a glance exchanged between Khrushchev and one of his aides. *They* knew what Watson was showing them, even if Watson didn't. I knew too, because I had read my Marx. I knew that the great goal of Communism, and hence of the Soviet system, was to abolish the distinction between blue and white collar, between physical and mental labor, to wipe out the historic divisions between the "toiling" class and the "exploiting" class. I had been in hundreds of Soviet factories and knew their grim, back-breaking nature. The distinctions were far from gone in the Soviet Union. A blue-collar family would make any sacrifice to lift its sons and daughters out of the "toiling" ranks and into the white-collar bureaucracy. But here in America, in the citadel of capitalism, the historic distinctions of blue and white collar had been obliterated so completely that there wasn't a person in the IBM plant who knew what they were. No one in the IBM plant or among the Americans accompanying Khrushchev had any notion that they were walking through a chapter in Marx's forecast of the future.

That was the nuance that underlay the quick glance passed between Khrushchev and his aide, and it told me more about the Soviet Union and the distance that separated it from its aspirations than a thousand words could.

Capitalism had achieved Marx's goal and didn't know it; Communism was so far distant from it that Khrushchev didn't dare talk about it.

Khrushchev's boyhood had been as close to poverty as his arguments with Nixon and Skouras suggested. He grew up in and near the mining and steel complex of Yuzovka, a Russification of Hughes, the name of the original Welsh entrepreneurs of this Donbas works. There was lots of foreign capital—English, French, Belgian and German—in the Donbas. Khrushchev, as I often heard him say, got no formal education in his childhood, but he worked for French, Belgian and German firms. Most of his education came after the Revolution, in *rab-fak,* workers' factory classes. He once said sadly that he was the only member of his family who couldn't speak English. As a young man, when he heard people in his boardinghouse talking about ballet, he didn't know, he said, whether it was a fish or a fowl, something to eat or to drink. When he read Zola's *Germinal,* he thought it was set in Yuzovka, the conditions were so similar to those he endured when he was growing up.

He was born in 1894 and from the beginning was tough, earthy, poking his nose into everything in response to his fierce curiosity.

Looking back on Khrushchev, it is difficult for me to see how he survived under Stalin. True, he was canny. He knew how to play the fool, and as he once said, when Stalin told him to dance the *gopak*—a Ukrainian folk dance—he danced the *gopak.* And when Stalin called him a *khokol,* a rude word for "Ukrainian," Khrushchev did not grimace. He jumped to obey Stalin's whim.

He played the fool and knew he was playing the fool and knew why he was doing it—to survive. As he was to recall after March 5, 1953: "Sometimes a man goes to see Stalin in the Kremlin and he does not know whether or not he will come home again." Khrushchev always came home.

I saw a good deal of Nina Petrovna Khrushcheva. She accompanied Khrushchev on his American tour, and the more I saw of her, the more I respected this warm, intelligent, shrewd, motherly former schoolteacher. She was the sheet anchor that kept Khrushchev's bark steady.

In the great family crises, it was Nina Petrovna who came to the fore. After Khrushchev was deposed, on October 12, 1964, she was seriously concerned. Khrushchev fell into deep depression. Nothing captured his interest. For weeks he dissolved in bathetic tears. She it was who arranged for the purchase of a German Leica and got him interested in taking pictures. She it was who had a greenhouse constructed and got Nikita Sergeevich to grow hothouse tomatoes and cucumbers, and she it was who managed to win him over to the notion of dictating his memoirs, a task facilitated when the family gave him a German tape recorder. It took Khrushchev some time to start using it. The family plied him with questions and insisted that he dictate the answers. This was how he fell into the habit of sitting on a bench in the garden (the noise of birds and of planes—the villa is not far from Vnukovo airport—is loud and clear on the tapes) and dictating his memories, which eventually were fashioned into two volumes edited by Strobe Talbot, a Time-Life correspondent. No one who knew Khrushchev can listen to those tapes, now at the Columbia University library, without an intense nostalgia. Here is the Khrushchev we knew so well, talking in his familiar style, grumbling that he doesn't feel so well this morning, wondering where he left off in yesterday's dictation, gradually warming up to his task and beginning to talk in the salty, frequently repetitive style to which we became so accustomed during his ascendancy.

The tale of how the tapes reached Time-Life has never been told, but I think I have pieced together most of it. Aleksei Adzhubei, Khrushchev's son-in-law and onetime editor of *Komsomolskaya Pravda* and later of *Izvestiya,* lost his post at the same time as his father-in-law, but he did not lose his connections with Komsomol leaders, some of whom had gone into the security apparatus.

I believe that the Khrushchev family sanitized the tapes, removing materials that would obviously cause state problems. Possibly Khrushchev refused to dictate material on high-level party matters. Certainly no such material is present in the tapes that reached the West. I think the family and Khrushchev wanted the materials to be published. Khrushchev probably had nothing to do with the complicated mechanism by which they were transmitted to the West, but I do not believe he objected to it and I know that the family had no criticism of the channels that were employed.

What was the route? I believe that Adzhubei played the key role. I think he turned the tapes over to one of his old friends in the police apparatus. The police may have made excisions in the tapes (careful examination of them makes it clear that whatever may have been taken out, nothing was added; Khrushchev's voice and manner are clear and unmistakable). The materials were then put into the hands of Victor Louis, a middleman-agent for the KGB who has often been used to convey materials (for profit) from Moscow to the West.

The first time I met Victor Louis, in 1959, he was just beginning his career. He had, I later learned from a friend who had been imprisoned with him, served a term in the camps, where he quickly acquired a cushy job in the commissary. His surname came from a French father who somehow became a Soviet citizen —so he said. When Victor emerged from the camps after Stalin's death, his first job was with the Moscow patriarchy. In 1959, he was a correspondent for the *London Evening News* and he had married a young Englishwoman named Jennifer. He invited me to his apartment in the new Cheryomukha quarter on Moscow's outskirts, very fashionable. Ostensibly, Victor wanted my advice on a motorists' travel guide which he and Jennifer had written after making an auto tour of Russia the previous summer. "You can imagine how many times we were arrested by local police," Victor said solemnly.

After we had talked about the guide, Victor rose with something of a flourish and started his record player. He pulled a fat sheaf of papers from his drawer and asked me in a conspiratorial voice whether I was interested in the transcript of the Writers'

Union plenary session that had expelled Pasternak. He was greatly disappointed when I said I wasn't interested (I knew Louis had sold the transcript to *Time* magazine a few days earlier; I wasn't going to buy a secondhand pup). He switched the subject to art. It was a moment when dissident artists had just appeared on the scene. I knew that Victor had introduced Western buyers to the artists (who were then often called in by the police). I didn't show much interest, so he brought out a portfolio of gouaches by an artist named Rabin, who was much in vogue among the diplomatic colony. When I didn't want to buy a Rabin, Louis was stunned. "You must have a Rabin," he said. "Everyone has one. I'll give you one." Hurriedly he shuffled out a half-dozen dreary-looking gouaches. "Here, take your choice." I selected one of the least obnoxious. Louis beamed. "That's a fine one," he said, examining it. Then he hastily pulled it back. "My God!" he said. "He forgot to sign it. You can't have an unsigned Rabin." He took out a pencil stub, wet it with his tongue and put a neat initial "R" in the corner.

Later Louis and I exchanged postcards from exotic parts of the world. He sent me one from Taipei. I sent him one from Lhasa. Once he sent me a series of letters. The first was on stationery imprinted: "On Her Majesty's Service: MI6." The next letterhead was boldly embossed: "CIA." The third and last: "KGB." He had picked them up, I deduced, in a novelty shop, perhaps in London's Soho. The letters were not, I was amused to see, mailed from Moscow. Victor had got someone to post them in Helsinki. I fancy he did not feel certain that the KGB would share his sense of humor.

Not all of Louis's gambits were so innocent. He was given a manuscript of Svetlana Alliluyeva's *Twenty Letters to a Friend,* which she had left behind in Moscow. He attempted to sell it in the West in an effort to cut into her royalties. He obtained an album of Svetlana's personal photographs which had also been left behind in Moscow, and sold them in the West. He made similar efforts to sell materials about Aleksandr Solzhenitsyn. He wrote a highly tendentious but revealing book which, in effect, laid out the rationale for a Soviet "liberating" attack on China. To Louis's outrage, the publishers commissioned me to do an introduction that would explain exactly who he was and what he was up to.

The motives of the police in the Alliluyeva, Solzhenitsyn and

China cases are obvious. But motivation is not so clear in the case of Khrushchev. If the caper was designed to destroy Khrushchev's reputation in the Soviet Union, it seems redundant. He had already lost his constituency there.

Nina Petrovna's strong hand was revealed in another family crisis. In the summer of 1969, Yelena, the youngest of the Khrushchev daughters, fell ill and the Kremlin physicians pronounced her dying of a medically irreversible disease, a rare form of cancer.

Nina Petrovna refused to accept this verdict. She set in motion an elaborate scheme to obtain for Yelena the best American treatment. A friend of the family who was attending a scientific meeting in Copenhagen took out a précis of the case and passed it to an American colleague, asking him to seek the top American specialist. The American brought the description back to the United States, where a friend put him in touch with Dr. A. McGee Harvey at Johns Hopkins. After two or three mysterious meetings with a first secretary of the Soviet embassy in Washington, Dr. Harvey agreed to go to Moscow. Until the night before he and his wife left New York, Dr. Harvey did not know the identity of his patient. The Harveys were met at Moscow airport by an Intourist representative and a pleasant, quiet, intelligent young scientist wearing Chekhovian steel-rimmed glasses—Sergei Khrushchev, whose identity was not known by the Intourist guide.

The Harveys were put up at the National Hotel. It was the beginning of November, cold and wintry weather. The first two days were spent in sightseeing, Sergei accompanying them despite the protests of the Intourist guide. On the second day, a Sunday, it was arranged to drive to the old Yusupov estate, about fifteen miles from town. There was a heavy snowfall and the guide didn't want to go, but Sergei insisted. They drove over slippery roads, and made a quick tour of the Yusupov palace. Then, leaving the guide, they got into Sergei's car and he drove them to the Khrushchev villa at nearby Petrovo Dalnye. They whizzed past the guards, through a gate in a green-painted fence, believing the guards did not spot them—probably a mistaken impression.

That snowy Sunday was a delight for the Harveys and for the Khrushchevs as well. Nikita and Nina Petrovna greeted the

American couple at the door. Khrushchev was seventy-five then, in apparent good health, and in fine spirits. The table was set for dinner. Most of the Khrushchev family, including grandchildren, were present and there was a holiday atmosphere. Nina Petrovna and Nikita Sergeevich took their guests for a tour of the house. Khrushchev proudly displayed the cucumbers and tomatoes that he had raised in his hothouse.

This was to be Khrushchev's last meeting with Americans— and possibly his last with any foreigners. He talked freely and easily, in his old style, of his life and career. He left no doubt of his continuing distaste for Richard Nixon, "a typical middle-class American businessman" (this was, of course, nearly four years before Watergate). He had warm words for Eisenhower, a man for whom he professed deep admiration, and for President Kennedy. He thought Kennedy had been inept at their Vienna confrontation, but believed he was learning fast, and he did not conceal his sorrow at Kennedy's untimely death.

As for his own political career, he dated the beginning of his fall to the shooting down of the American U-2 over Sverdlovsk on May Day, 1960. Never again, he insisted, did he regain full control over the government; he had to share power with those who believed that "only military force" would enable Moscow to deal with Washington.

Not everyone, myself included, would agree with Khrushchev's personal evaluation of how he lost power. I have spoken with men close to the Politburo, who challenge Khrushchev's analysis. They believe he lost his power because of overconfidence, a tendency to overplay his hand, the consistency with which he denigrated his fellow Politburo members (except for Mikoyan), his misjudgment of the character of men whom he advanced to high office, in particular, Frol Kozlov and KGB chief Semichastny, and his bad relations with the military. The military never forgave him for forcing the retirement of thousands of officers to half-pay pensions, with loss of cars, chauffeurs, aides, and perquisites.

But Khrushchev's version may, after all, be correct. The late Llewellyn Thompson, then U.S. ambassador in Moscow and, in a curious way, a man closer to Khrushchev than even Khrushchev's Politburo associates, once told me that on the day the U-2 incident was announced, he went to the Czech embassy for their national reception. The whole Politburo was there. Khrushchev took him aside and said, "I must talk with you." The two men went to a little side room. Khrushchev told Thompson: "This U-2 thing has put me in a terrible spot. You have to get me off it." Thompson promised that he would do everything he could. They rejoined the reception. Several Soviet marshals came up to Thompson, one after the other, each with the same message: We want to smooth this over. We don't want any war with the U.S.A. Thompson did his best to pour oil on the waters, but when Eisenhower insisted on taking personal responsibility for the overflight, the fate of the Eisenhower-Khrushchev summit in Paris and the Eisenhower visit to Russia was sealed.

The day after his dinner with the Khrushchevs, Dr. Harvey went to the Kremlin hospital. He examined Yelena and met with her doctors. He was, he thought, the first American physician to serve as a consultant in this hospital, reserved for the highest circles in Russia. He concluded that the diagnosis in Yelena's case was incorrect, and that she was suffering from a rare allergy. Nina Petrovna insisted that he write a detailed report on the disease and its treatment so there could be no possible confusion after he left. (In spite of the new regimen recommended by Dr. Harvey, Yelena died about two years later.)

The Harveys spent a week in Moscow. Sergei took them to the Zagorsk monastery, where the patriarch of the Orthodox Church presented them with a lovely icon. Nina Petrovna gave them an old samovar, a family heirloom. Sergei tried to get them tickets to watch the November 7 parade from Red Square, but he was not successful and they viewed it from outside the National Hotel in his company and that of the patriarch's physician.

Hardly had the party returned to their hotel suite than ten plainclothes security agents burst in. Everyone was ordered to remain exactly where he was. A three-hour examination ensued. The tiles from the bathroom were removed, electrical connections examined, walls tapped; the carpet was lifted, plumbing disconnected, furniture pulled apart. Mrs. Harvey was made to strip by two women operatives. Toothpaste was squeezed from tubes, every article of luggage was gone through, pockets were turned out. After three hours, a man whom Sergei identified as a deputy chief of the KGB arrived and the process was repeated for another hour.

The only explanation offered by the security detail was that the Harveys had entered the country for a purpose other than that described on their visas. The security men took away the icon, saying it could not be exported from the country. They also removed eight rolls of exposed color film. They said they would develop them, and if they were merely snapshots, return them. A lengthy "protocol" was written. Dr. Harvey insisted that every detail be put down. Later the film was brought back, except for one roll. At first Dr. Harvey thought it contained the pictures he had taken at the Khrushchev villa, but they were intact and he decided that the missing roll had simply been spoiled in development.

Sergei was mortified. He apologized repeatedly, but had no explanation to offer. Next day at customs, there was another fine-tooth examination, and the samovar was taken away. At length, the Harveys were permitted to board their plane, the last passengers to climb the staircase.

A couple of months later, Dr. Harvey had a call from *Life* magazine. The editors had acquired some photos of the Harveys' visit with the Khrushchevs. Harvey thought the pictures must be from his missing roll of film, but they were black-and-white shots made by one of the Khrushchev family. They had obviously made their way to *Life* by the same route as the tapes of the Khrushchev memoirs which *Life* had acquired earlier.

What Dr. Harvey told me of his adventure reinforced my belief that Khrushchev lived at the center of police intrigue, with more than one faction of KGB operatives active in the shadows around him. The extraordinary actions in the Harveys' hotel suite, conducted in Sergei's presence, seem to have been designed to ferret out any message or manuscript (the uncut version of his memoirs, for example) that Khrushchev might have entrusted to the Harveys to take to the West. They also demonstrated to Sergei the lengths to which the security apparatus was prepared to go to prevent the Khrushchev family from establishing *independent* contact with the West.

The fact that the black-and-white photos of the Harveys' Sunday with Khrushchev turned up in *Life*'s hands demonstrated that someone within the Khrushchev family was doing business-as-usual with the police. I think that individual was Adzhubei.

I believe Nikita Sergeevich Khrushchev was a flawed politician. Any politician growing up under Stalin was bound to be seriously damaged. The important thing about Khrushchev was not his flaws but his virtues. He was a bit like Fiorello La Guardia. He committed terrible blunders. But when he saw what he had done, he had the courage to admit it.

In 1962, he paid a visit to a famous exhibition of works of Moscow's young artists at the Menazhny Gallery, a visit organized by reactionaries to turn him against the young avant-garde by offending his middlebrow taste. A couple of months later, at a meeting of artists and writers, Khrushchev said to the sculptor Ernst Neizvestny, whose shoulders are slightly thickened by war wounds: "Only the grave will correct the hunchback." To which Yevgeny Yevtushenko interjected: "Surely, Nikita Sergeevich, we have come a long way from the time when only the grave straightens out the hunchback. Really, there are other ways." And he spoke of two Cuban partisans, one a constructivist, one a conventional painter, who died side by side fighting for the Revolution. Khrushchev joined those in the hall in applauding Yevtushenko.

After he retired, Khrushchev invited Neizvestny to his dacha, and apologized for his words. Following his death—at his specific wish—his widow commissioned Neizvestny to design the simple monument that stands at his grave in Novodeviche cemetery.

In his retirement, Khrushchev for the first time had leisure to read. He read everything Mikhail Sholokhov had written. Sholokhov had been his literary hero. When he finished his reading, he told his family: "The son of a bitch! He's written only one novel, *The Quiet Don.*"

When Pasternak's *Doctor Zhivago* appeared in the West and Pasternak was awarded the Nobel Prize, Khrushchev led the attack that resulted in Pasternak's expulsion from the Writers' Union.

Now, in his enforced leisure, Khrushchev read *Doctor Zhivago.* When he had finished, he burst out in a stream of Russian *mat',* that primitive Russian profanity constructed around the mother oath.

"Damn it," he said (his actual words were more bawdy). "Those bastards simply fooled me. They told me this was a terrible book, an anti-Soviet work, that it befouled our Revolution. They were just lying. There is nothing wrong with *Doctor Zhivago.* Sure, we might have cut out four or five lines—so what?

To create an international furor over this book and hold us up to ridicule and denunciation all over the world—it is just impossible."

He blamed himself and his lack of time. "I never should have paid attention to them." His family was kind. No one mentioned that when the Pasternak affair arose in 1956 and 1957, they had urged him to read the book and he had waved them away.

The fact was, of course, that Pasternak, Neizvestny and the rest of the intelligentsia were caught up in a political backlash that followed Khrushchev's attack on Stalin.

One of Khrushchev's strengths was old-fashioned stump oratory. He did not play by the rules. If he lost a vote in the Politburo—and, yes, questions are decided by recorded votes, as I learned from Nikita Sergeevich himself—he would carry the questions to the people. No one, not even Lenin, had acted like this and in the end Khrushchev paid a price for his freewheeling.

Putting the missiles into Cuba was a telltale indicator. His throw of the dice in favor of friendship with Eisenhower and partnership (which was what he really wanted) with the U.S.A. was another. Pulling out in one swoop thousands of Soviet specialists from China was another. Khrushchev thought he could bargain his Cuban missiles for a disarmament deal with the U.S. He thought he could bring China to her knees by pulling out the experts. He thought Eisenhower and he could divide the world (a peaceful reenactment, if you will, of the deal Hitler and Stalin laid on each other).

None of these gambles paid off. But behind the bravado Khrushchev was prey to a thousand fears. He had never been in a helicopter before Eisenhower invited him up to take a look at Washington as the government closing-hour rush jammed the highways. He was afraid it was a trick; he might crash or be hurled overboard. He wouldn't do it until Ike said he was going too. He was afraid to go to Camp David. What kind of trick did Ike have in store? After he went there, he basked in his intimacy with Eisenhower. When he sailed on the Soviet steamer *Baltika* in September 1960 to attend the United Nations session, he invited the Eastern European heads of state to come with him. Privately he worried that a U.S. submarine might torpedo his ship and sink the whole crew.

Because of the distortions of political life in the Soviet Union, Khrushchev was not always able to gauge practical political matters with accuracy. I watched him on his famous appearance at the United Nations. One day he had signified displeasure by pounding the table with his fists, rub-a-dub-dub. I think he had picked up this touch from what he'd heard about the prerevolutionary Duma, a most unruly parliament, and I think he thought his gesture would appeal to the third world nations. Foreign Minister Gromyko was sitting beside Khrushchev. Gromyko is a very formal man. A flicker of distaste crossed his face when he saw what Khrushchev was doing. But dutifully Gromyko doubled his fists and lightly tapped them on the table. Next day, the two again were sitting together. Khrushchev's fists went rub-a-dub. Gromyko followed his master's example. Then suddenly, hearing a new sound, he saw that Khrushchev had pulled off a shoe and was banging the table with it. Gromyko resolutely went quietly on with his fists. He would not take off his shoe for Khrushchev or anyone else.

Khrushchev's "proletarian" gesture backfired. It amused Americans, but third world politicians, who are nothing if not formal, thought Khrushchev gauche. The Soviet public thought the same thing. Twenty years later, Soviet men and women still cited Khrushchev's shoe-pounding as a vulgar act which brought contumely on the great Soviet state. "He made foreigners laugh at us," they say. He embarrassed the intelligentsia with his bad manners, his scruffy Russian speech, his baggy trousers (and later on, his too-tailored Italian suits). They thought him crude, rude, vulgar, ignorant. It was only when he was gone and replaced by Brezhnev and his faceless bureaucrats that they realized what they had lost.

Nothing made Khrushchev more angry than complaints that he and the Soviet Union were anti-Semitic. He was forever citing numerus clausus to demonstrate how fair Russia was in giving the Jews their appointed number of places in the university, in the academies, in the Bolshoi Theater Orchestra. But he would never explain why Jews were so rare in the upper ranks of the party, the army, the security service and the Foreign Office.

Even in retirement, when he seriously examined and reexamined his past, he never managed to get straight on the Jewish question. I think Khrushchev was so steeped in the conventional anti-Semitism of the Ukraine that he could not sense the virus in his system.

Khrushchev's strongest characteristic was an openness to new impressions, a willingness to change his mind based on physical observation. Again and again he harried the Russian bureaucrats to get out of their offices and into the streets to see for themselves. He pushed their noses into dirty, disordered, backward local conditions, bad plumbing, poor housing construction, inept planning, shoddy agriculture. He was like a cloud of bees when he descended on a provincial center where party bureaucrats preened themselves in cozy complacency.

Khrushchev respected American reporters. He delighted in banter with them and never missed an opportunity. He admired their open eyes and ready repartee, their frankness, their camaraderie and their hard work.

I spent two or three weeks in the autumn of 1960 at the corner of Park Avenue and Sixty-eighth Street in New York, where the Soviets then had their mission and where Khrushchev lived during his stay for the United Nations session. I was out on the pavement at 6 A.M. and I did not leave until midnight or 1 A.M. As soon as Khrushchev discovered the reporters on his doorstep, he began to perform, emerging on a balcony, ostensibly for a breath of fresh air, actually to banter with us, to speak into the microphones that the TV reporters hoisted up on long poles, and to indulge the whims of the photographers.

Khrushchev was a reporter's dream. All you had to do to get a story was wait. On weekends at Glen Cove, Long Island, where the Soviets had an estate, I would appear at the big iron gate with a dozen other reporters at 8 A.M. Sure as rain, Khrushchev would "accidentally" stroll down to the gate and discover us. He would repeat his "discovery" several times a day. I had the impression he was bored with his bureaucratic entourage and Eastern European companions, and found us better company.

He talked to me one evening as we strolled in the circular driveway at the entrance to the Glen Cove mansion. It was dusk and I could hardly make out his features, but he was very serious. He was talking about diplomacy, statesmanship and politics: the difficulty of politics, the difficulty of being a politician, the hard work. "You have no idea how hard it is," he said, and in the timbre of his voice I heard the echoes of the crises of the past. He had spent his life in Soviet politics. He had survived nearly twenty-five years, moving from the outer fringes of Stalin's clique to its very center. He knew politics at its most dangerous vortex. He knew what it meant when a casual word could cost you your life.

On another occasion, he told me that while he had not agreed with some of my articles, he thought others were objective and could provide a basis for the "peaceful coexistence" of our two countries. "So," he said, "if you were nominated for President, I would vote for you."

The next moment, he was listening to a reporter who suggested that he could have made a success in American politics even though the Communist party was not very strong in the U.S.A. Khrushchev said he might well have been a successful American politician, and had he been elected President, maybe many people would have wanted to join his party.

I like and enjoy politicians and I became fond of Khrushchev, as did most of the reporters. He had a good sense of humor and, what was most important, he was willing to learn and did learn. He did not bear grudges. I do not think he ever got over his inclination for quick fixes. One of his most disreputable moves was his short-lived restoration to favor of Trofim Lysenko, the quack agronomist whose mini-Stalinist purges destroyed Soviet genetics (the generation with which Hermann Muller had worked) and did terrible damage to Soviet science. Khrushchev's children strongly opposed his flirtation with Lysenko but could not halt it. Fortunately, Brezhnev brought a final end to Lysenko's influence. Far better and more wholesome was Khrushchev's friendship and fondness for the pragmatic but scientific farming practices to which he was introduced by the Coon Rapids, Iowa, farmer Roswell Garst. Garst knew what he was talking about and Khrushchev understood this. Garst brought into Soviet practice hybrid corn and the theory of the Iowa corn-hog economy, use of silage to produce beef and hogs, and mass production of poultry. It was Khrushchev who initiated the slow but certain Soviet transformation from a cereal diet to a meat economy.

On one of the first days of September 1971, Yevgeny Yevtushenko got a telephone call to come to the Khrushchev villa. It was a fine day, with sunshine and the scent of autumn in the air. Zhenya, as he told me, found Nikita Sergeevich, Nina Petrovna, Khrushchev's son Alexei and his daughter Rada there. They sat on benches in the garden and talked almost all day. Khrushchev had been ill and in the hospital, and he felt his end was approaching. He wanted to apologize to Yevtushenko and to the other writers he had criticized. He wanted to explain what had happened. When Yevtushenko had spoken to him in 1962 about the two painters, the conventionalist and the constructivist, who had died side by side, he had known that Yevtushenko was right.

"Then why did you shout at me, Nikita Sergeevich," Yevtushenko asked.

"Because I knew you were right," Khrushchev replied, "and I had to shout. You are very lucky. You are a poet. You can tell the truth. But I was a politician. You don't know what a terrible job it is to be a politician. I had to shout to hold my job."

Khrushchev said that after the 1956 Hungarian uprising, which was touched off by the Petöfi Circle of poets, the middle ranks of the Soviet party wrote many letters to him and to the Central Committee. They said that the Soviet intelligentsia were undisciplined, immoral, not reliable. They were like the Petöfi Circle; they had unbuckled their swords and were ready to strike.

Those bastards, said Khrushchev, referring to the party apparatchiki. The *svolochi!* They did not know what the Revolution was about. "We gave birth to them," said Khrushchev, "and they will kill us."

For hours, Khrushchev spoke with the poet he had once criticized. He went back over the events of his life, the tasks he had carried out for Stalin. Finally, they went inside and had a meal. It was dusk when Yevtushenko left the dacha, tired and drawn, tremendously moved by Khrushchev's talk. It was his *Areopagitica.*

A week later, Yevtushenko's telephone rang. It was Rada, the Khrushchev daughter: "Poppa died." Yevtushenko went to the service at the Kuntsevo funeral home. There were about fifteen members of the Khrushchev family, a few others: Julian Semenov, a writer; Sergo Mikoyan, son of Anastas, who brought a wreath from his father; perhaps twenty persons outside the family. There were one hundred police on hand, another one hundred plainclothesmen. Across the street from the funeral parlor, a hundred curious people stood, women with baby carriages, passersby. There was nothing to keep them from crossing the street. But no one did. Yevtushenko did not go on to the services at the cemetery. He was sick at heart and sick to the stomach. He went home and vomited.

Like Mikoyan, Khrushchev was denied his rightful place of burial in the Kremlin wall. He rests in Novodeviche cemetery under Neizvestny's monument. Each year the number of pilgrims to Nikita Sergeevich's grave grew. Each year more handfuls of flowers appeared on his grave. The pilgrims finally became too much for the Brezhnev administration. Now Russia has a *closed* cemetery along with all the other *closed* institutions—*closed* stores for the upper echelons, *closed* dacha communities for the *nomenclatura, closed* archives for the party priests, *closed* meetings for the party elite.

For five years, Novodeviche has been closed to the public, to visitors who might want to lay a flower on Khrushchev's grave. Only relatives of the dead who are buried there are now permitted.

I liked Nikita Sergeevich with all his faults, all his scary flights of fancy. I think he wanted a decent life for his people. I think he wanted to make a firm peace with Eisenhower. He had staked a lot on Eisenhower's promised trip in 1960. He had even, or so it was said, built a golf course in the Crimea and had taken some lessons himself, hoping to join his distinguished guest in this strange Scottish pastime which has never been played in Russia. There was talk of his building a Russian Disneyland. And I have seen the beautiful guesthouse Khrushchev built high over Lake Baikal, in which Eisenhower was to have spent his last night in Siberia on the eastward flight to Japan.

I am not so naive as to suppose that Eisenhower's trip would have resolved all the differences between the U.S.A. and the U.S.S.R. But I suspect the two men could have laid the basis for an evolving collaboration which by now might have given us two decades of serious investment in resolution of conflict rather than aggravation.

Nikita Sergeevich Khrushchev died at the age of seventy-eight on September 11, 1971, at his home, with his family at his side. The world first learned of the event through Victor Louis, who told foreign correspondents about it that afternoon. Not until two days later, on the morning of the funeral, did *Pravda* publish a brief notice. No official of party or government attended the

services. Thousands of police surrounded the Novodeviche cemetery and only members of the family, a few diplomats and correspondents were permitted to be present. His son Sergei spoke
over the grave. "An honest and brave man has died," he said. I
agree.

39 | A New Day Is Coming

I did not realize when I went into Russia in 1944 as a gawky agency reporter that the most important persons I would meet were not generals and front commanders and diplomats like Molotov and Litvinov, but writers like Ilya Ehrenburg and Konstantin Simonov. The sculptress Vera Mukhina was different. I knew the moment I saw her that I was in the presence of a woman who was strong and significant. I did not then know much about Russia, but I had the wit to sense that with her sculptor's hands, sorrow-haunted eyes and compassion, she represented that force which had, again and again, succored Russia after the agonies to which the Lenins, the Stalins, the Peters and the Ivans had subjected her. I sensed her fortitude and abhorrence of war (even as she hammered out the busts of marshals and generals); her contempt and even pity for the posturing Stalins, Molotovs, Kaganoviches and other pygmies of the Politburo. Mukhina and her sisters, I knew, were the life force of Russia.

I did not begin to perceive Ehrenburg's dimensions until his later days. I had no closeness with him until after Stalin's death. Stalin was still warm in his sarcophagus beside Lenin when Ehrenburg's novel *The Thaw* burst on the Soviet scene. For the first time, the forbidden topics of the purges, anti-Semitism, the squalor of the worker's life in the Soviet paradise, the greed of the party, the indecency of the Soviet literary world, were laid on the line. Ehrenburg gave the post-Stalin era its title. *The Thaw* was put together with cardboard and glue, the characters could hardly lift their heads off the page, but Ehrenburg's ears possessed perfect pitch. He knew what he was writing about. He was attacked by *Literaturnaya Gazeta*. All the old vendettas came to the surface. But he triumphed. The thaw had come. The old days were over. He plunged ahead with a doggedness that won my admiration.

I saw him when I went back to Moscow in 1959, and for the first time we began to talk as human beings. Though no less anti-

American than he had been in 1944, he did not feel that he had to prove it every time he opened his mouth. He was now well into the major work of his life, *People, Years, Life,* the memoir in which he sought single-handed to retrieve for future generations their cultural heritage: the writers whose lives Stalin had choked out, the novels and poetry Stalin had flushed down the Memory Hole, the intimate association of the Russian avant-garde and the French Impressionists and Postimpressionists, the cosmopolitan world of Europe, of which Russia was a part up to December 1934. He sought painstakingly, name by name, person by person, year by year, to restore to their historical places those bright talents whom Stalin had tortured and killed.

Whatever may have been Ehrenburg's sins, he compensated for them in *People, Years, Life.* No one in Russia produced anything like it. Nor did Ehrenburg spare himself. He squarely tackled the question of survival in his country, and if he did not explain it (I don't think anyone could), he at least faced the question. He was one of the survivors of the Jewish Anti-Fascist Committee. "I don't know why I am alive and the others are dead," he said. "I had a lucky ticket."

I drew close to this Ehrenburg. We exchanged confidences, and it was he who first gave me insight into the jungle of the Soviet literary world.

No one had had more contempt for "Jewishness," for the Jewish religion, for the notion of Jewish separateness, than Ehrenburg. He had deliberately insulted Golda Myerson, as she was still known, when she arrived in Moscow in 1948 as Israel's first ambassador. Mrs. Myerson gave an official reception at the Metropol Hotel. Paulina Zemchuzhina, Molotov's wife and head of the Soviet cosmetics industry, came up and said in rather formal Yiddish: "I'm a daughter of Israel." (Within weeks she was arrested in Stalin's 1948–49 anti-Semitic purge.) Ehrenburg approached at that moment and Mrs. Myerson greeted him in Yiddish. Ehrenburg turned on his heel, exclaiming (in Russian): "I don't care for American Jewesses who give themselves airs." He had never learned Yiddish and was not raised as a religious Jew. I don't know what he called himself during his life; an atheist, most probably. And yet . . . In the last years of World War II and the first months of peace, he and Vasily Grossman, a Jewish writer who was to be cruelly oppressed by Stalin, compiled the

famous *Black Book,* the encyclopedic record of Nazi extermination of 1,500,000 Jews on Soviet soil. However marred by verbi-
age about the noble Stalin, it is a faithful document of the fate of
Russia's Jews at Hitler's hands—Babi Yar, all the rest.

The fate of the *Black Book* was singular. Once compiled, set in
type and printed, it was ordered destroyed by Stalin, the type
scattered, the plates broken up. Not for thirty years, not until
after Ehrenburg's death, did it reappear like the phoenix, published in Israel in Russian and Yiddish, and then in an English-
language edition in the United States in 1982. The *Black Book*
has left a train of questions in its wake. Why did Stalin authorize its publication? Why, then, did he order it destroyed? Why
did Ehrenburg stand silent when it was consigned to the Memory
Hole? What, in fact, was Ehrenburg's role in this?

There is one clue to what Ehrenburg thought and what he believed he was doing. When in 1946 he visited the United States,
Ehrenburg brought with him a copy of the *Black Book,* just off
the presses, not yet put through the shredder. Ehrenburg presented it to Albert Einstein at Princeton on a fine day in late
May 1946. The two had their pictures taken looking at the copy.
I am certain Ehrenburg felt that by this act, the *Black Book*
would be preserved for future generations, whatever Stalin
might do. And he was right.

I was responsible for the publication in 1963 in the United
States of a collection of Ehrenberg's essays, including his
thoughts on rereading Chekhov and Stendhal. Ehrenburg had a
single theme in these essays, his message to younger writers: to
tell the truth. No matter how difficult. Tell the truth. I do not
think it accidental that his charge to the writers of Russia was
identical with that given to them by Simonov: to tell the truth.

Ehrenburg declared:

"We Russian writers must remember the precepts of our great
predecessors. Chekhov used to say that the writer's duty was to
defend man, that there was enough persecution without our joining in. The world has not known a more humanist literature than
the Russian. And I am proud to be a rank-and-file Russian
writer."

So it is not, perhaps, so surprising that on his seventieth birthday, Ehrenburg, speaking over Moscow radio to the whole country, for the first time publicly took his stand as a Jew.

"I am a Russian writer and so long as there is even a single anti-Semite in the world, I shall answer proudly to the question of nationality: I am a Jew."

It was Ehrenburg who put me onto Mikhail Sholokhov, the author of *The Quiet Don.* I heard tales of Sholokhov from the moment I arrived in Russia in 1944. I knew that he was Stalin's pet. I knew that he lived on an estate in the Don country in a manner not unlike that of the gentry of prerevolutionary days. I knew that he was reactionary, haughty and vituperative. When I came back to Russia in 1949, I discovered to my surprise that he did not necessarily show up at meetings where he was scheduled to speak, something unheard of in Stalin's Russia. People shrugged their shoulders and said, "He's having a night on the town."

I began to hear the rumors that had circulated since the days of his spectacular emergence in 1928, a young man of twenty-three who had written the masterful first volume of *The Quiet Don.* Or had he? There had been a fierce controversy, long since papered over, in which literary critics challenged his claims of authorship. But Stalin had resolved the question in Sholokhov's favor and he had become the "court" novelist of Stalin's regime.

I knew that he had steadily edited, re-edited and revised *The Quiet Don,* filing off the sharp edges, subtly shifting the character of his heroes (the original book had been remarkably sympathetic to the White cause during the Civil War in the Don country).

In the post-Stalin days, Sholokhov had come forward as Khrushchev's "court" novelist, champion of reaction, anti-Semitic, vulgar, profane in his contempt for new young writers or old "liberals" like Ehrenburg. I thought Sholokhov's philosophy remarkably resembled that of those Cossacks on whom Nicholas II relied to put down the revolutionaries.

Ehrenburg hated Sholokhov and the sentiment was returned by Sholokhov. After Khrushchev's "secret speech" against Stalin, Sholokhov led the chorus of hacks and time servers who wanted to put the cork back in the bottle. He denounced Ehrenburg and *The Thaw.* He spat upon the new poets, Zhenya Yevtushenko and Andrei Voznesensky. His comments on young writers like Vasily Aksionov were unpublishable. He would have sent

Dudintsev, author of *Not by Bread Alone,* to a hard-labor correction camp.

I sat with Ehrenburg in his apartment off Gorky Street, walls crowded with the trophies of long years in Paris—Légers, Matisses, Picassos, Modiglianis. I could see him as a young man, arguments raging at the Closerie des Lilas or the Dome, night after night, arguing over the future, whether there would be a future, and the role each would play in it.

As we sat there, Ehrenburg, smoking his inevitable Gauloise, the ashes dripping over his gray pullover as they had when I first met him in Room 346 of the Metropol, spoke of the new scandal surrounding Sholokhov. After thirty years, he had finally completed his second work, *The Virgin Soil Upturned.* The novel had been finished two years earlier, with a tragic but realistic ending. Davydov, the dedicated Communist hero, arrested by the secret police and flung into jail on false charges, takes his own life. It was an ending not unlike that of many dedicated Communists in Stalin's day.

Fair enough. But it was an ending that had touched off violent controversy within the party. It was not a *positive* ending. Party members did not commit suicide. Sholokhov, having made so many changes in *The Quiet Don* at Stalin's orders, put his back up. He would not change this ending. But, said Ehrenburg, the *svoloch,* the son of a bitch, has done it again. Nikita Sergeevich had flown to the Don and visited Sholokhov on his estate at Veshenskaya. There Khrushchev had persuaded him to change the ending; to give it a *positive* turn. Davydov in the new version did not fall victim to the police of the Soviet regime, to which he had dedicated his life, but to the underground anti-Communists.

I published this story in *The New York Times* on the eve of Khrushchev's arrival in September 1960. When Khrushchev landed, whom did he bring in his entourage but Sholokhov. My colleagues quickly raised the question of the "revised ending." Sholokhov responded like a true Cossack. He denied there was any truth in my story and said that the Cossacks had a way of settling such matters. They tied a man to the tail of a spirited pony, gave it a lash on the flanks and let it gallop over the steppes until the victim "had been taken care of."

Sholokhov is a small man, rather stocky, red-faced from years of vodka, and he made his punishment sound realistic. I let one of my associates write the story of "Sholokhov's Revenge." For the next two weeks, though I traveled with Khrushchev all over the country, I hardly caught a glimpse of Sholokhov. I kept hoping for a confrontation, but one never came. I don't know where he was. Maybe tied up with a bottle of vodka.

A few months later, the last episodes of *The Virgin Soil* began to appear in *Pravda*. My story about the new ending was confirmed. I wrote a follow-up for the *Times* and Sholokhov again exploded. This time he simply suggested that I be flogged.

Sholokhov had played a vicious role in attacking Pasternak as a "talentless Jew." Now he called the new generation of writers "giftless anti-party filth" and Solzhenitsyn "a traitor." Solzhenitsyn comes from the Don himself and knows it intimately. After leaving Russia, he gave his imprimatur to a scholarly study by a Soviet critic who signed himself "D." This book sought to demonstrate once again that Sholokhov was not the author of *The Quiet Don;* that it was, in fact, basically written by a White Russian officer and Don Cossack, an author of substantial prerevolutionary reputation, named Fedor Dmitrievich Krykov, who died in the last days of the Civil War.

Solzhenitsyn called for a critical study of Sholokhov's work; for the use of computer techniques to establish whether, as he believed, *The Quiet Don* contained evidence of being composed by more than one hand. His call stimulated the publication in the Soviet Union of a rash of studies designed to support Sholokhov's authorship. As yet, the study proposed by Solzhenitsyn has not been undertaken.

One fact has been established, however: Sholokhov is unwilling or unable to produce the original manuscript of his work. He has advanced various excuses. One is that his writings were lost when the Germans overran Veshenskaya during the war. Yet it is known that the original manuscript was carefully inspected in 1928, when the question of authenticity was first raised. The resultant studies are locked up in the archives. The Sholokhov manuscript is probably there too.

I got to Russia too late to meet the writers of the 1920s and 1930s—Babel, Mandelshtam, Tsvetaeva, Mayakovsky. They were all gone, all, in one way or another, victims of Stalin. And I was far too late for Blok, Bely, Ivanov and Merezhkovsky, whom I later learned to admire. I was not too late for Akhmatova, I suppose, but I was too ignorant in 1944 to know about her, and in the late Stalin era she was, of course, inaccessible. In the last years of her life, I felt too naive and too *American* to approach her.

I did catch a glimpse or two of Lila Brik, the woman with whom Mayakovsky was hopelessly infatuated. But it was very late in her life, at a time when the Soviet literary hit squads had taken to bushwhacking her, publishing articles insinuating that she was not Mayakovsky's femme fatale, that he had tossed her over for Tatiana Yakovleva (it was true Mayakovsky had fallen in love with Tatiana in Paris in the last year of his life); that Francine Grey, Tatiana's brilliant daughter, was actually Mayakovsky's daughter (a concoction which Francine repeatedly had to disprove by showing Soviet writers her passport and date of birth). In these times, Lila Brik lay back on the couch of her drawing room, the walls laden with magnificent works by Nikko Pirosmanishvili, the famous Georgian primitive, by Kandinsky, Tatlin and Picasso, and sometimes told how she had never permitted Mayakovsky to make love to her; how she would lock herself in the bedroom with Osip Brik and ignore Mayakovsky, who would bay in anguish, scratching at the door like a dog. She would tell her visitors, tell me, that had she been in Moscow in 1930, when Mayakovsky returned from Paris, "it never would have happened"—that is, Mayakovsky would not have shut himself into that cubicle of a room which he inhabited on Lubyanskaya Pereulok, just a prisoner's moan from the Lubyanka Prison itself, written a last poem to Lila, taken out his pistol and put a bullet through his heart.

A few hours with Lila Brik was not much, but it gave me a whiff of the wild emotions, despairs, delights, and exuberance of Russian life before Stalin put the poets into uniforms of gray and began, in Pasternak's words, to sell Mayakovsky to the people as Catherine the Great had sold the peasants on planting potatoes.

Of the galaxy of poets who witnessed the Revolution, there was only one whose life persisted long enough to touch mine—Pasternak. I went to meet him on Orthodox Easter of 1959, taking the suburban train to Peredelkino on a warm spring day, the train filled with shoppers returning from Moscow. I had no idea where to find Pasternak's dacha and I was certain there would be police sniffing around the station. Pasternak was still the center of international controversy over *Zhivago* and the Nobel Prize.

I had yielded to the entreaties of a young American woman and allowed her to come with me. No question but we would quickly be spotted. I noticed on the train a woman wearing a gray topcoat with a small gold pin. She was, I was certain, a writer or a writer's wife. If she got off at Peredelkino, I would see if she could tell me the way to Pasternak's. At Peredelkino, she rose and I asked her the question. She smiled. "Of course, I'll show you the way. I'm going to Fedin's [the writer Konstantin Fedin], just next door."

We started off and I saw a car beside the road, a man sitting in it. Sure enough, we were being followed, the car crawling along behind and a man ahead of us, casting a look back from time to time. Fortune favored us. We came to a large field and our guide suggested that we cut across it, directly to Pasternak's. By the time we got to the dacha, the *shpiks* had been outflanked.

A pleasant woman, possibly Pasternak's wife, Zinaida, answered my knock. I heard voices; an Easter feast was in progress. I didn't think she was too happy to see us. While we waited, a yellow dog, probably an Irish terrier, hobbled from an outbuilding. There was something wrong with its hindquarters and it brought a sick and fetid odor to the steps where we waited.

A moment later, Pasternak appeared, tall, lean, gaunt, high cheekbones, scraggly hair, a strong jaw, penetrating blue eyes, his profile more like that of an American Indian than I had imagined. I had brought him a small gift, a letter from Helen Wolff, his American publisher, a sheaf of reviews. We stood talking in the sunny courtyard, his clumsy hands—he was, or so he seemed to me, a clumsy man—encircling my companion's hands and mine. He apologized for not inviting us in. The house was full of guests, his sons and their wives. He was so sad not to receive us. But he had to be very careful. Things were going to be better, but now it was the government's wish that he live quietly.

I apologized for intruding. I said I had felt it was the most appropriate day to come, Easter Day. He smiled and accepted my remark. Pasternak had been born a Jew, but for years had been under the strong influence of the Orthodox faith. He talked a bit about how he worked: two hours in the morning, then he dusted his room, worked a bit in the garden, and back to his desk for two hours. He was deluged by mail. The dog—its name was Mishka—whimpered and the odor seemed to grow stronger. Pas-

ternak stood a moment, then released our hands. We said goodbye and walked to the gate, opened it, glanced back and saw him
still standing there. He gave a little wave and went inside.

Strolling slowly to the Peredelkino station, we passed a courtyard where three village girls were dancing and a boy played the
bayan. At the station, a handsome middle-aged man, red of face,
unsteady of gait, approached. He carried a red paper rose with
green paper leaves.

"Excuse me," he said. "This has been a wonderful day, a wonderful holiday. But now I am without money and, as you can see,
I need a shave. Can you kind people give me a ruble?"

I dug a rumpled paper ruble from my pocket. He leaned forward and kissed my companion's hand. "You are beautiful," he
said. "I've been drinking all . . . I don't know . . ." His words
slurred off. The train came in and we rode back to Moscow.

It had been a small meeting, it had no content, no poetic words,
no profound thoughts, but it lighted a candle in my heart which
will burn as long as I live.

I came back to Peredelkino on January 7, 1962, Christmas
Day, Orthodox Christmas, a snowy day, eighteen months after
Pasternak's death. I went to the blue, rose and white chapel of
the Church of the Assumption, which lies close to the meadow
before Pasternak's house. Hundreds of small candles sparkled at
the altars. Believers filled the church as the priests chanted the
services. I walked out into the world of snow, the world Pasternak had painted in "Christmas Star," one of the Zhivago poems:
"It was winter, the wind blew from the steppes, And it was cold
for the child in the cave of the hillside."

The world was white and great snowflakes sifted down from
gray skies. Youngsters tumbled off the electric trains from Moscow and crisscrossed the fields on their skis, in costumes of red,
yellow and blue. I made my way up to the ridge where Pasternak
was buried beneath two great pines, his gravestone hidden in
snow so that I could only see the words "Boris Leonidovich Pasternak." A fresh wreath lay there, together with a winter-frosted
bouquet of chrysanthemums and a spray of cedar. I was not the
first pilgrim of that snowy Christmas.

I can no longer remember when I first met Zhenya Yevtushenko, Andrei Voznesensky and Bella Akhmadulina. I mean the
exact circumstances. It must have been in the early sixties, but it
seems to me that I have always known them. You could not find

three persons more different, three who have been more close, three who have been more at odds, three who have quarreled and loved, and fought and cried and hated and loved again, three poets so poetic, three Russians so Russian, three persons so important to the life of their country for, amazingly the last twenty-five years! Three heroes, three friends whose friendship embraces me, warms me like a fire in winter and sometimes splashes me with the freezing water of Russian reality.

I cannot and will not in these few pages trace more than a few lines of what I believe Bella and Andrei and Zhenya mean to their country, to me and to the world. If there was anyone in Russia to whom Ehrenburg and Simonov addressed the admonition: "Tell the truth," it was to these three. Oh, yes, I know that these three would have told the truth in any event. You could have frozen Zhenya in the sixty-degree-below-zero mists of his beloved Lake Baikal and he would have told it so long as he could move his frozen jaws. The same for Bella. Even while her teeth are chattering as her imagination conjures up not unrealistic visions of the consequences of her candor, she speaks out the words that are in her heart. "I am not a heroine," she says, shaking her lovely russet head, "I am not brave." But she is the bravest, and God himself could not put a lock on her tongue. And Andrei, so slight, still with his schoolboy's posture, his head cocked to one side, squaring his shoulders and plunging ahead because there is no turning back . . . Three young poets of Russia. Young? Yevtushenko and Voznesensky are turning fifty and Bella is close behind—but they are still Russia's three young poets; younger voices have not appeared. They, with Joseph Brodsky, the Leningrad protégé of Akhmatova, who was compelled to leave Russia (like Solzhenitsyn) and has settled in the United States, constitute Russia's voice today.

What a voice! Any country would be blessed with one of them. It tells us something about Russia *in repression* that Bella, Zhenya and Andrei for all their difficulties (and they are real difficulties and often extreme) go on speaking, have never been silenced. It tells us of their courage and of the curious blend of permission and suppression that has marked Russia's years since 1953.

It has become the fashion in New York literary circles to disparage Yevtushenko. He has been criticized by certain intellectuals as being an instrument of the Soviet state, a propagandist for the regime, a carrier of anti-Semitism, a self-indulgent climber, a publicity hound—Lord knows all the things that have been said of Zhenya. Perhaps they even charge him with cowardice.

All this is spoken from the comfortable security of the barracks of the Upper West Side, from lazy beachheads at Southampton and on the pages of smart literary journals. This is said of the man who wrote "Babi Yar," that eloquent testament to the most savage crime against the Jews committed on Soviet soil, a crime which successive Soviet regimes, beginning with that of Stalin, sought to suppress from public knowledge. It was the "anti-Semite" Yevtushenko who spoke up for the martyrs of Babi Yar and whose poem was published by *Pravda*. When it had become apparent that Nikita Khrushchev was wavering on anti-Semitism, it again was Zhenya who spoke directly to Khrushchev in public and told him his regime was anti-Semitic; and it was he who in the Brezhnev days joined with Dmitri Shostakovich to create the "Babi Yar" symphony, music by Shostakovich, the stark, unlovely words from Yevtushenko's pen.

This poet who has been accused of pandering to the authorities is the man whose poem "Stalin's Heirs" remains the most dramatic warning to Russia, to its leaders and its people, that the danger of Stalin did not die with the old dictator, that Stalinism is alive and flourishing (as it is particularly in these days) and that the tomb of Stalin must be guarded with eternal watchfulness lest his evil spirit again spread over the land.

This is the poet whose lines have roused Russia's younger generation to new horizons, who has sought to give them a new consciousness of the world (not the stale old agitprop world but the contemporary world of rock and blues, the Beatles, the Beat generation and Watergate), never losing his taste for his homeland, Siberia, the Lena, the taiga, the free spirit of the generations that came by étape.

No, I have not lost faith in Zhenya. I know he can make a fool of himself, concocting silly stunts, confusing the Mongols with the Chinese in the xenophobic Russian fashion, taking himself seriously as a politician, not a wandering troubadour.

I have listened to Zhenya talk by the hour. I know his dreams, sometimes adolescent, sometimes soaring. I do not think he is Pushkin (whom he sometimes thinks he is); I don't know whether, as he believes, he has been shot at in Chile, plotted against in Moscow, targeted by the Mafia in New York. But I know he has moved Russia's conscience and sometimes even the conscience of Russia's rulers, and never, so far as I know, for any bad end. I know he has an ego as big as the Pamirs, but that is natural for a poet. I know that he wants the world to survive so that his two sons by his English wife can survive in peace.

I know that Andrei and Bella often criticize Zhenya, and I do too. But that's not bad. I feel uncomfortable with unanimous opinions. When others criticize Zhenya, you will usually find me at his side. I am glad that Zhenya exists. This is a better world for his living in it.

I know Andrei better than I know Zhenya. Perhaps we are more compatible. Zhenya is bigger than life, is forever dashing off to Alaska or the Congo or Vietnam or the South Seas or rafting down the Lena into the Arctic Ocean. God knows where he will turn up next. Of course, Andrei is no slouch at traveling. He has been to the North Pole and I would not be surprised to find him in outer space or on the moon. Andrei is a more *poetic* poet than Yevtushenko, whose style derives more from Mayakovsky, Russia's model of "civic"—that is, politically oriented—verse. Andrei was a protégé of Pasternak. He showed Pasternak each of his early verses and sat at the feet of that enigmatic man. It is no accident that Andrei has undertaken the burden of bringing Pasternak back into Russia's heritage. In 1980, he finally opened the way, or so I believe, for the publication of *Doctor Zhivago* in Pasternak's homeland. Andrei published in that year a long tribute to Pasternak, speaking as Pasternak's pupil. He succeeded in having included in an important anthology four of the religious poems from *Zhivago,* including "Christmas Star."

I know that I am prejudiced about Andrei. When I read his poetry, I hear his voice reciting from a bare stage in a crowded hall in Moscow or New York. I see him with his writing pad, alone beside a quiet pond in Connecticut. I am with him in a snowstorm in the Moscow countryside or sharing the ecstasy of a performance at the Taganka. I watch his face, like that of an impish child, his long pullover, his Oliver Twist cap, his wry grin, and his voice, extraordinarily and unexpectedly loud and resonant, roaring out the rhythm of "The Architectural Hall Is on Fire!" at a mass meeting of thousands of his Russian admirers. I hear him in the passenger lounge of a ferryboat, Allen Ginsberg beside him to translate, booming out his verses to a five o'clock commuting crowd between Manhattan and Staten Island. I am with him on a mountaintop in Connecticut, eating sandwiches and drinking wine; I am on the staircase at Tatiana Yakovleva Liberman's New York house, listening to Andrei read his new poems. We are drinking together late at night in a Moscow restaurant. Too many images, too many memories, warm, close, comradely. I cannot think of a line of Andrei's poetry with which I would argue.

Bella—well, I simply dissolve in Bella's presence. If Andrei is Pasternak's impish pupil, if Zhenya is Mayakovsky today, Bella is the child of Tsvetaeva and Akhmatova, a bit of one, a bit of the other, and very much Akhmadulina, offspring of hope, elfin, a woman of deep tragedy, carrying her fate in her lovely hands, seeing for herself a tragic end because tragedy awaits every Russian poet. I cannot believe it. I cannot believe that haunt will pursue Bella to the darkest corner of her life, but I see it in her eyes when she is sitting in a crowded room, everyone talking but she silent, her eyes far away, her mind far away, thinking perhaps of Tsvetaeva at Tarusa, thinking perhaps of Akhmatova in the queue with the other women at Kresty Prison, bearing a package for her son, telling her neighbor, yes, I will remember it all, I will remember everything, as she did and then wrote of it in "Poem Without a Hero." Akhmatova survived and remembered. Bella will survive and remember. Nor does she forget even now. Careless of herself, careless of reprisals, she goes into battle like Joan of Arc, but she insists, "I am not brave," "I am very frightened," and her eyes look like those of a doe. She is frightened but she does not halt. She cannot. She is a poet. There is no moderation for a poet; moderation is death; Bella is life.

How blessed, I think, that Russia has these poets; how great they are and how much of their greatness comes from the fact that they must fight to survive and they know what they must fight. The enemy is there, clear, obvious. They knew it even before the word was spelled out to them by the "fathers," the generation ahead of them, the Simonovs and the Ehrenburgs, the Mandelshtams, the Tsvetaevas, the Akhmatovas, all the rest. The poets know their mission. It is to tell the truth. Eternally to tell the truth. To make Russia listen to the truth. No matter how awful. To speak and speak again and to use every talent to make their voices heard. How I envy Russia these poets! How proud

Russia will be a hundred years from now of their voices, their
bravery, their honesty. No matter their little games, their feuds,
their fantasies.

No wonder they won crowds of thousands and tens of thousands when they took to the streets after 1956 and 1957 to read
in Pushkin Square and in Mayakovsky Square, to give their extravagant "concerts" at Dynamo, to fill the 100,000 seats of
Luzhniki stadium. Theirs were clear young voices speaking out
after decades of silence, of hypocrisy, of lies. They spoke the
truth, and if they didn't always get it straight, what did it matter? They would do better the next time. Their words flushed
away the stale and dangerous air after Stalin. They go on speaking, speaking, speaking, writing, writing, writing, sometimes
suppressed, sometimes silenced, revolting, finding new political
leverage, never ceasing to fight for a true Russia, an honest
Russia, a world in which people can live, not die.

I believe with William I. Thompson, who in *At the Edge of History* suggests that poets pre-view this world, that their sensitivity
presents to us a vision of the days ahead before those days yet
take form. Andrei Bely in *The Silver Dove,* ten years before the
event, published a terrifying blueprint of the Revolution and its
effect on the life of Russia. Bely understood with the fifth sense
of the poet that the elemental force in Russia, the peasant mass,
would rise and destroy the idealists who sought to overthrow the
Czar, replace him with a new order, rational, humanist, principled, and free the peasants. Instead, peasant violence carried all
before it. So Bely forecast and it came true. So William Butler
Yeats foresaw and perceived the terrible turning of brother
against brother in Ireland long before the guns spoke and the
dynamite went off.

So I believe the poets of Russia can tell us more of the future,
more of the state of their land, than analysts of think tanks,
strategists of security councils, and satellite scans by the CIA's
high tech. So I listen to the voices of the Akhmadulinas, the Voz-
nesenskys, the Yevtushenkos, the Brodskys. Above all, I listen to
the voice of Aleksandr Isayevich Solzhenitsyn.

Solzhenitsyn once said that a nation which possesses a good
writer is a nation which possesses "another government." I do
not know whether he was thinking of himself. He well might
have been. Aleksandr Isayevich is not merely the foremost writer

of Russia, the foremost writer of the world—he is "another government."

So it was, of course, with the giants of the nineteenth century —with Pushkin, Dostoyevsky, Tolstoy, Dickens and Thackeray, Heine, Hugo and Balzac. Perhaps even with Samuel Clemens. But I can think of no one in England, France or the United States today who speaks with a magisterial voice. Solzhenitsyn does. He towers above all. It is not unnatural that he is criticized, harassed, niggled at by poetasters in the salons of London, Paris and New York. But there is one government that does not underestimate the power of his mind and the weight of his pen. That is the Soviet government. (Russia possesses only one intellect of comparable power—that of Andrei Sakharov, and he has been deported into internal exile in the isolated city of Gorky.)

I did not know Aleksandr Isayevich in Russia. I shared in the excitement of his first published work, *One Day in the Life of Ivan Denisovich*—the event of that watershed year in Russia, 1962. In 1967, when I got back to Moscow, Solzhenitsyn had not yet crossed the line of contact with foreigners and correspondents. Not until he emerged from Russia, forcibly compelled to leave by the KGB, did our contacts begin, at first by letter and then, after he came to America, in person, meetings rare and precious.

Long before Solzhenitsyn left Moscow, I had, by chance, become privy to much of the secret side that led to the publication of *The First Circle* and, later, *The Gulag Archipelago,* works that, with *Ivan Denisovich* and *The Cancer Ward,* have changed the landscape, as we perceive it, of Russia and specifically of Russia in the Stalin years. I think no literary talent in the second half of this century has had a force comparable to Solzhenitsyn's. There is the meticulousness of his observation, the dense brushwork with which he fills his canvas, the philosophy that gives his work resonance. And there is his grasp of the character of the Russian man and the Russian world, which matches that of his greatest predecessors. If it can be said that Dostoyevsky changed our notion of the geography of the emotions, that Tolstoy gave us our moral values, then Solzhenitsyn has given new dimension to the architecture of the soul, its corruptibility, its nobility, its inscrutability.

Solzhenitsyn is not a man for the weak of heart. He does not spare himself, nor does he spare anyone. He is dedicated to a single purpose, the overthrow of Bolshevism and the restoration of a Russia faithful to the Orthodox Church and the traditions of the Russian ethos. He is a radical in a world of time servers. His words ring harshly in our ears. He has no mercy for the idolaters in the temple. He expects no mercy from Moscow, but is contemptuous of Moscow's ability to match his Cromwellian zeal. He has laid out his life like a military commander embarking on a long campaign behind enemy lines. He has provisioned himself for hard times, long sieges, unexpected assaults. He has total confidence in victory and in a Russia Redux.

If I make Aleksandr Isayevich sound formidable, even frightening, I have every intention of so doing. He is a man who believes he can bend kingdoms. I am not one to say he is wrong.

His face is familiar to the whole world, the deep-set eyes, wary with the experience of Gulag, fierce in conviction that faith will prevail over the Antichrist that has possessed the Russian spirit. His forehead seems to be marked by a deep scar. It is not. The strong line has been etched by resolution and will. He moves gracefully, like an animal, or, more plausibly, like a hunter slipping through the forest, conscious of every beast in the undergrowth, hardly rustling a leaf, deft as an Indian tracker. His figure is slight but muscular. He does not walk for miles every day, as he used to; he does not cut wood, as he once did; he does not carry heavy burdens on his back. But his muscles have not gone slack. There is a sense of steel in his close-knit frame. His beard is red and his eyes are blue. They see deep into you.

A fearsome man? No, a gentle man, but if he has you within the sights of his rifle, don't expect his shot to miss. He has a steady hand. Aleksandr Isayevich is a military man. I can see him in command of his artillery unit in East Prussia in World War II, following in the trail of his father, who fought over this land in World War I. A superior artillery officer, he is a man who knows his guns, his mathematics, his trigonometry, his discipline, a man whose company is smart, obeys swiftly, acts with precision.

Aleksandr Isayevich has programmed himself like a computer —his daily working schedule, his monthly writing quotas, his years of productive life, his series of historical novels, soon to come on line in a publication sequence that he worked out years earlier, and finally his great project for a new history of Russia to replace the classic Klyuchevsky and give a foundation on which to rebuild its nobility and respect—all this and more. Aleksandr Isayevich is not only a literary classic, he is a moral and political preceptor for the ages.

We sometimes try to fit Solzhenitsyn into an American iconostasis. It makes no sense. This man is a Russian, first and always. Every word he writes, every breath, every minute, is dedicated to one cause—Russia. If he criticizes American life (and he does), if he finds fault with our mores (and he does), if he is dismayed by our political life (and he is), if our press seems to him unruly and unprincipled (which it often is), if the policy of our Presidents and Congresses seems incomprehensible to him (as it may well to us), the basic and enduring reason is that Aleksandr Isayevich assesses all these from a single perspective—how do they affect his grand design, the resurrection of Russia, free of Communist influence, purged of modern decadence, arising again in the grandeur of ancient Rus, the Pravoslavnye Church and the purity of an earlier social contract.

Unless we understand this truth about Aleksandr Isayevich, we understand nothing.

I am afraid this picture presents the image of a forbidding man, a narrow man, a fanatical man. Nothing is further from reality. I judge a man not solely by his words, his goals, his public personality. I judge him by his private person, his interior life, the milieu he inhabits, the men and women about him, his family, the home he makes for them.

One winter day, Charlotte and I and two close friends visited Aleksandr Isayevich in his sunny, cheerful, invigorating house in the hills of Vermont, far from any city, set in a small forest, the great living room windows looking out on white birches, pines, distant snow-covered meadows, as Russian a vista as any to be found in the Ryazan *gubernia*. Here was a home that radiated life and cheer and *goodness*—that old-fashioned word, but I know no other—the goodness of Russian black bread, of the Russian word, of the bright Russian colors of a woman's dress. Here, in a house and working compound organized with exquisite attention to detail, Aleksandr Isayevich lives and works, with his wife, Natasha, their three blue-eyed, blond-haired Russian boys, Yermolai, then nine, Ignat, seven, and madcap Stepan, six, and his wife's mother, Ekaterina, in an atmosphere so Russian it brought tears to my eyes. Instantly I was transported back to the Russia of the last century, to the *Sovremennik* of Chernyshevsky and Dobrolubov, the bright dreams of the *narodniki,* the familiar pages of that companion of every Russian family of 1890, the illustrated weekly *Niva,* something like the *Harper's Weekly* of my father's youth, to that distant, intellectual, moral Russia which had already begun to disintegrate by 1900, not so much by the desiccation of the monarchy as by the battering rams of the new capitalists, the Morozovs, the Ryabushinskys, the Guchkovs and the others, who were demolishing the old Russian society with their new railroads, steel mills, coal mines and textile plants.

That evening, after a Russian dinner and toasts to those absent in prison and in exile, a toast which Russians have drunk for a hundred years, we seated ourselves in a small "ballroom" and the three boys, with their square-cut hair, their straight backs, their beautiful manners, their perfect English, their perfect Russian, distributed programs of their *konsert.*

Ignat played the piano, announcing his piece, a minuet by Bach, in proper Russian fashion before taking his seat at the Steinway. He played easily, confidently, a bit slowly. Aleksandr Isayevich said with a father's pride that Rostropovich thought the boy had talent. I think that is correct. Yermolai announced his piece, Lermontov's "Otchizna," and spoke the poem's words in confident Russian.

Stepan was next. He recited Mother Goose verses in English— "Fe, fi, fo, fum" and "Eeny, meeny, miney, mo," "Tom Thumb," "Jack and Jill" and "The Cat and the Fiddle," recited in his own rhythm: "Hey-y-y-y-y-y-y-y-y-y diddle, diddle."

Each boy stood straight as an arrow, head high, arms at sides, responding to applause with a little bow.

I asked Aleksandr Isayevich which of the boys he had most resembled in childhood. In appearance, he said, Yermolai, but in character, Stepan. I had been certain Aleksandr Isayevich had been bright, indulged by his parents, and in his youth mad for the theater, his ambition to be an actor, but cut off from that when a doctor told him his throat was not strong enough for an acting career. There was, I thought, still something of the actor in Aleksandr Isayevich. He could play the prophet, the thunderer, but the role in which he felt most congenial was that of paterfamilias, the head of a Russian family improbably planted in Vermont, as Russian as rye, as Russian as the Orthodox Church. They had their own little home chapel and icons, a priest who gave the youngsters instruction in religion, music and art. Aleksandr Isayevich taught them mathematics, Russian history and Russian literature, and conduct, and Natasha watched over them with motherly warmth.

Never in Russia had I been in so Russian a household, never in Russia had I met so Russian a family, so Russian a house, such Russian children, such Russian parents, and nothing so exquisitely nineteenth-century Russian as the children's *konsert*. It came from the pages of Chekhov or Turgenev, the shining faces of the boys, the quiet, confident parents. I was plunged back a hundred years in history, when all over Russia families lived like this, the children brought up in a close bond of morality, good literature, good works, companionship and religion.

When good night and *do svdaniye* was said by all and we went out into the star-sprinkled night with fresh snow on the ground, the Vermont hills dusted with diamonds in the distance, I felt that I was leaving the heart of Russia, the warm, beating heart of Russia, remarkably transported to New England. I realized that I had been on a visit not alone to the Russia of the 1880s but to the America of Longfellow and Hawthorne and Emerson.

It was a bracing moment, and as I looked back on it, I could not but share the faith of Aleksandr Isayevich. In truth, whatever their extremes of personality (and I know none of them who would welcome comparison with another), all of those in the company of this chapter share a single goal. They wish to see a better world and a better Russia, and if they differ widely as to how that goal is to be reached, they have one common bond: they believe that, one way or another, in the spirit of Herzen and in the words of Chernyshevsky, "a new day is coming," a day of truth.

And for all the pessimism which sometimes suffuses me, I share that belief and take strength and hope from these men and women of Russian courage.

40 | The Long Journey

I told the driver to take us to Saltykovka. He knew it well, he said. He was a *moskvich*—that is, he had been born in Moscow; his father, too, had been born in Moscow and worked at the Serp i Molot, the Hammer and Sickle, plant. He had grown up in the Baumansky *raion*. I said, "Then you know where Saltykovka is —out the Chaussée Entusiastov."

"I know," he said. "It used to be a terrible road." It had been, too.

I thought Saltykovka was a good place to start out. We were back in Moscow again, Charlotte and I, the Moscow I had first seen thirty-eight years before and she in 1967. It was the summer of 1982, and already I had found that the Moscow of World War II and the Stalin years had begun to fade from memories.

We had landed at Sheremetovo, an enormous airport that looks like every airport all over the world, and driven in through the new *kvartali,* the sprawl of apartment and factory complexes that fills the flat Moscow plain. We passed a concrete memorial supposed to mark the limit of Nazi penetration in the terrible autumn of 1941, but when we reached the old city limits at Khimki on the Moskva River, nothing denoted the spot where in 1944 I had seen the carcass of a light Nazi tank, one of those that had clawed through the barriers to the city itself. No one remembered that tank but me. Nor did anyone remember the old Tsentralnaya airport, where I had first landed in Moscow, just across Leningrad chaussée from the Sovetskaya Hotel, where our bus deposited us.

Inside the Sovetskaya, I took Charlotte to see its restaurant. This was, in fact, the famous Yar, where Rasputin had caroused, where young noblemen had flung their last gold rubles at the feet of the Gypsy dancers and walked out in the gray dawn to put a bullet through their brains. The Gypsies were long gone and a brassy band played hot jazz for the new elites, the upper middle class (yes, there now is in Moscow a powerful upwardly mobile middle class), the intelligentsia, the high bureaucracy. Not many of them had ever heard of the Yar.

I felt a bit of a survivor. I could not have guessed in January 1944 that I was only on the first leg of a long journey; that I would be coming back again and again; that Russia would, in fact, dominate so much of my adult life. I had traveled to the most remote parts, had seen more of the country than most Russians, and had lived with Russia through dramatic times and terrible troubles. Like it or not, Russia had been woven into the fabric of my life.

I found myself a bit uncomfortable in the Moscow of 1982. To be certain, I had hardly been comfortable in the Moscow of Stalin, with its deep shadows, its dangers, its despairs, its victims. I would never forget the icy winter of 1953, walking alone, night after night, to the Central Telegraph Office, past the frost-hoared windows, lights still burning, people up at 2 A.M., God knows what they were doing. Occasionally, a black car was parked beside the building. Were the jackboots echoing up the staircases, bursting in a door, ransacking a room, as the family huddled in terror, waiting for a father to disappear down the icy steps? Why did the *dezhurnayas* at the Metropol lower their eyes when I passed by?

I had known every street of that Moscow. I had walked them with Sytin's guide in hand, tracing my way through the Kitai *gorod* or the old Arbat, stopping at the houses, studying which Morozov, which Stroganov, which poet, had once lived there. Stalin's Moscow was a frightening Moscow, but it was *my* Moscow. I shared its fears. I might even, I sometimes thought, share its fate. But in the new Moscow I felt like a walk-on, looking from the outside at the endless march of construction that distorted my perspectives—the overpasses, the superhighways and the intricate traffic patterns.

Now we had reached the Chaussée Entusiastov. This was the old road out of Moscow to Siberia. Here the étapes began, the convoys of young revolutionaries, singing the forbidden songs, convicts with their begging chants, men and women in manacles, in leg irons, the hangdog Czarist guards turning their eyes when young girls pressed flowers on the prisoners, when housewives rushed out with loaves of new-baked bread and warm milk fresh from the cow's udder. The Chaussée Entusiastov had got its curious name in the early Soviet era to celebrate the enthusiasm of the young exiles, confident that in Siberia they would gain strength for the overthrow of the Czar and the building of a new order, fine, noble, pure. How naive!

On this warm August day, speeding along the divided six-lane highway, I turned to Charlotte and said: "There is not one thing here to remind me of my days in Moscow." There wasn't. No detours. No clouds of dust, no seas of mud. No endless waits for columns of trucks to pass. I kept watching for the old railroad bridge and the twisted lane we had followed while it was being rebuilt. All gone. I did spot the big chemical works, but huge cement ovoids had replaced the wooden coolers, dripping with water and enveloped in white steam, summer and winter, and the works were twice as big. Two-thirds of the way out, there had been a small NKVD camp, one of the camps from which Beria had drawn troops when he took over Moscow at the time of Stalin's death. Now the camp stretched for a mile or more along the highway. Everything was bigger.

When we got to Balashika, the textile town, I did not recognize the traffic-circle turn to the Ryazan chaussée, but the Ryazan road was familiar territory—wider, to be sure, but I was certain the old cobblestones lay under the new asphalt.

At the little bridge beside which the Vodopad restaurant had stood, Charlotte spotted a couple of picnic tables, but no trace of the pleasant tavern where the patrons had whiled away an afternoon eating crayfish and drinking beer.

The driver took us all the way to the Saltykovka railroad station. It was late afternoon now, but the *rynok,* the peasant market, was still open, cabbage and potatoes, carrots and onions for sale, some dried mushrooms, a few strawberries and one jovial farmer who insisted that I try a handful of huckleberries, tart and tasty. Of course, the Chinaman who had sold hot cross buns had vanished. So had the old lady with her bag of sunflower seeds and, hidden under her broad black skirts, a small stock of icons and religious books.

I was pleased. I had loved the Saltykovka *rynok,* the crowds of dachniki shopping on Sundays in their summer costumes of striped cotton pajamas and dressing gowns.

We decided to walk back along Dachnaya Street to the house that Tom and Juli and I had occupied thirty years before. We had taken this walk fifteen years earlier with our children, Ellen and Stephan, and Tom's daughter, Louise, and picnicked near the dacha. Then Dachnaya Street looked as I had first seen it, a greensward, the grass cropped by the goats of the dachniki, a broad avenue hardly touched by a wheeled vehicle.

Now the greensward had become a rutted track for the cars of the dachniki. No more goats. The lane was littered with *musor*— that is, paper, broken bricks, ashes, tin cans, bottle fragments, sometimes raked into untidy heaps, sometimes not. Many of the dachas that were so prosperous in 1967—painted in bright blues and greens by their owners, with neat gardens, fruit trees, berry patches, potato plots, zinnias, bachelor's buttons and nicotiana— sighed with neglect, porches tilting, steps broken, paint weathered off, grown up in weeds, with not even a bright clump of tall sunflowers in a sunny corner. I could not believe my eyes. Sadly Charlotte and I crossed the marshy stream where once six or seven fat geese had paddled in their whiteness, and headed for the dacha of the man who "stole" the Saltykovka well, the house now hidden and gray behind a decaying fence. Beside it I saw the well, what was left of it. Gone was the windlass, the rope, the bucket, the neat stone carapace. Instead I saw an iron hand pump, handle dangling, rusted, the well abandoned, falling in, no longer of use, not to the man who had "stolen" it, not to the women who had got it back. It broke my heart.

"What happened?" I asked a passing woman. "Oh," she said proudly, "we don't need a well anymore. They put in water mains several years ago, and sewers too; everything up to date."

Well, I guess it was up to date, but something had been lost. Indeed, as I saw a moment later, our dacha was gone too. The whole row was gone. "They were falling down," the woman said. "In terrible shape. So they replaced them with new dachas. About ten years ago."

In place of our dacha was another, not quite so large, no front porch, no colored panes of glass. It looked as though it had been there forever. When I told a Russian friend later, he shrugged: "All state property deteriorates very rapidly."

Our dacha was gone. So was that of the industrious Balakiryov family, so was that which the Hungarian diplomat had briefly rented. The tumbledown "barracks" where Dedya Petya and Natasha had lived still stood. We turned back to the station. On the path, Charlotte saw a scrap of bright blue paper, the wrapper from a jar of Pond's Beauty Shampoo. Saltykovka had entered the age of consumerism, and it didn't become her well.

As we drove back to Moscow, I thought of the years I had lived in Saltykovka. This was the most *Russian* period of my life, the time when I had lived more nearly as a Russian lived, entered more closely into the Russian spirit, sitting long hours in the garden, drinking tea from a samovar, endless philosophical discussions, hunting for mushrooms in the birch woods, days that came from the pages of Chekhov. I possess a strong sense of place, and the destruction of the Saltykovka dacha, like the destruction of my old house on Royalston Avenue, put a period to an epoch in my life. True, I might return again to Saltykovka (as I had to Royalston Avenue), but I would never *be* there again. Indeed, it would not surprise me if the next time I drove out the Chaussée Entusiastov I found Saltykovka gone, physically eradicated, the dachas and pleasant pines bulldozed away to make place for another of those industrial complexes that gird Moscow like fat inner tubes.

On another Moscow day, Charlotte and I made our way to Peredelkino. The last time we had been there, we had gone first to Pasternak's grave, and this we did again. We had a little trouble finding it—the cemetery on the hillside had grown and the grave was no longer at the edge of the meadow looking over to Pasternak's house. Half a dozen new lanes of graves had intruded into the field.

Hovered over the simple slab on which a bas-relief of Pasternak's head is impressed were three figures, two men and a woman, so engaged in discussion they did not notice us. They were past middle age, one man wearing a workingman's cap (probably a retired professor), another neatly dressed in a tweed suit (probably a minor critic) and a pleasant-looking woman (probably the widow of another literary personage). They were friends or enthusiasts of Pasternak and they were talking about an ugly scar on the Pasternak gravestone.

I asked how it had happened. Someone had bashed the monument with a stone, one of the men said. "Deliberately?" I asked. "Yes," he replied, "deliberately."

I could not but think of the blow struck against Pasternak when *Zhivago* was published, a blow dealt deliberately. But it had no more damaged Pasternak's reputation than had this casual stone damaged his memory. Let it stand, I thought, let it stand like the mud hurled by the official calumniators at the time of the Nobel Prize. It reflects not on Pasternak but on the perpetrators.

Now, again, I knew, the literary roughnecks were at work. Now their target was Pasternak's dacha. They wanted to evict his heirs, wanted to tear down the house where *Zhivago* was written and put up a "modern" dacha for some "modern" Soviet hack. They had told the Pasternaks: "Why should we preserve this house? Pasternak was not even a Soviet writer." They were trying to do the same thing to the dacha of Kornei Chukovsky.

We went over to Pasternak's house. A beautiful blue-eyed blond girl of sixteen or seventeen, wearing a simple blue cotton homespun dress, her hair in braids, was standing by the gate. She was Pasternak's granddaughter, and she took us inside the house and showed us Pasternak's working room on the second floor, devoid of most of its furniture because the house was undergoing a *bolshoi remont,* a major renovation ordered by Litfund, the writers' pension fund, which was trying to evict the Pasternaks. "The house seems safe for the time being," the girl said with a wry smile. "But no one knows what might happen next year."

We walked on to Kornei Chukovsky's dacha. Chukovsky had been a beloved figure, a children's writer, the A. A. Milne of Russia. Every child grew up on his tales, and when we visited him fifteen years before, he had shown us the children's library he had built with 250,000 rubles of his royalties, a fairy tale cottage of bright yellows, bright reds, greens, blues, splashed with pictures of animals and scenes from his stories, set in a garden of cockleshells and Canterbury bells. Within, we had found children reading their favorite books and playing games, eyes glistening at the sight of Chukovsky. Heaven, no less. Chukovsky was eighty-five years old that summer and Charlotte thought he was the most handsome man she had ever seen. "He looked the way I expected all Russian men to look," she wrote in her book, *Russian Diary.* She had known Serge Obolensky in New York and thought all Russians must look like him. Chukovsky fell in love with Charlotte at first sight. When I took their picture, he called her "My darling, my love, my bride." He had given refuge to Solzhenitsyn in the spring of 1967, when Aleksandr Isayevich was preparing his letter to the Writers' Union, calling for the abolition of censorship, and he pointed with pride to a snapshot of himself with Solzhenitsyn. He had, he said, been the first person after Aleksandr Tvardovsky, editor of *Novy Mir,* to read *One Day in the Life of Ivan Denisovich* and to support its publication. I thought he was more proud of his friendship with Solzhenitsyn than of his life's work. Chukovsky showed us his new toy, a lion from F. A. O. Schwarz. When he pulled a cord, it said: "I'm not a cowardly lion. I'm not a cowardly lion."

Now, as we pushed through the gate, we saw that the Chukovsky house needed paint, some windows were broken and there was debris scattered around the doorstep. Beside the door a little notice had been tacked up. It said: "Museum-House of Kornei Chukovsky," and gave the visiting hours, three days a week. We knocked, as we had fifteen years before. Then, Lydia Chukovskaya, Kornei's daughter, had greeted us, wearing a red dress, her black hair pulled up in a knot. We had only a glimpse of her as she ran upstairs, heels tap-tap-tapping, called to her father, hurried down, telling us to go up, and was off to town. She was, I knew, a strong woman. She had spent time in Stalin's camps, her husband and many friends had been killed by Stalin, she was close to Anna Akhmatova and had written of her. Kornei died in 1969. Five years later, Lydia had been excluded from the Soviet Writers' Union for her uncompromising support of those towering figures of contemporary Russia, Aleksandr Solzhenitsyn and Andrei Sakharov.

This was in my mind as the door opened and a woman appeared, ramrod-straight in long navy-blue cardigan, white shirtwaist and black skirt, a white net catching her gray hair. She wore heavy glasses. "I'm almost blind," she told us. This was Lydia Chukovskaya fifteen years later, worn but indomitable. She invited us into her kitchen, where we sat a long time, talking. She told us of the bureaucrats of Litfund who were trying to throw her out, to tear down the house and put up a new villa for some party-line writer. She had contempt for Litfund and more contempt for the cowards of the Writers' Union who would lift no voice in protest against the bully boys. Not that she was without support. The Society for the Preservation of Historical Monuments had come to her aid and even the *raion* party had sent a committee to inspect her house and, very polite and even sympathetic, to tell her they were on her side but, alas, had no power to overrule Litfund. Some of the foreign ambassadors, the American ambassador Arthur Hartman among them, had come to visit. There had been stories in the foreign press, but she was not reassured. She told us what had befallen the children's library. It had burned down a few years earlier, whether a random fire set by village hooligans or destroyed deliberately, who could say. It had been rebuilt, but without the charm of the original. The garden was unkempt. Worst of all was the woman who had been installed to run the place. She had turned it into an annex of agitprop, the joy and sunshine blotted out. Lydia would not set foot on the grounds. She lived alone and in fear that some night, vandals might break in, commit an outrage or set the house on fire. The roof leaked, the plumbing had rusted out, the plaster was falling. Litfund would do nothing. They had repaired the foundation only because they feared the house would tumble down.

We went upstairs to the cheerfully cluttered room where we had talked with her father. It was just as we had seen it—the snapshot of Solzhenitsyn, and on a nearby shelf the cowardly lion. I could not bear to ask whether the cowardly lion still spoke in that quavering voice which delighted Kornei Chukovsky.

I spoke a moment about Solzhenitsyn. I told Lydia that we had visited him in Vermont and talked a bit about his life and work in America. "He is," I said, "a very complicated man." "Don't I know it," she replied. "Remember he lived in this house."

Later we walked out past the little hut where Lydia wrote her books about Akhmatova, and we saw the miniature outdoor theater with its wooden benches and wooden platform where Kornei Chukovsky entertained children by the thousand, sometimes reading his books and poems, sometimes getting friends from Moscow to put on plays. Now it was growing up in weeds. No one in Moscow had the creativity or courage to endow the memory of the vanished Pied Piper by seeing that his fairy tales lived on.

We said goodbye to Lydia, hardly able to bear the thought that she must go back to this once lovely house which the gray bureaucrats had turned into a shabby ruin. As we went out the gate to the street, I saw the snout of a piggish *shpik* protruding from the children's playground, trying to spy out who was visiting Lydia Chukovskaya. When we got into our car, he ambled lazily back to the children's library, there, no doubt, to put in a telephone call or scribble a swinish report.

Ah, Russia, Russia, Russia! When will you change? When will decency and goodwill, brightness, imagination and an open heart, prevail over the dark forces that have stifled your spirit for so many centuries, one dynasty after another, from Ivan the Dread to Nicholas II, from Lenin to Brezhnev, from a stupid czar to a stupid commissar? Is there no path out for you, Russia, for your glorious lands, your amazing peoples, your treasures of talent, of culture, of genius, of wisdom—and your blank banality?

I know I sound like Herzen, Gogol, Dostoyevsky, Dobrolyubov, Chernyshevsky and even Amalrik, but the question has haunted Russia from the days of Catherine. What to do? What is to be done with this blundering giant of a nation, this blind colossus which threatens itself and threatens the world by its inability to manage its affairs with even a shadow of civility?

Do not expect an answer on these pages. There will not, I fear, be one in my day, nor, perhaps, for another century.

Years and years ago, I met a Russian who had thought deeply about his country. He is a man whom I saw in Moscow in the summer of 1982, a professional, a technician, not a man of politics or government, a man well read in Russian history, Russian literature, in the European classics—Pascal, Shakespeare, Ibsen, Goethe, Stendhal—not much American literature since school days, when he read James Fenimore Cooper, O. Henry and Mark Twain. He has little fondness for *partinost,* the party sensibilities of Moscow. He prefers the provinces, even with their dusty despots (although he lives in Moscow), and values the old Russian culture, is hostile to the new consumerism and cherishes a keen curiosity about the thinking of Aleksandr Solzhenitsyn. He reminds me a bit of my grandfather's generation in Minnesota, open-minded, inquiring, skeptical, confident of the ability of men to overcome nature's hardships, dubious of man's political capacity.

"We had a great chance in Russia," he told me one day. "A great chance for a new beginning. The Revolution wiped the slate clean. There was so much that needed to be done and so much enthusiasm, the young people especially. I keep wondering if, had Lenin lived, things might not have been different. He was a shrewd man and he knew before his death that it was not working out. Maybe he could have saved it. Once Lenin was gone, it was too late. I think the Revolution was too young, too new. It didn't understand Stalin. But Lenin did."

I don't know whether I agree with my friend. There is nostal-

gia in Russia today for this idealized Lenin, but I believe that
many of the evils in the Soviet system stem directly from Lenin,
from his fanatic insistence upon one-party rule, his pyramidal
party structure, which deprived those at the bottom of any more
voice in government than they had under the Czar—less, perhaps, since under the Czar they could protest and demonstrate
(often being shot down, to be sure, in the process) and sometimes
make their views felt. That hasn't been true since—well, since
Kronstadt in 1922, when Lenin with Trotsky's aid mowed down
the revolting sailors who were protesting that the Revolution had
lost its idealism.

What to make of a society that systematically and in each generation savagely wipes out its most talented souls—the roll is so
long it would take pages to list. Every literate person knows the
name of Aleksandr Blok. His long poem *The Twelve* epitomizes
the Revolution. Not long before Blok died, in 1921, his mind and
spirit broken, he wrote: "Dirty rotten Mother Russia has devoured me as a sow gobbles up her suckling pig."

So it has gone—Lev Gumilev, poet, husband of Akhmatova,
shot as an enemy of the Revolution; Isaak Babel, victim of Stalin; Ivan Bunin, driven to exile; Chagall, Rosanova, Kandinsky
and the others, fleeing to Berlin and Paris; Esenin a suicide;
Mayakovsky a suicide; Tsvetaeva a suicide; the poets, one after
the other, shooting themselves, slashing their wrists; Mandelshtam first driven mad and then to death in Stalin's camps. I
could go on and on; generation by generation, history repeats itself: Pasternak silenced; Solzhenitsyn driven abroad; Brodsky
driven abroad; Rostropovich and Baryshnikov choosing to de-
fect; the camp system revived—for street criminals and poets
whose thoughts do not fit the party pattern, camps for them, or
worse, insane asylums.

"That is what I most fear," a poet told me a few years back,
a poet I had known for years. Somehow he had got hold of
a revolver. "Don't worry," he said. "I'm all right. If they come
for me I will use it." Echoes of Maisky, of Litvinov, of
Mikoyan, men who kept a revolver not to fire at a robber or
to repel an attack but with which to end their own lives if
"they" came.

I think of a young man, son of an old friend in Moscow. He
has a good position, fine connections, a brilliant career. He does

not lead a dull life. His father often goes abroad. The family is well established, with all the consumer comforts: record players, tapes, cars, access to foreign films, a chance to travel to Hungary or Bulgaria almost anytime, once in a while to Western Europe. He reads and speaks English, knows what is published in the West, is happily married. But . . . "I don't know how much longer I can live here," he said. "It isn't any one thing. It is everything. My father has his career. I have a career too. But it doesn't absorb me. I could lead a different life somewhere else. And it isn't even that things are getting worse here. They are not. Life is better, far better, than when I was growing up."

But there was something about the air. He knew that life abroad would be difficult. He did not expect to be happy. But eventually, he thought, he would have to go. He had a Jewish grandmother. "That is a lifeline," he said. "Of course, they will make a fuss. But sooner or later I will leave."

Then there is Natasha, a beautiful, classic blond Russian girl, just out of the university, talented, a scholar in the literature faculty, fascinated by America, American literature, American life. She thought John Irving's *The World According to Garp* the funniest thing she had ever read. She read John Updike. She loved *Catch-22.* Kurt Vonnegut was her hero. She cried over Styron's *Sophie's Choice.* She had seen all of Tennessee Williams's plays (the latest Moscow rage) and she believed the Soviet Union the finest, most wonderful, most democratic country in the world. She hadn't a single negative thought about Russia, nor did she have many about America, except, perhaps, for questions about some American leaders whom she could not understand. It never entered her mind to challenge the validity of Soviet society. She had been to London, had spent four or five months at an English university, had enjoyed every moment, but could not understand the commercialism, as she saw it, of English cultural life. She thought English people sometimes went to Stratford-on-Avon not to see the plays but to enjoy a good dinner. She hated the ignorance of her fellow university students. "It's not that the English don't know anything," she said. "It's that they seem not to want to know anything. They never talk about art or literature or what one should do with one's life. All they talk about is football. All they like to do is drink beer."

Natasha never harangued anyone about Soviet morals or Communist philosophy. She did not belong to the Komsomols. She

just accepted what she believed were the human principles of Soviet society. She was too young, perhaps too sheltered, to have
encountered the swinish bureaucracy. She knew about Stalin (so
she thought—really she didn't know very much), but that was
"all behind us." It didn't concern her or her generation.

She was, I thought, the best bright hope of Russia. I saw in
her clear gray eyes a reflection of the eyes of the generation of
the sixties and seventies of the last century, that devotional generation which dedicated its lives to Russia's "black people," as
they were called, the youngsters of the "Going to the People"
movement, who went into the villages of the remote forests, trying to bring enlightenment, often paying with their lives when
the black Russian *narod,* suspicious of any stranger, did away
with them quietly, their bodies vanishing without a trace into the
bottomless bogs.

What would happen when those clear, honest eyes of Natasha
for the first time perceived the cant, the banality behind the
spiritual image of this country of hers? What then? Would the
young turn against the old? Perhaps, but it would be a long, long
road for them, as it was for the young people of the nineteenth
century.

These questions possessed my mind as I sat one night in the
comfortable house of another old friend, a man who had lived
through the Stalin days, who had known most of what had happened then, a man whose own life had been brushed by the tragedy of Stalin's crimes, a man who knew the good and the bad of
Soviet society and not a little about American life.

"We have come a long way," he said. "I know how discourag-
ing these times seem. I know how bad it was under Stalin. I
know the chances we missed with Khrushchev. It is true that
Brezhnev has not been imaginative. But we could have had something much worse. There are bad men here, but they have not got
control. I don't think they will when Brezhnev dies. You must
not lose hope—if you do, all is lost."

I thought his words wise. So many times in Russia it has
seemed that all hope was gone, perhaps never so clearly as in the
days of 1941 when I was still waking up to a 6 A.M. alarm clock,
struggling out of bed in Mamaroneck, catching the commuter
train to New York to write the story of the Wehrmacht pounding eastward, deeper and deeper into Russia, wondering if any

force on earth could halt Hitler. Not much hope in those days. Nor had there been much hope for Russia in 1916, before the February and October revolutions, when the Kaiser's armies were pressing Russia back upon itself, when the country was falling apart. Nor was there much hope after the Bolshevik coup, brother against brother, Russian army fighting Russian army, the Germans pressing on the west and the British, the French, the Americans and the Japanese landing on the perimeters, trying to stifle the newborn Revolution.

No, if Russia had taught me anything, it had taught that somehow, somehow we survive. How many times had I heard my Russian friends sigh: How hard it is to learn to live! How long it took me to understand that this was not Russian mysticism but plain truth. There was no shortcut to life. To the end of our days, life is a lesson imperfectly learned. But only in Russia had I heard the question discussed with the seriousness that life dictates.

I had brought to Russia my Minnesota mind. I asked sharp questions and looked for hard answers. I believed in dissent; I despised conformity. I was impatient, intolerant, scornful of theory. I was an aginner, and proud of it. I had little understanding of the difference between a Russian and a Communist; I did not know that the censorship had been coterminous with Czarist Russia and Communist Russia; that dictatorship was the Russian national tradition. I knew so little about Russian patriotism that I was amazed when White Czarist officers rallied to Stalin's side against the Nazis. I could not understand how Stalin could embrace the Orthodox Church during World War II and hang portraits of the 1812 generals Kutuzov and Suvorov in his Kremlin office in place of Marx and Engels.

I came back to Moscow in 1982 knowing that I would not find the Moscow of Sir Bernard Pares. I had never traveled as he had traveled, casually and intimately, all over Russia, friends in every town. I never would. I knew I would never find the Russia of George Kennan. I could not play a guitar and I would never knock at the door of a Russian cottage and ask for a room for the night. That Russia was long gone. My Russia was something else —the Russia I had built with my life, year by year, decade by decade; the Russia of far Siberia (which I loved so much, its clear streams and boundless forests like those of my native Minnesota); the Russia of the Volga and the slow steamboats that reminded me of my Mississippi; the Russia of the Kuban and the *chernozem,* the black earth, which spoke to me of the Dakotas, combines plowing the fields like red ships, spouting the grain into endless convoys of trucks. My Russia was the country of deep snow and silent pine woods, of wood smoke from the chimneys of small huts not so different from those of the Arrowhead.

And, yes, my Russia was the Russia of the battlefields, of wounded soldiers in freezing boxcars, of the bloated dead lying by the roadsides, of smashed houses, blackened cities, of the stockades and watchtowers of the concentration camps I had seen so often in Siberia and of their victims, of whom I had come to know so many. In my Russia there was a touch of the Bolshoi's Pushkin, of the magic of Galina Ulanova, a dream in human form. All this—and the miners one thousand feet below the Urals surface, the teenagers crowding from factory gates and fighting for a place in the vodka queue, women shoveling snow and the men I had seen atop Lenin's mausoleum, those I had met and those I had not: Stalin, Molotov (still plugging away in the summer of 1982 on the memoirs he would never see published), Khrushchev and Mikoyan, Marshals Voroshilov and Budenny and Zhukov and the others, Malenkov and Kaganovich and Beria with his pince-nez and belly-white face, Dekanozov and the Georgian Mafia, shot in the Lubyanka cellars where they had shot so many others, Zhenya Yevtushenko, Bella Akhmadulina and Andrei Voznesensky, Vasily Aksionov and Ernst Neizvestny, poets on streetcorners and artists in attics, Leningrad, Professor Varshavsky (and the brutal bureaucrat who mailed back to me the heart medicine I sent to save his life); Mikhail Dudin and Olga Berggoltz and Vera Inber and Dmitri Pavlov and all the survivors of the siege, Ehrenburg and Leonov, Simonov and Saava Dangulov and Estella Zapolskaya (whose grave I found a dilapidated ruin in Vvedenie cemetery in 1982), Olga Khludova and Ludmilla Nikolaevna, Dedya Petya and Maria Ivanovna, the party stalwarts like Yuri Zhukov and Nikolai Fedorenko, and— Lord, I cannot list all the names that mark the tapestry of my Russia, the names and the places, the times and the talk. George Kennan, Tom and Juli Whitney, all now fused together in some organic whole, part of me, part of my being, a Russian element in me along with the (hated) Welsh element, the passive Dutch element, the long, steady strain of English yeomen.

I can no longer sift it out and say what Russia has taught me, what it was that I brought to Russia. It has become an amalgam, for better or for worse.

I have written two novels set in Russia, only Russian characters, no Americans. The first is *The Northern Palmyra Affair,* and it takes place, for the most part, in Leningrad. After it was published, I had a letter from a Russian who had emigrated many years ago to Paris. He told me that he had known Irena, my heroine, when he was a young man in Petrograd. It was a precious compliment. Irena was the child of my mind. She had never existed until I gave her life in my novel. A few years later, I published *The Gates of Hell.* "How," a Russian said to me, "could you know about these things, you, an American?"

My hero in *The Gates of Hell* is a blend of Andrei Sakharov and Aleksandr Solzhenitsyn. His adversary is, under his own name, Yuri Andropov. I did not tell my Russian friend that I had been close to Sakharov for many years and had, in a way, introduced him to the American public, editing his first two books published here. Nor did I say that I counted myself a student of Solzhenitsyn, and more than that, his friend. As for Andropov, I had begun to study him the moment Brezhnev named him to head the KGB in 1967, and had intensified my research after Nicholas Nabokov, cousin of *Lolita*'s author, had given me some remarkable insights into his character back in 1971. When I went to Russia in the summer of 1982, I realized after conversations with a wide range of Russian friends that the succession to Leonid Brezhnev had been decided and that barring some extraordinary upset, Andropov, with his enigmatic fascination with things American, was about to become the fifth of Lenin's successors, following Stalin, Malenkov, Khrushchev and Brezhnev. This was a development of stellar magnitude, but because of one of those aberrations which sometimes strike *The New York Times,* I was unable to share my knowledge of Andropov with its readers until after Brezhnev died.

I suppose the true answer to the Russian's question about *The Gates of Hell* must be found in the long journey I have undertaken, a journey that continues to this day. I think of it as having begun in the wintry January of 1944, but perhaps it started in my childhood on that November day of 1917 when I stood guard at the Winter Palace on Royalston Avenue, or a bit later, as I listened to Nathan Rosen spin out for me his dreams of the Russian Revolution, of the new world that was being born in Petrograd, the new world that he believed would spread over Europe and even to America.

I have written here of that journey—of my Victorian boyhood, my early years as a newspaperman, World War II and the gradual shaping of my life by the long Russian experience. But there has been much more. Russia launched me upon other journeys, which took me into almost every part of the Communist world, particularly into capitals long barred to American journalists, into Southeast Asia and Vietnam, Hanoi behind the lines, into China and the remote Asian heartland, Mongolia, the countries of the Himalayas and Tibet.

The place where I would put to work most importantly the skills I learned in my Moscow days would be my homeland. I came back to America to confront a country that I had never really known. I set out from the first day I got my desk in the big *Times* city room, on a new voyage of discovery, to explore the U.S.A. with an appetite whetted by Moscow's frustrations. Ahead lay new conflict, new challenge, new goals, and, again and again, new tests of that rule which I had found to apply wherever I took out my reporter's notebook: Nothing is more difficult to report than the truth, and few, indeed, are those who want to read the tough, harsh words of reality. To be a reporter is no slick or easy task. If you are getting too many bouquets, too many words of praise—watch out! Something is wrong. You are not getting the whole story. If you are telling it all, and like it is, there will be brickbats mixed in with the bouquets, as I would find when I went to Birmingham, Alabama, and encountered Bull Connor during the civil rights struggle, or incurred the wrath of Lyndon Johnson over my trip to Hanoi.

But that is another story, one that will require another book for the telling. I have been on a long journey and now I know that I will always be a pilgrim in the same progress, an unending quest for knowledge—knowledge of Russia, whose shadow falls across the planet which in my lifetime has grown so small, so dangerous, so enigmatic; knowledge of America, so filled with promise, so shackled by frustration, yet still pregnant with hope for her people and for the world.

Index

ABOUT THE AUTHOR

Harrison E. Salisbury was born in Minnesota in 1908. He grew up in Minneapolis, attended the University of Minnesota and was expelled in 1930 in a row over his editorship of the student daily.

He began a newspaper career on the *Minneapolis Journal* while still in school, later working for the United Press in St. Paul, Chicago and Washington. After U.S. entry in World War II he was assigned to London as UP manager, covering the war in England, North Africa, the Middle East and Russia. He joined *The New York Times* in 1949 and was sent to Moscow where he spent nearly six years—the last of the Stalin era and the early Khrushchev period. As a specialist in Soviet affairs he has traveled to the most remote parts of Russia. He has spent much time in the People's Republic of China and has visited almost all of the Communist countries, writing extensive contemporary reports and several historical works.

In the years from 1955 onward he wrote widely for *The New York Times* in the political and social fields, covering the Civil Rights movement in the South and the turbulence of the 1960s. He served *The New York Times* as National Editor, Assistant Managing Editor and Associate Editor. He initiated the Op-Ed page and conducted it for several years. He is the author of some twenty books, including two novels.